INTERNATIONAL
BUSINESS

SECOND EDITION

To Miriam, Keshet, Joshua, and Rakefet; and to the memory of my parents, Bluma and Joshua Shenkar—OS

To my family, Cuihua, Edward, and Rosalie—YL

INTERNATIONAL BUSINESS

SECOND EDITION

ODED SHENKAR
Ohio State University

YADONG LUO
University of Miami

SAGE Publications

Los Angeles • London • New Delhi • Singapore

For information:

Sage Publications, Inc.
2455 Teller Road
Thousand Oaks, California 91320
E-mail: order@sagepub.com

Sage Publications Ltd.
1 Oliver's Yard
55 City Road
London EC1Y 1SP
United Kingdom

Sage Publications India Pvt. Ltd.
B 1/I 1 Mohan Cooperative Industrial Area
Mathura Road, New Delhi 110 044
India

Sage Publications Asia-Pacific Pte. Ltd.
33 Pekin Street #02-01
Far East Square
Singapore 048763

Printed in the United States of America

Library of Congress Cataloging-in-Publication Data

Shenkar, Oded.
International business / Oded Shenkar, Yadong Luo.—2nd ed.
    p. cm.
Includes bibliographical references and indexes.
ISBN 978-1-4129-4906-4 (pbk.)
    1. International trade. 2. International finance. 3. Investments, Foreign. 4. International business enterprises.
I. Luo, Yadong. II. Title.

HF1379.S536 2008
338.8'8—dc22   2007031736

This book is printed on acid-free paper.

08   09   10   11   10   9   8   7   6   5   4   3   2

Acquisitions Editor:	Al Bruckner
Developmental Editor:	Denise Simon
Editorial Assistant:	MaryAnn Vail
Production Editor:	Diane S. Foster
Copy Editor:	Tony Moore
Typesetter:	C&M Digitals (P) Ltd.
Proofreader:	Scott Oney
Indexer:	Molly Hall
Cover Designer:	Candice Harman
Marketing Manager:	Nichole M. Angress

BRIEF CONTENTS

DETAILED CONTENTS

Part IV International Business Strategies 273

10 · International Entry Strategies 275

11 · Organizing and Structuring Global Operations 309

12 · Building and Managing Global Strategic Alliances 331

13 · Managing Global Research and Development 355

PREFACE

International business impacts us much more significantly than ever before. In today's interconnected world, it is virtually impossible to understand and succeed in business without understanding the repercussions of global business realities and developments in countries other than your own. This book goes beyond a U.S.-centered perspective to take into consideration business realities in other countries and their unique cultures and practices and show how international business phenomena are perceived from their vantage point. Presenting the latest thinking in the field and immersed in recent trends and events around the world, this action-oriented approach helps students relate the material to current events as well as to their own daily lives. Most important, this approach will help broaden students' understanding of the global business environment and its influence on the role of the business executive.

This book is directed at both undergraduate and graduate students and is written so as to be accessible and motivational to both. We have done this by (a) presenting rigorously researched material in a readable form, (b) defining all new terms as they appear, (c) providing related knowledge, including that of current events, as necessary (rather than assuming knowledge, whether of basic geography or of recent world events), and (d) providing a balance as well as a clear link between theory and practice and between analytical frameworks and managerial solutions. These features also make the book accessible to students in the variety of disciplinary areas in which international business is taught and from which it draws. Relevant to all audiences around the world is the "real world" feel that conveys the excitement of cross-border business.

This book offers a fresh and unique perspective on international business: First, it takes a truly global rather than a U.S. perspective, providing balanced coverage. Second, it is written from an action-oriented, executive perspective, which helps students see the relevance of each topic to their future roles as managers and entrepreneurs. Third, the book offers an integrated approach that helps students make explicit connections across concepts and functions and develop the skills they need to address various international business issues and problems. Through this cross-functional prism, students gain a broad understanding of the environments, players, and policies at work in both the core and functional areas of international business. Fourth, we provide problem-solving strategies designed to give students the analytical skills and tools they need to meet the many challenges in today's global business environment. Finally, the book contains in-depth coverage of key topics such as culture, global e-commerce, global ethics and corruption, and international entrepreneurship, knowledge of which is essential for students entering the international business arena.

What's new in the second edition of **International Business?** In addition to updating each and every chapter in the first edition, the new edition adds new material that touches on emerging and critical topics that students should know. The second edition features a new chapter on international entrepreneurship, including the processes and strategies utilized by global start-ups or newborn global companies. The global competitive landscape is significantly shaped by unabated technological advancements, continuous reduction of entry barriers, and rapid development of virtual businesses around the world. This results in unprecedented opportunities for the growth of international entrepreneurship. In this chapter, students will find the guiding tools with which to develop strategies for leveraging cross-border opportunities for entrepreneurial development.

The second edition also features more prominently the internationalization of emerging-market multinationals. Businesses, both state-owned and private enterprises, from emerging economies (notably from China, India, Brazil, Mexico, Russia, and Turkey) are increasingly active in undertaking outward foreign investment in advanced markets and in other developing countries. In the new edition, we illustrate the unique motives, trajectories, and strategies underlying international expansion of these new multinationals. Students will find a comparison of emerging-market multinationals with those hailing from developed countries and those from newly industrialized economies such as South Korea, Singapore, and Hong Kong. Using this comparative lens, students learn that strategies, solutions, and actions in international business often diverge for different types of international firms.

The second edition is further improved by including new and updated case examples, company updates, and new data on world trade, foreign direct investment, and multinational enterprises, among other international business phenomena and players. This new material is found not only in respective sections but is also fully integrated throughout the book.

ORGANIZATION

The text begins with an introductory chapter providing the foundations of international business in the context of a quickly globalizing business environment. This sets the stage for the rest of the book and serves to align the expectations of students and their instructors.

The first main section of the book outlines what are arguably the core phenomena in international business—namely, trade and foreign direct investment, as well as the major players (i.e., the multinational and international firms that conduct international business). This section differs from what you might find in other books in at least three important ways. First, while many texts do not introduce these topics until later, we believe that it is essential to present them upfront so students begin to think as executives and seek relevance throughout the book. Second, this section integrates theory and reality by presenting them side by side and pinpointing when reality supports theory but also when it does not and why, a level of rigor rarely seen in other texts. Third, this section, like the rest of the book, reflects the most recent theoretical developments in international business as well as the most recent trends—for example, it does not merely offer coverage of the traditional multinational enterprise but also of the multinational from developing countries and the small international firm.

Part II introduces the environment of international business and has two prominent features. First, it starts with a unique chapter on country competitiveness, which ties environmental analysis with topics discussed earlier such as trade and comparative advantage and with topics to follow—for example, strategy. A second feature of this section is that it offers an extensive coverage of the cultural, political, and legal environments facing the multinational and international company and the challenges they represent. Most important, elements from these environments will show up again and again in later chapters and will be linked to topics appearing in this section, enabling true integration rather than a mere sequencing of topics.

The subsequent discussion on global business institutions—namely, monetary systems and financial markets—further serves to solidify this relationship between the international business environment and its firm and national actors. Here, too, the coverage is both extensive and integrative. For instance, the student will find coverage of almost every region of the world and the regions' regional integration rates, while also learning why integration occurs, using the terms and concepts introduced earlier in the text. Another unique feature is that we provide international managers with detailed strategic responses to economic integration and financial market changes, reinforcing the executive prism that runs throughout the book.

The next section deals with international business strategy. This too is a good illustration of the integrative approach taken in this book. This section includes chapters on strategy, organization design, and alliances, which are often dispersed in other books but have a key unifying theme. All four chapters have the firm's global strategy as a starting point, integrating learning of organization and human processes. For instance, Chapter 11 discusses organization design not as a standalone topic but also in relation to strategy, while Chapter 12 discusses both strategic and managerial aspects of alliances.

The section on functional areas enables the student to look at international business phenomena from the perspective of the functional expert, thus linking learning with prior functional courses as well as with the overall phenomena discussed earlier in the book. These chapters provide for extensive coverage of each functional area and also show how they fit together and how they link with other topics. For example, when covering global human resource management, we explain its control function and its relation to a firm's global strategy. In the chapters on international accounting, financial management, and taxation, we again integrate these key functional areas with global strategies and structures on the one hand and with facets of the international business environment on the other. For instance, we discuss the relation between cultural variables and accounting practices.

Finally, this book is unique in offering an extensive treatment of several emerging areas, including global e-commerce, global ethics and corruption, international entrepreneurship, and emerging-market multinational corporations. Each of these areas has received considerable attention lately, and the context here provides for an opportunity to make learning more realistic by linking it to current events.

FEATURES

- **Global Perspective:** Describes business realities and processes in many parts of the world, covering both developed and developing countries. Students will learn to look at the world from diverse perspectives, including those of small and midsize international companies and developing-country multinationals.
- **Currency and Relevance:** Presents the latest concepts and models, as well as recent events that help students relate the material to daily life. Spells out new developments in the global environment and shows how they impact the task of the business executive.
- **Integrated Approach:** Features an integrated approach that helps students make connections between different concepts and goes beyond the traditional silos that characterize much of current IB learning tools.
- **Cross-Functional Emphasis:** Students gain a broad, cross-functional understanding of the environments, players, and policies at work in both the core and functional areas of international business. At the same time, these functions are integrated through the lens of global strategic planning and corporate coordination.
- **Problem-Solving Strategies:** Outlines strategies, policies, and implementation tools for solving international business challenges, develops problem-solving aptitude and skills. Problem-solving actions and strategies are embodied not only in chapters focusing on international business strategies but also in other chapters, such as those on international economic organizations, financial markets, and multinational enterprises.
- **Cultural, Legal, and Environmental Coverage:** Highlights the role of these key elements in all aspects of international business. In addition to a chapter devoted to culture and one on the political and legal environment, these elements are fully integrated into other chapters. This enables students to link across areas and to develop executive-level thinking and action.
- **Opening Cases:** Each chapter begins with motivational questions followed by a brief case illustrating the core concepts presented in the chapter. This attunes the student to the material that follows, making subsequent reading more efficient.
- **Country and Industry Boxes:** Additional short cases in each chapter serve to illustrate and zoom in on phenomena that may at first look abstract, enabling the student to find relevance to their areas of interest. The use of these two boxes in every chapter enables a simultaneous use of country and industry lenses, a unique "hands-on" feature of this book.
- **Key Points Highlight:** The book summarizes the major points at the end of every section and at the end of every chapter. These key points enable the student to quickly grasp the most important ideas in every section and in every chapter and in most instances find the answer to each chapter's opening questions.

ANCILLARY PACKAGE

- *Instructor's Resource CD.* An Instructor's Resource CD makes teaching easier and more effective. This CD, prepared by Mernoush Banton at Florida International University, includes the following information for each chapter:
  - Chapter objectives
  - Detailed lecture outlines
  - Teaching notes and suggestions
  - Additional review and discussion questions
  - Suggested Web sites for further discussion

○ PowerPoint presentations
○ A test bank consisting of multiple-choice, true-false, and essay questions.

ACKNOWLEDGMENTS

In developing the second edition, we have benefited from the insightful comments and suggestions of many colleagues, to whom we remain indebted. We especially wish to thank the reviewers listed below for their invaluable feedback on the second edition.

Yusaf H. Akbar
Southern New Hampshire University

Prakash Dheeriya
California State University–Dominguez Hills

Stuart Graham
Georgia Institute of Technology

Rolf Hemmerling
Webster University

Terry Long
Marymount University

Mona Makhija
Ohio State University

James E. McConnell
University at Buffalo

Val Miskin
Washington State University

Sanela Porca
University of South Carolina–Aiken

Roberto Ragozzino
University of Central Florida

Manuchehr Shahrokhi
California State University–Fresno

Al Siu
Golden Gate University

Robert S. Spich
University of California–Los Angeles

Jeffrey Stone
California State University–Northridge

Heidi Vernon
Northeastern University

William Walker
University of Houston

INTERNATIONAL BUSINESS IN AN AGE OF GLOBALIZATION

DO YOU KNOW?

1. What is globalization? Why is globalization important even to firms that do not have any international involvement at present? How does globalization affect the consumer? The employee?

2. What are the benefits of globalization, and what are its threats, both real and perceived?

3. What do the terms *international business, international transaction, international trade,* and *international investment* mean? Can you distinguish between the multinational enterprise (MNE) and the international firm?

4. What are the differences between international business and domestic business? What is the source of these differences?

5. Why do firms expand globally? What do they hope to gain, and what hazards do they face? Does every firm seek identical goals or face the same obstacles and opportunities when expanding into international markets?

OPENING CASE

The Coca-Cola Company

Atlanta-based Coca-Cola Company, a manufacturer, distributor, and marketer of nonalcoholic beverages, is one of the first examples that come to mind when people think of a global company. With almost 400 beverage brands, and sales in more than 200 countries, few other companies can match Coca-Cola's worldwide presence or the visibility of its products, particularly its flagship, Coke, which has become the symbol of a global product. Studies show that the brand enjoys the highest name recognition in the world. The Coca-Cola Company ranked 89th on the Fortune 500 list for 2006 (up three slots from 2005), with roughly 23 billion U.S. dollars in revenue and 5 billion in profit. The company, which first sold trademark registered Coke in the United States in 1886, relied on international markets for 73% of its gallon volume in 2005. At 29.4% of the total, net operating revenue was highest for the European Union in the same year, followed by North America with 28.4%, and 19.5% for North Asia, Eurasia, and the Middle East (combined).

Coca-Cola normally sells concentrate to local bottlers that prepare the beverage and distribute it in their respective markets, but in some countries it does not grant bottlers full manufacturing rights. Unlike its domestic contracts, its international agreements are limited in time, allowing for termination at the company's discretion, and marketing support, while common, is not provided in all markets. True to the now famous slogan "Think globally, act locally," the company also preserves a coherent marketing theme yet adapts product taste as well as operations to local markets. The "Think globally act locally" slogan embodies what may be the central dilemma in international business: the need to maintain global strategic focus and leverage scale advantages, while allowing for adaptation to local circumstances in everything from product specifications to packaging and distribution. The company's most global function—advertising—avoids themes that would be controversial in local markets. This is in contrast to its rival Pepsi, which, for example, irked religious circles in Israel with ads showing monkeys as human ancestors.

Coca-Cola's global success has ruffled some feathers. A few years ago, the European Commission rejected its bid to acquire a French beverage maker, pointing out that it already had a majority share in the EU markets. The company's argument that it merely had a tiny share of the market—defined as all liquids consumed, including water—fell on deaf ears. Efforts to promote a global image did not prevent the company from being identified and labeled an

American icon, making it a lightning rod for criticism and attacks by anti-U.S. and antiglobalization activists. In 2001, Coca-Coca's facilities were bombed by Moslem rebels in India and by Maoist guerrillas in Nepal. Since that time, Coca-Cola has been the target of protests against U.S. policies in Serbia, Europe, and the Arab world, among others.

SOURCES: Coca-Cola Annual Report 2006; Fortune 500 annual list, 2006; media reports.

AN AGE OF GLOBALIZATION

Globalization has become one of the buzzwords of modern times. People see its manifestations all around them, from the Coke can in a small village store in Africa to McDonald's golden arches in a Chinese city; from an article in the local newspaper about the outsourcing of software maintenance to India to the shift of a call center to Canada. Opinions regarding the impact of globalization vary widely, ranging from praise for its association with rising living standards to condemnation of its ill effects, such as industrial pollution. On the evening news you may hear praise for globalization from a farmer who has just concluded a contract for a large shipment of soybeans to China, only to see it followed by coverage of an antiglobalization demonstration outside a trade conference. So what is globalization, and why does it generate such diverse and often emotional reactions?

In line with the diversity of opinion, globalization has been defined in numerous ways. In this book, we define **globalization** as the acceleration and extension of interdependence of economic and business activities across national boundaries. Simply put, this means that a development on one side of the globe will have consequences on the other. It is easy to see the impact within a particular industry—for instance, automotive. U.S.-based makers of auto parts, such as Delphi and Visteon, have been pushed to restructure by pressure from low-cost producers in Asia, Mexico, and Eastern Europe who can make the same automotive component for less. Volkswagen has demanded concessions from its German workforce as a condition for keeping production locally. Closer to home, the price you pay at the pump is partially determined by energy demand in other countries, with soaring consumption in China and India accounting for much of the doubling of oil prices between 2004 and 2006. This interdependence will not go away. The United States National Intelligence Council notices in its 2020 Project Report that "certain aspects of globalization, such as the growing global connectedness, are not likely to go away," and that this will have far-reaching consequences for the expansion of international business: "Interdependence has widened the reach of multinational business, enabling smaller firms as well as large multinationals to market across borders and bringing heretofore non-traded services into the international arena."[1]

What Does Globalization Mean to You?

To the consumer, globalization means more choices, generally lower prices (but not always, as the example of gas prices shows), and an increasingly blurred national identity for products and services. Send a package from New York to Chicago via DHL, and you have contributed to the revenue of the German

Postal Service. Buy a Swedish-made Saab, and you have increased the revenue of its U.S. owner, General Motors (GM). Buy a Jaguar, and you have contributed to the bottom line of the Ford Motor Company. Buy a Dodge, and you have purchased a product of German-based DaimlerChrysler, the product of a merger between German firm Daimler and U.S.-based Chrysler that is now being undone. Buy a foreign brand, and you may find out that it is manufactured in the United States—Honda Civics in Ohio, Mercedes M Class in Alabama, Nissan pickup trucks in Tennessee. If you prefer to buy Canadian, you can choose between a GM or a Ford vehicle manufactured in Canada; or you can settle for the Mercedes M class, made in the United States but advertised in Canada as "made by a Canadian"—alluding to the manager of a U.S. plant. If you are an Australian consumer who wants to buy a locally produced vehicle, you can select between three locally produced foreign brands: Holden (a GM brand whose design is influenced by its German subsidiary Opel), Ford, or Toyota. These Australian operations also export to other countries while facing more competition from imports as local tariffs are reduced.

Similar trends can be observed in the service sector. The mortgage on your U.S. property might be underwritten by Dutch bank ABN Amro; your life insurance by French insurer AXA. Your retirement funds might be invested in the stock of Swiss food giant Nestlé and Japanese electronics maker Sony (currently led by a U.S. executive) or managed by German-based Deutsche Bank. The advertisement enticing you to buy Cincinnati-based P&G's Pampers may have been conceived by the U.K.'s Saatchi & Saatchi, but the graphic work may have been done in India. If you buy at your local Wal-Mart, chances are that many of the products on the shelves are made outside the country; Wal-Mart imports from China, for instance, exceed those of the United Kingdom. Even the student sitting next to you may well be a foreign national, as might be the patient waiting next to you in the hospital clinic. You may take your next vacation in Mexico rather than in Florida—just remember to take your Chinese manufactured iPod along for the ride.

In addition to offering a dizzying array of consumer products and services, globalization affects your career prospects. At times, it will also limit your opportunities, as when the transcription of medical records is outsourced to India; at other times, especially if you are better educated, globalization will greatly expand your career choices and opportunities. It is increasingly possible that upon graduation you will join one of the many foreign firms in the United States or that you will be assigned to work in another country by a U.S., local, or third-country foreign firm. If you are considering employment with a foreign firm, you may want to know whether the recruiting company tends to open its senior-most ranks to other than its own nationals. If in doubt, look for foreign names on the list of members of the board of directors, which provides a good indication of how open the company is to nonnatives. Whether you work for a domestic or a foreign corporation, you not only will have to consider a foreign assignment but will spend time negotiating, entertaining, coaching, and learning from foreign executives and employees. How well you perform these tasks will determine the rest of your career, as companies are increasingly on the lookout for individuals who can successfully operate globally.

Interim Summary

1. Globalization is the accelerated interdependence of economic and business activities across national boundaries.

2. Globalization influences the availability and pricing of products and services around the world while often blurring their source and identity.

3. Globalization affects your career opportunities and the skills you will need to be successful.

THE FACE OF GLOBALIZATION

Countries differ greatly in their globalization levels. Exhibit 1.1 ranks the 20 most global countries according to their overall globalization level as well as according to the four components that make up the Globalization Index developed by A. T. Kearney, a consultancy, and *Foreign Policy* magazine:[2] economic integration, personal contact, technological connectivity, and political engagement. Economic integration scores are based on a country's trade and foreign investment, discussed later in Chapters 2 and 3 of this book. Technological connectivity scores are composed of the number of Internet users, hosts, and secure servers in a given nation. Personal contact scores are based on travel and tourism, international telephone traffic, and cross-border remittances. Finally, political engagement scores are a combination of membership in international organizations, contributions of staff and money to UN peacekeeping missions, the number of international treaties ratified, and government-to-government transfers.

Exhibit 1.1   The Global Top 20 Countries

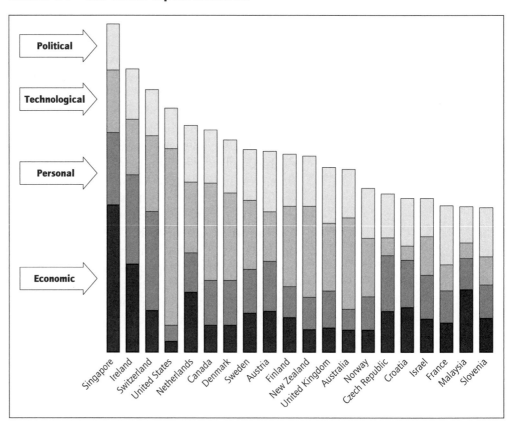

SOURCE: A. T. Kearney, "Globalization's Last Hurrah?" *Foreign Policy*, Jan/Feb. 2005.

Exhibit 1.2 provides the complete 2005 globalization scores for a broader group of 62 countries that together account for 96% of the world's GDP. Singapore is in first place, having displaced Ireland, which was ranked first in prior years. The United States advanced from seventh to fourth, its leadership in technological connectivity counterbalanced by low rankings on the other three globalization ingredients, in particular economic integration (typical of countries with large domestic markets). Indeed, one could argue that in a global environment, being large is sometimes a liability in the sense that it allows firms to neglect international markets for too long. The study did not find a strong relation between globalization and the propensity to suffer terrorist attacks on one's soil, discounting a speculation that opening to the outside world invites security risks. However the study did find a relation between globalization and public education spending, especially in the developing world. In other words, success in a global, knowledge-based economy depends on having an educated workforce. Elsewhere, a *New York Times* op-ed noted that countries that ranked high on the Globalization Index had higher economic and political stability (see Chapter 7), more flexible labor markets, better regulation, and less corruption (see Chapter 19).[3]

Exhibit 1.2   Globalization Index Rankings

2005 GI Rankings		Dimension				Item											
						Economic Integration		Personal Contact			Technological Connectivity			Political Engagement			
		Economic	*Personal*	*Technological*	*Political*	*Trade*	*FDI*	*Telephone*	*Travel*	*Remittances and Personal Transfers*	*Internet Users*	*Internet Hosts*	*Secure Servers*	*International Organization*	*U.N. Peacekeeping*	*Treaties*	*Government Transfers*
1	Singapore	1	3	11	32	1	1	1	5	47	10	9	11	29	3	41	47
2	Ireland	2	2	13	19	4	2	3	3	6	24	18	7	12	11	28	22
3	Switzerland	9	1	7	29	18	5	2	4	1	11	14	5	29	13	41	10
4	United States	60	40	1	43	61	42	19	34	58	4	1	1	1	28	57	38
5	Netherlands	5	11	8	4	8	4	6	13	45	9	4	13	5	17	6	6
6	Canada	27	8	2	10	26	23	4	22	60	5	11	2	2	22	6	28
7	Denmark	29	7	5	13	19	38	7	17	17	3	3	8	12	14	28	7
8	Sweden	12	10	9	16	21	6	9	6	43	1	10	9	17	12	6	40
9	Austria	10	5	14	2	14	12	11	2	31	16	15	14	12	2	6	8
10	Finland	15	20	6	15	33	7	17	12	42	8	2	10	12	7	28	13
11	New Zealand	36	16	3	21	39	27	5	23	53	7	8	3	29	23	6	20
12	United Kingdom	32	12	10	5	45	20	10	16	37	12	17	6	5	10	6	18
13	Australia	37	34	4	25	55	16	14	30	50	6	5	4	29	5	28	36
14	Norway	35	15	12	17	29	34	12	24	30	22	6	12	17	20	6	24
15	Czech Republic	11	4	24	35	5	24	25	1	25	25	22	26	17	42	28	15
16	Croatia	7	6	28	26	12	8	20	7	9	31	34	25	29	49	1	16
17	Israel	19	9	16	46	24	14	8	27	11	18	16	17	48	15	61	4
18	France	24	17	21	3	46	10	15	14	39	20	19	20	2	6	6	9
19	Malaysia	4	19	27	49	2	21	27	10	16	21	37	35	29	43	41	45
20	Slovenia	17	13	20	23	11	339	22	8	23	15	25	18	29	21	6	25
21	Germany	43	29	17	8	30	54	16	21	49	14	21	16	2	9	28	11

(Continued)

Exhibit 1.2 (Continued)

2005 GI Rankings		Economic	Personal	Technological	Political	Trade	FDI	Telephone	Travel	Remittances and Personal Transfers	Internet Users	Internet Hosts	Secure Servers	International Organization	U.N. Peacekeeping	Treaties	Government Transfers
		Dimension				Item											
						Economic Integration		Personal Contact			Technological Connectivity			Political Engagement			
22	Portugal	44	18	22	1	34	53	23	15	22	17	23	22	5	1	6	5
23	Hungary	6	32	26	22	6	15	34	9	36	28	20	29	17	35	1	30
24	Panama	3	47	34	34	9	3	33	37	40	46	41	23	48	56	1	26
25	Slovakia	8	38	30	7	3	37	30	33	21	26	26	34	29	4	1	53
26	Spain	22	28	23	11	42	11	24	18	29	29	24	19	5	25	6	14
27	Italy	47	27	25	6	50	40	18	20	44	23	33	24	5	18	6	12
28	Japan	62	58	15	18	62	52	40	45	61	13	12	15	29	8	6	49
29	Greece	55	23	32	9	48	58	21	11	38	33	29	27	5	24	28	3
30	South Korea	38	46	19	45	25	47	39	40	27	2	13	30	29	29	41	42
31	Poland	33	31	29	37	27	31	28	19	28	30	27	28	17	33	28	35
32	Philippines	28	14	49	42	16	55	41	51	2	49	48	47	17	51	28	41
33	Uganda	39	24	61	14	56	18	62	58	3	61	53	59	48	61	6	2
34	Chile	16	51	31	30	31	9	35	38	52	27	32	32	12	47	6	29
35	Romania	25	37	36	27	22	26	36	29	18	32	42	44	29	46	1	31
36	Taiwan	18	25	18	62	13	32	13	31	26	19	7	21	62	62	62	55
37	Tunisia	23	30	47	40	17	29	32	26	14	43	60	46	29	30	28	44
38	Botswana	30	39	51	12	20	41	31	25	33	51	46	50	48	57	6	1
39	Ukraine	13	41	45	41	10	41	42	32	19	44	43	49	48	37	28	21
40	Morocco	21	22	54	55	32	13	46	42	4	54	52	51	48	38	52	33
41	Senegal	40	36	55	24	35	44	48	47	12	55	58	56	29	26	6	17
42	Mexico	41	44	37	31	41	35	29	35	32	34	31	38	5	54	6	60
43	Sri Lanka	34	26	57	56	23	45	49	50	5	58	54	48	58	58	41	46
44	Nigeria	20	52	60	33	15	30	59	59	34	60	61	60	17	36	6	62
45	Saudi Arabia	45	21	46	57	28	62	26	28	8	45	47	45	48	45	52	54
46	Thailand	14	50	40	58	7	43	54	43	35	36	44	40	17	44	57	48
47	Argentina	58	56	33	20	53	49	47	44	55	35	28	37	17	16	6	39
48	South Africa	48	55	38	28	44	50	43	39	54	40	35	31	17	32	6	27
49	Kenya	52	42	58	38	43	56	61	55	13	57	50	57	48	27	28	32
50	Pakistan	53	33	59	52	54	36	53	62	7	59	55	55	48	31	52	19
51	Colombia	42	43	44	51	52	22	38	53	15	50	39	42	48	48	41	34
52	Russia	46	53	42	36	40	46	51	41	48	39	38	43	17	19	41	37
53	Peru	54	49	41	39	57	28	37	49	41	37	40	41	29	52	6	59
54	China	26	57	50	54	36	19	56	54	46	47	51	58	29	34	52	58
55	Venezuela	31	59	43	50	51	17	45	52	59	48	45	39	29	50	41	56
56	Turkey	49	54	39	47	38	57	44	36	56	41	36	36	29	41	41	43
57	Brazil	57	61	35	44	60	33	52	56	57	38	30	33	29	40	28	57
58	Bangladesh	61	35	62	53	58	61	60	60	10	62	62	62	58	39	41	50
59	Egypt	56	45	52	59	49	60	50	46	20	52	59	52	29	55	57	23
60	Indonesia	50	60	53	48	37	59	57	57	51	53	49	54	17	60	41	51
61	India	59	48	56	60	59	51	58	61	24	56	56	53	58	59	52	52
62	Iran	51	62	48	61	47	48	55	48	62	42	57	61	58	53	57	61

SOURCE: A. T. Kearney, "Measuring globalization," *Foreign Policy*, May/June 2005, p.52.

Who Benefits From Globalization?

One of the main arguments against globalization is that it confers benefits on rich nations at the expense of poor countries. Before we discuss this argument, let us take a look at the relationship between development level and globalization. It is evident from Exhibit 1.2 that some developed nations, such as Japan, obtain only moderate globalization scores, while some developing and emerging economies, such as the Czech Republic and Malaysia, obtain respectable scores. Still, the overall relationship is quite clear: The fourteen nations that score highest on globalization are all developed economies, while the bottom half of the list is occupied by developing and emerging economies. This does not mean that globalization brings no value to the developing world; on the contrary, integration into the global economy may well pave the route to economic growth and prosperity, as the case of Ireland, once Europe's economic laggard and now its fastest growing economy, shows clearly. In contrast, countries that fail to integrate into the global economy face the prospect of falling further behind.

The good news as we begin the 21st century is that the share of developing countries in world merchandise trade is rising to its highest level in more than 50 years, and the trade growth of the 49 least developed countries (LDCs) exceeds the global average. It is also important to realize that many of the manifestations of globalization in wealthy nations end up helping poorer economies. For instance, when a Singaporean tourist is visiting Laos, he is in effect increasing the export sales of Laos by purchasing such services as hotel stays and tours. And while wages in factories in a developing country are low by developed nation standards, employees of foreign affiliates in developing economies are paid, on average, far more than those employed by domestic firms. While some local firms are unable to compete with large foreign corporations and exit the market, others take advantage of the learning opportunities associated with multinational presence and upgrade their capabilities, thus positioning themselves to become future global players. If large multinational firms seem an exclusive club whose members come from rich nations, they are now joined by multinationals from developing economies. In 2000, for the first time ever, multinational firms from developing nations made it into the ranks of the top 100 global multinationals,[4] and new contenders, such as China-founded Lenovo, are growing rapidly.

The Impact of Globalization

A common lamentation against globalization is that it deprives nations of their sovereignty. This will supposedly occur because of the growing power of international institutions (see Chapter 8) such as the World Trade Organization (WTO) or the International Monetary Fund (IMF), whose officials are not elected by popular vote. Yet, while the WTO has assumed a conflict-resolution role that was previously the domain of bilateral negotiations, its resolutions are based on consensus, meaning that the vote of the smallest nation counts as much as that of the largest. Most important decisions regarding international trade are still made by governments, and trade relations are governed by bilateral agreements negotiated and monitored by sovereign governments. And while mega multinational corporations abound, small firms remain viable players that have a role in the global economy. As you will see in Chapter 4, small firms in the United States and in many other countries have actually increased their share of national exports over the last decade.

Another complaint against globalization is that it comes at the expense of the environment. Environmentalists accuse firms of relocating their operations abroad solely to escape tough pollution rules in their home countries, an argument often titled a "race to the bottom" in search of "the lowest common denominator." While there is no question that globalization increases pollution levels in rapidly industrializing economies such as Vietnam and China, rising living standards in those nations, in particular the purchase of automobiles, are at least partially to blame. And although some firms shed their environmental responsibilities in their quest for larger profits, others adhere to strict codes of environmental protection and make a positive contribution by introducing sophisticated environmental technologies in the developing world. For instance, Dow Chemical has been credited with environmental cleanup in Eastern Europe and the former East Germany. Further, the reality is that for most firms, environmental standards are only one of many criteria used in determining their investment and location decisions, meaning that the concept of "race to the bottom" does not always apply. Still, globalization poses huge environmental challenges, and firms and governments must maintain their vigilance. You will find further discussion of foreign direct investment in Chapter 3.

Throughout this book we will take the position that globalization is a complex phenomenon whose repercussions are often less than crystal clear. Globalization carries both promises and threats, and it produces winners as well as losers. Whether you view globalization as a blessing or a curse will often depend on your perspective and vantage point. For instance, while globalization is correlated with higher overall economic growth, this will probably be of little consolation to an employee who loses his job as a result of foreign competition. Keep in mind, however, that globalization is not the only factor influencing job loss and wage levels. Research shows that it is technology rather than globalization that puts the bulk of downward pressure on the wages of unskilled labor.[5] The challenge of globalization involves enhancing its benefits and mitigating its negative impact, maintaining a balance between the public and the individual interest.

Globalization can yield negatives at the national level as well. Global capital flow makes less regulated emerging economies such as Mexico, Thailand, and Argentina vulnerable to volatilities of international capital movements and foreign exchange markets and may contribute to a financial or currency crisis in these countries. Globalization exposes national economies to the uncertainties of the global economy, and, ironically, the most open economies are also the most at risk of a global slowdown. When prices of commodities, especially raw materials and natural resources, are undervalued owing to market control or influence by transnational cartels or by barriers imposed by importing nations, developing countries that export these commodities to developed countries lose many of the economic gains that would otherwise accrue. While asking for market access into developing countries, some developed nations themselves erect new barriers against developing-country imports, in particular farm products that are heavily subsidized in the European Union and, to a somewhat lesser extent, the United States.

To offer most of its benefits and mitigate some of the negatives, it helps to have a developed infrastructure for globalization. **Globalization infrastructure** is the institutional framework (e.g., multilateral agreements in trade, investment, and service) and market efficiency (e.g., efficiency of international capital markets or foreign exchange markets) that support fair and transparent transactions of products and services and streamline flows of commodities, capital, labor, knowledge, and information. As discussed in Chapter 8, international economic organizations such as the IMF, the World Bank, and the WTO play a vital role in facilitating such flows, as do firms, governments, and regional blocs, among others.

Interim Summary

1. It is useful to develop a balanced view on globalization, recognizing its positive and negative aspects, so as to focus attention on constructive solutions to the negatives while leveraging opportunities created by the positives.

2. International economic organizations such as the International Monetary Fund, the World Bank, and the World Trade Organization provide the infrastructure necessary to facilitate globalization.

GLOBALIZATION AND INTERNATIONAL BUSINESS

It is sometimes suggested that globalization means the advance of a homogeneous civilization and a uniform business system that would no longer require adjustment to different business environments. Nothing could be further from the truth. While globalization marches on, pressures to maintain national identity and solidarity are not subsiding. On the contrary, the growing interaction between different systems makes people more, rather than less, aware of the differences among them, often leading them to suspect foreign inputs as potentially threatening to their group identity. Unfortunately, the erroneous assumption regarding homogeneity might lead firms to believe that their strategies, practices, and products or services have universal applicability with no need to distinguish between domestic and international business. Instead, company executives should strive to learn the intricacies of the foreign environments in which they operate, because this is the only way to leverage their firms' global reach and scale. Globalization and localization may seem contradictory, but they are two sides of the same coin and are bound to live side by side in the future.

Throughout this book, you will learn about this simultaneous existence of global and local forces and their interaction in international business. The material will explore how to leverage the global resources of the multinational enterprise yet compensate for its unfamiliarity with the foreign environments in which it operates; how to extract economies of scale by selling a product in multiple locations while making product adjustments and adaptations to reflect different tastes and selling methods; and how to maintain a globally unified compensation system for employees while taking into account the vast differences in practices, values, standards of living, and taxation across the globe. Please note that we use the terms *country* and *nation* in this book to denote boundaries of economic and political units that are not necessarily sovereign states, such as Hong Kong, which is part of China but is a separate entity for foreign trade and investment purposes.

What Is International Business?

International business refers to business activities that involve the transfer of resources, goods, services, knowledge, skills, or information across national boundaries. The resources that make up this flow are raw materials, capital, goods, services, and people. Goods may be semi-finished and finished assemblies and products. Services include accounting, legal counsel, banking, insurance, management consulting, trade service, education, health care, and tourism, among others. Knowledge and skills include technology and innovation, organizational and managerial skills, and intellectual property rights such as copyrights, trademarks, and brand names. Information flows include databases and information networks, among others. The parties involved may be individuals (e.g., tourists and individual investors buying foreign stocks or bonds), companies (private or public), company clusters (e.g., alliances), government bodies (e.g., central banks), and international institutions (e.g., the World Bank, the IMF). Of these, companies are the dominant players. The firm is the primary economic agent facilitating and gaining (or suffering) from globalization. Firm activities and exchanges that involve the crossing of national boundaries are called international transactions. **International transactions** are manifested mainly in **international trade and investment**. International trade occurs when a company exports goods or services to buyers (importers) in another country. International investment occurs when the company invests resources in business activities outside its home country.

Any firm, regardless of size, that is engaged in international business is defined in this book as an **international firm**. A firm that has directly invested abroad and has at least one working affiliate in a foreign country (e.g., a factory, a branch office) over which it maintains effective control is defined in this book as a **multinational enterprise**, or **MNE**. Please note that there are multiple definitions of the MNE out there, most of which are rather arbitrary (for instance, one definition requires presence in at least six foreign locations; another that the firm has a presence in all major regions—North America, Europe, and Asia). For the sake of clarity, however, we use the standard working definition noted above.

International companies are the beneficiaries of, as well as the reason for, the growing interdependence among nations. Motorola has development, design, manufacturing, and sales facilities in multiple countries and derives most of its revenues from foreign operations. Companies like Motorola can be listed and raise capital in financial markets around the world, including New York, London, Paris, Zurich, Singapore, Tokyo, and Hong Kong. Both large and small firms can benefit from competitively priced labor, cheap resources, and enormous market opportunities by shifting their production facilities to emerging economies such as Vietnam, China, and India, while benefiting from the high skill level available in places such as Ireland and Israel to do development and design work. Levi Strauss jeans and other apparel are made by subcontractors in Bangladesh, China, and other locations and are then sold in markets throughout the world. IBM and Microsoft employ Indian software developers based in India and the United States, and both firms have development centers in Israel as well as in other foreign nations. Among service providers, U.S. architectural firms design buildings across Asia, while U.S. airlines compete for passengers on international routes with both foreign and third-party carriers. Such activities involve the movement of capital, people, knowledge, and products from one country to another. They are a consequence, as much as a generator, of globalization.

How can one measure the degree of globalization across various industries? One measure, which involves the industry's international linkages, gauges the extent to which a particular activity is concentrated in one country (low globalization) or in many countries (high globalization). The other measure is the integration of value-added activities—that is, whether most activities leading to a final product or service are done in one versus many countries. Together, these two measures tell us how global an industry is.[6] Other ways to measure industry globalization, such as the "transnationalization index," are mentioned in Chapters 2 and 3.

International Versus Domestic Business

Traditionally, international business has been the outgrowth of domestic business. In fact, most major corporations that are active in today's international scene started their operations in the domestic market. Leading Japanese automakers such as Toyota and Honda started their operations in their domestic market before beginning to export to other countries. As the magnitude of their operations grew, they found it profitable or otherwise necessary to build plants and facilities in other countries, most notably the United States. While many firms still follow the traditional route of domestic growth first, international expansion second, we increasingly see firms that target international markets when launching their operations. These firms are called **born global**, **global startups**, or **international new ventures** (INVs) and are discussed in Chapter 4 and especially in Chapter 20. NASDAQ-traded Israeli firm Checkpoint, a leader in the software security segment, is one such company. In addition, some companies engage in international activities without having a home base in the traditional sense. An example is the mainland operations of many Hong Kong investors whose "suitcase companies" do not have a presence in their home base.

Although international business is often an extension of domestic business, it is significantly different from the latter in **environmental dynamics** and **operational nature**. Environmentally, the diversity that exists between countries with regard to cultures, social customs, business practices, laws, government regulations, and political stability is among the many reasons for the complexity of international business. Therefore, international business is usually riskier than domestic business, although, on the whole, presence in multiple international markets provides a measure of diversification, which mitigates risk. Variations in inflation, currency, taxation, and interest rates among different nations have a significant impact on the profitability of an international firm. For a firm that is borrowing and investing in a foreign country, higher interest rates, tax rates, and inflation rates mean higher cost of operation and lower profitability. At the same time, for a firm that is depositing money in a foreign bank, higher interest rates mean a higher return. Similarly, when the euro goes down in value against the U.S. dollar, U.S. exporters to the European Union (EU) will receive (unless hedging their currency exposure) fewer dollars for their euro denominated transaction, while U.S. importers of EU goods will be able to either lower the cost of the imports or increase their profitability.

The Coca-Cola Company, described in the opening case, needs not only to hedge its currency risk but also navigate financial environments with different accounting and tax systems. It also needs to attend to different cultures and social system, different regulations, and different consumption patterns, among other factors. The competitive landscape can also be dramatically different in markets in which Coca-Cola is facing strong local competition (for example, from Wahaha in China), while in other markets the company must adjust for different rules (for instance, a ban on comparative advertising). Competition can spring from nowhere: for example, Mecca Cola emerged in the Middle East partially to take advantage of anti-American sentiment. The combined complexity entailed in operating in numerous markets that are different from each other and the uncertainty involved in the potential for a sudden change in any of those environments defines the essence of international business. This complex landscape creates opportunities (for instance, the opening of a new market such as Vietnam) but also poses risks and uncertainties. Broadly, **risk** refers to unpredictability of operational and financial outcomes. **Uncertainty** refers to the unpredictability of environmental or organizational conditions that affect firm performance. Uncertainty about environmental or organizational conditions increases the unpredictability of corporate performance and therefore increases risk. However, as earlier noticed, being in multiple markets also mitigates risk; for instance, in 2005 General Motors lost billions of dollars in North America, but its profits in China helped to somewhat narrow its overall loss.

Operationally, international business tends to be more difficult and costly to manage than business activities confined to a single country. Whatever benefits might be available from international operations, they will not be realized if the firm cannot run a complex business effectively. Local employees and expatriates (i.e., people who were sent to a foreign location from the home headquarters, as discussed in Chapter 17) may have trouble getting along because of cultural, linguistic, and managerial style differences. The cultural diversity encountered when operating in several countries may create problems of communication, coordination, and motivation. Organizational principles and managerial philosophies may differ widely, increasing the cost and difficulty of operation.

Why Do Firms Expand Internationally?

Generally speaking, the motivations for conducting international business include **market motives**, **economic motives**, and **strategic motives**. The motives vary from one business activity to another, producing multiple motivations for the international firm with a broad scope of activities in different parts of the globe.

Market motives can be **offensive** or **defensive**. An offensive motive is to seize market opportunities in foreign countries through trade or investment. Amway, Avon, and Mary Kay all entered China in the early 1990s in search of opportunities in the country's direct marketing business. Besides having the largest population and one of the fastest-growing economies in the world, China's strong culture of personal connections and the pervasiveness of close-knit families and friends helped make the country the world's biggest direct-selling market. That the Chinese government later outlawed direct selling altogether exemplifies the inherent risk in doing business abroad, although the companies found ways to adjust (for instance, Mary Kay has opened up customer "learning centers" as a substitute for direct door-to-door marketing and sales) until the ban was lifted years later.

A defensive motive is to protect and hold a firm's market power or competitive position in the face of threats from domestic rivalry or changes in government policies. Lenovo, now the world's third largest maker of personal computers, entered international markets via acquiring IBM's personal computers division partially to defend from growing encroachment into its domestic market by Dell and Hewlett Packard. Similarly, many North American and Asian companies in the computer and electronics industries invested heavily in European countries to bypass various barriers against imports from non–European Union members. Foreign automakers such as French conglomerate Peugeot-Citroën have established operations in China partially to offset inroads by their global competitors into this important market.

Photo 1.1 **China has become a magnet for international expansion.**

SOURCE: Jupiterimages.

Economic motives apply when firms expand internationally to increase their return through higher revenues or lower costs. International trade and investment are vehicles enabling a firm to benefit from intercountry differences in costs of labor, natural resources, and capital, as well as differences in regulatory treatments, such as taxation. For example, more than 2,000 plants have sprung up near the U.S-Mexico border to take advantage of low-wage Mexican labor to assemble American-made components for reexport to the United States. Some of the investors later relocated their plants to still cheaper China, Vietnam, and India. Fossil, a leading producer of wristwatches, opted to locate its overseas manufacturing headquarters in East Asia rather than in its home country, the United States. Firms such as Motorola, Boeing, Microsoft, Alcatel-Lucent, Intel, Kodak, Otis, and Coca-Cola established production facilities in China's special economic zones or open coastal cities to attain a significantly lower taxation rate than that applicable in the United States.

Strategic motives lead firms to participate in international business when they seek, for instance, to capitalize on distinctive resources or capabilities developed at home (e.g., technologies and economies of scale). By deploying these resources or capabilities abroad or increasing production through international trade, firms may be able to increase their cash inflows. Firms may also go international to be the first mover in the target foreign market before a major competitor gets in, gaining strategic benefits such as technological leadership, brand recognition, customer loyalty, and competitive position. Volkswagen was the second automaker to enter China and the first to locate in the all-important Shanghai market, gaining a virtual monopoly in that market for years. Additionally, firms may benefit from vertical integration involving different countries. For example, a company in the oil exploration and drilling business may integrate "downstream" by acquiring or building an oil refinery in a foreign country that has a market for its refined products. Conversely, a company that has strong distribution channels (e.g., gas stations) in a country but needs a steady source of supply of gasoline at a predictable price may integrate "upstream" and acquire an oil producer and refiner in another country.

Yet another strategic motive is to follow the company's major customers abroad (often termed "piggybacking"). Japanese tire maker Bridgestone found itself in the U.S. market when its customers—Japanese carmakers—exported their cars, with Bridgestone tires mounted on them, to the United States, and their customers needed replacement tires. Other suppliers of Honda, Nissan, and Toyota followed suit, many eventually locating manufacturing operations in the United States. Bridgestone, for instance, took over U.S. tire manufacturer Firestone to become the world's largest tire maker. Since responsiveness and product adaptation are becoming increasingly critical for business success, proximity to foreign customers is an important driver of overseas investment.

Interim Summary

1. International business is the conducting of business activities that involve the transfer of resources, goods, services, knowledge, skills, or information across national boundaries

2. International business is typically more complex and uncertain than domestic business owing to differences in environments and operational requirements.

3. If an international business is not run effectively, the benefit of doing business internationally may turn into a drawback because of the costs and difficulties associated with managing activities in multiple locations.

THE STRUCTURE OF THIS BOOK

This book is not about globalization per se but about conducting international business in a global and rapidly changing world environment. The book will help you learn the basic concepts, principles, procedures, and practices in international business and provide you with an understanding of the environments in which it is conducted and the institutions that oversee or otherwise play a role in international business activities. This should prepare you for a future in which you will effectively, responsibly, and ethically conduct international business, whether in your home country or in another.

The structure of this book is based on a vision of international business as a proactive managerial undertaking. Thus, the sequence consists of a description of the major international activities and the players that pursue them, the environments in which they operate, the institutions governing their transactions, their strategies and design, the various functional areas that conduct specialized international business activities, and the issues that currently top the agenda of international business practice and scholarship. A more detailed outline of the chapters follows.

Part 1 introduces three core topics in international business: international trade in Chapter 2 (imports/exports), foreign direct investment in Chapter 3 (e.g., establishing foreign subsidiaries), and the major players in international business in Chapter 4 (the more traditional multinational enterprises hailing from developing countries, the rising multinationals from developing economies, and the small- and medium-sized international companies).

Part 2 discusses the environment of international business. Understanding the environment is essential if we are to understand the motivations and nature of home and host country firms as well as explain the features that draw or inhibit trade and investment in a host country. We start with country competitiveness (Chapter 5), a key determinant of trade, foreign investment, and the operation and performance of the multinational firm; such competitiveness is also a product of the endowments described in this part and the strategies undertaken by nations, industries, and firms. We proceed with culture (Chapter 6), a somewhat intangible yet crucial facet of international business that is too often underestimated. We also discuss the political and legal environments that establish the ground rules within which international business operates (Chapter 7).

Part 3 focuses on global markets and institutions. It covers international economic integration and organizations (Chapter 8) and the international monetary system and financial markets (Chapter 9). These global institutions are key elements of the infrastructure of globalization. They affect either regulatory frameworks or market efficiency for cross-border transactions. Global institutions are part of the environments in which they operate, but they also participate in shaping the international business environment within which transactions take place.

Part 4 deals with international business strategies, the starting point for a firm's operations in international markets. This part begins with a chapter on international entry strategies (Chapter 10), followed by a chapter on the organization design of the multinational firm, explaining how this firm organizes its operations in order to execute its set strategy (Chapter 11). Chapter 12 focuses on building and managing global strategic alliances, an increasingly popular yet problematic type of organization. Finally, Chapter 13 focuses on global research and development (R&D), a progressively more crucial element in an increasingly knowledge-based economy.

Part 5 deals with the separate international business functions. The aim is to illustrate the main challenges international business poses to each of the functional business areas and the knowledge base necessary for effective performance in each of those areas. In this part, we include chapters on finance (e.g., raising capital; Chapter 14), accounting (e.g., transfer pricing issues; Chapter 15), marketing (e.g., advertising, pricing) and the supply chain (logistic issues such as distribution modes; Chapter 16), and human resource management (e.g., staffing subsidiaries; Chapter 17).

Part 6 highlights emerging issues in international business. One is global e-commerce (Chapter 18). After a much-hyped false start in the late 1990s, e-commerce has been growing rapidly. The nature of e-commerce challenges some key ways of doing business internationally as well as the regulatory systems that govern them; it also exposes firms that hitherto have engaged only in domestic business to the vagaries of international commerce. The second emerging topic, ethics and corruption (Chapter 19), has long been associated with international business, especially in developing economies. In recent years, this once taboo subject has become the subject of much debate in developing and developed markets alike. For instance, technological advances and increased globalization have opened the door to piracy, counterfeiting, and similar phenomena on an unprecedented scale. This assault on property rights can have a major influence on a firm's global strategy and operational performance. The third emerging topic, and the last chapter of this book (Chapter 20), deals with international entrepreneurship, a subject of great importance in an increasingly knowledge-based, innovation economy. The chapter covers both comparative (e.g., the motives of entrepreneurial activity in different countries) and international (e.g., European start-ups raising money in the United States) aspects of entrepreneurship.

Pedagogical Thrust

While providing an in-depth discussion of individual topics as described above, the emphasis in this book is on the integration of topical areas. For instance, although culture is discussed in a separate chapter, its impact on environments, institutions, and firms is apparent throughout the book. Thus, when we discuss accounting, we note that certain features of accounting and auditing systems tend to correlate with cultural patterns, and when we discuss human resource management, we examine the role of cultural differences in expatriate adjustment. The manager's challenge, after all, is about integration across functions and regions, and this book reflects this responsibility. In addition to offering topical cross-references across chapters, we utilize special integration mechanisms—the **country box** and the **industry box**—in each chapter. The country box provides a zoom-in to a particular national market and the industry box into a particular sector. Readers should use these boxes not only to learn about the country or industry being highlighted but also to ask, and attempt to answer, what would have been different in another country or industry.

To sum up, this book is based on an appreciation for the diversity of business systems around the globe and a belief that awareness of the changing and intensifying nature of globalization and global competition should be high on the agenda of the international manager. Whereas some observers see globalization as leading to a more homogeneous world, we view it as a continually changing mosaic whose diverse pieces come in more frequent contact with each other, affecting each and every piece in a unique manner. The role of management is to monitor, understand, and respond to this changing environment with sensitivity and respect for the differences encountered, with a realization that international business decisions influence a great variety of constituencies in multiple locations and, ultimately, the future and quality of life on the planet. This book is a reflection of this philosophy.

CHAPTER SUMMARY

1. Globalization enhances economic interdependence but does not necessarily make nations more similar; it is a complex phenomenon that carries both negative and positive consequences and produces winners and losers.

2. Globalization intensifies the ongoing tension between forces for standardization and consolidation on the one hand, and those pushing for localization and adaptation on the other. This tension represents one of the main challenges of doing business internationally.

3. International business consists of business activities and resources transferred across national boundaries. Firms that have directly invested in at least one foreign market are considered multinational enterprises (MNEs) in this book.

4. International business is more complex and unpredictable than domestic business and often requires different types and a different scale of resources and capabilities.

INDUSTRY BOX

SINOSTONE COMES TO ELBERTON

With 150 outfits turning out 250,000 gravestones every year, Elberton, Georgia, produces more granite monuments than any other place in the United States. Twenty percent of the local inhabitants are engaged in the granite business, carving gravestones from local quarries and from imported colored stone, unavailable locally. With the U.S. population aging and mortality rates on the rise, the industry was expecting robust sales. Then, a new company opened up in town. Unlike its local competitors, Sinostone, owned by China-based Wanli Stone Group, imported finished gravestones from China, offering them at half the going price. Ten-year-old Wanli has already exported its products to Japan and Europe and was now targeting the U.S. market. It decided to locate in Elberton because of the number of buyers who come there every year and the ready transportation to dealers across the United States. Assigned to oversee the new operation was Su Xian, a physician and the wife of a Wanli co-owner.

The local business community was not sure how to react. Some competitors spread the word that Sinostone's products were inferior and that the color on their gravestones would soon fade, an accusation the Chinese company strongly denies. The Elberton Granite Association has organized a "buy America" campaign from which Sinostone has been excluded. Others suggested to Mrs. Su that she should raise her prices. Still other competitors have traveled to Tianjin to look at the Wanli site, which is dedicated to U.S. exports. They noted that the operation, located next door to operations of Boeing and Motorola, was "ten years ahead" compared with other Chinese competitors, some of whom were "thirty years behind" their U.S. counterparts. Sinostone's U.S. competitors have now started to import finished gravestones from China, more than tripling China's exports to the United States in this category in three years.

SOURCE: Adapted from Neil King. "Grave reservations: Why Dr. Su's arrival rocks Georgia town." *Wall Street Journal*, July 23, 2002, A1; "The latest Chinese success story", *Fast Company*, 79, February 2004; "Destroying a community", *Small, Local Community*, 2005; Sinostone web site and publications, 2006.

Chapter Notes

1. United States National Intelligence Council. *The contradictions of globalization*, 2005.

2. A. T. Kearney. "Measuring globalization." *Foreign Policy*. May/June 2005: pp. 52–60.

3. Richard W. Fisher and W. Michael Cox. "Globalizing good government." *New York Times*, April 10, 2006, A25.

4. United Nations Conference on Trade and Development (UNCTAD). World Investment Report, 2000.

5. W. R. Cline, Institute of International Economics. Cited in the *Economist*, September 29, 2001: p. 9.

6. Mona V. Makhija, Kim Kwangsoo, and Sandra D. Williamson. "Measuring globalization of industries using a national industry approach: Empirical evidence across five countries and over time." *Journal of International Business Studies*, 1997, *28*, 4: pp. 679–710.

PART ONE

Concepts and Theories in International Business

INTERNATIONAL TRADE THEORY
AND APPLICATION

DO YOU KNOW?

1. What are the major theories of international trade?

2. How applicable are those theories in today's environment?

3. How do governments limit trade with other countries, and what are their reasons for doing so?

4. How does the level of development influence a country's trade relationships?

5. What is your country's balance of trade with its trade partners, and how might it affect you?

Photo 2.1 Bananas are a major export for many developing nations.

SOURCE: Jupiterimages.

OPENING CASE

The Banana Wars

In April of 1999, the World Trade Organization (WTO) ruled that the European Union (EU) violated international trade law by establishing quotas and tariffs on bananas from Latin America imported by U.S.-based Chiquita Brands International, Dole Foods, and Fresh Del Monte Produce. At the same time, the EU allowed licensed access for bananas from former colonies in Africa, Asia, and the Caribbean. According to the WTO ruling, the arrangement cost the United States $191 million in trade opportunities.

The banana business is hardly lucrative. Retail prices and sales of bananas have been falling for years, margins are narrow, the crop is susceptible to disease, and transportation is tricky. At 800 to 900 euros per ton, European banana prices are double those in the United States, but the growers barely benefit. The Center for International Economics in Canberra, Australia, estimates that only $150 million of the $2 billion this arrangement costs European consumers finds its way to the banana growers. The main beneficiaries are the firms that hold the banana import licenses. Still, bananas represent a major export for many developing nations. In the small Caribbean nation of St. Lucia, bananas bring in 56% of export revenues. Such nations find it difficult to substitute bananas' high output with other crops. Bananas are also labor-intensive, providing a crucial source of employment.

The Latin American nations whose banana exports have been restricted in Europe have been hopeful that the WTO ruling will eventually bear fruit. In 2001, during an all-night session during which a stunned WTO official kept murmuring "they are talking about bananas, they are talking about bananas," the United States and Ecuador reached an agreement with the EU to replace the quota structure with a preferential tariff regime by 2006, thus ending nine years of the Banana War. A 2005 United Nations report concludes that Banana growers in Africa, the Caribbean, and the Pacific will benefit from the shift, although some of the traditional exporters who have been renting quotas are expected to lose. The main losers from the new arrangement are expected to be the current banana distributors, while unexpected beneficiaries will be exporters to the United States—Guatemala and the Philippines—who will benefit from some South American exporters switching exports from the United States to the EU.

SOURCES: G. Fairclough and D. McDermott. "The banana business is rotten, so why do people fight over it?" *Wall Street Journal,* August 9, 1999; N. Dunne. "U.S. lists sanctions over bananas." *Financial Times,* April 10, 1999, p. 4; A. DePalma. "U.S. and Europeans agree on deal to end banana trade war." *New York Times,* April 12, 2001, C1; H. Cooper and G. Winestock. "Tough Talkers." *Wall Street Journal,* November 15, 2001, A1; United Nations Conference on Trade and Development. "Banana split: How EU politics divide global producers." Policy Series Issues #31, 2005.

INTERNATIONAL TRADE THEORIES

International (or foreign) trade is the exchange of goods and services across borders. Bananas, the subject of the opening case, are a major export commodity for some developing African, Caribbean, Pacific, and Latin American countries whose economies are therefore susceptible to international market conditions on bananas and other agricultural commodities. Industrialized countries such as EU members and the United States have markedly different export structures. Their primary exports are technology intensive (e.g., machine tools), knowledge intensive (e.g., software), capital-intensive (e.g., construction machinery and equipment), or a combination of all of the above (e.g., telecom products, pharmaceuticals, airplanes, and motor vehicles). You may wonder why export structures vary across countries, why nations do not mimic each other, and why they have different vulnerabilities to trade conditions and disruptions. The answers can be found in the international trade theories that are described below. Following their introduction, we will comment on the merits and limitations of each theory.

The Mercantilist Doctrine

Emerging in England in the mid-sixteenth century, **mercantilism** is the first (or preclassical) theory of international trade. The doctrine placed great faith in the ability of a government to improve the well-being of its residents using a system of centralized controls. Under mercantilism, the government had two goals in foreign economic policy. The first goal was to increase the wealth of the nation by acquiring gold. Mercantilists identified national wealth with the size of a nation's reserves of precious metals (which could then be used to hire mercenary armies). The second policy goal was to extract trade gains from foreigners through regulations and controls so as to achieve a surplus in the balance of trade through maximizing exports (e.g., subsidies) and minimizing imports (e.g., tariffs and quotas).

In modern economies, however, gold reserves are merely potential claims against real goods on foreigners. In addition, as demonstrated by David Hume in 1752, an influx of gold would increase the domestic price level and boost the price of exports.[1] Hence, the country holding the gold would lose the competitive edge in price that had enabled it to acquire the gold earlier by exporting more than it imported. In contrast, the loss of gold in the foreign nation would reduce prices there and reinforce its exports. Today, gold reserves represent a minor portion of national foreign exchange reserves.

Governments use such reserves to intervene in foreign exchange markets (e.g., selling some of these reserves in exchange for local currencies) to influence foreign exchange rates.

Mercantilism also overlooked other sources of a country's wealth accumulation such as the quantity of its capital, the skill of its workforce, and the strength of other production inputs such as land and natural resources. In Chapter 5 we explain in detail that a country's wealth today is accumulated mainly through superior competitiveness, which is in turn determined not only by the abundance of resources but also by national policies, industrial structure, firm efficiency, and individual productivity.

Absolute Advantage Theory

In his 1776 landmark treatise, *An Inquiry Into the Nature and Causes of the Wealth of Nations,* Adam Smith from the United Kingdom introduced the doctrine of **laissez-faire** to international trade.[2] Laissez-faire means literally "let make freely" or, more generally, "freedom of enterprise and freedom of commerce." Elimination of the ubiquitous regulation was the keystone of 19th-century liberalism. Smith argued that all nations would benefit from unregulated, free trade that would permit individual countries to specialize in goods they were best suited to produce because of natural and acquired advantages. Smith's theory of trade has come to be known as the theory of absolute advantage. This theory states that a nation's imports should consist of goods made more efficiently abroad while exports should consist of goods made more efficiently at home. According to this theory, Caribbean countries should export bananas (which have absolute advantage at home) and import apples from the state of Washington (which have absolute advantage in the United States).

Photo 2.2   Colombia remains a major grower of coffee.

SOURCE: Jupiterimages.

The absolute advantage theory holds that the market would reach an efficient end by itself. Government intervention in the economic life of a nation and in trade relations among nations (e.g., in the form of tariffs) is counterproductive. A nation would benefit from free trade simply because imports would cost less than domestic products it otherwise had to produce. Unlike the mercantilist doctrine that a nation could only gain from trade if the trading partner lost (i.e., zero-sum game), the absolute advantage theory argues that both countries would gain from the efficient allocation of national resources globally.

Exhibit 2.1 provides a simple illustration of how a country gains from free trade. It shows that the United States has an absolute advantage in producing wheat, whereas Colombia has an absolute advantage in producing coffee. It takes two labor hours to produce a unit of wheat in the United States, whereas it takes 10 hours to produce a unit of wheat in Colombia. Therefore, the United States should specialize in the production of wheat. Similarly it takes eight hours to produce a unit of coffee in the United States and two hours to produce a unit of coffee in Colombia. Therefore, Colombia should specialize in the production of coffee. Smith argued that in a situation such as this, both countries benefit from specialization and trade. World production would increase if both countries specialized in the production of the good in which they have an absolute advantage and then traded to obtain the other goods in which they have an absolute disadvantage.

Exhibit 2.1   Labor Hours Required to Produce One Unit of a Good

	Wheat (1 Unit)	Coffee (1 Unit)
United States	2	8
Colombia	10	2

Comparative Advantage Theory

The absolute advantage theory could not explain a situation in which, for example, one country is more efficient than another in producing *all* goods. Would it still pay for both countries to trade if one country were more efficient than the other in the production of all goods? David Ricardo, a 19th-century English economist, answered this question in his 1817 landmark book, *On the Principles of Political Economy and Taxation*. He stated that both countries would gain from trade even if one were more efficient in all goods.[3] Thus, it was the **comparative advantage** of a nation in producing a good relative to the other nation that determined international trade flows. To illustrate this, Ricardo used the example in Exhibit 2.2. In England a gallon of wine costs 120 and a yard of cloth 100 hours of work, while in Portugal the real cost (labor cost) of wine and cloth amounts to 80 and 90 hours of work, respectively. Portugal thus has an absolute advantage over England in the production of wine as well as in the production of cloth, because the labor cost of production for each unit of the two commodities is less in Portugal than in England.

To demonstrate that trade between England and Portugal will, even in this case, lead to gains for both countries, it is useful to introduce the concept of **opportunity cost.** The opportunity cost for a good X is the amount of other goods which have to be given up to produce one unit of X. Exhibit 2.3 shows the opportunity costs for producing wine and cloth in Portugal and England, based on the information given in Exhibit 2.2.

Exhibit 2.2   Labor Hours Required to Produce One Unit of a Good

	Wine (1 Gallon)	Cloth (1 Yard)
England	120	100
Portugal	80	90

A country has a comparative advantage in producing a good if the opportunity cost for producing the good is lower at home than in the other country. Exhibit 2.3 shows that Portugal has the lower opportunity cost of the two countries in producing wine, while England has the lower opportunity cost in producing cloth. Thus Portugal has a comparative advantage in the production of wine and England has a comparative advantage in the production of cloth. Once trade between the two countries is launched, England will export cloth and import wine. As long as the opportunity costs for the same commodities differ between countries, open trade will result in gains for each country through specialization in producing a commodity (or commodities) in which a country has comparative advantage vis-à-vis its trading partner(s).

Exhibit 2.3   Opportunity Costs for Producing Wine and Cloth

	Opportunity Cost for Wine	Opportunity Cost for Cloth
England	120/100 = 12/10	100/120 = 10/12
Portugal	80/90 = 8/9	90/80 = 9/8

It is important to understand the *sources* of comparative advantage. The immediate source of trade is a difference in the price of the same commodity between different countries, thus the difference in opportunity costs. But why does such a difference arise? Price is essentially determined by the interaction of supply and demand. Therefore, a price differential derives from differences in demand conditions, supply conditions, or both. On the demand side, differences in tastes and incomes will cause differences in patterns of demand and, hence, prices. When two countries share similar income levels and consumer tastes, however, income is unlikely to be a major source of demand differences. Similarly, differences in tastes are unlikely to account for significant demand differences—and thus for trade—between countries belonging to the same social–cultural matrix. On the supply side, we know that differences in supply patterns result from differences in the patterns of production costs.

Thus, in today's world economy, comparative advantage must be explained by reference to differences in **comparative production cost**, which further depend on the commodity's production process (especially the state of technology) and on the prices of **production factors** such as labor, land, capital, and natural resources. Factor prices, in turn, are related to the availability of those factors in the national economy. Economists refer to inputs to the production process as production factors. They then refer to conditions (availability and cost) of factors of production as the country's factor endowment. In today's global economy, quality levels of production factors (e.g., knowledge and productivity of workers or service and efficiency of a banking sector) become even more important for improving a country's exports or attracting foreign investments. In today's international business environment, therefore, factor endowment should also include the quality of production factors. However, because intercountry differences in technology were relatively minor in the 19th century, international variations in comparative advantage were attributed primarily to different national endowments in terms of availability and cost. This was the theoretical root of the **Heckscher-Ohlin theorem.**

Heckscher-Ohlin Theorem

The Heckscher-Ohlin (or H-O) theorem is named for its authors, Eli Heckscher and Bertil Ohlin, both Swedish economists. It explains the link between national factor endowments and comparative advantages of nations.[4] The theorem states that a country has a comparative advantage in commodities whose production is intensive in its relatively abundant factor and will hence export those commodities. Meanwhile, a country would import commodities whose production is intensive in the country's relatively scarce factor of production. Thus, differences in comparative advantage are attributed to the differences in the structure of the economy. A country is relatively more efficient in those activities that are better suited to its economic structure and does best with what it has most of. If, for example, the United States is more abundant in capital relative to labor than other countries, it will export such commodities (e.g., motor vehicles) whose production requires a greater use of capital than other products do and will import labor-intensive commodities (e.g., clothing).[5]

Several assumptions underlie the Heckscher-Ohlin theorem. First, it is assumed that countries vary in the availability of various factors of production. Second, while each commodity is assumed to have its own specific production function, the production function is assumed to be identical anywhere in the world. **Production function** shows the amount of output that can be produced by using a given quantity of capital and labor. In other words, this theorem assumes that the same amount of the same input will produce the same output in any country. Third, the theorem holds that technology is constant in all trading countries and that the same technology is used in all those countries. Finally, it assumes that the conditions of demand for production factors are the same in all countries. With identical demand conditions, differences in the relative supply of a factor of production will lead to differences in the relative price of that factor between the two countries.

The H-O theorem also implies international equalization of the prices of production factors under free trade—the so-called **Heckscher-Ohlin law of factor price equalization.** It argues that the exchange of goods between agricultural and industrial countries would result in an increase in the previously relatively low levels of land rents and a drop in the high level of industrial wages in the agricultural country. In the industrial country, however, the opposite change in factor prices occurs—an increase in industrial wages and a decrease in land rents. In addition to identical production factors across different countries, the theorem assumes other conditions under which free commodity trade equalizes factor prices: (a) free competition obtains in all markets, (b) transportation costs are absent, and (c) all commodities continue to be produced in both countries after free trade has begun.

The implications of the H-O theorem for world trade are highlighted below:

1. Trade as well as trade gains should be greatest between countries with the greatest differences in economic structure.

2. Trade should cause countries to specialize more in producing and exporting goods that are distinctly different from their imports.

3. Trade policy should take the form of trade restrictions rather than trade stimulation.

4. Countries should export goods that make intensive use of their relatively abundant factors.

5. Free trade should equalize factor prices between countries with fairly similar relative factor endowments but not between countries with markedly different endowments.

6. Factor prices should be nearly equal between countries with more liberal mutual trade.

7. International investment should be stimulated by differences in factor endowments, and international trade and international investment should be negatively correlated.

The Leontief Paradox

The central notion of the H-O theorem is that a country exports goods that make intensive use of the country's abundant factor and imports goods that make intensive use of the country's scarce factor. Wassily Leontief, the 1973 winner of the Nobel Prize in Economics, attempted in 1953 to test this proposition for the United States. Using input–output tables covering 200 industries and 1947 trade figures, he found that U.S. exports were apparently labor-intensive and its imports capital-intensive. Since this result contradicted the predictions of the H-O theorem, it has become known as the **Leontief paradox.** The Leontief study motivated further empirical research. The empirical evidence accumulated since then shows many paradoxical results and contains serious challenges to the general applicability of a factor-endowments explanation in other countries, such as Germany, India, Canada, and Japan.

Exhibit 2.4 shows the principal findings of Leontief's 1953 study. Since the ratio of imports to exports in terms of capital per worker-year (18,184/14,015) was about 1.30, U.S. exports were less capital-intensive (or more labor-intensive) Leontief showed that, instead of capital-intensive exports and labor-intensive import replacements, than U.S. import replacements, a representative bundle of U.S. import replacements required 30% more capital per worker-year to produce than a representative bundle of U.S. exports.

Exhibit 2.4   Capital Position in U.S. Exports and Imports

	Exports	*Import Replacements*
Capital (in 1947 $)	2,550,780	3,091,339
Labor (worker-years)	182	170
Capital per worker-year ($)	14,015	18,184

SOURCE: W. Leontief. "Domestic production and foreign trade: The American capital position reexamined." *Proceedings of the American Philosophical Society,* 97 (Nov. 1953): pp. 332–349.

The Leontief paradox stimulated a search for explanations, among them the following:[6]

- *Demand bias for capital-intensive goods.* The U.S. demand for capital-intensive goods is so strong that it reverses the U.S. comparative cost advantage in such goods.
- *Existence of trade barriers.* U.S. labor-intensive imports were reduced by trade barriers (e.g., tariffs and quotas) imposed to protect and save American jobs.
- *Importance of natural resources.* Leontief considered only capital and labor inputs, leaving out natural resource inputs. Because natural resources and capital are often used together in production, a country that imports capital-intensive goods may be actually importing natural resource-intensive

goods. For example, the United States imports crude oil, which is capital-intensive.

- *Prevalence of factor-intensity reversals.* A **factor-intensity reversal** occurs when the relative prices of labor and capital change over time, which changes the relative mix of capital and labor in the production process of a commodity from being capital-intensive to labor-intensive (or vice versa).

Human Skills and Technology-Based Views

The aforementioned explanations were subsequently found to have offered only a partial explanation of the Leontief paradox.[7] Searching for better explanations of the sources of comparative advantage, several scholars challenged the conventional theory of trade that assumed technology–human skills equivalence among different nations.[8] Rather than a separate theory, the human skills and technology-based view is regarded as a refinement of the conventional theory of trade. It added two new factors of production, namely **human skills** and **technology gaps**, to the explanation of comparative advantage sources.

Human skill theorists explained the source of comparative advantage in terms of the comparative abundance of professional skills and other high-level human skills. According to Donald B. Keesing, these include (a) scientists and engineers, (b) technicians and draftsmen, (c) managers, (d) other professionals, and (e) skilled manual workers. Keesing argued that U.S. export industries employ higher proportions of highly skilled labor than do import-competing industries. Thus, the United States exports more skill-intensive manufactures than do other countries. Studies treating professional and skilled human resources as capital reversed the Leontief paradox and found that U.S. exports were actually capital-intensive.[9] The relative abundance of professional and other highly skilled labor in the United States is thus a major source of its comparative advantage in manufacturing products.

Technology theorists argued that certain countries have special advantage as innovators of new products. They also postulated that there was an **imitation lag** that prevents other countries from immediately duplicating the new products of the innovating country. These two conditions gave rise to technology gaps in those products that afford the innovating country an export monopoly during the period of imitation lag.[10] In other words, for the duration of the imitation gap, the innovator is the only exporter on world markets. Similarly, when a firm discovers a different and more advanced production technique, it will enjoy a cost advantage and dominate the world market for a while (especially if its innovation is legally protected from imitators by the international patent system). For example, it was found that transportation, electrical machinery, instruments, chemicals, and nonelectrical machinery were the five strongest industries in the United States in terms of R&D, which performed 89.4% of U.S. total R&D, in 1962. These five industries accounted for 72% of U.S. exports of manufactures in the same year.[11] As long as technological progress is made, the technology gap would serve as a major source of comparative advantage. As such, technology, like human skills, is a separate factor of production whose relative abundance or scarcity in a country determines comparative advantage or disadvantage in technology-intensive products. This notion, despite being more than four decades old, still has strong implications for country competitiveness (as discussed in Chapter 5), competitive advantage of multinational enterprises (MNEs) (Chapter 4), and global R&D management (Chapter 13).

The Product Life-Cycle Model

Closely related to the technology gap view is the **product life-cycle model**, proposed by Raymond Vernon in the mid-1960s.[12] Vernon's theory further developed the imitation-gap approach by suggesting that changes occur in the input requirements of a new product as it becomes established in a market and standardized in production. As the product cycle develops, the cost advantage will change accordingly, and a comparative advantage in innovative capacity may be offset by a cost disadvantage. To explain the behavior of U.S. exports of manufactures, Vernon developed a four-stage model assuming that the export effects of product innovation are undermined by technological diffusion and lower costs abroad. This life-cycle model includes the following four stages:

1. The United States has an export monopoly in a new product.

2. Foreign production of this product begins.

3. Foreign production of this product becomes competitive in export markets.

4. The United States becomes an importer of this no-longer-new product.

Vernon postulated that U.S. producers are likely to be the first to exploit market opportunities for a technology-intensive new product. They will first produce this new product in the United States regardless of the costs of production inputs in other countries because of close proximity to customers and suppliers. In this first stage, U.S. producers have a monopoly in export markets, and they proceed to build up sales with no concern for foreign competition. During the second stage, producers in other industrial countries start to manufacture the product, whose design and production is now standardized. Consequently, the overall growth rate of U.S. exports declines. During the third stage, foreign producers displace U.S. exports in the remaining export markets. Finally, foreign producers achieve sufficient competitive strength arising from economies of scale and lower labor costs to export to the U.S. market.

Exhibit 2.5 graphically presents the product cycle model of international trade for the innovating country (e.g., the United States) and an imitating country (e.g., Germany or Mexico), respectively. As Exhibit 2.5 shows, the innovating country starts production of the new product at time 0, but it does not export that product until time A, when production exceeds domestic consumption. At time B, foreign production begins to compete against the innovating country's exports which, in turn, begin to fall. Exports come to an end at time C as the innovating country becomes an importer of this no-longer-new product.

Exhibit 2.6 shows that an imitating country starts to import the new product from the innovating country at time A'. If this imitating country is a high-income, advanced country (e.g., Germany), then time A' most likely coincides with time A in Exhibit 2.5. If, however, it is a low-income, developing country (e.g., Mexico), then time A' will come after time A. Local production begins at time B' when the local market grows to sufficient size and cost conditions favor production against imports. If the imitating country is an advanced country, then B' will coincide with B in Exhibit 2.5. If it is a developing country, B' will come after time B. At time C', when production begins to exceed consumption, the imitating country begins to export and may export first to third countries and later to the innovating country.

Vernon's theory also suggests that the product cycle model of international trade is associated with the life-cycle stage of the product itself. As the product

Exhibit 2.5   Product Cycle Model of International Trade—Innovating Country

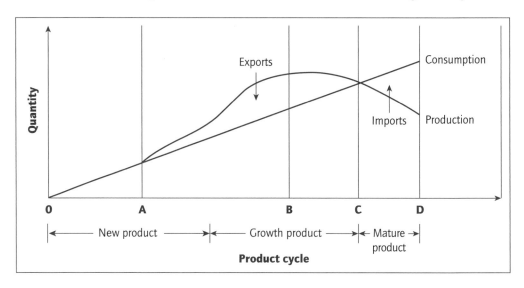

Exhibit 2.6   Product Cycle Model of International Trade—Imitating Country

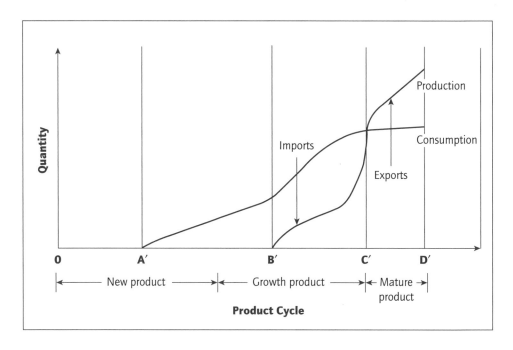

moves through its life cycle, the life cycle of international trade will change. The *new-product stage* is associated with the first production of the product in the innovating country (0–A) and the early portion of the export monopoly stage (A–B). During this stage, production functions are unstable and techniques used in production are rapidly changing. No economy of scale is reached. This phase is also characterized by a small number of firms and no close substitute products. The *growth-product stage* is associated with the later portion of the export monopoly (A–B) and the start of foreign production (C). During this stage, mass-production methods are used to exploit expanding markets, and therefore high returns are achieved from economy of scale and market growth. Finally, the *mature-product stage* is associated with the third and fourth stages of the product cycle model of international trade (C–D). This last stage is characterized by production of standardized products with stable techniques and intense price competition.

The product life-cycle theory helps to explain changes in production and trade in new product lines. It is generally true that the United States has been the principal innovator and production has spread rapidly to other countries that have been technically competent (e.g., Germany) and to those which have had a comparative advantage in terms of cheap labor (e.g., Mexico). It is also useful to remember that since the development of the model in the 1960s, the share of the United States in global GDP has declined substantially, with other countries, such as Germany and Japan, emerging as innovators. Also, some countries (e.g., the United Kingdom) were innovators of major products, such as the passenger jet, but failed to dominate the market for those products.

Several facts emerged in connection with product cycles:

1. The export performance of the mature, principal innovating country is better for new products than it is for products approaching maturity.

2. Technology is simplified as the maturing process continues, and products that are initially produced with skilled labor can later be produced by an increased use of automation combined with the use of unskilled labor.

3. The relationship between innovating and imitating countries changes over time. Countries that were once the principal innovators might fall into relative decline. Britain, for example, was the first country to build railways, at the time with a narrow gauge and small-goods wagons. Later, this investment proved to be a drag on progress, and subsequent imitators like Germany and the United States adapted their railways more successfully to new technological and economic conditions.

4. International trade may increase in the later stages of the product cycle. As a consumer good matures and income rises, products once seen as luxurles (e.g., cell phones) become necessities. General growth of per capita incomes broadens the market for mass production.

Linder's Income-Preference Similarity Theory

When you observe the actual pattern of international trade since the 1970s (described in the second part of this chapter), you will find a prominent feature: Developed countries trade more with other developed countries. Overall, developed countries among themselves generate about three-fourths of total world exports. This fact, by itself, is an indictment of Heckscher-Ohlin's factor-endowment theory. According to the H-O theorem, the incentive to trade is greatest among nations of radically different factor endowments. This means that trade would take place in larger part between developed manufacturing countries and developing countries producing primary products (e.g., natural resource commodities such as oil and petroleum) and labor-intensive goods.

Staffan B. Linder, a Swedish economist, divided international trade into two different categories: primary products (natural resource products) and manufactures.[13] Linder asserts that differences in factor endowments explain trade in natural resource–intensive products but not in manufactures. He argues that the range of a country's manufactured exports is determined by *internal demand*. International trade in manufactures takes place largely among developed nations because nations will only export those goods they manufacture at home and will only manufacture at home those goods for which there is a strong domestic demand. Note, however, that Chapter 4 on the MNE will introduce "born national" enterprises, whose very first products are destined for foreign markets.

Linder also contends that the more similar the demand preferences for manufactured goods in two countries (e.g., the United States and the United Kingdom), the more intensive is the potential trade in manufactures between them. If two countries have the same or similar demand structures, then their consumers and investors will demand the same goods with similar degrees of quality and sophistication, a phenomenon known as **preference similarity.** This similarity boosts trade between the two industrialized countries. To explain the determinants of the demand structure, Linder argues that average per capita income is the most important one. Countries with high per capita income will demand high-quality "luxury" consumer goods (e.g., motor vehicles) and sophisticated capital goods (e.g., telecommunications equipment and machinery), while low per capita income countries will demand low-quality "necessity" consumer goods (e.g., bicycles) and less sophisticated capital goods (e.g., food-processing machinery). Consequently, a rich country that has a comparative advantage in the production of high-quality, advanced manufactures will find its big export markets in other affluent countries where people demand such products. Similarly, manufactured exports of the poor countries should find their best markets in other poor countries with similar demand structures. Linder also acknowledged that the effect of per capita income levels on trade in manufactures may be constrained or distorted by entrepreneurial ignorance, cultural and political differences, transportation costs, and legislative obstacles such as tariffs.

INDUSTRY BOX

THE GLOBAL AUTOMOTIVE INDUSTRY

Global trade in the automotive industry is a century old. Almost as soon as the first products appeared, some of the manufacturers (e.g., the Ford Motor Company) began to export their cars. Today, the major exporters of automotive products are also the major importers (e.g., the United States, the European Union, Canada, Mexico, China), supporting Linder's income-preference similarity theory (see table on p. 31).

The largest volume of trade in automotive products involves trade among the countries of the European Union. The numbers are not necessarily balanced, however. For example, as noted earlier in this chapter, Japan exports to (and manufactures in) many more cars in the United States than the United States exports to and manufactures in Japan, suggesting the impact of other, nontariff barriers.

Although Mexico's increasing role as a car exporter seems to challenge the view of developed nations exporting to other developed nations, it is in line with the new trade theory, which suggests that intra-industry trade is driven mainly by increasing returns resulting from specialization within the industry. Mexican car exports to the United States contain a substantial content of components imported from the United States. The result, according to Lucinda Vargas of the Federal Reserve Bank of Dallas, is that "in some respects, each country is sending the other essentially the same product but at a different stage of production." China, which also imports sophisticated vehicle components, is currently a minor exporter of motor vehicles, but this is likely to change dramatically as the country's producers (many of them Foreign Invested Enterprises) rapidly enhance their capabilities.

	Exports				Imports		
	Value		Share		Value		Share
	1990 ($Mil)	2000 ($Mil)	2000		1990 ($Mil)	2000 ($Mil)	2000
world	31890	571320	9.2	Argentina	183	–	12.0
Argentina	200	–	7.7	Austria	5521	7745	11.3
Austria	3526	7789	12.2	Belgium-Luxembourg	18481	–	13.9
Belgium-Luxembourg	18046	–	14.2	Brazil	532	4314	7.4
Brazil	2034	4682	8.5	Canada	24640	46276	19.3
Canada	28442	60656	21.9	Finland	2595	2373	7.0
Finland	797	1257	2.8	France	21595	30532	10.0
France	26194	39885	13.4	Germany	30856	42241	8.4
Germany	69955	92167	16.7	Hungary	715	2481	7.7
Hungary	648	4765	17.0	Italy	18090	25314	10.9
Italy	13017	18363	7.7	Japan	7315	9957	2.6
Japan	66230	88082	18.4	Korea, Rep. of	929	–	1.2
Korea, Rep. of	2301	15368	8.9	Mexico	5268	18816	10.3
Mexico	4708	30645	18.4	Netherlands	8244	12606	6.4
Netherlands	4673	8655	4.1	Spain	10133	26308	17.1
Spain	11729	18127	24.7	Sweden	4585	7565	10.4
Sweden	7719	10771	12.4	Turkey	1177	5831	10.8
Turkey	153	1517	5.7	United Kingdom	22821	36078	10.9
United Kingdom	14087	25557	9.0	United States	79320	172727	13.7
United States	32547	67901	8.7				

SOURCES: WTO International Trade Statistics, 2005 (pp.165–167); "This trade deficit was made in the USA." *Wall Street Journal*, August 7, 2000, A1.

The New Trade Theory

The set of ideas sometimes referred to as the **new trade theory** was originally expounded in a series of papers by Dixit and Norman, Lancaster, Krugman, Helpman, and Ethier.[14] These theorists argue that countries do not necessarily specialize and trade solely to take advantage of their differences; they also trade because of *increasing returns,* which makes specialization advantageous per se. Although this theory is not totally "new," it makes several contributions to the understanding of international trade.

First, the new trade theorists introduce an industrial organization view into trade theory and include real-life imperfect competition in international trade. They argue that because of economies of scale, there are increasing returns to specialization in many industries. **Economy of scale** is reduction of manufacturing cost per unit as a result of increased production quantity during a given time period. For instance, manufacturing the 100,000th car is much cheaper than making the first. Because of the presence of substantial scale economies, world demand will actually support only a few firms in an industry (e.g., only Boeing and Airbus remain as makers of large passenger jets).

Second, the new trade theory suggests that *interindustry trade* (international trade between different industries in different nations) continues to be determined by factors of the Heckscher-Ohlin theory. In contrast, *intra-industry trade* (international trade involving the same industry) is largely driven by increasing returns resulting from specialization within the industry. This suggests that comparative advantage from factor endowment differences and increasing returns from economies of scale can coexist because they differ in the application of inter- versus intra-industry trade.

Finally, the new trade theory realizes the importance of externality in international specialization and trade. **Externality** occurs when the actions of one agent directly affect the environment of another agent. For example, firms that cause pollution or noise would have an adverse impact on local residents. In international trade, externalities include government policies, political relations between two countries, history of the importing or exporting country, consumption differences between different cultures, accident, and luck (e.g., first entrant of the industry), among others. The new trade theorists contend that these externalities could be the alternatives to comparative advantage as the factors influencing actual patterns of international trade.

The new trade theory has a number of implications. First, it helps explain the Leontief paradox by bringing in the economies-of-scale concept. The theory argues that firms engage in trade because they expect increasing returns from larger economies of scale; such economies may not necessarily be associated with factor endowment differences between importing and exporting countries. Scale economies will likely lead countries to specialize and trade with a similar country in terms of income level or consumption preference. Second, this theory helps explain intra-industry trade, which is a substantial two-way trade (i.e., import and export) that takes place with goods that belong to the same industry. Trade is intended to realize economies of scale and may not be correlated with differences in factor endowments. Finally, this theory helps explain intrafirm trade, which occurs when import and export activities take place between the subsidiaries of the same MNE. Driven by the prospect of increasing returns, MNEs see intrafirm trade as a facilitator of global integration of upstream and downstream activities. Chapter 4 discusses the MNE in more detail.

Theory Assessment

Although none of the theories is capable of explaining the entire range of motives for international trade, they collectively provide invaluable insights into why international trade occurs. With reference to the sources of comparative advantage, differences in factor endowments (i.e., the Heckscher-Ohlin theorem) survive as the most general explanation of the pattern of "old" trade (e.g., labor-intensive products). The comparative advantage theory, despite its diminishing power in explaining today's international trade, is still capable of explaining international trade in natural resource products such as bananas (see Opening Case). When we extend the factor endowments by including skilled labor and technologies, the Heckscher-Ohlin theorem applies to current import and export activities between developed and developing countries. As an example, let us look at trade between Europe and Southeast Asia. Major exports from Europe are technology intensive, including power-generation equipment, petroleum-processing machinery, medical equipment, and transportation equipment, whereas exports from Southeast Asia are mostly labor- or skilled-labor-intensive, such as garments, furniture, shoes, rubber products, arts and crafts, and standardized electric and electronics products.

Meanwhile, the technological gap (i.e., human skills and technology-based views) and the product life-cycle theories emerge as powerful explanations of trade in "new" products (i.e., manufactures made by a skilled workforce using technologies). These skills and technologies are the key stimuli to improving a country's terms of trade, the major concern of both developed and developing countries today. The **terms of trade** are the relative prices of exports—that is, the unit price of exports divided by the unit price of imports. The terms of trade improve if the country exports more goods that are associated with advanced human skills and technologies. In this case, the contribution of foreign trade to the nation's economic growth will be stronger. Although the product life-cycle model is less applicable today than at the time of its inception, it still explains key patterns in the evolution of international trade. A nation's import and export structures change over time. Similarly, every new product has its life stages in the global marketplace.

The Leontief paradox and Linder's income-preference similarity theory provide insights into the triggers of international trade for sophisticated manufacturing products and trade between regions with similar income levels and consumption preferences. These theories view market demand (income levels and demand structure) as important parameters of international trade. Indeed, international trade today is driven not only by national differences in factor endowments but also by national differences in market demand. Intraregional trade still accounts for a high proportion of world trade because of similarities in income levels and demand structures as well as efficiencies arising from reduced uncertainty and transaction costs. The limitation of these theories is that they did not illuminate how trade activities would take place between two nations sharing similar income levels but with different consumption preferences. Because of this weakness, they seem unable to explain the increasing trade between developed countries and newly industrialized (e.g., Singapore, South Korea, Taiwan, and Hong Kong) or emerging (e.g., China, Brazil, India, Russia, and Mexico) markets. These countries are not in the same region, nor do they share similar consumption preferences with the Western world. Increasing income and elevated purchasing power seem to be the key drivers of this trade phenomenon.

Finally, the new trade theory enriches our understanding of intra-industry and intrafirm trade. It links national factor endowments with firm behavior and firm incentives in explaining international trade. As Chapter 4 shows, this link is important because firms rather than countries conduct international trade and investment. The efficiency of international trade is maximized if both national factor endowment differences and economies-of-scale advantages of firms are combined and realized simultaneously. Since the MNE's role in international trade and investment is highly visible, the new trade theory has attracted more attention in recent years. The limitation of this theory, however, is that it overlooks other incentives beyond increasing returns from economies of scale. MNEs seek geographical diversification and accumulate knowledge about the target market from international trade. Chapter 4 articulates these issues in more detail.

Can we expect new theoretical developments concerning international trade in the future? We believe so. As the following sections of this chapter demonstrate, patterns and characteristics of today's international trade are quite different from those of trade activities in the last century and even those of two decades ago, a period when the last trade theory emerged. The most important thrust for a new line of theoretical development will be a shift from the analysis of country comparative advantages to the assessment of country capabilities (or competitiveness). Factor endowment conditions (including human resources, technology, and information) are a critical aspect of country competitiveness, and factor endowment differences between two nations remain an important foundation for international trade. However, other aspects of country capabilities also shape international trade. For example, an importing country's macroeconomic soundness, demand conditions, local competition, government policies, support of related industries (e.g., banking service and foreign exchange hedging systems) as well as culture are expected to affect trade activities. At the same time, an exporting country's infrastructure, business rivalry, openness, and innovation are important factors influencing the volume of, and gains from, export activities. Chapter 5 focuses on country competitiveness. A nation generally gains more from international trade if its competitiveness in the world market is higher than that of other countries. Japan, for instance, is not rich in terms of factor endowments, but its competitiveness in innovation, adaptability, and business management made it a major player in international trade.

Interim Summary

1. Many theorists have created models to show the reasons, rationales, gains, or complexities of international trade. Some older theories such as the mercantilist doctrine and the absolute advantage theory, while accurate for their time, are inaccurate in today's world, owing to drastic changes in technological diffusion, information exchange, and capital flow, as well as the enhanced role of MNEs.

2. The Heckscher-Ohlin theorem, the most general explanation of the "old" trade, is not entirely obsolete. By integrating advanced technology and a skilled workforce into systems of comparative advantage between countries, modern international trade can be modeled relatively accurately by the theorem.

3. When a new technology is created, the innovating country enjoys a trade advantage until the imitation gap is closed

4. The new trade theory explains intra-industry and intrafirm trade. Theories of international trade must be continually revised as new technology, and new political and economic realities, create a different global climate.

INTERNATIONAL TRADE PATTERNS

International Trade Volume and Growth

International trade continues to grow briskly, outpacing the growth in economic output. In 2004, global merchandise exports reached $8.9 trillion, boosted by both volume and price changes. Global exports of commercial services reached $2 trillion in 2004.[15] Between 2000 and 2004, both global merchandise and commercial services exports rose at an average annual rate of about 9%. From a historical perspective, however, it is useful to recall the late 19th century, when rapid trade growth was reversed by high tariff regimes raised in the name of domestic interests, in particular employment. This is a reminder of how trade is intertwined with other realities, such as domestic and global political interests, which will be explored later in this book.

Exhibit 2.7 shows the growth in international merchandise trade in 2004. The exhibit shows that the increase in merchandise trade has been more pronounced in manufacturing (especially exports of scientific and controlling instruments) than in agricultural products, a pattern partially explained by trade barriers discussed later in this chapter. Before 2000, world trade in manufacturing products had outgrown trade in mining products. This, however, has changed since then. The sharp rise in global demand for many primary commodities, including iron and steel, fuels, and other mining products, has resulted in tight markets and substantial price increases. While overall trade has been growing steadily, there has been, over time, a considerable change in the share of various world regions (see Exhibit 2.8). In exports, the Americas went from about half of the total in 1948 to less than one quarter in 2000, while Africa lost more than two-thirds of its already small share. In contrast, Asia and Western Europe increased their global share. In imports, Asia dramatically increased its intake while other regions had either small gains (North America) or substantial declines (Latin America). A noteworthy feature in recent years is that the two most populous countries in the world—China and India—recorded outstanding economic growth (9.5% and 7.3%, respectively, in 2004, and higher since then) and trade expansion. For many commodities, China has become the largest importer and for a number of manufactured goods, the largest supplier in the world.

Exhibit 2.7   World Merchandise Trade by Major Product Group, 2004

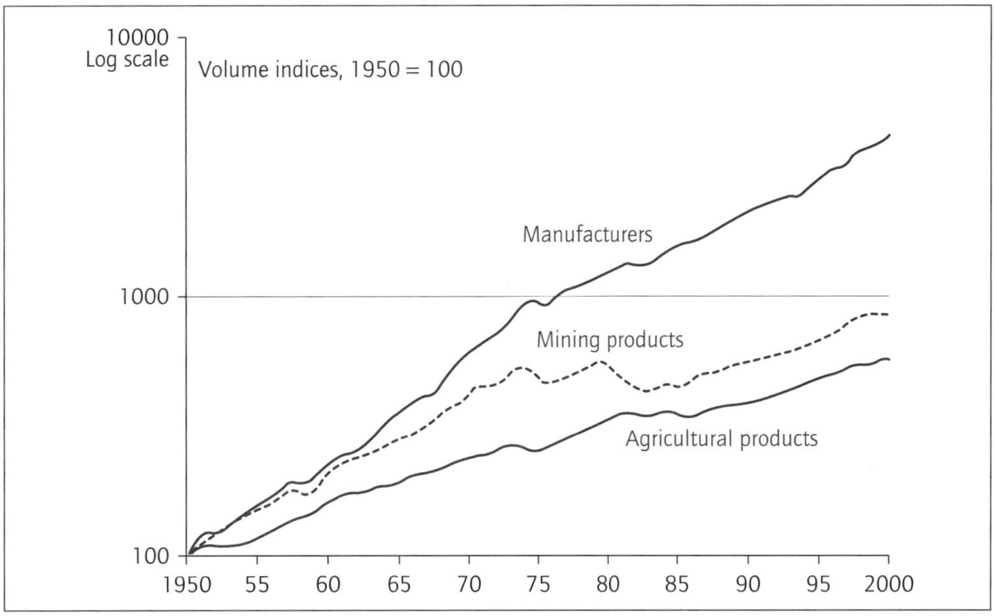

SOURCE: WTO International Trade Statistics, 2005, p. 4. Reprinted with permission by WTO Publications.

Service Trade

Trade in services currently accounts for about one-quarter of global trade, but as developed countries move toward service-based economies, its share is rapidly growing. **Service trade** encompasses the import and export of transportation services, travel, and other commercial services such as financial services, information services, the provision of education and training, health care, consulting and advisory services, and so on. Because of their advantage in services, developed countries tend to push much more aggressively for a removal of barriers to trade in services. In 2004, exports of transportation services, travel services, and other commercial services reached $500 billion, $626 billion, and $1 trillion, respectively. While developed countries, such as those of the European Union and the United States, enjoy their competitive advantages in exporting financial services, insurance services, computer and information services, education, and training and advisory services, some emerging economies, notably India and China, are establishing their competitive edge in exporting communications services (e.g., call centers) and technical support services.

Exhibit 2.8   World Merchandise Trade by Region and Selected Economy, 1953, 1963, 1973, 1983, 1993, and 2003

	1953	1963	1973	1983	1993	2003
	Export Value (US$ Billions)					
World	84.0	157.0	579.0	1838.0	3670.0	7342.0
	Share (%)					
World	100.0	100.0	100.0	100.0	100.0	100.0
North America	24.9	19.9	17.3	16.8	18.0	15.8
United States	18.8	14.9	12.3	11.2	12.7	9.9
South and Central America	9.8	6.3	4.3	4.4	3.0	2.9
Brazil	1.8	0.9	1.1	1.2	1.1	1.0
Argentina	1.3	0.9	0.6	0.4	0.4	0.4
Europe	34.9	41.4	45.4	38.9	43.5	46.1
CIS*	–	–	–	–	1.5	2.7
Africa	6.5	5.7	4.8	4.5	2.5	2.4
South Africa	1.7	1.5	1.0	1.0	0.7	0.5
Middle East	2.7	3.2	4.1	6.8	3.4	4.1
Asia	13.1	12.4	14.9	19.1	26.3	26.1
China	1.2	1.3	1.0	1.2	2.5	6.0
Japan	1.5	3.5	6.4	8.0	9.9	6.4
India	1.3	1.0	0.5	0.5	0.6	0.8
Australia and New Zealand	3.2	2.4	2.1	1.4	1.5	1.2
Six East Asian traders	2.7	2.4	3.4	5.8	9.7	9.4
GATT/WTO members	68.7	72.8	81.8	76.0	86.9	94.3
	Import Value(US$ Billions)					
World	84.0	163.0	589.0	1881.0	3768.0	7623.0
	Share (%)					
World	100.0	100.0	100.0	100.0	100.0	100.0
North America	20.7	16.2	17.3	18.5	21.5	22.7
United States	13.9	11.4	12.3	14.3	16.0	17.1
South and Central America	8.3	6.0	4.4	3.8	3.3	2.5
Brazil	1.6	0.9	1.2	0.9	0.7	0.7
Argentina	0.9	0.6	0.4	0.2	0.4	0.2
Europe	39.4	45.4	47.4	44.2	44.8	45.4
CIS	–	–	–	–	1.2	1.7
Africa	7.0	5.5	4.0	4.6	2.6	2.2
South Africa	1.5	1.1	0.9	0.8	0.5	0.5
Middle East	2.0	2.3	2.8	6.2	3.3	2.6
Asia	15.1	14.2	15.1	18.5	23.3	23.0
China	1.7	0.9	0.9	1.1	2.8	5.4
Japan	2.9	4.1	6.5	6.7	6.4	5.0
India	1.4	1.5	0.5	0.7	0.6	0.9
Australia and New Zealand	2.4	2.3	1.6	1.4	1.5	1.4
Six East Asian traders	3.4	3.1	3.7	6.1	9.9	8.1
GATT/WTO members	66.0	74.2	89.1	83.9	88.7	96.1

SOURCE: WTO International Trade Statistics, 2005, p. 32. Reprinted with permission by WTO Publications.

* Commonwealth of Independent States. Figures are significantly affected by changes in the country composition of the region and major adjustment in trade conversion factors between 1983 and 1993.

Exhibit 2.9 shows U.S. service exports and imports for 2000 and 2004. For 2004, U.S. service exports exceeded imports by more than US$58 billion. Service exports were mainly contributed by travel, transportation, royalties and license fees, and financial services. Imports were divided roughly equally between transportation, travel, and other services.

Trade Measurement

The United States has systematically recorded its imports and exports since 1821. Since 1989, it has used a harmonized system for classifying trade that facilitates comparability of data with the country's major trade partners. With the exception of Canada (where the United States is substituting Canadian import figures for U.S. exports), export data are compiled from Shipper's Export Declarations filed by exporters, forwarders, and carriers. Import data are compiled from U.S. customs forms. Trade data are used not only by governments but also by firms and research institutions to gauge such measures as market penetration and share.

While most trade statistics in this chapter appear in the aggregate, it is useful to remember that they are available for different categories—for example, domestic exports (produced or materially transformed in the United States) as opposed to reexports (commodities of foreign origin that have not been materially changed in the United States); or foreign imports (of foreign origin or those returned to the United States in their original form) as opposed to American

---

Exhibit 2.9   Trade in Commercial Services of the United States, 2004

	Exports			Imports		
	Value (US$ Billions)	Share (%)		Value (US$ Billions)	Share (%)	
	2004	2000	2004	2004	2000	2004
Total commercial services	318.3	100.0	100.0	260.0	100.0	100.0
Transportation	56.0	18.1	17.6	77.5	31.4	29.8
Sea transport	5.8	1.7	1.8	31.5	9.9	12.1
Air transport	25.9	9.3	8.1	28.4	13.6	10.9
Other transport	24.3	7.1	7.6	17.5	7.9	6.7
Travel	95.5	35.2	30.0	67.8	32.1	26.1
Other commercial services	166.8	46.7	52.4	114.7	36.5	44.1
Communication services[a]	6.1	1.5	1.9	5.3	2.8	2.1
Construction services[a]	3.7	0.9	1.2	1.3	0.2	0.5
Insurance services[a]	5.3	1.3	1.7	30.0	5.4	11.5
Financial services[a]	19.5	5.6	6.1	4.9	2.2	1.9
Computer and information services[a]	5.4	2.0	1.7	1.6	1.0	0.6
Royalties and licence fees	51.3	15.5	16.1	22.9	7.9	8.8
Other business services	67.7	17.6	21.3	48.3	16.9	18.6
Personal, cultural, and recreational services	7.7	2.3	2.4	0.4	0.1	0.1

SOURCE: WTO International Trade Statistics, 2005, p. 53. Reprinted with permission by WTO Publications.

[a]Excludes transactions between affiliates, which are recorded under "Other business services."

goods returned to the United States after processing or assembly. Additional data, for example, on transportation mode (see Chapter 16, Global Marketing and Supply Chain) are also available.[16]

Major Exporters and Importers

Exhibit 2.10 shows the largest exporters and importers of merchandise trade and commercial services, respectively. Not surprisingly, developed countries dominate imports and exports in both merchandise trade and commercial services. In merchandise trade, the top 10 exporters and importers are developed countries in Europe and North America, with the notable exception of China, which recently moved up as the world's third largest exporter and importer of merchandise trade. It is worth noting, however, that some developing economies, such as Korea (Republic of), Mexico, Russia, Singapore, Hong Kong (China), Taiwan, and Malaysia, are also emerging as important merchandise trade partners in both imports and exports (among the top 20). In commercial services, the top 10 importers and exporters are also developed economies, with China again being the exception. One reason for the gap between developed and developing economies in the trade of services is that many commercial services such as financial services, global transportation, consulting, and health care are knowledge intensive and hence less likely to be either produced or consumed in a developing economy. Nevertheless, some newly industrialized and emerging economies, such as India, Singapore, Korea (Republic of), and Russia, are rapidly advancing as important participants in commercial services trade (among the top 20).

Exhibit 2.10a   Top 10 Leading Exporters and Importers in World Merchandise Trade, 2004

Rank	Exporters	Value (US$ Billions)	Share (%)	Annual Percentage Change	Rank	Importers	Value (US$ Billions)	Share (%)	Annual Percentage Change
1	Germany	912.3	10.0	21	1	United States	1525.5	16.1	17
2	United States	818.8	8.9	13	2	Germany	716.9	7.6	19
3	China	593.3	6.5	35	3	China	561.2	5.9	36
4	Japan	565.8	6.2	20	4	France	465.5	4.9	17
5	France	448.7	4.9	14	5	United Kingdom	463.5	4.9	18
6	Netherlands	358.2	3.9	21	6	Japan	454.5	4.8	19
7	Italy	349.2	3.8	17	7	Italy	351.0	3.7	18
8	United Kingdom	346.9	3.8	13	8	Netherlands	319.3	3.4	21
9	Canada	316.5	3.5	16	9	Belgium	285.5	3.0	22
10	Belgium	306.5	3.3	20	10	Canada	279.8	2.9	14

SOURCE: WTO International Trade Statistics, 2005, p. 21. Reprinted with permission by WTO Publications.

U.S. Trade Partners

Exhibit 2.11 shows U.S. merchandise trade with various regions and countries. The EU, Canada, China, Mexico, and Japan are the United States' top five trade partners. How can these patterns be explained? With the exception of Mexico and

Exhibit 2.10b   Top 10 Leading Exporters and Importers in World Trade in Commercial Services, 2004

Rank	Exporters	Value (US$ Billions)	Share (%)	Annual Percentage Change	Rank	Importers	Value (US$ Billions)	Share (%)	Annual Percentage Change
1	United States	318.3	15.0	11	1	United States	260.0	12.4	14
2	United Kingdom	171.8	8.1	18	2	Germany	193.0	9.2	13
3	Germany	133.9	6.3	15	3	United Kingdom	136.1	6.5	14
4	France	109.5	5.1	12	4	Japan	134.0	6.4	22
5	Japan	94.9	4.5	25	5	France	96.4	4.6	18
6	Spain	84.5	4.0	11	6	Italy	80.6	3.8	10
7	Italy	82.0	3.9	17	7	Netherlands	72.4	3.5	11
8	Netherlands	73.0	3.4	16	8	China	71.6	3.4	31
9	China	62.1	2.9	34	9	Ireland	58.4	2.8	12
10	Hong Kong, China	53.6	2.5	18	10	Canada	55.9	2.7	12

SOURCE: WTO International Trade Statistics, 2005, p. 23. Reprinted with permission by WTO Publications.

China, three of the United States' five major trading partners are developed economies, a reality that supports Linder's income-preference similarity theory. Canada, the major partner of the United States, has additional advantages in terms of trade with the United States: geographic proximity, relative cultural similarity, and NAFTA membership. More than 100,000 U.S. companies export to Canada, more than double the number that exports to Mexico, the second-ranked destination. Mexico also benefits from its proximity to the United States and from NAFTA membership. Since NAFTA's establishment in 1994, Mexico's exports have grown threefold, with the United States and Canada accounting for much of the growth.

Following the Heckscher-Ohlin theorem, it is easy to see why U.S. eateries import agricultural products and processed foods from Mexico, where expenses are low and wages start at about $50 a week,[17] or why pencil imports, mostly from China, now account for half of the U.S. pencil market versus 16% just a decade ago.[18] Similarly, it is clear why Africa exports mostly mining products to North America but very few manufacturing products.[19] The overall trade picture, however, is more complex.

Let's start with the numbers. With increased globalization, more and more exported products contain a myriad of inputs from other countries, including those that end up importing the final product. The IBM plant in El Salto, Mexico, incorporates U.S. components in products that are then exported to the United States or sold in other export markets. They are registered as Mexican exports. Between 1995 and 1998, exports to countries other than the United States by the Mexican affiliates of U.S. corporations have tripled.[20] The same is true for information technology exports out of the Philippines, Malaysia, and Thailand, which represent a probable value added of no more than 20%, given the importation of semiconductors and other manufacturing inputs that go into the exported products.[21] Exports from China to the United States include manufacturing goods; however, many of those are made by firms from developed economies, including the United States, Japan, and the EU, which use China as an export platform and incorporate foreign inputs. In 2005, 58% of China's exports came from Foreign Invested Enterprises, a category that includes all

Exhibit 2.11   Merchandise Trade of the United States by Region and Economy, 2004

	Exports					Imports			
	Value (US$ Billions)	Share (%)		Annual Percentage Change		Value (US$ Billions)	Share (%)		Annual Percentage Change
Destination	2004	2000	2004	2004	Origin	2004	2000	2004	2004
World	818.8	100.0	100.0	13	World	1,525.5	100.0	100.0	17
North America	300.6	37.0	36.7	12	Asia	559.0	37.8	36.6	16
Asia	216.7	27.6	26.5	7	North America	417.7	29.4	27.4	14
Europe	188.8	23.6	23.1	12	Europe	317.5	20.3	20.8	13
South/Central America	60.7	7.5	7.4	18	South/Central America	105.2	6.2	6.9	26
Middle East	23.6	2.4	2.9	21	Middle East	40.3	3.9	3.2	23
Africa	13.5	1.4	1.6	26	Africa	48.3	2.3	3.2	43
CIS	4.8	0.4	0.6	31	CIS	14.9	0.8	1.0	43
Selected Economies					*Selected Economies*				
Canada	189.1	22.6	23.1	12	European Union (25)	290.9	18.6	19.1	12
European Union (25)	173.0	21.5	21.1	12	Canada	259.7	18.5	17.0	14
Mexico	110.8	14.3	13.5	14	China	210.5	8.5	13.8	29
Japan	54.4	8.3	6.6	4	Mexico	157.8	10.9	10.3	13
China	34.7	2.1	4.2	22	Japan	133.3	12.0	8.7	10

SOURCE: WTO International Trade Statistics, 2005, p. 51. Reprinted with permission by WTO Publications.

enterprises with an element of foreign equity. Vietnam stood to benefit only modestly from the abolition of U.S. tariffs on its textile exports, because those are made with imported raw material.

Exhibits 2.12a and b present the trade flow, by product, between the United States and Japan, a flow that has been described by some observers as one of the world's most important bilateral flows, both politically and economically. Some components of the flow are easily explained; for example, the flow of foodstuffs from the United States to Japan can be explained by factor endowments. Other components of the flow, however, are not easily explained. For example, Japanese vehicle exports to the United States are more than 10 times bigger than U.S. vehicle exports to Japan. Since the United States has the largest motor vehicle industry in the world and has (through its subsidiaries) a substantial share of competitive markets such as the EU, it is difficult to explain the large gap via comparative advantage or scale economy. Other factors must be at play, among them trade barriers (described in the next section) that limit the access of U.S. firms to the Japanese market, currency exchange rates that have made U.S. vehicles expensive in Japan, and externalities such as rising fuel prices that have made the more economical Japanese vehicles more attractive in the United States.

Recall that the new trade theory suggests that while interindustry trade was governed by the Heckscher-Ohlin theorem (trade between countries with different factor endowments), intra-industry trade was not. When we look at U.S. textile imports for 2005 and 2006, we see that they come mostly from the developing world, with China, Mexico, and India in top places, as one might expect from a labor-intensive product. Still, Canada and Italy remain important

Exhibit 2.12a   U.S. Exports to Japan (Top 10 Commodities)

Description	Millions of U.S. Dollars			% Share			% Change
	1997	1998	1999	1997	1998	1999	99/98
Total exports to Japan	33,587	29,408	28,288	9.89	8.59	8.40	−3.81
1 Machinery	5,346	4,267	4,114	15.92	14.51	14.54	−3.59
2 Electrical machinery	4,464	4,103	4,049	13.29	13.95	14.31	−1.31
3 Aircraft, spacecraft	2,054	2,526	2,612	6.11	8.59	9.23	3.39
4 Optic, NT B544; Med. instr.	2,613	2,495	2,458	7.78	8.48	8.69	−1.46
5 Meat	1,204	1,197	1,202	3.58	4.07	4.25	0.40
6 Cereals	1,555	1,254	1,165	4.63	4.26	4.12	−7.10
7 Vehicles, not railway	1,773	1,329	1,147	5.28	4.52	4.05	−13.69
8 Tobacco	955	991	1,001	2.84	3.37	3.54	1.00
9 Wood	1,427	790	791	4.25	2.69	2.80	0.15
10 Organic chemicals	791	623	656	2.36	2.12	2.32	5.28

SOURCE: U.S. Dept. of Commerce, Bureau of the Census.

Exhibit 2.12b   U.S. Imports From Japan (Top 10 Commodities)

Description	Millions of U.S. Dollars			% Share			% Change
	1997	1998	1999	1997	1998	1999	99/98
Total imports from Japan	59,272	60,427	61,883	14.23	13.59	12.93	2.41
1 Vehicles, not railway	15,079	16,272	18,276	25.44	26.93	29.53	12.31
2 Machinery	16,237	16,026	15,370	27.39	26.52	24.84	−4.09
3 Electrical machinery	12,135	11,540	11,970	20.47	19.10	19.34	3.73
4 Optic, NT 8544; Med. instr.	3,773	3,803	3,590	6.37	6.29	5.80	−5.60
5 Organic chemicals	1,267	1,353	1,138	2.14	2.24	1.84	−15.83
6 Special other	842	883	994	1.42	1.46	1.61	12.56
7 Toys and sports equipment	1,105	995	961	1.86	1.65	1.55	−3.38
8 Rubber	694	753	848	1.17	1.25	1.37	12.71
9 Plastic	741	791	772	1.25	1.31	1.25	−2.36
10 Aircraft, spacecraft	604	658	728	1.02	1.09	1.18	10.59

SOURCE: U.S. Dept. of Commerce, Bureau of the Census.

secondary sources, but the products they export to the United States are different, being of higher price and quality. In the case of Mexico, proximity and reexports account for much of the exports to the United States, but their importance markedly declined once tariff barriers started to come down.[22]

The Leontief paradox asks why the United States exported labor-intensive products when it had no advantage in labor rates. Labor migration is one reason. In this case, it is labor moving in the pursuit of capital rather than the other way around. Rather than moving south of the border, U.S. carpet manufacturers rely on Mexican migration to northwest Georgia to lower labor costs and remain competitive. While labor costs are still higher relative to Mexican plants, transportation costs to U.S.

customers are much lower, making domestic production cost-effective.[23] With the wages of U.S. trading partners rising as a percentage of U.S. wages (about doubling from 1960 to 1992),[24] wage differentials are not the only factor determining the location of production, although they remain a vitally important criterion.

Trade Balance

The **balance of trade** is calculated as exports minus imports of goods and services. The United States has by far the largest trade deficit of any country, although as a percentage of GDP, its deficit is much lower than that of many other nations (Exhibit 2.13). The U.S. deficit in merchandise trade has persisted since the early 1980s and was especially pronounced in trade with Japan during the 1980s and early 1990s and with China in the late 1990s and early 2000s. In both cases, considerable anxiety arose surrounding the possible repercussions of the deficit to U.S. competitiveness and national security.

In contrast to its deficit in merchandise trade, the United States enjoys a substantial surplus in services. In 2005, the U.S. deficit in merchandise trade approached $800 billion, roughly double the 1999 figure, but its service trade was in the plus column to the tune of more than $66 billion. This discrepancy explains why the United States is in the forefront of those fighting to reduce barriers in service trade. For instance, the United States has been a major proponent of "open skies" agreements that liberalize the markets for commercial aviation and has fought hard for the opening of hitherto closed markets (e.g., China) for financial services. India, a country that has been dramatically increasing its service exports, has become a center for software exports. This success played a role in the Indian government's decision to open up its own market to realize the benefits of free trade.

Knowledge is often the most valuable contribution toward a competitive advantage in services. This can be seen clearly in the distribution of U.S. service exports. The United States exports to Europe intellectual property (paid as royalties and license fees) and legal services, while in the Asia Pacific region it sells mostly educational and engineering services. U.S. freight services are sold mainly in the Asia Pacific and Africa/Middle East regions, while Latin America absorbs U.S. exports in advertising, insurance, communications, and travel services.[25]

Interim Summary

1. World trade levels have shifted dramatically in the last 50 years, with merchandise trade more pronounced in manufacturing than in mining and agricultural products. Also, the balance of trade between countries and regions has altered significantly.

2. Highly developed countries tend to have services as a major export. The United States is a prominent example.

3. The considerable U.S. surplus in service trade is outweighed by its much bigger deficit in merchandise trade, producing an overall deficit that has persisted for a quarter of a century.

OPPOSITION TO FREE TRADE

Generally speaking, trade theories show the benefits to be derived from international trade but dwell less on its potential drawbacks. This is particularly true for the theories of absolute and comparative advantage, which point out that trade allows for the efficient deployment of national resources from which everyone

Exhibit 2.13   Balance of Trade

Balance of Trade		2001
US$ billions (minus sign = deficit)		
Ranking		US$ billions
1	Germany	76.5
2	Japan	54.6
3	Russia	49.7
4	Canada	34.0
5	Ireland	32.5
6	Indonesia	25.5
7	Norway	25.5
8	China	23.1
9	Netherlands	22.0
10	Taiwan	15.7
11	Malaysia	14.1
12	Sweden	12.7
13	Finland	11.3
14	Belgium	10.9
15	Venezuela	9.8
16	Korea	9.5
17	Italy	7.5
18	Argentina	6.3
19	Denmark	6.3
20	Singapore	5.8
21	Thailand	4.0
22	Philippines	2.2
23	South Africa	0.6
24	Chile	0.5
25	Colombia	0.1
26	Brazil	−0.0
27	Australia	−0.5
28	New Zealand	−0.6
29	Iceland	−0.7
30	Slovak Republic	−0.8
31	Estonia	−0.8
32	Slovenia	−0.8
33	Switzerland	−2.0
34	Hungary	−2.1
35	Luxembourg	−2.5
36	Czech Republic	−3.1
37	France	−3.5
38	Austria	−3.6
39	Israel	−6.1
40	India	−6.7
41	Turkey	−9.2
42	Hong Kong	−11.6
43	Portugal	−13.9
44	Poland	−14.5
45	Greece	−16.1
46	Mexico	−17.6
47	Spain	−33.6
48	United Kingdom	−59.1
49	USA	−449.6

Balance of Trade		2001
Percentage of GDP		
Ranking		%
1	Ireland	30.91
2	Indonesia	19.61
3	Malaysia	16.15
4	Russia	16.04
5	Norway	15.57
6	Finland	9.31
7	Venezuela	7.85
8	Singapore	6.74
9	Sweden	6.06
10	Netherlands	5.78
11	Taiwan	5.55
12	Canada	4.86
13	Belgium	4.73
14	Germany	4.15
15	Denmark	3.85
16	Thailand	3.55
17	Philippines	3.10
18	Argentina	2.29
19	Korea	2.26
20	China	1.99
21	Japan	1.32
22	Chile	0.78
23	Italy	0.69
24	South Africa	0.52
25	Colombia	0.18
26	Brazil	−0.01
27	Australia	−0.14
28	France	−0.27
29	Switzerland	−0.81
30	New Zealand	−1.28
31	India	−1.51
32	Austria	−1.89
33	Mexico	−2.77
34	Slovak Republic	−4.05
35	United Kingdom	−4.14
36	Hungary	−4.15
37	USA	−4.41
38	Slovenia	−4.41
39	Israel	−5.53
40	Czech Republic	−5.57
41	Spain	−5.78
42	Turkey	−5.80
43	Hong Kong	−7.15
44	Iceland	−7.67
45	Poland	−8.27
46	Portugal	−12.12
47	Luxembourg	−12.76
48	Greece	−14.22
49	Estonia	−14.54

SOURCE: *IMD World Competitiveness Yearbook,* 2006. Some regional economies within a country (e.g., Zhejiang province in China) were also reported to illustrate such state- or province-level competitiveness.

benefits. At the same time, opponents of free trade have been wrangling for years, most recently in their strong opposition to "globalization." Most countries have taken the position that trade needs first and foremost to protect the interests of their citizens. For example, the U.S. Foreign Trade Anti-trust Improvement Act permits price-fixing agreements among exporters if neither U.S. consumers nor U.S. competitors are harmed.[26]

Opinion surveys (see also Chapter 7 on the political and legal environment) show that the American public is divided on the benefits of free trade. An opinion survey conducted for the Institute of International Economics shows that by a margin of 48% to 34% Americans believe that foreign trade is bad for the U.S. economy.[27] How can we reconcile the two views? One answer rests with the gap between the macro and micro views. Although trade may be good for the overall national economy, its impact varies across regional, occupational, and other lines. The aforementioned survey shows that unskilled workers are much less likely to support free trade, because they are threatened by a shift of their jobs to lower-cost locales. In contrast, skilled and highly educated people are more likely to benefit from trade, at least in the short term, and hence tend to support free trade. Other studies confirm that people with lower incomes tend to be more negatively disposed toward trade. This is ironic because, as the head of the WTO noted, poor people are more adversely affected by protectionism because it increases the price of consumer goods.[28] Union membership may not have much impact on attitudes toward trade, as is often assumed.[29] The schism between social groups regarding trade may in itself trigger opposition to trade on the part of governments that are worried about its economic, social, and political impact.

To deal with the uneven impact of trade, the U.S. government provides trade adjustment assistance in the form of extended unemployment benefits and retraining funds for workers who lose their jobs to overseas competition. Congress recently considered a bill that would provide wage insurance for workers who lose their jobs as a result of foreign competition, even when securing a new job at a lower pay level. It is estimated that an employee who loses his or her job to imports and gets another job will receive on average a 13% lower wage with a quarter suffering a 30% cut.[30]

The Sovereignty Argument

Another source of opposition to trade is the supposed threat it represents to national sovereignty. According to this argument, the shift in production to the most efficient location deprives a country of the base it needs to be a viable economic entity. In turn, this will make a country too dependent on nations that may challenge its national interests. This argument is particularly salient in industries considered key to national security, either directly (e.g., the arms industry) or indirectly (e.g., airlines). The United States, like many other countries, prohibits non-U.S. firms from acquiring a majority stake in a U.S. airline on the pretext that the aircraft need to be mobilized should an emergency occur. For similar reasons, countries sometimes curb the exports of certain products to designated countries.

Free trade sometimes is opposed as a threat to national culture and institutions. You will be reminded of that when you read about cultural industries in Chapter 6, The Cultural Environment. Some countries, notably France and Canada, impose restrictions on the introduction of foreign media under the pretext that open importation would endanger their culture and language. As we will see in our discussion of tariffs below, countries may establish particularly high tariffs on products that they see as essential to their way of life (e.g., rice in Japan).

The Lowest Common Denominator Argument

Still another source of opposition to free trade has to do with its potentially adverse consequences for the environment, safety, and such. This is the "lowest common denominator" argument whereby production will shift to nations with the least protection since they will offer the lowest cost base, but eventually everyone else will end up paying for the adverse impact in the form of environmental degradation, global warming, and such. As you may recall from Chapter 1, the lowest common denominator argument has been one of the main complaints lodged by the antiglobalization movement.

Trade Reciprocity

Although trade theories assume benefits even when a country opens its borders to free trade unilaterally, additional benefits can be gained from reciprocity. Those additional benefits are not only economic (e.g., the ability to export the goods and services in which it has a comparative advantage) but also political and social in that it is difficult to build domestic support for unilateral opening. For instance, if the U.S. government were to permit Chinese imports unilaterally, it might be supported by some consumer groups but opposed by almost everyone else. In contrast, the pressure it applied on China to open its borders to U.S. exports brought it the support of U.S. exporters. Reciprocity also appeals to our sense of fairness (itself a key U.S. value). In a *Business Week* survey, only 10% of respondents identified themselves as "free traders," 37% identified themselves as "protectionists," while the rest identified as "fair traders."[31]

Trebilcock and Howse distinguish between two kinds of reciprocity, passive and active. **Passive reciprocity** is a position taken by a country in which it refuses to lower or eliminate its barriers to trade until one or more other parties do the same. **Active or aggressive reciprocity** may be conducted through the threat of retaliation, such as the withdrawal of previous commitments and concessions or the undertaking of other retaliatory measures until the other party fulfills its obligations. An example is "super 301," which may be invoked by the United States in the case of "unreasonable and discriminatory" trade behavior by a foreign country.[32] Adam Smith suggested that retaliation should be considered a possible response to protectionism, although he was concerned that this could harm the retaliating nation as well.

Indeed, reciprocity and retaliation are an integral part of the international trade scene. Countervailing duties and subsidies are commonly used by nations to retaliate or compensate for the value produced by preferences provided to foreign manufacturers or service providers.

Interim Summary

1. Free trade and globalization are hot-button issues. Some constituencies believe that protectionism is the best stance, whereas most economists assert that free trade is the only path to a healthy economy in the long term.

2. There are many reasons for a nation to be cautious when entering into free trade with other nations. For example, a country must balance protection of its workforce, national security, and national culture and identity with the benefits brought about by free trade.

3. A major concern with free trade and globalization is the potential for environmental damage from firms operating in poorly regulated markets.

4. Trade reciprocity can bring about additional benefits to countries engaged in free trade.

TYPES OF TRADE BARRIERS

Barriers to trade are typically divided into tariff and nontariff barriers. **Tariff barriers** are official constraints on the importation of certain goods and services in the form of a total or a partial limitation or in the form of a special levy. **Nontariff barriers** are indirect measures that discriminate against foreign manufacturers in the domestic market or otherwise distort and constrain trade. While tariff barriers have been significantly reduced during the several decades of the General Agreement on Tariffs and Trade (GATT) regime, debate continues on whether similar progress has been made vis-à-vis nontariff barriers, which are by definition much more difficult to measure.

Although some nontariff barriers (e.g., subsidies) have been targeted and reduced, others have emerged in their place. Sometimes, both tariff and nontariff barriers are applied in tandem. India, which was once one of the most protective markets in the world, called the combination *swadeshi*, or "nationalist policies."[33] This meant, for instance, prohibiting foreign firms from bidding on strategic defense projects (a tariff barrier) while preventing those firms from winning less sensitive bids by failing to disclose essential requirements or by publicizing the bids in obscure local outlets unlikely to be scrutinized by foreign firms (a nontariff barrier).

Together, tariff and nontariff barriers pose a serious obstacle to international trade. In a survey of Minnesota businesses, regulations and tariffs were considered the most serious barriers to entry into international trade, ahead of lack of information, cost and financing, qualified employees, language, and culture.[34]

Tariff Barriers

Tariff barriers include mainly tariffs and quotas and their derivatives as well as export controls and antidumping laws.

Tariffs

Tariffs are surcharges that an importer must pay above and beyond taxes levied on domestic goods and services. Tariffs are transparent (listed in the Harmonized Tariff Schedule) and are typically set ad valorem—that is, based on the value of the product or service. Tariffs were used widely in the 19th century but were incrementally reduced over time. The Smoot-Hawley Act in 1930 reversed this trend, pushing tariffs to a level of almost 60% of import value. Predictably, these tariffs brought on retaliatory measures by major trade partners of the United States.

In the decades that followed, tariffs in the United States and later in other nations declined substantially, reaching single digits for most products. Nevertheless, U.S. tariffs on some products (e.g., sugar) remain very high. Examples of particularly high tariffs include a 300% tariff on butter in Canada, a 179% tariff on sweet powdered milk in the United States, a 215% tariff on frozen beef in the EU, and a 550% tariff on rice in Japan.[35] The Japanese tariff on rice is particularly interesting, since the Japanese government maintains that its rationale is to uphold a social and cultural way of life that is linked with rice cultivation. The more prosaic reason is the political strength of the farm lobby within Japan's ruling Liberal Democratic Party (LDP). The result, as trade theories would predict, is that the Japanese consumer pays much more for rice than do consumers in the United States and in most other countries.

Not surprisingly, tariffs had been on the agenda of virtually all rounds of trade negotiations through GATT (the predecessor of the WTO), and remarkable progress has now been made toward their elimination or reduction. Nevertheless, a hike in a tariff is not unheard of. The United States and other nations often use punitive tariffs as a way to retaliate or obtain reciprocity. India, while generally reducing tariffs, has increased tariffs on such goods as whiskey from an already high level of 104% to 220% to 550%.[36] Companies, on their part, have been investing efforts in circumventing tariffs. Heartland By-Products, a small Michigan firm, circumvents the high U.S. tariff on sugar by buying sugar-molasses from its Canadian sister company, which makes it from sugar bought at world prices; it then reverses the process and turns the molasses into sugar syrup it sells to U.S. makers of ice cream, cereals, and candy.[37]

With overall tariffs low, governments often attempt to shift a product into a higher tariff category while firms develop strategies to benefit from the lower tariff category. The EU imposes a 288% tariff on imported vegetables, which is geared toward protecting the farm lobby in the Union, and only a 20% tariff on sauces. The EU decided to apply the very high tariff to imported sauces that are more than 20% made up of "lumps of fruits and vegetables" only to face the ire of European firms such as Nestlé, whose own sauces have faced retaliatory tariffs in other countries.[38] Similarly, the United States imposes 12.5% (if water packed) and 35% (if oil packed) tariffs on imported tuna in cans or pouches but only 1.5% on cooked non-canned fish. Bumble Bee, a unit of ConAgra Foods, takes advantage of the gap by importing cooked tuna to automated processing plants in California and Puerto Rico, thereby qualifying for the lower tariff. Its rival Starkist, a unit of Heinz, which imports canned tuna from Ecuador, is fighting to reduce the tariff.[39]

Optimal Tariff

The **optimal tariff theory** assumes that by imposing a tariff, governments can capture a significant portion of the manufacturer's profit margin. In other words, assuming that the exporter cannot raise prices at will, domestic customers will not have to pay higher prices while their government manages to obtain part of the proceeds that otherwise would have been obtained by the exporter. The optimal tariff theory assumes, however, that the exporter can absorb the lower prices and will not simply shift its efforts into other markets. The theory also does not take into account the fact that high tariffs are likely to trigger smuggling (see Chapter 19, Social Responsibility and Corruption in the Global Marketplace), which eventually reduces government revenue. An example is the importation of cigarettes, traditionally a high-tariff item, where even the manufacturers themselves have been accused of rampant smuggling to circumvent tariffs.

Infant Industries

The **infant industry** argument for tariffs is that an industry new to a country, especially a developing one, needs to be protected by tariff walls or risk being squashed by established global players before it is given a chance to grow and develop. The argument was vigorously raised by the United States throughout the 19th century, by Japan after World War II, by Korea in the 1960s, and, more recently, by China. These countries wished to encourage the development of their domestic industry while generating revenues for the state, at the expense of foreign manufacturers. The interest of consumers, amply demonstrated by theories of international trade, was not considered. When U.S. motor vehicles were kept out of both Japan and Korea through high tariffs and other barriers, the result was higher local prices. The same was true for U.S. "voluntary quotas" set in the mid-1970s, which limited the number of Japanese cars sold in the United States and cost the U.S. consumer more than $1,000 per car. Here the argument was not one of infant industry (U.S. car manufacturers have been in business since early in the 20th century) but rather that the industry needed time to recuperate from the Japanese onslaught and restructure to produce more fuel-efficient cars. The "import surge" protection has since become an acceptable WTO protection.

COUNTRY BOX

THE UNITED STATES AND STEEL IMPORTS

The United States, once the world's major producer of steel, now trails both China and Japan in steel production. The United States now imports steel from other countries, including Japan, Russia, Ukraine, South Korea, and Brazil. The U.S. steel industry has been trying to mobilize support to curb steel imports.

One argument used by U.S. manufacturers to curb steel imports has gained more prominence in the wake of the September 11, 2001, terror attacks. According to this argument, steel is a vital input in armaments, and the United States can ill afford to become dependent on other nations for its supply. Steel is also a vital input in such industries as motor vehicles, so its price and availability would have a ripple effect in the economy.

The U.S. International Trade Commission recommended in early December 2001 to levy additional tariffs, ranging from 5% to 40%, on key steel products. The position was strongly supported by President Bush, who was also concerned with the political fallout in steel-producing states such as Ohio, Pennsylvania, and West Virginia. The EU trade commissioner, on his part, threatened to launch a complaint before the WTO. He has blamed the rising imports on the U.S. steel industry, whose outdated management and labor practices were behind the problems of the U.S. producers, in his opinion. In March 2002, the Bush administration imposed a 30% tariff on a range of steel imports, which was followed up by an EU plan for counter-sanctions. Most of the U.S. tariffs have since been gradually removed, some as recently as 2006, when an alliance of domestic and foreign U.S.-based auto manufacturers succeeded in convincing the Bush administration that cheaper imported steel was essential for them to remain competitive.

SOURCE: R. G. Matthews. "A big stick: The U.S. won't take 'no' for an answer at Paris steel summit." *Wall Street Journal*, December 14, 2001, A1; industry sources and press releases, 2006.

Quotas

Quotas are quantitative limitations on the importation of goods typically spelled in terms of units (e.g., 10,000 shirts) or value (ad valorem). Some quotas allow for a preset increase—for example, an annual increase of 3%. Some quotas allow for a preset incremental decrease, as contained in the NAFTA agreement and most recently in China's admission into the WTO, that will trigger stepwise tariff reductions. Quotas may also be established in terms of a market share, beyond which either tariff or cessation of imports is triggered. Quotas are widely used in the case of textile products, although they are by no means restricted to those.

Unlike tariffs, quotas hold the promise of definitive, quantifiable protection of domestic producers. They may, however, yield unintended consequences. The "voluntary" quotas capping Japanese auto imports at roughly 1.8 million units (set in terms of units rather than value) encouraged Japanese manufacturers to move beyond the entry-level cars they were exporting at the time into more expensive models so as to increase their dollar volume without violating the quotas. In contrast to tariffs, quotas do not have the potential to trigger the efficiencies that arise from the need to remain competitive with domestic producers. The unmet demand for Japanese cars was simply translated into higher margins for the dealers that sold them.

A good example of the impact of quotas is the Multifiber Arrangement, which has governed trade in garments for decades. Once the quota regime expired, on January 1, 2005, the composition of garment imports into the United States, the EU, and other markets changed dramatically. China had quickly overtaken Mexico as the largest source of garment imports into the United States, with the share of some developing nations, such as Lesotho, declining precipitously. Proponents of the regime's expiration have pointed out that the change has shifted production and exports toward the most efficient distributors, in the process lowering costs for domestic consumers, while opponents have pointed to the change as a vindication of their argument that many producers in the least developed nations will be wiped out.

Rule of Origin

Both tariffs and quotas are administered on the basis of their country of origin, for which the default is the first importing country. For example, a product that was manufactured in Belgium and exported to France and from there to the United States will be considered a Belgian product unless the product has undergone material change in France. It is also important to remember that **rule-of-origin** terms may differ between different types of tariffs and supports. For instance, under GSP (Generalized System of Preferences), only 35% of a product's value needs to be from a developing nation to be granted duty-free treatment, whereas under the Buy American Act, a product needs to be made in the United States from at least half U.S. content.

Rule of origin is often an issue of contention because the value added to the product in the transient country may be debatable. For instance, the French government once returned a shipment of U.S.-made Honda cars, arguing that the cars were in fact Japanese and hence fell under the quota for Japanese car imports into the country, which had already been exceeded. The U.S. government recently suspected that many garments imported from Hong Kong were in fact manufactured in Mainland China but had their origin concealed to circumvent the quota regime. The United States demanded that it be allowed to post inspectors at the Mainland–Hong Kong border, something the Hong Kong authorities (and China, who is the ultimate sovereign of the territory) saw as a threat to their sovereignty.

To remedy the problem, the WTO issued a first ever agreement on rules of origin. It requires that the rules be transparent, that they be applied in a consistent and impartial manner, that they be based on a positive rather than a negative standard (i.e., governments need to state what confers origin rather than what does not), and that they will not restrict, distort, or disrupt trade.

Export Controls

Many countries limit the type of products that can be exported to other countries, particularly those that are considered enemy nations or a security risk. **Export controls** are typically activated against products with a national security potential (e.g., armaments) but also may be applied to so-called dual-use products such as advanced computers or trucks that can have both security and civilian uses (e.g., trucks capable of having a heavy machine gun mounted on them). An example is the sale of aerospace equipment to China by McDonnell Douglas Corporation (which has since been acquired by Boeing). The company was fined $2.1 million by the Commerce Department because some of the machining tools it sold for use in a joint venture for the manufacturing of commercial aircraft parts were later found in a facility that manufactured military aircraft.[40] More recently, a number of U.S. companies have been prosecuted by the government for breaking rules on exports to Iran, a country high on the export control list because of its support for global terrorism.

In emergency situations, export controls can be used to prevent the export of goods that are vital to the domestic industry and armed forces—for example, oil. Export controls are different from most other trade barriers in that they are placed by the exporting country rather than by the importing one. Exporting companies often pressure their government to ease export controls, arguing that the importing country will get the products from a competitor whose country does not apply strict controls. Finally, export controls affect not only manufacturers in the home country but also those in a third country. This is especially relevant in the case of countries with a substantial surplus in technology balance of payments, such as the United States. For instance, the United States has asked Israel to guarantee that it does not use sensitive U.S. technologies incorporated into Israeli equipment when the equipment is exported to China and has forced Israel to cancel the sale of an early-warning aircraft to that country.

Dumping and Antidumping

Dumping is defined by the WTO as selling a product at an unfairly low price, with the "fair price" defined as the domestic price, the price charged by an exporter in another market, or a calculation of production costs. Because it distorts pricing, dumping interferes with free trade flow. Dumping undermines the principle of comparative advantage because it may cause the exporting country to specialize in a product or service in which it has no advantage over the importing country.

The WTO allows remedies against dumping but only where "material injury" to the domestic industry has been demonstrated. In theory, the extra duties, which can add up to 40% of product price, will bring the price back to a realistic level, restoring a level playing field and permitting the more efficient producers to sell their goods. The problem is that the retaliation, in the form of antidumping duties, is often used to protect inefficient domestic producers, thereby producing the opposite impact.

Whereas antidumping measures were once almost exclusively applied by developed nations fearing competition from developing and especially emerging economies, they are now taken by developed and developing nations alike. For example, India, which had no antidumping cases in 1993, became the number-one user of antidumping measures in 1999, with 68 cases, and its number-one target for antidumping measures was China, with 310 cases brought against it in the last decade.[41] It is easy to see why: The country has abundant low-cost labor and is a world leader in labor-intensive exports such as toys and apparel. The case of China also shows how antidumping can distort trade. Before signing NAFTA in 1992, Mexico imposed antidumping duties on 4,000 Chinese products, basically covering all Chinese-made goods, even goods for which there was no Mexican substitute. For 2002, the Mexican textiles and apparel industries extended antidumping tariffs of 557% on Chinese-made clothing and 1,100% on Chinese-made shoes, effectively keeping them off the retail shelf.[42]

With the recent growth of Chinese exports, a critical issue in antidumping complaints against Chinese manufacturers has been whether China had a market economy (in which case the price cited by Chinese producers for anything from raw material to labor would be accepted at face value as an indication of cost) or not (in which case comparable data from other, market economies would be used as a base). In general, the United States does not certify China as a market economy, although some other countries—for example, South Korea—now do.

However, the U.S. International Trade Commission ruled in 2005 that certain sectors of the Chinese economy were market based and thus assigned only a 10% tariff on Chinese household furniture imports rather than the 60% demanded by domestic competitors.

Interim Summary

1. Tariff barriers are an obvious and transparent means of controlling trade. Tariff barriers include quotas and their derivatives, as well as export controls.

2. In using tariffs, countries must account for the fact that rate increases will likely trigger retaliation.

3. Quotas and tariffs are applied to goods based on their country of origin. However, what defines a country of origin is subject to different interpretations. A clear designation of country of origin is difficult because in a global environment a product may pass through many countries and contain inputs from many others.

NONTARIFF BARRIERS

By definition, **nontariff barriers** are obstacles to trade, not anchored in laws and official regulations and therefore not transparent. It is difficult to fight nontariff barriers because the offending party is unlikely to admit that a barrier is in place and therefore will not enter into negotiations for its removal. Some barriers are especially difficult to detect and monitor. For instance, a change in domestic product standards will typically be publicized only in that country, with the result that foreign manufacturers may not be aware of it and may take a long time to make adjustments so that their products comply with the new standards. When a developing country limits the importation of used cars, the stated argument is safety, even though the imports may be safer than the vehicles currently on the road. The idea is to protect local manufacturers or to obtain the higher duties obtained from selling new vehicles or to reduce imports altogether, since most consumers cannot afford a new import.

There is great variety in nontariff barriers, and their combined effect can be substantial. For instance, Brazil's foreign minister, Celso Lafer, estimated that 60% of Brazil's exports to the United States face nontariff barriers.[43] The following section outlines some of the key barriers.

Administrative Barriers

Many administrative requirements result in the erection of barriers to trade. Often a government will use an administrative measure to block the entry of products while continuing to argue that no barrier exists. In one case, the French government tried to protect its domestic VCR manufacturer against Japanese competition by channeling those imports through a tiny customs station. This caused enormous delays and increased the cost of the Japanese exports without the French government having to accept responsibility for a policy violating trade agreements.

Labeling is one example of an administrative barrier. Most countries require product labels in the local language, which is a reasonable requirement but one that puts an additional burden on the small exporter who may not find it economically feasible to produce them. A U.S. requirement to list the nutritional value of a food product may seem simple and reasonable but may represent a substantial burden to a small exporter from a developing country where the requisite analysis of nutritional content is not easily obtained. Even for a large exporter, the need to make substantial adjustment in a small market may not make economic sense.

Another example of an administrative barrier—described in Chapter 16, Global Marketing and Supply Chain—is the United States barring Mexican trucks from entering the United States on safety grounds. This alleged violation of the NAFTA agreement not only hurts Mexican truck companies that are unable to export their services into the United States but also increases the cost to Mexican manufacturers (including the Mexican affiliates of U.S. firms) that export to the United States.

An interesting case of an administrative barrier involves the dispute-resolution mechanisms themselves. The Canadian government complained to the WTO that the United States was dragging its feet in appointing representatives to the WTO panel, which is supposed to investigate U.S. sanctions against soft wood imports from Canada.[44]

Production Subsidies

Subsidies are payments provided by a government or its agencies to domestic companies in order to make them more competitive vis-à-vis foreign competitors at home and/or abroad. A case in point is Airbus Industries, which receives subsidies from the EU and national governments to support the development of its aircraft. It has also been alleged that national airlines such as Air France received government support with the understanding that they would utilize Airbus products. Airbus countered that Boeing received subsidies as well through military procurement by the U.S. government. Airbus also accused Boeing of signing "exclusive supplier" agreements with some airlines (e.g., Continental) that were designed to keep Airbus out of the market. In 2005, the two companies submitted formal complaints against each other via their respective governments to the WTO, which has yet to issue a ruling on the dispute.

Subsidies introduce an artificial incentive into the production equation of domestic manufacturers, funneling resources away from their optimal deployment. In contrast to tariffs, subsidies do not distort consumer decisions because they do not raise prices beyond their global level.[45] The WTO distinguishes three types of subsidies: prohibited, actionable, and nonactionable. Prohibited subsidies require the recipient to meet export targets or to use domestic rather than foreign goods. Actionable subsidies are disallowed only when damage to national interests (of the complaining country) is demonstrated. Nonactionable subsidies include support for disenfranchised regions (e.g., China's western provinces), to help companies comply with more stringent environmental laws (up to one-fifth the cost), and R&D assistance not exceeding one-half (for basic research) or one-quarter (for applied research) of total R&D cost. Countervailing duties cannot be imposed on nonactionable subsidies.

Countervailing duties, designed to protect against the distortion of dumping and other forms of subsidies, often result in a barrier of their own. Such duties are set to counter the impact of the subsidies, thus leveling the playing field, but this can result in a recurring retaliatory game that is likely to dampen trade.

Emergency Import Protection

The WTO recognizes remedies against a **surge in imports**, defined as a sudden and dramatic increase in imports or in market share that can cause material damage to the domestic industry. Although the remedies cannot be targeted at a particular country, they establish a quota formula to allocate supply among different exporting countries. In general, developing countries are held to a lower standard in the application of remedies. A variation of emergency restrictions can be seen in the setting of "voluntary quotas." These quotas, such as those imposed by the U.S. government to stem the rising tide of Japanese auto imports in the 1980s, are often anything but voluntary, since the importing country typically threatens other measures if the quotas are not heeded. Although emergency import protection can be seen to disrupt the flow of free trade, it may be justified in that it can safeguard competition by preventing existing players from exiting the market because of a one-time surge, allowing them to regroup and remain viable competitors.

In the garment sector, import surge quotas have been used most recently in the United States (in 2005) and the EU (in 2006) to protect from a flood of Chinese imports that followed the expiration of the Multifiber Arrangement on January 1, 2005. In the EU, the surge quotas were set so swiftly that dozens of boats carrying Chinese imports were stranded in European ports, unable to unload their merchandise. Intensive negotiations between the EU, European retailers, and the Chinese government resulted in the release of the merchandise. It should be noted, however, that under the rules of China's accession to the WTO, anti-surge quotas in this sector are set to expire in 2008.

Foreign Sales Corporations

In February 2000, the WTO ruled in response to an EU complaint that the U.S. use of "foreign sales corporations" (FSCs) represented a subsidy to exports and that the United States had to remedy the situation or face sanctions. Such sanctions would take the form of retaliatory tariffs on U.S. products, producing an additional trade barrier in the opposite part of the trade flow. **Foreign sales corporations** are offshore corporations that market the products and/or services of firms in foreign countries. The benefit to the firms is that part of the income generated by the foreign sales corporation is excluded from U.S. taxes. The U.S. Treasury estimates that the arrangement saves U.S. firms more than $4 billion a year. Between 1991 and 1998, Cisco Systems saved $203.4 million. Boeing saved $230 million in 1999 alone. That reactions to the FSC issue are mixed is a testament to the complex reality of global business. For instance, British jet engine manufacturer Rolls-Royce was hurt by an FSC because it supported its U.S. rival Pratt & Whitney but also benefited from it through sales from its Illinois plant. Rolls-Royce was also worried by the specter of a global trade war that would severely harm its business.[46]

Attempts in the U.S. House of Representatives to replace the Extraterritorial Income Exclusion (meaning U.S. tax was not levied on sales made abroad) with other tax breaks encountered stiff opposition by large U.S. exporters such as Boeing, whose benefits from the break amounted to more than $1.2 billion between 1991 and 2000, and General Electric, whose benefits for the same period are estimated at more than $1.15 billion.[47] Still, after a long delay and after the WTO authorized the EU to undertake a number of retaliatory steps against imports from the United States, the U.S. Congress changed the tax law in 2005, replacing the tax break with changes in the corporate tax and a broad-based exemption for foreign-source income whether generated by exports or by foreign plants, comparable to exemptions granted by EU countries such as France and the Netherlands.

Embargoes and Boycotts

Embargoes and boycotts interfere with the free flow of trade by halting trade that would otherwise take place. Both seek to damage a country by withdrawing the benefits of international trade. An **embargo** is the prohibition on exportation to a designated country. In recent years, the United States has applied an embargo primarily to rogue states such as Iraq and Iran. In contrast to export controls, most embargoes are applied across the board. A **boycott** is the blank prohibition on importation of all or some goods and services from a designated country. The United States has antiboycott legislation that is seldom found in other countries. In one publicized case, Baxter, a U.S. medical equipment company, was fined for supporting the Arab boycott against Israel. Boycotts often constitute nontariff barriers as firms deny their existence. For instance, with the exception of Fuji Heavy Industries (manufacturer of Subaru cars), Japanese carmakers refused to sell their cars in Israel but argued that the decision was made for economic reasons (e.g., too small a market). As soon as one other major manufacturer entered Israel without triggering Arab retaliation, however, other manufacturers jumped into the market.

Boycotts are usually initiated by national governments. Examples are the U.S. embargo on Cuba or France's embargo on Israel after the 1967 war. They are sometimes also initiated by Nongovernmental Organizations (NGOs), such as business associations and consumer groups in the importing country. Supported by domestic growers, Japanese consumers organized protests against U.S. agricultural imports, at one time suggesting that U.S. oranges were sprayed with Agent Orange, an herbicide used during the Vietnam War that got its name from its coloring and had nothing to do with oranges.

Finally, **buy local campaigns** are efforts to curb all imports, regardless of the country of origin. Korean consumer groups have held frequent demonstrations suggesting that buyers of imported products were undermining the national interest. This was especially true during economic hard times and, whether organized by the producers or at a genuine grassroots level, had a chilling effect on imports. In the United States, "Buy American" campaigns are often launched, sometimes pointing out that the purchase of foreign products might put one's neighbors out of work. In all those cases, the campaigns constitute a nontariff barrier in that the free flow of trade is being interfered with, resulting in discrimination against foreign producers. Such campaigns should be distinguished from the Buy American Act, which obliges federal agencies and the recipients of certain federal support to purchase U.S. products and services unless no U.S. products are available (e.g., a flight to a destination not served by a U.S. carrier) and, in certain instances, unless the U.S. product is substantially more expensive. The act creates a tariff barrier in the sense that it establishes a transparent and formal constraint on the free trade in goods and services.

Technical Standards

Technical standards are provisions made by government agencies in various countries that pertain to a large array of areas—for example, safety, pollution, and technical performance. Companies that wish to sell in a particular country are then required to demonstrate that their products meet that country's standards. The existence of domestic standards that are at variance with those of other countries represents a trade barrier, whether intentional or not. A group appointed by the U.S. National Research Council and headed by Gary Hufbauer concluded the following:

(1) Standards that differ from international norms are employed as a means to protect domestic producers; (2) restrictive standards are written to match the design features of domestic products, rather than essential performance criteria; there remains unequal access to testing and certification systems between domestic producers and exporters in most nations; (3) there continues to be a failure to accept test results and certifications performed between domestic producers and exporters in most nations; (4) there continues to be a failure to accept test results and certifications performed by competent foreign organizations in multiple markets; and (5) there is significant lack of transparency in the systems for developing technical regulations and assessing conformity in most countries.[48]

An example of regulations that represent nontariff barriers are the EU's bans on the importation of hormone-treated beef and genetically modified corn and soybeans, which adversely affect U.S. producers. In both cases, the official reason for the ban is a potential health risk, although there is little in the form of scientific evidence to support it. On the contrary, the spread of mad cow and foot-and-mouth disease in Europe has made U.S. beef probably less risky than the domestic European variety. More recently, the EU banned the import of certain Chinese foods, arguing that they contained traces of a banned antibiotic. The Chinese, on their part, now require special safety permits for the import of genetically modified foods.[49] Recent safety concerns about Chinese goods have triggered import restrictions and additional inspections in the United States, the EU, and elsewhere, which the Chinese government has argued constitute nontariff trade barriers.

We should note that the WTO agreement "encourages" countries to use international standards where appropriate, but it does not obligate them to do so. The organization does, however, enforce import licensing procedures that require import licenses to be "simple, transparent, and predictable." The goal is to ensure that the administrative process will not in itself restrict or distort imports.

Corruption

Corruption, discussed separately in Chapter 19 of this book, is another barrier to trade. For instance, firms from countries with antibribery legislation such as the United States may refrain from doing business in a country where bribes are expected. Exporters may also refrain from selling in markets where intellectual property is not respected. For example, many U.S. publishers avoid selling books to Chinese customers, fearing that the books will be copied and then sold in bootlegged editions. Trebilcock and Howse argue that intellectual property is a case in which the interests of developed and developing countries do not coincide, challenging a key assumption in international trade theories that trade benefits all participants. They suggest that intellectual property protection serves the interests of innovating countries such as the United States but not the interests of economies such as Korea and Taiwan, which tend to be "imitators" of new knowledge developed elsewhere.[50] At the same time, the violation of intellectual property rights hurts developed-country manufacturers whose comparative advantage lies in innovation. Some U.S. manufacturers refuse to do business in China and other countries where intellectual property rights are often violated so as to prevent their technology from being compromised.

Ironically, the efforts to fight corruption can also represent trade barriers. An example is "pre-shipment inspection," a practice in many developing countries presumably aimed at preventing capital flight, tax evasion, and fraud by subjecting incoming imports to rigorous inspection by contracted private companies.

In many instances, such inspections are used to delay or block imports to protect domestic producers that may be associated with the inspectors.

Barriers to Service Trade

Barriers to trade in services are quite different from the barriers affecting merchandise trade. Because knowledge plays a key role in a service economy, any limitations on the free flow of information, including constraints on individual mobility (e.g., immigration controls), represent barriers to service trade. Some barriers to trade in services are similar in nature to tariff barriers. For example, the regulation of landing rights for airlines constitutes a tariff barrier governed mostly by bilateral treaties. Progress toward "open skies" has been made, especially within the EU and, more recently, between the EU and the United States, but elsewhere this remains a relatively distant goal.

Trebilcock and Howse note that in the absence of global standards and regulation, free trade in services may actually result in a reduction in global welfare. A case in point is lax regulation in the banking industry of one country that is damaging to depositors from another country, resulting in a net reduction in global welfare.[51] Opponents of globalization will argue that a similar situation exists in merchandise trade, where manufacturers transfer production to countries with lax environmental standards, resulting in global warming and other adverse consequences, with a net reduction in global welfare.

Interim Summary

1. Nontariff barriers to trade include government and business measures as well as other phenomena that discourage or interfere with trade between countries (e.g., culture).

2. Since nontariff barriers are not transparent, they may be much more difficult to respond to, and they offer an advantage to domestic businesses.

3. Barriers to service trade are different than those to merchandise trade—for instance, restrictions on individual mobility are an impediment to trade in services but less so for goods.

CHAPTER SUMMARY

1. International trade is the exchange of goods and services across borders. Theories explaining trade flows include the mercantilist doctrine, the absolute advantage theory, the comparative advantage theory, the Heckscher-Ohlin theorem, the product life-cycle model, Linder's income-preference similarity theory, and the new trade theory.

2. Although none of the theories is capable of explaining the entire range of motives for international trade, they collectively provide insights into why international trade occurs. Differences in factor endowments as explained by the Heckscher-Ohlin

theorem are still largely valid in explaining trade in labor-intensive or natural resource products, whereas theories of technological gap and product life cycle are more useful in explaining trade of technology-intensive products. The new trade theory distinguishes between intra-industry and intrafirm trade.

3. Further theoretical development for international trade is needed because many new factors that affect trade today have not been taken into account in extant theories. Examples of these factors include fast-paced flows of human, capital, information, and technological resources across nations and the

importance of country capabilities such as openness and innovation.

4. International trade has grown dramatically in recent decades; global trade in services is growing especially rapidly among the most developed nations and is likely to become more important with time.

5. International trade is becoming more difficult to measure and analyze as more products and services contain inputs that originate in a variety of nations.

Consequently, it is difficult to pinpoint the origin of a product or a service and the rules under which it is to be traded.

6. There are two types of trade barriers: tariff and nontariff. Tariff barriers include tariffs, quotas, export controls, and dumping regulations. Nontariff barriers are less transparent and include administrative barriers, technical standards, foreign sales corporations, and corrupt practices, among others. Because of their nature, nontariff barriers are difficult to argue and negotiate.

Chapter Notes

1. D. Hume. "Of the balance of trade." In *Essays, Moral, Political and Literary,* vol. 1. Oxford: Oxford University Press, 1973.

2. A. Smith. *An Inquiry Into the Nature and Causes of the Wealth of Nations,* Book IV, pp. 29–31. Oxford: Clarendon Press, 1869.

3. D. Ricardo. *On the Principles of Political Economy and Taxation.* New York: Dutton, 1948.

4. E. Heckscher. "The effects of foreign trade on the distribution of income." Reprinted in H. Ellis and L. Metzler (eds.), *Readings in the Theory of International Trade.* Homewood, IL: Irwin, 1949; Ohlin, B. *International and Interregional Trade.* Cambridge, MA: Harvard Economic Studies, 1933; revised edition, 1967.

5. W. Stolper and P. A. Samuelson. "Protection and real wages." *Review of Economic Studies,* vol. 9, November 1941: pp. 58–73.

6. R. E. Baldwin. "Determinants of the commodity structure of U.S. trade." *American Economic Review,* March 1971: pp. 126–146; J. Vanek, "The natural resource content of foreign trade, 1870–1955, and the relative abundance of natural resources in the United States." *Review of Economics and Statistics,* May 1959: pp. 146–153.

7. P. B. Kenen. "Nature, capital, and trade." *Journal of Political Economy,* October 1965: pp. 437–460; I. B. Kravis. "Wages and foreign trade." *Review of Economics and Statistics,* February 1956: pp. 14–30.

8. D. B. Keesing. "Labor skills and comparative advantage." *American Economic Review,* May 1966: pp. 249–258; R. E. Baldwin. "Determinants of the commodity structure of U.S. trade." *American Economic Review,* March 1971: pp. 126–146; W. H. Gruber, D. Metha, and R. Vernon. "The R&D factor in international trade and international investment of United States industries." *Journal of Political Economy,* February 1967: pp. 20–37; M. Posner. "International trade and technical change." *Oxford Economic Papers,* vol. 13, October 1961: pp. 323–341.

9. P. B. Kenen. "Nature, capital and trade." *Journal of Political Economy,* October 1965: pp. 437–460; R. E. Baldwin. "Determinants of the commodity structure of U.S. trade." *American Economic Review,* March 1971: pp. 126–146.

10. G. C. Hufbauer. *Synthetic Materials and the Theory of International Trade.* Cambridge, MA: Harvard University Press, 1966; M. Posner. "International trade and technical change." *Oxford Economic Papers,* vol. 13, October 1961: pp. 323–341.

11. W. H. Gruber, D. Metha, and R. Vernon. "The R&D factor in international trade and international investment of United States industries." *Journal of Political Economy,* February 1967: pp. 20–37.

12. R. Vernon. "International investments and international trade in the product life cycle." *Quarterly Journal of Economics,* May 1966: pp. 190–207.

13. S. B. Linder. *An Essay on Trade and Transformation.* New York: Wiley, 1961.

14. A. Dixit and V. Norman. *Theory of International Trade.* Cambridge, UK: Cambridge University Press, 1980; K. Lancaster. "Intra-industry trade under perfect monopolistic competition." *Journal of International Economics,* 1980, 10: pp. 151–175; P. Krugman. "Increasing returns, monopolistic competition, and international trade." *Journal of International Economics,* 1979, 9: pp. 469–479; P. Krugman. "Scale economies, product differentiation, and the pattern of trade." *American Economic Review,* 1980, 70: pp. 950–959; P. Krugman. "Intraindustry specialization and the gains from trade." *Journal of Political Economy,* 1981, 89: pp. 959–973; E. Helpman. "International trade in the presence of product differentiation, economies of scale, and monopolistic competition—A Chamberlinian-Heckscher-Ohlin approach." *Journal of International Economics,* 1981, 11: pp. 305–340; W. Ethier. "National and international returns to scale in the modern theory of international trade." *American Economic Review,* 1982, 72: pp. 389–405.

15. World Trade Organization Press Release, October 19, 2001.

16. U.S. Commerce Department. U.S. Trade Online, Guide to Foreign Trade Statistics.

17. J. Millman. "Mexico's newest export: Your meal." *Wall Street Journal,* January 19, 2000, B1.

18. A. Carrns. "A pencil icon tries to get a grip." *Wall Street Journal,* December 24, 2000, A1.

19. WTO, 2001 International Trade Statistics, p. 78.

20. "This trade deficit was made in the USA." *Wall Street Journal,* August 7, 2000, A1.

21. P. Bowring. "Pessimism unwarranted." *International Herald Tribune,* April 6, 2001, 17.

22. WTO. International Trade Statistics, 2001, p. 145; O. Shenkar. *The Chinese Century.* Wharton School Publishing, 2006.

23. J. Millman and W. Pinkston. "Mexicans transform a town in Georgia—and an entire industry." *Wall Street Journal,* August 30, 2001, A1.

24. International Labor Office. Yearbook of Labor Statistics, Geneva, Switzerland, 2000.

25. International Trade Administration. U.S. Services Trade Highlights, December 1999.

26. For a broader discussion, see M. J. Trebilcock and R. Howse. *The Regulation of International Trade.* London: Routledge, 2000.

27. D. S. Broder. "U.S. opinion on free trade is divided." *International Herald Tribune,* March 17–18, 2001, 10.

28. "The human face of globalization." *Economist,* 2000.

29. "Protests: Face of future or just a blast from the past." *Wall Street Journal,* December 2, 1999, A8.

30. "Trade balance: Tipping scales to help workers." *Wall Street Journal,* August 30, 2001, A1.

31. "Globalization: What Americans are worried about." *Business Week,* April 24, 2000, p. 44.

32. M. J. Trebilcock and R. Howse. *The Regulation of International Trade,* 2nd ed. London: Routledge, 2000.

33. P. Constable and R. Lakshmi. "India braces for flood of imports." *International Herald Tribune,* April 6, 2001.

34. "What business thinks." *Twin Cities Business Monthly,* August 24–27 Survey, 2000.

35. *Economist,* October 3, 1998.

36. P. Constable and R. Lakshmi. "India braces for flood of imports." *International Herald Tribune,* April 6, 2001, 13.

37. "Sugar solution." *Economist,* April 22, 2000, 58.

38. "One lump or two?" *Economist,* January 5, 2002, 61.

39. N. King, Jr. "Tale of the tuna: Grocery rivalry fuels tariff spat." *Wall Street Journal,* April 20, 2002, B1.

40. Y. J. Dreazen. "McDonnell Douglas to pay fine for problems with sale to China." *Wall Street Journal,* November 15, 2001, A4.

41. S. Sakuma. "What's unfair?—The WTO rules on dumping." *Japan Economic Currents,* Keizai Koho Center, No. 9, June 2001.

42. T. Beal. "A Mexican standoff with China—The Asian." *Wall Street Journal,* June 1–3, 2001, A6.

43. J. Karp. "Brazil to be vocal in America's trade talks." *Wall Street Journal,* April 19, 2001, A13.

44. I. Jacj and P. Morton. "Ottawa protests U.S. delays over lumber to WTO." *Financial Post,* January 23, 2002, FP6.

45. Trebilcock and Howse. *The Regulation of International Trade,* pp. 113–114. London: Routledge, 2000.

46. G. Winestock. "U.S., EU risk trade war over export tax shelters." *Wall Street Journal,* September 5, 2000, A26; [no author] "U.S. export subsidy has some fans in Europe." *Wall Street Journal,* September 29, 2000, A17.

47. J. D. McKinnon. "Exporters attack tax proposal." *Wall Street Journal,* May 1, 2002, A2.

48. Standards, Conformity Assessment, and Trade, cited in Trebilcock and Howse, p. 132.

49. "Is EU's vision of free trade blurred by protectionism?" *Wall Street Journal,* March 29, 2002, A10.

50. Trebilcock and Howse. *The Regulation of International Trade,* p. 311. London: Routledge, 2000.

51. Trebilcock and Howse, p. 274.

FOREIGN DIRECT INVESTMENT THEORY AND APPLICATION

DO YOU KNOW?

1. What are the various types of foreign direct investment (FDI)?

2. What are the strategic goals of multinational enterprises (MNEs) undertaking FDI? Do they vary by market and industry?

3. If you were the head of the investment authority of India, what benefits would you cite to MNE executives to attract them to establish operations in your country?

4. What drives FDI distribution and patterns—for instance, why is Africa left out of the FDI mix?

5. Do you believe the liberalization of FDI regimes will continue in the coming years?

OPENING CASE

Japan Changes Its Mind About FDI

Among the industrialized nations, Japan has attracted the lowest level of FDI by far. At the end of 2004, its inward FDI stock amounted to just 2% of GDP, compared with 13% in the United States and 33% in the United Kingdom. Historical suspicion of foreigners (the country was closed to foreigners for two centuries until the mid-19th century), restrictive regulation (for instance, from 1962 to 1974, foreign investors were by and large denied full ownership of Japanese firms and had to settle for a joint venture), high cost of doing business, and multiple entry barriers ranging from a fragmented retail system to nepotistic relations between domestic producers, suppliers, and distributors combined to limit FDI in the country despite the allure of access to the second

largest market in the world and the availability of a highly qualified workforce. Shintaro Abe, Japan's new prime minister, wants to change that. Building on the initiative of his predecessor, Junichiro Koizumi, he announced, in the fall of 2006, the "third opening" of the country (the first two followed the Meiji restoration in 1868 and the Second World War). The Japanese government has recently placed full-page advertisements in global newspapers calling on firms to invest in Japan not only via the establishment of new operations but also through mergers and acquisitions—the first time a Japanese government has done so.

Japan's change of heart regarding FDI was triggered by a number of factors, ranging from demographics (because of low birthrates, Japan is projected to suffer a declining population and labor shortage) to a growing realization that global competition from both emerging (e.g., China) and developed (e.g., the European Union) economies necessitates enhanced openness and the pooling of resources and talent from around the world. To create a more conducive investment environment, the government has identified 74 policy measures, covering (a) increased publicity of investment opportunities, (b) facilitating mergers and acquisitions, (c) improved administrative procedures, (d) better living arrangements for foreign workers, and (e) assigning a larger role in FDI to local governments, who now compete with each other in attracting FDI. A goal of FDI reaching 5% of GDP by 2010 has been set, and additional measures, including the establishment of Special Economic Zones, have been announced. To increase transparency, 180 laws pertaining to FDI have been translated into English.

SOURCES: Anthony H. Rowley. "New government aims to accelerate inward investment." *Asian Wall Street Journal*, October 27–28, p. 8; "Foreign firms put their funds into the 'new economy.'" *Wall Street Journal*, November 15, 2006, A17; Japanese government sources.

DEFINITION AND TYPES OF FOREIGN DIRECT INVESTMENT

As the opening case shows, increasing globalization has captured the attention of not only entrepreneurs and business-people but also government officials who are searching for international business advantages in an ever-changing world. The active pursuit of FDI for the first time in Japanese history is a signal that the rules of the game have changed under globalization. The message is clear: Markets are moving toward international competition, and to prosper, nations need to tap the resources and opportunities available beyond their borders. To this end, they need not only to attract FDI to their shores but also to engage in outward investment in foreign markets. However, as we will see in this chapter, as well as in Chapters 4, 6, 7, and 10, among others, investment in foreign markets is full of potential pitfalls. The complexities involved in controlling and coordinating foreign affiliates that are situated far from headquarters and from each other, and the uncertainty of operating in unfamiliar environments that differ from each other and from the home environment culturally, legally, and politically, represent major challenges to firms. Failed international expansions such as Swissair (which collapsed as a result) and Gateway Computers (which retreated to its domestic U.S. market) serve as reminders of the difficulty of investing and operating abroad.

Companies can enter a foreign market through either exporting or FDI. Exporting is a relatively low-risk and simple vehicle with which to enter a foreign market because it does not involve actual presence in the target market. While relatively low in risk, exporting does not enable a firm to maintain control over foreign production and operations nor benefit from opportunities available only through actual presence in a foreign market. **Foreign direct investment** (FDI) occurs when a firm invests directly in production or other facilities in a foreign country over which it has effective control. Manufacturing FDI requires an establishment of production facilities abroad (e.g., Coca-Cola has built bottling facilities in about 200 countries), whereas service FDI requires either the building of service facilities (e.g., Disneyland Hong Kong) or the establishment of an investment foothold via capital contribution and building office facilities (e.g., Citigroup's acquisition of the private banking and financial services firm Confia). Overseas units or entities are broadly called **foreign subsidiaries** or **affiliates**. The country in which a foreign subsidiary operates is termed the **host country**.

One needs to distinguish between the flow of FDI and the stock of FDI. The **flow of FDI** refers to the amount of FDI undertaken over a given time period (e.g., a year). The **stock of FDI** refers to the total accumulated value of foreign-owned assets at a given time (which takes into account possible divestment along the way). With regard to the flow of FDI, it is important to differentiate between outflow and inflow FDI. **Outflow of FDI** means the flow of FDI out of a country—that is, firms undertaking direct investment in foreign countries. **Inflow of FDI** means the flow of FDI into a country—that is, foreign firms undertaking direct investment in the host country. We will later present the patterns and characteristics of FDI flows and stocks involving major world nations.

FDI Versus Foreign Portfolio Investment

Foreign portfolio investment is investment by individuals, firms, or public organs (e.g., governments or nonprofit organizations) in foreign financial instruments such as government bonds, corporate bonds, mutual funds, and foreign stocks. In other words, portfolio investment is the investment in **financial assets** comprising stocks, bonds, and other forms of debt denominated in terms of a foreign country's national currency, whereas FDI is the investment in real or **physical assets,** such as factories and distribution facilities. As such, FDI involves control over foreign production or operations undertaken by the multinational enterprise (MNE), but portfolio investment does not. To understand foreign portfolio investment, one needs to be familiar with portfolio theory. **Portfolio theory** describes the behavior of individuals or firms administering large amounts of financial assets in search of the highest possible risk-adjusted net return. Fundamental to this theory is the idea that a guaranteed rate of return (say, 9% per year fixed over the next five years) is preferable to a rate of return that is higher on average but fluctuates over time (e.g., average 9.5% per year but with high volatility during this five-year period). The variability of the rate of return over time is referred to as the **financial risk** in portfolio investment. The key task of portfolio management is to reduce the variability (or risk) of a group of stocks so that the variability of the whole set is less than that of its component parts. If it is possible to identify some stocks whose yields will increase when the yields of others decrease, then, by including both types of securities in the portfolio, the portfolio's overall variability will be reduced. This is why some people interpret this theory as "putting eggs in different baskets rather than one basket." This logic also applies to the establishment of a conglomerate that diversifies into many product lines rather than specializing in a single line of products. A more detailed discussion of portfolio investment can be found in Chapters 9 and 14.

Types of FDI

We distinguish between horizontal and vertical FDI. **Horizontal FDI** occurs when the MNE enters a foreign country to produce the same product(s) produced at home (or offer the same service that it sells at home). It represents, therefore, a geographical diversification of the MNE's domestic product line. Most Japanese MNEs, for instance, begin their international expansion with horizontal investment because they believe that this approach enables them to share experience, resources, and knowledge already developed at home, thus reducing risk. If FDI abroad is to manufacture products not manufactured by the parent company at home, it is called **conglomerate FDI.** For example, Hong Kong MNEs often set up foreign subsidiaries or acquire local firms in Mainland China to manufacture goods that are unrelated to the parent company's portfolio of products. The main purpose is to seize emerging-market opportunities and capitalize on their established business and personal networks with the mainland that Western MNEs do not have. **Vertical FDI** occurs when the MNE enters a foreign country to produce intermediate goods that are intended for use as inputs in its home country (or in other subsidiaries') production process (this is called "backward vertical FDI"), to market its homemade products overseas, or to produce final outputs in a host country using its home-supplied intermediate goods or materials (this is called "forward vertical FDI"). An example of backward vertical FDI is offshore extractive investments in petroleum and minerals. An example of forward vertical integration is the establishment of an assembly plant or a sales outlet overseas.

The **liability of foreignness** represents the costs of doing business abroad that result in a competitive disadvantage vis-à-vis indigenous firms. An example of this liability is the lack of adaptation to European customs, from transportation models to food, by the Walt Disney Company when establishing its first park in Europe, Euro Disney (renamed Disneyland Europe since then). Utilizing established competencies abroad in the same product or business as that at home helps the firm overcome the liability of foreignness and thus reduces the risks inherent in foreign production and operations. Horizontal FDI enables the MNE to quickly establish its competitive advantage in the host country because the company's key competencies, whether technological or organizational, are generally more transferable. Conglomerate FDI involves more difficulties in establishing market power and competitive position in the host country. These difficulties arise from the firm's inability to share distinctive competencies developed at home. Finally, vertical FDI, whether backward or forward, can create financial and operational benefits (e.g., transfer pricing, high profit margin, market power, and quality control) but requires global coordination by the headquarters.

Entry Mode

The manner in which a firm chooses to enter a foreign market through FDI is referred to as **entry mode.** Entry mode examples include international franchising, branches, contractual alliances, equity joint ventures, and wholly foreign-owned subsidiaries. While Damon's restaurants, for example, used franchising to enter the Panama market, Lucent Technologies (now merged with the French firm Alcatel) preferred a contractual alliance (i.e., coproduction) to minimize investment risks when it entered this market. While U.S.-based General Electric and French company Snecma formed a joint venture to produce civilian jet engines, German-based DaimlerChrysler chose to establish a wholly owned subsidiary in Alabama to manufacture sport-utility vehicles. Once the entry mode is selected, firms determine the specific approach they will use to establish or realize the chosen entry mode. Specific investment approaches include (a) greenfield investment (i.e., building a brand-new facility), (b) cross-border mergers, (c) cross-border acquisitions, and (d) sharing or utilizing existing facilities. Entry modes and investment approaches are further detailed in Chapter 10.

The Strategic Logic of FDI

Different MNEs might have different strategic logic underlying FDI. **Resource-seeking FDI** attempts to acquire particular resources at a lower real cost than could be obtained in the home country. Resource seekers can be further classified into three groups: those seeking physical resources; those seeking cheap and/or skilled labor; and those seeking technological, organizational, and managerial skills. **Market-seeking FDI** attempts to secure market share and sales growth in the target foreign market. Apart from market size and the prospects for market growth, the reasons for market-seeking FDI include situations in which (a) the firm's main suppliers or customers have set up foreign producing facilities abroad and the firm needs to follow them overseas; (b) the firm's products need to be adapted to local tastes or needs, and to indigenous resources and capabilities; and (c) the firm considers it necessary, as part of its global production and marketing strategy, to maintain a physical presence in the leading markets served by its competitors. **Efficiency-seeking FDI** attempts to rationalize the structure of established resource-based or marketing-seeking investment in such a way that the firm can gain from the common governance of geographically dispersed activities. MNEs with this motive generally aim to take advantage of different factor endowments, cultures, economic systems and policies, and market structures by concentrating production in a limited number of locations to supply multiple markets. Finally, **strategic asset-seeking FDI** attempts to acquire the assets of foreign firms so as to promote their long-term strategic objectives, especially advancing their international competitiveness. MNEs with this intention often establish global strategic alliances or acquire local firms. Many MNEs today pursue pluralistic goals and engage in FDI that combines characteristics of several of the preceding categories. Procter & Gamble, for instance, has sales in over 140 countries and on-the-ground operations in over 70 countries. Its strategic aims behind product and geographical diversifications include better resources, larger markets, and higher efficiency.

Interim Summary

1. Although FDI involves a higher risk than exportation, it allows a company greater control over its products or services in foreign markets as well as access to specialized opportunities not available to exporters.

2. In addition to FDI in the form of subsidiaries and physical plants, many MNEs engage in foreign portfolio investment whereby they purchase foreign stocks, bonds, or other foreign financial instruments.

3. The strategic logic of FDI includes resource seeking, market seeking, efficiency seeking, and strategic asset seeking.

4. Horizontal FDI is a safe way to enter a foreign market because it produces the same product as the parent company, so experience and infrastructure are easily shared. If the investment produces a product unrelated to the parent's, it is a conglomerate FDI. Vertical FDI acts as an intermediary or finishing stage in the production process, offering either inputs to the parent or access to a foreign market.

HOW THE MNE BENEFITS FROM FOREIGN DIRECT INVESTMENT

Enhancing Efficiency From Location Advantages

In Chapter 2 we introduced the concept of comparative advantage of nations. Firms can realize these advantages not only through international trade but also through FDI. In fact, FDI is potentially a better vehicle than trade for firms in terms of leveraging factor endowment differences between home and host countries. This is because through FDI the firm owns and controls actual operations overseas and can consequently capture the entire profit margin that otherwise must be shared between an importer and an exporter. **Location advantages** are defined as the benefits arising from a host country's comparative advantages accrued to foreign direct investors. Firms are prompted to invest abroad to acquire particular and specific resources at lower real costs than could be obtained in their home country. The motivation for FDI is to make the investing firm more profitable and competitive in the markets it serves or intends to serve. In addition to natural endowments, location-specific advantages include created endowments such as economic systems and investment incentives. PepsiCo Inc., for example, invested heavily in Brazil, Argentina, and Mexico to seek out benefits resulting from economic liberalization in these economies. Generally, MNEs that use cost-leadership strategies will choose the location that minimizes total costs. Labor cost differentials, transportation costs, and tariff and nontariff barriers, as well as governmental policies (e.g., taxes affecting investment in a host country) are important determinants of location choice. MNEs use their knowledge and information-scanning ability to locate manufacturing activities in countries that are the most advantageous from the standpoint of cost or other strategic considerations.

Improving Performance From Structural Discrepancies

Structural discrepancies are the differences in industry structure attributes (e.g., profitability, growth potential, and competition) between home and host countries. Through FDI, MNEs are likely to achieve higher performance than firms operating domestically because they benefit from such structural discrepancies by investing those distinct resources that can enhance competitive advantages vis-à-vis their rivals in indigenous markets. Because national markets vary in industry life-cycle stages and in consumer purchasing power, market demand and sophistication are heterogeneous across borders. For instance, many emerging economies present vast market opportunities for MNEs to attain above-average returns from pent-up demand long stifled by government intervention.

Increasing Return From Ownership Advantages

Ownership advantages are benefits derived from the proprietary knowledge, resources, or assets possessed only by the owner (the MNE). The possession of intangible assets (e.g., reputation, brand image, and unique distribution channels) or proprietary knowledge (e.g., technological expertise, organizational skills, and international experience) confers competitive advantages on a firm's foreign owners. FDI serves as an instrument that allows firms to transfer capital, technology, and organizational skills from one country to another. FDI expands the market domain from which the MNE can deploy, exploit, and utilize its core competence developed at home. **Core competence** is the set of skills within the firm that competitors cannot easily match or imitate. These skills may exist in any of the firm's value-creation activities, such as production, marketing, R&D, and human resources. Such skills are typically expressed in product or service offerings that other firms find difficult to imitate; the core competencies are thus the bedrock of a firm's competitive advantage. They enable an MNE to reduce the cost of value creation or to create value in such a way that premium pricing is possible from product or service differentiation. FDI is hence a way of further exploiting the value-creation potential of skills and product offerings by applying them to new markets. IBM, for example, generates significant income from its voice-recognition software used by many Chinese. This software, first developed in the United States, did not generate sizable income until a Chinese version was developed by the company's subsidiary in Beijing.

Ensuring Growth From Organizational Learning

FDI creates the diversity of environments in which the MNE operates. This diversity exposes the MNE to multiple stimuli, allows it to develop diverse capabilities, and provides it with broader learning opportunities than those available to a domestic firm. Organizational learning has long been a key building block and major source of competitive advantages. Sustainable competitive advantages are only possible when firms continuously reinvest in building new resources or upgrading existing resources. FDI provides learning opportunities through exposure to new markets, new practices, new ideas, new cultures, and even new competition. These opportunities result in the development of new capabilities that may be applicable to operations in similar markets. For example, many early movers entering China, such as Motorola, Kodak, Philips, Sony, and Occidental Petroleum, realized that the relationship-building (personal ties with the local business community) skills they learned in China apply in their business in Vietnam, Egypt, Southeast Asia, and Latin America. Moreover, host country environments are often characterized by both market opportunities and tremendous uncertainties. This forces MNEs to learn how to respond to local settings. Further, through global alliances, FDI offers opportunities to acquire distinctive skills from foreign businesses or rivals. A global alliance can provide a firm with low-cost, fast access to new markets by "borrowing" a partner's existing core competencies, innovative skills, and country-specific knowledge. Chapter 12 discusses global alliances in detail.

The benefits suggested above are not guaranteed, however, since FDI is undertaken in a highly uncertain environment. Additional costs arise from unfamiliarity with the cultural, political, and economic dimensions of a new environment. The impact of a host country's regulatory and industrial environment on FDI is substantial. In an uncertain foreign environment, regulatory factors (e.g., FDI policies, taxation and financing regulations, foreign exchange administration rules, threat of nationalization, earnings repatriation, and price controls) are especially important. The effect of uncertainty is particularly significant in formerly centrally planned economies undergoing transition and emerging markets undergoing drastic privatization, despite their promising potentials.

Interim Summary

1. The location advantages of a host country are its comparative advantages for FDI in relation to other countries. These include cheaper and/or better-quality resources such as labor, capital, and natural resources (factor endowments) as well as investment incentives (created endowments) that affect cost.

2. National markets vary in their industry life-cycle stage, market growth potential, competition intensity, consumer purchasing power, and other factors. These variations can be used to the advantage of the MNE.

3. FDI expands the market domain in which an MNE capitalizes on its core competencies, generating more income from existing resources, capabilities, or knowledge.

4. FDI is also a vehicle for organizational learning. Being actively involved in FDI grants the MNE learning opportunities that would not have been available otherwise.

THE IMPACT OF FDI ON THE HOST (RECIPIENT) COUNTRY

The impact of FDI on national welfare is best assessed from the perspective of the home and host countries, although those too vary internally by region and constituency. While nationals of the Netherlands, Finland, and the United States find FDI and globalization the least threatening, those from Colombia, the Philippines, and Venezuela perceive it as a threat.[1] In Venezuela, the attitude toward inward FDI has turned much more negative in recent years. At the same time, many of the factors that may make FDI attractive to a host country may make it look detrimental to the home country. For instance, although FDI benefits employment in the host country, this is often accompanied by job losses in the home country. A case in point would be any labor-intensive industry in the United States (e.g., garments, furniture) that moved much of its operations first to Mexico and, later, to China.

Employment

When U.S. firms such as Xerox, Staples, and Cendant establish a customer-service call center in Canada, they do so to capitalize on that country's abundant and less expensive workforce.[2] While this enhances employment in Canada, the emphasis of most host governments today is placed on jobs requiring knowledge and high added value. Host governments are especially keen on attracting firms that will augment high-end employment, and home governments are especially worried about losing such jobs. One consequence of the increased diversity of functional areas for FDI is frequent criticism of FDI as a deployment of the less desirable segments of the production process abroad while retaining the most attractive portions, especially R&D, at home. Still, developed countries like the United States are concerned about the loss of those jobs and the resulting downward pressure on domestic wages. As noted in Chapter 2, when a job moves abroad, the displaced workers are unlikely to find a higher paying job than the one they lost. Recently, the more sophisticated parts of the value chain, including R&D, are also performed abroad, putting higher end jobs on the line in the home country.

FDI Impact on Domestic Enterprises

Thanks to their resource endowment, foreign invested enterprises are likely to be more productive than their local counterparts. The contribution of foreign affiliates to exports tends to be much higher than their proportional share in a national economy would suggest. For instance, firms with foreign equity (both wholly and partially owned) accounted in 2005 for roughly 58% of China's exports. FDI could adversely affect domestic enterprises. Its superiority is sometimes rooted in favorable treatment (e.g., lower taxation rates or tax breaks) offered by host governments but not accorded to local firms. Thus local firms may be institutionally discriminated against, resulting in lesser competition in the industry. Heightened competition contributed by FDI could hurt individual local firms who lose market share, resulting in layoffs, profit reduction, and/or the closure of facilities and factories. Such negative effects were felt in Nigeria when the oil MNEs of Shell (Anglo-Dutch), Chevron (U.S.), and Texaco (U.S.) started operations there. Local firms such as the Nigerian National Petroleum Corporation (NNPC) have yielded the market-leader position to those MNEs.

In response to the pressures of FDI, local enterprises seek to improve productivity and strengthen competitiveness on their own or through alliances with other local firms or with MNEs. Since the establishment of NAFTA, the number of Mexican firms undertaking outbound FDI has grown manifold. The Mexican food firm Bimbo used its supplier relationship with McDonald's to piggyback on the U.S. firm and establish supply bases throughout Latin America. Chinese manufacturers such as appliance-maker Haier are now exporting to both developing and developed markets and have begun to establish manufacturing plants abroad, a step that was inconceivable before a massive FDI flow into China changed work practices and standards there. As discussed in Chapter 4, FDI tends to create innovation and knowledge, which are eventually dispersed throughout the many levels of the local economy. The extent to which local firms can take advantage of this depends on a host of other factors (e.g., local infrastructure and government policies).

UNCTAD (United Nations Center for Trade and Development) documented the various relationships between MNEs and domestic firms, ranging from purchasing to joint ventures to various contractual relationships (Exhibit 3.1). The key point is that the spillover from FDI is substantial. In typical developed economies, for example, MNE affiliates realize between 10% and 20% of their input locally, and there is some evidence that local procurement increases over time. Such relationships are also important to MNEs in that they enable them to tap local resources while producing a beneficial outcome for the host country.

Exhibit 3.1   Backward Linkages Between Foreign Affiliates and Local Enterprises and Organizations

Form	Relationship of Foreign Affiliate to Local Enterprise			Relationship of Foreign Affiliate to NonBusiness Institutions
	Backward (Sourcing)	Forward (Distribution)	Horizontal (Cooperation in Production)	
Pure market transaction	• Off-the-shelf purchases	• Off-the-shelf sales		
Short-term linkage	• Once-for-all or intermittent purchases (on contract)	• Once-for-all or intermittent sales (on contract)		
Longer-term linkage	• Longer-term (contractual) arrangement for the procurement of inputs for further processing • Subcontracting of the production of final or intermediate products	• Longer-term (contractual) relationship with local distributor or end customer • Outsourcing from domestic firms to foreign affiliates	• Joint projects with competing domestic firm	• R&D contracts with local institutions such as universities and research centers • Training programs for firms by universities • Traineeships for students in firms
Equity relationship	• Joint venture with supplier • Establishment of new supplier–affiliate (by existing foreign affiliate)	• Joint venture with distributor or end customer • Establishment of new distribution affiliate (by existing foreign affiliate)	• Horizontal joint venture • Establishment of new affiliate (by existing foreign affiliate) for the production of same goods and services as it produces	• Joint public–private R&D centers/training centers/universities

Spillover	• Demonstration effects in unrelated firms
	  – Spillover on processes (including technology)
	  – Spillover on product design
	  – Spillover on format and on tacit skills (shop floor and managerial)
	• Effects due to mobility of trained human resources
	• Enterprise spin-offs
	• Competition effects			

SOURCE: UNCTAD, 2001.

Interim Summary

1. Job shift to the host country is one of the benefits of FDI to that country. Desirable jobs such as product design and R&D are usually retained in the home country, but this is starting to change.

2. MNEs are powerful competitors to local businesses. However, depending on the business environment of the host country, local companies may be able to learn from the MNE and become globally competitive.

CURRENT THEORIES ON FDI

Product Life-Cycle Theory

International product life-cycle theory (first introduced in Chapter 2) provides a theoretical explanation for both trade and FDI. The theory, developed by Raymond Vernon, explains why U.S. manufacturers shift from exporting to FDI. The manufacturers initially gain a monopolistic export advantage from product innovations developed for the U.S. market. In the new product stage, production continues to be concentrated in the United States even though production costs in some foreign countries may be lower. When the product becomes standardized in its growth product stage, the U.S. manufacturer has an incentive to invest abroad to exploit lower manufacturing costs and to prevent the loss of the export market to local producers. The U.S. manufacturer's first investment will be made in another industrial country where export sales are large enough to support economies of scale in local production. In the mature product stage, cost competition among all producers, including imitating foreign firms, intensifies. At this stage, the U.S. manufacturer may also shift production from the country of the initial FDI to a lower-cost country, sustaining the old subsidiary with new products.[3]

Vernon's theory is more relevant to manufacturers' initial entries into foreign markets than to MNEs that have FDI already in place. Many MNEs are able to develop new products abroad for subsequent sale in the United States, thus standing the product life-cycle model on its head. For example, Procter & Gamble employed more than 8,000 scientists and researchers in 2000 in 18 technical centers in nine countries. Many new products in the health care and beauty care segments were developed in these offshore research centers and subsequently marketed in the United States and other foreign countries. MNEs can also transfer new products from the United States directly to their existing foreign subsidiaries, thereby skipping the export stage. Otis Elevator, a wholly owned subsidiary of United Technologies Corp., offers its products in more than 200 countries and maintains major manufacturing facilities in Europe, Asia, and the Americas. Despite being headquartered in the United States, 80% of Otis's 2005 revenues of $9.6 billion were generated elsewhere. Most of Otis's new elevators, escalators, moving walkways, and shuttle systems were first developed in the United States and then transferred to and manufactured by its foreign subsidiaries in the target overseas markets, although the company increasingly engages in development work abroad.

Monopolistic Advantage Theory

The monopolistic advantage theory suggests that the MNE possesses monopolistic advantages, enabling it to operate subsidiaries abroad more profitably than local competing firms can.[4] **Monopolistic advantage** is the benefit accrued to a firm that maintains a monopolistic power in the market. Such advantages are specific to the investing firm rather than to the location of its production. Stephen H. Hymer found that FDI takes place because powerful MNEs choose industries or markets in which they have greater competitive advantages, such as technological knowledge not available to other firms operating in a given country. These competitive advantages are also referred to as firm-specific or ownership-specific advantages.

According to this theory, monopolistic advantages come from two sources: superior knowledge and economies of scale. The term *knowledge* includes production technologies, managerial skills, industrial organization, and knowledge of product. Although the MNE could possibly exploit its already developed superior knowledge through licensing to foreign markets, many types of knowledge cannot be directly sold. This is because it is impossible to package technological knowledge in a license, as is true for managerial expertise, industrial organization, knowledge of markets, and such. Even when the knowledge can be embodied in a license, the local producer may be unwilling to pay its full value because of uncertainties about its utilization. Given these reasons, the MNE realizes that it can obtain a higher return by producing directly through a subsidiary than by selling the license.

Besides superior knowledge, another determinant of FDI is the opportunity to achieve economies of scale. Economies of scale occur through either horizontal or vertical FDI. An increase in production through horizontal investment permits a reduction in unit cost of services such as financing, marketing, and technological research. Because each overseas plant produces the same product in its entirety, horizontal investment may also have the advantage of allowing the firm to even out the effects of business cycles in various markets by rearranging sales destinations across nations. Through vertical investment in which each affiliate produces those parts of the final product for which local production costs are lower, the MNE may benefit from local advantages in production costs while achieving maximum economies of scale in the production of single components. Such an international integration of production would be much more difficult through trade because of the need for close coordination of different producers and production phases.

Internalization Theory

Internalization theory holds that the available external market fails to provide an efficient environment in which the firm can profit by using its technology or production resources. Therefore, the firm tends to produce an internal market via investment in multiple countries and thus creates the needed market to achieve its objective.[5] A typical MNE consists of a group of geographically dispersed and goal-disparate organizations that include its headquarters and different national subsidiaries. These MNEs achieve their objectives not only through exploiting their proprietary knowledge but also through internalizing operations and management. **Internalization** is the activity in which an MNE internalizes its globally dispersed foreign operations through a unified governance structure and common ownership. Internalization theorists argue that internalization creates "contracting" through a unified, integrated intrafirm governance structure. It takes place either because there is no market for the intermediate products needed by MNEs (e.g., Falk, a global power transmission manufacturer, must use intermediate goods such as couplings and backstops produced by its Brazilian subsidiary owing to the unavailability from any outside source) or because the external market for such products is inefficient (e.g., IBM's speech-recognition technology is "transacted" internally among different units because the external market has not been developed enough to properly value and protect such expertise). The costs of transactions conducted at arm's length in an external market (i.e., a fair price in an open market) may be higher than transactions within an intraorganizational market. The incentives to internalize activities are to avoid disadvantages in external mechanisms of resource allocation or to benefit from an internally integrated and intraorganizational network.

Internalization theory also specifies that the common governance of activities in different locations (e.g., Rubbermaid's subsidiary in China uses materials supplied by its sister subsidiary in Thailand and then ships products to the United States, Europe, and Japan) is likely to result in transaction gains. In many industries, MNEs are no longer able to compete as a collection of nationally independent subsidiaries; rather, competition is based in part on the ability to link or integrate subsidiary activities across geographic locations. To summarize, internalization advantages include the following:

1. To avoid search and negotiating costs

2. To avoid costs of moral hazard (**moral hazard** refers to hidden detrimental action by external partners such as suppliers, buyers, and joint venture partners)

3. To avoid costs of violated contracts and ensuing litigation

4. To capture economies of interdependent activities

5. To avoid government intervention (e.g., quotas, tariffs, price controls)

6. To control supplies and conditions of sale of inputs (including technology)

7. To control market outlets

8. To better apply cross-subsidization, predatory pricing, and transfer pricing

Through internalization, global competitive advantages are developed by forming international economies of scale and scope and by triggering organizational learning across national markets. Operational flexibility can leverage the degree of integration. The allocation and dispersal of resources (both tangible and intangible) serve as a primary device for maintaining operational flexibility in global business activities. Essentially, by directing resource flows, an MNE may shift its activities in response to changes in tax structures, labor rates, exchange rates, governmental policy, competitor moves, or other uncertainties. Thus, resource flows are a necessary condition for achieving either location-specific or competitive advantages in global business. Resource flow requires internalization within an MNE network because it involves interdependence among subsidiaries. Internalization, in turn, requires centralized decision-making responsibility and authority. Nevertheless, control should be segmented by product line and distributed among different subsidiaries, depending on particular capabilities and environmental conditions.

The Eclectic Paradigm

The eclectic paradigm offers a general framework for explaining international production.[6] This paradigm includes three variables: ownership-specific (O), location-specific (L), and internalization (I), all identified in earlier theories of trade and FDI. The paradigm is also called the **OLI framework**. It stands at the intersection of a macroeconomic theory of international trade (L) and a microeconomic theory of the firm (O and I). It is an exercise in resource allocation and organizational economics. The key assertion is that all three factors (OLI) are important in determining the extent and pattern of FDI. Ownership-specific variables include tangible assets such as natural endowments, manpower, and capital but also intangible assets such as technology and information, managerial, marketing, and entrepreneurial skills, and organizational systems.

Location-specific (or country-specific) variables refer to factor endowments introduced in the preceding chapter as well as market structure, government legislation and policies, and the political, legal, and cultural environments in which FDI is undertaken. Finally, internalization refers to the firm's inherent flexibility and capacity to produce and market through its own internal subsidiaries. It is the inability of the market to produce a satisfactory deal between potential buyers and sellers of intermediate products that explains why MNEs often choose internalization over the market route for exploiting differences in comparative advantages between countries.

The eclectic paradigm distinguishes between structural and transactional market failure. Structural market failure is an external condition that gives rise to monopoly advantages as a result of entry barriers erected or increased by incumbent firms or governments. Structural market failure thus discriminates between firms in terms of their ability to gain and sustain control over property rights or to govern geographically dispersed valued-added activities. Transactional market failure is the failure of intermediate product markets to transact goods and services at a lower cost than that incurred via internalization.

Overall, the eclectic paradigm provides a more comprehensive view explaining FDI than do the product life-cycle theory, the monopolistic advantage theory, or the internalization theory. It combines and integrates country-specific, ownership-specific, and internalization factors in articulating the logic and benefits of international production. Although today's international business environment and MNE behavior are markedly different from what they were two decades ago, when the theory first emerged, the OLI advantages are still vital to explaining why FDI takes place and where MNEs' superior returns come from. The eclectic paradigm, like other theories of FDI, has some limitations, however. First, it does not adequately address how an MNE's ownership-specific advantages such as distinctive resources and capabilities should be deployed and exploited in international production. Possessing these resources is indeed important, but it will not yield high returns for the MNE unless they are efficiently deployed, allocated, and utilized in foreign production and operations. Second, the paradigm does not explicitly delineate the ongoing, evolving process of international production. FDI itself is a dynamic process in which resource commitment, production scale, and investment approaches are changing over time. The product life-cycle theory also falls short on explaining the dynamics of the FDI process. Third, the conventional wisdom seems inadequate in illuminating how geographically dispersed international production should be appropriately coordinated and integrated. The internalization perspective addresses how an MNE could circumvent or exploit market failure for intermediate products and services but does not discuss how a firm could integrate a multitude of sophisticated international production and balance global integration with local adaptation. To redress these deficiencies, several new theoretical perspectives have emerged in recent years. We introduce these perspectives next.

Interim Summary

1. The product life-cycle theory adequately describes how a new MNE develops a new product and then engages in FDI; however, it fails to describe the actions of existing MNEs with substantial FDI that may skip steps in the model or even reverse the process.

2. Monopolization theory suggests that the core competencies of an MNE are products over which it holds a monopoly. FDI occurs when it is more

cost-effective to directly exploit and market these monopolies than to license them to a local company.

3. Internalization theory states that one of the major reasons for MNEs to engage in FDI is to internalize most parts of the production process. This significantly reduces normal business risks and gives the MNE economy-of-scale advantages. The eclectic paradigm restates this concept and integrates it with corporate monopolization and national comparative advantage.

NEW PERSPECTIVES ON FDI

The Dynamic Capability Perspective

This perspective argues that ownership-specific resources or knowledge are necessary but insufficient for the success of international investment and production. This success depends not only on whether the MNE possesses distinctive resources but also on how it deploys and uses these resources in an efficient manner.[7] For example, IBM's breakthrough development in voice-recognition systems did not generate much income until this system was deployed and adapted to such markets as Singapore, Hong Kong, Taiwan, China, and Korea through its subsidiaries in those locations. FDI itself is not a single transaction, nor a one-step activity. Rather it is a dynamic process involving continued resource commitment. The ability of an MNE to thrive in today's turbulent international environment depends on its dynamic capabilities during international investment, production, and operations. **Dynamic capabilities** refer to a firm's ability to diffuse, deploy, utilize, and rebuild firm-specific resources in order to attain a sustained competitive advantage. Dynamic capability requires a capacity to extract economic returns from current resources (i.e., **capability exploitation**) as well as a capacity to learn and develop new capabilities (**capability building**). In other words, dynamic capabilities take MNE resources beyond their role as static sources of inimitable advantage toward aspects of sustainable, evolving advantage.

Resource deployment is the first step in efficient capability exploitation. Capability deployment involves both quantity- and quality-based resource commitment and allocation. **Quantity-based** deployment refers to the amount of key resources deployed in a target foreign market. **Quality-based** deployment involves the distinctiveness of resources allocated to a target market. To optimally deploy distinctive resources, MNEs need to know what factors affect the efficiency of deployment. Resources will generate stronger competitive advantages when they are applied through an appropriate configuration with external and internal dynamics in a competitive environment. Chapter 4 explains how this configuration should be made and how capability deployment may lead to competitive advantages for international expansion.

Resource deployment requires an MNE to transfer critical resources within a globally coordinated network. This transfer is the process whereby the MNE draws on some or all of its distinctive resources or capabilities from its home base or integrated network to give its operations in a foreign country a competitive advantage. **Transferability** is the extent to which MNE resources or knowledge developed at home can be transferred to a foreign subunit to result in competitive advantage or contribute to business success in the target foreign setting (industry, segmented market, or host country). Although foreign subsidiaries could rely on local resources or self-developed capabilities as needed in a local setting, this is usually inefficient because indigenous firms are already more effective at developing such capabilities. In other words, a foreign business can only gain an advantage if it is able to transfer critical capabilities unavailable to local players. For instance, McDonald's overseas success has been built on the firm's ability to rapidly transfer the capacity to operate its entire business system to foreign entrepreneurs. Similarly, KFC's superior knowledge in organizing and managing fast-food restaurants is transferable to its operations in foreign markets such as Australia and Russia.

Transferability may vary for different resources or capabilities. While Toyota's quality-control system applies well to all its global subunits, its just-in-time (JIT) system is problematic in locations where supply disruptions are common owing to such factors as inclement weather and labor strife. Technological capabilities are generally more transferable than organizational skills. For instance, in globalizing its R&D activities, Sony did not encounter difficulties transferring core technologies to overseas R&D units but was uncertain about which R&D management approach to use. Sony later realized that the top-down management approach used at home did not apply abroad and changed to a bottom-up approach. Furthermore, financial capabilities are more transferable than operational capabilities. Capital or cash flow management skills may be more mobile than workforce-related capabilities. Home country experience and reputation are also not easily transferred abroad, but international experience and global reputation are transferable across borders. Possession or control of a superior distribution network in the home market is another resource that cannot be shifted overseas. Knowing how to establish and manage a distribution network is, however, a critical capability that can be transferred to a foreign country. Finally, because environmental conditions differ across nations, transferability of the same resource or capability may also vary across nations. For example, Avon's direct-selling skills have been effective in Japan and Europe but not in China, whose government banned direct selling from the late 1990s until 2006.

The dynamic capability perspective holds that FDI requires resource commitment but also creates opportunities for acquiring new capabilities. Through FDI, an MNE becomes a social community that specializes in the creation and internal dissemination of knowledge. It uses relational structures and shared coding schemes to enhance the transfer and communication of new skills and capabilities within this community. FDI, especially by forming foreign alliances, also helps the MNE acquire external knowledge. Through alliances, the MNE increases its store of knowledge by internalizing knowledge not previously available within the organization. Within the MNE network or community, a firm may establish several centers of excellence with job rotation in and out of the center in order to transfer expertise among major regional headquarters. Centers of excellence are foreign units equipped with the best practice of managing knowledge. At the heart of each center of excellence is the leading-edge knowledge of a small number of individuals responsible for the continual maintenance and upgrading of the knowledge base in question. Other managerial actions to facilitate knowledge transfer within the community may include building more flexible and up-to-date information systems, encouraging external benchmarking and communications, and sharing information and success stories.

It is increasingly common to find FDI in a range of functions, from back-office activities (e.g., bookkeeping and cash management) to R&D. For example, many financial service MNEs use Ireland and India as places for conducting certain back-office operations, whereas high-tech firms such as Intel are locating R&D operations in Israel (although increasingly also in India and China). This enables MNEs an effective use of location advantages across the spectrum of corporate operations. Indeed, one of the main criticisms of the global corporation is that it places its activities wherever it is more economical to do so. One by-product of this trend is the increasing difficulty in determining company domicile and product country of origin, a phenomenon also discussed in other chapters (e.g., Chapters 2, 4, and 16).

INDUSTRY BOX

MNEs AND FDI IN THE AUTOMOTIVE INDUSTRY

The automotive industry was at the forefront of FDI early in the 20th century. Initially, FDI in automotives was mainly the result of high tariff barriers that prevented exportation into the host market. When the Ford Motor Company was founded in Detroit in 1903, it was aware of the promise of the neighboring Canadian market, but it was a 35% tariff that launched its joint venture with a Canadian firm to assemble cars in Windsor, Ontario, just across the water from Ford's U.S. base in Michigan. Today, Ford manufactures or distributes automobiles in 200 markets around the world.

Because of its visibility, automotive FDI has always triggered strong emotions. The investments made by Japanese automakers, starting with Honda and then continued by Nissan, Toyota, Mazda (a Ford affiliate), and others, prompted an initial outcry in the United States. Japanese carmakers were accused of bringing low-added-value jobs to the United States, while maintaining the production of sophisticated components, such as computer-controlled fuel injection systems, at home. On their part, Japanese manufacturers have worked to convey the impression that they are in essence local players contributing to the U.S. economy and trade balance and especially to the economies of the locales in which they have invested. Eager to expand employment, state governments from all around the United States have competed in recent years for automotive investment not only from Japan (e.g., Indiana won a new Honda plant in 2006) but also from Germany (DaimlerChrysler's Mercedes division and BMW) and South Korea (Hyundai) and have started to encourage the location of Chinese-owned parts makers in their states.

If automotive FDI was initially prompted by tariff walls, today's investments seek to realize advantages of economies of scale and tap host country competitive advantage, whether in labor costs, component availability, or proximity to market. As part of this evolution, R&D, finance, and other high-knowledge functions have now started to migrate to foreign locations. A number of Japanese car producers have major design studios in the United States. For instance, Toyota has a design studio in Newport Beach, California. It also has R&D centers in Ann Arbor, Michigan; Costa Mesa, California; and Timmins, Ontario. General Motors has opened a technical research center in China.

The Evolutionary Perspective

The evolutionary perspective of FDI views international investment as an ongoing, evolutionary process shaped by an MNE's international experience, organizational capabilities, strategic objectives, and environmental dynamics. At the core of the evolutionary perspective is the **Uppsala (or Scandinavian) model**, named after a group of scholars at Uppsala University of Sweden who published a series of articles about the international expansion process.[8] This perspective views international expansion as a process involving a series of incremental decisions during which firms develop international operations in small steps. The basic assumptions of the model are that lack of knowledge is an important obstacle to international operations and that the necessary knowledge can be acquired through time-based experience with operations abroad. Accumulated knowledge about country-specific markets, practices, and environments helps firms increase local commitment, reduces operational uncertainty, and enhances economic efficiency. The internationalization process stems from the interplay between the development of knowledge about foreign markets and operations, on the one hand, and an increasing commitment of resources to foreign markets, on the other.

Two kinds of knowledge are distinguished in the model: objective (which can be taught) and experiential (which can only be acquired through personal experience). A critical assumption is that market knowledge, including perceptions of market opportunities and problems, is acquired primarily through experience in current business activities in the market. Experiential market knowledge can bring in more business opportunities and is a driving force in the internationalization process. Experiential knowledge is also assumed to be the primary way to reduce market uncertainty. Thus, the firm is expected to make stronger resource commitments incrementally as it gains experience from current activities in a given market. This experience is to a large extent country specific and may not be applicable to other markets.

The internationalization process model explains two patterns of internationalization of the firm. The first pattern is that the firm progressively engages in a target market. During the first stage, export starts to take place via independent representatives (trading companies). During the second stage, sales subsidiaries are set up in the foreign market, specializing in marketing and promotion. During the third stage, manufacturing facilities are established overseas, involving a multitude of activities such as production, R&D, marketing, outsourcing, and reinvestment. This sequence of stages indicates an increasing commitment of resources to the market as well as market experience accumulation. While the first stage provides almost no market experience, the second allows the firm to receive fairly regular but superficial information about market conditions. The subsequent business activities lead to more differentiated market experience.

Kenich Ohmae extends this three-stage process by including a fourth ("insiderisation") and fifth stage (complete globalization). In the insiderisation stage, MNEs shift major functions such as engineering, R&D, customer financing, personnel, and finance from headquarters to local subsidiaries, which then become virtual microcosms in managing and running overseas activities. In the fifth (last) stage of internationalization, MNEs coordinate common functions such as global branding, information systems, corporate finance, and R&D, while foreign subsidiaries share common purposes, corporate missions, and corporate philosophies. This coordination substantially reduces fixed costs in research, development, and administration and fosters knowledge sharing among subsidiaries in different locations or businesses. At the same time, local activities and operations are fully decentralized, and local subsidiaries are totally autonomous in dealing with local markets and customers. The Industry Box shows some evolutionary experience of global automakers such as Ford and Toyota.

Another pattern stemming from the internationalization process model is that firms entering new markets involve successively greater psychic distance. **Psychic distance** is defined as differences in language, culture, political systems, and such, which disturb the flow of information between the firm and the market. Thus firms start internationalization in those markets where they can easily understand the environment, spot opportunities, and control operational risks. Overall, the model has gained some empirical support. This second pattern is an extension of **familiarity theory**, a theory that holds that a firm would rather invest in host countries that are relatively close to it culturally (see Chapter 6) and that it would likely be more successful in such relatively familiar environments.

The Integration–Responsiveness Perspective

For a large MNE, FDI is a complex process requiring coordinating subsidiary activities across national boundaries. Businesspeople often talk about "thinking globally but acting locally." Prahalad and Doz offer a theoretical framework on how such balance can be achieved.[9] The framework, known as the global integration (I) and local responsiveness (R) paradigm (or the **I–R paradigm**), suggests that participants in global industries develop competitive postures across two dimensions. These dimensions represent two imperatives that simultaneously confront a business competing internationally. The first dimension, **global integration**, refers to the coordination of activities across countries in an attempt to build efficient operations networks and maximize the advantage of similarities across locations. The second, **local responsiveness**, concerns response to specific host country needs. MNEs choose to emphasize one dimension over another or compete in both dimensions, resulting in three basic strategies: integrated, multifocal, or locally responsive. Integrated strategy requires strong worldwide coordination, whereas multidomestic strategy necessitates strong national adaptation. The required degree of internalization is highest for integrated strategy, followed by multifocal strategy, and finally by locally responsive strategy (for details, see Chapter 11).

Bruce Kogut enriched the I–R paradigm by incorporating the strategic flexibility view.[10] The view is composed of two related, complementary concepts: *operational flexibility* and *strategic options*. The key notion in operational flexibility is that the balance of global integration and local responsiveness lies less in designing long-term strategic plans than in instilling flexibility. Flexibility permits a firm to exploit future changes in competition, government policies, and market dynamics. This flexibility is gained by decreasing the firm's dependence on assets already in place. This suggests that managers will alter their decisions when such changes are justified by emerging conditions in an uncertain and dynamic environment. If a decision made now has a chance of being altered later in response to new information, then the economic consequences of such change should be properly accounted for when evaluating the current decision. For example, if the establishment of a joint venture with a local partner may lead to acquisition of the partner's stake in the future, the evaluation of the joint venture ex ante should take into account the economic impact of the possible acquisition. Kogut summarizes the five opportunities arising from strategic flexibility as follows:

1. Production movement. This permits the firm to respond to shifts in market and cost factors, especially exchange rates.

2. Tax avoidance. An MNE can adjust its markup on intracompany sales of goods in order to realize profits in a low-tax jurisdiction.

3. Financial arbitrage. MNEs can circumvent many host-government-instituted restrictions on finance, remittance, and foreign exchange balance with some innovative financial products.

4. Information transfer. Strategic flexibility enables MNEs to benefit from identifying more opportunities, scanning world markets to match sellers and buyers, and avoiding tariff and nontariff barriers to trade.

5. Competitive power. This flexibility enables MNEs to differentiate prices according to their world competitive posture. Different links in the international value-added chain also provide leverage on enforcing equity claims or contracts in national markets.

Interim Summary

1. According to the dynamic capability perspective, FDI is not a one-time occurrence but rather a dynamic attribute of adaptability that an MNE possesses in conjunction with an understanding of its own capabilities.

2. The evolutionary perspective suggests that as the company accumulates experience and know-how about foreign expansion, its pattern of FDI will change.

3. Global integration and local responsiveness are important in FDI so as to leverage both scale and ownership advantages on the one hand while permitting for local adaptation on the other.

PATTERNS OF FDI

In this section, we describe the patterns of FDI throughout the world. Our focus is on FDI rather than on portfolio investment. Before we begin, however, we should note that the U.S. portfolio investment liability, the largest in the world, is much larger than its portfolio of investment assets. In contrast, Germany, which has the second largest liability, has roughly the same amount in portfolio investment assets. This suggests that U.S. assets are more attractive to outsiders than foreign assets are to U.S. investors, but this is also the result of the large U.S. trade deficit described in the preceding chapter. Another observation regarding portfolio investment is that its high liquidity makes it less stable than FDI. For instance, FDI did not collapse in the aftermath of the Asian crisis.[11] Exhibit 3.2 shows that of all capital flows to developing nations, FDI constituted the largest component (and has been on the rise). In 2004, FDI inflows accounted for 51% of all resource flows to developing countries and were significantly higher than portfolio flows and commercial bank loan flows.

Exhibit 3.2   Total Resource Flows to Developing Countries, 1990–2003

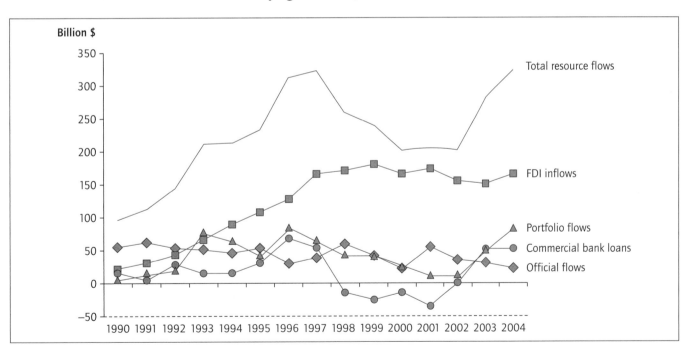

SOURCE: UNCTAD, World Investment Report, 2005, p. 7.

FDI continues to register dramatic growth. In 1980, the global FDI stock was 10% of global GDP; by 2000 it grew to over 30%. At the end of 2004, FDI outward stock stood at $9.73 trillion, compared to $1.78 trillion in 1990. In 1999 and 2000, FDI inflows had increased 55.2% and 18.2%, respectively.[12] In 2004, FDI inflows amounted to $648 billion. Between 1986 and 2000, FDI inflows and outflows had averaged an increase of more than 20% each year. This growth rate had declined between 2000 and 2003, but 2004 marked the end of the downturn. Exhibit 3.3 also shows the growth of selected FDI indicators from 1982 to 2004. Note, for instance, that between 1982 and 2004, FDI outward stock grew about 16-fold. Total assets and gross product of foreign affiliates grew more than sixfold.

Exhibit 3.3   Selected Indicators of FDI and International Production, 1982–2004

Item	Value at Current Prices (Billions of Dollars)		Annual Growth Rate (Percentage)					
	1982	1990	1986–2004	1990–1991	1995–1996	2000	2002	2004
FDI inflows	59	208	648	22.8	21.2	39.7	−13.3	2.5
FDI outflows	27	239	730	25.4	16.4	36.3	−12.3	18.4
FDI inward stock	628	1,769	8,902	16.9	9.5	17.3	8.2	11.5
FDI outward stock	601	1,785	9,732	18.0	9.1	17.4	11.0	11.5
Cross-border M&As	–	151	381	25.9	24.0	51.5	−37.8	28.2
Sales of foreign affiliates	2,765	5,727	18,677	15.9	10.6	8.7	14.6	10.1
Gross product of foreign affiliates	647	1,476	3,911	17.4	5.3	7.7	5.7	9.5
Total assets of foreign affiliates	2,113	5,937	36,008	18.1	12.2	19.4	41.1	11.9
Export of foreign affiliates	730	1,498	3,690	22.1	7.1	4.8	4.9	20.1
Employment of foreign affiliates (1,000)	19,579	24,471	57,394	5.4	2.3	9.4	10.8	7.9
GDP at factor cost	11,758	22,610	40,671	10.1	5.2	1.3	3.9	12.0
Gross fixed capital formation	2,398	4,905	8,869	12.6	5.6	1.6	0.5	12.9
Royalties and license fees receipts	9	30	98	21.2	14.3	8.0	7.5	5.0
Export of goods and nonfactor services	2,247	4,261	11,069	12.7	8.7	3.6	4.9	20.1

SOURCE: UNCTAD, World Investment Report, 2005, p. 14.

NOTE: The net differences between FDI inflows and outflows and between FDI inward stock and outward stock figures on the worldwide basis are not zero due to differences in measurement and recording by various countries (e.g., a recipient nation may record reinvestment from a foreign investor's retained earnings as FDI inflow but the firm's home country may not record it as FDI outflow).

The composition of FDI also continues to change. Increasingly, service investment in the form of financial services, tourism establishments, retail operations, health care centers, and the like is becoming more pronounced. Wal-Mart, the world's leading retailer, has a Mexican subsidiary with 520 stores and annual sales approaching $9 billion. Mexican operations bring in about one-third of the $1.1 billion annual operating profit that Wal-Mart earns abroad.[13] The University of Pittsburgh invested in a joint venture transplant center in Sicily, Italy. Citibank has opened a representative office in Israel and is looking forward to expanding its operations there when regulatory changes and political circumstances permit. In 2006, the bank, part of Citigroup, also bought a stake in a Chinese bank.

FDI OUTFLOWS

From the FDI theories described earlier in this chapter it should come as no surprise that developed countries account for most of the outflow of FDI. MNEs from developed countries are more likely to possess ownership or monopolistic advantages, more likely to be innovators (and hence place at the beginning of the product life cycle), more likely to be able to extract advantages from internalization, and more likely to have the dynamic capabilities necessary for successful venturing abroad. Indeed, in 2000 and 2004, respectively, the Triad countries (United States, Europe, and Japan) accounted for 80% and 82.7% of FDI outward stock, with much of their FDI outflow going to other Triad countries. **Concentration ratio**, which is the proportion of FDI outward stock held by the 10 top investor countries, was somewhat lower, however, in 2000 compared with 1985, at 81.2% and 89.8%, respectively.[14] FDI outflows increased in 2004 by 18% to $730 billion ($9.73 trillion FDI outward stock), of which $637 billion came from developed countries. These countries remain significant net capital exporters through FDI: Outflows exceeded inflows of developed countries by nearly $260 billion. In this year alone, FDI outflows from the United States increased by 90%, to $229 billion, its highest amount ever.

Exhibit 3.4 shows FDI outward stock for 2000 and 2004. The United States remains first in terms of FDI outward stock, with $1.3 trillion of outstanding FDI in 2000 and $2.02 trillion in 2004. Other leading countries in FDI outward stock include the United Kingdom ($1.38 trillion in 2004), Germany ($0.83 trillion), France ($0.77 trillion), and the Netherlands ($0.55 trillion). The EU, as a whole, had by far the highest FDI outflow, but this included FDI made by member countries in each other. In contrast, FDI outflows from Japan have declined,[15] and its FDI outward stock only marginally increased from 2000 to 2004.

The theory of familiarity suggests that MNEs prefer investments in countries and regions that are relatively similar to their own. In line with the theory, we can see that most FDI from Spanish firms targets Latin America, most outward FDI from Hong Kong targets Mainland China, and so forth. The first wave of FDI in many Eastern and Central European nations following the collapse of the Soviet Union was by Americans and European citizens of Hungarian, Polish, and Czech ancestry, who quickly spotted the opportunities available. These individuals and their small businesses had a competitive advantage in having acquired free market knowledge while being familiar with the investment target culture and language.

As you will recall from the theoretical discussion, the Scandinavian school suggests that FDI occurs incrementally, with firms gradually moving away from familiar to less familiar markets. Procter & Gamble is a good example. The company's first foreign operation, and for 15 years its only one, was in Canada, a destination especially close given P&G's location in Cincinnati, Ohio. The company's second foreign operation was established in 1930, in the United Kingdom, whose "psychic distance" from the United States is relatively small. The third investment, in 1935, was in the Philippines, then under U.S. control, followed by Puerto Rico (1947) and Mexico (1948).

Developing countries remain a secondary yet generally growing source of FDI. From 1980 to 2000, the share of developing countries in outflow FDI grew from 3% to 8%. Similarly, FDI outward stock from developing countries reached about 14% in 2000 and 11% in 2004 of the world's total outstanding FDI. Contributing to this outflow were mostly Asian firms, although Latin American firms also increased their FDI outflow.[16] In terms of outward FDI stock in 2004, the top developing country investors are Hong Kong, Singapore, Taiwan, Russia, Brazil, China, and South Korea. Many emerging-economy enterprises have recently started to expand internationally in an aggressive manner (e.g., through foreign acquisitions), which has spurred the wave of FDI outflows from these economies.[17] Chapter 4 discusses in detail the investment rationale and strategy of MNEs from developing countries. It notes that such MNEs rely on a different kind of competitive advantage and are often motivated by a search for knowledge rather than by a desire to leverage existing knowledge resources.

Exhibit 3.4 FDI Outward Stock, as of 2000 and 2004 (Billions of Dollars)

Economy	By 2000	By 2004
World	6,148.28	9,732.23
Developed Countries	5,257.26	8,610.15
Europe	3,324.13	5,658.81
Belgium	–	248.37
France	445.06	769.35
Germany	541.86	833.65
Netherlands	305.46	545.81
Portugal	17.26	45.56
Spain	166.06	332.66
Sweden	123.23	203.94
United Kingdom	897.85	1,378.13
United States	1,316.25	2,018.21
Japan	278.44	370.54
Developing Countries	868.92	1,035.68
Africa	45.41	45.60
Latin America & Caribbean	210.92	271.69
Argentina	21.28	21.82
Brazil	49.69	64.36
Chile	11.72	14.45
Mexico	7.54	15.89
Asia	612.59	718.39
China	27.77	38.83
Hong Kong	388.38	405.59
Singapore	56.77	100.91
Korea (Republic of)	26.83	39.32
Taiwan	66.66	91.24
India	1.86	6.59
Southeast Europe and CIS	22.10	86.41
Russia	20.14	81.87

SOURCE: UNCTAD, Key Data, 2006.

FDI INFLOWS

Similar to FDI outflow patterns, FDI inflows have been steadily growing in most years over the past three decades, reaching a peak in 2000 ($1.40 trillion) before easing and then climbing again. Developed countries dominated FDI inflows for the last decades, but this dominance has been gradually weakening since 2001. For instance, this group accounted for more than 80% of the world's total FDI inflows each year prior to the end of 2000, but this percentage has been reduced to below 60% since then. By contrast, FDI inflows into developing countries, especially major emerging economies, such as China, Brazil, Mexico, and India, have markedly increased, accounting for almost 40% of the world's total. This is congruent with the market-seeking logic we previously noted in that foreign emerging markets provide more market opportunities for developed-country multinationals to explore and exploit. Their monopolistic advantages may enable them to reap the benefits from

Photo 3.1   Africa remains a minor foreign investment target.

SOURCE: Jupiterimages.

these opportunities. Exhibit 3.5 shows FDI inflows and stocks in selected years. Notice the significant growth in overall FDI before 2000, and even more so in such regions as Asia and Latin America. As of the end of 2004, the world's stock of FDI inflows amounted to $8.90 trillion.

FDI inflows are generally correlated with economic growth. Most of the countries and regions with high economic growth rates over the past decades also recorded an increase in FDI inflows during the same period. A number of developing countries in Asia and Latin America, for instance, experienced a generally strong economic growth after the 1990s and, partly as a result, received significantly higher FDI inflows. In contrast, some EU countries that grew at slower rates saw declining or stagnating FDI inflows. In addition to economic growth, increases in FDI inflows may also have contributed to weakening host country currencies, meaning they were less costly to investors as evidenced by the wave of FDI inflows into the United States in the 1980s. A declining currency also improved the price competitiveness of local companies, therefore attracting efficiency-seeking FDI. The currency's depreciation boosts exports, which further stimulates FDI inflows. Rising exports are often accompanied by increasing FDI for improving distribution and marketing facilities for exports and for meeting the specific needs of exporters. Some institutional factors, such as reduced country risk, governmental support, regulatory transparency,

Exhibit 3.5   FDI Inflows in 1970, 1980, 1990, 2000, and 2004 (Billions of Dollars)

Economy	1970	1980	1990	2000	2004	Inward Stock as of 2004
World	13.43	55.11	207.88	1,396.54	648.15	8,895.28
Developed Countries	9.50	46.63	172.07	1,134.29	380.02	6,469.83
Europe	5.23	21.57	104.31	722.76	223.40	4,258.55
United States	1.19	16.92	48.42	314.01	95.86	1,473.86
Japan	0.09	0.28	1.75	8.32	7.82	96.98
Developing Countries	3.94	8.46	35.74	253.18	233.23	2,225.99
Africa	1.27	0.40	2.84	9.63	18.09	219.28
Latin America & Caribbean	1.68	7.49	9.59	97.52	67.53	723.75
Asia and Oceania	0.99	0.56	23.31	146.03	147.61	1,282.96
Southeast Europe and CIS	–	0.02	0.08	9.07	34.90	199.45

SOURCE: UNCTAD, Key Data, 2006.

increased market access, and business privatization also drive up FDI inflows. Interestingly, the above exhibits show that the curve for FDI inflows into developing countries increasingly tracks the curve for FDI outflows for those economies, suggesting that the general environment of those countries has an important impact on their FDI involvement as both home and host countries.

Exhibit 3.6 documents FDI inflows to the top 20 recipient economies, ranked by the components of FDI inflows. Generally, FDI is financed by equity capital, reinvested earnings, and intracompany loans. Equity capital is often the largest component of FDI financing (58% to 71% during the period 1995–2004), followed by intracompany loans (23% on average) and reinvested earnings (12% on average). Intracompany loans are particularly preferred when a host country's corporate income tax is high. For example, foreign investors may react to the high tax rate in Germany by preferring intracompany loans to equity financing for their investments in Germany. This practice allows the investors to record interest expense and thus pay less income tax. Although still accounting for a lower percentage, reinvested earnings have been rising substantially as a means of FDI financing (i.e., foreign affiliates' earnings not distributed as dividends to the parent company). For instance, many MNEs investing in emerging economies use their retained earnings to reinvest in their FDI projects and increase economies of scale and scope in host markets.

Exhibit 3.6   FDI Inflows to the Top 20 Recipient Economies, Ranked by Size of Different Financing Components, 2003 (Billions of Dollars)

Rank	Equity Capital		Reinvested Earnings		Intracompany Loans	
	Economy	Billions of Dollars	Economy	Billions of Dollars	Economy	Billions of Dollars
1	United States	87.0	Ireland	19.4	France	27.7
2	Luxembourg	80.9	Hong Kong, China	16.0	Spain	14.2
3	Germany	45.7	United Kingdom	12.2	Italy	8.8
4	China	37.4	China	7.2	Luxembourg	6.4
5	Belgium	26.2	Russian Federation	7.1	Belgium	5.9
6	France	17.0	Canada	6.7	Mexico	5.8
7	Netherlands	14.6	Australia	5.7	Switzerland	5.3
8	Spain	13.0	Netherlands	5.2	Sweden	3.2
9	Brazil	9.3	Italy	4.8	Angola	2.8
10	Switzerland	8.3	Luxembourg	3.7	Russian Federation	2.8
11	Portugal	7.7	Switzerland	2.9	United Kingdom	2.8
12	Japan	7.6	Malaysia	2.8	China	2.5
13	Ireland	6.0	Mexico	2.3	New Zealand	2.3
14	United Kingdom	5.4	Finland	2.3	Ireland	1.5
15	Poland	4.6	Czech Republic	2.2	Norway	1.4
16	Austria	4.4	Hungary	2.1	Austria	1.3
17	Thailand	4.1	Chile	1.9	Ecuador	1.3
18	Azerbaijan	3.3	Nigeria	1.9	Venezuela	1.2
19	Argentina	3.0	Spain	1.9	Chad	1.0
20	Israel	2.9	India	1.8	Kazakhstan	0.9

SOURCE: UNCTAD, World Investment Report 2005, p. 12.

It is also worth noting that the growing share of services in developed economies makes them ripe for investment in services, a sector representing a growing portion of total FDI. More than half of the outflow from major investor countries is in the service sector, whether by retailers such as Wal-Mart and Home Depot, airlines such as British Airways (which holds a 25% stake in Qantas, the Australian airline), Houston-based construction firm Hines, or financial institutions such as Deutsche Bank (which purchased U.S. Bankers Trust). Second, the decline in the value of labor and commodities in overall product price somehow erodes the competitive advantage of some developing economies that offer cheap labor pools. Meanwhile, as the global demand for fuels and other mineral resources has been drastically increasing, FDI inflows into these sectors in developing countries increase. Third, FDI flows into developing countries are concentrated in a relatively small number of countries, such as China in Asia or Poland, Hungary, and the Czech Republic in Central Europe. Inflows into Latin America and the Caribbean increased to $97 billion in 2000 ($67 billion in 2004). In contrast, the entire continent of Africa received only 1.2% of global FDI inflows, although investment in some countries (e.g., Angola) was high in relation to gross domestic capital formation.[18] New FDI targets have become prominent in recent years. Examples are Egypt, with its market and investment liberalization, and Israel, where much of FDI has been directed to the high-tech sector.

MNEs play an important part in FDI flows. Exhibit 3.7 shows that foreign assets, sales, and employment already account for about 50% of each category's total for the world's 100 largest MNEs. General Electric and Vodafone are leading MNEs, each with foreign assets of about $250 billion. Although more service companies have joined the top rankings, MNEs in traditional industries have remained in the highest rankings in terms of foreign assets, foreign sales, and foreign employment. In the petroleum industry, for instance, Shell and ExxonMobil are still among the top 10 MNEs in the world. Motor vehicle companies like Toyota, General Motors, and Ford are also still among the top 10. The largest MNEs remain geographically concentrated in a few home countries, such as the United States, France, Germany, Japan, and the United Kingdom.

Exhibit 3.7   Snapshot of the World's 100 Largest MNEs: Assets, Sales, and Employment, 2002 and 2003

Items	2002	2003	% Change
Assets ($ billion)			
Foreign	3,317	3,993	20.4
Total	6,891	8,023	16.4
Foreign as % of total	48.1	49.8	1.7
Sales ($ billion)			
Foreign	2,446	3,003	22.8
Total	4,749	5,551	16.9
Foreign as % of total	51.5	54.1	2.6
Employment (thousands)			
Foreign	7,036	7,242	2.9
Total	14,332	14,626	2.1
Foreign as % of total	49.1	49.5	0.4

SOURCE: UNCTAD, World Investment Report, 2005, p. 17.

Transnationality and FDI Performance of Individual Economies

When we account for the size of the economy in terms of output, employment, and the like, the impact of FDI looks quite different. UNCTAD calculated a **Host Economy Transnationality Index** as the average of four shares: FDI inflows as a percentage of gross capital formation, FDI inward stock as a percentage of GDP, value added of foreign affiliates as a percentage of GDP, and employment of foreign affiliates as a percentage of total employment. The results, presented in Exhibit 3.8, show the United States—the largest nominal recipient of FDI—near the bottom of the index, with only Greece, Italy, and Japan below it. When size of the economy is accounted for, Belgium and Luxembourg, Ireland, Estonia, the Netherlands, and Denmark are the top five developed economies in terms of national-level inward openness or internationalization. Among developing economies, Hong Kong ranks first, reaching 81.6% (highest among all economies in the world), followed by Singapore and Trinidad and Tobago.

The Inward FDI Performance and Potential indices, as well as the Outward FDI Performance index, were also introduced by UNCTAD to assess FDI performance of individual countries. The **Inward FDI Performance Index** is a measure of the extent to which a host economy receives inward FDI relative to its economic size. It is calculated as the ratio of a country's share in global FDI inflows to its share in global GDP. This compares FDI inflow levels across different countries when the GDP size is controlled for. According to this index, Azerbaijan, Belgium and Luxemburg, Angola, and Ireland are among the best performing countries, while Cameroon, Indonesia, Iran, Japan, Kuwait, Nepal, and Saudi Arabia are among the poorest performers. The **Inward FDI Potential Index** is based on several economic variables indicating a country's investment infrastructure and growth potential for foreign businesses. It is an average of scores (ranging from 0 to 1) on such economic conditions as GDP per capita, GDP growth rate, share of exports in GDP, telecoms infrastructure, commercial energy use per capita, share of R&D expenditures in gross national income, and country risk. The United States, Norway, the United Kingdom, Canada, and Singapore are among the best locations in terms of FDI potential. By comparing the Inward FDI Potential Index with the Performance Index, one gets an indication of how each country performs. Finally, the **Outward FDI Performance Index** is defined as the ratio of a country's share in global FDI outflows to its share in world GDP. Top outward FDI performers include Belgium and Luxembourg, Panama, Hong Kong, Azerbaijan, Iceland, and Singapore.

FDI flows and performance differ not only among countries but also across regions (states or provinces) within a large country. In most diversified host countries, the distribution of FDI is uneven, triggering criticism that only a few benefit from the investment and that the beneficiaries are concentrated in areas that are already relatively affluent. For example, in the United States, FDI projects are generally concentrated in a small number of states. California, Michigan, New Jersey, and Massachusetts have about a quarter of the manufacturing employment of Japanese affiliates in the United States and two-thirds (157 of 251) of these foreign investors' R&D facilities.[19] These states enjoyed the benefits of high-wage, knowledge-based employment of FDI much more than other states. FDI in services is even more skewed toward investment on the East Coast (primarily), followed by California and to a lesser extent Texas.[20] This

Exhibit 3.8   Transnationality of Host Economies, 2002 (Percentage)

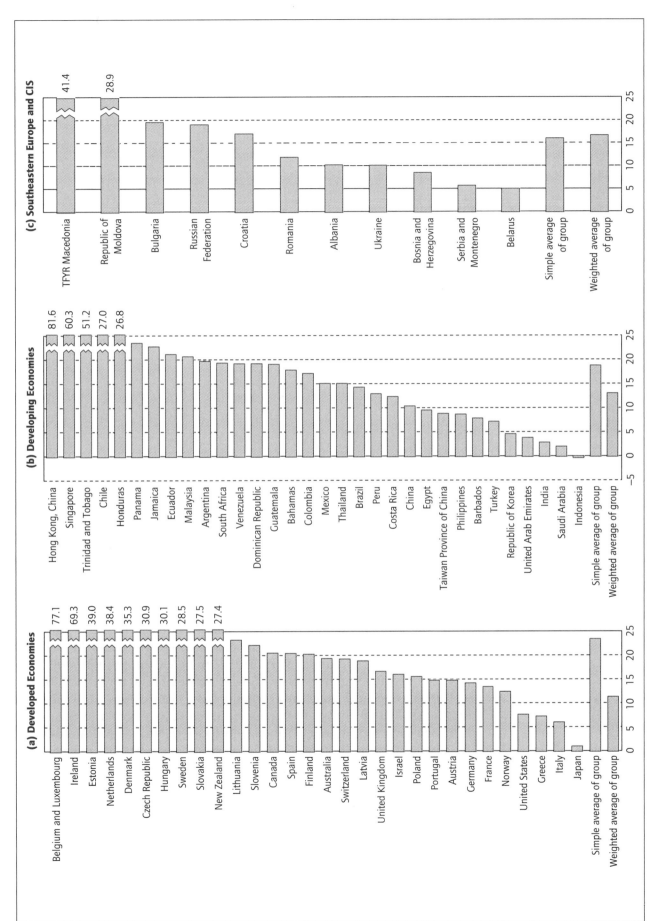

SOURCE: UNCTAD, World Investment Report, 2005, p. 16.

Exhibit 3.9   Cross-Border M&As With Values of Over $1 Billion, 1987–2004

Year	Value ($ Billion)	Percentage of Total M&As
1987	30.0	40.3
1988	49.6	42.9
1989	59.5	42.4
1990	60.9	40.4
1991	20.4	25.2
1992	21.3	26.8
1993	23.5	28.3
1994	50.9	40.1
1995	80.4	43.1
1996	94.0	41.4
1997	129.2	42.4
1998	329.7	62.0
1999	522.0	68.1
2000	866.2	75.7
2001	378.1	63.7
2002	213.9	57.8
2003	141.1	47.5
2004	199.8	52.5

SOURCE: UNCTAD, World Investment Report, 2005, p. 9.

reality explains some of the political undercurrents of trade and investment discussed in Chapter 7, The Political and Legal Environment.

In China, FDI was initially confined to special economic zones and still remains concentrated along coastal areas and in a small number of other regions. This pattern is beginning to change, however. The Chinese government, like many others, is offering special incentives to firms willing to invest in less developed regions. Such incentives to investment in disadvantaged regions are allowable under WTO rules. In Israel, the government offers extra incentives for foreign investors willing to locate in rural towns, as it did for Intel. In the United States, state governments have been competing with each other in offering FDI incentives in hopes of attracting investors into their state. Ohio provided such incentives to Honda, Tennessee to Nissan, and Alabama to BMW.

The location pattern of FDI is often correlated with the investor country of origin, which again may be predicted by the theory of familiarity. In China, much of the initial investment from Hong Kong (now a Special Administrative Region of China but a separate entity for investment purposes) was concentrated in Guandong province, which is adjacent to Hong Kong and shares a regional culture and dialect; Taiwanese investment was initially proportionally higher in Fujian province, which shares culture, language, and ethnicity with many Taiwan residents; and South Korea was more likely to invest in areas of China with large Korean minorities. As familiarity theory predicts, such investment gradually expanded into other regions.

FDI Entry Forms

Firms may enter host economies through greenfield investments or M&As (mergers and acquisitions). A **greenfield investment** occurs when a firm single-handedly (i.e., as sole owner) or jointly with another firm (i.e., in a joint venture) builds brand-new facilities from scratch in a host country. An **acquisition** occurs when a firm buys out a portion (i.e., partial acquisition) or the entire ownership (i.e., complete acquisition) of a target firm in a host country. The choice of entry form is influenced by industry-specific factors. For example, greenfield investment is more likely to be used as a form of entry in industries in which technological skills and production technology are key. The choice may also be influenced by institutional, cultural, and transaction cost factors, in particular, the attitude toward takeovers, conditions in capital markets, policies, privatization, regional integration, currency risks, and the role played by intermediaries (e.g., investment banks) actively seeking acquisition opportunities and taking initiatives in making deals. Chapter 10 explains these issues in greater detail.

In recent years, the proportion of M&As in total FDI has been growing at the expense of greenfield investments. Completed cross-border M&As rose in value from less than $100 billion in 1987 to more than $1 trillion in 2000. Moreover, as shown in Exhibit 3.9, the number of mega cross-border deals (with transaction values exceeding $1 billion) has been on the increase. The trend has been criticized by FDI opponents who say that M&As do not add to the capital stock and may stifle competition.[21] Proponents of FDI respond that acquisitions bring new technologies and better management that enable the acquired firm to survive and prosper under stiff global competition. They point out that, at least in transition economies, greenfield and acquisition investments do not substitute for each other but rather play different roles, the former providing new facilities and capacities, the latter contributing to the restructuring and improvement of existing facilities and capacities.[22]

Although the acquisition of major local firms in developing nations draws frequent media attention, the most common form of M&A is one originating in and targeting developed-country firms. Many large firms have embarked on multiple acquisitions. Examples are Ford Motor's acquisition of U.K.-based Jaguar and more recently Swedish company Volvo and the Land Rover division of the U.K.-based Rover group, formerly owned by German automaker BMW; the acquisition and partial acquisition of Chrysler and Mitsubishi by Daimler (later reversed); and the controlling interest taken in Nissan by French automaker Renault. This wave is not limited to the car industry. Swedish paper manufacturer Svenska Cellulosa acquired both Pennsylvania-based Tuscarora and an Atlanta-based unit of Georgia Pacific.[23] British utility National Grid completed three international acquisitions in 2000. In 2004, M&As between companies within the EU increase in value to almost $100 billion, accounting for 57% of the value of all cross-border deals in that region. Low interest rates and strategic needs for global expansion via M&As are among the major factors contributing to the rise in cross-border M&As, which resumed in 2006. In 2006, Japan's Toshiba acquired U.S.-based Westinghouse while French telecommunications maker Alcatel merged with U.S.-based Lucent.

Developing countries have attracted a larger number of greenfield investments than developed countries. This illustrates the tendency for developing economies to receive more FDI through greenfield projects than through M&As. Although acquisitions by developing-country MNEs are much less numerous than those by developed-country MNEs, they are increasing. Mumbai-based Silverline Technologies acquired New Jersey–based SeraNova in 2000 for $99 million. Like other Indian high-tech firms with recent U.S. acquisitions, the company sought to gain an understanding of the U.S. market, which increasingly sources software in India.[24] There was also a significant rise in cross-border M&A purchases in China and India in 2004, with a doubling of value in both countries, to record highs of $6.8 billion and $1.8 billion, respectively. China is now the largest target country for cross-border M&As in developing countries. As in the case of M&As, China and India also attracted significant numbers of greenfield investments, together accounting for nearly half of the total number in developing countries. Recent liberalization measures in India and strong economic growth in China, combined with the WTO access (see Chapter 8), contributed to this trend.

Interim Summary

1. FDI levels continue to increase while the companies engaging in FDI are becoming more diverse. However, FDI outflow is overwhelmingly from the Triad countries, mostly into other Triad countries.

2. The bulk of FDI entering into developing countries goes to a small number of nations with exceptionally attractive investment environments.

3. Recently, M&As outpaced greenfield investments, given their advantages such as quick access to local markets and better use of local firms' established supply and distribution channels. FDI tends to concentrate in limited areas within host countries, generating uneven benefits.

COUNTRY BOX

FDI IN ISRAEL

In 1994, foreign investment in Israel stood at roughly $500 million. By 2000, it grew 10-fold, reaching one of the highest per capita figures for any economy. How this transformation has come about reveals a lot about the factors that motivate FDI. Israel is a country that lacks natural resources, has a tiny land area, and has a relatively small population of about 7 million. However, Israel has a highly skilled workforce and one of the highest ratios of scientists and engineers in the world (almost double that of the United States), further boosted by the immigration of thousands of scientists from the former Soviet Union. Israel ranks third, after the United States and Japan, in the number of patents per capita. MNEs flocked to Israel to take advantage of this knowledge resource as well as Israel's sophisticated infrastructure and a supportive tax and investment environment. National Semiconductor, Cisco, and Motorola have all opened R&D facilities in Israel. Other firms investing in the country include Pratt & Whitney, Kimberly-Clark, Intel, and IBM (all from the United States); Siemens, Unilever, and British Telecom (Europe); and Sony, Toyo Ink, and Hutchison Telecom (Asia).

After growing considerably in the late 1990s, FDI in Israel fell in 2001, a decline that is attributed mainly to two factors: first, the global decline in the technology sector in which Israel has had a competitive advantage, and second, the deterioration in the security situation, which has devastated certain sectors such as tourism and lowered the country's appeal as a regional headquarters for the Middle East. The resulting uncertainty has kept many potential investors at bay, even in such industries as software that have not been directly affected. Still, FDI recovered quickly, reaching $6 billion in 2006 (among the highest per capita FDI ratios in the world), and was on course to pass the $10 billion mark in 2007. Much of the investment was in the form of acquisitions. For instance, Berkshire Hathaway, controlled by legendary investor Warren Buffet, has paid $4 billion to purchase an 80% stake in Iscar, an Israel-based toolmaker.

THE INVESTMENT ENVIRONMENT

With most nations keen on attracting FDI, market liberalization and openness to FDI have been on the increase. For instance, between 1991 and 2000, there were a total of 1,185 regulatory changes pertaining to FDI across the globe, of which 1,121 favored investors. In 1999 alone, 150 regulatory changes were made in 69 nations, and 147 of those were positive to FDI.[25] Many of the recently signed bilateral investment and double taxation treaties contain supportive FDI provisions.[26] The economies with the most liberal FDI environment in terms of freedom to control domestic firms are Luxembourg, Ireland, Argentina, and Hong Kong. The economies with the least open environment in this respect are China, Russia, Malaysia, and Slovenia. Russia offers by far the least protection for the foreign investor.[27] Still, recent data suggest a slowdown in the liberalization of FDI regimes: In 2003, 218 changes were favorable to FDI versus 24 unfavorable changes; however, the ratio changed to 234/36 in 2004 and 164/41 in 2005. While it is too early to say if this signals a fundamental change in direction, it is a reminder that the continued liberalization in the FDI environment should not be taken for granted.

Increased liberalization should also not be confused with the uncertainty that continues to characterize international operations in developing and transition economies (Country Box: FDI in Israel shows an example). Weak property rights, political upheaval, wild currency shifts, and the like make the international environment an uncertain terrain. However, liberalization means that FDI is less often made for the sole purpose of circumventing tariff barriers than for more fundamental economic and strategic reasons. With rapid globalization, product life-cycle assumptions have also been increasingly questioned. If in the past an MNE could simply utilize its older products in another, especially developing, market, it is now often demanded, or necessary (owing to internal efficiencies or competitive pressures), to transfer more technology to foreign affiliates at an early stage.

Global competition to attract FDI leads many countries to offer not only a liberalized investment market but also an array of incentives to the foreign investor. Such incentives include tax holidays, tariff concessions, direct and indirect financial subsidies, training support, infrastructure improvement, and capital repatriation rights. Countries offering the most attractive incentives to foreign investors include Ireland, Singapore, Luxembourg, and the Netherlands. Russia, Slovenia, New Zealand, and Venezuela offer the fewest investment incentives.

High-tech investment that involves substantial employment is particularly in demand, enhancing the bargaining power of the MNE. Intel was thus able to extract substantial concessions from governments in various parts of the world. In Costa Rica, Intel received an eight-year tax holiday (and several more years at a reduced rate), unlimited fund repatriation rights, and infrastructure support in the form of a power station supplying power to the Intel plant at a reduced rate. Advanced Micro Devices was similarly able to extract an array of incentives from the German government, especially since it agreed to locate its plant in the depressed eastern part of the country.[28]

FDI Decision Criteria

In the theory section, we discussed the location advantages of host countries as a major drive for FDI. We have noted that such advantages include natural endowments (e.g., mineral resources), creative endowments (e.g., consumer purchasing power, skilled workforce), and government incentives. We have also noted that these endowments vary by region and by industry and that they tend to shift over time. For example, many foreign firms that were enticed to invest in the United Kingdom as their EU base (the United Kingdom is the preferred EU entry point for Japanese firms, for example) have been rethinking their investment in the aftermath of the United Kingdom not joining the Euro Currency Zone. With the British pound appreciating vis-à-vis the euro, U.K.-made products sold in the EU have either become more expensive for consumers or less profitable for their producers.

Location factors may change in importance according to the industries involved. For instance, in industries based on monopolistic advantage, agglomeration in terms of existence of competitors is a negative rather than a positive. Low-tech, labor-intensive industries (e.g., most garment manufacturers) typically regard wages as a critical location factor. Similarly, tire manufacturers are much more concerned with transportation costs than electronic chip producers, for whom the value-to-weight ratio is much higher.

Nor is the relationship between cost of production and location simple. As you may recall from Chapter 2, the Leontief paradox showed that the United States, a country with high capital endowment, was also exporting many labor-intensive products. The United States is also domestically manufacturing low-tech products, despite wages that are often more than 10 times higher than in alternative locations. For example, most lightbulbs sold in the United States are made locally, sometimes by foreign firms such as German-based Siemens. The reasons are transportation costs, capital intensity (i.e., automation), the importance of quick delivery and on-site service, local tastes, trade barriers, skills that are not easily transferable, and the ability to quickly implement innovation.[29]

Similarly, Conference Board data show that U.S. manufacturers are more likely to choose a high- than a low-wage country for investment, and that this holds in North America, Asia, and Europe. For instance, Motorola chose to invest in Germany despite its having the highest labor costs and one of the highest tax rates in the EU. Quality and productivity supplemented by local incentives have turned the decision in Germany's favor.[30]

National boundaries do not always provide a good indication of key criteria for the location decision. As an example, wage costs can vary substantially across regions of the same country owing to varying levels of development (e.g., it is much more expensive to do business in Shanghai than in the Chinese inland) or to special arrangements in free trade zones or territorially contiguous areas. For instance, Ohio-based firm R. G. Barry opened a footwear plant in Laredo, Texas, thanks to the Twin Plant plan that allowed it to employ Mexican workers at a fraction of its U.S. domestic cost. The plant was, however, moved to Mexico in 2002 when the further wage savings were no longer offset by tariffs, thanks to the NAFTA agreement.[31] Chapter 10 provides a detailed framework with which to analyze location decisions.

Interim Summary

1. Global competition to attract FDI promotes liberalization of global markets and opening of the world economic environment. Many countries offer a host of incentives to foreign investors.

2. For investors in high-value-added products and services, FDI concerns are less related to natural endowments and more to creative endowments such as knowledge infrastructure, access to capital, consumer purchasing power, and government incentives.

CHAPTER SUMMARY

1. Foreign direct investment (FDI) involves investment in a manufacturing facility, service provision facility, or other assets in a foreign market over which the firm maintains control.

2. FDI can be horizontal (same product or service as the one produced or rendered in the home country) or vertical (investment in inputs preceding or following in the firm's value chain).

3. MNEs benefit from FDI by generating efficiencies from location advantages, leveraging structural discrepancies, generating returns from ownership advantages, and learning and leveraging their capabilities.

4. Among conventional perspectives, the monopolistic advantage approach suggests that MNEs possess monopolistic power, enabling them to operate subsidiaries abroad more profitably than local competitors can. The internalization perspective suggests that it is more efficient for MNEs to internalize overseas operations through a unified governance structure (e.g., through vertical integration) than otherwise to trade through open markets (if they exist). The OLI paradigm integrates these perspectives with country-specific comparative advantages.

5. Among emerging perspectives, the dynamic capability view suggests that global success depends not only on a firm's distinctive resources but also on how it deploys, uses, and upgrades those resources. The evolutionary perspective holds that internationalization is an evolutionary process, shifting from export, to building foreign branches, to relocating facilities overseas, to "insiderisation," and finally to globalization. The I–R paradigm addresses the balance between global integration and local responsiveness.

6. The United States has the highest stock of both outflows and inflows of FDI in the world. However, its share of the fast-growing pie of global FDI is shrinking, and today it is no longer the biggest investor.

7. In recent years, more FDI has been done via mergers and acquisitions than via "greenfield" investment.

8. The global investment environment continues to liberalize, reflecting increasing competition for investment dollars and a belief that FDI benefits outweigh its disadvantages; however, the rate of liberalization has slowed in recent years.

Chapter Notes

1. A. T. Kearney. Globalization Ledger, Global Business Policy Council, April 2000; "Measuring globalization." *Foreign Policy*, January/February 2001.

2. L. M. Greenberg. "Canada answers the call for U.S. firms." *Wall Street Journal*, October 1, 1999, A13.

3. R. Vernon. "International investments and international trade in the product life cycle." *Quarterly Journal of Economics*, May 1966: pp. 190–207.

4. The first systematic presentation of this theory was made by S. H. Hymer in his doctoral dissertation in 1960. See S. H. Hymer. *The International Operations of National Firms*. Cambridge, MA: The MIT Press, 1976. Follow-up efforts to reiterate this theory include C. P. Kindleberger. *American Business Abroad*. New Haven: Yale University Press, 1969; R. Z. Aliber. "A theory of direct foreign investment." In *The International Corporation: A Symposium*, edited by C. P. Kindleberger. Cambridge, MA: The MIT Press, 1970; and R. E. Caves. "International corporations: The industrial economics of foreign investment." *Economica*, February 1971: pp. 1–27.

5. P. J. Buckley and M. Casson. *The Future of the Multinational Enterprise*. New York: Holmes and Meier, 1976; A. M. Rugman. *Inside the Multinationals*. New York: Columbia University Press, 1981.

6. J. H. Dunning. "Toward an eclectic theory of international production: Some empirical tests." *Journal of International Business Studies*, 11, 1: pp. 9–31; J. H. Dunning. *International Production and the Multinational Enterprise*. London: Allen and Unwin, 1981; J. H. Dunning. *Explaining International Production*. London: Unwin Hyman, 1988.

7. D. J. Collis. "A resource-based analysis of global competition: The case of the bearings industry." *Strategic Management Journal*, 1991, 12: pp. 49–68; Y. Luo. "Dynamic capabilities in international expansion." *Journal of World Business*, 2000, 35, 4: pp. 355–378; S. Tallman. "Strategic management models and resource-based strategies among MNEs in a host market." *Strategic Management Journal*, 1991, 12: pp. 69–82; U. Zander and B. Kogut. "Knowledge and the speed of the transfer and imitation of organizational capabilities." *Organization Science*, 1995, 6, 1: pp. 76–92; D. J. Teece, G. Pisano, and A. Shuen. "Dynamic capabilities and strategic management." *Strategic Management Journal*, 1997, 18, 7: pp. 509–533.

8. See J. Johanson and J. Vahlne. "The internationalization process of the firm: A model of knowledge development and increasing foreign market commitment." *Journal of International Business Studies*, 1977, 8: pp. 23–32; R. Luostarinen. *Internationalization of the Firm*. Helsinki,

Finland: Helsinki School of Economics, 1980. Follow-up efforts include W. Davidson. "The location of foreign direct investment activity: Country characteristics and experience effects." *Journal of International Business Studies*, 1980, 11: pp. 9–22; B. Kogut. "Foreign direct investment as a sequential process." In C. P. Kindleberger and D. Audretsch (eds.), *The Multinational Corporation in the 1980s*, pp. 35–56. Cambridge, MA: MIT Press: O. Andersen. "On the internationalization process of firms: A critical analysis." *Journal of International Business Studies*, 1993, *24*, 2: pp. 209–231; S. J. Chang. "International expansion strategy of Japanese firms: Capability building through sequential entry." *Academy of Management Journal*, 1995, 38: pp. 383–407; Y. Luo and M. W. Peng. "Learning to compete in a transition economy: Experience, environment, and performance." *Journal of International Business Studies*, 1999, *30*, 2: pp. 269–296, among others.

9. See C. K. Prahalad and Y. Doz. *The Multinational Mission: Balancing Local Demands and Global Vision*. New York: The Free Press, 1987. Contributions to this perspective also come from C. A. Bartlett and S. Ghoshal. *Managing Across Borders*. Boston: Harvard Business School Press, 1989; K. Roth and A. J. Morrison. "An empirical analysis of the integration-responsiveness framework in global industries." *Journal of International Business Studies*, 1991, *21*, 4: pp. 541–564; S. J. Kobrin. "An empirical analysis of the determinants of global integration." *Strategic Management Journal*, 12 (Summer 1991): pp. 17–32; G. S. Yip. *Total Global Strategy*. Englewood Cliffs, NJ: Prentice-Hall, 1995.

10. See B. Kogut. "Designing global strategies: Comparative and competitive value-added chains." *Sloan Management Review*, Summer 1985: pp. 15–27; B. Kogut. "Designing global strategies: Profiting from operational flexibility." *Sloan Management Review*, Fall 1985: pp. 27–38; B. Kogut. "Joint ventures and the option to expand and acquire." *Management Science*, 1990, *37*, 1: pp. 19–33; B. Kogut. "Options thinking and platform investments: Investing in opportunity." *California Management Review*, Winter 1994: pp. 52–71.

11. See O. Shenkar and M. Serapio (eds.). "Tamed tigers: Restructuring, liberalization and changing business systems in the East Asian economies." *Management International Review*, 1999, 4.

12. United Nations Conference on Trade and Development (UNCTAD). World Investment Report, 2000 & 2001.

13. D. Luhnow. "Crossover success: How NAFTA helped Wal-Mart dominate the Mexican market." *Wall Street Journal*, August 31, 2001, A1.

14. UNCTAD. World Investment Report, 2001, p. 9.

15. UNCTAD. World Investment Report, 2001, pp. 29, 35.

16. UNCTAD. World Investment Report, 2000, p. 16.

17. IMD International. *The World Competitiveness Yearbook*, 2000, p. 388.

18. UNCTAD. World Investment Report, 2000.

19. UNCTAD. World Investment Report, 2001, p. 82.

20. L. Nachum. "Economic geography and the location of TNCs: Financial and professional service FDI to the US." *Journal of International Business Studies*, 2000, *31*, 3: pp. 367–385.

21. UNCTAD. World Investment Report, 2000, pp. 14–15.

22. UNCTAD, *Transnational Corporations*, 2000, *10*, 3.

23. C. Terhune. "Swedish concern to expand in the U.S. through two deals." *Wall Street Journal*, January 23, 2001.

24. J. Pesta. "Indian companies buy passage to U.S." *Wall Street Journal*, January 22, 2001, A16.

25. UNCTAD. World Investment Report, 2001, p. 6.

26. UNCTAD. World Investment Report, 2000.

27. International Institute for Management Development. *The World Competitiveness Yearbook*, 2000, p. 390.

28. C. M. Yee. "Let's make a deal." *Wall Street Journal*, September 25, 2000, R10.

29. "The strange life of low-tech America." *Economist*, October 17, 1998, 73.

30. C. Rhoades. "A contrarian Motorola picks Germany." *Wall Street Journal*, October 10, 1997, A18.

31. J. Millman. "Mexican workers suffer as plants relocate south of the border." *Wall Street Journal*, March 26, 2002, A20.

THE MULTINATIONAL ENTERPRISE

FOUR

DO YOU KNOW?

1. Who are the players in the international business arena?

2. How can you tell the degree of a firm's internationalization?

3. What advantages and disadvantages do MNEs (multinational enterprises) have, compared to local firms, when they operate overseas, and what are the essential capabilities with which a successful MNE must be equipped?

4. What are the typical features of developing-country MNEs, and how do they differ from those of developed-country MNEs?

5. What would you recommend to a small international firm seeking to compete with an established MNE?

OPENING CASE

Johnson & Johnson

Incorporated in 1886, Johnson & Johnson is the world's most comprehensive manufacturer of health care products as well as a provider of related services for the consumer, pharmaceutical, medical devices, and diagnostics markets. Consisting of more than 230 operating companies located in 57 nations, the company sells its products throughout the world. About half of its US$50.5 billion in sales in 2005 have been derived from international sales, and almost 60% of its 100,000-strong workforce resides outside the United States. Johnson & Johnson has been conducting international operations for decades. The company established its first

affiliate in Canada in 1919, followed by the United Kingdom in 1924. Affiliates were established in Australia in 1931, Sweden in 1956, Japan in 1961, South Korea in 1981, and Egypt in 1985. In 1990, Shanghai Johnson & Johnson Limited, a joint venture, was opened in China, followed the next year by Johnson & Johnson China Ltd. By 1995, the company already had five companies in China. 1990 also saw the establishment of the first offices in Hungary, Poland, and the former Yugoslavia, and in the Czech Republic the following year. Johnson & Johnson used both greenfield investment and acquisitions to expand its global reach. It acquired Belgian pharmaceutical firm Janssen Pharmaceutica in 1961, German sanitary protection manufacturer Dr. Carl Hahn in 1974, German baby toiletries maker Penaten in 1986, and French skin-care firm RoC, S.A. in 1993. In 1998, the company consolidated its manufacturing, until then done purely on a local basis, along regional lines. In 2001 it acquired the 40% it did not previously own in its Japanese joint venture, and in 2002 it bought the Belgian firm Tibotec-Virca. In 2005, Johnson & Johnson announced it is an official partner in the 2008 Beijing Olympics.

The company has made significant strides in its efforts to leverage its global reach. In Europe, for example, it has moved to establish "global platforms" consolidating production facilities in one country from which neighboring countries are served. It also embarked on a global human resources strategy, ranging from international recruitment to global management development. Many challenges remain, however, including how to expand in emerging markets while sustaining growth in established locations, how to coordinate the global network of member companies with different national and corporate cultures, and how to respond to changes such as health care regulatory reforms in the multiple environments in which it operates. For a number of years, a strong dollar weighed heavily on the profitability of Johnson & Johnson's overseas operations by depressing its earnings when converted from foreign currencies into U.S. dollars; however the dollar reversed direction around 2004, boosting the company's profits from international operations.

SOURCES: Johnson and Johnson 2005 Annual Report and company Web site.

WHAT IS A MULTINATIONAL ENTERPRISE?

When reading about international business, you will encounter many terms describing a company with significant international operations and presence. These include the following:

The **internationally committed company** is a firm with at least one majority-owned plant or a joint venture abroad but which lacks representation in all major regions of the world, which include Asia, Europe, and the Americas.[1]

The **internationally leaning** firm is one with foreign sales and possibly a representative office and/or a licensing agreement, but no ownership of foreign production sites.[2]

The **multidomestic** firm is an enterprise with multiple international subsidiaries that are relatively independent from headquarters.

The **global** firm consists of closely integrated international subsidiaries controlled and coordinated from central headquarters.

The **transnational** firm consists of subsidiaries that fulfill varying roles, with some subsidiaries playing a strategic role that in the global firm is reserved for headquarters.[3] Some scholars, as well as the United Nations Conference on Trade and Development (UNCTAD), use this term to refer to the most global of companies; however, in this book we prefer to use the more commonly used term *multinational*.

The multinational firm, or MNE, according to the OECD (Organization for Economic Co-operation and Development), is "an enterprise that engages in FDI and owns or controls value-adding activities in more than one country." An MNE typically

1. Has "multiple" facilities around the globe. According to the Conference Board, to merit the title of an MNE, a firm needs to own a majority stake in plants in the three key regions of North America, Europe, and the Pacific Rim.

2. Derives a "substantial" portion of revenues from foreign operations.

3. Runs subsidiaries that possess a common strategic vision and draw from a common pool of resources.

4. Places foreign nationals or expatriates at the board level and/or in senior management posts.

Firms such as Johnson & Johnson, Ford Motor Company, and Nestlé meet all of those criteria. Others may meet some or most or do so only partially, but they are still commonly referred to as MNEs. For instance, French dairy producer Danone has only two foreign nationals on its board; however, it has a vast global presence and a common vision, and revenues from foreign operations make up a substantial portion of its overall revenues.

Throughout this textbook we use the term **multinational enterprise (MNE)** to denote a firm with foreign direct investment (FDI), whether in manufacturing or in services, over which it maintains effective control. A firm might have investment in only one foreign market, but if this investment is controlled by it, we will classify it as an MNE. A firm engaged in trade activities but without an FDI component will be called an **international firm**. For example, a U.S.-based company that specializes in import and export management services such as export logistics, or an Italian firm that is exclusively an importer or exporter of, say, handbags, is referred to in this book as an international firm. A firm that has a small (less than 10%) equity stake in a single foreign investment and has no control over its operation and management is also an international rather than a multinational enterprise.

In this chapter, we first discuss "traditional" MNEs—that is, large firms based in developed nations, such as those of the European Union (EU), and having activities in most parts of the world. Johnson & Johnson belongs to this group. The second group consists of MNEs from developing and emerging economies (DMNEs), such as China and South Korea. The third group includes small and midsize enterprises engaged in international business. Most of these firms do not have FDI and hence do not qualify as MNEs under our definition. In this book, they will be called **small and midsize international enterprises**, or SMIEs.

The Degree of Internationalization

The level of MNE internationalization can be gauged by the **Transnationality Index (TNI)** used by UNCTAD. This index is calculated as the average of three ratios: (a) foreign assets to total assets, (b) foreign sales to total sales, and (c) foreign employment to total employment.[4] Exhibit 4.1 shows the average TNI for the world's largest MNEs. While the average has been rising over the years (especially for the top 50 firms), it remains under 60%, indicating that even the largest of multinationals are still dependent on their home country for much of their sales, assets, and human resources. Empirical evidence has been inconclusive regarding the possible link between TNI level and corporate performance. This may be because despite their obvious prowess, even the most global firms face daunting challenges in such realms as coordination and oversight of far-flung operations, establishment of a complex global supply chain, and the management of a diverse workforce. Also, as we will discuss elsewhere in the book, TNI is not the only measure of firm internationalization. For instance, in Chapter 11 we will mention that truly global companies do not retain all of their high-value-added activities in the home country, while in Chapter 17 we will point to the presence of foreign nationals on the board of directors as an indicator of how global a firm truly is.

History of the MNE

The MNE is not a new phenomenon. In their book *The Birth of the Multinational*, Moore and Lewis trace the origin and evolution of the MNE during the Phoenician, Carthaginian, Greek, and Roman empires. Formed as stock ownership companies, these firms appeared in Assyria shortly after 2000 B.C. They deployed their resources from the capital Ashur into foreign markets using both domestic and foreign employees engaged in value-adding activities. These early firms had to overcome many of the same obstacles facing current MNEs, such as tariffs and nationalist opposition to foreign trade and investment, but they used their competitive advantage and market power to prevail.[5] MNEs have continued to flourish and expand their reach in modern times. In the 18th and 19th centuries, the British-based East India Company took advantage of England's colonial rule and control of shipping lanes to become a formidable force in Asia.

Exhibit 4.1 **Average TNI* of the 100 Largest MNEs in the World and of the 50 Largest MNEs From Developing Countries, 1993–2003**

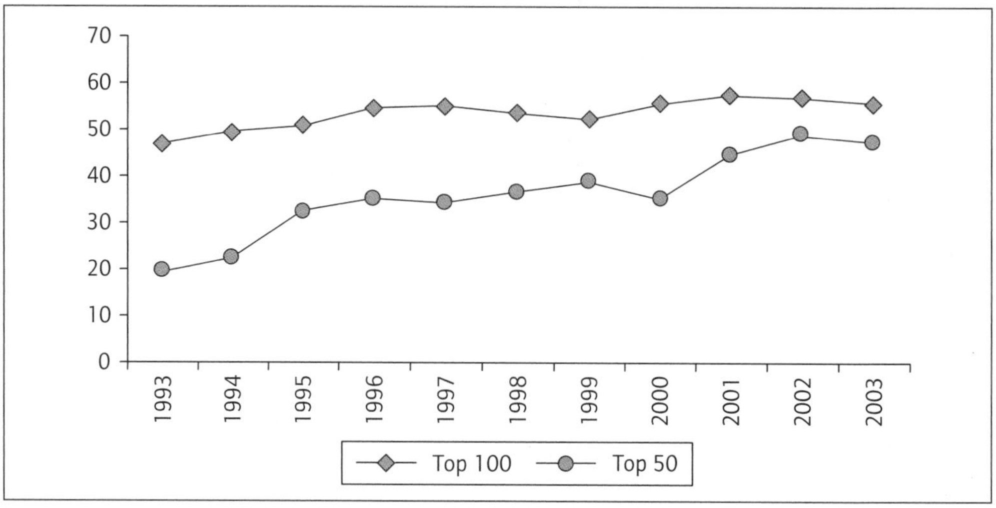

SOURCE: UNCTAD World Investment Report, 2005/Erasmus University database.

* A simple average value is used. It is the sum of the TNI values of all the companies, divided by the total number of companies.

When the company lost its monopoly on trading with China in the 1830s, competitors quickly emerged. Jardine Matheson, formed in Canton (today's Guangzhou), China, at that time opened an office in the newly established colony of Hong Kong. A decade later it became the first foreign trading firm to open an office in Japan. Jardine is now a diversified MNE listed in Bermuda but conducting most of its business in Asia from its Hong Kong base.

In recent decades, the number of MNEs has expanded dramatically. The same 15 developed countries that had 7,276 MNEs at the end of 1960 were home to 39,650 multinationals by the second half of the 1990s. Today, the MNE is a key player in the global economy. Consider this:

> The world's largest 1,000 industrial firms, most of which are MNEs, account for roughly 80% of global industrial output.[6]

> In a Conference Board survey of 1,250 publicly listed large firms, MNEs represented only 13% of the sample but had 53% of total sales.[7]

> Roughly 40% to 50% of world trade is conducted between MNEs and their affiliates. One-third of U.S. trade consists of internal transfers among units of the same MNE.

> At the beginning of the 21st century, the annual sales of each of the 10 largest industrial MNEs exceeded the tax revenues of Australia.[8] In Ireland, foreign firms account for two-thirds of national output and roughly 50% of employment.

Interim Summary

1. There are many different types of international companies and multiple definitions of a multinational firm. In this book, we use the term *multinational enterprise* (MNE) to refer to any company that has control over a foreign investment.

2. One indicator of the degree of an MNE's internationality is its TNI score.

3. While the MNE is not a new phenomenon, recent decades have seen a significant growth in the number and reach of such firms.

THE WORLD'S LARGEST MNEs

Exhibit 4.2 shows the top 50 nonfinancial MNEs for 2004, ranked by foreign assets. As the exhibit shows, the top 10 on the list are a diverse group led by General Electric (which, although classified as an electronics firm under the UNCTAD classification, is a diversified firm) and dominated by automakers Ford (U.S.), General Motors (U.S.), and Toyota (Japan) and energy and telecommunications companies. With the exception of Hong Kong–based Hutchison, all of the top 50 hail from developed economies in North America, Western Europe, or Japan.

Exhibit 4.2   The Top 50 Nonfinancial MNEs, Ranked by the UNCTAD Spread Index, 2004

Ranking 2004 by

Foreign Assets	TNI	Corporation	Country	Industry
1	68	General Electric	United States	Electronics
2	4	Vodafone Group Plc	United Kingdom	Telecommunications
3	67	Ford Motor Company	United States	Motor vehicles
4	90	General Motors	United States	Motor vehicles
5	10	British Petroleum Company Plc	United Kingdom	Petroleum expl./ref./distr.
6	38	ExxonMobil	United States	Petroleum expl./ref./distr.
7	25	Royal Dutch Shell Group	UK/Netherlands	Petroleum expl./ref./distr.
8	62	Toyota Motor Corporation	Japan	Motor vehicles
9	20	Total	France	Petroleum expl./ref./distr.
10	66	France Télécom	France	Telecommunications
11	49	Volkswagen AG	Germany	Motor vehicles
12	16	Sanofi-Aventis	France	Pharmaceuticals
13	61	Deutsche Telekom AG	Germany	Telecommunications
14	60	RWE Group	Germany	Electricity, gas, and water
15	19	Suez	France	Electricity, gas, and water
16	81	E.on	Germany	Electricity, gas, and water
17	13	Hutchinson Whampoa	Hong Kong, China	Diversified
18	39	Siemens AG	Germany	Electrical and electronic equipment
19	3	Nestlé SA	France	Food and beverages
20	92	Électricité de France	France	Electricity, gas, and water
21	29	Honda Motor Co Ltd	Japan	Motor vehicles
22	52	Vivendi Universal	France	Diversified
23	48	Chevron Texaco	United States	Motor vehicles
24	34	BMW AG	Germany	Motor vehicles
25	93	DaimlerChrysler	United States/Germany	Motor vehicles

(Continued)

Exhibit 4.2 (Continued)

Ranking 2004 by				
Foreign Assets	TNI	Corporation	Country	Industry
26	79	Pfizer Inc	United States	Pharmaceuticals
27	65	ENI	Italy	Petroleum expl./ref./distr.
28	41	Nissan Motor Co Ltd	Japan	Motor vehicles
29	54	IBM	United States	Computer and related activities
30	85	ConocoPhillips	United States	Petroleum expl./ref./distr.
31	40	Hewlett-Packard	United States	Computer and related activities
32	87	Mitsubishi Corporation	Japan	Wholesale trade
33	76	Telefonica SA	Spain	Telecommunications
34	14	Roche Group	Switzerland	Pharmaceuticals
35	94	Telecom Italia Spa	Italy	Telecommunications
36	23	Anglo American	United Kingdom	Mining and quarrying
37	55	Fiat Spa	Italy	Motor vehicles
38	9	Unilever	UK/Netherlands	Diversified
39	58	Carrefour	France	Retail
40	46	Procter & Gamble	United States	Diversified
41	47	Sony Corporation	Japan	Electrical and electronic equipment
42	71	Mitsui & Co Ltd	Japan	Wholesale trade
43	97	Wal-Mart Stores	United States	Retail
44	89	Deutsche Post AG	Germany	Transport and storage
45	26	Compagnie de Saint-Gobain SA	Japan	Nonmetallic mineral products
46	50	Veolia Environment SA	France	Water supply
47	7	Philips Electronics	Netherlands	Electrical and electronic equipment
48	12	Lafarge SA	France	Nonmetallic products
49	72	Repsol YPF SA	Spain	Petroleum expl./ref./distr.
50	30	Novartis	Switzerland	Pharmaceuticals

SOURCE: UNCTAD, World Investment Report, 2006.

NOTE: TNI rankings are within the 100 largest.

Exhibit 4.3 provides information on the top U.S.-based MNEs. Unlike the UNCTAD list of the world's multinationals, this list includes financial services firms, which populate nearly half of the top 10 firms, led by Citigroup.

The Growth of Service MNEs

Recent years have seen a significant growth of MNEs in media, education, transportation, information services, travel, tourism, health care, and professional services. There are several reasons for the growth, as follows:

Economic transformation. As developed nations have shifted into service economies, their service firms have sought to leverage their scale and resources

Exhibit 4.3   The 10 Largest U.S. MNEs

Rank	Company	Industry ($Bil)	Sales ($Bil)	Profits ($Bil)	Assets ($Bil)	Market Value
1	Citigroup	Banking	120.32	24.64	1,494.04	230.93
2	General Electric	Conglomerates	49.70	16.35	673.30	348.45
3	Bank of America	Banking	85.39	16.47	1,291.80	184.17
4	American Intl Group	Insurance	106.98	11.90	843.40	172.24
5	ExxonMobil	Oil & Gas Operations	328.21	36.13	208.34	362.53
6	JPMorgan Chase	Banking	79.90	8.48	1,198.94	144.13
7	Wal-Mart Stores	Retailing	312.43	11.23	138.17	188.86
8	Chevron	Oil & Gas Operations	184.92	4.10	124.81	126.80
9	Berkshire Hathaway	Diversified Financials	76.33	6.74	196.71	133.67
10	Procter & Gamble	Household & Personal Products	61.68	7.79	136.52	197.12

SOURCE: The Forbes 2000, March 2006. Reprinted by permission of *Forbes* magazine © 2007 Forbes Media LLC.

toward new growth venues in foreign markets. For instance, large U.S. airlines such as United, Delta, and Continental have expanded their international route network to serve the increasingly global destinations of their customers and to capture the better profit margins as compared with domestic routes.

Globalization and liberalization of regulatory systems. Because many service MNEs are "location bound"—that is, production and consumption must take place in the same location—they are especially dependent on global regulatory regimes as well as on the domestic regulations in each market in which they operate. New "open skies" aviation agreements have allowed carriers to serve more foreign markets and have opened domestic markets to foreign competition. The globalization of accounting standards has made it possible for large U.S.-based accounting firms to operate abroad. The relaxation of the "Big Store" law in Japan has permitted Toys 'R' Us to operate the large-scale retail operations it has come to master in the United States.

Communications advances. Progress in communications and computer technologies have enabled service MNEs to coordinate knowledge-intensive operations across borders. As an example, consulting firms can now exchange information and transfer knowledge quickly and efficiently among far-flung subsidiaries, making coordination easier and better.

The growth of service MNEs has been especially pronounced in the United States, which is regarded as having the most competitive service sector as a result of relative openness and intense domestic competition in comparison with the European and Japanese service industries. As noted in Chapter 2, the United States runs a substantial trade surplus in services vis-à-vis a chronic deficit in its merchandise trade. U.S. firms do not dominate all service sectors, however. Exhibit 4.4 shows the list of the world's 20 largest banks by assets in 2004. Only one U.S. bank (Citigroup) is among the top 10, while two more (JPMorgan Chase and Bank of America) are in the second tier. Although this is partly the result of U.S. limitations on interstate banking, it does provide a sense of how competitive this sector is globally.

Exhibit 4.4   The World's Top 20 Banks, 2004 (Based on Total Assets, $M)

Rank	Bank Name	Country	Assets
1	Mizuho Financial Group	Japan	1,285,471
2	Citigroup	U.S.	1,264,032
3	UBS	Switzerland	1,120,543
4	Crédit Agricole Groupe	France	1,105,378
5	HSBC Holdings	UK	1,034,216
6	Deutsche Bank	Germany	1,014,845
7	BNP Paribas	France	988,982
8	Mitsubishi Tokyo Financial Group	Japan	974,950
9	Sumitomo Mitsui Financial Group	Japan	950,448
10	Royal Bank of Scotland	UK	806,207
11	Barclays Bank	UK	791,292
12	Credit Suisse Group	Switzerland	777,849
13	JPMorgan Chase & Co.	U.S.	770,912
14	UFJ Holdings	Japan	753,631
15	Bank of America Corp.	U.S.	736,445
16	ING Bank	Netherlands	684,004
17	Société Générale	France	681,216
18	ABN Amro Bank	Netherlands	667,636
19	HBOS	UK	650,721
20	Indust. & Commercial Bank of China	China	637,829
21	HypoVereinsbank	Germany	605,525
22	Dresdner Bank	Germany	602,461
23	Fortis Bank	Belgium	535,462
24	Rabobank Group	Netherlands	509,352
25	Commerzbank	Germany	481,921

SOURCE: *The Banker,* July 2004.

In advertising, U.S. and European agencies are the leaders, whereas the Japanese lag behind. Dentsu—Japan's dominant advertising agency—still generated only a modest portion of its revenue from foreign sources. This is not for lack of trying. Dentsu opened a New York office in 1959, and in 1999 it took a 20% stake in U.S.-based Bcom3 Group, a merger of Leo Burnett and D'arcy Masius Benton & Bowles. In many service sectors, however, U.S. firms face tough competition. As you can see in Exhibit 4.5, U.S. carriers are among the largest airlines in terms of passenger traffic, but this is mostly the result of the size of the U.S. domestic aviation market. When it comes to service reputation, U.S. firms lag behind foreign carriers, in particular Singapore Airlines and Hong Kong–based Cathay Pacific, which have been occupying the top spots in global surveys.

Interim Summary

1. With a few exceptions, the largest MNEs are based in the Triad of the countries of Europe, the United States, and Japan.

2. The annual revenues of the largest MNEs are higher than the tax incomes of some countries.

Exhibit 4.5   Top 20 Airlines—System Traffic, January–August 2006

Rank	Airline	RPKs (000)
1	American	153,841,431
2	Air France KLM	131,782,000
3	United	128,433,154
4	Delta	127,340,427
5	Continental	86,637,730
6	Northwest	79,031,359
7	British Airways	77,387,000
8	Southwest	73,523,562
9	Lufthansa Group	73,221,000
10	US Airways	69,794,246
11	Singapore	57,519,100
12	Qantas	53,582,000
13	Japan Airlines	52,359,188
14	Air Canada	49,776,000
15	Cathay Pacific	47,321,604
16	Emirates	40,967,044
17	Thai Airways	36,796,083
18	Iberia	34,761,000
19	SAS Group	25,693,000
20	Alitalia	21,708,300

SOURCE: ATW Research. Reprinted with permission from the January–August 2006 issues of *Air Transport World*.

3. Service MNEs are growing rapidly, the result of a shift toward service economies in developed nations, changes in regulatory regimes, and the availability of modern means of communication.

4. U.S. MNEs are competitive in many areas but face intense competition from other global players in sectors such as banking.

THE IMAGE OF THE MNE

The MNE in the Public Eye

Over the years, the MNE has been both lauded and vilified for its impact on its host (especially) and home countries. If the MNE was criticized as a monopolistic player representing a threat to national sovereignty in the 1970s, in the 1980s it was labeled a cumbersome dinosaur unable to adapt to change and hence doomed. In the 1990s, the MNE emerged as a relatively benevolent provider of knowledge and capital, whose technology and expertise contribute to national productivity and export performance.[9] For instance, in 2005 foreign invested enterprises (FIEs) accounted for 58% of China's exports. MNEs were also positively cited for being agents of change, introducing new ways of doing business that would eventually be adopted by local firms. For example, the first industrial robots were introduced to Singapore by MNEs, with local firms adopting the technology later. Finally, MNEs have been noted for creating jobs. In Turkey, MNEs increased their staffing at a double-digit level in an otherwise stagnant labor market, and those jobs have been paying more than double the average wage.[10]

At the dawn of the 21st century, MNEs are once again seen in some circles as a threat to national sovereignty. The *Economist* suggests that this is because the MNE is the most visible symbol of globalization. Developing nations expect the MNE to bring in capital and technology but refrain from bringing in foreign ideas. The MNE is accused of having an unfair advantage, exploiting incentives granted exclusively to foreign firms to shift production to ever lower-cost locations. It is also criticized for limiting knowledge transfer to "intermediate" technologies, constraining the host country's ability to become a global competitor. For instance, Motorola has been criticized for limiting its R&D efforts in Brazil to the adaptation of its existing technology to Latin American markets rather than creating new technologies.[11] A related criticism is that MNEs generate low-paying, low-tech jobs in the host country while keeping high-value-added jobs at home. In China, there are now many voices calling on the government to curb the rising influence of foreign MNEs.

The image of the MNE varies, among other factors, by country, industry, market orientation, and the constituency affected. The impact of the MNE in developed countries is assessed using different yardsticks than in developing countries. MNEs in extraction industries (e.g., oil, mining) are scrutinized more closely than those engaged in manufacturing, and those that bring advanced technology are often treated differently from those that provide mere assembly ("screwdriver plants").[12] In the public eye, MNEs and host country governments involve both cooperation and bargaining elements in their interdependent relationships. The two cooperate by contributing complementary resources. An MNE's technological resources, capital investment, global distribution, and managerial expertise add critical value to local economies, especially to developing countries. MNEs need support from local governments in developing investment infrastructure, creating a better environment for fair competition, and improving the quality of production factors such as labor (through training and education), information (through advancing the information technology industry), and capital (through improving the banking sector). When a particular MNE's strategic goals are not compatible with those of the host country government, bargaining ensues. The government may want to control critical natural resources demanded by the MNE or safeguard an infant local industry by posing many entry or operational barriers against the MNE. We further discuss MNE–government relations in Chapter 7.

Feelings toward the MNE in its home country are also often ambivalent. On the one hand, it is often recognized that the MNE brings resources that are unavailable in the home country, lowering prices for domestic consumers and helping a nation sustain its global competitiveness. Another plus is that the MNE's successes in foreign markets allow suppliers and other host country firms to "piggyback" on the MNE, thus increasing national output and job creation at home. At the same time, MNEs are criticized for shifting production and investment from their home base to foreign locations, undermining employment and "hollowing out" the production and knowledge base of the home country.

The Borderless Corporation: Myth or Reality?

The rise of the borderless, transnational corporation, which owes allegiance to no one, has been a major theme in the popular media. According to this view, the MNE establishes its headquarters anywhere it sees fit, shifts its operations at will to wherever it can garner the highest return, and adopts the form of governance and management that it finds most suitable in terms of profitability rather than in terms of social responsibility or other broader considerations. Proponents of this thesis point out that it is increasingly difficult to pinpoint country of origin for firms engaged in international business. DaimlerChrysler, the result of the acquisition of U.S.-based Chrysler by German automaker Daimler Benz, is headquartered and registered in Germany, although it maintains a U.S. headquarters for its North American operations and its shares are traded on the New York Stock Exchange, with a large block held by U.S. investors. Rhombic Corp. was founded in Nevada; is based in Vancouver, Canada; while the highest turnover of its shares is in Hamburg, Germany.

Opponents of this thesis argue that the borderless corporation is a myth; that most MNEs maintain a clear national base and that enduring national and political realities shape their governance, financing, R&D, FDI, and intrafirm trading strategies.[13] MNEs based in different countries utilize various competitive advantages developed in response to factor and product market circumstances in their home countries.[14] Most MNEs still produce more than two-thirds of their output and employ two-thirds of their workforce in their home countries.[15] For instance, a recent study suggests that there remain significant differences among Triad firms in product strategy. While U.S. firms compete on "economy" (lower price, lower quality), Japanese MNEs highlight the superior value of their products (a combination of higher quality and lower prices), whereas Europeans emphasize the premium nature of their product (higher quality, higher price). In the study, companies that aligned their global strategy with the national stereotype performed better than those that did not.[16]

Interim Summary

1. The image of MNEs varies by time, country, and industry.

2. The level of MNEs' contribution to the local economy is affected by whether MNEs and the local government share goals and contribute complementary resources; MNEs and the government both cooperate and bargain with each other.

3. Despite a heightened tendency toward borderless activities and a growing contribution from foreign production and sales, most MNEs retain their home country roots and characteristics.

THE COMPETITIVE ADVANTAGE OF THE MNE

When McDonald's opened its first restaurant in Moscow, the MNE increased the number of customers served there more than 20-fold over the number served in the Soviet-era cafeteria that occupied the site before. Thanks to its global scale and experience, the MNE has a large capital, human, brand, and technological resource base that it can effectively leverage in multiple countries. As the chairman and CEO of Toronto-based Four Seasons Hotels justifies its drive for foreign expansion, "We can double the size of the company, and then can double it again, without changing the product or brand."[17] Procter & Gamble's operations in some 140 countries allow it to spread development, manufacturing, and marketing costs. With almost five billion customers worldwide, the company can monitor the performance of each of its 100 brands and apply lessons from one market to another. Global spread also permits the MNE an effective response to trade and investment barriers.

PepsiCo was able to profitably sell its cola in the Soviet Union despite the lack of a convertible currency by taking Russian vodka as payment and then using its U.S. distribution channels to market it. Similarly, KFC used its China revenues to commission uniforms for its branches in other Asian countries.

Global spread also provides MNEs with diversification, allowing them to compensate for low performance or uncertainties such as currency fluctuations in certain markets. This allows them to overcome entry barriers in the form of high start-up costs and be early entrants in emerging markets where return is often not realized for many years. One of the most successful MNEs in China, Procter & Gamble, entered the country in the 1980s but did not turn a profit until the mid-1990s. Automotive MNEs had not made money in China during many years of operation, but most of them now enjoy high profitability in this market. Although the performance of MNEs varies by company and markets, as a group they have been consistently more profitable than their local counterparts. However, this higher rate of return must be considered against the higher risk associated with foreign investment.[18] In contrast, the returns for internationally committed and internationally leaning firms were found to be quite comparable with those of domestic companies. Despite the reputation of developing markets as being a difficult place to do business, profitability was higher for firms operating in those markets than for those in developed markets, a spread especially pronounced for internationally leaning firms.[19] One reason is that monopoly profits are often easier to obtain in developing markets that are less regulated and have lesser competition.

The MNE's Capabilities

In Chapter 3 we introduced the dynamic capability theory. It suggests that, to prosper in today's turbulent international environment, the MNE cannot merely rely on its existing resources; it must develop "dynamic capabilities" to create, deploy, and upgrade resources in pursuit of sustained competitive advantage. It must instill its capabilities within its global operating units. If superior knowledge is the main source of its competitive advantage, the MNE must have an organization that extends and exploits its knowledge throughout its global operations.

MNE Capabilities

Firm capabilities include familiarity with national culture, industrial structure, and government requirements, as well as relationships with customers, suppliers, and regulators. These and various other aspects of doing business locally give a domestic business a potential edge over a foreign competitor. The MNE must have strategic and organizational capabilities to mitigate this disadvantage. Such capabilities include resources that are unique to the firm, difficult to imitate, and able to generate economic returns and competitive advantage. Coca-Cola's vast number of bottling facilities worldwide is less critical than its ability to coordinate such a system. Its formulas (syrups and concentrates), however, are a key asset that gives the firm a leading edge.

Strategic capabilities include technological assets such as patents, trade secrets, proprietary designs, product development, and process innovation. IBM's Chinese speech-recognition system, ViaVoice, has dominated the greater China market for years. The system uses IBM's most advanced voice recognition technology and can be adapted to standard Mandarin and a number of special dialects. The Body Shop's franchising skills with international retail operations, Merrill Lynch's relationships with Japanese financial institutions, and Kodak's extensive networking with Chinese government agencies have significantly contributed to each firm's success.

Managerial skills are an important component of MNE capabilities. Such skills are manifested in global human resource management as well as in information, organization design, and control systems. Kodak's skills in recruiting, evaluating, motivating, and training its overseas employees provide a distinct advantage. Coca-Cola's ability to propagate a common human resources philosophy and develop a group of internationally minded midlevel executives also constitutes an advantage. Colgate's system of recruiting MBAs who speak at least one foreign language and have lived outside the United States is another example. Colgate does not assign foreign-born trainees to their native countries for initial postings, but rather to a third country.

International experience is essential to strategic and organizational capabilities. Gillette's 20-plus years' experience in emerging markets and a century of experience in its industry has helped the company become a global leader. This experience allows Gillette (now part of Procter & Gamble) to select and enter foreign markets successfully. The same is true for Starbuck's Coffee, which leveraged its first experience in foreign forays into Tokyo in 1996 to expand into other foreign markets. Starbuck's is now present in 36 foreign markets, from Bahrain to the Philippines.

Capability Deployment

To be successful, the MNE must transfer critical capabilities unavailable to local players. McDonald's and KFC's overseas success has been built on their ability to rapidly transfer the capacity to operate their entire complex business system to foreign entrepreneurs. Leveraging capabilities across markets is difficult, however. As market conditions in other countries vary, so does the effectiveness of those skills. Toyota's "Just in Time" (JIT) system yields benefits globally, but the risks associated with reduced inventory levels are greater in countries where change and disruptions—from weather conditions to strikes—are common.

Technological and financial capabilities (e.g., cash flow management) are generally more transferable than organizational skills. Among strategic capabilities, both a superior market position and an oligopolistic market power are competitive edges that are not immediately transferable. The same is true for home-country experience and reputation, although some firms and brands—for example, the Four Seasons hotel chain—possess a global reputation that can be leveraged. A superior distribution network cannot be easily replicated overseas; however, knowing how to establish and manage a distribution network is transferable. Nestlé's experience with promotion and distribution in China was helpful in other emerging markets, such as Vietnam and Russia.

Capability Upgrading

Learning capability is the capacity to generate ideas and acquire new knowledge. It is generally more transferable than firm resources. Firms with the capacity to learn can gain more from experience and apply what they have learned to other relevant situations. This capacity helps mitigate the "liabilities of foreignness" during international expansion. To translate learning into competence, the MNE must convert it into firm-specific resources. This involves acquisition, sharing, and utilization. Knowledge acquisition accrues through internal development or external learning. Some MNEs offer seminars in which senior managers regularly share their best practices and knowledge about foreign markets across functional, divisional, and geographical boundaries.

Measuring, benchmarking, tracking, and rewards for knowledge enhancement may also increase learning. Centers of excellence that represent the best practice of managing knowledge are another learning mechanism. An MNE can put together a list of best practices in core marketing activities; for example, the best database marketing is done in London, the best distribution logistics can be found in Singapore, and the best account management is in New York. Many MNEs have gained ideas and experience from foreign businesses that were early movers in a host-country market. Next, firms must be able to generate innovative ideas useful in international expansion through competency acquisition, experimentation, and spanning boundaries. When learning through competency acquisition is coupled with a high capacity for change, MNEs tend to be more innovative, proactive, and willing to take risks. They react to market changes in different countries more quickly.

External knowledge acquisition through alliances is also an important vehicle for upgrading capabilities. Starbuck's takes a 20% stake in many of its overseas stores with the hope of learning about the local market and eventually increasing its stake.[20] Alliances enable firms to run product development programs in conjunction with their own internal development efforts or to broaden their access to new skills and insights. Motorola licensed some of its microprocessor technology to Toshiba and in return Toshiba licensed some of its memory chip technology to Motorola. The alliance experience can trigger learning but can also expose the MNE to technology loss. In the alliance between GE and Snecma to build commercial aircraft engines, GE tried to reduce the risk of excess transfer by walling off certain sections of the production process. This modularization was supposed to cut off transfer of what GE felt was key competitive technology, but complete separation was found to be impractical and detrimental to the effectiveness of the venture. Chapter 12 is focused on the opportunities and challenges associated with global strategic alliances.

Sharing and disseminating newly acquired knowledge among different subunits of an MNE will determine the efficiency of capability upgrading. Once new knowledge is acquired, firms integrate it with their existing skills. The integration depends on having an effective information transfer system, an incentive structure promoting external learning and experimentation, and an organizational implementing mechanism. Sharing experiences and mindsets through training programs, efficient communications systems, and clear information transfer is crucial, as is a governance structure that facilitates learning diffusion.

Interim Summary

1. MNEs have many advantages over local firms: They can draw on larger financial knowledge and human resources, have broader experience than most local firms, and can afford to operate at a loss in unfavorable markets for a longer time before turning a profit. However, local firms enjoy superior knowledge of their home market and are often supported by their governments.

2. It is relatively easy to transfer capital and equipment to a new operation but much more difficult to transfer knowledge, skills, and experience. It is crucial for the MNE to be able to disseminate knowledge to new operations and to integrate information acquired from those operations into already existing

procedures. Effective knowledge transfer is the most important capability for an MNE to develop.

THE MNE FROM EMERGING/ DEVELOPING ECONOMIES (DMNE)

For years, the term *MNE* was synonymous with the likes of General Motors, Coca-Cola, Siemens, and Matsushita—large firms from developed nations, mostly from the United States, Europe, and Japan. Firms from emerging and developing nations were rarely in a position to amass the resources and knowledge necessary for extensive forays into foreign markets. Although MNEs from developed nations still dominate global business, **developing nations' MNEs** (DMNEs), especially those from emerging economies, have become global competitors and sometimes leaders in their field. Taiwan-based Acer is a leader in notebook computers. Thai conglomerate Charoen Pokphand is a major force in food production and processing in Asia.[21] Philippines' brewer San Miguel and Singapore Telecom are also global players.

The rise of DMNEs is intertwined with the increase in outward FDI from developing countries. In 1960 the stock of FDI from developing countries amounted to a mere 0.8% of the global FDI stock, whereas it reached 1.2% in 1975 and 3.2% in 1992, with a growth rate about double that of FDI from developed nations.[22] In Asia and Eastern Europe, DMNEs represent a considerable proportion of FDI. Hong Kong and Taiwan are the largest foreign investors in Mainland China, while Singapore and South Korea are major investors there.

Photo 4.1   Hong Kong is a regional headquarters for many multinationals as well as a major center for small international firms.

SOURCE: Jupiterimages. Used with permission.

The Largest Developing-Country MNEs

Exhibit 4.6 lists the top 50 DMNEs in 2004, led by Hutchison Whampoa, a diversified Hong Kong–based conglomerate with interests ranging from shipping to mobile phone networks. While these firms come from many countries, the list is dominated by Asia-based companies, a reflection of the rapid economic growth in this part of the world. The industry base of those DMNEs is also quite diverse, ranging from energy to shipping to telecommunications, and including a number of highly diversified conglomerates.

Exhibit 4.7 shows the country and industry distribution of the 100 largest DMNEs. The list is dominated by Chinese economies, including China, Hong Kong (a Special Administrative Region of China), Taiwan (which China views as a renegade province), and Singapore. Together, these economies, which are sometimes labeled as "Greater China," hold more than 60% of the top DMNEs. In terms of industry composition, the most common are diversified companies, a unique feature of DMNEs, particularly in Asia.

Exhibit 4.6   The 50 Largest MNEs From Developing Economies, 2004

Ranking by Foreign Assets	TNI	Corporation	Economy	Industry
1	28	Hutchison Whampoa, Ltd.	Hong Kong, China	Diversified
2	80	Petronas–Petroliam Nasional Bhd	Malaysia	Petroleum expl./ref./distr.
3	32	Singtel, Ltd.	Singapore	Telecommunications
4	54	Samsung Electronics Co., Ltd.	Republic of Korea	Electrical and electronic equip.
5	86	CITIC Group	China	Diversified
6	30	Cemex S.A.	Mexico	Construction
7	11	LG Electronics, Inc.	Republic of Korea	Electrical and electronic equip.
8	62	China Ocean Shipping (Group) Co.	China	Shipping
9	75	Petróleos de Venezuela	Venezuela	Petroleum expl./ref./distr.
10	37	Jardine Matheson Holdings, Ltd.	Hong Kong, China	Diversified
11	66	Formosa Plastic Group	Taiwan Province of China	Industrial chemicals
12	96	Petroleo Brasileiro S.A.–Petrobras	Brazil	Petroleum expl./ref./distr.
13	94	Hyundai Motor Company	Republic of Korea	Motor vehicles
14	33	Flextronics International, Ltd.	Singapore	Electrical and electronic equipment
15	45	Capitaland, Ltd.	Singapore	Real Estate
16	63	Sasol, Ltd.	South Africa	Industrial chemicals
17	90	Telmex	Mexico	Telecommunications
18	55	América Móvil	Mexico	Telecommunications
19	79	China State Construction Engineering Corporation	China	Construction
20	43	Hon Hai Precision Industries (Foxconn)	Taiwan Province of China	Electrical and electronic equipment
21	19	Shangri-La Asia, Ltd.	Hong Kong, China	Hotels and motels
22	77	New World Development Co., Ltd.	Hong Kong, China	Diversified
23	27	Sappi, Ltd.	South Africa	Paper
24	100	China National Petroleum Corporation	China	Petroleum expl./ref./distr.
25	60	Companhia Vale do Rio Doce	Brazil	Mining and quarrying
26	97	Oil and Natural Gas Corporation	India	Petroleum and natural gas
27	71	Kia Motors	Republic of Korea	Motor vehicles
28	59	Sinochem Corp.	China	Wholesale trade
29	88	CLP Holdings	Hong Kong, China	Electricity, gas, and water
30	6	Asia Food & Properties	Singapore	Food and beverages
31	5	Guangdong Investment, Ltd.	Hong Kong, China	Diversified
32	58	YTL Corp. Berhad	Malaysia	Diversified
33	56	Metalurgica Gerdau S.A.	Brazil	Metal and metal products
34	31	Orient Overseas International, Ltd.	Hong Kong, China	Transport and storage
35	24	China Resources Enterprises	Hong Kong, China	Petroleum expl./ref./distr.
36	23	Star Cruises	Hong Kong, China	Transport
37	69	Quanta Computer, Inc.	Taiwan Province of China	Computer and related activities
38	15	Neptune Orient Lines, Ltd.	Singapore	Transport and storage
39	81	United Microelectronics Corporation	Taiwan Province of China	Electrical and electronic equipment
40	44	City Developments, Ltd.	Singapore	Hotels
41	52	MTN Group, Ltd.	South Africa	Telecommunications

Ranking by				
Foreign Assets	TNI	Corporation	Economy	Industry
42	74	Taiwan Semiconductor	Taiwan Province	Computer and related activities
43	48	Steinhoff International Holdings	South Africa	Household goods
44	35	TCL Corporation	China	Electrical and electronic equipment
45	49	Misc Corp. Berhad	Malaysia	Transport
46	83	Singapore Airlines, Ltd.	Singapore	Transport and storage
47	92	China National Offshore Oil Corp.	China	Petroleum and natural gas
48	1	First Pacific Company, Ltd.	Hong Kong, China	Electrical and electronic equipment
49	57	Barloworld, Ltd.	South Africa	Diversified
50	82	FEMSA–Fomento Economico Mexicano	Mexico	Food and beverages

SOURCE: UNCTAD, World Investment Report, 2006.

Exhibit 4.7   Country/Industry Composition of the 100 Largest DMNEs From Developing Economies, 2004 (Percentage)

Economy/Industry	Top 100
Number of economies	14
Share in total	
Hong Kong, China	25
Taiwan Province of China	15
Singapore	13
China	10
Mexico	8
South Africa	10
Number of industries	25
Share in total	
Diversified	16
Electrical/electronics	11
Petroleum	8
Transport and storage	9
Food and beverages	7
Telecommunications	6
Computers	9
TNI (Transnationality Index)	50.7

SOURCE: United Nations Conference on Trade and Development (UNCTAD).

COUNTRY BOX

AN ISRAELI FIRM BECOMES THE WORLD'S LARGEST GENERIC DRUG MAKER

Israel-based Teva was established in Jerusalem in 1901 as a drug distribution agency and started its pharmaceutical operations in the 1930s as a small-scale producer competing with foreign imports. Taking advantage of the immigration-driven growth in its domestic market as well as of the cessation of imports during wartimes, the company grew rapidly and then merged with its domestic competitors Asia and Zori and embarked on exports as a major thrust. Teva solidified its entry into the U.S. market via a joint venture with W. R. Grace in 1985 and the acquisition of Lemmon in 1986. In the 1990s, Teva embarked on an aggressive acquisition strategy in the United States and Europe, eventually gaining a berth among the world's 50 largest pharmaceutical companies. By 2001, the company was the world's largest maker of generic drugs, a position solidified by additional acquisitions in subsequent years. It has also emerged as a developer of new drugs in a number of areas. The company shares are trading on the NASDAQ, the Tel-Aviv Stock Exchange, the Seaq International in London, and the Frankfurt Stock Exchange.

Like Teva, many DMNEs start by competing on price, using "intermediary" technology that is not cutting-edge but still represents sufficient improvement over local standards in developing markets. South Korean firms such as Samsung and Daewoo (which eventually collapsed) expanded in Southeast Asia, Eastern Europe, and the (former) Soviet republics, where their products were superior to those available locally yet competitively priced. Today, South Korean conglomerates LG and Samsung sell their consumer electronics in the United States and the EU, while China-based Haier dominates the small refrigerator market in the United States. Brazilian regional jet manufacturer Embraer has been holding its own in this very competitive market contested by developed market players such as Canadian-based Bombardier. In the wake of the U.S. presidential election impasse in 2000, Brazilian Procomp (acquired by Ohio-based Diebold) offered electronic voting machines superior to those currently in use.

Obstacles Facing MNEs From Developing Economies

DMNEs face a number of obstacles in entering foreign markets, including the following:

Resource Constraints. Teva initially focused on generic drugs, partly because it could ill afford the huge capital investment involved in the development of new drugs. Lack of reputation and brand recognition are other obstacles faced by DMNEs.

Lack of Knowledge.[25] For Teva, the complex process involved in obtaining FDA approval in the United States—a prerequisite for selling pharmaceutical products in many markets—was a major hurdle. DMNEs lack experience in foreign operations and may lack the production, marketing, and management skills that are necessary in competitive international markets.

A Sheltered Environment. Teva was initially protected by duties on the foreign drugs with which it competed. Many DMNEs have been sheltered in their domestic market for a long time. They have often benefited from a domestic monopoly or enjoyed a cost advantage thanks to protectionist measures. International activities (if any) were mediated by specialized governmental or quasi-governmental agencies (e.g., China's foreign trade corporations), which prevented those firms from developing the knowledge and expertise that result from conducting international business directly (e.g., feedback from international clients).

Exhibit 4.8 shows the top nonfinancial DMNEs from southeastern Europe and the CIS countries. The list is dominated by energy firms from Russia, a country endowed with tremendous oil and mineral deposits.

Exhibit 4.8   The Top 10 Nonfinancial MNEs From Southeastern Europe and the CIS,* Ranked by Foreign Assets, 2004

Rank	Corporation	Country	Industry	Sales Foreign / Total	TNI
1	Gazprom	Russian Federation	Petroleum and natural gas	24,536 / 36,422	
2	Lukoil	Russian Federation	Petroleum and natural gas	26,408 / 33,845	37.8
3	Norilsk	Russian Federation	Mining and quarrying	5,968 / 7,033	32.3
4	Novoship Co.	Russian Federation	Transport	350 / 419	58.9
5	PLIVA Pharmaceuticals industry	Croatia	Pharmaceuticals	939 / 1,130	62.9
6	Rusal	Russian Federation	Metal and metal products	4,412 / 5,436	33.7
7	OMZ	Russian Federation	Motor vehicles	271 / 524	42.9
8	Energoprojekt	Serbia and Montenegro	Heavy construction	108 / 172	57.3
9	Severstal	Russian Federation	Metal and metal products	3,954 / 6,664	25.0
10	Mechel	Russian Federation	Metal and metal products	2,203 / 3,636	25.6

SOURCE: UNCTAD, World Investment Report, 2006.

*Based on survey responses and annual reports.

DMNE Advantage in Global Markets

Obstacles notwithstanding, DMNEs develop some unique advantages that position them well in the competition with established MNEs. Among these advantages are the following:

Home Government Support. DMNEs enjoy the backing of their home governments to an extent that may compensate for their ownership and location disadvantages.[26] A major reason for the support is the impact of the DMNE on its national economy. One form of indirect support and subsidy is local government procurement: Embraer accounts for 50% of the Brazilian Air Force fleet. In Thailand, government support for commercial chicken farming assists the animal feed business of Charoen Pokphand. Many DMNEs benefit from monopolized access to a natural resource, such as oil. They have access to low-cost capital, subsidies, and incentives as well as to competitively priced labor, although their wage advantage tends to erode as their home economies develop. When that happens, exchange rates become less favorable, and DMNEs move production to other low-cost locations. This is what is happening today in China, where a number of garment makers have been shifting some production to Laos and Cambodia.

Government support is a two-edged sword. It shields the firm from the marketplace, thereby acting as a damper on its capability development, and the price for the support is often government interference in such key decisions as the domain and location of investment, limiting the strategic leeway of the firm. One reason for the development of "bogus blue-eyed" ventures in mainland China—ventures that are funded by the Chinese firms themselves through a foreign-registered entity—is to circumvent government control and involvement.

Flexibility. While reducing scale advantages, the lower production scale of the DMNE permits the flexibility and adaptation that are critical in international markets. DMNEs tend to have less investment sunk in older plants and technologies and can leapfrog into cutting-edge technologies. They develop a competitive advantage in their ability to "mediate" technologies for use in developing markets by downscaling, simplifying, and substituting local inputs and by increasing the labor intensity of production.[27] DMNEs also have experience in customizing technologies and products, capabilities that serve them well, especially in other developing markets.[28]

Typical Features of DMNEs

DMNEs differ along national lines. For example, Li found that, compared with their Taiwanese counterparts, South Korean MNEs put more emphasis on market share or revenue growth than on profit margins (although the Asian crisis has probably narrowed the differences) and focused more on cost reduction than on value maintenance and enhancement. While Korean MNEs favored mass and domestic markets, Taiwanese MNEs favored niche and international markets, relied more on core competencies, and were less centralized than their Korean counterparts.[29] Because many of these differences can be attributed to cultural and institutional factors, it is reasonable to assume that as DMNEs mature, they will follow a different path.

At the same time, some generalities seem to hold for most DMNEs, as follows:

Internationalization Patterns. Some of the motivations of DMNEs are similar to those of MNEs from developed economies. Both groups seek to exploit their firm-specific advantages, overcome obstacles to exports in the form of tariff and nontariff barriers, escape stringent environmental limitations at home, and obtain lower-cost production bases. Although both groups seek to enter new and promising markets, DMNEs have a number of unique reasons to pursue foreign trade and investment:

1. To develop ownership advantages. Although traditional MNEs move abroad to exploit their ownership and skill advantages, DMNEs often do so to develop and gain such advantages.[30] A survey of outward FDI by Chinese enterprises found that learning manufacturing and marketing techniques was a key reason for internationalization.[31] DMNEs also seek to exploit their advantage in intermediate technologies.

2. To serve as intermediaries. DMNEs mediate the flow of technologies from industrialized to developing countries.[32] For instance, Korean VCR makers relied on Japanese technology to develop low-cost VCRs, which they then exported to developing (and also developed) markets.

3. To overcome import quotas in developed markets.[33] By locating FDI in developed markets or in a developing market that has a trade agreement with a developed country, quota barriers can be overcome.

4. To reduce risk via diversification.[34] By shifting assets abroad, DMNEs based in regions characterized by political risk and volatility can reduce risk exposure and protect some of their capital base. FDI in this case serves as a substitute for portfolio investment that is limited owing to foreign exchange controls in many developing countries.

Focus on Other Developing Markets. DMNEs are more likely to have a greater share of FDI in other developing markets where their combination of intermediary technology and low cost provide a competitive advantage. For instance, Brazilian companies sell arms to other developing countries. However, DMNEs often find it necessary to eventually enter developed markets to increase scale and improve learning.

Reliance on Third Parties. To compensate for their limited resource base, DMNEs tend to rely on other entities in their international activities, whether alliance partners, export intermediaries, or government organizations.

Governance. DMNEs are less likely to be publicly traded and are often tightly controlled by a founding family or the government. For instance, Hong Kong–listed Lippo is controlled by the founding Riady family, Indonesians with overseas Chinese roots. Some DMNEs eventually evolve into market entities, however. Embraer (Empresa Brasiliera de Aeronáutica) was founded in 1969 as a government company with the purpose of developing a local aircraft industry. Privatized in 1994, it was purchased by Bozano Simonsen, one of Brazil's biggest investment firms, and by the country's two largest pension funds, PREVI and SISTEL. In 1999, Embraer formed a strategic alliance with a group of French aerospace companies—Aerospatiale-Matra, Dassault Aviation, Snecma, and Thomson-CSF—which jointly acquired 20% of Embraer's voting shares.

Industry Domain. When not diversified, DMNEs are likely to be in manufacturing, starting with labor-intensive production and gradually moving into technological and marketing-intensive products often based on imported technology.[35] Some emerging-market MNEs can be found in services (e.g., Singapore Airlines, consistently ranked at the top of the industry in terms of service and profitability).

Bargaining Power. DMNEs are less likely to export from their foreign affiliates, and when they do they are less likely to target their home markets.[36] DMNEs lack bargaining power in the host country. Although their home governments are very supportive, they usually cannot offer much assistance in the form of pressuring the host government to purchase the DMNE's products or to accord it favorable investment terms. DMNEs sometimes have bargaining power intraregionally (e.g., a Brazilian firm investing in Venezuela). A DMNE advantage is that it is often perceived in other developing economies to be less intimidating than developed country MNEs.

Strategy. DMNEs are more likely to compete on price than on product differentiation.[37] Activity often begins with manufacturing for private brands and continues with low-end branded products.

DMNEs also tend to pursue niche strategies. Having already entered other developing markets, China-based Haier has entered the U.S. market for small office refrigerators, a product line abandoned by most domestic manufacturers such as GE and Amana because of its low profitability. Embraer specializes in regional aircraft ranging from 30 to 108 seats, one of the fastest-growing segments in the industry, but one in which Boeing and Airbus currently do not compete. DMNEs are less likely to be innovators but rather quickly offer a lower priced version of an original product introduced in a developed market. With the entry of competitors from less developed markets, however, DMNEs seek to go up the value chain. This is what happened to Taiwanese TV and computer makers with the advance of Mainland Chinese firms. Taiwanese computer maker Acer started by selling components that were used in computers sold by such firms as Hitachi and Siemens but then proceeded to also sell them under its own name. Korean electronics maker LG (then Lucky Goldstar) started by selling under private label but eventually developed its own brand name and now sells most of its products under it. When Korean firms first began selling TV sets in the United States, they focused on the low end, offering limited-feature sets priced substantially below their Japanese and U.S. competitors. However, rises in wages and the currency exchange rate in their home country put pressure on costs and forced Korean firms to move up-market.

DMNEs are also less likely to be vertically integrated than MNEs from developed economies.[38] This strategy has been viewed as an advantage in changing global markets and has been adopted to a considerable extent by established MNEs. DMNEs are more likely to establish alliances and to take a minority stake both for lack of resources and because of a lesser need to protect proprietary technology.

Craig and Douglas outline six strategies that DMNEs can pursue: (a) low-cost commodity, where a firm competes only on price and exports out of its domestic base; (b) manufacture for private label, where a company manufactures a product but sells it under a retailer's brand name; (c) component manufacturing, where a company manufactures inputs to be assembled and marketed by the developed country firm; (d) low-cost leader, where the emerging-market MNE sells an assembled product but competes mostly on cost; (e) first-generation or market-specific technology, where the emerging market firm focuses on a market with characteristics similar to its domestic market; and (f) a specialized niche, whether in a given country or region or worldwide.[39] Some DMNEs continue with the same strategy for a long period. For example, Mexican cement maker Cemex continues to compete on cost, whereas others move through those strategies as they mature.

For the DMNE, the shift away from cost leadership implies developing its own technological base, emphasizing profitability, expanding foreign sales, locating production abroad, and moving toward a product-based organization structure.[40] In the wake of the Asian financial crisis, Samsung and LG divested entire subsidiaries and product lines at home and abroad to reduce their debt load and sharpen their competitive advantage. Both companies have now achieved a leadership position in newer technologies such as HD plasma TVs. DMNEs must also contend with the threats to competitiveness that accompany development and liberalization. Higher wages erode their competitive advantage at home, with lower priced competitors from "new tigers" such as Malaysia and Indonesia and especially China threatening their lower end products. Greater openness at home means that the home market is not as well protected as it was and cannot serve as an assured base from which to launch foreign expansion. Rapid changes in technology require capital investment that is more difficult to obtain as home-base creditors have become more careful in scrutinizing investment projects.

Interim Summary

1. DMNEs are increasingly competitive with developed-country MNEs, and many enhance their competitive position over time.

2. Compared with traditional MNEs, DMNEs are smaller and more diversified.

3. DMNEs tend to lack the capital resources of other MNEs as well as experience in dealing with foreign institutions and the rigors of international competition; however, they have some unique advantages—for instance, flexibility in taking advantage of new products, technologies, and market opportunities.

THE SMALL AND MEDIUM-SIZED INTERNATIONAL ENTERPRISE (SMIE)

Small and medium-sized enterprises (SMIEs) have been major participants in international business since at least the 1920s. According to the U.S. Department of Commerce, a total of 218,382 SMIEs exported from the United States in 2003, accounting for 97% of all U.S.

exporters. The SMIE share of U.S. merchandise exports has recently hovered around 30%. SMIEs were responsible for 27.2% of goods exports in 2003, down slightly from 28.8% in 1999, 29.5% in 1992, and 30.8% in 1997.

What Is a SMIE?

There are numerous definitions of small and medium-sized enterprises. A common definition of "small" business in the United States is a firm with fewer than 100 employees and less than $5 million in annual revenues. Midsize firms, according to the Conference Board, are firms with annual revenues in the range of $100 million to $500 million. Although this may sound like a lot, keep in mind that large MNEs are in a different league. IBM, for instance, has annual revenues in excess of $90 billion. The 24 million U.S.-based SMIEs represent 99.7% of all employers in the country and employ 53% of the private workforce in both manufacturing and services. They account for approximately 50% of U.S. GDP and, remarkably, 55% of technological innovations, providing almost all of the nearly 20 million net new jobs added between 1992 and 1997 in the U.S. economy. The SBA notes that every $1 billion in exports of manufactured goods creates an estimated 15,000 new jobs; two to three times that number of additional jobs emerge to support the new products and personnel (e.g., restaurants, housing). SMIE exporters pay 15% higher wages and 11% higher benefits than their counterparts that do not export, are 20% more productive, and 9% more likely to stay financially solvent. They also experience a 20% greater job growth than nonexporters.[41]

The importance of the SMIE sector varies by country. For example, they are a formidable force in Taiwan and Korea, where they account for more than 40% and 46% of output, respectively.[42] In contrast, in Indonesia and the Philippines, SMIEs account for less than 10% and 13% of output, respectively; in Singapore, SMIEs account for 15%. The contribution of SMIEs to national exports also varies. In France and Italy, the export contribution of SMIEs approaches that of large MNEs. In Italy, 45% of exports were attributed to SMIEs.[43] In Korea, SMIEs accounted for 42.6% of total merchandise export in 1998.[44] In contrast, Japanese SMIEs contributed merely 13% of the country's merchandise exports in 1990.[45]

SMIE involvement in international business is likely to grow rapidly in the coming years, especially in services and technology-related areas, the fastest growing sectors in the economy, where SMIEs tend to be concentrated. Their potential is still largely untapped. Just a shade over 200,000 of the 24 million U.S. SMIEs are currently exporting. In 1999, 205,577 SMIEs with fewer than 100 employees and 18,104 medium-sized (100 to 499 employees) firms were exporters. SMIEs account for 47% of total domestic sales but only 31% of total exports. Nearly two-thirds of SMIEs send their products to just one country, with total exports of less than $1 million.[46]

A study by PricewaterhouseCoopers found that access to international markets was viewed as an important benefit by SMIEs from many nations.[47] The Internet may lower entry barriers into international markets (see also Chapter 18, Global Internet and E-Commerce). Technological developments such as flexible manufacturing systems are also making it possible for a small firm to profitably produce relatively small batches of goods. Developments in financial services have had a similar effect.

Size and Internationalization

In one study, only a quarter of SMIEs considered their size a constraint.[48] Indeed, the fastest export growth occurred among very small businesses—those with fewer than 20 employees. These firms made up 65% of all U.S. exporting firms in 1997, up from 59% in 1992. Even among firms with sales of $1,000 to $99,000, almost half were exporting.[49] Other studies, however, have suggested that size matters. Even among small international firms, the larger the firm, the more likely it was to engage in international business and to have an international strategy. Size was significantly correlated with exports; 82% of larger (more than $50 million in sales) firms were exporters versus 48% of the small firms.[50]

Midsize firms ($100 million to $500 million annual sales) seem to have an especially appropriate balance of size and agility for international operations. The Conference Board found that such firms reported a significant percentage of foreign sales and early manufacturing presence overseas. Foreign sales accounted for 22% of total annual turnover for firms in the midsize category. Small international firms grew three times as fast as companies their size that did not internationalize and twice as fast as the large MNEs. Those with sales below $100 million grew at an annual rate of 67% with a 35% annual return in the 1986–1991 time period.

Obstacles to SMIE Internationalization

Exhibit 4.9 lists entry barriers to international trade identified in a survey of SMIEs in Minnesota. Note that some of the obstacles noted in the exhibit (e.g., culture) are not different, in principle, from those encountered by established MNEs. However, much of the challenge presented by SMIE entry into international markets involves the unique character of the smaller enterprise.[51] A study examining the concerns of U.S.-based SMIEs expanding into Europe found that their concerns differed considerably from those of large MNEs. For example, managing foreign exchange risk was ranked the most minor concern of the large MNE but is a concern for the SMIE, which lacks the resources to effectively manage risk or geographical diversity. Similarly, international communications was an important concern for smaller firms but not for the larger ones. In contrast, developing a manufacturing strategy was a concern for large MNEs but not for the SMIEs, possibly because of lack of awareness of the need for formal planning on the SMIEs' part.[52]

A UN report states that internationalizing SMIEs face problems relating to management, training, and quality control as well as market and infrastructure

Exhibit 4.9   Entry Barriers to International Trade for Minnesota SMIEs

	A Serious Obstacle	Somewhat of an Obstacle	A Minor Obstacle	Not an Obstacle
• Integration with a country's business culture	10.4%	31.2%	24.4%	29.2%
• Lack of information	16.0%	30.0%	26.4%	24.8%
• Cost and financing	15.6%	24.8%	24.4%	32.0%
• Qualified employees	14.8%	26.8%	19.6%	36.4%
• Regulations and tariffs	21.2%	37.2%	23.6%	15.6%
• Language	12.4%	35.2%	26.4%	25.2%
• Lack of expertise	10.4%	28.8%	21.2%	34.8%
• Brokers	2.8%	12.8%	14.8%	61.6%
• Partners	5.2%	20.0%	17.6%	52.0%
• Port of entry	4.4%	16.0%	19.2%	55.6%

SOURCE: *Twin Cities Business Monthly.* "What business thinks." August 2001: p. 14.

problems, such as the lack of capital and intense competition. However, it considers the greatest obstacle the barriers created or permitted by governments, such as regulatory impediments or corruption. Some of the main obstacles for the internationalizing SMIE are listed below.

Scale and Transaction Constraints

The small scale and limited reach of the SMIE constrain its production and service delivery options and costs. The transaction costs of the SMIE are substantially higher than those of the large MNE, which internalizes much of its operations. While large MNEs conduct much of their trade via internal networks, SMIEs have to go through the complex process of cross-border trade flow, which can add as much as 10% to the final value of goods.[53] Relying on export intermediaries is an option, but it is costly and implies distance from the customer.

Access to Capital

An important roadblock on the internationalization route for the SMIE is shortage of capital[54] and its correlates (e.g., inability to obtain reliable market information and lack of training for traders and expatriates). Public institutions judged financial strength the single most important problem for internationalizing SMIEs.[55] Much of the problem has to do with lack of access. The SBA reports that only 150 to 200 of the 9,000 banks operating in the United States offer significant financing for SMIEs.[56] At the same time, the globalization of financial services is rapidly changing the patterns of access to capital and opening new opportunities for raising capital. This is true not only in the United States, where venture capital has created many opportunities for SMIEs (especially in high tech), but also in countries like Japan where in the past banks would rarely extend loans to SMIEs.

Lack of Knowledge

A critical resource for SMIEs entering foreign markets is knowledge.[57] Lacking a track record in exporting and experience in foreign investment, such firms usually do not possess the relevant knowledge, ranging from how to conduct market research in foreign locations to how to address currency fluctuations. Tiny Hatteras Yachts was hard-hit when the euro declined in value against the U.S. dollar (it has strongly rebounded since) because it did not employ sophisticated hedging techniques and lacked the ability to source globally.[58] SMIEs also face problems when having to transfer their knowledge to foreign recipients. More than in large MNEs, the knowledge possessed by SMIEs tends to be less codified and more tacit and embedded. Combined with weak information processing, SMIEs find it hard to "level the playing field" with larger players.[59]

To compensate for its knowledge deficiency, the SMIE is often compelled to look to others for assistance. UNCTAD recommends that governments assist SMIEs with information on market conditions, opportunities, and government regulations and requirements. Channels include commercial attachés and embassies, trade missions, trade shows, networking systems, chambers of commerce, international agencies, technology-exchange programs, international forums and conferences, Web sites, market-research consultants, and national trade promotions. A U.S. Chamber of Commerce survey shows that 66% of SMIEs utilized at least one form of government export assistance, while 50% used two or more agencies.

Another way to compensate for knowledge deficiency is by learning from the experience of others in a similar situation in the industry.[60] An important source is the knowledge shared by executives with experience in foreign markets. SMIEs with internationally experienced management teams obtained foreign sales more quickly than those without such teams.[61]

Lack of Market Power

Lack of market power is another key deficiency for smaller firms, which often find themselves powerless against trade barriers. They are too small to bargain with local governments and cannot produce the large quantities that would trigger local suppliers to manufacture to their specifications.[62] They are also vulnerable to trade barriers. The SBA is required to promote the interests of U.S. small business in international trade under the Small Business Export Promotion Act of 1980.

Vulnerability to Intellectual Property Violations

U.S. SMIEs are very concerned with intellectual property rights such as patents, copyrights, and trademarks. This issue is particularly important to SMIEs because they are overrepresented in high-tech areas but lack the resources to pursue violators across the globe or the political muscle to pressure host governments to protect their rights. A number of U.S.-based SMIEs had to withdraw from the Chinese market because their product designs had been copied and they lacked the contacts and resources to fight the violators.

SMIE Advantages in Internationalization

The many obstacles noted notwithstanding, SMIEs have been successful in the global marketplace owing to a number of distinct advantages. Innovativeness, creativity, entrepreneurial spirit, lower overhead costs, and the ability to move fast to take advantage of new opportunities are all important factors in the global marketplace and are relatively common at SMIEs. Some of the advantages noted for DMNEs, such as lack of investment in outdated technologies and hence the ability to "leapfrog" technologically, also apply to SMIEs.

SMIE Internationalization Features

Internationalization Motivation

An UNCTAD survey identified a number of drivers of SMIE internationalization, including "push" factors, "pull" factors, management factors, and chance. The push factors are competitive pressures in the SMIE's domestic market, which "push" the SMIE to increase the scale of its operations via exports so as to reduce unit cost, or to reduce its labor costs by moving operations to low-cost countries. Another push factor is decline in domestic demand. For instance, facing an economic downturn in the 1990s, architectural firms in Hawaii doubled their efforts to penetrate Asian markets. Pull factors make foreign locations more attractive (e.g., rapidly expanding markets, growth potential, or lower production costs). Management factors include managerial commitment and resources devoted to international activity. Finally, chance factors are unforeseen circumstances that create internationalization opportunities. According to the survey findings, when SMIEs invest in other small firms, management and chance factors are the most important, followed by push factors. For larger enterprises investing in foreign SMIEs, management and pull factors are the most important, whereas push factors are relatively less important.[63]

　　Brush[64] found that the manager's personal knowledge of markets, personal contacts, and expertise were important factors influencing the export decision of young firms. However, these factors were linked to the perceived market opportunity in terms of demand and growth potential, an opportunity often expressed in the form of unsolicited orders from foreign customers. Personal contacts, owner/manager's expertise and competencies (often acquired earlier in another venture or another firm), product innovation, and foreign market information were key factors behind internationalization. For established SMIEs, perceived market demand and managerial factors were less instrumental than the desire for expansion and growth. Host country transportation and distribution were also more important for established firms than for newer firms. Established firms were also more likely to use export intermediaries or piggyback on large exporters and investors. They tended to sell more products to a wider array of countries and derive more overall revenues from export than the younger firms. Exhibit 4.10 lists FDI motivations by SMIEs of different world regions.

Exhibit 4.10 Motivations for Foreign Direct Investment by Small and Medium-Sized Corporations, by Host Region, 1998 (Percentage)

	Motivation	Host Region				
		North America	Europe	Asia	Latin America	World
(1)	Outside proposal (initiative in this venture came from outside the firm in host country, host-country governments, or third party, such as international organizations, etc.)	1.9	1.3	3.2	50.0	3.3
(2)	To secure raw materials	9.6	3.8	14.0	50.0	11.2
(3)	To secure supply of materials (intermediate goods)	3.9	6.3	6.5	16.7	5.8
(4)	Low-cost labor in host country	3.9	3.8	31.2	16.7	14.5
(5)	Protection measures by host-country government	3.9	3.8	17.2	–	9.9
(6)	Expectation of growth in local market	5.8	44.3	52.7	16.7	50.0
(7)	Access to and growth in third-country markets	15.4	24.1	29.0	33.3	24.4
(8)	Lower production costs for exporting to third countries and to home country	3.9	2.5	21.5	–	9.9
(9)	Information gathering	28.9	22.8	16.1	–	20.6
(10)	Presence of other foreign firms or firms of the same home country in the same industry in the host country	11.5	11.4	10.8	–	11.2
(11)	Small market in home country	5.8	20.3	8.6	–	11.2
(12)	Risk diversification	3.9	16.5	9.7	–	10.7
(13)	High return in host country	–	2.5	6.5	16.7	5.0
(14)	Home-country government incentives	–	1.3	–	–	0.4
(15)	Host-country government incentives	–	2.5	11.8	–	5.4
(16)	To acquire technology	7.7	1.3	2.2	–	2.9
(17)	To acquire managerial expertise	–	–	1.1	–	0.4
(18)	To diversify production lines	3.9	2.5	7.5	–	5.0
(19)	To strengthen competitive capacity	25.0	29.1	31.2	16.7	27.3
(20)	To strengthen financial capability (fund-raising)	–	1.3	2.2	–	1.2
(21)	Favorable tax schemes (tax holiday)	–	1.3	15.1	–	7.0
(22)	Others	7.7	10.1	4.3	–	6.6
	Number of foreign affiliates observed	52.0	79.0	91.0	6.0	242.0

SOURCE: M. Fujita. *The Transnational Activities of Small and Medium-Sized Enterprises.* Boston: Kluwer, 1998. With kind permission of Springer Science and Business Media.

Internationalization Patterns

Controlling for industry, significant differences have been found between the foreign expansion strategies of large and small firms.[65] SMIE internationalization is often not incremental. Newer, small high-tech firms in particular tend to "leapfrog" into international markets before gaining a foothold in their domestic markets. This has been found to be the case for small software firms.[66] Other SMIEs go through a number of stages but follow a different route than that of large MNEs, often starting with inward investment before moving to outward investment.

More than large MNEs, SMIEs rely on exports rather than on FDI. This is understandable in light of the SMIE resource constraints, as well as the fact that SMIEs are often in an early phase of the internationalization process. SMIEs are also more likely to rely on export intermediaries such as export agents, export merchants, export management firms, and export trading firms. Like their larger counterparts, SMIEs often use foreign markets as an export platform to third countries.[67] This is probably more accurate for Japan and other high labor cost countries faced with a decline in their export competitiveness at home. Indeed, manufacturing SMIEs are more likely to internationalize in the more labor-intensive areas of textiles, clothing, and mechanical equipment.

SMIE Exporter Profile

Nonmanufacturing companies dominate exporting by SMIEs. In 2003, wholesalers and other nonmanufacturing firms made up 68% of all SMIE exporters and generated 60% of total SMIE exports. Because many exports consist of intracompany transfers within subsidiaries of the same MNE, the proportion of SMIEs in intercompany exports is considerably larger. According to the U.S. Central Budget Office, small exporters were more likely to export 50% or more of their product than large exporters. Some 22.8% of self-employed exporters (i.e., with no hired employees) exported half or more of their product, compared with 3.7% of the exporters with 100 or more employees. Canada is by far the most popular export destination for SMIEs. In 2003, some 87,596 SMIE exporting companies registered sales to Canada—an increase of 94% over 1992. Mexico ranked second, receiving merchandise exports from 33,408 U.S. SMIEs. Other popular markets for SMIE exporters were the United Kingdom, Japan, and Germany. The position of Canada and the United Kingdom shows that as in the case of traditional MNEs, cultural familiarity is a major factor in determining where SMIEs choose to invest. In the same vein, many French firms entering the North American market start with Quebec, the French-speaking province of Canada. This reality may be changing, however. Certain markets are among the fastest-growing customers for SMIEs. From 1992 to 2003, SMIE exports to China surged by 416%, while exports to Malaysia increased by 259%, sales to Ireland increased by 227%, and sales to Brazil rose by 152%. This record is especially impressive since China is considered one of the most difficult markets for foreign investors.

Foreign investment by SMIEs is at present relatively small (which is why, as you may recall, most of these firms do not qualify as MNEs). In Japan, it accounts for more than half of the cases but only about 10% of the value of outward FDI. In the United States, SMIEs account for 6% of the number and 3% of the assets of foreign affiliates.[68] Still, as far back as 1988, American SMIEs controlled US$15 billion in FDI stock. Western Europe is by far the largest target for U.S. SMIE foreign investment. In Singapore, Taiwan, and Vietnam, SMIEs are the recipients of FDI by large foreign MNEs. "Small-package FDI" (>$1 million) accounts for 5% to 20% by value in Myanmar and less than half a percent in Vietnam. In the Philippines, it accounts for more than 60% of projects but only about 2% to 10% by value. In recent years, FDI by SMIEs has been growing, often at a more rapid pace than FDI overall. A UN survey of Asian SMIEs found that factors considered important for their internationalization include improving the quality of products and services, local management and staff training, and government relations. SMIEs were found to be three times more likely than MNEs to regard training of unskilled staff as very important to strategic success, more than twice as likely to regard the introduction or improvement of products or services as very important, and more than 50% more likely to regard local managers' training and increase in foreign earnings as very important.

SMIEs' exports and FDI are often not systematically planned strategic moves but rather responses to an incidental opportunity. In a survey of 100 U.S. entrepreneurial technology firms commissioned by the U.S. firm Protégé, 82% of CEOs acknowledged that their foreign expansion was not part of a broader strategy but rather an opportunistic pursuit of clients and an inexpensive way to achieve internationalization.[69] Chances for internationalization include, for example, a customer expanding into a foreign location ("piggybacking"). The piggybacking may occur at the initiative of an MNE that needs supply, components, and such for its international operations. For example, Japanese automotive suppliers followed Japanese auto manufacturers to the United States.[70] Pico Rivera, a shelving company that once sold only in the United States and Canada, followed its customer Disney to Eastern Europe and other countries where Disney wanted to install the same shelves that it has in the United States.[71]

Nature of FDI by SMIEs

Emphasis on Developed Markets. When engaging in FDI, SMIEs are more likely to invest in developed rather than developing markets. In one study, 80% of SMIEs located in developed countries. Host country red tape, economic instability, hard currency restrictions, procurement difficulties, and lack of domestic bank support were among the reasons SMIEs avoided investment in developing markets. Japanese, Australian, and Hong Kong firms are an exception, probably because most markets in their areas are developing.[72] The trend is also true for medium-sized firms. Conference Board data show that firms with more than 20 overseas plants were much more likely to invest in developing countries than firms with fewer than 10 foreign plants.[73] SMIEs are also more likely to establish new operations (greenfield investments) than to acquire existing operations. This is largely a product of their resource limitations.

Selective Globalization. SMIEs tend to focus on one link in the supply chain (e.g., manufacturing) as well as on a selected market.[74] In one study, 17% of the large firms exported to more than 50 countries versus none among the small and medium-sized firms.[75] In a Conference Board study, very large firms ($5 billion and over) had an average of 36 plants in 14 foreign countries, compared with 13 plants in six countries for firms with $1 billion to $5 billion in annual sales. Companies with sales of less than $100 million had one to three overseas plants.

Strategy. SMIEs often adopt niche strategies, pursuing areas that are not covered by large firms because of neglect, lack of expertise, or high cost structure.[76] In making investment decisions, SMIEs are unlikely to be motivated by host country incentives,[77] which is not surprising given their lack of market power.

However, SMIE investment is less likely to trigger the visibility and the resentment that sometimes accompanies FDI.

SMIEs rely more on cooperative strategies, often as a result of the local partner initiative to compensate for a resource shortfall. This is particularly true for those with experienced management.[78] In the UN survey, SMIEs are shown to engage a local partner in a joint venture in more than half of the cases. When Canadian Sleeman Brewing entered the highly competitive U.S. market, it teamed up with the Boston Beer Company, whose beer was already being sold in Canada, to launch a U.S. brand.[79]

Namiki lists effective export strategies for small firms as follows: competitive pricing and brand identification, specialty product manufacturing, technological advantage, and superior customer service. Exploiting niche markets is also very important.[80] Smaller firms often went abroad to avoid direct competition with large MNEs. This led them to develop in-depth narrow expertise that may be useful in developing "deep niche" strategies.[81]

The UNCTAD report recommends that governments encourage cross-border alliances between SMIEs. Governments can create a pool of suitable partners, initiate introductions, and resolve conflicts. They can encourage investment and trade missions, conferences, and investment/trade shows designed to encourage business matching, electronic business-matching services, chambers of commerce and other facilitators, and clustering programs.

INDUSTRY BOX

INVESTMENT BANKING AND THE SMIE

Recent surveys of client satisfaction with service placed Geneva (Switzerland)-based Pictet at the top of the league in providing financial custodian services. The bank, which calls itself "a Swiss bank with an international presence," has substantial presence in Europe (Switzerland, Italy, Germany, England, Spain, and Luxembourg) and Asia (Singapore, Japan, and Hong Kong) as well as one subsidiary in North America (Montreal). Pictet offers personalized service to high-net-worth individuals around the globe. The two-centuries-old bank actually views its size as an advantage. "We offer the size and breadth of experience to offer a quality service. But we are still small enough to offer a service tailored to each client's specific needs," says Judith Webster, a client relationship manager. Pictet is taking advantage of the consolidation in the financial service industry to expand its reach by appealing to smaller clients who seek the personal service they feel is unavailable from the increasingly large and diversified providers.

Pictet is a niche player that builds on its strengths. The firm is active mostly in the pension fund market, where it feels it has a competitive advantage. It also tries to minimize administration and coordination costs by staying closer to its home base in Geneva and using a network of contracted providers in their home countries. Only 5 of its 17 subsidiaries are outside Europe.

SOURCE: "Small business proves worthy challenger." *Financial Times*, July 14, 2000, III; company Web site, 2007.

Born International

Some firms develop an international orientation very early. Those include "international market makers"—namely, multinational traders or import/export start-ups and "geographically focused start-ups," which utilize their knowledge of a particular world area. The most advanced form is the "global start-up," or **"born international**," a "business organization that from inception seeks to derive significant competitive advantages from the use of resources and sale of output in multiple countries."[82] While "born international" firms existed for many years (e.g., the East India Company, established in 1600), the phenomenon is associated mainly with the last two decades, particularly in the high-tech sector. Examples of "born international" are European and Israeli high-tech start-ups that generate most, and sometimes all, of their revenues abroad from the very start.[83] Oviatt & McDougall provide this interview with a United Kingdom executive:

> We did not succeed because we tried to sell the product by starting up in England and then selling in the U.S., and by that time it was too late. We should have developed our products first of all for the U.S. market and then sold it back into England.[82]

In his subsequent venture, this executive targeted the United States and Japan before turning his attention to the United Kingdom and Continental Europe. According to the authors, successful global start-ups have global vision from inception; internationally experienced management; strong international business networks; use of preemptive technology or marketing, building on a unique intangible asset; incremental, closely linked extensions in product or service; and tight worldwide coordination. You will find a broader discussion of "born global" firms in Chapter 20, International Entrepreneurship.

Interim Summary

1. Although each SMIE is small, collectively they are a force to be reckoned with in international business.

2. SMIEs face many of the same difficulties that DMNEs experience in internationalization and make up for their disadvantages with adaptability, innovation, and partnering with other firms.

3. SMIEs usually develop niche market strategies when going international, often "piggybacking" on an established client base.

4. "Born global" firms plan on exporting from the very beginning without developing a local market until after they have found success abroad.

CHAPTER SUMMARY

1. The "players" in the international business scene include a great variety of companies, but only those with foreign direct investment (FDI) over which the company maintains effective control are called, in this book, multinational enterprises (MNEs).

2. MNEs, whether in manufacturing or service sectors, need strong competitive advantages to compete with established local firms. They need to effectively and efficiently build, deploy, exploit, and upgrade distinctive capabilities (technological, organizational, operational, and financial) if they want to prosper.

3. MNEs from developing and emerging economies (DMNEs) and small and medium-sized international

companies (SMIEs, which include "born international" firms) play an important role in global business. The MNE, DMNE, and SMIE significantly differ in their internationalization patterns, resources, and obstacles to international expansion.

4. DMNEs suffer from resource constraints, lack of knowledge, and a sheltered environment. However, they enjoy unique advantages such as flexibility and home government support.

5. SMIEs emphasize export rather than FDI owing to their resource limitations. They either export directly to a foreign market or sell through export intermediaries.

Chapter Notes

1. The Conference Board. *U.S. Manufacturers in the Global Marketplace*. Report #1058-94-RR, 1994.

2. The Conference Board.

3. C. A. Bartlett and S. Ghoshal. *Managing Across Borders: The Transnational Solution*. Cambridge, MA: Harvard Business School Press, 1989.

4. United Nations Conference on Trade and Development (UNCTAD). World Investment Report, 2000.

5. K. Moore and D. Lewis. *Birth of the Multinational*. Copenhagen Business School Press, 2000.

6. "The world view of multinationals." *Economist*, January 29, 2000, 21.

7. The Conference Board, *U.S. Manufacturers in the Global Marketplace*. Report #1058-94-RR, 1994.

8. "The world view of multinationals." *Economist*, January 29, 2000, 21.

9. R. E. Caves. *Multinational Enterprise and Economic Analysis*. Cambridge, MA: Cambridge University Press, 1996.

10. "The world view of multinationals." *Economist*, January 29, 2000.

11. P. Druckerman. "The foreign invasion." *Wall Street Journal*, September 25, 2000, R21.

12. L. T. Wells. "Multinationals and the developing countries." *Journal of International Business Studies*, 1998, *29*, 1: pp. 101–114.

13. P. N. Doremus, W. W. Keller, L. W. Pauly, and S. Reich. *The Myth of the Global Corporation*. Princeton, NJ: Princeton University Press, 1998.

14. D. J. Lecraw. "Performance of transnational corporations in less developed countries." *Journal of International Business Studies*, Spring/Summer 1983: pp. 15–33.

15. "The world view of multinationals." *Economist*, January 29, 2000, p. 21.

16. M. S. Roth and J. B. Romeo. "Matching product category and country image perceptions: A framework for managing country-of-origin effects." *Journal of International Business Studies*, 1997, 3: pp. 477–497.

17. E. Cherney. "Four seasons hotels has plans for huge overseas expansion." *Wall Street Journal*, October 20, 2000, A22.

18. D. J. Lecraw. "Performance of transnational corporations in less developed countries." *Journal of International Business Studies*, Spring/Summer 1983: pp. 15–33.

19. The Conference Board. *U.S. Manufacturers in the Global Marketplace*. Report #1058-94-RR, 1994.

20. J. Ordonez. "Starbuck's to start major expansion in overseas markets." *Wall Street Journal*, October 27, 2000.

21. P. Pananond and C. P. Zeithaml. "The international expansion of MNEs from developing countries: A case study of Thailand's CP group." *Asia Pacific Journal of Management*, 1998, 15: pp. 163–184.

22. H. W. C. Yeung. "Transnational corporations from Asian developing countries: Their characteristics and competitive edge." *Journal of Asian Business*, 1994, *10*, 4: pp. 17–58; UNCTAD, World Investment Report, 2001.

23. Company publications.

24. J. Karp. "Procomp hopes to bring Brazilian efficiency to Floridian chaos." *Wall Street Journal*, November 13, 2000, A27.

25. D. J. Lecraw. "Performance of transnational corporations in less developed countries." *Journal of International Business Studies*, Spring/Summer 1983: pp. 15–33.

26. R. Aggarwal and T. Agmon. "The international success of developing country firms: Role of government directed comparative advantage." *Management International Review*, 1990, *30*, 2: pp. 163–180.

27. L. T. Wells. *Third World Multinationals: The Rise of Foreign Investment From Developing Countries*. Cambridge, MA: MIT Press, 1983.

28. H. Vernon-Wortzel and L. H. Wortzel. "Globalizing strategies for multinationals from developing countries." *Columbia Journal of World Business*, Spring 1988.

29. P. P. Li. "Strategy profiles of indigenous MNEs from the NIEs: The case of South Korea and Taiwan." *International Executive*, 1994, *36*, 2: pp. 147–170.

30. D. J. Lecraw. "Outward direct investment by Indonesian firms: Motivation and effects." *Journal of International Business Studies*, 1993, 3rd quarter: pp. 589–600.

31. H. Zhang and D. Ven den Bulcke. *International Management Strategies of Chinese Multinational Firms*. University of Antwerp, E/17, 1994.

32. S. Tallman and O. Shenkar. "International cooperative venture strategies: Outward investment and small firms from NICs." *Management International Review*, 1994, 34: pp. 75–91.

33. D. J. Lecraw. "Direct investment by firms from less developed countries." *Oxford Economic Papers*, *29*, 3: pp. 442–457.

34. Lecraw. "Direct investment."

35. Lecraw. "Direct investment."

36. Lecraw. "Direct investment."

37. Lecraw. "Direct investment."

38. H. Vernon-Wortzel and L. H. Wortzel. "Globalizing strategies for multinationals from developing countries." *Columbia Journal of International Business*, Spring 1988: pp. 27–35.

39. C. S. Craig and S. P. Douglas. "Managing the transnational value chain—Strategies for firms from emerging markets." *Journal of International Marketing*, 1997, 3: pp. 71–84.

40. Y. H. Kim and N. Campbell. "Strategic control in Korean MNCs." *Management International Review*, 1995, 1: pp. 95–108.

41. U.S. Small Business Administration, Office of International Trade: A report. November 1999.

42. M. Fujita. *The Transnational Activities of Small and Medium-Size Enterprises*. Boston: Kluwer, 1998.

43. Z. Acs, R. Morck, M. Shaver, and B. Yeung. "The internationalization of small and medium-size enterprises." In Z. Acs and B. Yeung (eds.), *Small and Medium-Size Enterprises in the Global Economy*. Ann Arbor: The University of Michigan Press, 1999.

44. Korea Federation of Small Business (KFSB).

45. M. Fujita. *The Transnational Activities of Small and Medium-Size Enterprises*. Boston: Kluwer, 1998.

46. U.S. Department of Commerce, August 17, 2001.

47. PricewaterhouseCoopers. *Transforming a Business*. 2000.

48. M. Fujita. *The Transnational Activities of Small and Medium-Size Enterprises*. Boston: Kluwer, 1998.

49. The Conference Board. *U.S. Manufacturers in the Global Marketplace*. Report #1058-94-RR, 1994.

50. J. L. Calof. "The relationship between firm size and export behavior revisited." *Journal of International Business Studies*, 1994, *25*, 2: pp. 367–387; S. Baird, M. A. Lyles, and J. B. Orris. "The choice of international strategies by small business." *Journal of Small Business Management*, January 1994: pp. 48–59.

51. J. C. Shuman and J. A. Seeger. "The theory and practice of strategic management in smaller rapid growth companies." *American Journal of Small Business, 11*, 1: pp. 7–18; N. E. Coviello and A. McAuley. "Internationalization and the smaller firm." *Management International Review*, 3: pp. 223–256.

52. R. Klassen and C. Whyback. "Barriers to the management of international operations." *Journal of Operations Management*, 1994, 11: pp. 385–397.

53. UNCTAD. World Investment Report, 1993.

54. G. Fairclough and M. Murray. "Small banks expand their trade financing for exports." *Wall Street Journal*, February 24, 1998, B2.

55. M. Fujita. *The Transnational Activities of Small and Medium-Size Enterprises*. Boston: Kluwer, 1998.

56. G. Fairclough and M. Murray. "Small banks expand their trade financing for exports." *Wall Street Journal*, February 24, 1998, B2.

57. P. Liesch and G. A. Knight. "Information internalization and hurdle rates in small and medium enterprise internationalization." *Journal of International Business Studies, 30*, 1: pp. 383–394.

58. C. Cooper. "Euro drop is hardest for the smallest." *Wall Street Journal*, October 2, 2000.

59. E. Prater and S. Gosh. "The globalization process of U.S. small and medium-sized firms: A comparative analysis." Working paper #97-005. DuPree School of Management, Georgia Institute of Technology.

60. Prater and Gosh.

61. A. R. Reuber and E. Fischer. "The influence of the management team's international experience on the internationalization behaviors of SMIEs." *Journal of International Business Studies*, 1997, *28*, 4: pp. 807–825.

62. M. Fujita. *The Transnational Activities of Small and Medium-Size Enterprises*. Boston: Kluwer, 1998.

63. UNCTAD. World Investment Report, 1999.

64. C. A. Brush. *International Entrepreneurship: The Effect of Firm Age on Motives for Internationalization*. New York: Garland, 1995.

65. J. W. Ballantine, F. W. Cleveland, and C. T. Koeller. "Characterizing profitable and unprofitable strategies in small and large businesses." *Journal of Small Business Management*, April 1992: pp. 13–24.

66. H. Boter and C. Holmquist. "Industry characteristics and internationalization processes in small firms." *Journal of Business Venturing*, 1994, 11:

pp. 471–487; B. M. Oviatt and P. P. McDougal. "Toward a theory of international new ventures." *Journal of International Business Studies, 25*, 1: pp. 45–64; Bell, J. "The internationalization of small computer software firms—A further challenge to stage theories." *European Journal of Marketing, 29*, 8: pp. 60–75.

67. M. Fujita. *The Transnational Activities of Small and Medium-Size Enterprises*. Boston: Kluwer, 1998.

68. M. Fujita. *The Transnational Activities of Small and Medium-Size Enterprises*. Boston: Kluwer, 1998.

69. C. Fleming. "U.S. tech firms press on with global expansion." *Toronto Globe and Mail* (by agreement with the *Wall Street Journal*), August 17, 2001, B7.

70. K. Banejri and R. Sambharya. "Vertical Keiretsu and international market entry: The case of the Japanese automobile ancillary industry." *Journal of International Business Studies*, 1996, *27*, 1: pp. 89–113.

71. S. Doggett and A. Haddad. "Global savvy." *Los Angeles Times*, February 21, 2000.

72. M. Fujita. *The Transnational Activities of Small and Medium-Size Enterprises*. Boston: Kluwer, 1998.

73. The Conference Board. *U.S. Manufacturers in the Global Marketplace*. Report #1058-96-RR, 1994.

74. K. Roth. "International configuration and coordination archetypes for medium-sized firms in global industries." *Journal of International Business Studies*, 3: pp. 533–549; P. W. Beamish, A. Goerzen, and H. Munro. "The export characteristics of Canadian manufacturers: A profile by firm size." Working paper #824, School of Business and Economics, Wilfred Laurier University, 1984.

75. J. L. Calof. "The relationship between firm size and export behavior revisited." *Journal of International Business Studies*, 1994, *25*, 2: pp. 367–387.

76. D. L. Balcome. "Choosing their own paths: Profiles of the export strategies of Canadian manufacturers." International Business Research Center Report 06-86, Conference Board of Canada, 1986.

77. M. Fujita. *The Transnational Activities of Small and Medium-Size Enterprises*. Boston: Kluwer, 1998.

78. B. Gomes-Casseres. "Alliance strategies of small firms." In Acs and Yeung, *Small and Medium-Sized Enterprises in the Global Economies*. Ann Arbor: The University of Michigan Press, 1999.

79. E. Cherney. "Canadian brewery seeks export success to U.S. market." *Wall Street Journal*, July 24, 2001, B2.

80. N. Namiki. "Export strategy for small business." *Journal of Small Business Management*, 26, April 1988: pp. 32–37.

81. N. Namiki, B. Gomes-Casseres, and T. Kohn. "Small firms in international competition: A challenge to traditional theory?" In P. Buckley et al., *International Technology Transfer by Small and Medium-Size Enterprises: Country Studies*, pp. 280–296. New York: St., Martin's Press, 1997.

82. B. M. Oviatt and P. P. McDougal. "Toward a theory of international new ventures." *Journal of International Business Studies*, 1994, *25*, 1: pp. 45–64.

83. T. Almor. "Ownership structure of small high tech global companies: The case of Israel." Discussion paper #99.8, The College of Management, Tel-Aviv, Israel, 1999.

PART TWO

Endowments and Environments of International Business

COUNTRY COMPETITIVENESS

DO YOU KNOW?

1. Why do countries differ in their overall competitiveness in the global marketplace?

2. Why is a country's competitiveness more salient in some industries? For example, why do Swiss watches or pharmaceuticals dominate the world market, as do German upscale cars or Italian gold and silver jewelry?

3. What roles should firms and individuals play in shaping country competitiveness? For example, can Japanese firms' total quality management improve their country's competitiveness?

4. How does a foreign country's competitiveness influence the strategies and decisions of MNEs (multinational enterprises)?

Photo 5.1 **The Raffles Statue was officially unveiled on June 27, 1887, to commemorate the founder of modern Singapore.**

OPENING CASE

Singapore's Competitive Advantage in the Hard Disk Drive Industry

Singapore is known as one of the most competitive nations in the world. Between 1995 and 2001, the country ranked second in the national competitiveness scoreboard released by Swiss-based IMD (International Institute for Management Development). Hard disk drive (HDD) production in Singapore reached about $10 billion and accounted for approximately 70% of the world's production of HDDs in 1999.

HDDs are highly standardized and easily transportable. Demand is primarily driven by their technical and operating characteristics. This allows manufacturing to be located in distant locations away from consumers. Many world MNEs (multinational enterprises) and domestic companies use Singapore as their platform of HDD manufacturing and as the gateway to international markets, particularly to other Asian countries. Seagate, a world leader in the industry and the largest industrial employer in Singapore, has built a $130 million facility there for assembling disk drives and making printed circuit boards.

Singapore's workforce was rated the best in the world by Business Environment Risk Intelligence (BERI), based on such factors as relative productivity, worker attitude, technical skills, and legal framework. Although not rich in natural resources, Singapore is situated in a strategic location on a major trading route across continents and is a focal point for Southeast Asian shipping routes. Singapore is also a thriving financial center served by 149 commercial banks, 77 merchant banks, and eight international money brokers. Additionally, Singapore has first-class infrastructure in telecommunications and communications. The National Science and Technology Board (NSTB) was established in Singapore in 1991 to promote R&D through a financial assistance program, coordinating with several research institutions such as the Institute of Microelectronics (IME) and the Institute of Manufacturing Technology (IMF).

To promote growth and productivity in the electronics industry, the Singaporean government established several major agencies. Apart from the NSTB, the Economic Development Board (EDB) devises incentives to attract competitive companies into the nation's electronics sector. In addition, the National Computer Board (NCB) was created to drive Singapore to excel in the information age and to exploit the information technology (IT) niche. The NCB spearheads the implementation of Singapore's national IT master plan—IT2000. The government also initiated eight large-scale industrial parks in China, Indonesia, India, and Vietnam. These flagship projects, each of which is geographically concentrated in the same area, are positioned as premier investment locations, not only for Singaporean investors but also for other foreign firms and local enterprises. Singapore is increasingly dependent on the value-added edge that a highly skilled workforce brings. Therefore, through research aid and program development, the government assists higher-education institutions in providing a skilled workforce.

DEFINING COUNTRY COMPETITIVENESS

The preceding chapters explained that MNEs are a dominant force in today's international business activities (Chapter 4) and that activities such as trade and FDI are largely determined by comparative advantages of nations (Chapters 2 and 3). So how are MNEs and comparative advantages of nations linked? How do national advantages in a foreign country influence MNE strategies? If these advantages are important to national wealth, social welfare, and business operations, then how are these advantages determined, established, and maintained? We explain these issues from a country competitiveness perspective.

Competitiveness is the relative strength that one needs to win in competition against rivals. **Country competitiveness** is the extent to which a country is capable of generating more wealth than its competitors do in world markets. It measures and compares the effectiveness of countries in providing firms with an environment that sustains the domestic and international competitiveness of those firms. In the opening case, the Singaporean government created several institutions and offshore zones to help local businesses excel in international competition in the information industry. The core of country competitiveness centers on productivity. **Productivity** is the value of the output produced by a unit of labor or capital. It is the prime determinant of a nation's long-term standard of living and is the root source of national per capita income. The level of productivity depends on both the quality and features of products and services and the efficiency with which they are produced or provided. As such, increasing productivity is key to enhancing country competitiveness. Many factors (such as a nation's educational and scientific strengths) influence productivity, which in turn determines a country's capabilities.

Country competitiveness is associated with, but different from, country comparative advantages. As introduced in Chapter 2, conventional wisdom suggests that comparative advantages of nations are based on factor endowment conditions (abundance and costs of production factors such as labor, land, natural resources, and capital). The resultant conclusion is that a nation's competitiveness is high if it possesses an abundance of labor, capital, and or natural resources at low prices.[1] This theory falls short of explaining the reality that we see today: There are many countries with abundant resources that are characterized by poor economies, and vice versa. Germany, Switzerland, and Sweden have prospered, despite having high wages and labor shortages. Similarly, Japan, South Korea, and Singapore have limited natural resources but are very successful in maintaining their high competitiveness. In today's world where raw materials, capital, and even labor move across national borders, endowed resources can influence, but in and of themselves do not fully determine, a nation's competitiveness. Country comparative advantages (e.g., cheap land and labor in developing countries) may influence the level of competitiveness in industries that are labor-intensive or cost sensitive. However, a nation's comparative advantage in production factors alone is far from sufficient in determining its international competitiveness—that is, its competitive advantage in the global marketplace.

International trade and investment can both improve a nation's competitiveness and threaten it. They increase national productivity by allowing a nation to specialize in industries in which its companies are more productive and to import where its companies are less productive. No nation can be competitive in everything. The ideal is to deploy the nation's limited human and other resources into their most productive use. Yet, international trade and FDI are likely to threaten productivity growth because they can expose a nation's industries to the test of international productivity standards. A country's industry will suffer if its productivity is not sufficiently higher than a foreign rival's productivity. If a nation loses the ability to compete in a range of high-productivity industries, its standard of living is threatened. In several industrialized countries, the rapid development of information technology has led to increased productivity and higher economic growth. Meanwhile, large disparities in the global economy continue to exist. Of major concern to international managers is why such national disparities exist and how companies should respond to them.

Interim Summary

1. Country competitiveness measures and compares how effective countries are in providing firms with an environment that sustains the domestic and international competitiveness of those firms. Productivity is the core of country competitiveness.

2. Country competitiveness is associated with, but different from, country comparative advantages. Germany, Switzerland, and Sweden have all prospered, despite having high wages and labor shortages.

COUNTRY COMPETITIVENESS AND MNEs

In a world of increasing global competition, nations have become more, rather than less, influential in international business operations. Differences in national values, culture, economic structures, institutions, and histories all contribute to competitive success. The national environment influences national competitiveness through the development of particular profiles of resources and capabilities (e.g., Italian footwear and textiles or Japanese semiconductors and electronics). The national environment also influences national competitiveness through its impact on the conditions for innovation. For example, as concern for product safety has grown in many industrialized countries, Volvo, originally based in Sweden, has succeeded by anticipating the market opportunities in this area. The impacts of country competitiveness on MNEs are fourfold.

First, *country competitiveness affects an MNE's selection of its global operations location.* Nike, for example, utilizes China as one of its major offshore production centers to benefit from cheap labor, abundant materials, and large market demand.

Second, *country competitiveness affects an MNE's industry selection.* For diversified MNEs, it is important to choose a foreign industry that will fit with the firm's global product portfolio and benefit from industry structure differences between home and host countries. A country's competitiveness is industry specific, meaning that no nation can, nor should, maintain high competitiveness in every industry. Japan, for example, while very competitive in motor vehicles, has large sectors of its economy (e.g., aircraft, chemicals, and banking) that lag far behind the world's leading competitors. Thus, a more important question that concerns international managers is which industry of the target country is superior in terms of environment and competitiveness.

Third, *country competitiveness affects an MNE's innovation and capability building.* Trade and FDI patterns often reflect the sectors favored by a country's organizing and technological strengths (e.g., Japan's VCRs and Singapore's hard disk drives), and these patterns promote further expansion and investment in these capabilities. The variations in country competitiveness pertain to differences in organizational and institutional capabilities. By investing and operating in a country with superior organizing and technological strengths, MNEs can learn more from local partners and the business community.

Finally, *country competitiveness affects an MNE's global strategy.* A country's competitiveness is reflected in different elements, including rich resources, strong market demand, efficient governmental administration, and superior infrastructure for innovation. This diversity enables MNEs to globally differentiate their dispersed functions and businesses to leverage the advantages of various countries' competitiveness. Several Taiwanese companies (e.g., Acer) have greatly benefited from this differentiated process, in which R&D is located in Taiwan and the United States, products are manufactured in Mainland China, financing is obtained in Hong Kong, and worldwide distribution is channeled through Singapore or Hong Kong.

Interim Summary

1. Country competitiveness affects an MNE's location selection and industry selection. For example, Nike chose China because it benefits from cheap labor and abundant resources needed for its production.

2. Country competitiveness affects an MNE's capability building and global strategy. For example, India has lured many software MNEs because it offers a favorable environment for developing software, which is then marketed globally.

COUNTRY-LEVEL DETERMINANTS

Country competitiveness improves via increased productivity, which is driven by a large array of *country-level, industry-level, firm-level,* and *individual-level* factors. Sustained productivity growth requires that an economy continually upgrade itself. International managers search for those decisive characteristics of a nation that allow its companies to create and sustain competitive advantage in particular fields (industries or sectors). Country competitiveness necessitates competitive strength across all these four levels (see Exhibit 5.1).

Economic growth and stability cannot be sustained without political and social stability, a well-constructed and -enforced legal system, and sound macroeconomic conditions. This chapter emphasizes economic essentials required for country competitiveness and leaves the discussion of the importance of the

Exhibit 5.1   Determinants of Country Competitiveness

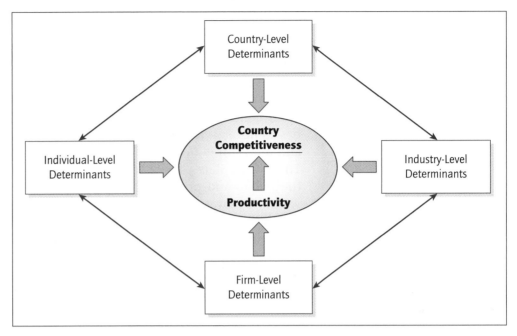

social and cultural and political and legal environments to the next two chapters. Economic fundamentals have long been considered the cornerstone for economic development. As summarized in Exhibit 5.2, these country-level fundamentals include (a) science, education, and innovation; (b) economic soundness; (c) finance; and (d) internationalization.

Exhibit 5.2   Country-Level Determinants of Country Competitiveness

Science, Education, and Innovation

Technological innovation has long been seen in all economies as central to the process of raising productivity and thus improving country competitiveness. By increasing the range of choices with respect to new products and production processes, technological progress raises the potential for economic expansion and, in general, fosters human and economic development. Conversely, technological deficiencies are one of the major reasons for low incomes in some developing countries. To build and maintain a strong record of innovation, a country has to develop and promote science and education. Technological innovation and diffusion is a complex process, requiring support from a set of institutions. The United States, for example, has developed a rich set of institutions in both the public and private sectors to support a high level of technological innovation. Innovation depends on a complex interplay between basic science and new technologies and on commercialization of those technologies in new products and production processes. Basic science is not exclusively a market-driven activity, because it is difficult to ensure payoff. Thus, nonmarket institutions usually carry out most projects in basic science. Examples include government laboratories (such as the National Institutes of Health in the United States) and academic centers such as universities. Some corporations sponsor basic scientific research in their laboratories as well.

The level of technological innovation depends largely on the commercialization of new products and processes. Several developing countries, most notably Russia, China, and India, have a large number of world-class scientists in basic science. However, because they lack a developed commercialization system, the competitiveness of these countries remains low. An effective commercialization process requires several ingredients:

1. There must be a close interface between basic scientists and R&D managers in the corporate world. In the United States, the education system has allowed scientific faculty to participate in private-sector R&D undertakings and has allowed universities to own patents for products developed by their faculty. This pattern of close business–university linkage is quite distinct from the situation in Poland or Ukraine, for instance, in which universities belong to state institutions and have minimal contact with industry sectors.

2. There must be strong support for developing intellectual property rights to encourage enterprises to make large outlays in R&D activities before a product is introduced to market. About 1% of the U.S. GDP is provided as the seed money for basic science in many crucial areas such as information technology, biotechnology, and material sciences.

3. The economy must be flexible enough to support the rapid adoption and diffusion of new technologies. For example, venture capital funds should be available to innovative firms to commercialize new technologies.

Apart from commercialization, technological innovation can also be improved by adopting and assimilating technology from foreign countries. There are several channels through which this can be done. First, a country can attract investments from MNEs, thereby bringing advanced technological innovation into its economy. For example, Mexico has dramatically upgraded its production technology through the rapid inflow of U.S. investments in key sectors such as motor vehicles, electronics, textiles, and pharmaceuticals. International joint ventures with MNEs (discussed in Chapter 12) are a quick and effective means for the host country to acquire foreign technologies and innovation expertise. Second, technology (e.g., robots) can be bought from a foreign country or licensed from a foreign patent holder for use in the borrowing country. In fact, international trade in technology via licensing, franchising, export, or lease has been growing since the early 1990s. Finally, the technology can be engineered by an adopting country and suitably modified by local engineers for domestic production and use. Generally, knowledge acquisition from foreign firms is a better strategy for relatively small but newly industrialized countries, since they usually lack the scientific and technological base to innovate on their own, yet they still have the ability to absorb technologies introduced in advanced countries. The competitiveness growth of the four mini-dragons—namely, Singapore, South Korea, Taiwan, and Hong Kong—largely subscribes to this strategy.

It is difficult to think about competitiveness and technological innovation without considering education. Education has become the prerequisite for entry into the knowledge-based economy, while technology has become the prerequisite for bringing education to society. The excellence in basic skills required in a good primary and secondary school system is important but by itself is not very helpful in pushing countries up the ladder of country competitiveness if it is not matched by superior higher education in technology and management. Vietnam, for example, is one of the top-ranking countries with regard to the math skills exhibited by its elementary and high school students. Its weakness in higher education, however, hampers the nation's competitiveness. The executives of the 21st century require not only business savvy, but also strong technical, communication, project-management, and human resource management skills. This is the new formula for grooming leaders who can handle the business world's increasingly complex problems.

Macroeconomic Soundness

Economic soundness is the key economic foundation and a major source of country competitiveness. It occupies an important place in the assessment of country competitiveness because it influences an economy's capacity to grow, the health of the trade sector, the balance of payments, and the attractiveness of investment by foreign businesses. **Economic soundness** can be defined as the extent to which an economy has been equipped with all the economic prerequisites for sustained economic growth. Macroeconomic soundness concerns both economic growth and economic stability, which are two distinct, but not mutually exclusive, fundamentals of the macroeconomic environment. An economy may be stable, but the policies that are in place may not be conducive to growth. Long-term growth and sustained competitiveness can be accomplished only if economic stability is maintained. Generally, economic stability is reflected in a low rate of inflation. In high-inflation situations, the loss of competitiveness and the emergence of balance-of-payments difficulties may interrupt economic growth. Rising public expenditures and the resultant budget deficits are often a principal cause of inflation. Expansionary public policies may initially stimulate economic growth, but as capacity limits are reached, output fails to keep up with rising expenditures, which eventually results in increased difficulty in financing the deficits.

Specific elements of economic soundness include *investment, consumption, real income level, economic sectors' performance,* and *infrastructure development.* First, investment by domestic firms and foreign businesses plays an important role in stimulating economic growth. Investment does not just augment a factor of production; it is also the means by which new technologies are put into practice. In addition, investment in one sector stimulates investment in others and encourages technological progress. When an economy slows down, investments from public or private sectors are important forces driving economic growth. In the late 1990s, for example, the United States, Japan, and most European nations employed a more favorable policy toward such investments.

Second, real income per capita and consumption per capita levels are also important because an economy's sustained growth depends partly on its citizens' final consumption. "Real" means that inflation has been subtracted from this indicator. The real interest rate is a key component linking the real income and consumption levels because this rate acts to adjust consumption relative to savings. The Federal Reserve, the central bank of the United States, for example, cut this rate several times in 2001 in an effort to stimulate domestic consumption.

Third, the performance of economic sectors, including both the manufacturing and service sectors, is a driving force for country competitiveness because it represents the strength of economic development. This performance consists of many facets such as innovativeness, efficiency, profitability, stability, and quality of products and service. The reason that the competitiveness of many developing countries (especially those in Africa) is relatively low is that their manufacturing and service sectors have not yet been developed, nor are they performing well.

Finally, the development levels of basic infrastructure (e.g., transportation, utility, and energy) and technological infrastructure (e.g., telecommunications and university graduates in science and engineering) influence country competitiveness because they are key segments of the external environment in which businesses operate. The supportiveness of these infrastructures affects production and business operations. The high growth rate of the Chinese economy in the 1990s, for example, was supported by its infrastructure improvement. Foreign investors there previously complained about an inadequacy of electric power and freight transportation, but today these infrastructure elements have expanded to a point where capacities are actually underutilized in some provinces.

Building on the preceding criteria, the *World Competitiveness Yearbook,* prepared and published by the International Institute for Management Development (IMD), based in Lausanne, Switzerland, reported the country rankings in terms of economic soundness between 2002 and 2006 (see Exhibit 5.3).

Finance

Finance is an important macroeconomic fundamental affecting economic stability and growth, and thus country competitiveness. Specific finance indicators that affect competitiveness include *currency valuation, solvency of the banking system,* and *short-term external debt.* First, **currency valuation** concerns the extent to which a country's home currency is valued or priced properly to reflect the situation of market supply and demand pertaining to this currency. The price level in one country naturally rises along with this country's income. A country with a price level exceeding its income level is said to have an *overvalued currency.* A country with an income level exceeding its price level is said to have an *undervalued currency.* High overvaluation or undervaluation can be a source of instability and is unhealthy for long-term economic growth (see Chapter 9 for details). One of the factors leading to the collapse of the Thai baht and the Korean won in 1997 involved overvaluation of their currencies.

Second, a weak banking system can be a source of instability as well. The nature of banking itself—borrowing short and lending long—always leaves

Exhibit 5.3   Macroeconomic Strength of Domestic Economy, 2002–2006 (Top 20 Ranking)

Country	2002	2003	2004	2005	2006
United States	1	1	1	1	1
Luxembourg	2	2	3	2	2
China Mainland	4	3	2	3	3
Singapore	18	7	5	5	4
Hong Kong	22	29	11	4	5
Iceland	14	20	15	17	6
India	17	22	12	12	7
United Kingdom	6	9	14	14	8
Ireland	8	8	6	6	9
Zhejiang (China)	–	12	10	13	10
Malaysia	29	25	16	8	11
Estonia	24	21	29	16	12
Canada	13	11	8	11	13
Australia	16	23	19	22	14
Japan	28	28	17	21	15
Chile	36	42	35	24	16
France	9	10	13	9	17
Netherlands	7	5	7	10	18
Maharashtra (India)	–	34	30	28	19
Norway	10	16	26	27	20

SOURCE: The International Institute for Management Development (IMD). *The World Competitiveness Yearbook, 2006,* p. 54. Lausanne, Switzerland: IMD. Reprinted with permission.

banks vulnerable to abrupt and unanticipated losses on deposits. This can happen internationally just as it can happen domestically. If the creditors of the bank happen to be foreign, then perceptions of exchange rate vulnerability can interact with perceived banking vulnerability to produce a particularly volatile mixture. While the Netherlands, Luxembourg, and Australia are considered to have the most solvent banks, banks in Indonesia and Thailand are considered the most vulnerable, which is one of the major causes of the banking crisis that began in the region in 1997 (see Chapter 9 for details).[2]

The last indicator of financial vulnerability is a high amount of short debt in relation to the hard currency reserves of a country's central bank. This indicator is more relevant for a country defending its fixed exchange rate. If foreign creditors discover that a country does not have enough hard currency to meet its short-term liabilities, then the country is at risk of a bank-run situation, where each creditor wishes to get its money out before the hard currency runs out. Taiwan, for example, was not considered high risk during the Asian financial crisis because its central bank had enough hard currency reserves to cover these liabilities. Hong Kong, although recognized as one of the world's most expensive cities, still remains competitive thanks to its solid financial system, its advanced financial markets, and its position as one of the largest financial centers in the world. Hong Kong also enjoys very high foreign exchange reserves and also benefits from the high reserves held by Mainland China.

Internationalization

Internationalization associated with country competitiveness refers to the extent to which the country participates in international trade and investment. (As you may recall from Chapter 1, this participation is one of the key indicators on the Globalization Index). This internationalization is influenced by a nation's strength in the following areas: (a) exports (both goods and services) and related current account balance (see Chapter 9), (b) exchange rate systems, (c) foreign investment (both FDI and portfolio investment), (d) foreign exchange reserves, and (e) openness of the economy. A high degree of competitiveness requires a high degree of internationalization of an economy, because competitiveness measures a nation's competitive advantage in an international marketplace compared with other countries. A strong domestic economy may or may not translate into a strong international competitiveness; it depends on the economy's openness and strength of foreign trade and investment as reflected in its current account and foreign exchange reserves. This openness is in turn dependent on a nation's economic soundness as well as the government's policies pertaining to foreign trade, investment, and exchange rate. A country's **openness** refers to the extent to which its national economy is linked to world economies through the flow of resources, goods, services, people, technologies, information, and capital. In a competitive nation, this flow means both inflow and outflow. The inflow of goods, capital, services, and the like is determined not only by an economy's attractiveness but also by the extent of its national protectionism. **National protectionism** reflects the level of barriers that foreign goods, capital, services, and other inputs of production are confronted with when moving into the focal country. As introduced in Chapter 2, examples of these barriers include import tariffs, quotas, voluntary export restraint, and commodity inspection standards, among others. For developing countries in which economic foundations and systems are underdeveloped, a certain degree of protectionism during an early stage of economic development is necessary for ensuring trade balance and economic stability. For this reason, the World Trade Organization (WTO) permits a few developing country members—for example, Poland, Hungary, and the Czech Republic—to have a higher bar against foreign imports.

Interim Summary

1. Country competitiveness is determined by four levels of factors: country level, industry level, firm level, and individual level. They affect competitiveness individually as well as jointly.

2. Country-level determinants include (a) science, education, and innovation; (b) macroeconomic soundness; (c) finance; and (d) internationalization.

3. Macroeconomic soundness is determined by investment, consumption, real income level, economic sectors' performance, and infrastructure development.

INDUSTRY-LEVEL DETERMINANTS

Sound country-level foundations such as macroeconomic fundamentals and science and innovation are necessary for enhancing country competitiveness. However, they are not sufficient to ensure a prosperous economy. Although country-level determinants influence overall competitiveness of a nation and are important to improving national productivity, no country can build and maintain high competitiveness in every industry. Within a country, different industries are not the same in terms of comparative advantages. Economically, it is neither necessary nor realistic to expect high competitiveness in every industry of the economy. This industry-specific perspective is especially important for international managers because it is often a target country's *industrial,* rather than national, environment that directly impacts firm decisions and operations. Of course, for a nation's government, the more industries with high international competitiveness, the greater the overall country competitiveness. Governments should devote more resources to improving infrastructures of those industries (or sub-industries) in which their nations are potentially already competitive.

When you look closely at any national economy, you will see enormous differences among a nation's industries in the area of competitive success. International advantage is often concentrated in particular industry sectors or segments within a given economy. For example, U.S. commercial aircraft and defense industries have dominated the world market, while Japanese semiconductors and VCRs have led as well. In the automobile industry, German exports are heavily skewed toward high-performance cars, whereas Korean exports are clustered at the low end of the market. The assessment of country competitiveness therefore is about competitive advantage of a nation in particular industries or industry segments. To help assess this competitiveness, classical theory explains the successes of nations in certain industries based on production factors (or inputs) such as land, labor, and natural resources. A nation gains comparative advantages in industries that make intensive use of the factors it possesses in abundance. This classical view, however, has been overshadowed in advanced industries and economies by the globalization of competition and the power of technology. A new perspective called the "diamond framework," developed by Michael E. Porter, offers an analytical tool for international managers to appraise a country's competitive advantage in particular fields.[3]

According to Porter's diamond framework, there are four broad attributes, which individually and collectively constitute the diamond of national advantage in particular fields:

1. *Factor Conditions.* This concerns the nation's position in factors of production, including basic factors such as labor, capital, land, and natural resources and sophisticated factors such as skilled workforce, scientific base, infrastructure, and information. Each country may be abundant in certain factors while lacking in others. For example, Hungary's optical instrument industry is abundant in skilled workers but lacks a well-developed supplier infrastructure. The same is true for China's copy-machine industry. Low design costs and growing market demand for copier machines are also major considerations luring foreign companies such as Xerox to invest there. Country competitiveness is likely to be higher in industries in which the country has superior factors of production. Basic factors are generally important in obtaining competitive advantage in labor-intensive industries but do not constitute an advantage in knowledge-intensive industries that require sophisticated factors of production. The contribution of factor conditions to country competitiveness changes over time. The stock of factors that a nation enjoys at a particular time is less important than the rate and efficiency with which it creates, upgrades, and deploys them in particular industries.

2. *Demand Conditions.* This involves the nature of market demand for the industry's product or service. International companies often enter a foreign market because of promising opportunities arising from strong market demand. Strong market demand drives an economy's gross domestic product (GDP) upward and facilitates the improvement of productivity in a competitive environment. In

addition to the size of market demand, the character of demand is also critical. Nations can gain competitive advantage in industries where the market demand gives their companies a clearer or earlier picture of emerging buyer needs as well as where demanding buyers pressure companies to innovate faster and achieve more sophisticated competitive advantages than their foreign rivals. If domestic buyers are the world's most sophisticated and demanding buyers, then a nation's companies in this sector are more likely to gain competitive advantage through constantly improving and upgrading their products or services. As an example, Japanese firms have pioneered compact, quiet air-conditioning units powered by energy-saving rotary compressors. This is largely because the firms have responded to the needs of Japanese consumers, most of whom live in small, crowded homes in a country where humid summers are the norm.

3. *Related and Supporting Industries.* This refers to the presence and support level of a nation's suppliers or other related industries. For foreign investors, the availability and supportiveness of local suppliers as well as other related industries such as banking, foreign exchange services, and infrastructure services are fundamental to their routine operations. For the country itself, the competitiveness of related industries provides benefits of information flow and technical interchange among related industries, which in turn speeds up the rate of innovation and upgrading. For example, Switzerland's success in pharmaceuticals evolved from previous international success in the dye industry. Having home-based suppliers that are internationally competitive can create advantages in downstream industries. Italian gold and silver jewelry companies lead the world in part because other Italian companies supply two-thirds of the world's jewelry-making and precious-metal recycling machinery. In addition, suppliers and end users located near each other can take advantage of short lines of communication, quick and constant flow of information, and an ongoing exchange of ideas and innovations. Through close working relationships, companies have the opportunity to influence their suppliers' technical efforts and can serve as test sites for R&D work, accelerating the pace of innovation. When suppliers, manufacturers, and even distributors are located near each other or concentrated in the same area (a city or part of a city), we call this geographical concentration a **cluster.** Examples include Silicon Valley in California for the semiconductor and software industry, Milan in Italy for fashion garments, Hamamatsu in Japan for motorcycles and musical instruments, Pusan in South Korea for footwear products, and Zhongguanchun in Beijing for electronics.

4. *Rivalry and Business Practice.* This entails the nature of domestic rivalry in addition to the conditions governing how businesses are organized, managed, and operated in a nation. International investors may select a country in which local rivalry is low. However, in terms of competitiveness, the presence of strong local rivals is a powerful stimulus to the creation and persistence of national competitive advantage. This is especially true for small countries such as Switzerland, where the rivalries among its pharmaceutical companies—Ciba-Geigy, Sandoz, and Hoffman-La Roche—contribute to global leadership. Domestic rivalries exert pressure on companies to innovate and improve. Local rivals force each other to lower costs, improve quality and service, and create new products and processes. Domestic rivals compete not only for market share but also for people, for technical excellence, and more important, for product quality, customer responsiveness, and innovation. Business and management practice is relevant to country competitiveness because competitiveness in a specific industry results from convergence of management and business policy with the sources of competitive advantage in the industry. In industries where Italian companies

are among the world's leaders—such as lighting, furniture, footwear, woolen fabrics, and packaging machines—a company strategy that emphasizes customized products, niche marketing, rapid adaptation, and great flexibility fits well, both with the dynamics of the industry and with the character of the Italian management system. Successful Italian international competitors also tend to be small or medium-sized companies (SMEs) that are privately owned and operated like extended families. In Germany, companies tend to be hierarchical in organization and management practices, and top managers usually have technical backgrounds. This system works well in technical or engineering-oriented industries (e.g., optics, chemicals) in which complex products demand precision manufacturing as well as a highly disciplined management. Germany's success, however, is quite limited in consumer goods and services in which image marketing and product innovation are important to competition. In the greater China region, including the P.R.C., Taiwan, Hong Kong, Macao, and Singapore, successful companies are technologically innovative as well as skillful in cultivating and developing personal ties with government officials and with top managers of other firms. Personal relations (or *guanxi,* in Mandarin) may be conducive to improving competitiveness in such industries where the regulatory environment is highly unpredictable.

Exhibit 5.4 highlights the diamond framework of national competitive advantage. The four determinants in this framework create the national environment into which companies are born and in which they learn to compete. Each point on the diamond—as well as the diamond itself as a system—produces essential ingredients for achieving international competitive success. In general, companies gain a competitive advantage when a national environment (a) permits and supports the

---

Exhibit 5.4   Industry-Level Determinants of Country Competitiveness

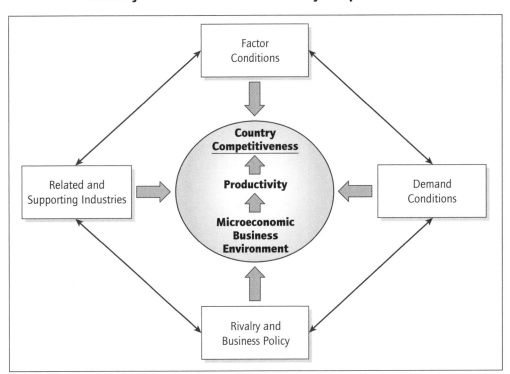

SOURCE: Adapted from M. E. Porter. "The competitive advantage of nations." *Harvard Business Review,* March–April 1990: pp. 73–93.

most rapid accumulation of specialized assets and skills, (b) affords better ongoing information and insight into product and process needs, and (c) pressures companies to innovate and invest. It is also important to note that the diamond factors create an environment that may promote competitiveness of other related industries. Japan's strength in consumer electronics, for example, drove its success in semiconductors toward the memory chips and integrated circuits these products use.

The four diamond attributes together serve as the microeconomic business environment that affects country competitiveness. Exhibit 5.5 lists the top 20 countries in terms of the strength of their microeconomic business environments from 2001 to 2005, appraised using the preceding diamond framework. Unless there is appropriate improvement at the microeconomic environment, the country-level determinants (i.e., macroeconomic business environment) as discussed earlier will not bear full fruit.[4] National productivity is ultimately set by the productivity of a nation's companies. Companies need appropriate conditions for rapid and sustained productivity growth. The country-level determinants create the potential for improving national prosperity, but wealth is actually created at the microeconomic (industrial) level—in the ability of firms to create valuable goods and services productively. A country's economy cannot be competitive unless the companies operating within it are competitive, whether they are domestic or foreign company subsidiaries. To conclude, the improvement of country competitiveness is a process of successive upgrading, in which a

Exhibit 5.5   The Microeconomic Competitiveness Scoreboard (Top 20)

Economy	2001 Rank	2003 Rank	2005 Rank
United States	2	2	1
Finland	1	1	2
Germany	4	5	3
Denmark	8	4	4
Singapore	9	8	5
United Kingdom	7	6	6
Switzerland	5	7	7
Japan	10	13	8
Netherlands	3	9	9
Austria	11	17	10
France	13	10	11
Sweden	6	3	12
Canada	12	12	13
Taiwan	21	16	14
Australia	14	11	15
Belgium	15	15	16
Iceland	16	14	17
New Zealand	20	18	18
Ireland	22	21	19
Hong Kong	18	19	20

SOURCE: M. E. Porter. "Building the microeconomic foundations of prosperity." In *The Global Competitiveness Report 2005–2006*, p. 52. Geneva, Switzerland: World Economic Forum.

nation's business environment evolves to support and encourage increasingly sophisticated and productive ways of competing and innovating. This chapter's Industry Box illustrates how e-business may shape country competitiveness in the future. Chapter 18 provides more detailed information on global e-commerce.

INDUSTRY BOX

E-COMMERCE AS AN ELEMENT OF COUNTRY COMPETITIVENESS

E-commerce capabilities can help boost a country's competitiveness in many ways. First, the Internet is a global network, enabling people and businesses to connect to the rest of the world. Second, the Internet provides easy access to the global market, matching buyers and sellers across national boundaries. Third, the Internet is an efficient distribution tool, saving transaction costs. Fourth, the Internet lets small businesses play in the big business arena. Finally, the Internet shortens a company's time to market.

However, many countries lag behind in the e-business race, and in many cases, the e-business laggards are at the bottom of the competitive rankings. The reasons are three-fold: language, education, and technical infrastructure. But many governments are taking steps to address these issues because they understand that the Internet presents developing nations the opportunity to bolster their competitiveness and economy. Asia-Pacific Economic Cooperation Forum (APEC) leaders, for instance, acknowledged during their meetings in Vancouver on November 25, 1997, the need to promote Asian economies to construct and utilize a global information infrastructure. For governments, adequate regulations and supervision also need to be in place to ensure that private enterprises are playing their part in innovating and implementing the global systems and needed infrastructure. International companies such as GE Capital and Infotech Global have made investments in emerging markets. For example, both companies have announced expansion of their services in India.

SOURCE: Adapted from E. Sprano and A. Zakak. "E-commerce capable: Competitive advantage for countries in the new world e-economy." *Competitiveness Review*, 2000, *10*, 2: pp. 114–131.

Interim Summary

1. It is neither possible nor necessary to expect *every* industry in a country to be competitive. Industry-level fundamentals determine a country's microeconomic business environment.

2. The "diamond framework" is often used to assess country competitiveness in particular industries or fields. This framework consists of four factors—factor conditions, demand conditions, related and supporting industries, and rivalry and business practice.

3. A cluster is a geographical concentration in which suppliers, manufacturers, and even distributors are located near each other. Clusters can help improve country competitiveness.

FIRM-LEVEL DETERMINANTS

An economy's product competitiveness stems from companies within that nation. Firms produce products and provide services. Thus, country competitiveness is also associated with firm-level factors that can characterize country-unique organizational, innovational, and operational strategies employed by most firms of that nation. These strategies, principles, or approaches should differentiate one country's firms from those of other countries and, more important, create competitive advantages for both the nation and firms to which they belong. For example, most Japanese firms have obtained their competitive advantages vis-à-vis American and European companies through superior process innovations, quality control systems, and unique manager–employee relationships. These firm-level policies have become Japan's national standards and have been widely applied by most Japanese firms. Country competitiveness can thus be partly explained by differences in country capabilities in terms of technologies and organizing principles. These technologies and organizing principles diffuse more slowly across borders than within a nation. In other words, these unique firm-level factors are virtually embedded in Japanese firms. This embeddedness helps Japan maintain strong country competitiveness.

Organizing principles of technological innovation and production are particularly important because they are not easily diffused across nations. National economic leadership of a country is not driven by technological investments alone but also by the efficiency of a country's dominant organizing principles.[5] The superiority of U.S. competitiveness in relation to that of European countries is attributable not only to the country's creation of technologies (as measured by patents) but also to its adoption of new methods of management. Although the basic research skills of Japanese firms are generally inferior to those of U.S. firms, organizing principles such as lean flexible production, total quality management, just-in-time manufacturing, and multi-sourcing strategy used by Japanese firms add substantial value to the international competitiveness of Japanese products.

The contribution of technologies and organizing principles to creating competitive advantages for both firms and the country cannot last forever. Technology, and even organizing principles, are inevitably diffused across nations and eventually imitated by foreign rivals. Through technology transfer, foreign direct investment, and global strategic alliances, one nation's firms can learn both technologies and organizing principles that were developed and employed by counterparts in another nation. This suggests that firms ought to continuously upgrade their technological skills and organizing approaches if they wish to sustain competitive advantages that help maintain their country's competitiveness in the long run. Constant and rapid technological progress, rather than one single innovation, is the secret to retaining competitive advantage.

Firms can also influence the environment that impacts country competitiveness. Companies do not simply accept the status quo of factor development in the nation but instead seek to upgrade it. For example, Italian industry associations invest in marketing information, process technology, and common infrastructure in such industries as woolens, ceramic tiles, and lighting equipment. Swiss and German firms widely participate in apprenticeship programs. In Britain, successful industries such as chemicals and pharmaceuticals are characterized by close ties with universities and government research institutes. Firms can, and must, invest directly in factor creation through their own training, research, and infrastructure building. Internal efforts at factor creation lead to the most specialized, and often most important, factors. Competitive firms often have well-developed internal training programs and, compared with their rivals, set aside higher amounts of resources for R&D. Large U.S. and Japanese companies usually have their own universities or schools. Yamaha, for example, faced a shortage of skilled piano technicians in Japan, so it founded its own educational program for acoustics training that is now highly regarded internationally. The benefits flow to Yamaha as well as to the entire Japanese industry.

Firms can also join with, or participate in, the efforts of governmental entities, educational institutions, and local communities to influence factor creation or improvement. Nestlé, for example, founded and supports Geneva-based IMI, which has become a leading European business school. Nestlé has benefited from a steady flow of talented management as well as ongoing management training. German chemical companies have established relationships with all of the major German universities and also sponsor institutes devoted to chemical research, contributing to advancements in the industry. In addition, they sponsor students or their staff to study at the universities. They also play an active role in helping institutions identify the needs of the industry by assisting with planning curriculum, placing graduates, and providing financial support for facilities and scholarships. Exhibit 5.6 outlines the firm-level determinants of country competitiveness.

Exhibit 5.6   Firm-Level Determinants of Country Competitiveness

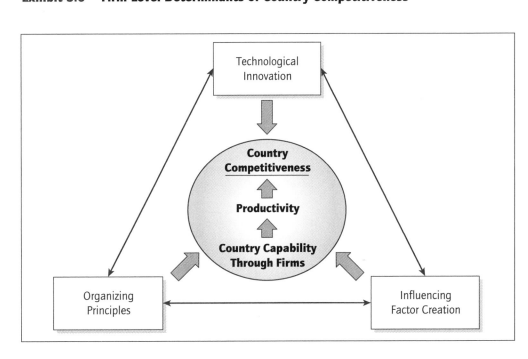

Interim Summary

1. It is firms that directly create national wealth, and thus the productivity of firms is central to country competitiveness.

2. Technologies and organizing principles (e.g., process innovation and quality-control systems) are two firm-level fundamentals. When unique and productive organizing principles and technological skills become national standards or permeate throughout the nation, they will substantially heighten country competitiveness.

INDIVIDUAL-LEVEL DETERMINANTS

Individual-level determinants are people or human resources associated with country competitiveness. They include workers, entrepreneurs, professional managers, designers and engineers, educators and intellectuals, and politicians and government officials (see Exhibit 5.7). Human resources affect productivity (the core of country competitiveness) by shaping the environment for developing competitiveness and by combining and arranging the preceding physical competitiveness determinants at both the country and industry levels.

Exhibit 5.7   Individual-Level Determinants of Country Competitiveness

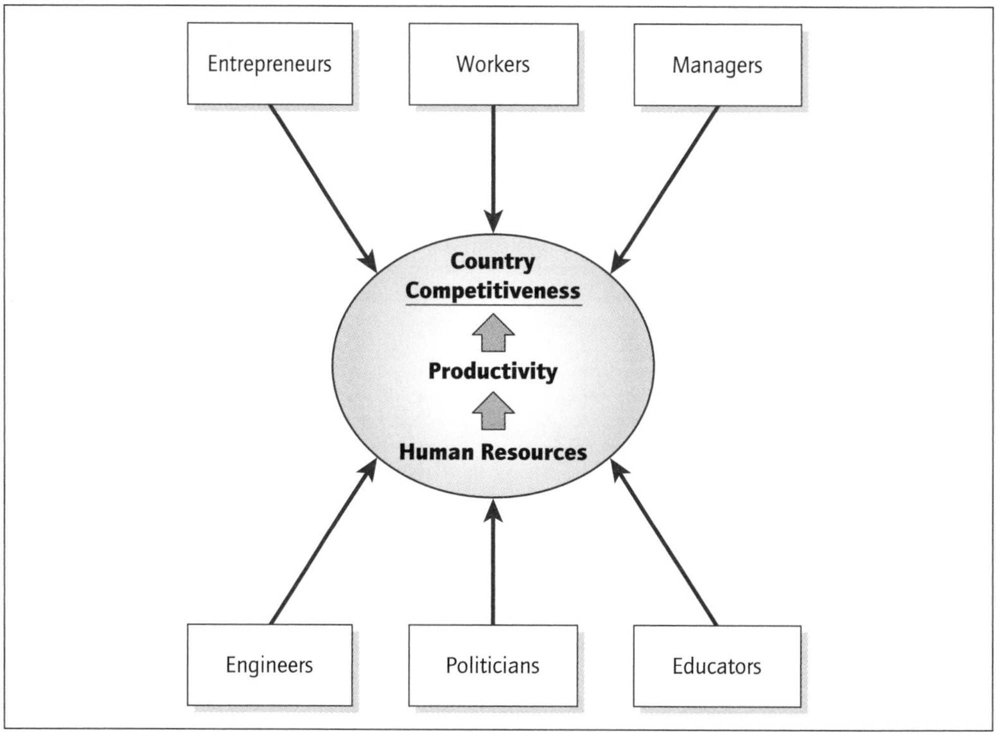

Workers: Workers' productivity affects country productivity. For example, skillful and diligent workers in Singapore are an important force in improving that nation's country-level productivity. In addition to the wage level and the size of the labor pool, other important factors associated with worker productivity include educational level, loyalty to organizations, passion for work, self-motivation, learning skills, and discipline. In Denmark, Finland, and Sweden, superior education and passion for work are important reasons for the superior productivity of workers. In Japan, workers' loyalty to organizations and learning skills are partly responsible for their employers' competitiveness.

Entrepreneurs: **Entrepreneurs** venture into new businesses despite a high degree of risk arising from uncertainty about the future. They are a special group of businesspeople taking risks in the development of new products, new markets, or new technologies. They create new businesses, stimulating a nation's economic development. A nation's competitiveness is strengthened in the course of its entrepreneurs' efforts and commitments to take high risks and maximize returns. Singapore's high level of competitiveness can in large part be attributed to the high percentage of entrepreneurs in its total population.

Managers: Experienced and skillful managers in various enterprises, whether public, private, or state-owned, play an important role in increasing country competitiveness. Production and operation processes are becoming increasingly complex and interrelated among different value-chain activities (e.g., from inbound logistics and operations to outbound logistics, marketing, and service; or from human resource management to technological development and procurement). As a result, a country with a large pool of educated and experienced managers who are well versed in production, operation, and organization will have a much better chance of creating and sustaining high competitiveness. Several newly industrialized economies such as South Korea and Taiwan have successfully secured and retained a large number of Western-educated and experienced managers. This greatly helps to raise the level of national competitiveness in these countries.

Engineers: Engineers and designers stand at the forefront of country competitiveness. They are key players in improving a nation's productivity because they create value through production innovation and process innovation. A country's expertise in these two types of innovations is a crucial element for elevating its competitiveness. Because international competitiveness involves worldwide consumers, it is important for engineers and designers to have a global vision. Engineers in Switzerland and the Netherlands have a strong educational background, industrial experience, and global vision, which in turn help stimulate the competitiveness of these nations.

Educators: Educators and intellectuals represent a prime force for strengthening education and science. High competitiveness of an economy requires the creation and dissemination of knowledge needed for improving productivity. Although intellectuals are the major source of knowledge creation, educators at various levels (from elementary to higher education) are a prominent source for knowledge dissemination. For countries moving to knowledge-based economies, growth depends heavily on the contributions of educators and intellectuals. A country's productivity and competitiveness are generally positively correlated with the salary level or, more broadly, living standards of educators and intellectuals.

Politicians: The role of politicians and government officials in supporting competitiveness cannot be underestimated simply because government policies and administrative efficiency exert a significant effect on other determinants of country competitiveness. Nations with politicians who select economic development as a priority or are willing to give up their political ambitions for their nations' economic development tend to create competitiveness. South Korea in the 1970s is a manifestation of how a national economy can benefit from political leaders with a strong commitment to economic growth even under a nondemocratic regime. Government officials apply policies to the economy. Their role can be compared to that of an automobile's transmission: The most efficient transmission would convey the power with minimum loss of power. Officials who can implement politicians' policies in the most efficient way can enhance their nation's competitiveness.[6]

Interplay of the Four Levels of Determinants

The preceding four levels of determinants are not exclusive of each other. Country-level determinants provide an overall national foundation for developing country competitiveness. This foundation provides a general economic and technological environment, which can directly or indirectly influence industrial, organizational, and individual determinants of competitiveness. For example, a nation's education system (a country-level determinant) affects the qualifications of workers, managers, and engineers (individual-level determinants). Conversely, politicians and officials (individual-level determinants) have the power to change country-level determinants such as economic policies and financial systems. Industry-level determinants jointly create a microeconomic business environment that impacts companies' productivity. They are a central force linking a nation's comparative advantage with firms' competitive advantages in wealth creation. While country-level and industry-level determinants together provide a context for improving country competitiveness, firm-level and individual-level determinants are direct "hands" in creating and improving this competitiveness. These "hands" can be stronger or weaker, depending on both country-level and industry-level conditions. This chapter's Country Box provides an illustrative case in which Italy's country competitiveness is jointly influenced by various determinants at the individual level (e.g., politicians, entrepreneurs, workers), firm level (e.g., flexibility, cluster, small size), industry level (competition, factor conditions, related industries), and country level (infrastructure, education, legal system, economic soundness).

COUNTRY BOX

ITALY: CAN BERLUSCONI RENEW THE NATION?

Hundreds of thousands of anxious entrepreneurs voted on May 13, 2001, for media baron Silvio Berlusconi in the hope that this new prime minister would carry out his promise to reverse Italy's declining competitiveness. The country's entrepreneurs survived and even thrived by remaining small and nimble. In the northern industrial districts, manufacturers of the same products, such as textiles or shoes, clustered together like virtual keiretsu, purchasing supplies jointly, for example, but skirting inflexible labor laws by employing fewer than 15 workers each. They bridged the gaps in skills or education with extensive in-house training. The result has been an army of small and midsize companies that boast global strength in fashion, industrial design, machinery, and other niche sectors.

But now, Italy's stalwart exporters face a series of obstacles that is proving insurmountable for many of them. They are caught in the middle of two new forces: Cheap Asian goods of steadily improving quality are flooding global markets, posing competition Italians have never experienced, and the rest of Europe is leaping ahead into the digital economy, with companies producing some of the most sophisticated software and telecom products in the world. And Italy? Its businesses, by and large, simply lack the size and research muscle to go against bigger competitors in these technology-driven industries.

Meanwhile, in Italy, taxes, labor costs, and labor-market regulation have become even more burdensome and restrictive over the past 15 years. Aging roads and railroads are obstacles to growth. Half-hearted liberalization has left markets in the grip of former monopolies. Worst of all is a serious deterioration in the quality of education at every level and the power of courts to function properly.

SOURCE: Adapted from G. Edmondson, K. Carlisle, and S. Pierce. "Italy: Can Berlusconi renew the nation?" *Business Week*, May 28, 2001: p. 46.

Interim Summary

1. Individual-level determinants are people or human resources that affect country competitiveness. They include workers, entrepreneurs, managers, engineers and designers, educators and intellectuals, and politicians and government officials.

2. Human resources affect country competitiveness in such a way that they determine a country's expertise, creativity, and efficiency.

3. Multilevel fundamentals also interactively affect country competitiveness. Country- and industry-level determinants provide an important context in

which firms and individuals directly create national wealth. Firms and individuals are also able to reshape this context so that macro- and microeconomic business environments become more favorable for productivity.

GOVERNMENT ROLE

Government plays an important role in shaping country competitiveness. It can affect all four levels of determinants outlined previously. Through policy making and intervention, government can impact investment, savings, and trade. Through a combination of trade liberalization and exchange rate adjustment, government can strengthen the balance of payments and improve international competitiveness. The experiences of several newly industrialized nations in the early 1980s suggest that a certain amount of governmental control over macroeconomic problems is necessary. In that particular instance, when macroeconomic fundamentals grew seriously out of line, governments acted promptly to bring the situation under control. They were also committed to export expansion rather than import substitution as a means of relieving balance-of-payment constraints.

Governments can also exert influence on the microeconomic business environment and on human resource development. Such influence is normally exerted through a set of industrial policies. **Industrial policies** can be defined as all forms of conscious and coordinated government interventions to promote industrial development. Such forms include, but are not limited to, import protection, financial subsidies, regulatory changes, and interventions in capital, labor, technology, and natural resource markets. For example, a government can shape factor conditions through its training and infrastructure policies. Factor conditions are also affected through subsidies and policies aimed at the development of capital markets. Furthermore, market demand conditions are influenced by regulatory standards and processes, government purchasing, and openness to imports. Governments are often a major buyer of many products, including defense goods, telecommunications equipment, and aircraft for a national airline. Governments can shape the circumstances of related and supporting industries through control of advertising media and also through regulation of supporting services such as banking and foreign exchange. Finally, government policy also influences competition and business practices through such means as capital market regulation, tax policy, and antitrust laws.

The effect of government policies on country competitiveness can be positive (stimulating competitiveness) or negative (obstructing competitiveness). Too much dependence on direct help or interference from the government may hurt companies in the long run and only lead to them becoming more dependent. On the other hand, a government that has a hands-off policy may miss out on the benefits of shaping the macro- and microeconomic business environment and institutional structure that can stimulate companies to gain competitive advantage. Thus, the appropriate role that a government should play is one of a catalyst and challenger—it should encourage, or even push, companies to aspire to higher levels of competitive performance, even though this process may be difficult. Governments cannot directly create competitive industries; only companies can do that. Government policies that succeed are those that create an environment in which companies can gain competitive advantage.

There are several principles that governments should embrace in order to play a supporting role in national competitiveness:

1. *They should emphasize competitiveness infrastructure.* Governments have critical responsibilities for developing and improving infrastructure such as education, science, research, transportation, and information technology.

2. *They should enforce strict product, safety, and environmental standards.* Stringent standards for product performance, product safety, and environmental control pressure companies to improve quality, upgrade technology, and provide features that respond to consumer and social demands.

3. *They should deregulate competition.* Regulation through maintaining a state monopoly, controlling entry to industry, or fixing prices hampers rivalry and innovation.

4. *They should adopt strong domestic antitrust policies.* These policies, especially when applied to horizontal mergers, alliances, and collusive behavior, are fundamental to innovation. Government policy should generally favor new entry over acquisition.

5. *They should boost goal setting that leads to sustained investment.* Governments can indirectly affect the goals of investors, managers, and employees though various policies. For instance, the tax rate for long-term capital gains is a powerful tool for adjusting the rate of sustained investment in industry as it affects the level of new investment in corporate equity.

This chapter concludes with the World Competitiveness Scoreboard, 1998–2006 (Exhibit 5.8), identified in the *World Competitiveness Yearbook*. This yearbook ranks nations' environments according to their ability to provide an environment in which enterprises can compete. Similar to the aforementioned determinants at multiple levels, the yearbook assesses country competitiveness based on eight competitiveness input factors: domestic economy, science and technology, people, firm management, internationalization, infrastructure, finance, and government. Since 2001, these factors have been regrouped into four main categories, including economic performance, government efficiency, business efficiency, and infrastructure.

Interim Summary

1. Government is a critical force impacting country competitiveness and can influence virtually all determinants discussed previously.

2. To improve country competitiveness, governments should be committed to upgrading competitiveness infrastructures; encouraging competition; enforcing strict product, safety, and environmental standards; and motivating firms and individuals for better innovation and creativity.

Exhibit 5.8   The World Competitiveness Scoreboard, 1998–2006

Economy	1998 Rank	2000 Rank	2002 Rank	2004 Rank	2006 Rank
USA	1	1	1	1	1
Hong Kong, China	5	12	9	6	2
Singapore	2	2	5	2	3
Iceland	18	9	12	5	4
Denmark	10	13	6	7	5
Australia	12	10	14	4	6

Economy	1998 Rank	2000 Rank	2002 Rank	2004 Rank	2006 Rank
Canada	8	8	8	3	7
Switzerland	9	7	7	14	8
Luxembourg	3	6	3	9	9
Finland	6	4	2	8	10
Ireland	7	5	10	10	11
Norway	11	17	17	17	12
Austria	24	15	13	13	13
Sweden	16	14	11	11	14
Netherlands	4	3	4	15	15
Bavaria (Germany)	–	–	–	20	16
Japan	20	24	30	23	17
Taiwan	14	20	24	12	18
China (Mainland)	21	30	31	24	19
Estonia	–	–	21	28	20
United Kingdom	13	16	16	22	21
New Zealand	17	18	19	18	22
Malaysia	19	27	26	16	23
Chile	27	25	20	26	24
Israel	25	21	25	33	25
Germany	15	11	15	21	26
Belgium	23	19	18	25	27
Ile-de-France (France)	–	–	–	32	28
India	38	39	42	34	29
Scotland (UK)	–	–	–	36	30
Czech Republic	37	40	29	43	31
Thailand	41	35	34	29	32
Zhejiang (China)	–	–	–	19	33
Catalonia (Spain)	–	–	–	27	34
France	22	22	22	30	35
Spain	26	23	23	31	36
Maharashtra (India)	–	–	–	38	37
South Korea	36	28	27	35	38
Slovak Republic	–	–	37	40	39
Colombia	45	45	44	41	40
Hungary	28	26	28	42	41
Greece	33	34	36	44	42
Portugal	29	29	33	39	43
South Africa	42	43	39	49	44
Slovenia	–	36	38	45	45
Jordan	–	–	–	48	46
Bulgaria	–	–	–	–	47

(Continued)

Exhibit 5.8 (Continued)

Economy	1998 Rank	2000 Rank	2002 Rank	2004 Rank	2006 Rank
São Paulo (Brazil)	–	–	–	47	48
Philippines	32	37	40	52	49
Lombardy (Italy)	–	–	–	46	50
Turkey	39	42	46	55	51
Brazil	35	31	35	53	52
Mexico	34	33	41	56	53
Russia	43	47	43	50	54
Argentina	30	41	49	59	55
Italy	31	32	32	51	56
Romania	–	–	–	54	57
Poland	44	38	45	57	58
Croatia	–	–	–	–	59
Indonesia	40	44	47	58	60
Venezuela	46	46	48	60	61

SOURCE: The International Institute for Management Development (IMD). *The World Competitiveness Yearbook.* Lausanne, Switzerland: IMD. Reprinted with permission.

Note that this source may differ from the Global Competitiveness Report published by World Economic Forum concerning the above rankings. For instance, the latter ranked the U.S. sixth in world competitiveness in 2006 (first place in 2005) after taking into account the nation's macroeconomic concerns, such as huge defense and homeland security spending, long-term potential costs from health care and pensions, low savings rate, and record-high current account deficits.

CHAPTER SUMMARY

1. Country competitiveness is the extent to which a country is capable of generating more wealth than its competitors in world markets. The central force for improving country competitiveness is productivity. There are four levels of specific determinants of country competitiveness: country level, industry level, firm level, and individual level.

2. Country competitiveness can be analyzed by governments for consummating competitiveness infrastructures, by local firms for selecting a more favorable environment in which sustained competitive advantages can be developed, or by MNEs for electing optimal foreign locations and industries.

3. Country-level determinants of competitiveness comprise (a) science, education, and innovation; (b) economic soundness; (c) finance; and (d) internationalization. These fundamentals are the cornerstone for economic development and the building blocks of macroeconomic business environment for country competitiveness.

4. Industry-level determinants of competitiveness comprise (a) factor conditions, (b) demand conditions, (c) related and supporting industries, and (d) rivalry and business practice. They affect country competitiveness individually as well as collectively. MNEs operating in foreign countries are often impacted more directly by these industry-level determinants than by country-level determinants.

5. Firm-level determinants are country-unique organizational, technological, or operational strategies, policies, and practices employed by most firms in a particular nation. Country competitiveness can be partly explained by differences in national capabilities in terms of technologies and organizing principles (e.g., lean flexible

production, total quality management, just-in-time manufacturing, and multi-sourcing strategy used by Japanese firms).

6. Individual-level determinants are human resources that shape the environment for developing competitiveness. Major players include workers, entrepreneurs, managers, engineers, educators, politicians, and government officials. Country competitiveness is positively correlated with the productivity or creativity of these individuals.

7. Governments significantly shape country competitiveness through industrial policies and the development of a competitiveness infrastructure. Governments should serve as catalysts in providing a stimulating environment for companies to gain a competitive advantage in international markets.

Chapter Notes

1. B. Ohlin. *Interregional and International Trade.* Cambridge, MA: Harvard University Press, 1952; W. W. Leontief. "Domestic production and foreign trade: The American capital position reexamined." *Proceedings of the American Philosophical Society,* 1953.

2. *The Global Competitiveness Report 1999,* pp. 14–27. Geneva, Switzerland: World Economic Forum, 1999.

3. M. E. Porter. *The Competitive Advantage of Nations.* New York: The Free Press, 1990; also see Porter, "The competitive advantage of nations." *Harvard Business Review,* March–April 1990: pp. 73–93.

4. M. E. Porter. "The current competitiveness index: Measuring the microeconomic foundations of prosperity." In *The Global Competitiveness Report 1999.* Geneva: World Economic Forum.

5. B. Kogut. "Country capabilities and the permeability of borders." *Strategic Management Journal,* 1991, 12 (summer special): pp. 33–47.

6. D. S. Cho. "From national competitiveness to bloc and global competitiveness." *Competitiveness Review,* 1998, 8, 1: pp. 11–23.

THE CULTURAL ENVIRONMENT

DO YOU KNOW?

1. Does culture influence international investment and trade?

2. Does culture influence strategy? Does it have an impact on marketing, human resource management, and other functional areas?

3. What are the similarities and differences between "national culture," "industry culture," and "corporate culture"?

4. Is it possible to define and measure culture? How?

5. Is it possible to measure differences between cultures? How, and what are the pitfalls?

OPENING CASE

The Goodyear–Sumitomo Alliance

When Ohio-based tire manufacturer Goodyear, among the world's largest tire companies, acquired a majority stake and took control of the tire operations of Japanese manufacturer Sumitomo in 1999, it took pains to portray the transaction as an alliance of equals rather than as a partnership dominated by the U.S. firm. Why has Goodyear been willing to term the deal "a global alliance" while in effect it was taking control of Sumitomo's tire operations? By presenting the alliance as a

Photo 6.1   Culture is apparent in many features of life.

SOURCE: Jupiterimages.

marriage of equals, Goodyear prevented its Japanese partner from "losing face." If Goodyear were to appear as the controlling partner in the alliance, it would imply an acknowledgment of failure on Sumitomo's part. Further, letting the U.S. firm appear to be in charge of running the operations would position the Japanese firm as the junior partner in the venture, something embarrassing in a culture that puts great emphasis on hierarchy.

Several years later, in 2003, Goodyear reduced to 10% the Sumitomo Group's stake it had previously acquired as part of the alliance between the two firms. The relationship, however, remains solid. The two firms continue to cooperate today via six joint ventures, building on the trust they have accumulated over years of cooperation. Japan—Sumitomo's base—is the only Asian Pacific market where Goodyear does not have direct presence. Executives from both Goodyear and Sumitomo as well as those who work for partner firms in other long-running U.S.-Japanese joint ventures and alliances (e.g., Fuji Film–Xerox, Toyota–General Motors, Ford Motor–Mazda) identify understanding the national and corporate culture of their partners as a long and challenging process but an essential ingredient in the success of their respective ventures.

SOURCES: Based on "From Egypt to Europe to Ohio, a CEO finds his home." *Wall Street Journal,* December 22, 1999, A1; "Goodyear reduces holdings in Sumitomo Rubber Industries." Goodyear Press Release, April 8, 2003; Goodyear Web site 9/2006.

The concept of "face," introduced in the opening case, is deeply ingrained in the culture of many Asian societies and has ramifications for many facets of international business. In conducting negotiations, for example, Japanese buyers will rarely inform a vendor when they are not interested in his or her product, but rather will say that they "will think about it." The idea is not to offend their counterparts; however, those who are unaware of this cultural imperative may end up with just that feeling. For instance, Americans, misinterpreting the indirect response by Japanese executives, will often complain that the Japanese are "beating around the bush," that is, wasting time and effort by not providing a clear and straightforward answer. In the human resources area, "face" implies that negative performance feedback is rarely provided in Asian societies such as China except indirectly (e.g., through a trusted third person and not in the presence of peers and subordinates).

WHAT IS CULTURE?

The *Oxford Encyclopedic English Dictionary* defines **culture**—in the sense of its usage in this book—as the art and other manifestations of human intellectual achievement regarded collectively; the customs, civilization, and achievement of a particular time or people; the way of life of a particular society or group. Culture has been defined in literally hundreds of ways[1]—a testament both to its importance and to its elusive and intangible nature. Huntington, a political scientist, distinguishes "culture" from "civilization"— both civilization and culture refer to a people's way of life, values, norms, and modes of thinking; however, a civilization is the broadest cultural entity.[2] Among modern management scholars, Hofstede defines culture as "the collective programming of the human mind," whereas Trompenaars and Hampden-Turner define culture as "the way in which people solve problems and recognize dilemmas."[3] Whitely and England synthesized more than 100 definitions of culture to arrive at this working definition, which is also the definition we use in this book:[4]

The knowledge, beliefs, art, law, morals, customs and other capabilities of one group distinguishing it from other groups.

Different definitions notwithstanding, there is a broad consensus regarding the main features of culture, as follows:

- *Culture is shared.* It is not an individual but a group property. Multiple group affiliations (e.g., with a nation, a firm) create multiple cultural memberships. Individuals vary, however, in the extent to which they adhere to cultural prescriptions.
- *Culture is intangible.* Culture is not only about "things," be they products or customs, but, importantly, about meaning. Meanings are not very visible; thus, many aspects of culture must be inferred.[5]
- *Culture is confirmed by others.* To understand a culture, you need to step back and look at it from the outside. This is why some of the most astute observers of a given culture are members of another culture.

CULTURE AND INTERNATIONAL BUSINESS

The importance of culture to international business cannot be overestimated. For instance, culture is a key ingredient in the "liability of foreignness" described earlier as an obstacle to the MNE's success abroad. The impact of culture at the firm level ranges from strategy formulation to FDI and organization design.[6] As the Goodyear case shows, culture

Photo 6.2   Hierarchy is a key feature of Japanese culture.

SOURCE: Jupiterimages.

can influence how strategic moves are presented; however, culture can also impact the decisions themselves. Organization behavior processes such as perception, motivation, and leadership as well as human resource management are also influenced by culture, as are management style, decision making, and negotiations. Not surprisingly, more that 70% of the articles on international organization behavior and international human resource management used the concept of culture.[7] As you will discover throughout this book, the impact of culture is not limited to management, however. Marketing, the management of the supply chain (see Chapter 16), accounting and taxation (see Chapter 15), and virtually all other functions of business are influenced by culture. Culture also plays a key role in international alliances and mergers, corruption, and entrepreneurial behavior (see Chapters 12, 19, and 20).

According to Huntington, the role of culture will not be reduced in the global era; on the contrary,[8]

In this new world the most pervasive, important and dangerous conflicts will not be between social classes, rich and poor, or other economically defined groups, but between people belonging to different cultural entities.

Culture, says Huntington, "is both a divisive and a unifying force." It is a force of cohesion among members but a source of friction between them and others. Culture can also be a source of internal friction, where strict adherents struggle with others whom they see as betraying the cultural heritage. Often, foreign cultural imports such as movies and TV programs are a subject of contention in such disputes (please refer to the Industry Box on cultural industries in this chapter).

Culture Does Not Explain Everything

Although we should not ignore the important role culture plays, we should not commit the opposite error of treating culture as a "residual variable"—namely, as the explanation for anything that is different. Uncertainty of what drives the strategy of a foreign competitor makes it tempting to conclude that culture is behind it. But the strategy could well be the result of other factors, be they economic, political, social, or otherwise. In the 1980s, the ascent of Japan and later that of the "four tigers" of Taiwan, Korea, Hong Kong, and Singapore was attributed by many to Confucian values of frugality and discipline. The bestsellers that drove this explanation forgot to mention that Confucianism also contains elements that can be considered negative for progress, such as support for the status quo and low regard for economic activity. As for the Japanese, many of them overplayed the role of culture in their economic success and as a result failed to make the governance and structural adjustments that could have salvaged Japan from a decade of stagnation.

To avoid the pitfall of treating culture as a residual variable, it is essential to consider the possible impact of other, noncultural environmental variables. The research design in Exhibit 6.1 shows how this can be done.

In addition to comparing Japanese Americans with Anglo-Americans and Japanese managers, Kelley and his associates also compared Japanese, Chinese,

Exhibit 6.1   Research Design for the Isolation of Culture

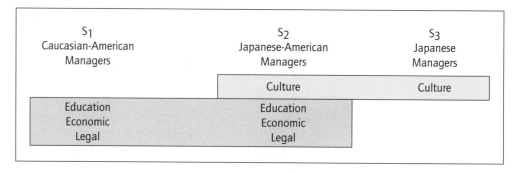

SOURCE: L. Kelley, A. Whately, and R. Worthley. "Assessing the effects of culture on managerial attitudes: A three-culture test." *Journal of International Business Studies*, 1987, *18*, 2: pp. 17–31. Reprinted with permission.

and Mexican managers with their ethnic American counterparts.[9] Shenkar and Ronen compared managerial values in Mainland China, Hong Kong, Taiwan, and Singapore, so as to isolate the role of culture from that of political, economic, and social variables.[10]

CORRELATES OF CULTURE

Culture is correlated with other variables that vary cross-nationally (e.g., language and religion). It is useful to remember, however, that culture often cuts across linguistic and religious boundaries, and that the latter cut across national borders. For example, Switzerland, Belgium, Singapore, Israel, and Nigeria are all countries with multiple official languages. South Korea has a large Christian minority (although this does not necessarily imply that this minority has developed a meaningful subculture), while upward of 8% of French citizens are Moslems. Lebanon has a large Christian minority, while Northern Ireland has both Protestant and Catholic communities.

Language

Webster's Dictionary definition of **language** is "a systematic means of communicating ideas or feelings by the use of conventionalized signs, gestures, marks, or especially articulate vocal sounds." Language is one of the defining expressions of culture. It instills basic socialization themes and determines how values and norms are expressed and communicated. Just as culture is both a unifying and a dividing force, so is language. Exhibit 6. 2 shows the major families of languages and the number of speakers of the most commonly spoken languages.

Because of fundamental differences between languages in structure and in the usage of slang and dialects, language blunders are common. Such mistakes as launching a hair product by the name of "Mist Stick" in Germany, where "mist" is slang for manure, are humorous, but the consequences for the manufacturer may be dire. Coca-Cola was originally translated into Chinese as "bite the wax tadpole," only to be outdone by Pepsi, whose jingle "[Pepsi] comes alive" was translated into "brings your ancestors from their burial place." Name

Exhibit 6.2   Numbers of Speakers of Major Languages of the World (Estimated)

Language Family	Major Language	Number of Speakers (Millions)
Indo-European	English	405
	Spanish	300
	Hindi	300
	Bengali	195
	Russian	205
	Portuguese	165
	German	100
	Punjabi	90
	French	90
	Italian	60
Sino-Tibetan	Chinese	1,160
	Thai	50
	Burmese	35
Japanese–Korean	Japanese	125
	Korean	75
Afro-Asiatic	Arabic	170
Dravidian	Telugu	80
	Tamil	75
Malay–Polynesian	Indonesian	150

SOURCE: From H. J. de Blij and A. B. Murphy. *Human Geography*. New York: John Wiley & Sons, 1999. Reprinted with permission of John Wiley & Sons, Inc.

evaluation, where natives get an opportunity to comment on the proposed product or service name prior to its launch, is a simple way to mitigate the problem.

Differences in grammatical and structural format produce radically different types of discourse between languages. For instance, in contrast to the preference for subject–predicate format in English and other European languages, most Chinese utterances are of the topic-comment type (i.e., the topic precedes the comment). Young's recording of a budget meeting illustrates the point (literal translation from the Chinese original):[11]

Chairman: So by purchasing the new machine, do you think we need to recruit additional workers or our existing workforce will cope with our requirement?

Subordinate: I think that with this new machine, the production time will be shortened or will become more efficient. And the number of staff required, I think we can utilize the existing staff for the time being, and no more new staff is necessary. So that we can solve the problem in recruiting the new staff.

And, again in the following example from the same source:

One thing I would like to ask. Because most of our raw materials are coming from Japan and this year is going up and up and, uh, it's not really

I think an increase in price but, uh, we lose a lot in exchange rate and secondly I understand we've spent a lot of money in TV ads last year. So, in that case I would like to suggest here: Chop half of the budget in TV ads and spend a little money on *Mad* magazine.

Note that the "punch line" does not appear until the last minute, which is typical of Chinese discourse. This is contrary to Western discourse, which tends to start with a preview statement providing tone and direction for the rest of the conversation. Young notes that the main points were often lost on native English speakers listening to these examples. This explains why patience and listening skills are promoted as key negotiation skills with the Chinese. Listening patiently is especially critical because the most important points will come at the end rather than at the beginning of a conversation.

Finally, nonverbal language is an important means of communication that varies across languages and cultures and is more important in some cultures than in others. Variations in the meaning of nonverbal cues may lead to embarrassing gaffes. For instance, the hand gesture used in many Western cultures to implore someone to come over is reserved in Korea for pets—not a good way to leave a positive impression on a Korean executive.

The Emergence of English as "Lingua Franca"

The term **lingua franca** comes from the Franks—people originating in southern France who traded with other people in the Mediterranean who spoke a variety of languages—Arabic, Italian, Greek, Spanish, and Portuguese. The Franks developed a language that was a mixture of the preceding languages and became the language of commerce in the Mediterranean. Today, the term *lingua franca* denotes any knowledge shared by people of different national and linguistic origins.

English has become the business world's lingua franca, the number-one foreign language taught in non-English-speaking countries. Germans and French speakers are more likely to converse with each other in English than they are in each other's language. Only 20% or so of Germans learn French as a foreign language, whereas roughly 60% choose English. This is resented in some countries as "cultural imperialism." France is an example. In 1975, the country banned the use of foreign words in commercials as well as in TV and radio broadcasts. In 1992, the constitution was amended to declare French the official language, and in 1994, the use of foreign words was banned. In 1988, Quebec, a province of Canada with a French majority, enacted a law requiring the use of French in all commercial signs.

The dominance of English does not imply that knowledge of other languages is not necessary. On the contrary, knowledge of foreign languages is often viewed as a distinct advantage. Much has been said of the advantage enjoyed by Europeans, who typically master at least one foreign language. Utah has become attractive to international firms because of the abundance of multilingual residents. Moncton in New Brunswick, Canada, has become the call center of choice in Canada because it enjoys bilingual (English and French) fluency, while Canada's Maritime Provinces attract U.S. firms with the "neutral accent of their residents."[12] However, multilingualism also has its drawbacks. Multilingual states such as Belgium (where Flemish and French are official languages) and Canada are often ripe for tension and conflict. Indeed, there tends to be a correlation between multilingualism and political risk.

While English is a lingua franca, its adoption might have a symbolic and even a strategic meaning. When Korean car manufacturer Daewoo Motor was acquired by General Motors, the Korean executives quickly embarked on the study of English, figuring that it would now be the enterprise's working language.[13] The adoption of English as a working language in an Italian–British joint venture helped the British get the upper hand because it meant adopting their working routines.[14] And English is not the only language vying for international acceptance: Recently, the Chinese government embarked on an effort to expand the study of Chinese as a foreign language, joining France and Germany, among others, who have already established cultural centers around the world devised for, among other roles, spreading their native languages around the globe.

Religion

Religions contain key values and norms that are reflected in their adherents' way of life. The impact of religion extends to the secular segment of the population, albeit to a lesser extent. Globally, Christianity claims the most adherents, while Islam is the fastest growing. De Blij and Murphy term the two together with Buddhism "global religions," whereas religions that dominate a single national culture are termed "cultural religions" (see Exhibit 6.3).

Exhibit 6.3   Adherents to Major World Religions, by Geographic Region, 1996 (in Millions)*

Religion	Americas			Europe	N. Africa/ Sub-Saharan Africa	Southwest Asia	Asia			Russia	Pacific	Totals
	North	Middle	South				South	Southeast	East			
Christianity	208.1	140.8	296.2	409.6	253.1	5.0	24.7	90.5	50.0	110.7	15.3	1,604.0
R. Catholic	94.7	128.6	281.8	255.3	109.1	0.3	5.5	69.7	13.0	4.9	6.9	969.8
Protestant	107.4	12.1	14.2	107.2	114.6	4.3	19.2	20.8	37.0	9.1	7.9	453.8
Orthodox	6.0	0.1	0.2	47.1	29.4	0.4	–	–	–	96.7	0.5	180.4
Islam	6.1	0.2	0.3	13.9	171.9	401.3	327.1	182.6	29.3	3.2	0.2	1,136.1
Sunni	6.0	0.2	0.3	11.9	164.5	260.4	319.4	180.1	29.3	3.2	0.2	975.5
Shiite	0.1	–	–	2.0	7.4	140.9	8.7	2.5	–	–	–	160.6
Hinduism	1.0	0.3	0.4	0.7	1.7	2.3	741.3	5.9	0.3	–	0.4	754.3
Buddhism	0.6	0.1	0.4	0.3	–	0.1	22.5	168.7	151.2	0.9	–	343.9
Chinese religions	0.1	–	0.1	0.1	–	–	0.1	9.1	253.0	–	–	262.5
Sikhism	0.3	–	–	0.2	–	–	20.1	–	–	–	–	20.6
Judaism	7.4	0.2	0.7	2.1	0.1	5.1	–	–	–	2.5	0.1	18.2

SOURCE: From H. J. de Blij and A. B. Murphy. *Human Geography.* New York: John Wiley & Sons, 1999. Reprinted with permission of John Wiley & Sons, Inc.

*Figures from 1996 data.

Religion influences international business in many ways. National institutions (in particular) and business firms try to adopt practices that will satisfy religious decrees without undermining modern business practice. For instance, because bank interest is generally prohibited under Islamic law, banks in Moslem countries issue shares to depositors and charge borrowers fees and commissions to maintain profitability without charging interest. Religion and its associated customs also influence marketing. In China, birthrates tend to rise during the year of the dragon in the Chinese 12-year calendar, creating opportunities for manufacturers of children's clothes and toys. In Moslem countries from Saudi Arabia to Indonesia, believers do not eat during daylight hours during the month of Ramadan, curtailing lunch business at restaurants but creating opportunities for traditional buffet dinners after dark.

Interim Summary

1. Culture plays an important role in international business. Culture affects not only how employees behave and interact but also the strategy that firms and business units employ.

2. Language and religion often create communication and coordination challenges within the MNE, but diversity is also a source of strength because it brings about different and new opinions and ideas from which the firm can benefit.

NATIONAL CULTURAL CLASSIFICATIONS

To international business scholars and practitioners, nation is the most visible layer of culture. This is not to say that culture and nation are synonymous—cultural and national boundaries overlap only partially—but the national unit represents a convenient way of assessing culture together with other environmental sectors such as the economic and the political. The following are the key classifications of national culture.

Hofstede's Dimensions of Culture

By far the most used (and, some would say, abused) work on culture is that of Hofstede, who studied more than 100,000 IBM employees throughout the world.[15] The study, controlling for employee function and level, was also noteworthy for its attempt to correlate its findings with a host of other predictors (e.g., climate). Hofstede's survey yielded four underlying dimensions: power distance, uncertainty avoidance, individualism/collectivism, and masculinity/femininity.

Power Distance

Power distance (PD) is the extent to which hierarchical differences are accepted in society and articulated, for example, in the form of deference to senior echelons. Exhibit 6.4 shows a number of countries that are very high or very low on PD as well as the organizational implications of their position on the construct.

PD should not be confused with the actual distribution of wealth and power in a nation. For instance, Israel is very low on power distance although its income inequality is among the highest in the developed world. In contrast, Japan is relatively egalitarian in terms of wealth and income distribution (although this is changing and some Japanese already describe Japan's "middle-class society" as a myth) yet is relatively high on power distance.

COUNTRY BOX

KOREA: POWER DISTANCE IN THE COCKPIT

A chilling example of the potential influence of power distance comes from descriptions of past crashes of Korean Air's planes: "Did aspects of Korean national culture, such as respect for authority, play a role in the crash by preventing lower-level crew members from challenging the captain's decisions?...South Korean military discipline pervaded many Korean Air cockpits. Even after altitude alarms sounded in their cockpit, the co-pilot and flight engineer on a Korean Air Boeing 747 that eventually crashed, killing 228 people, didn't insist the pilot abort his landing until just six seconds before impact. Discipline can be enforced physically: The report cites an incident in which a captain hit his co-pilot with the back of his hand for making a mistake....A Korean Air official disputed suggestions that the Korean tradition of respecting authority played a role in the crash. But he also announced that the airline had extensively revised pilot training to encourage co-pilots to speak up and offer advice to the captain....The airline now teaches co-pilots to repeat their concern if a captain ignores them...." To correct the recurring problem that at some point led to the suspension of Korean Air from the Skyteam global alliance, the airline has hired outside experts from Western cultures where the problem is less common and who are likely to enjoy a high hierarchical standing based on their experience and expertise. The airline's more recent safety record has been excellent.

The authority problem has not been unique to the South Korean airline. "Veteran pilots and industry experts say the problems described in the Korean Air report can be found in varying degrees at airlines throughout Asia.... Some Asian airlines need to address the hierarchical culture in the cockpit, where no one questions the pilot even if he's making a mistake," said Ross Hamony, manager of the FAA's Asia Pacific flight-standards office in Singapore.

SOURCES: Adapted from "Korean airlines faulted on safety by internal study." *Wall Street Journal*, April 8, 1999; "Korean Air sees no culture link in Guam crash." *International Herald Tribune*, March 27, 1998, A6 (see also November 3, 1999, A6; April 8, 1999, A15); Korean Air Press, Skyteam press releases, and various aviation reports, 2003–2006.

Exhibit 6.4   Power Distance: Country Examples and Organizational Implications

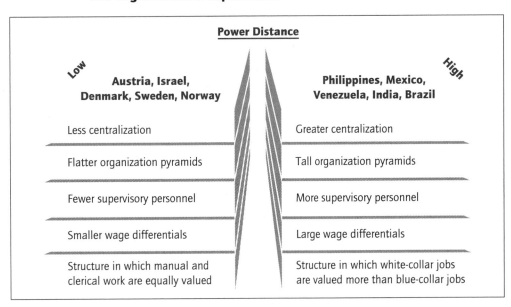

SOURCE: Adapted from G. Hofstede. *Culture's Consequences*. Thousand Oaks, CA: Sage, 1980.

Uncertainty Avoidance

Uncertainty avoidance (UA) refers to the extent to which uncertainty and ambiguity are tolerated. Exhibit 6.5 includes country examples and organizational implications of uncertainty avoidance. Japan's high score on uncertainty avoidance is reflected in the attempt to standardize behavior and rules, as in the following example:

> The design and construction of Japanese parks is highly regulated. The rules cover not only how many trees each park must contain, but how many of them must be small, medium-sized and large, and at what density they should be planted.[16]

Exhibit 6.5   Uncertainty Avoidance: Country Examples and Organizational Implications

Low — Uncertainty Avoidance — High	
Denmark, Sweden, Great Britain, United States, India	**Greece, Portugal, Japan, Peru, France**
Less structuring of activities	More structuring of activities
Fewer written rules	More written rules
More generalists	More specialists
Variability	Standardization
Greater willingness to take risks	Less willingness to take risks
Less ritualistic behavior	More ritualistic behavior

SOURCE: Adapted from G. Hofstede. *Culture's Consequences*. Thousand Oaks, CA: Sage, 1980.

Hofstede believes that uncertainty avoidance is probably the most critical dimension for foreign investment because of its implication for risk taking and investment. MNEs from cultures high on uncertainty avoidance are likely to take a more incremental approach to internationalization. For instance, Japanese car manufacturers such as Nissan lagged behind their European and U.S. counterparts in establishing production facilities in China.

Individualism/Collectivism

Individualism/collectivism (I/C) refers to the extent to which the self or the group constitutes the center point of identification for the individual. To some scholars, this is the most important dimension of culture. High collectivism does not mean that individuals do not seek self-interest. Rather, it means that the pursuit is conducted within acceptable group frameworks with group norms guiding individual behavior and with group harmony being an important endeavor. Gannon et al. distinguish between different types of collectivism—for example, the Chinese family altar and the Israeli kibbutz.[17]

Exhibit 6.6 shows examples of countries high or low on individualism as well as some key organizational implications. Of all the countries surveyed, the United States received the highest score on individualism.

Exhibit 6.6   Individualism/Collectivism: Country Examples and Organizational Implications

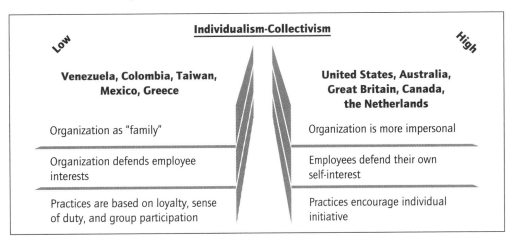

SOURCE: Adapted from G. Hofstede. *Culture's Consequences*. Thousand Oaks, CA: Sage, 1980.

McClelland used children's literature to study national cultures. He assumed that such literature helps us learn about the patterns of acculturation—the process by which the basic values of a culture are instilled in its members. The following illustration, taken from a Chinese children's book, shows how collectivism is weaved into a story:

"What are you looking for, Mom?"

"A sweater for you to take to kindergarten. It may be windy today."

"Two new friends have come to our class . . . They won't know about the wind."

Mom nods and smiles. She puts three sweaters in Qin's satchel.

"Good child," says the teacher. "So little, but you already know about helping others."[18]

MNEs from highly collectivistic cultures—for example, Taiwan's Acer—tend to be more paternalistic. For instance, they are less likely to lay off employees during a downturn. However, such protection does not always extend to overseas subsidiaries.

Masculinity/Femininity

Masculinity/femininity (M/F) describes the extent to which traditional masculine values such as aggressiveness and assertiveness are emphasized. Exhibit 6.7 shows the organizational implications of masculinity ratings. However, there are implications in other domains, such as marketing. De Mooij found that masculinity/femininity explained differences in consumer behavior. For instance,

Exhibit 6.7   Masculinity/Femininity: Country Examples and Organizational Implications

Masculinity-Femininity

Low | *High*

Sweden, Denmark, Thailand, Finland, Yugoslavia	Japan, Austria, Venezuela, Italy, Mexico
Sex roles are minimized	Sex roles are clearly differentiated
Organizations do not interfere with people's private lives	Organizations may interfere to protect their interests
More women in more qualified jobs	Fewer women are in qualified jobs
Soft, intuitive skills are rewarded	Aggression, competition, and justice are rewarded
Social rewards are valued	Work is valued as a central life interest

SOURCE: Adapted from G. Hofstede. *Culture's Consequences*. Thousand Oaks, CA: Sage, 1980.

consumers in feminine European cultures preferred coupé cars in 1990 and hatchbacks in 1996.[19]

MNEs from feministic cultures—for example, carmakers Volvo and Saab (now owned by Ford and General Motors, respectively)—tend to emphasize social rewards and benefits in the workplace that are sometimes viewed as excessive by their parent firms.

Long-Term Orientation

Originally termed **Confucian Dynamism**, this dimension has been renamed **long-term orientation (LTO)** to connote its underlying meaning and business ramifications. The LTO dimension represents such values as thrift and persistence as well as traditional respect of social obligations. In high LTO cultures, organizations are likely to adopt a longer planning horizon, with individuals ready to delay gratification. MNEs that hail from cultures high on LTO are more likely to be willing to defer return on investment for a long time. This tendency, however, has often led to disregard of basic principles of economic return, as in the case of Korean conglomerates prior to the Asian financial crisis. Firms from high LTO cultures may also find it difficult to operate in a way that challenges deeply rooted traditions and practices.

The LTO is *not* one of the original dimensions unveiled in Hofstede's 1980 book. Rather, it is the result of his cooperation with Michael Bond and his associates (known as the Chinese Cultural Connection) who developed the **Chinese Values Survey (CVS)**. The Connection used an innovative technique: A group of Chinese social scientists was asked to name at least 10 "fundamental and basic values for Chinese people." Supplemented by readings of Chinese philosophy and social science, this produced a list of 40 values that made up the survey. The survey was then distributed to students in 22 countries. Country rankings on LTO are shown in Exhibit 6.8.

Exhibit 6.8   Country Scores on Confucian Dynamism (Long-Term Orientation)

Score Rank		Country or Regional Score
1	China	118
2	Hong Kong	96
3	Taiwan	87
4	Japan	80
5	South Korea	75
6	Brazil	65
7	India	61
8	Thailand	56
9	Singapore	48
10	Netherlands	44
11	Bangladesh	40
12	Sweden	33
13	Poland	32
14	Germany	31
15	Australia	31
16	New Zealand	30
17	United States	29
18	Great Britain	25
19	Zimbabwe	25
20	Canada	23
21	Philippines	19
22	Nigeria	16
23	Pakistan	0

SOURCE: Chinese Cultural Connection. "Chinese values and the search for culture-free dimensions of culture." *Journal of Cross-Cultural Psychology,* 18: pp. 143–164. Reprinted with permission.

Criticism of Hofstede

Over the years, Hofstede's work received considerable support. Sondergaard[20] reviewed the empirical studies that used Hofstede's framework and concluded that Hofstede's results were generally confirmed and the dimensions validated. The individualism/collectivism dimension received the broadest support, followed by power distance, then uncertainty avoidance, and lastly masculinity/femininity. Hoppe replicated Hofstede's masculinity/femininity dimension among business elites in 19 countries and obtained a rank order that was strongly correlated with Hofstede's results.[21]

In recent years, however, Hofstede's work has come under growing criticism, with his measures, data, and methodology coming under attack for lacking rigor or for misdirected analysis. For instance, Michael Bond suggested that a proper analysis would not have shown the United States and Japan being on the opposite side of the individualism/collectivism dimension.[22] Exhibit 6.9 lists some of the main criticisms of Hofstede's classification.

Exhibit 6.9   Criticisms of Hofstede

- **A single company's data:** Hofstede's survey was conducted at IBM, an MNE with a strong corporate culture. IBM employees might not be representative of their compatriots in other firms and industries. A counterargument is that the use of single-firm data permits control of corporate culture, allowing for an equivalent intercountry comparison. Also, finding significant national variations in a firm with a strong corporate culture shows the importance of national culture.
- **Time-dependent results:** Hofstede's results are an artifact of the time of data collection and analysis. Data were collected between 1967 and 1973 and analyzed in the late 1970s. Most subsequent studies confirmed the results.
- **Business culture, not values:** A number of scholars argue that the dimensions reflect business culture rather than underlying values. The counterargument is that it is precisely this layer that is of interest to business scholars and practitioners and that business behavior is embedded in broader societal values.
- **Nonexhaustive:** Schwartz argues that Hofstede's dimensions do not cover the entire spectrum of the culture phenomenon. This is true, but the framework is meant to provide a mere blueprint of some of culture's main building blocks. Such dimensions as time and spatial orientation are not included in Hofstede's dimensions.
- **Partial geographic coverage:** Hofstede covered only a portion of the world's countries, possibly missing other dimensions' underlying cultures. But over the years, information has been collected on additional countries.
- **Western bias:** The meaning of items used in Hofstede's instrument might vary from one culture to another and therefore be culturally biased. The work of the Chinese Cultural Connection shows this concern to be partially valid.
- **Attitudinal rather than behavioral measures:** This general criticism of attitudinal classifications of culture objects to the making of inferences from attitude to behavior.
- **Ecological fallacy:** The interpretation of Hofstede's national-level data as if it were about individuals is questioned here. This criticism applies more to the interpretations and uses of Hofstede than to the original framework.

Schwartz's Classification

Originating in psychology, this framework has been used to a limited extent in the business literature but is now becoming more popular. Schwartz arrived at his classification by a conceptualization of values prior to their sampling and measurement. His data are more recent than Hofstede's, having been collected in the 1980s and 1990s. Schwartz has collected data on a fairly large number of countries (including subregions).[23]

Schwartz identifies three polar dimensions of culture, producing the following dimensions:

    I. Embeddedness Versus Autonomy
      (1) Embeddedness (conservatism) implies emphasis on social relationships and tradition.

      (2) Autonomy implies finding meaning in one's own uniqueness and being encouraged to express one's own attributes.

There are two kinds of autonomy:

        (a) Intellectual autonomy—self-direction, creativity
        (b) Affective autonomy—the pursuit of stimulation and hedonism

    II. Hierarchy Versus Egalitarianism
      (3) Hierarchy means legitimacy of hierarchical role and resource allocation.

      (4) Egalitarianism means transcendence of self-interests and promoting others' welfare.

    III. Mastery Versus Harmony
      (5) Mastery implies mastering the social environment via self-assertion (success, ambition).

      (6) Harmony implies being "at peace" with nature and society. Organizations are viewed as part of the broader social system.

Exhibit 6.10   Sample Country Rankings on Schwartz's Dimensions

	Embeddedness	Affective Autonomy	Intellectual Autonomy	Hierarchy
High	Singapore Taiwan Poland Turkey	France Switzerland Germany Denmark	Switzerland France Slovenia Spain	China Thailand Turkey Zimbabwe
Low	Japan United States Brazil China	Turkey Brazil China Hungary	Hong Kong Poland Greece Turkey	Italy Slovenia Denmark Greece

	Egalitarianism	Mastery	Harmony
High	Estonia Mexico Australia Hungary	Hong Kong Switzerland Brazil Spain	Italy Mexico Finland Spain
Low	Thailand China Malaysia Taiwan	Finland Estonia Slovenia France	Israel Malaysia Hong Kong United States

SOURCE: L. Sagiv and S. H. Schwartz. "A new look at national culture: Illustrative applications to role stress and managerial behavior." In N. N. Ashkanasy and M. F. Peterson (eds.), *The Handbook of Organizational Culture and Climate.* Thousand Oaks, CA: Sage, 2000. Reprinted with permission.

Exhibit 6.10 presents some examples of countries that are very high or very low on Schwartz's dimensions. You will notice that there is partial overlap between Schwartz's classification and that of Hofstede. For instance, autonomy in Schwartz's model is close to Hofstede's individualism/collectivism dimension, whereas hierarchy is similar to Hofstede's power distance. Mastery is close to masculinity in that both emphasize goal achievement. Harmony is relatively similar to uncertainty avoidance; Schwartz found positive correlation between them. Egalitarian commitment overlaps with femininity; a positive correlation was found between the two.

The GLOBE Classification

The GLOBE classification was originally devised to measure perceptions and attitudes vis-à-vis organizational leadership but later became a way to broadly conceptualize and measure cross-national differences in culture. Data were collected by a large group of researchers between 1994 and 1997. GLOBE has classified cultures according to their scores on nine cultural dimensions—namely, future orientation, gender equality, assertiveness, humane orientation, in-group collectivism, performance orientation, power distance, institutional collectivisim, and uncertainty avoidance. Here, too, you will note the partial overlap with Hofstede's dimensions. Leadership behavior was classified separately, according to six dimensions—namely, charismatic-value based, team oriented, participative, humane oriented, autonomous, and self-protective.[24] The GLOBE framework has been used in a number of subsequent studies, most often in the "micro" area (i.e., motivation, leadership, and the like).

Trompenaars and Hampden-Turner's Classification

This classification found followers especially in the practitioner community, although it has not been often applied in scholarly studies. The classification consists of seven dimensions largely drawn from previous literature, in particular work by the eminent sociologist Parsons, but validated, according to the authors, by large-scale practitioner surveys.

- *Universalism versus particularism* (rules versus relationships): In universal cultures, rules are assumed to apply in all situations and legal solutions are prominent. Countries high on universalism include the United States, Canada, the United Kingdom, the Netherlands, Germany, and the Scandinavian countries. Cultures high on particularism (e.g., Arab) typically provide more benefits to employees in return for commitment.
- *Communitarianism versus individualism* (the group versus the individual): In individualistic cultures, people see themselves primarily as individuals, whereas in communal cultures they see themselves as members of a group. Countries high on individualism are Israel, Canada, Nigeria, Romania, the United States, the Czech Republic, and Denmark. Countries high on communitarianism are Egypt, Nepal, Mexico, India, and Japan.
- *Neutral versus emotional:* In neutral cultures, interactions are impersonal and objective; in emotional cultures they are laden with emotions. Countries high on neutral expression include Ethiopia, Japan, Poland, and New Zealand; they prefer indirect, nonconfrontational response and emphasize control. Countries high on emotional expression include Kuwait, Egypt, Oman, and Spain; they prefer direct, emotional response and avoid social distance.
- *Diffuse versus specific:* In specific cultures, interaction is confined to a narrow domain and private life is kept separate from work. Countries high on specific involvement—the United States and Germany—allow more outspoken expression and encourage transparency. Countries high on diffuse involvement include Japan, Mexico, and France. Such cultures have no clear separation between different life domains. Response is situational, depending on the person and other circumstances.
- *Achievement versus ascription:* In achievement cultures, status is based on achievement and people are evaluated by performance. In ascriptive cultures, status is bestowed by birth, kinship, and age. Countries high on achievement—the United States and Canada—permit individuals to make commitments in the name of their company and make use of detailed technical data to support their positions. Countries high on ascription—Kuwait and Saudi Arabia—make ample use of titles and show respect for superiors.
- *Attitudes to time:* Countries emphasizing the short term—the United States, Ireland, and Brazil—plan for a shorter time horizon than countries with long time horizon—Portugal and Pakistan. Countries with orientation toward the past—Hong Kong, Israel, and China—emphasize heritage and reputation more than the present or future. Countries with sequential time perception, such as the United States, adhere to planning more than those with synchronic culture, such as Italy and Spain.

- *Attitudes toward the environment:* Countries geared toward controlling the environment—the United States, Israel, and Spain—appreciate control and dominance, whereas countries not geared toward such control—Venezuela, Nepal, and Russia—accept that many life events cannot be controlled.

Trompenaars and Hampden-Turner's classification also bears partial resemblance to Hofstede's model. The long- versus short-term orientation is similar to the fifth dimension (LTO) in Hofstede's model. The communitarianism versus individualism dimension is similar to Hofstede's collectivism versus individualism. There is no equivalent in Hofstede's scheme to the specific/diffuse dimension; however, in individualistic cultures, interpersonal relationships tend to be more specific, whereas in collectivist cultures they tend to be diffuse. Achievement versus ascription has no direct match in Hofstede's model; however, people with achievement orientation are likely to emphasize success and goal attainment, whereas high-power-distance cultures are more likely to contain ascriptive assumptions.

Other Dimensions of Culture

The classifications presented here do not cover all aspects of culture. For instance, Hall distinguishes cultures as being "high context" or "low context." High-context cultures such as Japan do not emphasize verbal communications, tend to require a strong leader, and have a polychromatic perception of time (i.e., they will handle various issues and groups at the same time). In contrast, low-context cultures, such as the United States, have a monochronic time perspective (i.e., they usually attend to various issues sequentially).[25] Thus, it remains difficult if not impossible to capture all aspects of culture via a single lens.

National Culture Clustering

Culture clustering is the grouping of cultures based on their relative similarity. Based on historical and political observations (although not quantitative empirical research), Huntington distinguishes seven civilizations: Sinic, Japanese, Hindu, Islamic, Western, Latin American, and African[26] (see Exhibit 6.11); there, Sinic includes Orthodox, Confucian, and Buddhist civilizations). Huntington's grouping has received considerable attention since September 11, 2001, partly because of the probable clash he sees between Western and Islamic civilizations. Most of the studies mentioned earlier have also produced country clusters, but those, while empirically assisted, have usually been formed on the basis of historical and political assumptions but have not been statistically validated.

The Ronen and Shenkar Clustering

The Ronen and Shenkar classification is based on a statistical synthesis of all earlier clustering studies (see Exhibit 6.12). Please note that the degree of similarity between countries is relative—that is, countries are more similar in their culture to countries that are members of the same cluster than to countries that are found in other clusters. Note also that language, religion, and geography are all correlated with cluster affiliation, albeit to a limited extent. For instance, note that the Anglo cluster includes countries from three continents—namely, North America, Europe, and Australia/New Zealand. It is interesting to note that the 2006 clustering is remarkably similar to clustering published by the authors in

Exhibit 6.11   Huntington's Civilization Clustering

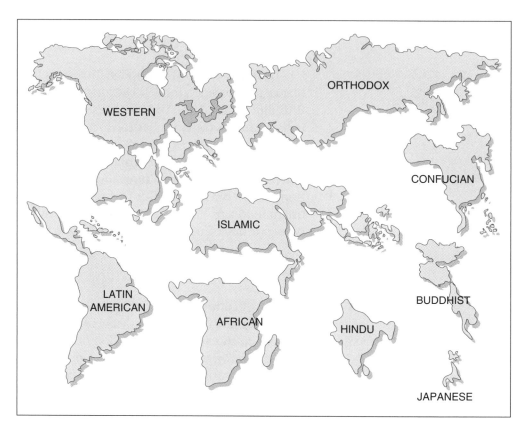

1985, suggesting considerable continuity and stability in culture clustering.[27] Like Hofstede's classification, Ronen and Shenkar's scheme was utilized to predict MNE strategies (e.g., entry mode, as in Chapter 10) and organization design (see Chapter 11).

Measuring Cultural Differences

Researchers and practitioners of international business often face the need to evaluate just how different certain cultures are. For instance, you may want to know whether the difference between the cultures of the United States and the United Kingdom is smaller than the difference between, say, the cultures of the United States and France; this would imply, for instance, that the liability of foreignness of an American company doing business in the UK would be lower than when doing business in France. Currently, this is assessed by a popular index called "**cultural distance**," a measure of the extent to which one culture differs from another. Devised by Kogut and Singh, the index sums up the differences on Hofstede's original four cultural dimensions, producing a number that presumably reflects the extent to which two cultures are different.[28]

The Kogut and Singh index has come under serious criticism in recent years. Hofstede himself suggested that some of his dimensions were more important than others for certain purposes. For instance, as mentioned earlier, he forecasted uncertainty avoidance to be the most important dimension for FDI because it involved different perceptions of risk.[29] Other studies confirmed the variability in

Exhibit 6.12   The Ronen and Shenkar 2006 Clustering

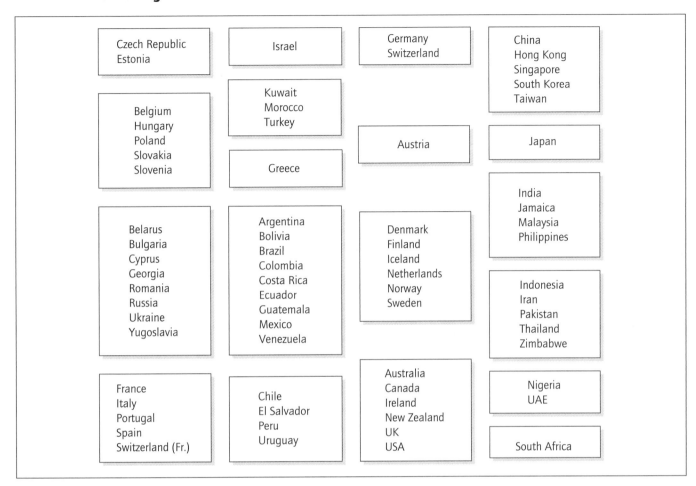

the impact of various dimensions.[30] Trompenaars and Hampden-Turner elaborated on the encounters of different cultures and the problems likely to arise from such encounters.[31] In a more recent paper, Shenkar observed that most of the assumptions underlying the cultural index measure are questionable; for instance, the measure assumes symmetry (meaning, say, a U.S. firm entering France faces the same cultural distance as a French company entering the United States), an assumption that goes against empirical evidence.[32] Besides, he noted that there are various ways in which "cultural distance" can be narrowed. These include international experience (of an individual or a company), socialization ("learning the ropes" of another culture), education, and training.

To improve the measurement of cultural differences, it is highly recommended to use multiple measures (e.g., use both the GLOBE and Schwartz's measure described earlier). To avoid attributing all differences to culture, it is important to control for differences in economic and technological development, among others. It is also advisable to add another measure, "institutional distance," which gauges the difference between the institutional environments of countries, thus going beyond culture in treating the national environments in which firms operate in diverse countries.[33]

Despite measurement issues, cultural differences are an important factor in MNE strategies and foreign investment. Recall, for instance, familiarity theory (discussed in Chapter 3), which suggests that firms incrementally invest in culturally distant locations. Cultural distance also affects entry mode (see Chapter 10) and alliance performance (see Chapter 12), among other things.

Interim Summary

1. There are multiple systems for classifying national cultures, including those by Hofstede, Schwartz, GLOBE, and Trompenaars and Hampden-Turner.

2. The most widely applied, but also the most criticized, framework has been the one produced by Hofstede.

3. Culture clustering enables a comparison of cultures based on their relative similarity.

4. Measuring the difference, or "distance," between national cultures is a complex endeavor, and the usefulness of measurement tools is limited at this point; still, it is essential to understand how different cultures are, as this can influence the liability of foreignness and how firms approach the challenge.

CORPORATE CULTURE

Corporate culture is the culture adopted, developed, and disseminated by a company. It is of vital importance, for instance, for an MNE that adopts a global strategy and uses corporate culture as an integrator of its various units. Corporate culture can deviate from the "national norm." For example, Honda is often described as being different from the "typical" Japanese firm in that it is less immersed in tradition and more open to change. Hofstede points out that corporate culture is more superficial than national culture, because the imprints on the latter alone reside in deeply embedded values. While national culture forms values through early socialization, corporate culture involves the subsequent acquisition of organizational practices and symbols in the firm.

Hofstede and his colleagues who studied corporate cultures in two countries, the Netherlands and Denmark, found differences in values but more considerable differences in practices among the firms they studied. They proposed that national and corporate cultures are distinct—if related—constructs.[34] Laurent proposes that corporate culture can modify (a) behavior and artifacts and (b) beliefs and values, but the deeper level of underlying assumptions is derived from national culture.[35] Laurent found that national differences in beliefs regarding firm practices were considerably greater in a single MNE than in multi-firm samples, leading Schneider to suggest the existence of "a paradox that national culture may play a stronger role in the face of a strong corporate culture. The pressures to conform may create the need to reassert autonomy and identity, creating a national mosaic rather than a melting pot."[36]

Classifications of Corporate Culture

Two of the authors who provided classifications of national cultures did the same for corporate culture. Exhibit 6.13 presents the classifications.

Other Layers of Culture

Ethnicity

Significant ethnic communities exist in many countries. In the United States, Hispanic and various Asian communities have been growing rapidly, creating

Exhibit 6.13   Corporate Culture Classifications

Hofstede et al.:

I. Value dimensions (factors):

Need for security

Work centrality

Need for authority

II. Practices

Process oriented vs. results oriented

Employee oriented vs. job oriented

Parochial vs. professional

Open system vs. closed system

Loose control vs. tight control

Normative vs. pragmatic

SOURCE: G. Hofstede, B. Neuijen, D. D. Ohayv, and G. Sanders. "Measuring organizational cultures: A qualitative and quantitative study across twenty cases." *Administrative Science Quarterly*, 35, 1990, 286–316. Reprinted with permission of *Administrative Science Quarterly*.

Trompenaars and Hampden-Turner:

a. The Family: Personal, hierarchical, power oriented

b. The Eiffel Tower: Specific relations, ascribed status, rational authority

c. The Guided Missile: Egalitarian, impersonal, and task oriented

d. The Incubator: Individual self-fulfillment, personal and egalitarian relations

SOURCE: F. Trompenaars and C. Hampden-Turner. *Riding the Waves of Culture: Understanding Diversity in Global Business.* New York: McGraw-Hill, 1998.

subcultures within the U.S. culture. In Asia, Chinese have long constituted much of the business elite in countries such as Thailand, Malaysia, and Indonesia. Such variations must be recognized by the MNE, as they are likely to affect a myriad of issues, from consumption patterns to employee relations.

Industry

While relatively little researched, industry is clearly an important layer of culture. For instance, the high-tech industry is considered flexible, informal, and innovative. It is also probably the most "global" industry in the sense of people having shared values and (albeit electronic) interaction. Profession also provides an important source of cultural affiliation. Common values and norms shared by, say, marketers across the markets in which the MNE operates can facilitate global integration.

Demographics

Hofstede et al. found that education, age, seniority, and hierarchical level strongly affected differences in values, although not differences in practices.[37] For instance, Ralston et al.[38] found the new generation of Chinese managers to be considerably more individualistic and to adhere less to Confucianism than the previous generation. These subcultures also vary geographically, making the country unit less homogeneous and making the MNE's integration challenge more complex.

Ideology

An important though less stable layer of culture is ideology. In China, for example, Maoist ideology provided many of the beliefs and values in the country from the mid-1950s to the mid-1970s. Ideologies are not always consistent with cultures and can vary through time and across regions.

McClelland, the motivational theorist mentioned earlier in this chapter, studied the strength of achievement, affiliation, and power motivations during different periods and locations in Chinese history: Republican (or Nationalist) China, which existed between 1911 and 1949; Taiwan, which has been ruled by the Nationalist regime since 1949; and Mainland Communist China.[39] (see Exhibit 6.14). The differences could be attributed, among other factors, to changes in the prevailing ideologies—for example, between relatively free-market Taiwan and the Communist Mainland. Ideological as well as political and legal differences between the Chinese Mainland and Taiwan imply that countries with a similar culture may still require the MNE to adopt different operational modes and practices.

Exhibit 6.14   Motive Scores in Chinese Societies

	Republican China	Taiwan	Mainland China
Achievement	.86	1.81	2.24
Affiliation	.38	.43	1.05
Power	1.29	1.00	1.81

SOURCE: D. C. McClelland. "Motivational patterns in Southeast Asia with special reference to the Chinese case." *Social Issues*, 1963, 19: pp. 6–19. Reprinted with permission of Blackwell Publishing, Ltd.

Interim Summary

1. Corporate culture is embedded in national culture but is also notably different. Corporate culture is less deeply imprinted than national culture. Essentially, corporate culture is an add-on to national culture, which overlays the basic cultural patterns.

2. Culture is composed of many layers in addition to corporate culture. These layers, such as ethnicity and demographic backgrounds of employees, are all modifiers of the base culture of the individual.

3. The various layers of culture affect MNE strategy and operations in both the home and host country.

KEY CULTURAL ISSUES

Cultural Etiquette

Each culture has values, beliefs, and norms that distinguish it from other cultures. **Cultural** or **business etiquette** is the set of manners and behavior that are expected in a given situation, be it business negotiations, a supervisor–subordinate discussion of a raise, or activities outside the workplace and after business hours. Violation of business culture is considered more offensive in some cultures, especially those that are high on uncertainty avoidance and that emphasize ritualistic behavior.

Cultural Stereotypes

Our view of other people's culture is a function of our perceptions and stereotypes. To an extent, we are all **ethnocentric**—that is, we look at the world from a perspective shaped by our own culture and upbringing. Ethnocentrism, in turn, shapes our **mental maps**—namely, our perceptions of the world around us and even our perceptions of geographic realities. Note the following interview with a Japanese executive on how his firm made its site location selection in the United States:

> In picking a site . . . companies like Mazda or Nissan look for areas in which the population is relatively well educated, and where there is not a lot of competition for labor. Asked which part of America the Japanese were eyeing now, he replied, "the Northeast."—The Northeast? Where land is expensive and the demand for skilled labor particularly intense? "No, no," he replied, "I mean up around Washington, Oregon, around there . . ." The Northeast, that is, viewed from Tokyo, Beijing, and Seoul.[40]

Although we may not always believe our culture is superior, we use it as an anchor when looking at ourselves as well as when interacting with others. **Stereotypes** are our beliefs about others, their attitudes and behavior. **Auto-stereotypes** are how we see ourselves as a group distinguished from others. The following are auto-stereotypes of U.S. culture, according to Adler and Jelinek:[41]

1. Distrust of others combined with a belief that individual change is possible

2. Man mastering a predictable environment; situations are problems to be resolved

3. The individual above all else—hence, impermanence of relationships

4. Emphasis on doing rather than on being

5. A present to slightly future orientation; immediate gratification but change is constant

According to Graham and Sano, Americans are[42]

Informal—not bound by rules

Materialistic

Nondeterministic

Egalitarian

Individualistic

Achievement/action oriented

Open/direct

Practical/efficient

Litigious

Culturally ignorant/monolingual

Hetero-stereotypes are how we are seen by others. In Exhibit 6.15, Americans are described by Chinese observers. Note that the Chinese tend to notice precisely those elements that are different in their culture. For instance, the "me first" attitude is salient to someone who comes from a collectivistic culture.

Stereotypes are important because they affect how MNE staff at headquarters and in various locations perceive other MNE employees. For instance, if headquarters staff believe that employees in a given country are not self-motivating, they may be reluctant to delegate authority to that subsidiary.

Exhibit 6.15   Americans From A to E

> A. Americans are Westerners.
> B. Busy folks, whether blue- or brown-eyed.
> C. Competition in business.
> D. Dollars are an uncommonly common goal.
> E. Enter and exit human relations quickly.

SOURCE: G. Hofstede, B. Neuijen, D. D. Ohayv and G. Sanders. Measuring organizational cultures: A qualitative and quantitative study across twenty cases. *Administrative Science Quarterly, 35*, 1990, 286–316. Copyright © Johnson Graduate School of Management, Cornell University.

In Exhibit 6.16, a group of U.S. employees protest, using their stereotype of Japanese firms.

Exhibit 6.16   Nikko Hotel Pamphlet

> To: The General Public
> From: Hotel Employees & Restaurant Employees International Union 1216 28th Street N.W. Washington D.C. 30007
>
> Japanese Airlines (JAL) owns the Nikko Hotel in Chicago. The Nikko Hotel signed a neutrality agreement with Hotel Employees and Restaurant Employees Union Local 1, in Chicago.
>
> Essentially, the agreement provided that Nikko Workers would have the right to Join Local 1, if they so choose, without any interference from the company. Moreover, if a majority of the workers joined Local 1, the Nikko would recognize Local 1 as the bargaining agent and would begin negotiating a labor contract.
>
> However, when the workers began signing union cards, the Nikko blatantly broke their word to the Union by doing all it could to discourage the workers from organizing.
>
> We thought the Japanese companies honored their agreements as part of their culture. Apparently, we Americans were wrong.
>
> Please don't patronize JAL or the Nikko Hotel.
>
> *From a leaflet distributed by picketing workers in New York City, August 8, 1988*

SOURCE: Nikko Hotel pamphlet.

Convergence and Divergence

The debate surrounding "convergence" versus "divergence" presents two competing theses: The **convergence hypothesis** assumes that the combination of technology and economics is making countries more alike, and that with global integration of markets and the diffusion of MNC practices, convergence will accelerate.[43] The **divergence hypothesis** assumes that countries will continue to maintain their distinctive characteristics, and that those differences may even be accentuated over time. The case for convergence is often made in terms of the proliferation of "global products" that are widely recognized throughout the world and sold with little or no adaptation; examples are McDonald's and Coca-Cola, though, as you will see in Chapter 16, even those products are tinkered with in different markets. Trompenaars and Hampden-Turner suggest that even "global goods" are subject to cultural variations. This is because these products and services have different meanings to the people in each culture. Nor do global products imply harmony among diverse cultures and civilizations. John Bolton has pointed out in the *Washington Times* that the Kosovo conflict punctured the myth that "no two countries which both have a McDonald's will ever go to war with each other."[44]

INDUSTRY BOX

CULTURAL INDUSTRIES

Cultural industries—movies, radio and television programming, book publishing and distribution, and so forth—are especially susceptible to protectionism in countries that see their culture endangered by a dominant and close neighbor (Canada) or by a dominant language (France; the Canadian province of Quebec). For example, Canada has a heritage minister, whose role is to protect the national heritage of the country and restrict foreign ownership of cultural industries. The Canadian government tried to limit the sale of U.S. magazines without "sufficient" Canadian content, but publishers, who in the past have had their trucks stopped at the border, used new technology to beam the content to their print plants in Canada. Most recently, Canada's supreme court ruled that foreign satellite television signals could not be picked up legally in the country. The French government has been concerned for a long time with the permeation of English terms such as "le weekend" and with the decline in consumption of the famous French baguette. Among other things, the French limit the foreign content of TV broadcasting. Canada and France have worked together to exempt cultural industries from the Multilateral Agreement on Investment. Maude Barlow, chairwoman of the Council of Canadians, called the Agreement "the largest threat to Canadian culture ever."

At the same time, France and Canada (as well as other nations) are working hard to promote exports of their cultural industries, which they see not only as a way to generate export earnings but also as a way to spread their culture and influence abroad. For instance, the Canadian government has established the "Trade Routes" program, which provides market entry support for Canadian cultural industries via a network of advisers in Canada and major foreign markets. Especially targeted are SMEs in crafts, design, film/video, heritage, new media, publishing, sound recording, television/ broadcasting, and the performing arts.

SOURCE: Adapted from M. Heinzl. "Foreign satellite-TV signals barred by Canada's high court." *Wall Street Journal*, April 29, 2002, B5; *Wall Street Journal*, February 4, 1998; R. Tamburri. "Canada considers new stand against American culture." *Wall Street Journal*, February 4, 1998, A18; Canada's Ministry of Cultural Heritage, 9/2006.

There are of course also strong forces for convergence. Those include migration, developments in communications (especially the Internet), transportation, and travel. It is useful to remember, however, that at the end of the 19th century, many countries were doing almost as much trade as a proportion of GDP as they do today, yet cultures remained highly differentiated. According to Huntington, the world is moving toward greater divergence: "Global politics has become multipolar and multicivilizational." Rather than taking over, the West, currently the most powerful civilization, is gradually losing power to non-Western civilizations.[45] The events of September 11, 2001, have focused much attention on that view.

Interim Summary

1. Cultural stereotypes are an important force in international business. For instance, they influence how headquarters and subsidiary staff perceive each other.

2. The issue of convergence versus divergence is vital for firms as they try to forecast the business environments they will face in the future and prepare accordingly.

CHAPTER SUMMARY

1. Culture is a very important force in international business. However, culture does not explain everything, and we should not attribute all differences observed across nations to culture.

2. When interacting with other cultures, individuals and firms use their own culture as an anchor.

3. Language and religion are correlates of culture that also exert direct influence on international business strategies and operations.

4. There are various classifications of national culture, including those of Hofstede, Schwartz, GLOBE, and Trompenaars–Hampden-Turner. Using the Ronen and Shenkar framework, it is possible to cluster countries according to the relative similarity of their cultures.

5. While it is possible to calculate the "cultural distance" among countries, this requires more sophistication than that provided by most current approaches.

6. In addition to the national level, we should be aware of corporate culture as well as of differences in culture by industry, ethnicity, and ideology, among other factors.

7. Key cultural issues include stereotypes (e.g., how we see others) and convergence/divergence.

8. The question of difference between cultures is not as important in an international business context as is the question of what happens when those cultures interact.

9. "Cultural industries" (e.g., media) are typically more sensitive to cultural issues—for example, to criticism of "colonization" by a foreign culture.

Chapter Notes

1. R. S. Bhagat and S. J. McQuaid. "The role of subjective culture in organizations: A review and direction for future research." *Journal of Applied Psychology Monograph*, 1982, *67*, 5: pp. 635–685.

2. S. P. Huntington. *The Clash of Civilizations and the Remaking of World Order*. New York: Simon & Schuster, 1996.

3. G. Hofstede. *Culture's Consequences*. Thousand Oaks, CA: Sage, 1980; F. Trompenaars and C. Hampden-Turner. *Riding the Waves of Culture: Understanding Diversity in Global Business*. New York: McGraw-Hill, 1998.

4. W. Whitely and G. W. England. "Managerial values as a reflection of culture and the process of industrialization." *Academy of Management Journal*, 1977, *20*, 3: pp. 439–453.

5. C. Geertz. "Thick description: Towards an interpretive theory of culture." In *The Interpretation of Culture*. New York: Basic Books, 1973.

6. S. Ronen. *Comparative and Multinational Management*. New York: Wiley, 1986.

7. N. J. Adler and S. Bartholomew. "Academic and professional communities of discourse: Generating knowledge on transnational human resource management." *Journal of International Business Studies*, 1992, *23*, 3: pp. 551–569.

8. P. Huntington. *The Clash of Civilizations and the Remaking of World Order*. New York: Simon & Schuster, 1996.

9. L. Kelley and R. Worthley. "The role of culture in comparative management: A cross-cultural perspective." *Academy of Management Journal*, 1981, *24*, 1: pp. 164–173; L. Kelley, A. Whately, and R. Worthley. "Assessing the effects of culture on managerial attitudes: A three-culture test." *Journal of International Business Studies*, 1987, *18*, 2: pp. 17–31.

10. O. Shenkar and S. Ronen. "Structure and importance of work goals among managers in the People's Republic of China." *Academy of Management Journal*, 1987, *30*, 3: pp. 564–576.

11. L. W. Young. "Inscrutability revisited." In J. J. Gumperz (ed.), *Language and Social Identity.* New York: Cambridge University Press, 1982.

12. M. Greenberg. "Canada answers the call for U.S. firms." *Wall Street Journal,* October 1, 1999, A13.

13. Ki-tae Kim. "Daewoo Motor staff engrossed in English learning." *Korea Times* On-Line, September 29, 2001.

14. J. Salk and O. Shenkar. "Social identities in an international joint venture: An exploratory case study." *Organization Science,* 2001, *12,* 2: pp. 161–178.

15. G. Hofstede. *Culture's Consequences.* Thousand Oaks, CA: Sage, 1980.

16. "A land fit for consumers." *Economist,* November 27, 1999, 16.

17. M. J. Gannon. *Understanding Global Cultures: Metaphorical Journeys Through 28 Countries.* Thousand Oaks, CA: Sage, 2003.

18. S. Wang. *Three Sweaters.* Beijing: Foreign Languages Press, 1976.

19. M. De Mooj. "Masculinity/femininity and consumer behavior." In G. Hofstede, with W. A. Arrindell, *Masculinity and Femininity: The Taboo Dimension of National Cultures.* Thousand Oaks, CA: Sage, 1998.

20. M. Sondergaard. "Hofstede's consequences: A study of reviews, citations and replications." *Organization Studies,* 1994, *15,* 3: pp. 447–456.

21. M. H. Hoppe. "Validating the masculinity/femininity dimension on elites from 19 countries." In G. Hofstede, with W. Arrindell, *Masculinity and Femininity: The Taboo Dimension of National Cultures.* Thousand Oaks, CA: Sage, 1998.

22. M. Bond. "Reclaiming the individual from Hofstede's ecological analysis—A 20-year odyssey: Comment on Oyserman et al." *Psychological Bulletin,* 2002, *128,* 1: pp. 73–77.

23. S. H. Schwartz. "A theory of cultural values and some implications for work." *Applied Psychology: An International Review,* 1999, 48: pp. 23–47.

24. R. J. House and M. Javidan. *Overview of GLOBE.* In R. J. House, R. J. Hanges, P. J. Javidan, P. W. Dorfman, and V. Gupta (eds.), *Leadership, Culture, and Organizations: The GLOBE Study of 62 Societies.* Thousand Oaks, CA: Sage, 2004.

25. T. Hall. *Beyond Culture.* New York: Doubleday, 1976; *The Silent Language.* Greenwich, CT: Fawcett, 1959.

26. S. P. Huntington. *The Clash of Civilizations and the Remaking of World Order.* New York: Simon & Schuster, 1996.

27. S. Ronen and O. Shenkar. "Clustering countries on attitudinal dimensions: A review and synthesis." *Academy of Management Review,* 1985, *10,* 3: pp. 435–454; S. Ronen and O. Shenkar. "The new cultural geography." Keynote address at the 26th International Congress of Applied Psychology, Athens, July 2006.

28. B. Kogut and H. Singh. "The effect of national culture on the choice of entry mode." *Journal of International Business Studies,* 1988, *19,* 3: pp. 411–432.

29. G. Hofstede. "Organizing for cultural diversity."*European Management Journal,* 1989, 7: pp. 390–397.

30. O. Shenkar and Y. Zeira. "Role conflict and role ambiguity of chief executive officers in international joint ventures." *Journal of International Business Studies,* 1992, 23: pp. 55–75.

31. F. Trompenaars and C. Hampden-Turner. *Riding the Waves of Culture: Understanding Diversity in Global Business.* New York: McGraw-Hill, 1998.

32. O. Shenkar. "Cultural distance revisited: Towards a more rigorous conceptualization and measurement of cultural differences." *Journal of International Business Studies,* 2001, *32,* 3: pp. 519–535.

33. T. Kostova. "Country institutional profile: Concept and measurement." *Academy of Management Best Papers Proceedings,* 1997: pp. 180–184.

34. G. Hofstede, B. Neujen, D. D. Ohayv, and G. Sanders. "Measuring organizational cultures: A qualitative and quantitative study across twenty cases." *Administrative Science Quarterly,* 1990, 35: pp. 286–316.

35. A. Laurent. "The cross-cultural puzzle of international human resource management." *Human Resource Management,* 1986, *25,* 1: pp. 91–102.

36. S. Schneider. "National vs. corporate culture: Implications for human resource management." *Human Resource Management,* 1988, *27,* 2: pp. 231–246.

37. G. Hofstede, B. Neujen, D. D. Ohayv, and G. Sanders. "Measuring organizational cultures: A qualitative and quantitative study across twenty cases." *Administrative Science Quarterly,* 1990, 35: pp. 286–316.

38. D. A. Ralston, C. P. Egri, S. Stewart, R. H. Terpstra, and Y. Kaicheng. "Doing business in the 21st century with the new generation of Chinese managers: A study of generational shifts in work values in China." *Journal of International Business Studies,* 1999, *30,* 2: pp. 415–428.

39. D. C. McClelland. "Motivational patterns in Southeast Asia with special reference to the Chinese case." *Social Issues,* 1963. 19: pp. 6–19.

40. *Newsweek,* February 22, 1988: p. 14.

41. N. J. Adler and M. Jelinek. "Is 'organization culture' culture bound?" *Human Resource Management,* 1986, *25,* 1: pp. 73–90.

42. J. L. Graham and Y. Sano. *Smart Bargaining: Doing Business With the Japanese.* Cambridge, MA: Ballinger, 1984.

43. J. T. Dunlop, F. H. Harbison, C. Kerr, and C. A. Myers. *Industrialism and Industrial Man Reconsidered.* Princeton, NJ: Princeton University Press, 1975; K. Ohmae. *The Borderless World.* New York: Harper Row, 1990; F. Mueller. "Social effect, organizational effect, and globalization." *Organization Studies,* 1994, 15: pp. 407–428.

44. Cited in "That thing that won't go away." *Economist,* July 31, 1999: p. 8.

45. S. P. Huntington. *The Clash of Civilizations and the Remaking of World Order.* New York: Simon & Schuster, 1996.

THE POLITICAL AND LEGAL ENVIRONMENT

DO YOU KNOW?

1. How do geopolitical factors and internal politics affect international trade and foreign investment? Can you distinguish between different types of political risk?

2. How can an MNE (multinational enterprise) constructively engage the political organizations and constituencies that most affect its operations and performance?

3. What are the challenges of working in countries whose legal systems are different from that of the MNE's home country?

4. How do different national laws regarding competition, product liability, and the like affect the MNE's operations?

OPENING CASE

Bolivia Nationalizes Natural Gas

Just a few months into his election as president in December 2005, Bolivia's Evo Morales announced that in line with his campaign's promise, he was nationalizing the country's natural gas industry. Declaring that "the time has come" for Bolivia to retake "absolute control" of its natural resources, the Bolivian leader decreed that natural gas becomes the property of the state as soon as it is extracted. The foreign MNEs that previously owned and continue to operate the fields, mainly Brazil's Petrobras and Spain's Repsol, will receive, from now on, 18% of the natural gas the fields produce.

The move by the Bolivian president was not entirely unexpected; prior to his election he had led a rebellion against a $6 billion pipeline project that would have pumped natural gas to Chile, a country hated in Bolivia since their 19th-century war. The nationalization act also mimics earlier moves by Mr. Morales' Venezuelan counterpart, Hugo Chavez, to assert control over his country's oil industry. Mr. Chavez has forced foreign multinationals to accept a minority stake in oil fields they had previously controlled outright while paying higher royalties and taxes to the Venezuelan government. Multinational executives have been worried that the nationalization drive would rapidly expand throughout the region. Just prior to the Bolivian decision, Ecuador enacted a law limiting the profits of foreign crude oil producers, and its newly elected leader suggested he might follow in the footsteps of Venezuela and Bolivia; however, recent close wins by the right in Peru and Mexico have made the prospect of similar measures in those countries more distant.

In the meantime, it remains to be seen whether the steps taken by Bolivia will not come back to haunt a nation that has seen many of its rich minerals disappear for centuries without much to show for it. Analysts express worries that foreign investment will dry up following the recent measures, leading to lower production and less revenue for the state; while the government admitted that the local energy company had neither the expertise nor the capital to take over from foreign MNEs if they decided to pull out completely. Indeed, the fear is that, like Venezuela, which saw a significant decline in oil output once it restricted foreign investment, Bolivia will produce less natural gas in the years ahead.

SOURCE: Adapted from D. Luchnow and J. de Cordoba. "Bolivia's president Morales orders nationalization of natural gas." *Wall Street Journal*, May 2, 2006, A1.

The political and legal environment provides a critical context for the MNE at home and abroad. As the opening case illustrates, political factors, including political risk, are part and parcel of conducting business across national boundaries. Such factors are geopolitical (namely, concerned with the relations among nations and their relative bargaining power in the world) as well as internal (namely, related to domestic constituencies and their position regarding trade, investment, and other international business issues). As the opening case illustrates, these two sets of factors are interrelated—for instance, the ideological affinity between the current leaders is a major reason behind the mimicking of Venezuela's approach to FDI (foreign direct investment) by Bolivia. Historical factors, such as the animosity between Bolivia and Chile, are shown to retain their importance in affecting current affairs more than a century later. The MNE, on its part, must not only respond to the pressures exerted by political factors but also be proactive in anticipating their repercussions, responding to multiple constituencies and continuously reassessing its options in a changing market.

If the political environment identifies key constituencies and determines the sensitivity and vulnerability of MNE operations, the legal environment sets the "rules of the game" as well as the range within which legitimate business activity is conducted. Since, at least in democratic systems, laws are enacted by elected legislative bodies, political processes both determine legal issues and are guided by them. While the MNEs caught up in the Bolivian nationalization have few legal options at present, they may still undertake legal action at some point, especially should they decide to pull out of the country altogether. For instance, they may attempt to seize Bolivian funds held in other countries on the argument that those represent revenues from gas fields for which the MNEs claim ownership.

THE POLITICAL ENVIRONMENT

Political behavior is defined as "the acquisition, development, securing, and use of power in relation to other entities, where power is viewed as the capacity of social actors to overcome the resistance of other actors."[1] While not unique to international operations, the political processes faced by the MNE—compliance, evasion, negotiation, cooperation, coalition building, and cooptation[2]—are more complex and problematic than is typically the case for domestic operations. The number of political constituencies—governments, political parties' interest groups, unions, and public opinion—is multiplied in the international business environment, where the MNE is often viewed as a foreign implant, prompting coalitions of domestic forces to unite against the "foreign invasion." Geopolitics also plays an important role in the international context; for instance, Venezuela's repeated efforts to build a counterweight to U.S. influence in the hemisphere is also behind its encouragement and support for the Bolivian nationalization drive, even though the main companies affected are not American. As part of this effort, Venezuela has been subsidizing oil exports to Cuba and Bolivia and has negotiated deals with Chinese energy companies. Similarly, the U.S. government resists efforts by South Korea to cover exports from its Kaesong special zone in North Korea under the free trade agreement that the two countries have been negotiating.[3]

Political processes are viewed by economists as constraints on the free flow of production factors, intermediary and final goods, that distort supply and demand. Political processes do not represent only constraints, however.[4] Government incentives, preferential subsidies, and other political acts alter the transaction costs of the firm and influence its strategic decisions. For instance, high import tariffs imposed by a government may lead an MNE to launch foreign investment that it would not have otherwise pursued. At other times, a host government may protect a foreign firm by limiting the access of other foreign players into its market. Being politically astute—having superior political intelligence and influence skills[5]—is a key capability for MNEs, many of which have placed "government liaison" executives in senior positions.

The nature of international business activity influences the political constraints and the political agenda. For instance, while importers are typically concerned with achieving such goals as tariff reduction, exporters may seek to reduce limitations on high-technology exportation. Foreign investors, on their part, seek a more favorable investment climate in a host country. Domestic firms utilize political pressure to keep foreign competitors off of their home turf or to create obstacles to their operation. Certain industries are more sensitive to political pressures than others; for instance, industries that are viewed as having a national strategy role, in particular national security, are especially susceptible to political interference, as is the case for firms regarded as "national champions." However, the ability to garner domestic political support by the firm's constituencies (e.g., owners, employees, unions) in the home and host country is not less important in determining the outcome of a political process.

The Institutional Context

The historical landscape of political institutions and relations both between and within countries constitutes a crucial layer of the political environment. Some 40 years after the end of French colonial rule, former colonies in western Africa still import most of their needs from France. Air France enjoys a virtual monopoly on many West African routes that as a result have been very lucrative for the French state-owned airline. In Latin America, Spanish banks dominate foreign investment in the financial industry. In addition to linguistic and cultural affinity, personal relationships, and knowledge of the local market (hence lower "liability of foreignness"), the trade and investment dominance of former colonial powers is the result of political pressure, often in the form of economic aid packages tied to spending in the donor's country. The endurance of political ties is also evident in the "banana war," in which European governments devised a tariff regime to protect former colonies and present allies in Africa and the Caribbean. This triggered a backlash on the part of the United States, whose firms dominate Latin American banana plantations and who is more closely aligned with Latin American nations (see the Opening Case in Chapter 2).

Affinity or **animosity** between nations reflects how closely aligned, or estranged, nations are based on history and political reality, which is an important determinant of international business relations.[6] Nations that share a historical bond and political affinity, such as the United States and the United Kingdom, tend to have high levels of mutual trade and investment. In contrast, trade and investment among hostile countries are often prohibited. U.S. firms are not allowed to invest in Cuba, and Syrian citizens are prohibited from doing business with Israel. Even where trade and investment are not legally banned, animosity can still have a serious effect. Trade and investment flows between Turkey and Greece are much smaller than they would be if not for the historical hostility between the two nations. However, animosity—and trade barriers in general—also creates opportunities for those that act as middlemen between the foes or that have special access to one of the trading partners. Prior to the opening of the Chinese mainland, Hong Kong benefited from its position as gateway to China. Jordan benefits from transferring Israeli goods to and from countries such as Indonesia that do not permit direct trade with Israel.

Political considerations also influence third countries. The U.S. administration successfully lobbied the Israeli government to cancel the sale of airborne aircraft-warning systems to China, threatening to withhold economic aid to Israel if it were to consummate the deal. The pressure reflected geopolitical considerations—the United States feared the equipment could tempt China to mount an attack on Taiwan. Israel argued that the intervention was aimed at protecting U.S. firms from competition and that another foreign supplier would emerge in the event it withdrew from the deal. Israel finally caved in to U.S. pressure and had to face an angry Chinese government that became less enthusiastic about promoting Israeli trade and investment. Trade is also used to influence political outcomes. Such is the effort by some EU members to deny duty-free access to Israeli products made in the territories held by Israel since 1967.[7]

Political relations among nations not only influence trade and investment but are also influenced by them. According to John Bolton of the American Enterprise Institute, the myth that no two countries that both have a McDonald's will go to war with each other has exploded with the Kosovo crisis[8] (and, more recently, with the Israel–Lebanon conflict). Still, a study showed that countries belonging to the same preferential trade agreement (PTA) were 30% to 45% less likely to become involved in military disputes than countries that did not have such agreements. When PTA members did have military disputes, they were less likely to go to war over them. Only 2% of such disputes led to war among signatories of PTA agreements versus 11% for nonsignatories. When not accompanied by a PTA, trade flows did not contribute to reduced hostilities, however.[9]

THE MNE–GOVERNMENT RELATIONSHIP

The relationship with governments in its host and home countries is probably the most important political challenge facing the MNE. Governments affect the economic and legal environment in which the MNE operates—for example, via setting monetary and tax policies; setting price controls; enacting, endorsing, and enforcing intellectual property legislation; and influencing labor relations. Governments are also responsible for trade and investment policies, capital and exchange controls, and transfer-pricing regulations.[10] In some countries, they have a broader role than in a parliamentary democracy.[11] For instance, in Vietnam, the government is a regulator, a competitor, a customer, and a potential partner. With no clear separation of the executive and the judiciary, the Vietnamese government also influences legal procedures and plays the key role in enforcement decisions.

The MNE Relationship With the Host Government

Three models have been used to describe the government–MNE relationship, *sovereignty at bay, dependency,* and *neo-mercantilism.* All three assume a powerful MNE at odds with the government of a weaker, developing nation over market access or broader sovereignty issues. The sovereignty at bay model goes the furthest by viewing the MNE as a threat to the national sovereignty of the host country. The dependency model also sees a cooperative relationship but only between the MNE and its home government.[12]

At the beginning of the 21st century, the nature of the relationship between MNEs and host governments can perhaps be best described as **"coopetition,"** that is, a combination of cooperation and competition. Cooperation reflects mutual accommodation and collaboration, with the government and the MNE seeking joint payoffs and goal accomplishment from their interdependent activities or resources. Competition reflects bargaining or control and related conflicts with the government and the MNE, each seeking private gains at the expense of the other's interests. From a government's viewpoint, increasing pressure for global integration, heightened competition for inbound FDI, decelerated economic growth, and a stronger need for upgrading economic structure all encourage cooperation with MNEs. From an MNE's viewpoint, foreign operations increasingly depend on the educational, technological, industrial, and financial infrastructure built by host governments. Whether a host government provides a stable set of rules for business players to act accordingly and whether the rules can be adapted to changing conditions have become increasingly crucial for firm growth and international expansion. However, despite the liberalization of foreign investment regimes (see Chapter 3), the MNE and the government are often at odds and end up bargaining over control of resources and/or market access.

MNE Political Objectives in the Host Country

Typically, the key political goal of the MNE in the host country is the establishment of a favorable trade and investment environment. This means nondiscrimination—namely, equal (if not preferential) treatment of the foreign firm. Except where it seeks to block the entry of other MNEs, the MNE strives to remove limits on foreign ownership, to open access to local markets (i.e., to face few or no tariff and nontariff barriers), and to have as few regulatory hurdles as possible. In short, it wishes to remove any obstacles that interfere with its freedom to locate, manufacture, and sell where it can deploy its resources most effectively and obtain the highest return. MNEs also wish to reduce mandatory requirements for product or service adaptation, especially where they judge adaptation to be unnecessary in terms of competitive advantage or customer preferences.

Another important goal for the MNE in the host environment is to obtain **legitimacy.** Legitimacy is the acceptance of the MNE as a natural organ in the local environment. It is not transferable across borders,[13] and acceptance in one market may even constitute a liability in another. The MNE will often try to convince political constituencies that it operates as a domestic company, contributes to the local economy, and takes social responsibility seriously. Airbus often buys full-page advertisements in U.S. newspapers to highlight its use of U.S. suppliers, as do Toyota, Honda, and Nissan. When McDonald's opened its first Russian restaurant, children from a local orphanage were invited to head the customer line. In Saipan, part of the Northern Marianas (a U.S. commonwealth), MNEs improved roads and local schools. Research shows that such positive corporate citizenship is a good investment that improves the MNE's bargaining power.[14]

Pressure for good citizenship can also come from outside the host country and is particularly strong when the MNE operates under regimes with poor political records. Canadian oil firm Talisman's operations in Sudan bring the host government revenues are being used to fund a civil war with the southern part of the country. To pacify the critics, Talisman funds community programs in Sudanese villages, builds hospitals, and digs watering ponds for cattle.[15] Similarly, Apple had been criticized for the conditions under which its iPod devices are manufactured in China, although the company argued its review has found only marginal violations of labor standards.

Host Government Objectives

Host governments are primarily interested in protecting national interests, especially where "vital interests" such as national security are concerned. In Venezuela, the dependence on oil as the major foreign exchange earner means considerable government intervention in the form of taxation, government participation in the industry, and the protection of external markets and prices.[16] Host governments have been found to discriminate against MNEs, especially during the later stages of industry competition.[17] Today, when competition for FDI is keen, host government efforts are directed at technology transfer and exports, and there are often instances in which foreign investors receive terms that are more favorable than those of domestic players—for example, a lower tax rate.

Increasingly, local governments are also concerned with protecting their environment from pollution, unsustainable logging, and the like. Host nations, especially (but not only) developing economies, are also concerned with MNE interference with the political process either directly (for example, via lobbying) or by way of introducing foreign values and lifestyles that erode the standing of current political actors and tip the balance. MNEs are often criticized for aligning with elite segments of society that do not necessarily express the interests of the vast majority of the people.

The Bargaining Power of the MNE and the Host Government

When the political objectives of the MNE and the host nation diverge, their relative bargaining power will, to a significant extent, determine the outcome. When a nation offers an attractive environment that is unmatched by other locations, its bargaining power is high, especially when competition among investors is intense.[18] For instance, when the price of oil tripled in world markets, competition for investment in Russia heated up and the government offered less generous terms than initially contemplated. In contrast, some 15 years earlier when investment opportunities emerged in Eastern and Central Europe following the collapse of the Soviet Union, the Chinese government relaxed its investment requirements to remain an attractive investment target. When the country later became the location of choice among emerging markets, it withdrew some of the special incentives. In the end, however, the outcome of the bargaining also depends on the success of the parties in building political coalitions that will enlist support for their cause in both the host and the home country.

The bargaining power of the MNE tends to be greater when it offers a differentiated, technologically advanced product that others cannot or are unwilling to provide but that is vital to the host economy (for instance, it constitutes a nation's major source of foreign currency). Extractive industries usually provide the foreign investor with considerable leverage with both home and host government, but this advantage fast erodes once the investment has been consummated because the investment is by and large irreversible. The MNE also has a stronger bargaining position when the subsidiary is complex to operate and manage, when its volume of exports is large, and when the ratio of expatriates is high.[19]

While "traditional" MNEs operating in developing markets command substantial marketing power vis-à-vis their host governments, developing country MNEs (DMNEs) do not. DMNEs are usually not in a position to pressure host governments for concessions and favorable investment terms, although they can insist on reciprocity in host countries that are substantial investors in their home market. For small and midsize international firms (SMIEs), the probability of pressuring host governments is even lower, although they may build alliances and coalitions that will build such pressure. Some of the liabilities of SMIEs and DMNEs can be seen as advantages, however. Both types of firms are considered less of a menace to national sovereignty than traditional MNEs and are less likely to arouse nationalist sentiments in the host country; as a result, such firms are more likely to be granted access to a market where local sensitivities run high.

Government Investment Support

In an era of keen competition for FDI, governments compete with each other and are willing to bargain with the MNE over the provision of investment incentives. These incentives typically are administered by a designated investment agency whose main roles are to solicit potential investors, weigh project feasibility and contribution to national goals, and assure compliance with investment requirements. Incentives range from outright grants and investment allowances to subsidies for infrastructure development, preferential tax treatment (tax holidays, reduced rates, accelerated depreciation), import duties exemptions, loans and loan guarantees, and interest subsidies.[20] For example, it is estimated that to entice Mercedes-Benz to invest in Alabama, the state offered the automaker $253 million—$169,000 for every job the company promised to create.[21] More recently, Indiana has won out over Ohio as a location for a new Honda plant, among other reasons, by offering a more generous incentive package.

Special support is often provided to MNEs willing to invest in troubled areas, such as Northern Ireland, or in disadvantaged regions, such as the former East Germany, China's western provinces, and inner-city neighborhoods in the United States. Such preferences are permitted under the World Trade Organization (WTO) rules. The WTO also makes sure that foreign MNEs are not discriminated against; however, domestic firms sometimes complain that they are being shortchanged by not being offered the support and incentives available to the foreign investor. To counter, domestic firms build political coalitions to counterbalance incentives granted to foreign firms or decide to invest in their home country via a foreign entity. An example is "bogus blue-eyed" ventures, domestic Chinese firms disguised as foreign investors by registering a Hong Kong entity.

Investment incentives are more likely to be offered when competition among potential sites is intense, when the investment at stake is considered vital, and when a country perceives itself to be at a disadvantage owing to worsening economic conditions or political and social turmoil. Research conducted in the Caribbean shows that the attractiveness of various FDI incentives offered by host governments varies with market orientation and the type, size, and location of the investment; its timing; and the type of product involved. Import duty concessions were seen as the most desirable by exporters in that region because of the high ratio of imported components in the exported product.[22]

The MNE and Its Home Government

Globalization notwithstanding, the MNE remains firmly grounded in its home environment.[23] The state continues to charter and steer the MNE and shape its operating environment and is the only entity to conduct international affairs, including international trade and investment policies. For example, the long-simmering dispute between U.S. aircraft maker Boeing and its European competitor Airbus is arbitrated and negotiated in the WTO on behalf of the governments of the United States and the European Union, respectively. Nor is the government role in international business diminishing. In developed nations, the ratio of government expenditure as percentage of GDP now stands at five times the World War I level. MNEs are engaged in lobbying their home governments in support of their cause, as U.S. MNEs did in the 1990s when they sought to end the trade embargo on Vietnam and lift the restrictions on investment there.

The home government plays an important role in facilitating MNE political objectives. When Saudi Arabia had to choose between buying aircraft from Boeing or Airbus, President Clinton personally called the Saudi king on behalf of Boeing. Years later, China used the occasion of a visit by President Bush to announce a large airplane purchase from Boeing, while ordering Airbus planes on the occasion of a visit by the president of France. Understandably, not every deal is accorded such high-level treatment. The larger the magnitude and visibility and the bigger the perceived threat to a country's MNE, the more likely are political leaders to intervene. The stated rationale for the intervention is usually to protect the national interest and preserve jobs, goals that have broad political appeal at home. In contrast, when

French cheeses were included on the list of U.S. retaliatory measures in the "banana war," the president of the French Cheese Association lamented, "We represent the flower of French gastronomy, but we have no political clout."[24]

While political pressure is often applied in the opening of foreign markets, it can also be exercised to obtain the closure of the home market to foreign competition. In the late 1970s and 1980s, U.S. car manufacturers sought to limit Japanese imports to the United States. The media decried the "buying up of America," suggesting that the United States was becoming a low-tech platform for Japanese firms, which were keeping high-value-added production at home. As a result, the U.S. government was persuaded to set "voluntary" quotas on Japanese car imports. In South Korea, activist groups pressured their government not to open its market to foreign goods, stalling international efforts to open the country's economy.

Coalition Building and Influence Tactics

Nations and governments are not unitary entities but rather collections of individuals, political parties, interest groups, and agencies that negotiate internally as much as externally to define and achieve their agendas. Singapore, Finland, and Ireland are examples of governments with more policy consensus than the United States; Slovenia, the Philippines, and Russia have a much lower policy consensus.[25] In the United States, elite groups are more favorably disposed toward trade, whereas lower income groups tend to support mercantilism.[26] Political interests influence not only the general approach toward trade but also the treatment of specific goods and services. In the aftermath of September 11, the United States abolished tariffs on the importation of cotton yarn from Pakistan and eased restrictions on the importation of bed linen from that country. The U.S. government refused, however, to do the same for textiles, fearful of angering the House Ways and Means chairman, whose congressional district includes a large textile manufacturer.[27] U.S. political activities—constituency building, political action committee contributions, advocacy advertising, lobbying, and coalition building[28]—have all been used at one time or another in the service of international business objectives. For example, dozens of foreign countries have registered lobbyists in the United States representing their interests.

The appointment of executives with political experience and contacts is evidence of the importance of political activities. For example, Boeing appointed Thomas Pickering, former U.S. undersecretary of state for political affairs, as senior vice president for political affairs. To build political goodwill, firms channel investment into regions and industries supported by a political party or an influential constituency. Political contributions are made with a similar purpose, even though they are prohibited or restricted in many nations. Coalition building also involves bringing on board local constituencies, sometimes in the form of alliance partners. For instance, the Italian company Finmeccanica aligned with Boeing in hopes of winning a Pentagon bid for a new cargo aircraft and sought to win points with the U.S. administration by criticizing its European competitor, EADS, for selling planes to Venezuela.[29]

Economic Freedom

A major factor of variation among political environments as they relate to business is economic freedom, or the degree to which the government interferes with free enterprise in a variety of ways, from selecting winners and losers to the ability of firms to engage in various lines of business. Exhibit 7.1 provides the 2006 rankings on economic freedom. Note that first place Hong Kong is not a

INDUSTRY BOX

MANAGING POLITICS IN THE AUTOMOTIVE INDUSTRY

The automotive industry, which includes the manufacturing, service, and sales of vehicles and their component parts, is one of the most important to both developed and developing nations, from the United States and Germany to Thailand and Malaysia. For instance, in China, the automotive industry is classified as a "pillar industry," which means that it gets priority in resource allocation, whether steel or access to low-cost capital. Many other industries are dependent on the automotives in one way or another; for instance, the industry is the largest buyer of research and development.

U.S. automakers, in particular the "big three" (General Motors [GM], Ford, and Chrysler, which is now part of German-based DaimlerChrysler), have been under considerable pressure in their domestic market, where they continue to lose market share, and, to a lesser extent, in some world markets (e.g., the EU). The big three have often sought the help of the U.S. government, which bailed Chrysler out from bankruptcy some 25 years ago, seeking support ranging from import quotas on Japanese cars (in the 1980s) to the establishment of fuel economy standards that were conducive to their interests. They also negotiated with states where their plants are located over various supports and concessions, although foreign car markers, from BMW to Hyundai, seem to achieve more significant concessions. In 2006, the big three again appealed to the U.S. government for help, but this has not been forthcoming.

At the same time, GM and Ford have been successful in some emerging markets, in particular China. GM, which now competes for the number-one spot in that growing market, manufactures Buicks in Shanghai via a joint venture with Shanghai Automotive Industry Corporation (SAIC), which is partially owned by the Shanghai government. GM has sought the help of both the Chinese and U.S. governments in a dispute over the alleged copying of one of its models by a Chinese competitor, which is still outstanding in court.

country but a Special Administrative Region of a nondemocratic country, China, a reminder that economic and political freedom need not go hand in hand.

Political Risk

Political risk is the probability of disruption to an MNE's operations from political forces and events and their correlates. The risk may come from the actions of government, as the opening case illustrates, or from other directions. For instance, with the increasing separatist sentiment in the Aceh province in Indonesia, ExxonMobil's gas field there came under guerrilla attack. Political risk is not only about political stability; it is also about a steady society, a stable economic and regulatory climate, policy continuity, and the likelihood of unforeseen problems for the trader and investor. An arbitrary change in investment conditions (e.g., retroactive change in investment rules) and the undermining of property rights by the court system are also examples of political risk.

Political risk is a problem for foreign traders and investors since they like to have a stable environment in which to plan and operate. Firms undertaking FDI are more vulnerable to political risk since foreign investors commit more resources to the host country and are much more likely to place staff on the ground. Political risk narrows the decision-making span of the foreign investor, in effect transferring power to the host government or other entities. A high political risk ranking, or even the perception of political risk, may lead the MNE to refrain from investing in a country or in a particular region in that country or to seek a high premium to compensate for the extra risk (e.g., in the form of extra incentives). A country does not need to be democratic to rank low on political risk. Nor is political risk the exclusive realm of developing countries. Prospects for the breakup of Canada triggered by Quebec's possible secession

Exhibit 7.1   Index of Economic Freedom (2006)

2006 Index of Economic Freedom

HOME | COUNTRIES | SCORES | DOWNLOADS | PRESS | USER GUDES | FAQs | ABOUT

Countries

Country Rank (Score)

Hong Kong	1 [1.28]		Tajikistan	137 [3.76]
Singapore	2 [1.56]		Yemen	139 [3.84]
Ireland	3 [1.58]		Angola	139 [3.84]
Luxembourg	4 [1.60]		Bangladesh	141 [3.88]
United Kingdom	5 [1.74]		Vietnam	142 [3.89]
Iceland	5 [1.74]		Congo, Republic of	143 [3.90]
Estonia	7 [1.75]		Uzbekistan	144 [3.91]
Denmark	8 [1.78]		Syria	145 [3.93]
Australia	9 [1.84]		Nigeria	146 [4.00]
United States	9 [1.84]		Haiti	147 [4.03]
New Zealand	9 [1.84]		Turkmenistan	148 [4.04]
Finland	12 [1.85]		Laos	149 [4.08]
Canada	12 [1.85]		Cuba	150 [4.10]
Chile	14 [1.88]		Belarus	151 [4.11]
Switzerland	15 [1.89]		Venezuela	152 [4.16]
Cyprus	16 [1.90]		Libya	152 [4.16]
Netherlands	16 [1.90]		Zimbabwe	154 [4.23]
Austria	18 [1.95]		Burma	155 [4.46]
Germany	19 [1.96]		Iran	156 [4.51]
Sweden	19 [1.96]		Korea, North	157 [5.00]

 *The* Heritage Foundation   HERITAE BOOKSTORE   THE WALL STREE JOURNAL

represent a political risk for investors, who may find their investment located in a different political entity than the one they initially targeted for investment.

The events of September 11, 2001, drew attention to the risk of terrorism, which is now becoming a more acute concern for companies. Terrorism not only puts a company's own workforce at risk but also endangers its business prospects. Understandably, some industries are more vulnerable than others; for instance, tourism is much more sensitive than high tech to terrorist attacks, as the cases of Israel and India clearly show. At the same time, firms in countries that are vulnerable to terrorism learn early on how to deal with the phenomenon and are therefore also more open to invest in world regions that are considered risky by other investors.

The Measurement of Political Risk

The inherent problem in the measurement of political risk is that the political landscape is notoriously difficult to forecast. Change may come as a result of election, as in the opening case, but it can also come with a decision by an autocratic ruler, such as Saddam Hussein's invasion of Kuwait. It may be a political misstep; for instance, Credit Suisse First Boston Corp. was removed from a foreign underwriting team for a lucrative share offering in China after company executives hosted conferences attended by senior Taiwanese officials.[30] Political risk can also occur as a result of a shifting power balance. Coca-Cola partnered with the son-in-law of the president of Uzbekistan, who became the president of its local bottling company. When the son-in-law separated from the president's daughter, the company found itself harassed by the authorities, with its operations shut for a period of 18 months.[31] In the opening case, we described how regime change in Latin America has dramatically altered the treatment of FDI in both Bolivia and Venezuela.

The importance of political risk creates demand for its assessment. The various ways to measure the risk can be roughly classified into five categories: (a) qualitative approaches, (b) aggregates of expert opinions, (c) scenario approaches, (d) decision-tree methods, and (e) quantitative techniques that result in political risk indices. Many MNEs use their own customized instruments to gauge political risk; others rely on independent assessments (e.g., by the Economist Intelligence Unit, Business International, and Eurasia).

Exhibit 7.2 shows the risk of political instability according to the *World Competitiveness Yearbook.*

Types of Political Risk

The three types of political risk include ownership risk, operational risk, and transfer risk. **Ownership risk** represents a threat to the current ownership structure or to the ability of the MNE to select or shift to a given governance structure. Its extreme form is outright expropriation—namely, the forced divestment of assets as a result of a host government decision to nationalize or otherwise transfer ownership. Such divestment may or may not carry compensation, but even when it does, this rarely compensates the MNE for actual damages, especially in opportunity cost. Expropriation risk has been traditionally higher in extractive industries such as oil, natural gas, and mining. Milder forms of ownership risk include pressure being applied or a formal change in investment rules that forces firms to reduce their stake (e.g., sharing ownership with the government or a local firm). In the early 1970s, the Indian government established such rules, which resulted in a strategic shift toward unrelated diversification and eventually to the exodus of many foreign MNEs.[32] Ownership risk has lessened in recent years because of competition for investment dollars and because of the development of institutions such as the WTO, which make such

Exhibit 7.2   Risk of Political Instability

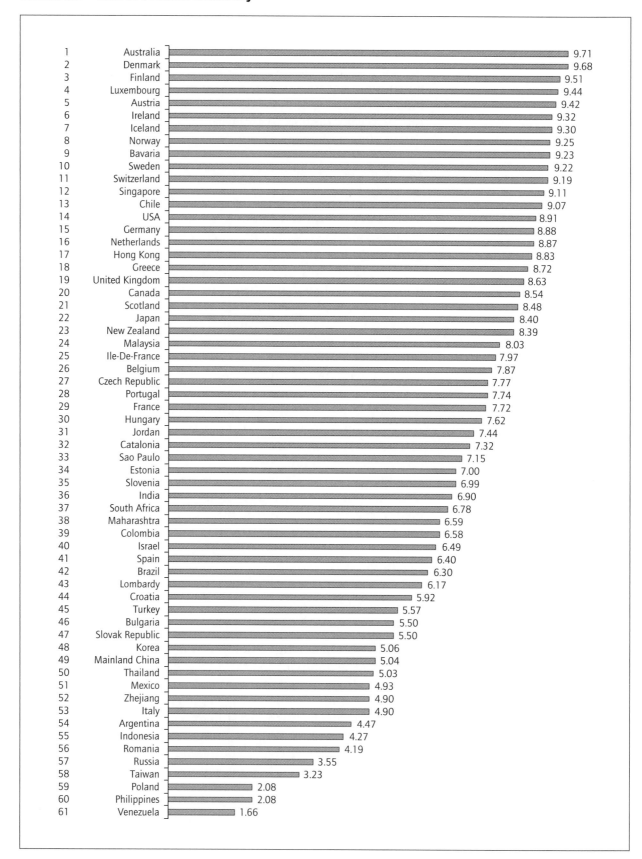

1	Australia	9.71
2	Denmark	9.68
3	Finland	9.51
4	Luxembourg	9.44
5	Austria	9.42
6	Ireland	9.32
7	Iceland	9.30
8	Norway	9.25
9	Bavaria	9.23
10	Sweden	9.22
11	Switzerland	9.19
12	Singapore	9.11
13	Chile	9.07
14	USA	8.91
15	Germany	8.88
16	Netherlands	8.87
17	Hong Kong	8.83
18	Greece	8.72
19	United Kingdom	8.63
20	Canada	8.54
21	Scotland	8.48
22	Japan	8.40
23	New Zealand	8.39
24	Malaysia	8.03
25	Ile-De-France	7.97
26	Belgium	7.87
27	Czech Republic	7.77
28	Portugal	7.74
29	France	7.72
30	Hungary	7.62
31	Jordan	7.44
32	Catalonia	7.32
33	Sao Paulo	7.15
34	Estonia	7.00
35	Slovenia	6.99
36	India	6.90
37	South Africa	6.78
38	Maharashtra	6.59
39	Colombia	6.58
40	Israel	6.49
41	Spain	6.40
42	Brazil	6.30
43	Lombardy	6.17
44	Croatia	5.92
45	Turkey	5.57
46	Bulgaria	5.50
47	Slovak Republic	5.50
48	Korea	5.06
49	Mainland China	5.04
50	Thailand	5.03
51	Mexico	4.93
52	Zhejiang	4.90
53	Italy	4.90
54	Argentina	4.47
55	Indonesia	4.27
56	Romania	4.19
57	Russia	3.55
58	Taiwan	3.23
59	Poland	2.08
60	Philippines	2.08
61	Venezuela	1.66

SOURCE: The International Institute for Management Development (IMD). *The World Competitiveness Yearbook, 2006.* Lausanne, Switzerland:. IMD. Reprinted with permission.

unilateral steps prohibitively difficult. Still, as the opening case shows, owner-ship risk exists and is unlikely to disappear in the foreseeable future.

Operational risk includes any change to the "rules of the game" under which the foreign firm operates (e.g., new and arbitrary taxation), especially when foreign firms are singled out. Operational risk is less tangible than owner-ship risk but may be equally damaging should it limit strategic freedom and autonomy. For example, Amway faced an effort on the part of the Japanese and the Chinese authorities to curb the direct-selling practices that are at the core of its business model. Finally, **transfer risk** involves impediments to the transfer of production factors (e.g., newly imposed capital controls). The three risk types are interrelated. For instance, if a government prohibits the placement of expatri-ates in key positions, this may present an operational risk compromising effi-cient operation and technology protection.

While host governments have been moving away from a confrontational stance to a partnership in which bargaining is focused on the value-added activ-ities of the MNE,[33] the level of risk in many nations remains substantial. Furthermore, owing to increased global integration, problems in one location can adversely influence operations in another: If a strike shuts down your Polish operations, for instance, you may be unable to complete product assembly in the UK. MNE operations in one market can be used as leverage by political groups at home or in third countries. For instance, U.S.-based Apple has been targeted by European protest groups over the employment practices of its Chinese suppliers. Political risk also affects outward investment. Firms and indi-viduals in high political risk nations often seek "safe haven" investment loca-tions such as the United States as a way of protecting capital.[34] This trend is more apparent for portfolio investment than for FDI, because it is much easier to shift capital than to start actual operations in a foreign location.

Finally, as in other facets of business, risk can be associated with opportunities. U.S.-based AES is fueling much of its growth acquiring utilities in global hot spots, many of them in Latin America, where its competitors are reluctant to tread. AES relies on cultivating close relationships with host governments and their leaders, as it did in Venezuela, where it bought the leading utility.[35] A similar strategy has been adopted by Taiwan-based Grace T.H.W. Group when seeking a semiconduc-tor venture in Mainland China, whose investors included the son of then presi-dent Jiang Zemin.[36] Obviously such strategies entail their own risk—for example a change in government that renders a past relationship obsolete (or when a new regime does not look kindly on its predecessor).

Strategies for Managing Political Risk

Despite the decline in expropriation, political risk remains a vital concern for the MNE. The successful MNE is not only educated about political risk but also knows how to proactively manage it. To manage political risk, the MNE can do the following:

- Minimize outright investment, leasing rather than buying and relying on government incentives, where available.
- Sign bilateral or multilateral treaties that protect foreign investment.
- Identify or create reciprocal settings in which investment from the host country can be seized in case of expropriation.
- Avoid high-visibility acquisitions, especially if firms or their key assets are viewed as national icons.
- Reduce capital exposure by utilizing host country financing.
- Accelerate profit repatriation.

- Develop a staggered technology transfer policy.
- Source locally, reducing the host country incentive to harm the foreign firm.
- Opt for strategic alliances with a local partner, reducing the foreign investor outlays and pacifying nationalist sentiment.
- Utilize agencies such as the Overseas Private Investment Corporation (OPIC), which insure companies against political risk.
- Build political support at home and in the host nation through lobbying, public relations, and a proactive social responsibility.
- Monitor political and economic development so as to prepare, avoid, or counter intervention.

Regional-Level Politics

Although the national government is typically the most influential in the political arena, it is not the only one to exert power over incoming foreign investment. Above the state level, regional and federated organizations are partners to the dialogue with the MNE. This is especially apparent where economic integration is accompanied by political integration, as is the case in the European Union (see Chapter 8). Global industry organizations such as the airline association IATA also play a role in this dialogue—for instance, by negotiating industry standards.

Below the national level there are also relevant political entities with whom the MNE interacts. For instance, Hong Kong has its own trade and investment agreements with foreign countries that are separate from those of its national sovereign, China. We have already mentioned the incentives offered by various American states to lure foreign car manufacturers such as Mercedes-Benz, Toyota, Nissan, BMW, and Hyundai. Most American states maintain trade and investment offices in foreign countries and often compete with each other on attracting FDI. In Canada, provincial governments play a substantial role in trade and investment regulation. In China, provincial governments often act as quasi-independent fiefdoms with powers often beyond the reach of the central government. In India, U.S. power producers in Tamil Nadu found out that the state government could not pay for the electricity their multimillion-dollar investment had produced. In Indonesia, Freeport-McMoran Copper & Gold has a land-rights agreement with the Amungme and Kamoro tribes in the West Papua province, which exists side by side with its contract with the Indonesian government.[37] Finally, Nongovernmental Organizations (NGOs) are increasingly involved in dialogue and negotiations with MNEs—for instance, over environmental and employment standards. In the United States, student groups (e.g., at the University of Michigan) have sought to boycott Coca-Cola because of the alleged use of pesticides in its beverages sold in India (something the company has strenuously denied).

Microregion Political Processes

Entities smaller than the state or province (e.g., municipalities) are also part of the political landscape for international business. A conference of mayors from France, Germany, and the United States convened in Lyons, France, to discuss the problems and opportunities stemming from globalization. They concluded that like nations and firms, cities were now in a global competition for investment and skilled employees. According to Alain Juppe, the mayor of Bordeaux and a former French prime minister, "governments are too small to deal with the big problems and too big to deal with the small problems. Cities are now competing with each other to attract people who can choose to live where they wish, but also cooperate and establish alliances with each other."[38]

Interim Summary

1. The political environment for international business includes both geopolitics (country-to-country relations) and internal political processes.

2. The MNE's main political relationship is with the host government, and its bargaining power will vary by location, time, and industry.

3. Among the three types of political risk, ownership risk, including possible nationalization, is more severe than operational and transfer risk.

4. Entities below the state level are important players in the political environment of the MNE.

THE LEGAL ENVIRONMENT

The Institutional Context

History, colonization, migration, and related phenomena combine to define the nature of the legal system used in a country. The United States and other former British colonies such as Australia and New Zealand rely on a **common law** system, which originated in England. Common law is associated with an independent judiciary relying on case precedents. Some U.S. politicians are decrying the use of foreign court precedents by U.S. courts, who are thus basing their decisions "on the fads, the cultural environment, the laws, the constitutions and the biases of foreigners," as argued by Representative Tom Feeney,[39] a reminder that legal systems too are correlated with variations in culture and institutions as well as subject to political processes.

In contrast to the Anglo system of precedents, most of Continental Europe and Latin America use a **civil law** system that originated in the Roman Empire. Civil law relies almost exclusively on the legal code and is applied universally. It is therefore considered less flexible than the common law system. The implications of those differences are substantial. For instance, in common law, ownership rights are affected by actual use and are generally better protected. Common law limits the range of events that justify noncompliance to "acts of God" such as a natural disaster and, generally speaking, is less receptive to government intervention than civil law. An additional type of legal system is **theocratic law**, which relies on religious code. Among the countries using theocratic law are Iran and Saudi Arabia, which rely on Islamic law as the basis of their legal system. Countries such as Indonesia and Malaysia use limited elements of Islamic law (e.g., in family-related matters).

Another fundamental difference between legal systems is the status of the judiciary versus the executive and legislative branches. Even in civil law

Photo 7.1   Legal institutions are a major facet of the national environment.

SOURCE: Jupiterimages.

systems, where the law is administered by public officials, there is a clear separation of powers. In contrast, in China and Vietnam, "rule by man and not by law" has been a longtime tradition, and although these nations have now developed the contours of a modern legal system, much of that tradition lives with the judiciary lacking real independence. A judiciary that lacks independence will often act not on the merits of the case but in accordance with the desire of the political echelon. The Canadian insurer Manufacturers Life Insurance had great difficulty enforcing its ownership rights after its bankrupt Indonesian partner protested the sale of its stake. Furthermore, it was targeted by Indonesian police and was prevented from obtaining effective recourse from the Indonesian justice system[40] (see Country Box). In Ukraine, a small investor in a pharmaceutical factory won a legal battle to recover assets pillaged by his joint-venture partner only to have the ruling overturned following pressure by the country's president, who, in a televised visit to the factory, said the following:

> "I often say . . . we must obey the law. But there is something slightly higher than the law: The country's national interest. And this means the interests of our people, not someone else's."
>
> "This is no longer a legal case, this is a political case," said the exasperated investor.[41]

Judiciary systems that lack independence also tend to have an enforcement problem, meaning that even if a company were to obtain a favorable ruling, there is no certainty that the ruling would actually be acted upon. Plaintiffs in such countries as China, Vietnam, Nigeria, and Russia are often unable to collect won damages or to force a violator of intellectual property rights—say, a Starbuck's look-alike—to cease operations.

COUNTRY BOX

MANUFACTURERS LIFE WEATHERS THE STORM IN INDONESIA

First entering the Indonesian market in 1985, Canadian insurer Manufacturers Life Insurance Company (Manulife) established a joint venture in Indonesia in 1995. By the end of 1999, this largest joint venture in Indonesia accounted for 7% of the life insurance market there, with over 70 branches in more than 30 cities in the country. When its local partner became insolvent, Manulife offered to buy his 40% stake in a bankruptcy auction. During the auction, the local partner presented documentation that a company registered in the British Virgin Islands had already bought the same shares from a western Samoan firm. The judge ruled that the Virgin Islands company had no title to the shares and approved Manulife's bid. This did not resolve Manulife's problems, however. The Indonesian partner launched criminal complaints with the Jakarta police, leading to the arrest of senior executives at Manulife. Although they were never charged, some executives were held in custody for weeks while others received harassing phone calls. In February 2002, the company was cleared of any wrongdoing, and it urged the Indonesian authorities to take action against those responsible for the share scam.

Having weathered the crisis and with Indonesia moving toward democracy and a stable and less corrupt government, the business of Manulife has thrived. In 2005, celebrating two decades of business in the country, Manulife had 950,000 customers served by 5,000 employees and full-time agents from 139 branch offices in 36 cities across the country. It has become the country's top mutual fund firm, second pension provider, and third in life insurance.

SOURCES: Adapted from T. Mapes. "Manufacturers Life learns Indonesian hardball." *Wall Street Journal*, December 11, 2000, A32; company press releases 2000–2006.

Finally, legal environments differ in the tendency to rely on courts as the primary conflict-resolution mechanism. In the United States, which is considered one of the most litigious societies in the world, it is taken for granted that disputes are often settled via the court system. Japan, in contrast, is a "noncontractual" society, relying more on such mechanisms as third-party mediation to resolve conflicts. Unlike in the United States, in Japan a signed contract reflects mostly general understanding that is subject to change should circumstances so demand.

Exhibit 7.3 shows country rankings on the fair administration of justice, based on survey results, according to the *World Competitiveness Yearbook*. At the bottom of the list you will find mostly developing and emerging economies.

Legal Jurisdiction

When a supersonic Concorde crashed outside Paris, victims' families filed suit in the United States because the plane, manufactured in France and the United Kingdom and flown by national carrier Air France with mostly German passengers on board, was bound for New York, and because a Continental Airlines jet was implicated in the investigation. The more generous awards meted out by U.S. courts were an additional incentive to file suit in New York, but it is the nature of the service that provided the opportunity to argue for American jurisdiction in an otherwise French and German affair.

Legal jurisdiction is the legal authority under which a case can be adjudicated. It is often difficult to determine legal jurisdiction in international business. The MNE is subject to the laws of both its home and host countries and, less often, to the laws of a third country. These laws may be in conflict—compliance in one legal jurisdiction could invoke noncompliance or violation in the other. As an example, the 2002 corporate governance law known as the Sarbanes-Oxley Act requires U.S. companies to establish hotlines for potential whistle-blowers; however, doing this in their French subsidiaries will most likely violate French privacy laws.[42] As Chapter 18 illustrates, jurisdictional issues come to the fore even more prominently in electronic trade, where it is especially difficult to determine the origin of manufacturing, distribution, and consumption.

Jurisdictional Levels

At the international level, a firm is subject to international law and to a rapidly internationalizing regulatory system often run by global organizations. The WTO, for one, has become more proactive in deciding matters of jurisdiction and contradictory laws. For instance, it has ruled that a U.S. law denying protection to trademarks held by businesses confiscated in Cuba contradicted WTO trade rules, thereby allowing Pernod Ricard to sue a U.S. firm over the rights to Havana Club rum.[43] A firm may also be subject to the laws and regulations of a regional entity, such as the EU, or of a trade framework such as ASEAN. Generally speaking, the more integrated the region, the more important are the laws enacted at that level (see Chapter 8). Still, the national level, whether of a home or host country, or sometimes a third country, remains the most important and relevant for the MNE.

International Jurisdiction. Because international law relies on customs and treaties but has no government behind it, it is rarely enforced. The International Court of Justice in The Hague (Netherlands) is a UN institution that has no jurisdiction in most cases unless the governments involved agree to submit the

Exhibit 7.3   Fair Administration of Justice

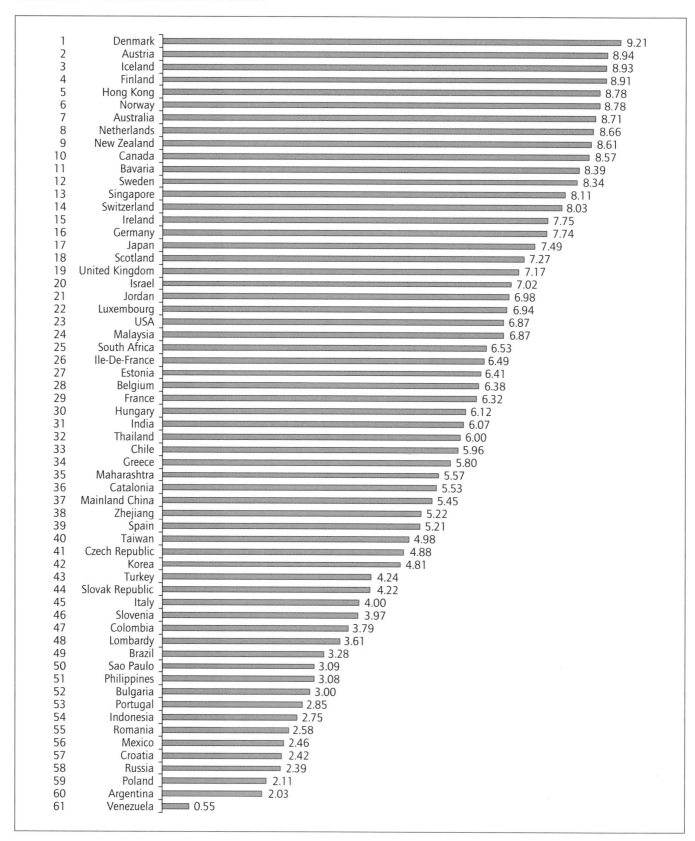

1	Denmark	9.21
2	Austria	8.94
3	Iceland	8.93
4	Finland	8.91
5	Hong Kong	8.78
6	Norway	8.78
7	Australia	8.71
8	Netherlands	8.66
9	New Zealand	8.61
10	Canada	8.57
11	Bavaria	8.39
12	Sweden	8.34
13	Singapore	8.11
14	Switzerland	8.03
15	Ireland	7.75
16	Germany	7.74
17	Japan	7.49
18	Scotland	7.27
19	United Kingdom	7.17
20	Israel	7.02
21	Jordan	6.98
22	Luxembourg	6.94
23	USA	6.87
24	Malaysia	6.87
25	South Africa	6.53
26	Ile-De-France	6.49
27	Estonia	6.41
28	Belgium	6.38
29	France	6.32
30	Hungary	6.12
31	India	6.07
32	Thailand	6.00
33	Chile	5.96
34	Greece	5.80
35	Maharashtra	5.57
36	Catalonia	5.53
37	Mainland China	5.45
38	Zhejiang	5.22
39	Spain	5.21
40	Taiwan	4.98
41	Czech Republic	4.88
42	Korea	4.81
43	Turkey	4.24
44	Slovak Republic	4.22
45	Italy	4.00
46	Slovenia	3.97
47	Colombia	3.79
48	Lombardy	3.61
49	Brazil	3.28
50	Sao Paulo	3.09
51	Philippines	3.08
52	Bulgaria	3.00
53	Portugal	2.85
54	Indonesia	2.75
55	Romania	2.58
56	Mexico	2.46
57	Croatia	2.42
58	Russia	2.39
59	Poland	2.11
60	Argentina	2.03
61	Venezuela	0.55

SOURCE: The International Institute for Management Development (IMD). *The World Competitiveness Yearbook, 2006.* Lausanne, Switzerland:. IMD. Reprinted with permission.

matter to the court (this is beginning to change, however, in regard to war-related violations). Parties to international business contracts often agree in advance to an arbitration authority, such as the International Court of Arbitration, the Inter-American Commercial Arbitration Commission, or the Canadian-American Commercial Arbitration Commission, each specializing in arbitrating between firms from their region and U.S. companies. Parties can also choose a body such as the International Center for Settlement of Investment Disputes, which specializes in FDI.

Recent years saw a rapid globalization in international business regulation, evolving around a number of key principles, chief among them transparency.[44] The United States and the EU have been the most active supporters of the globalization of regulation, while other countries and firms have been active in niche areas. For instance, Lloyd's of London has been a major driving force behind the globalization of marine insurance. International organizations also play a major role in the globalization of regulation. Much of the global regulatory work takes place in technical committees of such organizations as the WTO (see Chapter 8).

In the aircraft and airline industries, the United States has often taken the regulatory lead. National regulators typically await certification by the U.S. Federal Aviation Administration (FAA) before sending in their teams to Boeing's Seattle facilities, largely to rubber-stamp the FAA's decision. Similarly, although inspection orders issued by the FAA are binding only for U.S. carriers and, in some instances, for aircraft flying to the United States, they are often followed by other carriers wishing to uphold safety and sustain their reputations. Similarly, while approval by the Federal Food and Drug Administration is required for any drug sold in the United States, authorities in many other countries require such approval as an indication of product safety and effectiveness.[45]

Regional Jurisdiction. Increasingly, regional bodies are taking responsibility for the enactment and enforcement of laws. At times, considerable uncertainty prevails as to whether regional jurisdiction supersedes national jurisdiction. For example, the European Court of Justice ruled that no EU country could limit trade in a product imported into the EU. In this case, the court found that French rules prohibiting such trade were incompatible with European laws.[46]

National Jurisdiction. While the MNE must comply with domestic jurisdiction at home and foreign jurisdiction abroad, many of its foreign operations fall under domestic jurisdiction as well. One example is the Foreign Corrupt Practices Act, which holds U.S. MNEs responsible for bribery and related activities in their foreign operations (see Chapter 19). Recently, activist groups in the United States resurrected a 1789 law enacted to protect foreigners from sea pirates to prosecute U.S.-based MNEs accused of unethical business practices. In one case, 18 U.S.-based retailers and garment manufacturers were sued on behalf of 50,000 garment workers in Saipan.[47] Such alien-tort precedents may mean that in the future, MNEs will become more vulnerable to suits filed at home concerning their foreign operations.

Legal Issues of Interest to the MNE

Legal issues that are of particular concern to the MNE include the protection of corporate and individual property, contract law (the United Nations Convention on Contracts for the International Sale of Goods sets standards for the formulation and enforcement of contracts among its signatories), and restriction on foreign asset ownership. For instance, the United States does not permit foreign entities to own a majority share in a U.S. airline, in case its aircraft are needed for emergency deployment of American troops. This rule was used to block British Airways' attempt to acquire a controlling stake in US Air, a U.S. carrier. In a related case, the United States ordered an immediate halt to the operations of Discovery Airlines, a Hawaii-based interisland carrier, when it was discovered that the airline owner, while U.S. registered, was a Japanese corporation. Limitations on foreign ownership together with historical and regulatory factors explain why the global airline industry has not consolidated like many other industries (e.g., automotive). Also on national security grounds, the United States does not permit foreigners to own television and radio stations. Rupert Murdoch, an Australian citizen and owner of News Corporation (which operates the Fox television network), overcame the restriction by becoming a naturalized American citizen.

Rule-of-Origin Laws

Knowing **product origin** is important for determining duties or for measuring local content, a frequent requirement in trade and FDI. Local content is an especially important issue in developing economies. For instance, India and China, among others, require substantial local content for cars produced domestically by foreign manufacturers. Determining product origin is increasingly complex, however. The U.S. Federal Trade Commission determined that for a product to be labeled "Made in the USA," it must be "all or virtually all" made in the United States and should contain "no—or negligible—foreign content"; however, it is unclear what "negligible" means. The EU, on its part, uses 60% local value as a threshold.

Competition Laws

Antitrust Legislation and Enforcement

Antitrust and takeovers are one area in which legal provisions vary significantly, even within the EU. Take the case of France Telecom, which recently purchased a 54% stake in Equant NV. Because Equant was incorporated in the Netherlands, France Telecom did not have to make the same or better offer to all shareholders, as it would have to do if the acquired firm were located in the United Kingdom or Germany.[48] U.S. antitrust legislation is among the most advanced and a model emulated by several countries. For example, Japan's antitrust legislation dates back to its occupation by U.S. forces, and its American heritage is evident. In contrast to the United States, however, antitrust laws are seldom enforced in Japan. The United States poses the most stringent transparency requirements and is willing to enforce its authority abroad. For instance, the Securities and Exchange Commission filed a suit alleging fraud on the part of German-based, U.S.-traded E.On for failing to disclose merger intentions.[49] Chrysler's biggest shareholder sued DaimlerChrysler for allegedly concealing its takeover of Chrysler as a "merger of equals." Nevertheless, when asked whether competition laws prevented unfair competition in their country, respondents from Finland, the Netherlands, Germany, and Norway gave their legal systems a better grade than that of the United States, as did respondents in 15 other countries. Indonesia, Argentina, and Russia ranked lowest.[50]

In recent years, the European Commission has become an aggressive enforcer of antitrust legislation. The commission derailed the purchase of a French beverage company by Coca-Cola on the grounds that it would give the Atlanta-based company a monopoly position in the European market. The commission has also investigated Coca-Cola's sales and distribution practices following allegations by its U.S. archrival PepsiCo that Coca-Cola is paying retail outlets to refrain from stocking Pepsi's products. The commission also derailed the acquisition of Honeywell by General Electric, both U.S. companies, arguing that it would lower competition in the European aviation market. The United States has undertaken a major effort to adopt a global approach to antitrust regulation and enforcement. It proposed the establishment of an independent international agency to oversee mergers and acquisitions, whose increasingly global scope involves multiple jurisdictions. The EU endorses the idea but would like to see such an agency operate within the WTO.[51]

Subsidies

EU rules prohibit government subsidies that give an unfair edge to a firm from one country over another. The commission tried (but failed) to prevent the French government from providing a hefty subsidy to Air France, the then-ailing national French carrier. The commission seems less concerned, however, with infringements detrimental to non-EU firms. Boeing contends that Airbus, a European consortium, holds an unfair advantage because it has been receiving subsidies from the German, French, Spanish, and British governments of its partner firms. Airbus counters that the award of military contracts to Boeing by the U.S. government amounts to a subsidy because it permits the company to use research and development and manufacturing techniques developed for the military in their civilian aircraft production. The case is now before the WTO.

Marketing and Distribution Laws

National laws determine allowable practices in distribution, advertising, and promotion. For instance, TV cigarette advertising is prohibited in many countries. Norway does not permit two-for-one promotions. In France, a manufacturer cannot offer a product it does not manufacture as an inducement to buy one of its products. In Germany, comparative advertising (arguing that product A is superior to product B) is prohibited; in China, it is prohibited if the comparison reflects negatively on the other product (e.g., suggesting that the competing product is unsafe). Of special interest to MNEs, especially in the EU, is a ruling by the European court in favor of San Francisco–based Levi Strauss & Co. The court ruled against British retailer Tesco, which imported Levi's jeans from outside the EU, where they are cheaper, and undercut the prices charged by Levi Strauss in the EU (see also Chapter 16).[52] This decision is important to the strategy of MNEs, which often position their brands differently in different locations.

Product Liability Laws

Product liability laws are stringent in the United States and the EU and many other developed countries but are lax or not enforceable in some economies. In Japan, product liability cases are rarely brought to court, partly because it is more difficult to prove negligence. When a case is brought to court outside the United States, restitution rarely includes the punitive damages that are common in the United States and can increase an award manifold. The Bridgestone/Firestone tire controversy revealed just how much the United States and Japan differ on product liability enforcement. Where the United States had 47 people in the National Highway Traffic Safety Administration working on tire issues, Japan had only two, and they lacked authority to investigate and press for recalls.[53]

Since U.S. laws are considered among the most stringent, numerous countries accept U.S. certification of product safety as a substitute for their own, making it easier for U.S. firms to export their products into those markets. Some countries (e.g., Japan) often do not accept U.S. or EU product certification, however, making it necessary for foreign firms to go through costly testing and product adaptation and at times abandon the export idea altogether. At the same time, the lesser rigor and enforcement of product liability legislation in developing-country markets sometimes presents firms with a temptation to sell lower standard products in those markets, an unethical behavior in the case of safety standards, such as the use of fire-retardant material.

Patent Laws

Patent registration is nation based, meaning that a patent issued in the United States does not provide protection from infringement in other countries. Separate patent applications must be made in each country, a costly and time-consuming investment. Most patent systems outside the United States operate on a "first to file" rather than the "first to invent" principle that underlies U.S. patent laws. A **first to invent** system grants patent or trademark protection to the person, or entity, who first invented the technology or the product. A **first to file** principle means that the first to file a patent in a given country is awarded the patent without the need to prove he or she is the inventor. Some countries, notably Japan, require such detailed disclosure as part of the application process that the technology may be compromised. Finally, patents are granted for a limited number of years, which varies from one country to another, providing "arbitrage" opportunities.

Treaties

Treaties are agreements signed by two (bilateral) or more (multilateral) nations. In the United States, treaties require Senate approval, but **executive agreements** do not. A multilateral treaty that is ratified by many countries with a joint interest in the issue at hand is called a **lawmaking treaty.** Some of the international institutions described in Chapters 8, 17, and others, such as the International Labor Office (ILO), have their origins in multilateral treaties. **Treaties of friendship, commerce, and navigation** grant firms from signatory countries rights and privileges enjoyed by domestic businesses. Many of those treaties contain a **most favored nation** clause that entitles the signatory nation to a treatment as favorable as that provided to other countries (see Chapter 8). The UN Convention on the Recognition and Enforcement of Foreign Arbitration Awards facilitates the enforcement of arbitration rulings. When a judgment is issued and not performed, the plaintiff can pursue a court judgment in a foreign or domestic court, although an award by the latter may have little impact unless the company in question has substantial assets in the home country that can be seized.

Two international treaties govern patent protection. The first is the Paris Convention for the Protection of Industrial Property, which has been ratified by many countries but not by some newly industrialized economies that are among the main violators of such rights. The Convention guarantees equal treatment of applicants from member countries. It sets a one-year grace period from the time of application in one country during which the filer enjoys priority in registering patents in other signatory countries. It also prevents automatic expiry of patents in all member countries when a patent has expired in one. The second international treaty governing patent protection is the Patent Cooperation Treaty, which permits a one-stop application for patents in all signatory countries.

Other treaties of importance include those involving the protection of intellectual property rights—for example, the Paris Convention for the Protection of Intellectual Property, the Berne Convention, the Madrid Trademark Convention, the Universal Copyright Convention, and the Geneva Phonograph Convention. The Berne Convention for the Protection of Literary and Artistic Work automatically extends protection of a copyright holder in one signatory country to all others, so that the copyright needs to be registered in only one office of a signatory country. For work done on or after January 1, 1987, protection is typically extended for up to 50 years after the death of the author (and may be extended to 70 years in the future). The Paris Convention for the Protection of Industrial Property recognizes the use of a trademark in one signatory country as a substitute for its use in another signatory country. For instance, because both the United States and Canada are signatories to the Convention, a Canadian firm that has used a trademark in Canada will be granted the use of the same trademark in the United States without having to show prior use of this trademark in the United States. One of the obstacles for a smaller firm, especially one that lacks substantial resources, is that trademark information is often available only in the native language.

Interim Summary

1. Legal systems in different countries vary in their underlying principle (common, civil, or theocratic) as well as in judiciary independence, transparency, and enforcement.

2. The nation remains the most potent level for legal jurisdiction, although regional and international entities have become important in recent years.

3. MNEs study, adapt, and leverage national variations in competition, product liability, marketing, and rule-of-origin laws, among others, to further their competitive advantage.

CHAPTER SUMMARY

1. The political environment in the home and host countries greatly influences international trade and investment.

2. The institutional context is an imprint of history and political relations that represents both a constraint and an advantage for MNE operations in a given market.

3. Managing the relationship with the home and host governments is probably the most important political challenge for the MNE.

4. Political risk is the probability of disruption to MNE operations; however, the MNE has numerous strategies at its disposal with which to mitigate its effects.

5. The type of legal system used in a country— common, civil, or theocratic—determines, for instance, the protections available to an MNE's assets.

6. Jurisdictional issues are more complex in international compared to domestic business. MNEs face conflicting demands from overlapping jurisdictions but can also vary jurisdiction to further their interests.

7. Among the main legal issues in international business are rule of origin, competition, marketing and distribution, product liability, treaties, and patent laws.

Chapter Notes

1. W. G. Astley and P. S. Sachdeva. "Structural sources of interorganizational power: A theoretical synthesis." *Academy of Management Review*, 1984, 9: pp. 104–113.

2. J. J. Boddewyn and T. L. Brewer. "International business political behavior: New theoretical directions." *Academy of Management Review*, 1994, 19: pp. 119–143.

3. G. Hitt. "North Korea complicates trade talks." *Wall Street Journal*, July 10, 2006, A4.

4. J. J. Boddewyn and T. L. Brewer. "International business political behavior: New theoretical directions." *Academy of Management Review*, 1994: pp. 119–143.

5. J. J. Boddewyn. "Political aspects of MNE theory." *Journal of International Business Studies*, Fall 1988: pp. 341–363.

6. S. B. Tallman. "Home country political risk and foreign direct investment in the United States." *Journal of International Business Studies*, Summer 1988.

7. H. Keinon. "Israel fighting EU on duty-free products." *Jerusalem Post Internet Edition*, November 14, 2001.

8. American Enterprise Institute, 2001 press release.

9. E. D. Mansfield, J. C. Pevehouse, and D. H. Bearce. "Preferential trading arrangements and military disputes." *Security Studies*, 9, January 2, 2000.

10. T. L. Brewer. "Government policies, market imperfections, and foreign direct investment." *Journal of International Business Studies*, 1993, 1: pp. 101–120.

11. A. Hillman and G. Keim. "International variation in the business-government interface." *Academy of Management Review*, January 1995.

12. T. L. Brewer. "An issue area approach to the analysis of MNE-government relations." *Journal of International Business Studies*, 1998, 2: pp. 295–309.

13. J. N. Behrman, J. J. Boddewyn, and A. Kapoor. *International Business–Government Communications.* Lexington, MA: Lexington Books, 1975.

14. W. C. Kim. "The effects of competition and corporate social responsiveness on multinational bargaining power." *Strategic Management Journal*, 1988, 9: pp. 289–295.

15. T. Carlisle. "For Canadian firm, an African albatross." *Wall Street Journal*, August 17, 2000, A19.

16. M. V. Makhija. "Government intervention in the Venezuelan petroleum industry: An empirical investigation of political risk." *Journal of International Business Studies*, 1993, 3: pp. 531–555.

17. K. W. Chan. "Industry competition, corporate variables, and host government." *Management International Review*, 1988.

18. W. C. Kim. "Industry competition, corporate variables, and host government intervention in developing nations." *Management International Review*, 1998, *28*, 2.

19. N. Fagre and L. T. Wells. "Bargaining power of multinationals and host governments." *Journal of International Business Studies*, Fall 1982: pp. 9–23; T. A. Poynter. "Government intervention in less developed countries: The experience of multinational companies." *Journal of International Business Studies*, Spring/Summer 1982: pp. 9–25.

20. R. Mudambi. "Multinational investment attraction: Principal-agent considerations." *International Journal of Economics and Business*, February 1999.

21. R. Brooks. "How big incentives won Alabama a piece of the auto industry." *Wall Street Journal*, April 3, 2002, A1.

22. R. J. Rolfe, D. A. Ricks, M. M. Pointer, and M. McCarthy. "Determinants of FDI incentive preferences of MNEs." *Journal of International Business Studies*, 1993, 3: pp. 335–355.

23. P. N. Doremus, W. W. Keller, L. W. Pauly, and S. Reich. *The Myth of the Global Corporation.* Princeton, NJ: Princeton University Press, 1998.

24. G. Winestock. "Why U.S. trade sanctions don't faze Europe." *Wall Street Journal*, September 8, 2000, A15.

25. International Institute of Management Development (IMD). *The World Competitiveness Yearbook, 2000.* Lausanne, Switzerland: IMD.

26. R. K. Herrmann, P. E. Tetlock, and M. N. Diascro. "How Americans think about trade: Combining ideas about politics and economics." Working paper, The Mershon Center, Ohio State University.

27. H. Cooperm and G. Winestock. "Domestic interests limit U.S., EU bargaining at WTO." *Wall Street Journal*, November 12, 2001, A24.

28. G. D. Keim and C. P. Zeithaml. "Corporate political strategy and legislative decision making: A review and contingency approach." *Academy of Management Review*, 1986, *11*, 4: pp. 828–843.

29. J. Karp. "Boeing joins team competing for U.S. military plane contract." *Wall Street Journal*, April 28, 2006, B4.

30. "CSFB pays a steep price for offending Beijing." *Wall Street Journal*, August 31, 2001, A4.

31. S. LeVine and B. McKay. "Coke finds mixing marriage and business is tricky in Tashkent." *Wall Street Journal*, August 21, 2001, A1; E. Alden. "Bottled up: Why Coke stands accused of being too cozy with the Karimovs." *Financial Times*, June 14, 2006, 11.

32. Y. L. Doz. "How MNEs cope with host government intervention." *Harvard Business Review*, March–April 1980: pp. 149–157.

33. J. H. Dunning. "An overview of relations with national governments: New political economy." *Abingdon*, July 1998.

34. S. B. Tallman. "Home country political risk and foreign direct investment in the United States." *Journal of International Business Studies,* Summer 1988.

35. P. Druckerman. "How to project power around the world." *Wall Street Journal,* November 13, 2000, A23.

36. R. Flannery. "Chip plant venture discussed by firms in China, Taiwan." *Wall Street Journal,* August 21, 2000, A13.

37. C. Cummins. "Freeport signs accord with Indonesian tribes." *Wall Street Journal,* August 21, 2000, A10.

38. "Mayors not stopping at city limits." *International Herald Tribune,* April 8–9, 2000, 1.

39. J. Bravin. "Congress may fight court on global front." *Wall Street Journal,* March 21, 2005, A4.

40. T. Mapes. "Manufacturers Life learns Indonesian hardball." *Wall Street Journal,* December 11, 2000, A32; company press releases.

41. T. Warner. "Lessons for foreign investors in Ukraine." *Wall Street Journal,* August 16, 2000, A18.

42. D. Reilly and S. Nassauer. "Tip-line bind: Follow the law in U.S. or EU?" *Wall Street Journal,* September 9, 2005, C1.

43. "WTO panel says U.S. trademark law violates trade rules." *Wall Street Journal,* August 7, 2001, A11.

44. J. Braithwaite and P. Drahos. *Global Business Regulation.* Cambridge, UK: Cambridge University Press, 2000.

45. J. Braithwaite and P. Drahos. *Global Business Regulation.* Cambridge, UK: Cambridge University Press, 2000.

46. "Trade ban fails trademark test." *Financial Times,* March 25, 1997.

47. "Go global, sue local." *Economist,* August 14, 1999: p. 54.

48. A. Raghavan. "Netherlands remains cool to investors' concerns." *Wall Street Journal,* December 22, 2000, C1.

49. V. Fuhrmans. "Foreign firms trading in U.S. get a warning on deception." *Wall Street Journal,* September 29, 2000, A12.

50. International Institute of Management Development (IMD). *The World Competitiveness Yearbook, 2000,* p. 418. Lausanne, Switzerland: IMD.

51. B. Mitchener. "U.S. endorses a global approach to antitrust." *Wall Street Journal,* September 15, 2000, A15.

52. *The Plain Dealer,* November 21, 2001, C1.

53. P. Dvorak and T. Zaun. "To grasp the tire case, pay a visit to Mr. Seki, a very mild regulator." *Wall Street Journal,* September 8, 2000, A1.

PART THREE

Global Markets and Institutions

INTERNATIONAL ECONOMIC INTEGRATION AND INSTITUTIONS

DO YOU KNOW?

1. Why have world markets become more integrated today? How has this integration taken place? Why, for example, did the U.S. government push hard to form NAFTA with Canada and Mexico?

2. What roles do the WTO, the World Bank, and the IMF play in the world economy? Are they "clubs" of rich nations? If not, why did thousands of people in Seattle protest against the WTO meeting?

3. Why do people debate whether regional blocs (e.g., the European Union or MERCOSUR) are compatible with globalization? If you are an export manager in an Australian company, would you like to see the advent of more blocs in other regions?

4. How should MNEs strategically respond to regional integration? Why, for example, have Siemens and Nokia proactively diversified their geographical presence throughout Europe since 1992, while Hitachi and Toshiba have substituted FDI in Europe for export to Europe?

OPENING CASE

3M's Response to European Market Integration

3M, a U.S. supplier of branded industrial and consumer products, derives about one-quarter of its total revenues from its European operations. 3M integrated its

Europe-wide production network in the early 1980s, specializing each plant to manufacture certain products for the entire European market. Even before the European Union was announced, the company had already integrated its upstream activities (e.g., outsourcing, supply base, and inbound logistics) to attain economies of production scale on a regional level. However, its downstream activities—marketing, sales, distribution, and after-sale service—remained fragmented, with local sales forces and advertising geared toward a national, rather than a regional (European), market. By removing many costly barriers to cross-border flows of goods, information, capital, and services (such as advertising and after-sale support), the harmonized market program in Europe makes it possible for 3M to achieve scale economies not just in production but in customer-related activities as well. 3M took advantage of this development by consolidating the company's downstream activities within Europe. The manager of marketing communications at 3M Europe calls the company's new marketing approach "Pan-European communication," in which marketing and selling expenses are spread over a regional customer base, creating economies of scale in advertising and distribution. Part of the strategy involves creating Euro-brands and uniform products and services whose brand image, packaging, attributes, and advertising are standardized throughout Europe. The reason 3M is able to pursue such a strategy is that it sells relatively standardized products. Moreover, many of 3M's products enjoy high brand-name recognition. Substantial competitive advantages can accrue to the market leaders in this type of market segment—through significant economies of scale—after a large share of the market has been captured. 3M is in a position to take advantage of globalizing its operations—selling a single, standardized product to global markets—thereby maximizing profitability through worldwide economies of scale.

INTERNATIONAL ECONOMIC INTEGRATION

The preceding case suggests that MNEs (multinational enterprises) are facing a new landscape in the international market: increasing economic integration among countries. International managers must understand the influence of such integration on their worldwide operations and, more importantly, strategically respond to this integration as 3M did. International economic relations are governed by a variety of institutions and a complex web of principles, most of which have been established by treaties and agreements signed since World War II. These institutions (e.g., the International Monetary Fund and the World Bank), treaties, and agreements (e.g., the General Agreement on Tariffs and Trade, or GATT, and the International Multifiber Arrangement) have helped boost global economic integration and erase barriers to free trade, investment, and services among nations. Meanwhile, many regions or subregions, from Europe and North America to Latin America and the Caribbean, have established harmonized blocs within their respective territories. Intraregional trade and investments significantly increase as a result of reduction or elimination of various trade barriers. While MNEs have to realign international expansion strategies with increasingly integrated environments, they themselves are also a critical force steering international economic integration. MNEs are more committed today to intraorganizational trade and global vertical integration. This intra-MNE activity heightens cross-border and interregional flows of products, services, capital, technology, and human resources. Consequently, the world is entering a new era of economic integration that is simultaneously altering global political and social systems. This integration is characterized by high levels of both globalization and regionalization.

Economic integration is concerned with the removal of trade barriers or impediments between at least two participating nations and the establishment of cooperation and coordination between them. Economic integration helps steer the world toward globalization. As explained in Chapter 1, **globalization** refers to the growing economic interdependencies of countries worldwide through the increasing volume and variety of cross-border transactions in goods and services and of international capital flows, as well as through the rapid and widespread diffusion of technology and information. The following forms of economic integration are often implemented:

1. **Free trade area** involves country combination, where the member nations remove all trade impediments among themselves but retain their freedom concerning their policy making vis-à-vis nonmember countries. The Latin American Free Trade Area (LAFTA) and the North American Free Trade Agreement (NAFTA) are examples of this form.

2. **Customs union** is similar to a free trade area except that member nations must conduct and pursue common external commercial relations such as common tariff policies on imports from nonmember nations. The Central American Common Market (CACM) and the Caribbean Community and Common Market (CARICOM) are examples of this form.

3. **Common market** is a particular customs union that allows not only free trade of products and services but also free mobility of production factors (capital, labor, technology) across national member borders. The Southern Common Market Treaty (MERCOSUR) is an example of this form.

4. **Economic union** is a particular common market that involves unification of monetary and fiscal policies. Participants introduce a central

authority to exercise control over these matters so that member nations virtually become an enlarged single "country" in an economic sense.

5. **Political union** requires the participating nations to become literally one nation in both an economic and a political sense. This union involves the establishment of a common parliament and other political institutions.

Along the above list, the degree of economic integration increases sequentially. One form may shift to another over time if all the participating nations agree. For example, the European Union, or EU, started as a common market and shifted over the years to an economic union and now to a partial political union (e.g., citizens vote for both national and European parliaments).

The above forms reflect economic integration between or among nations within a region. Global economic integration also occurs through **multilateral cooperation** in which participating nations are bound by rules, principles, or responsibilities stipulated by common agreement. Unlike the preceding five forms that all lead to regional economic integration, multilateral agreements are largely used to promote worldwide economic exchanges. They may be designed to govern general trade, service, and investments (e.g., the World Trade Organization); capital flows and financial market stability (e.g., the World Bank and the International Monetary Fund); or specific areas of trade such as dealings in particular commodities (e.g., the International Coffee Agreement).

Economic integration has the potential to generate economic gains for participating nations. Efficiency in production may be enhanced by increased specialization in accordance with the law of comparative advantage.[1] The increased size of the market improves economies of scale, which in turn elevates production levels. Further, the collective bargaining power of member nations is increased vis-à-vis nonparticipating nations. This power may lead to better terms of trade—that is, lower prices on imports from the nonparticipating countries and higher prices on products exported to those countries.[2] It should be noted, however, that these gains are not guaranteed, nor will each member country benefit equally from integration. The unification of monetary and fiscal policies, for instance, may exert a different impact on participating countries that experience different macroeconomic conditions and varying levels of economic growth. Free mobility of production factors such as labor and capital may create different pressures on employment levels, inflation rates, income distribution, or trade balance for nations that are in different economic stages or have a varying dependence on the goods and services of other nations. Although there are legitimate reasons for possible economic gains from integration, integration in and of itself is not a panacea for all economic ills.

International economic integration is propelled by three levels of cooperation: *global, regional,* and *commodity.* Global-level cooperation occurs mainly through international economic agreements or organizations (e.g., the WTO); regional-level cooperation proceeds through common markets or unions (e.g., NAFTA); and commodity-level cooperation proceeds through multilateral commodity cartels or agreements (e.g., OPEC). To international managers, it is important not only to understand how economic integration impacts their international expansion but, more important, to realign their resources and strategies to cope with increasingly borderless regions. Exhibit 8.1 lists these issues, which are described in detail in the following sections.

Exhibit 8.1   Forces Stimulating International Economic Integration

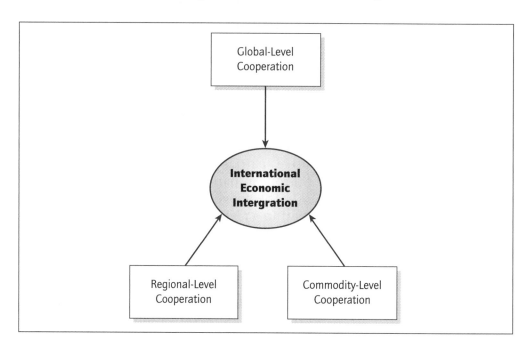

Interim Summary

1. World markets are more integrated today because of (a) the formation of regional blocs such as the European Union and NAFTA; (b) the contribution of international economic organizations such as the WTO, the IMF, and the World Bank; and (c) increased intraorganizational investments, trade, and production undertaken by MNEs.

2. International economic integration takes several forms, including free trade area, customs union, common market, economic union, political union, and multilateral cooperation. Economic integration occurs at three levels: global, regional, and commodity.

3. Economic integration is likely to generate economic gains for participating nations. However, these gains are not necessarily equally distributed to all participating nations, nor will every individual or organization within a participating nation be equally impacted by integration.

GLOBAL-LEVEL COOPERATION AMONG NATIONS

The **World Trade Organization (WTO)**, the World Bank, and the International Monetary Fund (IMF) are the three fundamental institutions affecting the global-level cooperation of nations. While the World Bank and IMF serve as the institutional foundation of the international monetary and financial system, the WTO represents the institutional foundation of the international trade system.

The World Trade Organization (WTO)

Background and Structure

The WTO is a multilateral trade organization aimed at international trade liberalization. It came into being on January 1, 1995, as the successor to the

Exhibit 8.2   Multilateral Negotiations Under GATT/WTO

Round	Year	No. of Members	Average Tariff Cut (%)
Geneva Round	1947	23	35
Annecy Round	1949	13	na
Torguay Round	1950–51	38	25
Geneva Round	1955–56	26	na
Dillon Round	1961–62	45	na
Kennedy Round	1963–67	62	35
Tokyo Round	1973–79	99	33
Uruguay Round	1986–94	117	36
Doha Round	2001–	149	na

General Agreement on Tariffs and Trade (GATT), which was established in the wake of World War II. GATT was the result of the first round of tariff negotiations at the 1947 Geneva conference on the proposed International Trade Organization (ITO). GATT evolved through periodic rounds of multilateral negotiations on tariff cuts and nontariff reductions. Exhibit 8.2 summarizes these negotiations.

Prior to the Kennedy Round, early negotiations dealt primarily with reducing tariffs. These tariff cuts facilitated postwar trade liberalization, pushing average trade growth to 8.1% per year. By the end of the Tokyo Round in 1979, the need to confront the increasing use of nontariff barriers, particularly by developed countries, led to the adoption of a number of codes dealing with specific practices. The Uruguay Round sought to broaden the scope of GATT and reintroduced the idea of a comprehensive international trade organization to coordinate international economic activities including those involving a large number of developing countries. The Uruguay round led to the WTO's creation.

Taking effect in 1995, the Uruguay Round agreement specified several liberalization measures that affected the opportunities and threats for international companies. First, members agreed to slash domestic agricultural price supports by 20% and export subsidies by 36%. These subsidy reductions have benefited major food exporters such as Australia, Canada, New Zealand, Thailand, and the United States. Second, the Uruguay Round instituted several principles concerning trade in services. For instance, one principle held that government controls on services trade should be administered in a nondiscriminatory manner. Third, the Uruguay Round agreement substantially strengthened the protection of intellectual property rights, which include patents, copyrights, trademarks, brand names, and expertise.

Negotiations continued after the end of the Uruguay Round. In February 1997, agreement was reached on telecommunications services, with 69 governments agreeing to wide-ranging liberalization measures that went beyond the agreements reached in the Uruguay Round. Also in this year, 40 governments successfully concluded negotiations for tariff-free trade in information technology products, and 70 members concluded a financial services deal covering more than 95% of trade in banking, insurance, securities, and financial information. From 2000 on, new talks started on agriculture and services. These were incorporated into a broader agenda launched at the fourth WTO Ministerial Conference in Doha, Qatar, in

November 2001. The Doha Development Agenda (DDA) adds negotiations and other work on nonagricultural tariffs, trade and environment, WTO rules such as antidumping and subsidies, investment, competition policy, trade facilitation, transparency in government procurement, intellectual property, and a range of issues raised by developing countries as difficulties they face in implementing the present WTO agreements. Owing to the lack of progress, the General Council decided to suspend the Doha negotiations at its meetings in July 2006 and May 2007, and a new deadline to conclude the negotiations has not yet been reached.

As successor to GATT, the WTO's main objective is the establishment of trade policy rules that help international trade expand and raise living standards. These rules foster nondiscrimination, transparency, and predictability in the conduct of trade policy. The WTO pursues these objectives through the following measures:

- Administering trade agreements
- Acting as a forum for trade negotiations
- Settling trade disputes
- Reviewing national trade policies
- Assisting developing countries on trade policy issues, through technical assistance and training programs
- Cooperating with other international organizations

The WTO had 150 members as of July 2007, accounting for about 95% of world trade. About 30 applicants are negotiating to become members. Russia is not yet a member of the WTO. In November 2001, China's membership was officially approved, ending 15 years of marathon negotiations with WTO members (most notably the United States). As required by the WTO, China slashed import tariffs to 8% from 21% and reduced subsidies for farmers and state-owned enterprises (see the Country Box for more details). Decisions on admission into the WTO are made by the entire membership, not by the WTO itself.

The WTO's top-level decision-making body is the Ministerial Conference, which meets at least once every two years. In the intervals between sessions, the highest-level WTO decision-making body is the General Council, where member nations are usually represented by ambassadors or the heads of delegations. The General Council also meets as the Trade Policy Review Body and the Dispute Settlement Body. Reporting to the General Council are the Goods Council, Services Council, and Trade-Related Aspects of Intellectual Property Council. In addition, numerous specialized working groups or committees deal with individual agreements and other important areas such as the environment, development, membership applications, regional trade agreements, trade and investment, trade and competition policy, and transparency in government procurement. Electronic commerce is also being studied by various councils and committees.

Functions and Measures

In addition to reduction in import duties, which is the dominant function of the WTO, the organization has several other functions. The first function is the *elimination of discrimination*. The two main principles designed to eliminate discrimination are the *most-favored-nation* treatment and the *national treatment*. The **most-favored-nation (MFN) treatment** means that any advantage, favor, or privilege granted to one country must be extended to all other member countries. For example, if Canada reduces its tariff on imports of German cars to

20%, it must cut its tariffs on cars imported from all other member nations to 20%. The **national treatment** means that once they have cleared customs, foreign goods in a member country should be treated the same as domestic goods.

Several exceptions to the MFN principle should be noted. First, the WTO allows members to establish bilateral or regional *customs unions* or free trade areas. For example, following China's admission into the WTO, the Association of Southeast Asian Nations (ASEAN) and China embarked on a plan to form the world's largest free trade area (1.7 billion in population) within a decade. Members in such unions or areas may enjoy more preferential treatment than those outside the group. Second, the WTO allows members to *lower tariffs to developing countries* without lowering them to developed countries. For example, the United States offers such treatment to developing countries (they must be WTO members) through what is called the *Generalized System of Preferences (GSP)*. Because of this system, U.S. companies that are more vulnerable to import competition from developing countries face greater pressure on cost reduction. If a developing country is not a WTO member, it cannot enjoy such preferences. The third exception is the *escape clauses* permitted by the WTO. **Escape clauses** are special allowances permitted by the WTO to safeguard infant industries or nourish economic growth for newly admitted developing countries. These countries may (a) withdraw or modify concessions on customs duties if this is required for the establishment of a new industry that will improve standards of living; (b) restrict imports to keep the balance of payments in equilibrium and to obtain the necessary exchange for the purchase of goods for the implementation of development plans; and (c) grant governmental assistance if this appears necessary to promote the establishment of enterprises. The purpose of escape clauses is to help developing-country members safeguard their economies. The term *safeguard* is used to denote government actions in response to imports that are believed to cause serious "harm" to the importing country's economic or domestic competing industries.

The second function of the WTO is to *combat various forms of protection and trade barriers*. In addition to the reduction of import duties, as shown in Exhibit 8.2, the WTO is devoted to the elimination of quantitative restrictions (i.e., quotas) maintained for agricultural products or for balancing foreign exchange reserves by a member government. Quantitative restrictions are also levied on industrial products by slapping an antidumping duty on them. **Dumping** is the sale of imported goods either at prices below what a company charges in its home market or at prices below cost. Other forms of protection include import deposit without interest, customs valuation, excise duties, subsidies, and countervailing duty (see Chapter 2 for more details). The Uruguay Round was particularly effective in combating nontariff barriers. The WTO's Trade Policy Review Body regularly monitors the trade policies of its members. These efforts significantly enhance the degree of market access to members' markets.

The third function of the WTO is to *provide a forum for dealing with various emerging issues* concerning the world trade system such as intellectual property, the environment, economic development, regional agreements, unfair trade practices, government procurement, and special sectors such as agriculture, telecommunications, financial services, and maritime service. Many new rules have been derived from such forum discussions. For example, the Trade-Related Intellectual Property Agreement (TRIP) brings new discipline to the protection of patents, copyrights, trade secrets, and similar intellectual property components.

Finally, the WTO functions as a *united dispute-settlement system for members* through its Dispute Settlement Body (DSB), consisting of representatives from every WTO member. The DSB has the sole authority to establish dispute-settlement panels for cases, to adopt panel reports, to monitor the implementation of its rulings, and to authorize suspension of rights if its rulings are not acted upon by the member(s) in a timely fashion. Since the WTO's obligations extend only to member governments, nonmembers may not take advantage of the WTO and are not subject to its requirements. In this regard, the WTO's judicial reach differs from that of the International Court of Justice, in which nonmembers of the United Nations may be parties as applicant, respondent, and perhaps intervenor. For example, the DSB established a panel to examine the European Union's complaint against Section 304 of the U.S. Trade Act of 1994. Section 304 is often used by the United States to redress trade policies not covered by the WTO. The EU claimed that Section 304 violates WTO principles because it allows the U.S. Trade Representative Office to unilaterally decide whether another WTO member has violated WTO rules *before* the DSB has ruled on the matter.

The WTO, and its predecessor, GATT, have been viewed as the "club of rich nations" by some developing countries. While beneficial to world trade as a whole, benefits depend in large part on the bargaining power of a member nation or a group of nations. Developing countries often believe they are victims of unfair trade policies and practices adopted by rich nations. Developing countries have long been asking affluent nations to honor commitments to open more markets or to remove unfair treatments. At the WTO's ministerial meeting in Doha, the capital of Qatar, in November 2001, several developing countries, such as Malaysia and India, voiced the opinion that rich nations have no right to call for a new round of talks until they have honored past commitments.

COUNTRY BOX

CHINA JOINS THE WTO

China, one of the 23 original contracting parties of GATT, has rejoined the world trade forum. It signed the accession agreement at the WTO's fourth Ministerial Meeting in Doha on November 10, 2001. This accession process took 15 long and difficult years, beginning with its application in July 1986. The road was so arduous that some people even called the WTO the "World Torture Organization" for the process that applicants must go through.

Because China is the world's largest consumer market and fastest growing economy, its entry is viewed with both optimism and caution. Since 1978, the Chinese economy has registered a growth rate of 10% annually and doubled its per capita income every 10 years. This record has not been matched by any other country. Under the WTO, MNEs will enjoy nondiscriminatory treatment. Barriers to imports will fall. China will limit its domestic subsidies on agriculture to 8.5% of the aggregate value of farm output. Import duties on cars will fall drastically to 25%. Foreign investors will also be allowed to enter China's infrastructure sector (e.g., railways). Foreign banks can handle both foreign exchange and Chinese yuan (RMB) transactions for Chinese companies and individuals. China will also open other service industries such as telecommunications, insurance, and tourism. MNEs have already made their move. South Korea's LG group launched a new joint venture with Changhong Electronics in a bid to become China's leading manufacturer of household appliances. Nissan initiated a new partnership with Dongfeng Automobile in an effort to make China its largest manufacturing and export base.

It remains to be seen, however, whether China will honor all its obligations. China has a long history of according priority to its own national interests. It is also a leading international competitor in labor-intensive products. Current members of the WTO are obligated to phase out quantitative restrictions against Chinese goods in accordance with a mutually agreed-upon timetable. Above all, China's accession provides a new impetus for worldwide trade and investment growth.

The International Monetary Fund (IMF)

The IMF and the World Bank together are often called the Bretton Woods Institutions, because they were both established at Bretton Woods, New Hampshire, in July 1944. The overall objectives of the IMF are to promote international monetary cooperation and expansion of international trade and to reduce the disequilibrium in members' balances of payments. To accomplish these goals, the IMF seeks to promote exchange stability, maintain orderly exchange arrangements, avoid competitive exchange depreciation, and provide confidence to member states by placing the general resources of the Fund at the disposal of nations facing an economic crisis, subject to adequate safeguards. As the key institution in the international monetary system, the IMF was established to render temporary assistance to member countries trying to defend their currencies against cyclical, seasonal, or random fluctuations. It also assists countries having structural trade problems if they take adequate steps to correct their problems. If persistent deficits occur, however, the IMF cannot save a country from eventual devaluation.

The IMF is headed by a board of governors, composed of representatives from all member countries (185 as of July 2007). To facilitate the exchange of goods, services, and capital, and to provide conditions necessary for financial and economic stability, the IMF requires all members to collaborate with the Fund in promoting a stable system of exchange rates. Each member should avoid manipulating exchange rates for the purpose of preventing effective balance-of-payments adjustments or as an attempt to gain an unfair competitive advantage. Although members may apply the exchange arrangements of their choice, they must follow exchange policies compatible with these undertakings. While the financing role played by the IMF has diminished for industrial countries, this role remains significant for the vast majority of developing countries.

The world community has been increasingly using the IMF as an important forum for multilateral surveillance and coordination of national fiscal and monetary policies. Developing countries have a particularly strong stake in this process: It is only in a multilateral forum that major countries' policies are likely to be coordinated in a manner that accords due weight to the impact and implications of these policies on the rest of the world community.

The growing integration of the world's money and capital markets and the inevitable increased role of private capital can at times greatly complicate the task of orderly economic management, particularly in developing countries with limited policy instruments at their disposal. As demonstrated by the Asian financial crisis, one has to take particular note of the volatility and unpredictability of portfolio capital flows. The world needs credible international safety nets, while preserving the freedom of capital markets, to protect the integrity of national development programs in the face of sudden outflows of private capital. In a rapidly changing and uncertain world, the IMF has already begun, and should continue, to develop greater flexibility to respond purposefully and quickly to constantly changing economic conditions.

To carry out the tasks of monitoring the international monetary system and supplementing foreign exchange reserves, the IMF created the **special drawing right (SDR).** As an international reserve asset, SDR serves as a unit of account for the IMF and other international and regional organizations and is also the base against which some countries peg the rate of exchange for their currencies. Defined initially in terms of a fixed quantity of gold, the SDR was later the weighted value of currencies of the five IMF members that had the largest exports of goods and services: U.S. dollar (39%), German mark (21%), Japanese yen (18%), French franc (11%), and British pound sterling (11%).

SDRs are not circulated internationally. Individual countries hold SDRs in the form of deposits in the IMF. These holdings are part of each country's international monetary reserves, along with each country's official holdings of gold, foreign exchange, and reserve position at the IMF. Members may settle transactions among themselves by transferring SDRs.

The World Bank Group

The World Bank refers to the International Bank for Reconstruction and Development (IBRD). The World Bank, together with its three affiliates, the International Development Association (IDA), the International Finance Corporation (IFC), and the Multilateral Investment Guarantee Agency (MIGA), are sometimes referred to as the **World Bank Group.** The common objective of these institutions is to help raise standards of living in developing countries by channeling financial resources to them from developed countries.

Established in 1945, the World Bank is owned by the governments of 185 countries (as of July 2007). Its capital is funded from the subscription of its member countries. The World Bank finances its lending operations primarily through its own borrowing in the world capital markets. A substantial contribution to the World Bank's capital resource also comes from its retained earnings and the flow of repayments on its loans. World Bank loans generally have a grace period of five years and are repayable over 15 to 20 years. Loans are geared toward developing countries that are in relatively more advanced stages of economic and social growth. The interest rates on these loans are calculated based on the cost of their borrowing, which makes them lower than market interest rates.

The World Bank's charter spells out basic rules that govern its operations. It must lend only for productive purposes and must stimulate economic growth in the recipient developing countries. It must pay due regard to the prospects of repayment. Each loan is made to a government or must be guaranteed by the government concerned. The use of loans cannot be restricted to purchases in any particular member country.

While the World Bank has traditionally financed all kinds of capital infrastructure (such as roads and railways, telecommunications, and port and power facilities), the centerpiece of its development strategy emphasizes investment that can directly affect the well-being of the masses of impoverished people in developing countries by making them more productive and by integrating them as active partners in the development process.

The IDA, established in 1960, concentrates on assisting the least-developed nations. The terms of IDA credits, which are traditionally made only to governments, are 10-year grace periods, 35- or 40-year maturities, and no interest. The IFC was established in 1956 for the purpose of assisting the economic development of developing countries by promoting growth in the private sector of their economies and helping to mobilize domestic and foreign capital for this purpose. Finally, the MIGA established in 1988, specializes in encouraging equity investment and other direct investment flows to the developing countries through the mitigation of noncommercial investment barriers. To carry out this mandate, the MIGA offers investors guarantees against noncommercial risks, advises developing-country governments on the design and implementation of policies concerning foreign investments, and sponsors a dialogue between the international business community and host governments on investment issues.

Since the late 1990s, cooperation between the WTO, the IMF, and the World Bank has increased significantly. This includes participation at meetings, information sharing, contacts at staff level, and the creation of a High Level Working Group on Coherence that oversees the process and prepares an annual joint statement on coherence. In 1998, the WTO secretariat cooperated with the staff of the IMF and the World Bank to assist developing countries in stimulating their foreign trade and their participation in the multilateral trading system. Such cooperation was also addressed in a joint statement by the director-general of the WTO, the managing director of the IMF, and the president of the World Bank, which was issued at the time of the Seattle Ministerial Conference. The Joint Statement calls upon ministers to make substantial progress on all three fronts, noting that such efforts represent the essence of adopting a more coherent approach to global economic policy making.

Other International Economic Organizations

The Organization for Economic Cooperation and Development (OECD)

The Organization for Economic Cooperation and Development (OECD), established in December 1960, replaced the former OEEC (the Organization for European Economic Cooperation) and includes non-European countries such as the United States, Canada, Japan, Australia, New Zealand, and Mexico. The OECD consists of 30 member countries (as of July 2007) that share a commitment to democratic government and the market economy. With active relationships with some 70 other countries, nongovernmental organizations, and civil society, it has a global reach. Its mission is to aid in the achievement of the highest and soundest possible growth in economies of member countries and also of nonmember states. Its emphases are placed on economic development, employment expansion, living standard improvement, financial stability, and extension of world trade on a multilateral and nondiscriminatory basis. Best known for its publications and its statistics, its work covers economic and social issues from macroeconomics to trade, education, development, and science and innovation. The Council is the highest authority in the OECD. In the past, the OECD has made efforts to lower barriers to the exchange of goods, services, and capital; stabilize financial fluctuations that may endanger economies of members or those of other countries; and promote scientific research and vocational training. The OECD, however, does not have specific provisions on the liberalization of goods, invisible transactions, and capital. Thus, the OECD has not made many concrete decisions, although it has issued many publications on international business. Coordination of economic policies of all developed countries became the principal aim of the OECD after the European Union was formed.

The United Nations Conference on Trade and Development (UNCTAD)

Prior to the first United Nations Conference on Trade and Development (UNCTAD), held in Geneva in June 1964, most international economic organizations concerned the economic interests of the developed countries. UNCTAD is in many ways a forum for an examination of economic problems plaguing developing countries as well as for formulating, negotiating, and implementing measures to improve the development process for these countries. This forum is essential to achieve the demand for "a new international economic order" involving more trade and capital concessions on the part of developed countries, which have generally benefited more from global trade and investment. Specifically, developing countries hope to solve three problems via UNCTAD:

1. Their share in world trade is decreasing and their terms of trade with developed countries are deteriorating.

2. Markets of developed countries are not sufficiently open to manufactured products of developing countries.

3. Although the aid given by developed countries has increased, it remains inadequate. In fact, many developing countries are still struggling with a huge burden of foreign debts.

Exhibit 8.3 summarizes other international economic organizations by their function or objective.

Exhibit 8.3   Summary of Specialized International Economic Organizations

Special Area	Name of Organization	Major Function/Objective
Food	Food and Agriculture Organization (FAO) of the United Nations, founded in 1945	Collect, analyze, interpret, and disseminate information on nutrition, food, and agriculture
Health	World Health Organization (WHO), founded in 1946	Assist all people in achieving the highest level of health
Labor training	International Labor Organization (ILO), founded in 1919	Promote employment, higher living standards, better working conditions, and social security
Standardization	International Organization for Standardization (ISO), founded in 1947	Promote the development of standardization to facilitate exchange of goods and services throughout the world
Intellectual property	World Intellectual Property Organization (WIPO), founded in 1967	Promote the protection of intellectual property through cooperation among nations and intellectual property unions
Tourism	World Tourism Organization (WTO), founded in 1970	Promote and develop tourism to contribute to economic growth, international understanding, and peace
Environment	United Nations Environment Program (UNEP), founded in 1972	Preserve the environment and natural resources through international cooperation

Interim Summary

1. The WTO, IMF, and World Bank are the three major international economic organizations affecting global-level cooperation of nations. The WTO aims to facilitate trade through reducing trade barriers and eliminating discrimination, whereas the IMF and the World Bank focus on the monetary (currency stability) and fiscal (financial funding) systems, respectively.

2. Although these organizations are supposed to help raise standards of living in member countries, developing countries often find their voices weak in these organizations, especially the WTO, and ask affluent nations to remove unfair trade policies or honor commitments for further opening their markets.

REGIONAL-LEVEL COOPERATION AMONG NATIONS

Multilateral trade liberalization after World War II has been paralleled by a process of integration through regional agreements.[3] The vast majority of WTO members are party to one or more regional trade agreements. A total of 250 agreements were reported to the GATT/WTO from 1947 through 2003, of which over

Exhibit 8.4   Selected Regional Integration Agreements (as of September, 2006)

EUROPE

European Union (EU)

Austria	Belgium	Bulgaria	Cyprus	Czech Republic	Denmark
Estonia	Finland	France	Germany	Greece	Slovakia
Hungary	Ireland	Italy	Latvia	Lithuania	
Luxembourg	Malta	Poland	Portugal	Romania	
Slovenia	Spain	Sweden	The Netherlands	United Kingdom	

EC free trade agreements with

Estonia	Latvia	Norway
Iceland	Liechtenstein	Switzerland
Israel	Lithuania	

EC association agreements with

Bulgaria	Hungary	Romania
Cyprus	Malta	Slovak Republic
Czech Republic	Poland	Turkey

NORTH AMERICA

Canada–United States Free Trade Agreement (CUFTA)
North American Free Trade Agreement (NAFTA)

LATIN AMERICA AND THE CARIBBEAN

Caribbean Community and Common Market (CARICOM)
Central American Common Market (CACM)
Latin American Integration Association (LAIA)
Southern Common Market (MERCOSUR)
Andean Free Trade Area (Andean nations)

MIDDLE EAST

Economic Cooperation Market (ECO)
Gulf Cooperation Council (GCC)

ASIA

Australia–New Zealand Closer Economic Relations Trade Agreement (CER)
Asia-Pacific Economic Cooperation Forum (APEC)
Association of Southeast Asian Nations (ASEAN)
Great China Circle

OTHER

Central America–U.S. Free Trade Agreement (CAFTA)
Israel–United States Free Trade Agreement

170 regional trade agreements are currently in force. These agreements have, for the most part, involved countries in the same geographic region (see Exhibit 8.4).

Postwar Regional Integration

Three features characterize postwar regional integration. First, postwar regional integration has been centered primarily in Western Europe. The creation of the European Economic Community (EEC) in 1958 and of the European Free Trade Association (EFTA) in 1960 initiated a process of enlarging the scope of regional integration among European countries and with other countries. Integration through preferential trade agreements has also been a significant feature of the trade policies of non-European countries. If APEC's (Asia-Pacific Economic Cooperation Forum) objective of achieving open trade and investment by the year 2020 is formalized as a free trade area, all WTO members will be parties to at least one trade agreement. In other words, all WTO members will simultaneously be insiders to at least one trade agreement and outsiders to other agreements.

Second, many developing countries, particularly in Latin America and Asia, have renewed their interest in regional integration since the Uruguay Round began. As part of their adoption of outward-oriented policies, regional integration can help broaden the openness and internationalization of developing economies while avoiding overdependence on world markets. Moreover, continued economic reforms, especially more developed macroeconomic and exchange rate policies, suggest that the overall policy environment has become more conducive to regional integration objectives.[4]

Third, the level of economic integration varies widely among different agreements. Most regional integration agreements involve free trade areas, and the number of customs union agreements is small. Among free trade agreements, it is useful to distinguish between *reciprocal agreements* and *nonreciprocal agreements*. In a reciprocal agreement, each member agrees to reduce or eliminate barriers to trade. In a nonreciprocal agreement, some developed countries may reduce trade barriers, allowing more exports from some developing countries without a request for reciprocity from the latter.

North America: The North American Free Trade Agreement (NAFTA)

The leaders of Canada, Mexico, and the United States signed a historic trade accord, the North American Free Trade Agreement (NAFTA), on December 17, 1992, creating a trinational market area of more than 360 million people with a combined purchasing power of approximately $6.5 trillion. NAFTA is the first ever reciprocal free trade accord between industrial countries and a developing nation (Mexico), which explains why this pact is of special interest to developing countries, particularly those located in Latin America. NAFTA helps enhance the ability of North American producers (especially U.S. companies) to compete globally. By improving the investment climate in North America and by providing companies with a larger market, NAFTA also helps increase economic growth, despite the fact that this increase is not equal among the three members.

NAFTA went into effect on January 1, 1994, uniting the United States with its largest (Canada) and third-largest (Mexico) trading partners. Based on the earlier U.S.–Canada Free Trade Agreement, NAFTA dismantled trade barriers for industrial goods and included agreements on services, investments, intellectual property rights, and agriculture.

NAFTA also includes side agreements on labor adjustment, environmental protection, and import surges. The side agreement on labor adjustment came in response to American workers' concerns that jobs in the United States would be exported to Mexico because of Mexico's lower labor wages, weak child labor laws, and other conditions that afford Mexican labor an economic advantage over its American counterpart. The side agreement is an attempt to manage the terms of the potential change in labor markets. The agreement involves such issues as restrictions on child labor, health and safety standards, and minimum wages. In addition to signing the labor side agreement, the Mexican government has pledged to link increases in the Mexican minimum wage to productivity increases.

The side agreement on environmental cooperation explicitly ensures the rights of the United States to safeguard the environment. NAFTA upholds all existing U.S. health, safety, and environmental standards. It allows states and cities to enact even tougher standards, while providing mechanisms to encourage all parties to raise their standards. The side agreement on import surges creates an early-warning mechanism to identify those sectors where a sudden, explosive trade growth may do significant harm to the domestic industry. It also establishes that, going forward, a working group can provide for revisions in the treaty text based on the experiences with the existing safeguard mechanisms. During the transition period, safeguard relief is available in the form of a temporary retreat to pre-NAFTA duties if an import surge threatens to seriously damage a domestic industry. These three side agreements were negotiated to alleviate the fears of U.S. labor and industry groups that felt threatened by the possible immediate adverse impact on their members.

With the integration of the Canadian, U.S., and Mexican markets, many companies have changed their business strategies and plans to serve the integrated North American market more efficiently. Many companies in Mexico, the United States, and Canada closed inefficient plants and concentrated production where it could generate highest possible returns. Whether it is the Mexican company Cemex, the Canadian company Alcan Aluminum, or the American company Ford, each can take advantage of cheaper labor or resources for certain components and products. In the foreseeable future, assuming that Mexican worker productivity is equal to or close to that of the U.S. or Canadian worker, one would expect that labor-intensive production would be performed in Mexico, where workers' hourly wages are less than half of those in the United States.

Photo 8.1 **The European Union represents 25 countries (as of September 1, 2006), the largest regional block in the world.**

SOURCE: Jupiterimages.

Europe: The European Union (EU)

The postwar efforts to establish the European Union have been a long process, beginning with the formation of the European Economic Community (EEC) in 1957. After three enlargement efforts ended on January 1, 1995, the European Community (EC) was formed, consisting of 15 member states: Belgium, the Netherlands, Luxembourg, France, Germany, Italy, Denmark, Ireland, the United Kingdom, Greece, Spain, Portugal, Finland, Sweden, and Austria. These EC member states constitute the core as well as the deepest level of the European economic integration. The outer tier of trade and economic liberalization within the European Union is composed of countries in Central and Eastern Europe (e.g., the Czech Republic, Hungary, Poland), as well as Mediterranean countries (e.g., Slovenia, Malta). As of July 2007, there were 27 member states in the EU (see Exhibits 8.4 and 8.5,) with Croatia, Macedonia, and Turkey as candidate countries. The EU has about half a billion people—surpassed only by China and India.

The most fundamental step in strengthening economic and political ties among EC member states occurred with the Treaty on European Union (or the "Maastricht" Treaty). Signed in February 1992, the treaty was enforced in November 1993. This treaty not

Exhibit 8.5   European Union

SOURCE: © European Communities, 1995–2007.

only promotes economic and trade expansion within a common market but also embraces the formation of a monetary union, the establishment of a common foreign and security policy, common citizenship, and the development of cooperation on justice and social affairs. Its significance was marked by the adoption of the new name "European Union" (EU). The Maastricht Treaty contains several high-impacting provisions, including the following:

1. It creates a common European currency, known as the European Currency Unit (ECU).

2. Every citizen in each member state in the EU is eligible to obtain a European passport, which bestows the right to move freely from one country to another within the Union.

3. It contains provisions on cooperation in the fields of justice and domestic affairs.

4. It empowers the Union to play a more active role in areas such as trans-European transport and environmental protection.

5. It increases the power of the European Parliament to enact legislation.

6. It removes all restrictions on capital movements between member states.

7. Finally, it establishes a European Central Bank, responsible for monetary policy, and transforms the European Union into the European Economic and Monetary Union (EMU), under which the currencies of the member states are tied irrevocably to one another at the same exchange rate.

The ECU, or euro, is a "basket" of specified amounts of each EC currency. The amounts are determined in accordance with the economic size of the member countries and are revised every five years. The value of the ECU is determined by using the spot market rate of each member currency. The ECU has become a popular unit for international payment, bond issuance, security investment, bank deposits, commercial loans, and traveler's checks since it was created in 1999.

The EU is run by five institutions, each playing a specific role:

- European Parliament (elected by the people of the member states)
- Council of the Union (governments of the member states)
- European Commission (executive body)
- Court of Justice (compliance with the law)
- Court of Auditors (lawful management of the EU budget)

Apart from the European Union, there are several other trade unions in Europe. For instance, in December 1992, several Central and Eastern European countries (the Czech Republic, Slovakia, Hungary, and Poland) created the Central European Free Trade Agreement (CEFTA), which provided for the establishment of a free trade area by the end of 1997. Also in 1992, Finland, Norway, Sweden, and Switzerland concluded free trade agreements with each of the Baltic states (Estonia, Latvia, and Lithuania).

Asia-Pacific

The Asia-Pacific Economic Cooperation Forum (APEC), founded in 1989, consists of 21 economies (as of September 2006), including Australia, New Zealand, Canada, Mexico, the United States, Chile, China, Hong Kong, Japan, South Korea, Papua New Guinea, Chinese Taipei (Taiwan), Indonesia, Malaysia, Peru, the Philippines, Russia, Singapore, Thailand, Brunei, and Vietnam. APEC member economies work together to sustain economic growth through a commitment to open trade, investment, and economic reform. In the 1994 summit declaration, members agreed to build on the commitments they made in the Uruguay Round of GATT, by accelerating their implementation and broadening and deepening these commitments. By progressively reducing tariffs and other barriers to trade, imports and exports between member economies have expanded dramatically. Compared with other regional unions or areas, APEC is cross-regional, spanning Asia, North and South America, and the Pacific. Moreover, APEC is unique in terms of the mix of members involved, encompassing large and small, rich and poor, as well as politically divergent nations (see Exhibit 8.6). APEC member economies generate nearly 70% of global economic growth, and the APEC region consistently outperformed the rest of the world, even during the Asian financial crisis.

APEC operates as a cooperative, multilateral economic and trade forum. It is unique in that it represents the only intergovernmental grouping in the world committed to reducing trade barriers and increasing investments without requiring its members to enter into legally binding obligations. The forum aims to promote dialogue and equal respect for the views of all participants and decision making based on consensus to achieve its free and open trade and investment goals. APEC members take both individual and collective actions to open their markets and promote economic growth. Each year, one member economy plays host to APEC meetings and serves as the APEC chair. The APEC host economy is responsible for chairing the annual Government Leaders' Meeting, selected Ministerial Meetings, senior officials meetings, and the APEC Business Advisory Council and also fills the executive director position at the APEC secretariat. The Forum has several special committees, including the Committee on Trade and Investment, the Economic Committee, Special Task Groups, and the Budget and Management Committee, working for the above meetings.

Exhibit 8.6   The Asia-Pacific Economic Cooperation (APEC)

SOURCE: The Asia-Pacific Economic Cooperation Fourm (APEC).

Relative to APEC, the Association of Southeast Asian Nations (ASEAN) is much older, established on August 8, 1967, by Indonesia, Malaysia, the Philippines, Singapore, and Thailand (Brunei joined in 1984). The aim of ASEAN is to promote peace, stability, and economic growth in the region. Since January 1995, member countries have earmarked products for low-duty status from a list of 3,141 items. To become a free trade zone by the year 2003, when the average tariff was reduced to 2.6%, ASEAN countries had cut the tariffs on various products such as cement, ceramics, chemicals, pharmaceuticals, and dozens of others. Although located in the same region, ASEAN members are diverse in terms of economic, geographical, political, and cultural backgrounds. This diversity sometimes increases the difficulty in achieving the specific goals or implementing plans set by ASEAN members.

Accounting for one-fifth of world trade, Asia is distinctive in several ways. First, many countries in the region have accelerated their trade liberalization at the subnational level by authorizing export processing zones or special investment areas within each country. In China, for instance, the Standing Committee of the National People's Congress approved in August 1980 the establishment of four special economic zones: Shenzhen, Zhuhai, Shantou, and Xiamen. Thailand, Vietnam, Indonesia, Malaysia, India, Bangladesh, and the Philippines, to name a few, also established such zones within their own territories.

Second, many geographically proximate neighbors in Asia reached less formal trade agreements. For example, members of the South Asian Association for Regional Cooperation (SAARC)—Bhutan, India, the Maldives, Nepal, Pakistan, and Sri Lanka—concluded a trade agreement in April 1993. Similarly, the China Circle is now an extremely dynamic region exerting substantial influence on world trade and investment. This circle, which includes Hong Kong, Macau, Taiwan, and Mainland China, comprises—from the standpoint of degree of economic integration—three concentric layers. The core consists of the Hong Kong–Guangdong economic nexus; the inner layer, "Greater South China," embraces Hong Kong, Guangdong, Fujian, and Taiwan; and the outer layer, "Greater China," includes Hong Kong, Taiwan, and China. Hong Kong is the pivot for integration of the China Circle and plays a role in each of its three layers.

Finally, numerous subregional economic zones have emerged. Intense trade and investment flows have grown among geographically contiguous but politically separated border areas, taking advantage of the complementarity in factor endowment and technological capacity among countries at different stages of economic development. These zones are alternately called *transnational export processing zones, natural economic territories,* or *growth triangles.* They include the Tumen River Area Development Project in northeast Asia, composed of the Russian Far East, Mongolia, northeast China, the Korean Peninsula, and Japan; the Baht Economic Zone, encompassing Thailand and the contiguous border areas of southwest China, Myanmar, Laos, Cambodia, and Vietnam; the Mekong River Basin Project, involving the riparian countries of Thailand, Myanmar, Vietnam, Laos, Cambodia, and southwest China; and three growth triangles in ASEAN— the Southern Growth Triangle (Singapore, the Johor state in Malaysia, and Batam Island in Indonesia), the Northern Growth Triangle (western Indonesia, northern Malaysia, and southern Thailand), and the Eastern Growth Triangle (Brunei, eastern Indonesia, southern Philippines, and Sabah and Sarawak in eastern Malaysia).

Latin America

Attempts to form free trade blocs in Latin America were made as early as 1960 when the Latin American Free Trade Association (LAFTA) (involving Argentina,

Bolivia, Brazil, Chile, Colombia, Ecuador, Mexico, Paraguay, Peru, Uruguay, and Venezuela) and the Central American Common Market (CACM) (consisting of Costa Rica, El Salvador, Guatemala, Honduras, and Nicaragua) were initiated. Both failed to achieve their objectives because of different economic conditions and economic policies among member countries that worked against regional economic integration.

LAFTA was superseded in 1980 by the Montevideo Treaty, which established the Latin American Integration Association (LAIA). Its goal was to increase bilateral trade among its member countries, carried out on a sectoral basis. In 1991, Argentina, Brazil, Paraguay, and Uruguay signed the Southern Common Market Treaty (MERCOSUR), which called for a common market among the four countries with free circulation of goods, services, capital, and labor. The member countries also aimed to coordinate macroeconomic policy and to harmonize legislation to strengthen the integration process. Since January 1, 1995, MERCOSUR members have used a common tariff structure and common external tariff rates.

Other LAFTA members, including Bolivia, Colombia, Ecuador, Peru, and Venezuela, formed the Andean Free Trade Area in 1992 with a common external tariff. Since 1995, these members adopted a four-tier external tariff structure of 5%, 10%, 15%, and 20% when trading with other members of this agreement. The CACM reactivated its objectives and established a customs union on January 1, 1993. Countries in the Caribbean region started the Caribbean Community and Common Market (CARICOM) in 1973. The major objective of this treaty is to achieve economies of scale in the regional production of services, such as transportation, education, and health, and to pool financial resources for investment in a regional development bank. This treaty also targets the coordination of economic policies and development planning (see Exhibit 8.7).

Exhibit 8.7   Free Trade Blocs in the Americas

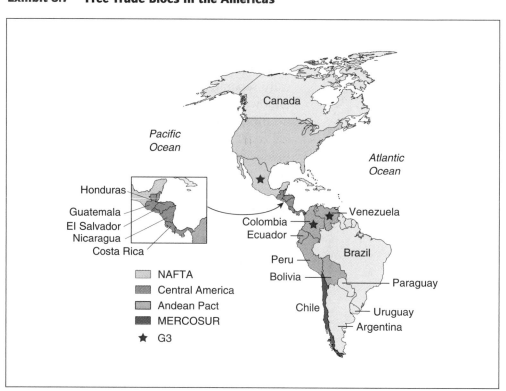

Africa and the Middle East

The Economic Community of West African States (ECOWAS), established in 1975, is composed of Benin, Burkina Faso, Ivory Coast Mali, Mauritania, Niger, Senegal, Guinea, Liberia, Sierra Leone, Cape Verde, Gambia, Ghana, Guinea-Bissau, Nigeria, and Togo. ECOWAS eliminated duties on unprocessed agricultural products and handicrafts in 1981 and implemented free trade for all unprocessed products in 1990. Other activities of the community have included progressive liberalization of industrial products, steps to avoid the use of hard currencies in intramember trade through a regional payments-clearing system, and cooperation on industrial and agricultural investment projects.

Established in 1966 in former French Africa, the Central African Economic and Customs Union (UDEAC) consists of Congo, Gabon, Chad, the Central African Republic, Equatorial Guinea, and Cameroon. EDEAC provides a framework for the free movement of capital throughout the area and for the harmonization of fiscal incentives, as well as the coordination of industrial development. A common external tariff was introduced in 1990 by four members of the community—Cameroon, Congo, Gabon, and the Central African Republic.

In former British East Africa, the establishment of the East African Economic Community (EAEC) in 1967 by Kenya, Tanzania, and Uganda formalized the common market. The EAEC was dissolved in 1979 and the three members later joined with other states (Angola, Burundi, Comoros, Djibouti, Ethiopia, Lesotho, Malawi, Mauritius, Mozambique, Namibia, Rwanda, Somalia, Sudan, Swaziland, Zambia, and Zimbabwe) to establish the Preferential Trade Area (PTA) for eastern and southern African states in 1981. Its goals include the establishment of a common market and the promotion of trade and economic cooperation among its members.

In the Middle East, Kuwait, Saudi Arabia, Bahrain, Oman, Qatar, and the United Arab Emirates established the Gulf Cooperation Council (GCC) in 1981. A free trade area covering industrial and agricultural products (excluding petroleum products) was established. In 1989, the Arab Maghreb Union was also established by Algeria, Libya, Mauritania, Morocco, and Tunisia to lay the foundations for a Maghreb Economic Area.

Regionalization Versus Globalization

Does regionalization work? Let us look at how the preceding regional blocs or agreements have actually contributed to the increased share of intraregional trade. Indeed, intraregional trade increased in Western Europe (e.g., from 53% in 1958 to 70% in 1999), as it has done in North America. For example, Canada expanded its exports to the United States by 18% between 1997 and 1999, and Mexico's exports and imports, heavily linked to the U.S. market, grew by 20% over 1997–1999. This seems to support a view that regionalization can increase the share of regional trade. However, the uniqueness of the European Union and NAFTA—in terms of the structure and commitment to carry integration—differs markedly from what has been envisaged in other regional integration agreements. Caution is required in generalizing the unique experiences of NAFTA and the European Union to other regional agreements (e.g., MERCOSUR experienced a contraction of its intratrade by about one-quarter during 1997–1999). In fact, many developing countries encountered problems when implementing these agreements. Moreover, as Asia's experience indicates (e.g., despite absence of any bilateral trade agreements, China's trade with Japan and Korea has steadily increased in the late 1990s), regional integration agreements are not a prerequisite for rising share of intraregional trade. Economic growth, commodity structure, and demand–supply situations seem to be more profound factors affecting the level of intraregional exchanges.[5]

Many people, from government officials and corporate executives to labor union leaders and business instructors, ask whether regionalization is compatible with globalization. To answer this question, we first need to know how the WTO rules regulate regionalization.

Both regional integration agreements (regionalization) and multilateral trading systems (globalization) share the general objective of achieving, within their respective spheres, substantial reduction of tariffs and other barriers to trade. The WTO requires that (a) under the MFN (most favored nations) rule, any privilege promised to another regional member as specified in a regional agreement must extend unconditionally to all other WTO members (bilateral or regional obligations thus transform into multilateral or global obligations); (b) members of a regional integration agreement must have a common trade policy with respect to third countries (outsiders), and this policy should not be more restrictive than policies of individual members prior to the agreement; and (c) the WTO's dispute-settlement mechanisms provide a platform to solve disputes between members concerning discrepancies between regional agreements and global trading rules. For WTO members, these rules make it possible for regional integration and global trading systems to mutually support (rather than conflict with) each other in reducing tariffs and other trade barriers.

The complementarity between regionalization and globalization in dismantling trade barriers is also manifested in other areas. With the exception of the EU, few regional agreements have specified the rules of nontariff barrier reduction, intellectual property protection, and service trade. Multilateral trading systems such as the WTO, however, serve as an important framework for them to follow in these areas. In other words, members of regional agreements still benefit from the enhanced transparency and procedural guarantees for dealing with these issues in intraregional trade as well as in trade with third countries as covered under the WTO agreements in which they participate. On the other hand, implemented policies or measures taken by certain regional integration agreements (e.g., environmental rules, competition regulations, and investment policies enacted by the EU) help lay the foundation for progress in multilateral trading systems. Finally, the WTO has been provided with a strengthened dispute-settlement system and a monitoring function, which together bring increased transparency and predictability to trade and economic policies. As a result, parties to regional integration have ensured—by virtue of being members of the WTO—the adoption of an enhanced set of policies and procedures for their trade and economic relations.

The preceding complementarity, however, holds true for WTO members only under the assumption that the multilateral trading rules will be fully enforced. For non-WTO members, regionalization of foreign markets may increase the barriers to their foreign trade, thus conflicting with their efforts toward global integration. Rules and procedures for trade-related policies are the essence of the world trading system. If these rules are not completely and strictly implemented by all members, the compatibility between regionalization and globalization will be obstructed.

Interim Summary

1. Regionalization, such as the formation of NAFTA and the European Union, is a prominent feature of the world economy today. In the near future, all WTO members will simultaneously be insiders of at least one regional bloc or agreement and outsiders of others.

2. Regional integration takes several different forms, including common markets (e.g., the European Union and MERCOSUR), free trade areas (e.g., NAFTA and LAFTA), customs unions (e.g., CACM and CARICOM), economic cooperation forums (e.g., APEC and GCC), and economic and political associations (e.g., ASEAN).

3. Regionalization is generally compatible with globalization. However, insiders gain many more benefits than outsiders from economic integration.

COMMODITY-LEVEL COOPERATION AMONG NATIONS

The emergence of many international commodity agreements and organizations is a natural development in international economic relations. Countries may also cooperate with one another to control the production, pricing, and sale of goods that are traded internationally. A **commodity cartel** is a group of producing countries that wish to protect themselves from the wild fluctuations that often occur in the prices of certain commodities traded internationally (e.g., crude oil, coffee, rubber, cocoa). Cartel members may also seek higher, as well as more stable, prices for their goods. By assigning production quotas to individual countries and limiting overall output, a commodity cartel can raise the price of its goods in international markets. The two most important commodity cartels influencing the world economy are OPEC and the Multifiber Arrangement.

Organization of Petroleum Exporting Countries (OPEC)

The most notable and critical commodity cartel today is the Organization of Petroleum Exporting Countries (OPEC). OPEC is not a commercial entity but an intergovernmental organization. Its members are Iran, Iraq, Kuwait, Saudi Arabia, Venezuela, Algeria, Indonesia, Libya, Nigeria, Qatar, and the United Arab Emirates. OPEC is the strongest collective force influencing prices in the international oil market. OPEC controls the price of oil in world markets by assigning to its members production quotas that limit the overall amount of crude oil supplied internationally. This organization successfully augmented oil prices for the benefit of its members in the 1970s and successfully overcame crises facing it in the 1980s. Currently, OPEC members control more than 40% of the world's oil production and nearly 80% of the world crude oil reserves (see Exhibit 8.8).

The world lives on oil. The bulk of OPEC oil reserves are located in the Middle East, with Saudi Arabia, Iran, and Iraq contributing 57% to the OPEC total. Total world oil demand in 2000 was about 76 million barrels per day. But as world economic growth continues, crude oil demand will rise to more than 90 million barrels per day in 2010 and more than 100 million barrels per day in 2020, according to the OPEC prediction. On the price side, crude oil prices react to the balance of demand and supply in the short run and the rate of investment in the longer term. Sentiment is also an important factor: If traders in the oil

Exhibit 8.8   OPEC Share of World Crude Oil Reserves (2004)

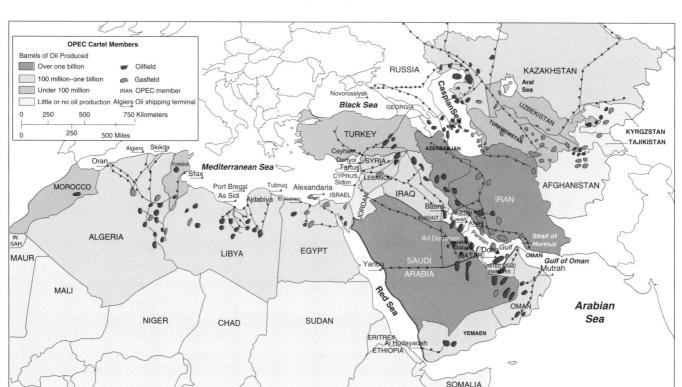

SOURCE: OPEC.

market believe there will be a shortage of oil suppliers, they may raise prices before a shortage actually occurs. Other factors influencing the price of crude oil include accidents, bad weather, increasing demand, halting transport of oil from producers, labor disputes, and other disruptions to production including war and natural disasters. The price of oil is reflected in most of the things we do. It affects the price of transport, the cost of goods and services, and the availability of many products, including food, water, and shelter. If oil prices are too high, then these goods and services become more expensive and economies experience inflation.

OPEC became a catalyst for action by developing countries to ensure remunerative export earnings from their raw materials and tropical products. For instance, the International Bauxite Association (IBA) and the Intergovernmental Council of Copper Exporting Countries (CIPEC) were formed in the 1970s by the major developing countries producing these commodities, both following the model of OPEC.

The Multifiber Arrangement (MFA)

The Multifiber Arrangement (MFA), originally signed in 1972, was an agreement between exporting and importing countries to control exports of textiles and apparel from developing countries to developed countries. The MFA took advantage of an exemption in GATT rules that allows individual importing countries to establish quotas and other restrictions on textile and apparel exports on a country-by-country basis. About two-thirds of textile and apparel products that are traded internationally were covered by the MFA. The United States currently imposes quotas on imports from 41 countries.

The MFA has been renewed several times for lack of a better solution to the conflict between developing and developed nations over the textile and apparel trade. For example, the United States and China renegotiate yearly over the quota (restricted quantity) of Chinese exported textiles and garments. The process is lengthy because of conflicts over issues on which neither party is willing to compromise. Generally, this type of conflict results from the nature of the production of these goods: It requires much labor, little capital, and simple technology. Thus it presents one of the major opportunities for less developed, low-wage countries to export manufactured goods to developed countries. Yet, because it is labor-intensive, domestic political forces in developed countries often organize to protect domestic jobs from low-wage foreign competition. As a result, many developed countries have imposed high tariffs or low quotas on the importation of textiles and apparel, thereby severely restricting trade. The MFA's complex barriers to trade expired in 2005 as a result of the Uruguay Round.[6]

Other multilateral commodity agreements include the Wheat Trade Convention (WTC), the International Sugar Agreement (ISA), the International Coffee Agreement (ICA), the International Cocoa Agreement (ICCA), the International Tin Agreement (ITA), and the International Natural Rubber Agreement (INRA).

Interim Summary

1. International economic integration also occurs at the commodity level via the establishment of commodity cartels (e.g., OPEC and CIPEC) or multilateral arrangements (e.g., MFA and ISA).

2. OPEC is an intergovernmental organization and the strongest collective force impacting supply and price in the international oil market.

STRATEGIC RESPONSES OF MNEs

International economic integration profoundly affects the operations of MNEs. So how should MNEs properly respond to, and further benefit from, increasing integration? As a result of heightened integration of the world economy, national boundaries have become increasingly irrelevant in the definition of market and production spaces, while at the same time regions, rather than countries, are emerging as the key economic policy arenas.

Economic integration triggers MNE activities, which then increase FDI in the integrated region. This is not surprising, because MNEs quickly make adjustments to the new environment in which intraregional trade barriers have been eliminated.[7] Three strategies can be identified in response to regional economic integration. The *defensive export substituting investment* is a strategy by which MNEs defend their preexisting market share achieved through exports by switching to direct production inside the region. Many Japanese MNEs, such as Sony and Nissan, employed this strategy in response to European market integration in the early 1990s, in part to protect themselves against the possibility of future barriers to Japanese exports. In comparison to U.S. MNEs, Japanese MNEs were latecomers to the European market and had a trade-based rather than an investment-based commercial relationship with the European community. As a result of defensive export substituting investment, Japanese MNEs are now in a strong position to compete in the EU. As another example, both Du Pont and Dow Chemical increased investments in their Canadian export-oriented operations in reaction to NAFTA.

The *offensive export substituting investment* is a strategy by which MNEs choose to ensure market penetration by investing directly in the region before the region is officially integrated. This strategy is intended to gain early position in the market, which is anticipated to grow rapidly as a result of an integration program. To gain an early foothold in the European market, Coca-Cola, which has an 80% share of the European cola market, used this strategy and invested more than $100 million in new European plants. Similarly, Campbell Soup and Quaker Oats have used this strategy to expand their operations in Canada. Aggressive acquisition activities by these U.S. MNEs in the Canadian market occurred in response to the passage of NAFTA.

The *rationalized foreign direct investment* is a strategy by which MNEs increase investment in, and heighten resource commitment to, the integrated region in pursuit of greater economic efficiency through scale economies and market expansion. IBM, for example, has been operating in Europe for about eight decades and is the industry leader in the European data-processing market. It used rationalized FDI strategy in response to European market integration by establishing 12 new manufacturing plants, nine R&D facilities, seven scientific centers, and a network of local sales and support offices. To benefit from NAFTA, IBM also invested more than $1 billion to upgrade its Canadian facilities and now exports all high-technology components and software manufactured in Canada to overseas markets.

Finally, the *reorganization investment* is a strategy by which MNEs realign their organizational structures and value-added activities to reflect a regional market. Firms realign investment capital among members of the trading bloc once protective barriers have been removed altogether. Under this strategy, an MNE's cross-border investment activity within the region increases, while the aggregate level of investment stock may not necessarily increase. Several European MNEs, for example, used this strategy to respond to European market integration. Philips, one of Europe's largest MNEs in the electronics industry, was reorganized as a collection of autonomous national subsidiaries. It restructured to create an integrated set of Europe-wide, product-based companies. To prepare for a single European market, Siemens launched a radical corporate reorganization in 1987, with plans to concentrate on high-growth segments of its core electronics/electrical businesses, while expanding geographically throughout Europe through a series of acquisitions (see the Industry Box for details). In North America, Gillette and Whirlpool closed some of their Canadian facilities as a response to free trade in the region. They committed more production to their home markets and then exported to Canada from the United States.

As shown in the preceding examples, strategic choice depends on a company's current position in the regional market, the length of time it has had a presence in the region, and the industry to which it belongs. In response to economic integration, MNEs, including those from developing economies such as South Korea, Taiwan, Singapore, and Brazil, have been actively employing cross-border strategic alliances. These alliances allow them to enter a new market far more rapidly than do mergers and acquisitions. Brazil, for example, is now one of the largest investors in the Portuguese economy, mostly with joint ventures in industries such as construction, textiles, and shoes.

INDUSTRY BOX

SIEMENS SHARPENS ITS FOCUS TO RESPOND TO THE SINGLE MARKET

Siemens, Germany's largest electronics firm, is an example of an MNE from the European community that was forced to reorganize and expand geographically in the region. Before the single market was formed, Siemens was highly dependent on government purchases and concentrated in regulated markets such as telecommunications equipment, nuclear power and energy, and defense-related equipment. After 1992, Siemens and other former "national champions" in Europe faced deregulated markets in which they competed with MNEs such as AT&T, GE, and IBM. In response, Siemens diversified its geographical presence in Europe and refocused its product lines on those that had competitive advantages. It chose the United Kingdom and France as locations for major new markets in Europe. It integrated vertically to produce end products that shared a common core in advanced semiconductor technology in high-growth sectors. Siemens decentralized from seven product-based divisions to 15 smaller independent units, making the company more flexible in a fast-changing environment. It acquired Plessey of the United Kingdom, which gave it a foothold there and a 10% world market share for public branch exchange products. Siemens also entered into alliances with BASF in mainframes, Bendix in automotive electronics, and Westinghouse in factory automation and controls. All of these efforts helped Siemens become a premier MNE in Europe in the electronics, semiconductor, computer, and software industries.

Interim Summary

1. MNEs need to respond strategically to economic integration, whether at the regional or global level, if they want to survive in an increasingly competitive environment.

2. MNEs can emphasize one of the three strategies to cope with economic integration: defensive export substituting investment, offensive export substituting investment, and rationalized FDI. The selection of this strategy depends on an MNE's goals, experience, and capabilities.

3. MNEs, whether insiders or outsiders, can expand their presence within a regional bloc through acquisitions, alliances, or the building of new facilities.

CHAPTER SUMMARY

1. International economic integration involves the discriminatory removal of all trade impediments as well as the establishment of some elements of cooperation among several nations. This integration fosters globalization.

2. Economic integration takes several forms, including free trade area, customs union, common market, economic union, political union, and multilateral cooperation and occurs at three levels—global, regional, and commodity.

3. Global-level cooperation among nations proceeds through international economic organizations such as the WTO, the IMF, and the World Bank. While the WTO sets the institutional foundation for the global trading system, the IMF and the World Bank serve as the foundation of the global monetary and financial systems.

4. The WTO attempts not only to reduce tariff and nontariff barriers in trade (commodity and service) but also to help solve problems associated with economic development, intellectual property, environmental protection, unfair practices, and dispute settlement.

5. Regional integration has become a prominent characteristic of the world economy. From the EU to NAFTA, APEC to LAFTA, GCC to ECOWAS, most countries already belong to at least one regional bloc or agreement. Within a regional bloc, subregional

integration such as a free trade area or a common market becomes increasingly pervasive.

6. From the world economy perspective, regionalization is an integral part of globalization. From the firm perspective, regionalization substantially benefits insiders but not outsiders. Outsiders may shift exports to FDI because an actual investment within the region bypasses trade barriers against outsiders' exports and enables these firms to gain from free flows of products, capital, services, or human resources within the integrated region.

7. Commodity-level cooperation is reflected in commodity cartels or arrangements. The most important cartel is OPEC, which controls more than 40% of the world's oil production.

Chapter Notes

1. M. A. G. Van Meerhaeghe. *International Economic Institutions*. Boston, MA: Martinus Nijhoff Publishers, 1985; A. M. El-Agraa. *Economic Integration Worldwide*. New York: St. Martin's Press, 1997.

2. B. Hoekman and M. Kostechi. *The Political Economy of the World Trading System: From GATT to WTO*. Oxford, UK: Oxford University Press, 1995; J. Groome. *Reshaping the World Trading System: A History of the Uruguay Round*. Geneva: World Trade Organization, 1996.

3. *Regionalism and the World Trading System*. Geneva: World Trade Organization, 1995.

4. J. H. Jackson. *The World Trading System*. Cambridge, MA: MIT Press, 1997; B. Hettne, A. Inotai, and O. Sunkel. *Globalism and the New Regionalism*. New York: St. Martin's Press, 1999.

5. Organization for Economic Cooperation and Development (OECD). *Regionalism and Its Place in the Multilateral Trading System*. France: OECD, 1996; R. Gibb and W. Michalak (eds.). *Continental Trading Blocs: The Growth of Regionalism in the World Economy*. Chichester, UK: Wiley, 1994.

6. M. R. Mendoza, P. Low, and B. Kotschwar (eds.). *Trading Rules in the Making: Challenges in Regional and Multilateral Negotiations*. Washington, DC: Brookings Institution Press, 1999; B. Colas (ed.). *Global Economic Cooperation: A Guide to Agreements and Organizations*. Cambridge, MA: Kluwer Law and Taxation Publishers, 1994.

7. N. A. Phelps. *Multinationals and European Integration: Trade Investment and Regional Development*. London: Jessica Kingsley Publishers, 1997; H. Mirza. *Global Competitive Strategies in the New World Economy*. Cheltenham, UK: Edward Elgar, 1998.

THE INTERNATIONAL MONETARY SYSTEM AND FINANCIAL MARKETS

DO YOU KNOW?

1. What exchange rate systems are available today? Why don't nations use the same exchange rate system? For example, why does Cameroon peg its currency (CFA franc) to the French franc, whereas Romania allows its currency (leu) to independently float?

2. Why do some currencies fluctuate more than others? Why do some currencies depreciate while others appreciate? How do you determine and predict the foreign exchange rate?

3. What constitutes international financial markets? How do speculators earn profits from international foreign exchange markets? Is this speculation one factor that led to the Asian financial crisis? How do MNEs (multinational enterprises) finance global operations via international capital markets?

Photo 9.1   Along with globalization, more foreign firms are listed and traded in international stock markets.

SOURCE: Jupiterimages.

OPENING CASE

Foreign Exchange Crisis in Mexico

Mexico experienced a financial crisis during 1994–1995. Mexico's exchange rate regime was modified a number of times, but it was consistently aimed at price stabilization. It started as a strict peg to the U.S. dollar in 1988 and shifted to a crawl policy in early 1989. Beginning in 1992, an asymmetrical band was adopted, allowing for gradual depreciation but placing a ceiling on the peso in relation to the dollar. Although steady from mid-1992 to early 1994, the Mexican peso became overvalued. The real effective exchange rate appreciated steadily as inflation exceeded the rate of the peso's depreciation. Between 1990 and December 1993, the peso depreciated by about 17% in nominal terms. However, consumer price inflation amounted to 56% from 1990 to 1993. Thus, the real effective exchange rate rose by nearly 35% over that period. The result was an increase in the current-account deficit from $7.5 billion in 1990 to $29.4 billion in 1994, which amounted to 7% of Mexico's GDP.

The year 1994 was an election year and a period of political mishaps in Mexico. Both the presidential candidate and the secretary-general of the majority party were assassinated. These and other events led to a slowdown in capital inflow and withdrawals of capital that had been invested in short-term government securities (*cetes*). Reserves decreased by $11 billion in April 1994. The government then issued short-term peso obligations (*tesobonos*) with interest and principal linked to the dollar. The interest rate on these securities was considerably lower than it was on peso securities without a dollar link. Many Mexican residents shifted out of pesos into dollars, further escalating the peso devaluation. This crisis differs slightly from the one that occurred during the 1980s. In the previous crisis, Mexico fought to keep the peso fixed to the U.S. dollar. To discourage investors from withdrawing funds from Mexico to avoid losses when the devaluation eventually occurred, the Mexican government had to maintain high interest rates. These high rates were the indirect consequence of fixed exchange rates, and they consequently stifled investment and job creation. The problem of high interest rates attributable to delayed devaluation with fixed exchange rates became known as "the peso problem."

HISTORY OF THE INTERNATIONAL MONETARY SYSTEM

The preceding case shows that a country's currency value is not always stable, and therefore its exchange rate with other countries' currencies can change. International businesses operate in an uncertain environment in which exchange rates have been increasingly volatile over the past quarter century. Volatile exchange rates increase risk for international companies. To manage foreign exchange risk, management must first understand how the international monetary system works. As the opening case demonstrates, there are many new terms associated with this system (e.g., peg or crawl policies, nominal or real exchange rate). This chapter is designed to explain these concepts and related monetary system and financial markets.

The **international monetary system** refers primarily to the set of policies, institutions, practices, regulations, and mechanisms that determine foreign exchange rates. This system comprises currencies from individual countries as well as some composite currency units such as the European currency unit (ECU) and the special drawing right (SDR), as illustrated in Chapter 8. **Foreign exchange** refers to the money of a foreign country, such as foreign currency bank balances, banknotes, checks, and drafts. A **foreign exchange rate** (or simply, exchange rate) is the price of one currency expressed in terms of another currency (or gold). If the government of a country (e.g., Iraq) regulates the rate at which the local currency (e.g., the Iraqi dinar) is exchanged for other currencies, the system is classified as a **fixed** or **managed exchange rate system.** When a country's currency (e.g., the Iraqi dinar) is tied or fixed to another country's currency (the U.S. dollar), this is called a **pegged exchange rate system.** The rate at which the currency is fixed is often referred to as its **par value.** If the government does not interfere in the valuation of its currency, it is classified as **floating** or **flexible exchange rate system** (e.g., the U.S. dollar). The **real exchange rate** is the exchange rate after deducting an inflation factor. The **nominal exchange rate** is the exchange rate before deducting an inflation factor.

Changes in exchange rates may move in one of two directions. Associated with the fixed or managed exchange rate system, **devaluation** of a currency refers to a drop in the foreign exchange value of a currency that is pegged to another currency or gold. In other words, the par value is reduced. The opposite of devaluation is **revaluation**. Associated with the floating exchange rate system, **depreciation** (or weakening, deterioration) means a drop in the foreign exchange value of a floating currency. The opposite of depreciation is **appreciation** (or strengthening), which means a gain in the exchange value of a floating currency. The media often use the terms *devaluation* and *depreciation* (or *revaluation* and *appreciation*) interchangeably, without distinctions, which is incorrect.

The choice of foreign currencies used by international companies affects their cash flows and even their income levels. For example, firms in countries with soft currencies often use hard foreign currencies in export businesses. A **soft** or **weak currency** is one that is anticipated to devaluate or depreciate relative to major trading currencies. Conversely, a currency is considered **hard** or **strong** if it is expected to revalue or appreciate relative to major currencies. In daily life, the term *hard currency* is also used to denote the fully convertible currency of a major developed country (e.g., the U.S. dollar, the U.K. pound, or the Japanese yen).

A brief review of the history of the international monetary system can help us better understand the present monetary system and also appraise the strengths and weaknesses of different foreign exchange systems.

The Gold Standard Period: 1876–1914

Since the days of the pharaohs (about 3000 B.C.), gold was used as a medium of exchange and a store of value. The gold standard gained acceptance as an international monetary system in the 1870s. Under this system, each country pegged its money to gold. For example, if the German Bank fixed the price of gold at 50 deutsche marks (DM) per ounce of gold, it effectively stood ready to buy and sell gold at this rate. The same applied to the United States if the U.S. Federal Reserve (the Fed) fixed the price of gold at $20 per ounce. The exchange rate, then, is simply the ratio of the two prices: DM50/$20 means an exchange rate of DM2.5 per U.S. dollar.

The government of each country using the gold standard agreed to buy or sell gold on demand at its own fixed parity rate. Thus, the value of each individual currency in gold terms and the fixed parities between currencies remained stable. Under this system, it was very important for a country to maintain adequate gold reserves with which to back its currency's value. The gold standard worked adequately until the outbreak of World War I interrupted trade flows and the free movement of gold. As a result, the major trading nations suspended the gold standard.

The Interwar Years and World War II: 1914–1944

During World War I and the early 1920s, currencies were allowed to fluctuate over fairly wide ranges in terms of both gold and other currencies. This created arbitrage opportunities for international speculators. Such fluctuations hampered world trade in the 1920s, thereby contributing to the Great Depression in the 1930s.

The United States returned to a modified gold standard in 1934, when the U.S. dollar was devalued to $35/ounce of gold from the $20.67/ounce price in effect prior to World War I. Although the United States returned to the gold standard, gold was traded only with foreign central banks, not with individual citizens. From 1934 to the end of World War II, exchange rates were determined, in theory, by each currency's value in terms of gold. During World War II and its immediate aftermath, however, many of the main trading currencies lost their convertibility into other currencies. The dollar was the only major trading currency that continued to be convertible.

The Bretton Woods System: 1944–1973

This period, commencing a year prior to the end of World War II, was characterized by a fixed exchange system. Under the provisions of the Bretton Woods Agreement, signed in 1944, the government of each member country pledged to maintain a fixed, or pegged, exchange rate for its currency vis-à-vis the dollar or gold. Because one ounce of gold was set equal to $35, fixing a currency's gold price was equivalent to setting its exchange rate relative to the dollar. For example, the deutsche mark was set equal to 1/140 of an ounce of gold, meaning it was worth $0.25 ($35/DM140). Participating countries agreed to try to maintain the value of their currencies within a 1% band by buying or selling foreign exchange or gold as needed. Devaluation was not to be used as a competitive trade policy, but if a currency became too weak to defend, a devaluation of up to 10% was allowed without formal approval by the IMF.

During this period, the U.S. dollar was the main reserve currency held by central banks and was the key to the web of exchange rate values. Unfortunately, the United States ran persistent and growing deficits on its balance of payments. A heavy capital outflow of dollars was required to finance these deficits and to meet the growing demand for dollars from investors and businesses. Eventually the heavy overhang of dollars held abroad resulted in a lack of confidence in the ability of the United States to meet its commitment to convert dollars to gold. On August 15, 1971, the United States responded to a huge trade deficit by making the dollar inconvertible into gold. A 10% surcharge was placed on imports, and a program of wage and price controls was introduced. Many of the major currencies were allowed to float against the dollar. The dollar then began a decade of decline.

Under the Smithsonian Agreement, which was reached among the world's leading trading nations in Washington, D.C., in December 1971, the United States agreed to devalue the dollar to $38 per ounce of gold. In return, the other countries present agreed to revalue their own currencies upward in relation to the dollar by specified amounts. Actual revaluation ranged from 7.4% by Canada to 16.9% by Japan. Furthermore, the allowed floating band around par value was expanded from ± 1% to ± 2.25%.

Because of high inflation in the United States, the dollar devaluation remained insufficient to restore stability to the system. By 1973, the dollar was under heavy selling pressure even at its devalued rates. By late February 1973, a fixed-rate system appeared no longer feasible given the speculative flows of currencies. The major foreign exchange markets were actually closed for several weeks in March 1973. When they reopened, most currencies were allowed to float to levels determined by market forces.

The Post–Bretton Woods System: 1973–Present

This period is characterized by a floating exchange rate system. Since March 1973, exchange rates have become much more volatile and less predictable than they were during the "fixed" exchange rate period. The system became increasingly volatile as it approached the oil crisis of the fall of 1973. As mentioned in the preceding chapter, October 1973 marked the beginning of successful efforts by the Organization of Petroleum Exporting Countries (OPEC) to raise the price of oil. By 1974, oil prices had quadrupled. Several nations, most notably the United States, tried to offset the effect of higher energy bills by boosting spending. The results were high inflation and vast deficits in the balance of payments, which eventually caused the dollar crisis of 1977–1978.

Although the U.S. dollar strongly rebounded during 1981–1985, largely because of President Reagan's economic policies (high interest rates, foreign capital inflow, and economic expansion), the dollar resumed its long downhill slide. The slide was attributed mainly to changes in U.S. government policy and a slowdown in the U.S. economy. Believing that the dollar had declined enough, the United States, Japan, West Germany, France, Britain, Canada, and Italy—also known as the **Group of Seven** (or G7)—met in February 1987 and agreed to slow the dollar's fall. This agreement, also known as the **Louvre Accords**, called for the G7 nations to support the falling dollar by pegging exchange rates within a narrow, undisclosed range. They agreed that exchange rates had been sufficiently realigned and pledged to support stability of exchange rates at or near their current levels. Although the dollar declined further during 1987, it rallied in early 1988, thereby ending for the moment its dramatic volatility during the period 1980–1987. The U.S. dollar fell again in 1990 but then stayed basically flat during 1991–1992. It began falling again in 1993, especially against the Japanese yen and DM.

The turmoil that rocked Asian foreign exchange markets starting in June 1997 was the third major crisis of the 1990s. Its two predecessors were the crisis in the European Monetary System (EMS) of 1992–1993 and the Mexican peso crisis of 1994–1995 (see Opening Case). The collapse of the Thai currency, the baht, started the Asian crisis in June 1997. In one month, the baht lost 20% of its value against the dollar. The currencies of the Philippines, Malaysia, and Indonesia all weakened as well. Malaysian prime minister Mahathir Mohamad blasted "rogue speculators." Later he called billionaire hedge-fund manager George Soros a "moron" for betting against Asian currencies. In August 1997, Indonesian authorities were forced to allow the national currency, the rupiah, to move freely against other currencies. In December 1997, the IMF put together a $58.4 billion international bailout for Korea, the largest ever. The Koreans decided to let the won float. Faced with rapidly deteriorating foreign currency reserves, the Russian authorities devalued the ruble in August 1998. The U.S. Federal Reserve responded to fear of a U.S. credit crunch by lowering interest rates three times in quick succession during the course of the fall, including a rare unilateral move by former Fed chairman Alan Greenspan. Other industrialized countries, such as Canada, Japan, and most of the European nations, also eased monetary policies in September 1998. In October 1998, the world's rich nations, the G7, endorsed a U.S. plan to allow the IMF to lend to countries before they get into financial difficulties. Exhibit 9.1 lists major events related to the international monetary system during 1973–2006.

Interim Summary

1. The international monetary system has gone through several phases, including the gold standard period (1876–1914), the interwar years and World War II (1914–1944), the Bretton Woods system (1944–1973), and the post–Bretton Woods system (1973–present).

Exhibit 9.1 World Currency Events 1973–2006

Date	Event	Impact
February 1973	U.S. dollar devalued	Devaluation pressure increases on U.S. dollar forcing devaluation to $42.22/oz. of gold.
February–March 1973	Currency markets in crisis	Fixed exchange rates no longer considered defensible; speculative pressures force closure of international foreign exchange markets for nearly two weeks; markets reopen with floating rates for major industrial currencies.
June 1973	U.S. dollar depreciation	Floating rates continue to drive the new free-floating U.S. dollar down by about 10% by June.
Fall 1973–1974	OPEC oil embargo	Organization of Petroleum Exporting Countries (OPEC) imposes an oil embargo, eventually quadrupling the world price of oil; because oil prices are stated in U.S. dollars, the U.S. dollar recovers some of its former strength.
January 1976	Jamaica Agreement	IMF meeting in Jamaica results in the "legalization" of the floating exchange rate system already in effect; gold is demonetized as a reserve asset; IMF quotas are increased.
1977–1978	U.S. inflation rate rises	Rising U.S. inflation causes continued depreciation of the U.S. dollar.
March 1979	EMS created	European Monetary System (EMS) is created, establishing a cooperative exchange rate system for participating members of the EEC.
Summer 1979	OPEC raises prices	OPEC nations raise oil prices once again.
Fall 1979	Iranian assets frozen	President Carter responds to Iranian hostage crisis by freezing all Iranian assets held in U.S. financial institutions.
Spring 1980	U.S. dollar begins rise	Worldwide inflation and early signs of recession coupled with real interest differential advantages for dollar-denominated assets contribute to rising demand for dollars.
August 1982	Latin American debt crisis	Mexico informs U.S. Treasury that it will be unable to make debt service payments; Brazil and Argentina follow suit; the debt crisis begins.
February 1985	U.S. dollar peaks	U.S. dollar peaks against most major industrial currencies, hitting record highs against the deutsche mark and other European currencies.
September 1985	Plaza Agreement	Group of Five members, meeting at the Plaza Hotel in New York, sign an international cooperative agreement to control the volatility of world currency markets and establish currency target zones.
February 1987	Louvre Accords	Group of Seven members state they will "intensify" economic policy coordination to promote growth and reduce external imbalances.
September 1992	EMS crisis	High German interest rates induce massive capital flows into Germany and deutsche mark–denominated assets, eventually causing the withdrawal of the Italian lira and British pound from the EMS's Exchange Rate Mechanism (ERM).
July 31, 1993	EMS realignment	EMS adjusts allowable deviation band to +/− 15% for all member currencies (except the Dutch guilder); U.S. dollar continues to weaken against other major currencies; Japanese yen reaches ¥100.25/$ in August 1993.
1994	EMI founded	European Monetary Institute, the predecessor to the European Central Bank, is founded in Frankfurt, Germany.
December 1994	Peso collapses	Mexican peso suffers major devaluation as a result of increasing pressure on the managed devaluation policy; peso falls from Ps3.46/$ to Ps5.50/$ within days. The peso's collapse results in a fall in most major Latin American exchanges (tequila effect).
August 1995	Yen peaks	Japanese yen reaches an all-time high versus the U.S. dollar of ¥79/$; yen slowly depreciates over the following two-year period, rising to over ¥130/$.

Date	Event	Impact
June 1997	Asian financial crisis	First afflicting Thailand in June 1997, then quickly spreading to South Korea, Indonesia, Malaysia, the Philippines, and other Southeast and East Asian countries.
August 1998	Financial turmoil in Russia and Latin America	Influenced by the Asian crisis, Russia devaluates the ruble and unilaterally restructures its debts. The situation worsens following the devaluation in Brazil in January 1999.
January 1, 1999	Euro launched	Official launch date for the single European currency, the euro. Participating states' exchange rates will be irrevocably locked; European Monetary Institute will be succeeded by the European Central Bank, establishing a single monetary policy for Europe.
January 1, 2002	Euro coinage	Euro coins and notes are introduced in parallel with home currencies; transition period to last no more than six months.
July 2005	RMB revaluation	The Chinese government increased the value of the country's currency, renminbi (RMB), by 2.1% and has continued to do so since. China's main trading partners, especially the United States, pressure the Chinese government for a change, saying that RMB is undervalued and is making the country's exports artificially cheap.

2. The fixed exchange rate system was a staple of the international monetary system prior to March 1973, and the floating exchange rate system was dominant after March 1973.

CONTEMPORARY EXCHANGE RATE SYSTEMS

Fixed-Rate System

Under a **fixed-rate system**, governments (through their central banks) buy or sell their currencies in the foreign exchange market whenever exchange rates deviate from their stated par values. A purely fixed-rate system is employed currently by only a few centrally planned economies, such as Cuba and North Korea. In these economies, it is generally mandatory that a local firm's foreign exchange earnings be surrendered to the central bank, which in return pays the firm a corresponding amount in local currency. The central bank often allocates these foreign exchange incomes to state-owned users on the basis of governmental priorities. Exhibit 9.2 presents typical foreign exchange control measures used by governments under fixed or managed foreign exchange systems.

Exhibit 9.2 Frequently Used Foreign Exchange Control Measures

1. Import restrictions such as license or quota systems
2. Restrictions on remittance of foreign exchange such as profit, dividends, or royalties
3. Surrender of hard-currency export earnings to the central bank
4. Mandatory government approval for using a firm's retained foreign exchange earnings
5. Predeposit of foreign exchange expenditures for import businesses in interest-free accounts with the central bank for a certain period
6. Credit ceilings for foreign firms
7. Restriction or prohibition on offshore deposit or investment of hard currencies
8. Use of multiple exchange rates simultaneously for different items of the balance of payment

Despite drawbacks such as resource misallocation, distortion of foreign exchange demand and supply, and a drag on company performance, the fixed-rate system may help economies stabilize their economic environment, emphasize priority projects that need foreign exchange, and control foreign exchange reserves. In a broader, international context, fixed rates provide stability in international prices for the conduct of trade, which in turn lessens risks for international companies.

Crawling Peg System

The peg system is situated between the fixed-rate and float-rate systems. The **crawling peg** is an automatic system for revising the exchange rate, establishing a par value around which the rate can vary up to a given percentage point. The par value is revised regularly according to a formula determined by the authorities. Once the par value is set, the central bank intervenes whenever the market value approaches a limit point. Suppose, for example, that the par value of the Mexican peso is 3,000 pesos for one dollar, and that it can vary ±2% around this rate, between 3,060 pesos and 2,940 pesos. If the dollar approaches the rate of 3,060 pesos, the central bank intervenes by buying pesos and selling dollars. If the dollar approaches 2,940 pesos, the central bank intervenes by selling pesos and buying dollars. If it hovers around a limit point for too long, causing frequent central bank intervention, a new par value closer to this point is established. Suppose the dollar were hovering around 3,060 pesos. The government might then establish the new par value at 3,060 pesos with new limit points at 3,121 and 2,999.

A government can peg its currency either to another single currency (see the Country Box for illustration) or to a "basket" of foreign currencies. Today, 62 of the 167 members of the IMF peg their currency to some other currency. The U.S. dollar is the base for 20 other currencies (e.g., Argentina, Iraq, Panama, Venezuela, Dominica, and Hong Kong). The French franc is the base for 14 currencies (all issued by former French colonies in Africa). Similarly, six of the new countries created with the breakup of the Soviet Union peg their currency to the Russian ruble.

Other countries peg their currency to a composite basket of currencies, where the basket consists of a portfolio of currencies of their major trading partners. The base value of such a basket is more stable than any single currency. Under this regime, a country can peg its currency to the standard basket such as the special drawing rights (SDR; e.g., Libya and Myanmar), or to its own basket, designed to fit the country's unique trading and investing needs (e.g., Bangladesh, Cyprus, the Czech Republic, Iceland, Jordan, Kuwait, Nepal, Thailand, and Morocco). In the latter approach, the basket normally contains currencies of major trading partners, weighted according to trading relations with the focal country.

The peg system is not a panacea. When pegged rates become overvalued, countries are forced to deplete their foreign exchange reserves to defend the currency peg. With reserves depleted, countries try to manipulate interest rates but are often eventually forced to devalue, repegging at a lower rate or giving up the peg altogether. With a floating rate system, countries can maintain their foreign reserves and thereby maintain a defense against financial panic, which often plagues pegged exchange regimes. Foreign creditors understand that the central bank has sufficient reserves to repay short-term debts, thereby eliminating the possibility of a self-fulfilling creditor panic. Also, governments are not forced to break their word when international or domestic events force change in market exchange rates. For example, in April 2002, undergoing economic meltdown and five changes of president in two weeks, Argentina (under the floating regime) declared the world's largest debt default and devalued its peso by more than 70%.

COUNTRY BOX

CAN THE HONG KONG DOLLAR RETAIN THE FIXED PEG TO THE U.S. DOLLAR?

Many analysts question whether Hong Kong can retain the fixed peg to the U.S. dollar. Several factors are in Hong Kong's favor. First, in addition to Hong Kong's foreign exchange reserves of some US$75 billion, the Chinese government is also prepared to use its US$140 billion of reserves to defend the HK dollar. China has a vested economic and political interest in preserving Hong Kong's exchange rate and financial stability. Second, the overall economy of Hong Kong remains strong, as reflected in recurring fiscal and balance-of-payments surpluses, an extremely long foreign debt service ratio (1.3%), and an efficiently regulated and supervised banking system. Nonperforming loans account for less than 1% of advances, and capital adequacy ratios are over 13%. The risk is that coming off the peg now would lead to more frequent and intense speculation in the future in both the foreign exchange and equity markets, given the openness of these markets and the lack of exchange controls. A very small economy like Hong Kong, which serves as a regional financial and trading center, needs stability and certainty, which the peg provides. With the manufacturing sector accounting for less than 10% of GDP, the benefits of devaluation would be minimal. The peg system was established in 1984 to counter the uncertainty following the UK–PRC declaration of 1997 handover.

SOURCE: Adapted from *Accountancy* (International Edition), First Quarter 1998: pp. 27–29.

Target-Zone Arrangement

Target-zone arrangement is virtually a joint float system cooperatively arranged by a group of nations sharing some common interests and goals. Under a target-zone arrangement, countries adjust their national economic policies to maintain their exchange rates within a specific margin around agreed-upon, fixed central exchange rates. Such an arrangement exists for the major European currencies participating in the European Monetary System (EMS). Members of the European Union have a cooperative agreement to maintain their currencies within a set range against other members of their group. The **EMS** is, in essence, a peg of each country's currency to all the others, as well as a joint float of all member currencies together against non-EMS currencies. The target-zone arrangement helps minimize exchange rate instability and enhance economic stability in the group (zone).

Let us use the EMS to illustrate this type of arrangement. As part of the EMS, the members established the ECU (and later the euro), which plays a central role in the functioning of the EMS. Taking effect January 1, 1999, the **euro** is a composite currency for European Union countries (Denmark, the United Kingdom, and Sweden have not joined the euro yet), with foreign exchange rates of the participating national currencies being irrevocably fixed against one another and against the euro. The new member states (e.g., the Czech Republic, Estonia, Cyprus, Latvia, Lithuania, Hungary, Malta, Poland, Slovakia, and Slovenia) will adopt the euro only when they fulfill certain economic criteria—namely, a high degree of price stability, a sound fiscal situation, stable exchange rates, and converged long-term interest rates.

Today, the euro functions as a unit of account, a means of settlement, a reserve asset for the members of the European Union, and a real currency. At the heart of the EMS is an exchange-rate mechanism that allows each member to determine a mutually agreed-upon central exchange rate for its currency; each rate is denominated in currency units per euro (e.g., DM2.05853 per euro). Central rates establish a grid of cross-exchange rates between currencies. For example, 2.05853 deutsche marks per euro, divided by 6.90403 French francs per euro, equals 0.29816 DM per French franc. Member nations pledged to keep their currencies within a ±2.25% margin around their central cross-exchange rates (Spain has a 6% margin).

The **European Central Bank** (ECB), based in Frankfurt and established in June 1998, is the central bank in the euro zone. It is as powerful in Europe as the Federal Reserve is in the United States. This central bank sets interest rates for the euro zone. However, the ECB is not a duplicate of the U.S. Fed. One of the most important differences between the two is their respective mandates. The Fed's goal is to balance the objectives of price stability with those of employment and economic growth. The ECB, on the other hand, has a narrower focus patterned on the Bundesbank (Germany's former central bank). It is only responsible for keeping prices stable. In addition, the Fed deals with only one government, whereas the ECB is faced with all member governments, each with its own fiscal policies. Finance ministers from the currency-union members hold informal meetings regularly to coordinate fiscal policies.

The target-zone arrangement is not without problems. Owing to the divergence of national policies, the level of economic development, and the trade structure, it is difficult for every member to maintain the central exchange rate for a long period of time. Moreover, when currency speculators attack one of the zone currencies, defense is more costly. In fact, the euro's exchange rate mechanism had to be realigned in 1992, as a result of attacks by speculators against the Nordic currencies (Finland, Sweden, and Norway) as well as the French franc, British pound, and Italian lira, successively.

Managed Float System

The **managed float**, also known as a "dirty float," is employed by governments to preserve an orderly pattern of exchange rate changes and is designed to eliminate excess volatility. Each central bank sets the nation's exchange rate against a predetermined goal but allows the rate to vary. In other words, rate change is not automatic but is based on the government's view of an appropriate rate in the context of the country's balance-of-payments position, foreign exchange reserves, and rates quoted outside the official market. Rather than resist the underlying market forces, the authorities occasionally intervene by buying or selling domestic currency to smooth the transition from one rate to another. At other times they intervene to moderate or counteract self-correcting cyclical or seasonal market forces. The rationale for the managed float is to improve the economic and financial environment by reducing uncertainty. For instance, government intervention may reduce exporters' uncertainty caused by disruptive exchange rate changes. Currently, about 40 countries (e.g., Brazil, China, Egypt, Hungary, Korea, Israel, Poland, Turkey, and Russia) maintain a managed float system. The challenge behind this approach is to define just what is meant by "excess volatility." It is also questionable if governments are more capable than markets in determining what is fundamental and what is temporary and self-correcting.[1]

Independent Float System

Approximately 55 countries currently allow full flexibility through an **independent float**, also known as a *clean float*. Under this system, an exchange rate is allowed to adjust freely to the supply and demand of one currency for another. Consequently, there is usually no need for an economy to undergo the painful adjustment process set in motion by a decrease or increase in the money supply. This category contains currencies of both developed (e.g., the United States) and developing (e.g., Peru) countries. Central banks of these countries allow exchange rates to be determined by market forces alone. Although some central banks may intervene in the market from time to time, such intervening usually attempts to alleviate speculative pressures on their currency. Further, central banks intervene only as one of many anonymous participants in the free market in an occasional, noncontinuous manner. Exhibit 9.3 shows sample countries and their exchange rate systems.

Advantages and Disadvantages of the Floating System

The floating-rate system, whether managed or independent, is the dominant system at the beginning of the 21st century, utilized by about 100 countries. The flexible exchange rate system provides a less painful adjustment mechanism to trade imbalances than do fixed exchange rates and prevents a country from having large persistent deficits. Unlike the fixed-rate system, which requires a recession to reduce real (inflation-adjusted) income or prices when trade deficits arise, flexible exchange rates will only lower the foreign exchange value of the currency. In a fixed-rate system, reducing local currency income (wages) is likely to be painful for political and social reasons, even though this reduction (and thus the decline in the value of this nation's currency) can improve the trade balance.[2]

Moreover, flexible exchange rates do not require central banks to hold foreign exchange reserves because there is no need to intervene in the foreign exchange market. This means that the problem of insufficient liquidity (foreign exchange reserves) does not exist with truly flexible rates. Further, flexible exchange rates avoid the need for strict import and export regulations such as tariffs, foreign exchange control, and import restrictions. These regulations

---

Exhibit 9.3   Sample Countries Using Different Exchange Rate Systems

Independent Float	Managed Float	Target Zone	Crawling Peg	Fixed
United States	Singapore	Austria	Argentina	North Korea
Peru	Afghanistan	Belgium	Iraq	Cuba
Philippines	Brazil	France	Panama	
Romania	Australia	Germany	Hong Kong	
South Africa	China	Ireland	Cameroon	
Yemen	Canada	Luxembourg	Chad	
Zambia	India	Netherlands	Togo	
Denmark	Japan	Portugal	Estonia	
Yemen	Israel	Spain	Libya	
Zimbabwe	Korea	Finland	Bangladesh	
Paraguay	Malaysia	Italy	Czech Republic	
Sudan	Poland	Greece	Kuwait	
Tanzania	Russia	United Kingdom	Iceland	

are not only costly to enforce but also prone to criticism and even retaliation from trade partner countries.

Finally, floating exchange rates can help ensure the independence of trade policies. For example, if the United States allows rapid growth in the money supply, this will tend to raise U.S. prices and lower interest rates (in the short run), the former causing a deficit or deterioration in the current account and the latter causing a deficit or deterioration in the capital account. If, for example, the Canadian dollar were fixed to the U.S. dollar, the deficit in the United States would most likely mean a surplus in Canada. This would put upward pressure on the Canadian dollar, forcing the Bank of Canada to sell Canadian dollars and hence increase the Canadian money supply. In this case an increase in the U.S. money supply would cause an increase in the Canadian money supply. However, if exchange rates were flexible, the U.S. dollar would simply depreciate against the Canadian dollar.

The role of flexible rates, however, is limited in balancing trade after a certain period of time. A depreciation or devaluation of currency will help the balance of trade if it reduces the relative prices of locally produced goods and services. However, after a short period of time, domestic prices of tradable goods will rise following depreciation or devaluation. This will increase the cost of living, which puts upward pressure on wages.[3] For example, if 1% depreciation raises production costs by the same percentage point, and if real wages are maintained, then nominal wages must rise by the amount of depreciation or devaluation. If wages rise 1% when the currency falls by 1%, the effects are offsetting, and changes in exchange rates will be ineffective. In addition, flexible rates could make it more difficult for governments to control inflation and also create less motivation for governments to combat it.[4] Finally, free-float rates may cause more uncertainty, which may in turn hamper the growth and stability of economies vulnerable to international financial and export markets. Under the floating system, international speculators can cause wide swings in the values of different currencies. These swings are the result of the movement of "hot money chasing better returns and the enormous speed of capital flows whose scale dwarfs that of trade flows."[5]

Interim Summary

1. Countries utilize the crawling peg system, target-zone arrangement, managed float system, or independent float system in a rising sequence of flexibility and volatility.

2. Countries select different exchange rate systems because they have different goals, different levels of internationalization, and different capabilities of managing foreign exchange volatility.

DETERMINATION OF FOREIGN EXCHANGE RATES

The determination of a national currency's exchange rate should answer two basic questions: (a) *How is the base rate between this nation's currency and foreign currencies determined?* That is, what is the underlying criterion used to determine the base level (*stocks*) of exchange rate of a currency vis-à-vis others? and (b) *How does a nation's exchange rate change over time (flows)?* That is, what are the conditions under which the exchange rate should change, and how?

Under the gold standard regime (1876–1914), the base level of a currency's exchange rate was determined by the stated value of gold per unit of the currency. Assume, for example, that one deutsche mark is worth 0.02 ounce of gold while one U.S. dollar is worth 0.048 ounce of gold. The gold equivalent then becomes the underlying criterion used in determining the base rate of the deutsche mark against other currencies, such as the U.S. dollar (DM2.4/$1 in this case).

Under other foreign exchange regimes, however, there is no direct way to value one currency against others in terms of both stocks and flows. Moreover, the present international monetary system is characterized by a mix of free-floating, managed-floating, pegged or target zone, and fixed exchange rates. No single general theory is available to forecast exchange rates under all conditions. Nevertheless, it is widely agreed that the purchasing power parity principle helps explain both the stocks and the flows of exchange rates. Other principles or approaches to analyze foreign exchange movements include interest rate parity and international Fisher parity. The purchasing power parity approach emphasizes the role of prices of goods and services in determining exchange rates, whereas the **interest rate parity** focuses on the role of capital movements. Although these two perspectives are insufficient to explain exchange rate changes, they are useful building blocks of foreign exchange determination.

Purchasing Power Parity

The **purchasing power parity (PPP) principle** suggests that the exchange rate between two currencies should, in the long run, reflect purchasing power differences—that is, the exchange rate should equalize the price of an identical basket of goods and services in the two countries. This principle has absolute and relative perspectives toward purchasing power parity. **Absolute PPP** states that the exchange rate is determined by the relative prices of similar baskets of goods or services. In other words, the ratio of one currency's price of a bundle of goods and services to another currency's price of the same bundle should be the exchange rate between the two. For example, if the identical basket of goods cost ¥1,000 in Japan and $10 in the United States, the PPP-based exchange rate would be ¥100/$1.

The PPP principle in the absolute, or static, form offers a simple explanation for exchange rate determination. However, it is difficult in practice to compute the price indices. Different baskets of goods are used in different countries, given the different demand structures and consumption behaviors. To avoid this deficiency, **relative PPP** focuses on the relationship between the change in prices of two countries and the change in the exchange rate over the same period. The relative PPP suggests that if the exchange rate between two countries starts in equilibrium, any change in the differential rate of inflation between them tends to be offset over the long run by an equal but opposite change in the exchange rate. If the domestic inflation level is rising faster than the foreign inflation level, the exchange rate is depreciating. If the foreign inflation level is rising faster than the domestic inflation level, the exchange rate is appreciating. If the exchange rate does not change in this situation, the country's exports of goods and services will become less competitive with comparable products produced elsewhere. Imports from abroad will also become more price competitive than higher-priced domestic products.

The PPP principle offers an economic foundation for determining and adjusting the exchange rates. In the real business world, however, PPP conditions may not always hold. The exchange rates are thus not always determined by the purchasing power parity. Reasons for departures from PPP include the following:

1. The PPP principle assumes that goods or services can move freely across borders. In practice, however, we see many restrictions on movement of goods and services (e.g., tariff and nontariff barriers). These barriers affect both the price and quantity of exports and imports.

2. Many of the items that are often included in the commonly used price indices do not enter into international trade (e.g., land and buildings). These nontraded items can allow departures from PPP to persist.

3. The PPP principle fails to consider cross-border transportation costs, which enlarge the PPP deviations.

4. The PPP principle fails to consider the reality that different items have different weights in various nations' price indices.

Interest Rate Parity

The PPP principle focuses only on goods and services and omits the importance of capital flows in the determination of exchange rates. To redress this limitation, the **interest rate parity (IRP) principle** provides an understanding of the way in which interest rates are linked between different countries through capital flows. The IRP principle suggests that the difference in national interest rates for securities of similar risk and maturity should be equal to, but opposite in sign of, the forward rate discount or premium for the foreign currency. A **forward rate** is the rate at which a bank is willing to exchange one currency for another at some specified future date. If this exchange takes place immediately, this rate is called a spot rate. A forward rate discount (premium) measures the percentage by which the forward rate is less (or more) than the spot rate at a specific date. The IRP implies that the interest rate differential between two countries will be matched by the forward premium of the exchange rate. This relation holds owing to efficient arbitrage in risk-free assets. It can be applied to international investments as well as to international lending. The rationale underlying the IRP is that for investment projects, investors compare the return from the domestic market with the return from the foreign market; the latter is the return from the foreign asset plus the forward premium. For financing projects, borrowers compare the costs from the domestic market with those from the foreign market. Equilibrium will be achieved when interest parity is established.

Consider, for example, the case in which the one-year interest rate in New York is 8.75%, and in London 11.75%. This seems to suggest that investors will earn an excess return of 3% if the funds are invested in the London bond market (or that borrowers will acquire funds more inexpensively in New York). However, if the prevailing current spot rate is \$1.6375/£1 and the one-year forward rate is \$1.5883/£1, then investors who convert their proceeds back to U.S. dollars will have to pay a 3% forward discount on the pound sterling in the forward market. We see that the interest rate advantage is offset by the forward discount on the pound. If the investors did not use the forward market, they may suffer a loss greater than 3%, because the actual spot rate between dollar and pound a year later may drop more than 3%.

Like PPP, IRP also faces deviations owing to transaction costs and tax factors in financial markets. Political risks can also cause deviations from interest parity between countries because investors expect to be compensated for the greater risk of investing in a foreign country. The forward market and related terms will be discussed in detail later in this chapter.

The IRP is generally applicable to securities with maturities of one year or less, since forward contracts are not routinely available for periods longer than one year. Similar to the IRP principle but involving securities with maturity that could be longer than one year, the **international Fisher effect** addresses the relationship between the percentage change in the spot exchange rate over time and the differential between comparable interest rates in different national capital markets. Specifically, the international Fisher effect states that the spot exchange rate should change in an equal amount but in the opposite direction to the difference in interest rates between two countries. For example, if a dollar-based investor buys a 10-year yen bond earning 4% annual interest, compared with 6% interest available on dollars, the investor must be anticipating the yen to appreciate vis-à-vis the dollar by at least 2% per year during the 10 years.

Implications for MNEs: Foreign Exchange Forecasting

Because future exchange rates are uncertain, participants in international financial markets can never know for sure what the exchange rate will be one month or one year ahead. As a result, forecasts must be made. Some forecasters believe that for the major floating currencies, foreign exchange markets are "efficient" and forward exchange rates are unbiased predictors of future spot exchange rates. However, empirical studies have rejected this hypothesis.[6] Although referencing the forward rate (see next section) is still necessary and useful, and can be viewed as a baseline in forecasting a foreign exchange rate, international managers should take into account many economic and noneconomic factors in predicting foreign exchange rates, especially long-term rates (over one year).

Economic fundamentals that influence long-term exchange rates include balance of payments, foreign exchange reserves, relative inflation rates, relative interest rates, and the long-run properties of purchasing power parity. The strength of a focal country's economy, which is often reflected in its GDP (gross domestic product), GNP (gross national product), national income, investment growth, and export growth, among other measures, also influences the country's long-term exchange rates. Because governments differ in the extent to which they exert influence on foreign exchange rates, even under the floating system, managers should be aware of government declarations and agreements regarding exchange rate goals. Noneconomic fundamentals that may affect exchange rates include political or social events, bilateral relations between the two countries, market speculations against the currency, the confidence of market participants, and natural disasters.

In emerging markets with foreign exchange control set by the government, there often exist foreign exchange black (or parallel) markets in which buyers and sellers exchange foreign currencies using the market rate, which is generally different from the official rate. Because this "market" rate is often a "shadow" price that reflects the demand and supply equilibrium in the foreign exchange market, it is often used as the reference rate in predicting managerial floating exchange rates. In predicting exchange rates, international managers also look at the country's foreign exchange rate system. If, for example, a country pegs its currency to that of another major trade partner, then the exchange rate prediction will emphasize the partner country's currency. To predict a long-term fixed rate, managers also need to see if the government is capable of controlling domestic inflation, to generate hard currency reserves to use for intervention and to run trade surpluses. To predict a long-term floating rate, managers must focus on inflationary fundamentals and PPP as well as indicators for economic health such as growth and stability.

Time-series analysis of prior years, together with anticipated new factors about future changes, is a widely applied technique for predicting foreign exchange rates, particularly short-term trends. The accuracy of these forecasts depends on whether the foreign exchange market is efficient. The more efficient the market, the more likely it is that exchange rates are "random walks" (e.g., with past price behavior providing no clues to the future). The less efficient the foreign exchange market, the higher the probability that forecasters will find a key pattern that holds, at least in the short run. If the pattern is truly consistent, however, others will soon discover it and the market will become efficient again with respect to that information.

Interim Summary

1. The purchasing power parity (PPP) principle holds that the exchange rate between two currencies is determined in the long run by the price of an identical basket of goods and services. The interest rate parity (IRP) principle holds that the interest rate differential between two countries will be matched by the premium of their forward exchange rate.

2. To predict or forecast foreign exchange rates, international managers analyze both economic and noneconomic fundamentals, while making reference to forward or black-market exchange rates.

THE BALANCE OF PAYMENTS

The exchange rate system is a necessary tool for international transactions involving different currencies. The national goal of these transactions is to accomplish gains from trade and investment activities, which are recorded in the balance-of-payments account. The **balance of payments** is an accounting statement that summarizes all the economic transactions between residents (individuals, companies, and other organizations) of the home country and those of all other countries. That is, it reports the country's international performance in trading with other nations and the volume of capital flowing in and out of the country. Balance of payments accounting uses the system of **double-entry bookkeeping**, which means that every debit or credit in the account is also represented as a credit or debit somewhere else. On a balance-of-payments sheet, currency inflows are recorded as *credits* (plus sign), whereas outflows are recorded as *debits* (minus sign).

A standard balance of payments includes the *current account, capital account,* and *official reserves account.* Each category is made of several subcategories. To maintain the balance of the total credit and total debit, the statistical discrepancy is also included in a balance of payments. Statistical discrepancy reflects net errors and omissions in collecting data on international transactions. Exhibit 9.4 illustrates the United States' balance-of-payments sheet for 2000 and 2005.

Current Account

The **current account** records flows of goods, services, and unilateral transfers (gifts). It includes exports and imports of merchandise (trade balance) and service transactions (also known as invisible items). The service account includes various service income and fees (e.g., interest, dividends, and royalties). Tourism income, financial charges (e.g., banking and insurance), and transportation charges (e.g., shipping and air travel) are part of service income. The investment income account separates investment income from service income, and it records income

Exhibit 9.4   The U.S. Balance of Payments, 2002 and 2005 (in Billions of Dollars)

	2000	*2005*
CURRENT ACCOUNT		
Goods		
Exports	+772.21	+894.63
Imports	−1224.42	−1677.37
Balance of merchandise trade	−452.21	−782.74
Services		
Exports	+293.49	+380.61
Imports	−217.02	−314.60
Balance of services trade	+76.47	+66.01
Investment income		
Received	+352.87	+474.65
Paid	−367.66	−463.35
Balance of investment income	−14.79	+11.30
Unilateral transfer (net)	−54.14	−86.07
Balance on current account	−444.67	−791.51
CAPITAL ACCOUNT		
Portfolio investment		
New investment/lending in United States	+736.56	+1102.50
New U.S. investment/lending abroad	−428.22	−436.18
Foreign direct investment		
New FDI in United States	+287.66	+109.75
New U.S. FDI abroad	−152.44	−9.07
Balance on capital account	+443.56	+767.00
OFFICIAL RESERVES ACCOUNT	−0.29	+14.10
Gold	0	0
SDRs	−0.72	+4.51
Reserve in the IMF	+2.31	+10.20
Foreign currencies	−1.88	−0.61
ERRORS AND OMISSIONS	+1.40	+10.41
NET BALANCE	**0**	**0**

SOURCE: Bureau of Economic Analysis, U.S. Department of Commerce, Washington, D.C. www.bea.gov.

receipts on the country-owned assets abroad and income payments on foreign-owned assets within the country. Unilateral transfers include pensions, remittances, and other transfers for which no specific services are furnished.

Capital Account

The **capital account** records private and public investment or lending activities and is divided into portfolio (short- and long-term) and foreign direct investment. Foreign branches, wholly owned subsidiaries, and joint ventures are typical forms of direct investments. Foreign bonds, notes, or mutual funds are examples of portfolio investment insofar as they confer no management or voting rights on their owners. The portfolio account includes both short-term (e.g., cash, deposits, and bills) and long-term investments or lending (e.g., securities with a maturity longer than one year, bank loans, and mortgages). Government borrowing and lending are also included in the capital account.

Official Reserves Account

The **official reserves account** records net holdings of the official reserves held by a national government. Reserves include gold, special drawing rights (SDRs), reserve positions in the IMF, and convertible foreign currencies. To most countries, foreign currency is by far the largest component of total international liquidity. Each government normally keeps foreign exchange reserves in the form of foreign treasury bills, short-term and long-term government securities, euros, and the like.

Note that the implications of the balance of payments, especially a trade deficit or surplus under current account, may change over time and is subject to interpretation. Today many imports are actually "exported" by the country's own companies operating in a trading partner country. But, statistically, they are still "imports" recorded in the balance of payments. The United States had, for example, a $52.67 billion merchandise trade deficit with China, followed by $45.67 with Japan, $37.57 with Canada, and $19.86 with Mexico, as of August 2001. However, a sizable percentage of imports entering the United States were in fact "exported" by American companies (e.g., RCA, HP, Pepsi, GE, Xerox, and Rubbermaid) investing and operating in these partner countries. One-third of China's total exports ($249 billion in 2000), for instance, are undertaken by foreign investors in the country. From a wealth creation perspective, these "imports" may be viewed as a plus, rather than minus, sign in the balance of payments.

Interim Summary

1. The balance of payments records economic transactions between one country and the rest of the world. It contains the current account, capital account, and official reserves balance.

2. A nation's trade deficits (such as those in the United States) may be reinterpreted if a large number of MNEs from this nation invest abroad and export back their products.

INTERNATIONAL FOREIGN EXCHANGE MARKETS

The international monetary systems introduced earlier are not the only influence on foreign currency movements. International financial markets also play a crucial role. International monetary systems and international financial markets are inherently linked such that the former affect company decisions or firm operations through the latter. International firms face many opportunities as well as threats arising from the international financial markets, which are determined at least partly by the monetary systems. International financial markets are composed of *international foreign exchange markets* and *international capital markets*. International capital markets further include (a) international money markets, (b) international stock markets, (c) international bond markets, and (d) international loan markets (see Exhibit 9.5).

Exhibit 9.5   International Financial Markets

	International Capital Markets			
International Foreign Exchange Market	International Money Market	International Stock Market	International Bond Market	International Loan Market

Landscape of the International Foreign Exchange Market

The **foreign exchange market** is where foreign currencies are bought and sold. It is the physical as well as institutional structure through which currencies are exchanged, exchange rates determined, and foreign exchange transactions completed. A **foreign exchange transaction** is an agreement between a buyer and seller for the delivery of a certain amount of one currency at a specified rate in exchange for some other currency. The 1999 survey of foreign exchange markets conducted by the BIS (Bank of International Settlements) illustrated that average daily turnover in the international foreign exchange market was about $1.5 trillion. The U.S. dollar was the most actively traded currency, reflecting its liquidity, its use as a settlement currency, and its predominance in trade-related transactions. The dollar was involved in over 80% of all foreign exchange transactions in 2001. The second and third most traded currencies were the deutsche mark and Japanese yen, respectively.

The global foreign exchange business is concentrated in four centers, which together account for about two-thirds of total reported turnover. These four centers are London, New York, Tokyo, and Singapore. Other important exchange markets are located in Paris, Frankfurt, Hong Kong, Amsterdam, Milan, Zurich, Toronto, Brussels, and Bahrain. A larger share of U.S. dollar turnover is conducted in London than in New York. The foreign exchange market is dominated by dealers and is becoming increasingly automated and concentrated.

Market Participants and Functions

A market for foreign exchange consists of individuals, corporations, banks, and brokers who buy or sell currencies. Currency trading in each country is conducted through the intermediation of foreign-exchange brokers, who match currency bids and offers of banks and also trade directly among themselves internationally. Banks in each country and throughout the world are linked together by telephone, Internet, telex, and a satellite communications network called the **Society for Worldwide International Financial Telecommunications (SWIFT)** based in Brussels, Belgium. Despite the long distance separating market participants, this computer-based communication system makes all significant events virtually instantaneous everywhere in the financial world. This in turn contributes to a worldwide market with narrower spreads for participants.

Although the market is global, the exchange market in each country has its own identity and institutional and regulatory framework. An efficient communication system can substitute for participants' need to convene in a specific location (bourse). Indeed, the UK–U.S. type of market is based on communication networks, whereas the European approach remains traditional, based on the physical meeting of the participants, usually at the bourse. Daily meetings take place in some markets such as those in Frankfurt and Paris, where representatives of commercial banks and central banks meet and determine a rate, known as the fixing rate. In those countries, the posted fixing rates serve as a guide for pricing small to medium-sized transactions between banks and their customers. Among major industrial countries, Japan, Germany, France, Italy, and the Scandinavian and the Benelux countries have a daily fixing. The United Kingdom, Switzerland, Canada, and the United States do not.

Foreign exchange is traded in a 24-hour market. As the market in the Far East closes, trading in the Middle Eastern financial centers has been going on for a couple of hours, and trading in Europe is just beginning. As the London market closes, the one in New York opens. A few hours later, the market in San Francisco opens and trades with the East Coast of the United States and the Far East as well. Banks dominate the foreign exchange market, with about 90% of foreign-exchange trading constituting interbank trading. Nonbank participants in foreign-exchange trading include commodities dealers, multinational corporations, and nonbank financial institutions.

The foreign-exchange market performs three major functions:

1. It is part of the international payments system and provides a mechanism for exchange or transfer of the national currency of one country into the currency of another country, thereby facilitating international business.

2. It assists in supplying short-term credits through the Eurocurrency market (see next section) and swap arrangements.

3. It provides foreign-exchange instruments for hedging against exchange risk. Although most commercial banks handle actions for their clients, many banks also act as market makers, with each prepared to deal with other banks at any time. This activity constitutes the interbank market, where portfolio positions are adjusted and exchange rates determined.

Foreign-exchange trading expanded sharply under the floating exchange rate system, and the number of banks participating in the market increased significantly as they entered the market to service their corporate clients. Increased hedging by companies of their cash flows and balance sheets was accompanied by the entry of new corporate participants into the market.

Foreign Exchange Rate Quotations

A foreign exchange quotation is the expression of willingness to buy or sell at a set rate. There are several pairs of quotations being used in foreign exchange businesses. Correctly interpreting the meaning of these quotations is important, as they are easy to confuse.

Direct and Indirect

A **direct quote** is a home currency price of a foreign currency unit (e.g., C$1.489/US$1 in Canada), whereas an **indirect quote** is a foreign currency price of a home currency unit (US$0.67182/C$1 in Canada). Under a direct quote, an increase of the exchange rate (e.g., from C$1.489 to C$1.589 per dollar) means depreciation of the home currency (C$) or appreciation of the foreign currency (US$). Conversely, under an indirect quote, an increase of the exchange rate (e.g., from US$0.67182 to US$0.68182 per Canadian dollar) means the appreciation of the home currency (C$) or depreciation of the foreign currency (US$). In most countries, banks use a direct quote.

Bid and Offer

A **bid** is the exchange rate in one currency at which a dealer (usually a bank) will buy another currency. An **offer** (also referred to as *ask*) is the exchange rate at which a dealer (usually a bank) will sell the other currency. The difference between the bid and offer prices, also known as the **bid-ask spread**, is the compensation for transaction cost for the dealer. For example, a Canadian bank's quotation for the U.S. dollar (US$/C$) may be 0.6718 (bid) and 0.6748 (offer). For widely traded currencies such as the U.S. dollar, euro, yen, or pound, the spread ranges from 0.05% to 0.08%.

Spot and Forward

This pair of quotes is used for foreign exchange transactions between dealers in the interbank market. A **spot rate** is the exchange rate for a transaction that requires almost immediate delivery of foreign exchange (normally before the end of the second business day). A **forward rate** is the exchange rate for a transaction that requires delivery of foreign exchange at a specified future date (e.g., 30-day, 90-day, or 180-day). See Exhibit 9.6 for some examples.

Exhibit 9.6   Spot and Forward Quotations Between the U.S. Dollar and Deutsche Mark (DM)

	American Terms ($/DM)		European Terms (DM/$)	
	Bid	Offer	Bid	Offer
Spot	0.6396	0.6400	1.5625	1.5635
Forward—1 month	0.6419	0.6424	1.5567	1.5579
Forward—3 months	0.6466	0.6472	1.5450	1.5466
Forward—6 months	0.6536	0.6543	1.5283	1.5301

NOTE: 1 euro = DM1.95583 (euro fixed exchange rate).

Cross Rates

The **cross rate** is the exchange rate between two infrequently traded currencies, calculated through a widely traded third currency. For example, an Argentine importer needs the Hong Kong dollar to pay for a purchase in Hong Kong. The Argentinean peso is not quoted against the Hong Kong dollar. However, both currencies are quoted against the U.S. dollar, which yields the following ratios:

Argentinean peso:	Arg$0.998/US$1
Hong Kong dollar:	HK$7.798/US$1
Cross Rates Between Arg$ and HK$:	Arg$0.998/HK$7.798 = Arg$0.128/HK$
	or HK$7.798/Arg$0.998 = HK$7.814/Arg$

Transaction Forms

Spot Transactions

Spot transactions include banknote transactions for individuals and spot transactions between banks. Banknote transactions such as currency changes for individuals are exchanged for each other instantaneously over the counter. Spot transactions between banks, however, are normally settled on the second working day after the date on which the transaction is concluded. The interbank foreign exchange market is by far the world's largest financial market. On the settlement date (also referred to as value date), most dollar transactions in the world are settled through the computerized **Clearing House Interbank Payments System (CHIPS)** in New York, which provides for calculation of new balances owed by any one bank to another and for payment by 6:00 P.M. the same day in Federal Reserve Bank of New York funds. This system, owned by large New York clearing banks, has more than 150 members, including the U.S. agencies and subsidiaries of many foreign banks. It handles over 150,000 transactions a day, together worth hundreds of billions of dollars. Similar systems also exist in other major foreign exchange centers where currencies other than the U.S. dollar are settled.

When a company (or individual) needs foreign exchange to be paid to a foreign company, it can use either customer drafts or international wire transfers through a bank. The bank sells this company a foreign exchange draft payable to the stated foreign company. For example, if a U.S. business needs to make a Japanese yen payment to a Japanese company, it can buy a yen draft from a U.S. bank, where this draft is drawn against the U.S. bank's yen account at a Japanese bank. A wire transfer is the fastest settlement for international companies, paying foreign exchange to their foreign creditors. Under a wire transfer, the payment instructions are sent via SWIFT or similar electronic means.

Forward Transactions

A **forward transaction** occurs between a bank and a customer (company, broker, or another bank), calling for delivery at a fixed future date, of a specified amount of foreign exchange at the fixed forward exchange rate. This exchange rate is established at the time of agreement, but payment and delivery are not required until maturity. Customers such as international companies may either buy a foreign currency forward from a bank (e.g., in an import business) or sell a foreign currency forward to a bank (e.g., in an export bank). If the initial transaction represents an asset or future ownership claim to foreign currency, this position is described as a **long position**. If the cash market position represents a liability or a future obligation to deliver foreign currency, this position is described as a **short position**. Chapter 14 will describe forward transactions to avoid foreign exchange risks for MNEs.

Swap Transactions

A **swap** is an agreement to buy and sell foreign exchange at prespecified exchange rates where the buying and selling are separated in time. In other words, a **swap transaction** involves the simultaneous purchase and sale of a given amount for two different settlement dates. Both purchase and sale are carried out by the same counter-party. Two common types of swap transactions are spot-forward swaps and forward-forward swaps.

In a **spot-forward swap,** an investor sells forward the foreign currency maturity value of the bill and simultaneously buys the spot foreign exchange to pay for the bill. Since a known amount of the investor's home currency will be received according to the forward component of the swap, no uncertainty from exchange rates exists. Similarly, those who borrow in foreign currency can buy forward the foreign currency needed for repayment of the foreign currency loan at the same time that they convert the borrowed foreign funds on the spot market.

A **forward-forward swap** involves two forward transactions. For example, a dealer sells £1,000,000 forward for dollars for delivery in three months at US$0.94/euro and simultaneously buys £1,000,000 forward for delivery in six months at US$0.94/euro. The difference between the buying price and the selling price is equivalent to the three-month interest rate differential between the euro and the U.S. dollar.

The two preceding types of swaps are particularly popular with banks, because it is difficult for them to avoid risk when making a market for many future dates and currencies. For some dates and currencies, a bank may be in a long position, which means that it has agreed to purchase more of the foreign currency than it has agreed to sell. For other dates and currencies, the bank may be in a short position, which means that it has agreed to sell more of these currencies than it has agreed to buy. Swaps help the bank to balance its position and reduce financial risk.

Foreign Exchange Arbitrage

In the foreign exchange market, price information is readily available through computer networks, which makes it easy to compare prices in different markets. As such, exchange rates tend to be equal worldwide, but temporary discrepancies do exist. These temporary discrepancies provide profit opportunities for simultaneously buying a currency in one market (at a lower price) while selling it in another (at a higher price). This activity is known as **arbitrage.** Arbitrage will continue until the exchange rates in different locales are so close that it is not worth the costs incurred in further buying and selling.[7]

For example, suppose Citibank is quoting the German mark/U.S. dollar exchange rate as 1.4445–55 and Dresdner Bank in Frankfurt is quoting 1.4425–35. This means that Citibank will buy dollars for 1.4445 marks and will sell dollars for 1.4455 marks. Dresdner will buy dollars for 1.4425 marks and will sell dollars for 1.4435 marks. This presents an arbitrage opportunity. We could buy $10 million at Dresdner's ask price of 1.4435 and simultaneously sell $10 million to Citibank at their bid price of 1.4445 marks. This would earn a profit of DM0.0010 per dollar traded, so DM10,000 would be the total arbitrage profit. If such a profit opportunity exists, the demand to buy dollars from Dresdner will cause it to raise its ask price above 1.4435, while the increased interest in selling dollars to Citibank at its bid price of 1.4445 marks will cause it to lower its bid. In this way, arbitrage activity pushes the prices of different traders to levels where no arbitrage profits are earned.

Arbitrage could also involve three or more currencies. Let us temporarily ignore the bid–ask spread and associated transaction costs. Suppose that in London $/£ = 2.00, while in New York $/DM = 0.40, then £/DM = 0.40/2.00 = 0.2. If we observe a market in which one of the three exchange rates—$/£, $/DM, £/DM—is out of line with the other two, there is an arbitrage opportunity. Suppose that in Frankfurt the exchange rate is £/DM = 0.2, while in New York $/DM = 0.40, but in London $/£ = 1.90. A trader could start with dollars and use $1.9 million to buy £1 million in London since $/£ = 1.90. The pounds then could be used to buy marks at £/DM = 0.2, so that £1,000,000 = DM5,000,000. DM5 million could then be used in New York to buy dollars at

$/DM = 0.40, so that DM5,000,000 = $2,000,000. Thus the initial $1.9 million could be turned into $2 million with the triangular arbitrage action earning the trader $100,000.

Black Market and Parallel Market

As a result of government restrictions or legal prohibitions on foreign exchange transactions, illegal markets in foreign exchange exist in many developing countries in response to business or private demand for foreign exchange. These illegal markets are known as **black markets.** Such illegal markets exist openly in some countries (e.g., Brazil and Venezuela), with little government interference. In some other countries, however, foreign exchange laws are strictly enforced and lawbreakers receive harsh sentences when caught (e.g., China before 1985).

Often, governments set an official exchange rate that deviates widely from that which the free market would establish. If a government will purchase foreign exchange only at the official rate, but private citizens are willing to pay the market-determined rate, there will be a steady supply of foreign exchange to the black market. Obviously, government policy creates the black market. The demand arises because of legal restrictions on buying foreign exchange, and the supply exists because government-mandated official exchange rates offer less than the free-market rate. Ironically, governments defend the need for foreign exchange restrictions based on conserving scarce foreign exchange for high-priority uses. But such restrictions work to reduce the amount of foreign exchange that flows to the government as traders turn to the black market instead.

When the black market is legalized by the government, this market is referred to as the **parallel market** and operates as an alternative to the official exchange market. In many countries facing economic hardship, the parallel markets allow normal economic activities to continue through a steady supply of foreign exchange. For instance, Guatemala had an artificially low official exchange rate of one quetzal per dollar for more than three decades; however, a black market where the exchange rate fluctuated daily with market conditions was allowed to operate openly in front of the country's main post office. In Mexico, this parallel market thrived during times of crisis when the official peso/dollar exchange rate varied greatly from the market rate. For instance, in August 1982, the Mexican government banned the sale of dollars by Mexican banks. Immediately, the parallel market responded. The official exchange rate was 69.5 pesos per dollar, but the rate on the street ranged from 120 to 150 as the parallel market demand increased with the ban on bank sales. Private currency trades between individuals were legal, so trading flourished at the Mexico City airport and other public places.

Interim Summary

1. A foreign exchange market consists of individuals, corporations, banks, and brokers who buy or sell currencies. Major foreign exchange markets in the world include London, New York, Tokyo, and Singapore. International foreign exchange markets offer spot transactions, forward transactions, and swap transactions.

2. It is possible to earn profits from foreign exchange arbitrage—simultaneously buying a currency in one market at a lower price while selling it in another market at a higher price. This type of activity escalates volatility in international foreign exchange markets.

INTERNATIONAL CAPITAL MARKETS

International Money Markets

International money markets are the markets in which foreign monies are financed or invested (e.g., Hitachi and Matsushita borrowed U.S. dollars from several U.S. banks in Tokyo to finance their worldwide operations). MNEs use international money markets to finance global operations at a lower cost than is possible domestically. They borrow currencies that have low interest rates and are expected to depreciate against their own currency. They incur the risk that the currencies borrowed may appreciate, however, which will increase their cost of financing. Investors, on the other hand, may achieve substantially higher returns in foreign markets than in their domestic markets when investing in currencies that appreciate against their home currency. However, if these currencies depreciate, the effective yield on the foreign investments will likely be lower than the domestic yield, and may even be negative. Investors attempt to capitalize on potentially high effective yields on foreign money market securities, while reducing the exchange rate risk by diversifying the investments across currencies.

Often, transactions in international money markets are conducted via the Eurocurrency market. The **Eurocurrency market** consists of commercial banks that accept large deposits and provide large loans in foreign currencies (e.g., banks in Zurich lend U.S. dollars or banks in Frankfurt provide loans in Japanese yen). Those banks offering Eurocurrency services are either local banks or foreign bank subsidiaries in a host country. Growing international trade and capital flows as well as cross-border differences in interest rates are the primary reasons for the growth of the Eurocurrency market. In this market, Eurodollar deposits are intensively transacted.

Eurodollars represent U.S. dollar deposits in non-U.S. banks. When interest rate ceilings were imposed on dollar deposits in U.S. banks, corporations with large dollar balances often deposited their funds overseas to receive a higher yield. These deposits were used by local banks to provide loans to other corporations that needed U.S. dollars. Eurodollar deposits are not subject to reserve requirements, so banks can lend out 100% of the deposits. For these reasons, the spread between the interest rate paid on large Eurodollar deposits and the rate charged on Eurodollar loans is relatively small. Deposits and loan transactions in Eurodollars are typically $1 million or more per transaction.

Two popular Eurodollar deposits are Eurodollar fixed-rate certificates of deposit (CDs) and Eurodollar floating-rate certificates of deposit. Investors in fixed-rate Eurodollar CDs receive guaranteed interest but are adversely affected by rising market interest rates. To neutralize this problem, floating-rate Eurodollar CDs provide the rate that is adjusted periodically to the London Interbank Offer Rate (LIBOR)—the rate charged on interbank dollar loans. The floating-rate CDs allow the borrower's cost and investor's return to reflect prevailing market interest rates.[8]

International Bond Markets

International bond markets are the markets where government bonds or corporate bonds are issued, bought, and sold in foreign countries (e.g., China International Trust and Investment Corporation, or CITIC, issued its corporate bonds in Japan, Europe, and the United States during the 1980s and 1990s). The growth of international bond markets is attributed to some unique features offered by international bonds that are not offered by domestic bonds (see the Industry Box). The development of international bond markets is partially attributed to tax law differentials across countries. Until 1984, foreign investors who purchased bonds that were placed in the United States paid a 30% withholding tax on interest payments. However, various tax treaties between the United States and other countries reduced the withholding tax. Interest payments to non-U.S. investors were exempt from the withholding tax, triggering lower interest rates and allowing U.S. firms to issue bonds at a higher price. The withholding tax on U.S.-placed bonds was eliminated in 1984, causing an even larger increase in the foreign demand for U.S.-placed bonds.

Bonds placed in international bond markets are typically underwritten by a syndicate of investment banking firms. Many underwriters in the Eurobond market (i.e., bonds in one foreign currency are issued in the country that uses this currency) are subsidiaries of U.S. banks that have focused their growth on non-U.S. countries, since they were historically banned by the Glass-Steagall Act from underwriting corporate bonds in the United States.[9] Some recent issuers of bonds in the Eurobond market include DaimlerChrysler Financial, Citigroup, General Motors Acceptance Corp., and the World Bank. DaimlerChrysler Financial Corp. now obtains about one-fourth of its funds from the Eurobond market. Its bonds have been denominated not only in dollars but also in Swiss francs, German marks, and Australian dollars. Citigroup now borrows about half of its funds overseas.

INDUSTRY BOX

FOREIGN COMPANIES BORROW IN CHEAP U.S. BOND MARKET

Foreign companies are turning to U.S. debt markets to borrow funds they would have had trouble raising at home. They are attracted by low U.S. interest rates and the fact that American money managers are groping for higher returns and more diversified portfolios. A prime example is triple-B-rated Philips Electronics NV's recent $500 million offering of so-called Yankee bonds, which are foreign companies' debt sold in the United States. In a two-part underwriting led by Goldman, Sachs & Co., the large Dutch consumer electronics company sold $250 million in 10-year notes and $250 million in 20-year bonds. Philips had an investment grade credit rating from Standard & Poor's and it was able to borrow large sums at long maturities in a public bond offering. U.S. capital markets (bond, loan, and equity), the world's largest, offer foreign companies a chance to diversify their funding sources and borrow at longer maturities than those usually available in either the Euromarket or their home markets. By contrast, roughly 95% of all Eurobonds mature in 10 years or less. In addition, many European companies, including Philips, have traditionally relied on bank borrowing for most of their funding.

SOURCE: Adapted from Michael R. Sesit. "Foreign companies borrow in cheap, hungry U.S. markets." *Wall Street Journal*, September 14, 1993, C1, C15.

International Stock Markets

International stock (or equity) markets are where company stocks are listed and traded on foreign stock exchanges (e.g., Nokia of Finland issued stock on the New York Stock Exchange [NYSE]). Firms in need of financing use foreign stock markets as additional sources of funds. Investors use foreign stock markets to enhance their portfolio performance. This financing source allows MNEs to attract more funds without flooding their home stock market, avoiding a decline in share price. A large number of MNEs also issue stock in foreign markets to circumvent regulations, since regulatory provisions differ among markets. Firms may also believe that they can achieve worldwide recognition among consumers if they issue stock in various foreign markets. Further, listing stock on a foreign stock exchange not only enhances the stock's liquidity but also increases the firm's perceived financial standing when the exchange approves the listing application. It can also protect a firm against hostile takeovers because it disperses ownership and makes it more difficult for other firms to gain a controlling interest. For instance, when Daimler-Benz AG announced its listing on the New York Stock Exchange, its share price quickly increased by 30%.

The Euroequity market (e.g., issuing U.S. dollar-denominated stocks on non-U.S. exchanges) has developed and grown at a rapid pace since the 1980s. The stocks issued in the Euroequity market are specifically designed for distribution among foreign markets. They are underwritten by a group of investment banks and purchased primarily by institutional investors in several countries. Many of the underwriters are U.S.-based investment banks, such as First Boston (now part of Credit Suisse First Boston), Merrill Lynch, and Salomon Brothers.

The ability of firms to place new shares in foreign markets depends partially on the stock's perceived liquidity in that market. A secondary market for the stock must be established in foreign markets to enhance liquidity and makes newly issued stocks more attractive. There are some costs of listing on a foreign exchange, such as translating a company's annual financial report from the local currency into the foreign currency and making financial statements compatible with the accounting standards used in that country.

International Loan Markets

International loan markets involve large commercial banks and other lending institutions providing loans to foreign companies. Unlike international money markets that deal only with foreign money, loan markets are not restricted to foreign currency transactions. As regulations across Europe, Japan, and the United States are becoming standardized, the markets for loans and other financial services are becoming more globalized. As a result, some financial institutions are attempting to achieve greater economies of scale on the services they offer. Even financial institutions that are not planning global expansion are experiencing increased foreign competition in their home markets. U.S. banks have been particularly interested in foreign markets because U.S. regulations restrain banks from spreading across state lines.

Banks from all countries perceive *international lending* as a means of diversification. A portfolio of loans to borrowers across various countries is less susceptible to a recession in the bank's home country. International lending also allows banks to develop relationships with foreign firms, which creates a demand for the banks' other services. In addition, a large portion of international lending is to support *international acquisitions*. Commercial banks and investment banks serve not only as advisers but also as financial intermediaries by placing stocks and bonds or by providing loans. One common form of participation has been to provide direct loans for financing acquisitions, especially for leveraged buyouts (LBOs) by management or some other group of investors. Since LBOs are financed mostly with debt, they result in a large demand for loanable funds. Many LBOs are supported by debt from an international syndicate of banks. In this way, each bank limits its exposure to any particular borrower. Because the firms engaged in LBOs are often in diversified industries, a problem in any given industry does not create a new lending crisis. In addition, the debt of each individual firm is relatively small, so that most borrowers would not have sufficient bargaining power to reschedule debt payments. For this reason, international bank financing of LBOs is perceived to be less risky than providing loans to governments of developing countries, another group of major borrowers in international loan markets.

Lending to developing countries often requires credit checking. International commercial banks and other lending institutions do so based on analysis by credit rating agencies such as Standard & Poor's and Moody's. Notably, political risk and overall pressures on the balance of payments and macroeconomic conditions are the focus of analysis (see also Chapter 7). Exhibit 9.7 provides an illustrative example.

Exhibit 9.7   Factors Used in Sovereign Rating by Standard & Poor's

Political Risk
1. Form of government and adaptability of political institutions
2. Extent of popular participation
3. Orderliness of leadership succession
4. Degree of consensus on economic policy objectives
5. Integration into global trade and financial system
6. Internal and external security risks

Economic Factors
1. Income and economic structure
2. Economic growth prospects
3. Fiscal flexibility
4. Public debt burden
5. Price stability
6. Balance-of-payments flexibility
7. External debt and liquidity

Issuer Credit Ratings (or ICR) are offered by credit-rating agencies based on the preceding analysis. ICR apply to both Corporate Credit Service (company level) and Sovereign Credit Ratings (country level). Under the Standard and Poor's system, the long-term issuer credit ratings are classified into the following:

AAA   An obligor (debtor) has extremely strong capacity to meet its financial commitments.

AA   An obligor has very strong capacity to meet its financial commitments. It differs from the highest-rated obligor (AAA) only in small degree.

A   An obligor has strong capacity to meet its financial commitments but is somewhat more susceptible to the adverse effects of changes in circumstances and economic conditions.

BBB   An obligor has adequate capacity to meet its financial commitments. However, adverse economic conditions are more likely to weaken this capacity.

BB   An obligor is less vulnerable in the near term than other lower-rated obligors. However, it faces major ongoing uncertainties and exposure to adverse business, financial, or economic conditions that could lead to the obligor's inadequate capacity to meet its financial commitments.

B   An obligor is more vulnerable than in the case of BB but currently has the capacity to meet its financial commitments. Adverse business, financial, or economic conditions will likely impair the obligor's capacity or willingness to meet its financial commitments.

CCC   An obligor is currently vulnerable and is dependent on favorable business, financial, and economic conditions to meet its financial commitments.

CC   An obligor is currently highly vulnerable.

The preceding ratings may be modified by the addition of a plus or minus sign to show relative standing within each rating category.

Interim Summary

1. MNEs can finance their global operations from international money markets, bond markets, equity markets, and loan markets. They can borrow money from money markets or loan markets or issue corporate bonds (in bond markets) or stocks (in equity markets).

2. Banks and corporations actively participate in Eurocurrency markets (e.g., banks in Amsterdam lend U.S. dollars), Eurobond markets (e.g., issue U.S. dollar bonds in Brussels), and Euroequity markets (e.g., issue U.S. dollar stocks on the Singapore Stock Exchange) to benefit from interest rate differentials or regulatory differences.

THE ASIAN FINANCIAL CRISIS

The Asian financial crisis shows how a crisis can occur in international financial markets (foreign exchange market, stock market, money market, and loan market) and how this crisis relates to businesses (domestic and foreign), governments, financial institutions, and international financial markets. First afflicting Thailand in June 1997, the Asian financial crisis quickly spread to South Korea, Indonesia, Malaysia, the Philippines, and other Southeast and East Asian countries. The crisis initially took the form of a financial meltdown, with currencies, stock markets, and property prices tumbling across the region. Economic aftershocks ensued. The crisis was soon to affect markets and economies across the world from Europe to Latin America. The nations of East and Southeast Asia, accustomed to high single- or double-digit growth rates, shifted to slow or negative growth. These poor economic conditions prevailed in most of these nations until early 1999. Explanations concerning the causes of the crisis fall into three broad perspectives:[10] (a) financial, (b) political/institutional, and (c) managerial.

The Financial Perspective

The financial perspective views the Asian financial crisis as resulting primarily from financial-sector weakness and market failure. From a financial perspective, two interrelated factors stand out as having contributed to financial-sector weakness and market failure. The first is the maintenance of pegged exchange rates that came to be viewed as implicit guarantees of exchange, constraining monetary remedies. The second is excessive private-sector short-term and dollar-denominated borrowing. For example, Thailand pegged its currency to the U.S.

dollar, prompting dollar-denominated borrowing underpinned by higher interest rates for baht-denominated loans. From 1988 to 1994, international bank loans to Thai borrowers more than doubled. By the end of 1997, Thai foreign debt reached $89 billion, of which $81.6 billion was owed by private corporations. About half of the debt carried a maturity date of under a year. In 1997, the value of private-sector foreign liabilities was estimated at 25% of GDP. Thailand's weakening exports, growing current account deficit, and exploding dollar-denominated short-term private company debt began to weigh on foreign investors and lenders in late 1996. Attacks by currency speculators in the first half of 1997 were followed by loan defaults by several property companies, a downgrade of Thailand's long-term debt, and the unraveling of the Thai stock market. The situation quickly deteriorated, and on June 27, 1997, the government floated its currency (the baht).[11]

The financial perspective additionally emphasizes the effects of contagion on the crisis. Contagion fueled the crisis through the dynamics of competitive devaluation and the so-called wake-up-call effect. The former pertains to the pressures faced by Asian countries to devalue their currency to match devaluation by neighboring Asian countries. The latter explains the tendency of most foreign investors to treat all Asian countries as one and pull out investments from a country regardless of its economic or market fundamentals. Undoubtedly, contagion played a major role in accelerating the pace by which the crisis spread from Thailand to South Korea, Indonesia, and Malaysia and throughout Southeast and East Asia.

The Political/Institutional Perspective

Political/institutional-based explanations contend that the causes of the Asian crisis extend much deeper than financial sector weaknesses and market failure, the latter often seen as symptoms rather than causes. The political/institutional perspective points to crony capitalism, irresponsible domestic governance, weak national and political institutions, corruption in the public and private sectors, a misguided and poorly enforced regulatory environment, and other political and institutional-related factors as the principal forces behind the crisis.

The crisis exposed key weaknesses in the political/economic systems and institutions of several Asian countries. The widespread practice of crony capitalism and the incestuous relationship between government, banking, and business in such countries as Indonesia, Malaysia, and Thailand led to an overextension of credit to undeserving companies with close ties to the political and military leadership. In addition, politicians and government bureaucrats have been largely ineffective in responding to the crisis owing to conflicting business interests. In the case of Indonesia, for example, the Suharto government backpedaled in implementing the IMF reforms because of their possible adverse impact on the business interests of the ruler's extended family and cronies.

The IMF noted three political and institutional-related considerations as contributing forces to the Asian financial crisis:[12]

1. In financial systems, weak management and poor control of risks, lax enforcement of providential rules and inadequate supervision, and government direct-lending practices led to a sharp deterioration in the quality of banks' loan portfolios.

2. Problems of data availability and lack of transparency hindered market participants from maintaining a realistic view of economic fundamentals and at the same time added to uncertainty.

3. Problems of governance and political uncertainties exacerbated the crisis of confidence, the reluctance of foreign creditors to roll over short-term loans, and the downward pressure on currencies and stock markets.

The Managerial Perspective

The third group of explanations maintains that micro-mismanagement was at the heart of the crisis. Encouraged by a booming economy in the 1990s, many industrial companies in East and Southeast Asia pursued risky overdiversification. To fund their expansion, these companies relied heavily on short-term debt financing. In 1996, the five largest South Korean conglomerates, or *chaebols* (i.e., Samsung, Hyundai, Lucky Goldstar, Daewoo, and Sunkyong), controlled over 250 subsidiaries in more than four dozen (mostly unrelated) lines of business. The combined liabilities of the five amounted to about 70% of South Korea's gross domestic product in 1996.

Overdiversification and extended leveraging created a vicious cycle for many companies. Firms pursued risky ventures in order to earn larger returns on their investments and service their expensive, short-term debt. When these risky projects failed, they turned to more borrowing to keep their operations afloat. These companies were able to maintain this practice for as long as banks were willing and able to extend credit. When the financial crisis hit, and banks refused or were unable to roll over their loans, many of these industrial companies, particularly the undercapitalized firms, were forced into bankruptcy.

Rising labor costs, falling commodity prices, contracting export markets, and other external pressures compounded the problems faced by industrial companies during the months preceding the financial crisis. Instead of addressing these external pressures by improving productivity, cutting costs, and focusing on the bottom line, the large majority of companies opted for growth and diversification into unrelated businesses. This strategy proved costly when the financial crisis hit and funds dried up. In contrast, firms that remained focused on their core competencies—and that enhanced productivity, cut costs, and focused on profitability—were able to weather the storm. Most notable among them are South Korea's Pohang Steel Company and Ayala Land Corporation in the Philippines.

Banks and financial institutions extended credit to undeserving companies. When those companies were unable to repay, the banks agreed to roll over the loans and extend new credit. The financial perspective views the process as a market failure but hardly explains its roots. The political/institutional perspective blames the decision to overextend credit on such factors as direct government lending, crony capitalism, close relationships between banks and industrial companies, and lack of transparency in financial reporting. The management perspective attributes such overextension of credit to the lack of management sophistication, as well as the absence of the administrative apparatus to conduct proper analysis and oversight. In addition, the management perspective sees a behavioral process of escalation, with banks increasing credit to justify earlier credit decisions.

Interim Summary

1. The Asian financial crisis provides an illustrative case of how a financial crisis is reflected simultaneously in international foreign exchange markets and international capital markets.

2. The Asian financial crisis derived from political, financial, and managerial factors. This crisis is a reminder that the growth of an emerging economy

requires strong economic fundamentals, an efficient banking sector, transparent political institutions, counter-fluctuation capabilities, and clearly defined business–government relations.

CHAPTER SUMMARY

1. The international monetary system is made up of the policies, institutions, regulations, and mechanisms that determine foreign exchange rates. Most countries today use the peg system, managed-float system, target-zone system, or free-float system.

2. Each foreign exchange system has its merits and drawbacks. The floating exchange rate is less costly for the government and its central bank to adjust trade imbalances and can facilitate independence of trade policies. It may lead, however, to immense market fluctuations that hamper economic growth, and it cannot help the country balance trade for a long period.

3. In the long run, the purchasing power parity (PPP) tends to be a proper foundation to determine the foreign exchange rate. In the short run, the demand and supply in the foreign exchange market are crucial in determining changes in the floating rate.

4. The balance of payments summarizes a country's currency inflows and outflows and documents current account, capital account, and official reserves. Official reserves are made of gold, special drawing rights (SDRs), and foreign currencies. Many imports are actually "exported" by a nation's own companies investing abroad, making current account balance statistically less meaningful.

5. International financial markets consist of international foreign exchange markets and international capital markets. International capital markets in turn comprise money markets, bond markets, equity markets, and loan markets.

6. Foreign exchange markets perform three functions, including international payment, short-term supply of foreign currencies, and hedging against foreign exchange risks. These markets also offer opportunities for foreign exchange arbitrage.

7. International money markets are where foreign capital (such as Eurodollars) is financed or invested. Eurodollars are U.S. dollar deposits in non-U.S. banks. International loan markets deal with loans in any international currency provided by large commercial banks that must assess corporate credit or sovereign credit ranked by credit rating agencies.

8. International stock (or equity) markets are the places where company stocks are listed and traded on foreign stock exchanges. International bond markets are the places where corporate or government bonds are issued and traded in foreign countries. These markets not only provide financing for global operations but can also improve organizational recognition.

9. The Asian financial crisis demonstrates that international foreign exchange markets and capital markets can present risks destabilizing emerging economies that depend on international markets. This crisis also reveals the importance of transparent and efficient institutions (governments, the banking sector, and legal systems) that govern financial markets.

Chapter Notes

1. See T. Agmon, R. G. Hawkins, and R. M. Levich. *The Future of the International Monetary System*. Lexington, MA: Lexington Books, 1984; R. N. Cooper. *The International Monetary System: Essays in World Economics*. Cambridge, MA: MIT Press, 1987.

2. E. Sohmen. *Flexible Exchange Rates: Theory and Controversy*. Chicago: University of Chicago Press, 1969; I. Friedman. *Reshaping the Global Money System*. Lexington, MA: Lexington Books, 1987.

3. W. J. McKibben and J. D. Sachs. "Comparing the global performance of alternative exchange agreements." *Journal of International Money and Finance*, 1988, *7*, 4: pp. 387–410; J. R. Shafer and B. E. Loopesko. "Floating exchange rate after ten years." *Brookings Papers on Economic Activity*, Washington, DC: Brookings Institution, 1983.

4. G. Dufey and I. H. Giddy. *The International Money Market*, 2nd ed. Englewood Cliffs, NJ: Prentice-Hall, 1994; V. Koromzay, J. Llewellyn, and S. Potter. "The rise and

fall of the dollar: Some explanations, consequences, and lessons." *Economic Journal,* March 1987: pp. 23–43.

5. R. I. McKinnon. "The rules of the game: International money in historical perspective." *Journal of Economic Literature,* March 1993: pp. 1–44; E. Sohmen. *Flexible Exchange Rates: Theory and Controversy.* Chicago: University of Chicago Press, 1969.

6. G. Dufey and I. H. Giddy. *The International Money Market,* 2nd ed. Englewood Cliffs, NJ: Prentice-Hall, 1994.

7. R. M. Kubarych. *Foreign Exchange Markets in the United States.* New York: Federal Reserve Bank of New York, 1983.

8. K. A. Chrystal. "A guide to foreign exchange markets." *Federal Reserve Bank of St. Louis Review,* March 1984: pp. 5–18.

9. R. G. F. Coninx. *Foreign Exchange Dealer's Handbook.* Homewood, IL: Dow Jones-Irwin, 1986; I. Gregory and P. Moore. "Foreign exchange dealing." *Corporate Finance,* October 1986: pp. 33–46.

10. M. G. Serapio and O. Shenkar. "Reflections on the Asian crisis." *Management International Review,* April 1999 (Special Issue): pp. 3–10; "Deep impact: The Asian crisis" (Special Report). *Far East Economic Review,* July 16, 1998: pp. 40–52.

11. "Deep impact: The Asian crisis" (Special Report). *Far East Economic Review,* July 16, 1998: pp. 40–52.

12. International Monetary Fund. *World Economic Outlook,* Washington, DC, May 1998.

PART FOUR

International Business Strategies

INTERNATIONAL ENTRY STRATEGIES

TEN

DO YOU KNOW?

1. What factors should managers take into account in choosing locations for FDI projects? Why has Rio de Janeiro in Brazil lured hundreds of large MNEs to invest there? How should location selection be associated with the firm's goals and experience? Why does Nike often locate its projects in underdeveloped areas but Oracle does not?

2. How do MNEs benefit when they enter foreign markets as first movers? What challenges do early movers normally face? Why have some early movers, such as Motorola and Siemens, been quite successful in China whereas other early movers there, such as Peugeot and Occidental Petroleum, have not?

3. What entry modes are available to companies interested in investing in another country? How do such entry modes vary in terms of expected risks and returns as well as required commitment? If you are concerned with organizational control over overseas operations, what entry modes would you elect?

OPENING CASE

DuPont's Entry Strategies Into China

DuPont is one of the oldest and largest industrial corporations in the world. Since 1989 DuPont has set up 12 joint ventures, four wholly owned subsidiaries, and four representative offices, with a total investment of more than $300 million in China. Joint-venture examples include partnerships with Shanghai Photomask Precision Company to produce photomasks and with China Worldbest

Development Corporation to manufacture Lycra spandex fiber. It has also formed joint ventures there with other foreign companies such as BASF Aktiengesellschaft. DuPont's use of joint ventures was aimed at garnering greater loyalty by Chinese consumers. Joint ventures also allowed DuPont to overcome trade barriers and gain access to distribution channels. Meanwhile, the company set up wholly owned subsidiaries to produce those products that involve very sensitive technologies and require strong control over production and chemical patent protection.

DuPont was an early entrant to China's chemical and energy industries. As an early entrant, it was able to establish strong market power and create entry barriers for followers. It faced little competition because there were only a few companies in the country that participated in the same industry. DuPont also had the advantage of being the first company to make use of some of China's raw materials. DuPont took advantage of these factors to build a strong foundation for itself while increasing its presence in China, gaining technological leadership, and establishing its brand name. Of course, the company also faced many operational risks as an early entrant. DuPont had to deal with high anti-imitation costs. In 1991, a local entrepreneur took one of DuPont's fiber formulas and started a rival firm to produce the same product. It was not until 1993 that new laws were introduced to supplement and strengthen China's patent regulations, extending patent protection from 10 to 20 years and requiring patents to be registered in China.

DuPont chose China for its low labor costs, high demand, and abundant raw materials. It selected areas such as Shenzhen, Shanghai, and Guangdong, where the tax rates were lower. Shenzhen and Guangdong, for example, are coastal cities offering tax rates of only 15%. Shanghai was chosen because it is a major industrial and financial center. Shanghai and other eastern coastal provinces such as Jiangsu, Shandong, and Zhejiang form the heart of China's chemical industry. A new chemical industrial zone is being built on the outskirts of Shanghai at Caojing on Hangzhou Bay. In 1998, DuPont formed DuPont (China) Ltd. in Beijing to coordinate its operations in China.

INTERNATIONAL LOCATION SELECTION (*WHERE*)

The preceding case illustrates that several important decisions have to be made when entering a foreign market. **International entry strategies** concern where (location selection), when (timing of entry), and how (entry-mode selection) international companies should enter and invest in a foreign territory during international expansion. These entry strategies are important because they determine an MNE's investment environment, operation treatment, resource commitment, and evolutionary path. In the opening case, DuPont views China as a strategic location not only in terms of being the primary offshore market but also by virtue of being the major manufacturing center of products marketed elsewhere. Even though it encountered tremendous uncertainty in the early 1980s, DuPont decided to enter this market as an early mover seeking market leadership. The company's ambitious investments, however, were incremental. DuPont started with exports to China, followed by minority joint ventures, then majority joint ventures, and eventually wholly owned subsidiaries. This evolutionary entry path balances well its experience and capability with the risks and hazards it has faced in the past. This chapter details these issues, beginning with international location selection (e.g., for DuPont, why China? And why Shanghai and Shenzhen within China?).

International location selection involves country selection *and* regional selection (e.g., state, province, or city) within the chosen country for an MNE's foreign direct investment project(s). The country selection determines the macroenvironment for operations in a specific site. Siemens, for example, chose Brazil as an important platform for Latin America and the Caribbean nations. The company selected the city of Rio de Janeiro, rather than São Paulo, as its major production base since Rio de Janeiro provides cheaper and more abundant resources (labor and supplies) and a superior infrastructure. Similarly, Motorola chose the city of Tianjin instead of Beijing or Shanghai as its major production base in China. This location strategy seems to have worked well, because the sales revenue generated by this base accounted for more than 10% of its worldwide revenue in 2002. To select an appropriate country and a region within that country, international managers should first appraise locational determinants that are likely to influence future operations and expected returns. These determinants as well as the decision framework elaborated below are generally applicable to both country selection and region (city or province) selection. The only distinction between them is that the breadths of locational determinants differ. Country selection should emphasize nationwide factors, whereas site selection should focus more on related factors that are specific to that region.

You may recall that we discussed country competitiveness in Chapter 5 and explained the relevance of country competitiveness to an MNE's location selection. The analysis of country competitiveness helps us better understand a host country's national environment and is thus valuable to country selection. Nevertheless, location selection requires analyses and comparisons of specific factors (i.e., locational determinants) associated with the costs and revenues of investment in a specific site. For this purpose, we outline specific locational determinants managers need to consider when they calculate expected costs and payoffs from a potential foreign location.

Locational Determinants

Locational determinants can be categorized into the following groups: (a) cost and tax factors, (b) demand factors (c) strategic factors, (d) regulatory and economic factors, and (e) sociopolitical factors. The importance of each of these factors to a specific firm depends on the firm's objectives and the business nature of the FDI project. For instance, high-tech FDI may depend more on strategic factors while labor-intensive projects may be more susceptible to cost and tax factors. Local market-focused investments may rely more on demand factors, whereas export market-focused investments may be affected more by cost and tax conditions.

Cost and Tax Factors

1. *Transportation costs:* For country selection, MNEs should consider the costs incurred in transporting materials from a home (or foreign) country to a host country or transporting products from a host country to a home or international market. When an MNE's home country is the source of product components as well as the market for finished products, transportation costs associated with this two-way flow become even more important. For site selection, MNEs need to calculate the convenience and costs of the various transportation channels (air, sea, railway, and highway) from the candidate site to destinations of major local and foreign customers. When the Ford Motor Company entered the United Arab Emirates, it chose Dubai because of its convenience and low-cost connections to the rest of the country and the world.

2. *Wage rate:* Labor costs constitute a substantial proportion of total production costs. Foreign production is more likely to occur when production costs are lower abroad than at home. Labor costs sway investment location decisions, particularly for firms in labor-intensive industries. The decision by many MNEs to locate assembly plants in developing countries is heavily influenced by prevailing wages. Nike located its 13 footwear and 14 apparel factories along the Pearl River Delta in China because of the low wage rate of workers relative to their productivity.

3. *Availability and costs of land:* Availability of suitable plant sites, the cost of land, space for expansion, and local government policy on renting or purchasing land have been recognized by international managers as critical factors in the early stages of project development and late stages of project operation. In some cases, this consideration may overwhelm other location factors, since it influences other costs such as transportation and construction. Mercedes-Benz selected Alabama in 1993 as its site for producing its sport-utility vehicles because the Alabama state government provided the company with 1,000 acres of land between Tuscaloosa and Birmingham.

4. *Construction costs:* This cost accounts for a substantial part of capital investment. Different sites vary in the cost of construction materials, labor, land, equipment rental, and quality of construction. Burger King had opened 1,640 restaurants in Europe by the end of 2001, 1,397 of which were franchise-owned operations. A major factor behind the franchise strategy is high construction costs in Europe.

5. *Costs of raw materials and resources:* MNEs are increasing the percentage of local outsourcing in total production. This localization reduces foreign exchange risks from devalued currencies and improves relationships with local governments and indigenous firms. Under these circumstances, the costs of local

materials and resources needed in production will affect the firm's gross profit margin. Ikea, a leading furniture MNE based in Sweden, buys 90% of what it sells from closely monitored suppliers in many countries—mostly developing countries such as Poland and China. One of the major reasons the company chose these countries is the relatively low cost of raw materials.

6. *Financing costs:* The cost and availability of local capital are major concerns for MNEs because local financing provides much of the capital needed for mass production and operations. Financing by local banks and financial institutions also helps an MNE mitigate possible financial risks arising from fluctuations in foreign exchange rates and uncertain foreign exchange policies as well as political risk in a host country. Merck entered Brazil, sited specifically in São Paulo, Rio de Janeiro, Recife, Curitiba, and Campinas, because local banks are very supportive in financing Merck's investments or expansion.

7. *Tax rates:* Both statutory and effective tax rates influence a firm's profitability. The **statutory tax** rate determines the general level of the tax burden shouldered by firms. The **effective tax rate** on corporate income, which is the statutory corporate rate adjusted for all other taxes and subsidies affecting an MNE's taxable income, determines the company's net return from its revenues. Depending on the extent of these subsidies and other taxes, the statutory corporate tax rate may differ substantially from the effective corporate tax rate because the latter is adjusted to include tax-related incentives such as investment tax credits, tax breaks, and accelerated depreciation. MNEs need to assess both the statutory and the effective tax rate. Because regions within diverse nations such as Brazil, China, and Indonesia may vary in terms of the statutory or effective rates, investors should compare these rates at both the country and regional level. Since FDI projects are still subject to import or export tariffs when importing regulated materials or export licensed products, firms should also be aware of the level of these tariffs.

8. *Investment incentives:* Many countries, especially developing ones, are competing to attract FDI to support their domestic economies. In so doing, they often offer preferential incentives to foreign investors. Although these are country specific, an array of investment incentives that attract FDI include the following (see also Chapter 3):
   a. Tax breaks or reductions on corporate income taxes
   b. Financial assistance such as preferential terms of financing, wage subsidies, investment grants, or low-interest loans
   c. Tariff concessions including exemption from or reduction of duties on imports, additional duties on imports of competing goods, or rebates of duties on imported inputs
   d. Business assistance such as employee training, research and development support, land grants, site improvements, and site selection assistance
   e. Other incentives such as infrastructure development and access, legal services, business consultation, and partner selection assistance[1]

9. *Profit repatriation:* Repatriation restrictions have a negative impact on the net income or dividends remitted to foreign headquarters. Restrictions can involve a remittance tax on the cash repatriated to a home country or a ceiling on the cash amount. In other cases, investors must obtain approval from the central bank or foreign exchange administration department to repatriate dividends. These restrictions can become a deterrent to FDI. Today, profit repatriation restrictions have been gradually

removed in many developing countries. Nonetheless, restrictions on foreign exchange flows still abound (e.g., currency conversion at formally set exchange rates in Russia, China, and India).

Demand Factors

1. *Market size and growth:* Although different MNEs may not emphasize the same level of marketing in a host country, it is rare for them not to consider local consumers. At the national level, the size and growth rate of markets signal market opportunities and potentials. Pfizer selected India to produce multivitamins targeting India's 300 million middle-class consumers. In 1990, Toys "R" Us chose Japan, whose retail market expanded greatly in the 1980s as a result of the strong Japanese economy and increased consumer spending. At the subnational level, per capita consumption and the growth rate of consumption in respective regions (state, province, city) may be more accurate parameters for measuring market potential and growth. Average income growth among consumers in a target region is also an appropriate measure (see also Chapter 16).

2. *Presence of customers:* MNEs may find it desirable to locate their manufacturing sites in the area where they have long-standing customers. The closer operations are to major buyers, the better the cost efficiency and marketing effectiveness. Coca-Cola and PepsiCo both selected east coast provinces of China as project sites because the majority of their consumers are located there. Similarly, UPS (United Parcel Service) elected Cologne in Germany and Taipei in Taiwan as its European and Asia-Pacific air hubs, respectively, because of the ease of reaching customers.

3. *Local competition:* The intensity of competition in a host country or specific region is important because it directly impacts a firm's market position and gross profit margin from local sales.[2] In general, MNEs locate sites in places where competition is relatively low unless they have sufficient advantages to ensure their competitive edge in the market. Competition may come from local rivals as well as from other foreign rivals. When Coca-Cola made substantial new investments to strengthen its market position in east coast provinces of China in the early 1990s, PepsiCo began to expand to inland provinces to pioneer in this new territory.

Strategic Factors

1. *Investment infrastructure:* Today, MNEs attach increasing importance to infrastructure conditions. This is especially true for companies investing in knowledge- or technology-intensive projects. Singapore attracted many of those MNEs mainly because of its ideal infrastructure. Major infrastructure variables include transportation (highways, ports, airports, and railroads), telecommunications, utilities, and governmental efficiency. The infrastructure also includes the availability of international seaports and import/export facilities since most FDI projects have operational linkages with home and other international markets. When Hewlett-Packard entered Mexico, it did not choose Mexico City but instead Ciudad Juarez, near the metropolitan area, which has excellent infrastructure conditions (access to roads and airports, strong support from local authorities, a superb export-processing environment, and the availability of an information-technology industry).

2. *Manufacturing concentration:* One of the major determinants of location selection is the strength of existing manufacturing activities. Cost savings can

result from manufacturers locating in close proximity. A country or region with a strong concentration of manufacturing activity in certain industries or products is more likely to have an adequate labor pool and supply network supporting production or operations.[3] Just-in-time systems require a supplier base that is capable, reliable, and physically close. Otis opted for Leningrad as its primary manufacturing center in Russia because it has a well-established supply network for materials and components and has many skilled laborers and technicians for producing elevators and escalators.

3. *Industrial linkages:* The nature and quality of complementary industries and special services (distribution, consulting, auditing, banking, insurance, marketing services, etc.) are also important, as MNE operations interact actively with these sectors in a host country. Industrial linkages with these businesses affect the firm's ability to pursue value creation and addition. Mary Kay Cosmetics located its business center in Buenos Aires, which serves Argentina, Uruguay, and Chile, having considered the favorable industrial linkages in this city.

4. *Workforce productivity:* As a result of increasing technological permeation and process innovation, international production requires high workforce productivity and superior labor skills. The labor requirements of new systems and techniques are driving the need for a better educated direct-labor workforce. Just-in-time and total quality management systems place greater importance on the flexibility of workers and their ability to operate under growing autonomy. The increasing sophistication of product and process technologies has also increased skill requirements. The availability of a skilled managerial, marketing, and technical workforce is also crucial, because they are primary forces in gaining competitive advantages in the market.

5. *Inbound and outbound logistics:* Typical inbound (input) logistics include proximity to suppliers and sources of raw materials and inputs. Since MNEs have a tendency to rely more on local input sources, this type of logistics should be among the critical considerations for international managers. Outbound (market) logistics are based largely on proximity to major buyers and end consumers. This factor can heavily influence the effectiveness of customer responsiveness. When the firm pursues market penetration and product specialization strategies, the firm's profitability will be strongly associated with market logistics. A main reason why Procter & Gamble (P&G) chose Mexico City as its major production base for North America was the effective inbound and outbound logistics, which satisfy P&G's needs for production and marketing.

Regulatory and Economic Factors

1. *Industrial policies:* In many countries, industrial policies are used to control new entrants (both foreign and local firms), net profit margins, degree of competition, structural concentration, and social benefits. Typical industrial policies include antitrust rules, project approval and registration, categorization of industries and treatment differences among categories, and varying value-added tax, among others (also see the last section of Chapter 4). In selecting a location, MNEs need to make sure that the target country or region allows foreign business entry and that industrial policies are reasonably favorable or at least not a hindrance. Industrial policies generally have a more direct impact on MNE operations than do macroeconomic policies of a host government.[4]

Lucent Technologies moved into Brazil after the Brazilian government announced the "Real Plan" in 1994, which devalued its currency (the *real*), privatized telecom services, and offered more favorable treatments to new entrants into the telecom infrastructure sector.

2. *FDI policies.* In considering a foreign location (country and region), MNEs need to learn how FDI policies there will affect their plans and payoffs. First, they should know what entry mode(s) are allowed. They might be allowed to enter into certain sites or industries only through certain entry modes such as minority joint ventures. Second, a host government may require MNEs to locate projects in certain geographical regions to help boost regional economies. Projects in different locations may be taxed differently. Third, MNEs should check content localization requirements. A foreign company is often required to purchase and use local materials, parts, semi-products, or other supplies made by indigenous firms for the production of its final outputs. The required level of localization varies across countries and industries. Fourth, MNEs need to identify any geographical restrictions imposed on the breadth of the market. For example, prior to China's entry into the WTO, foreign banks were allowed to provide services only in the city in which they were located. Finally, MNEs must appraise foreign exchange control measures in a host country. These measures may hinder the free inflow and outflow of foreign capital and income.

3. *Availability of special economic zones:* One way many countries (especially in the developing world) attempt to attract FDI is through the establishment of special zones such as free trade zones, special economic zones, economic and technological development zones, high-tech development zones, open economic regions, bonded areas, and so on. In general, these zones provide preferential treatment in terms of taxation, import duties, land use, infrastructure access, and governmental assistance to MNEs. However, many of these zones are regulated regarding eligibility for preferential treatment. For instance, MNEs located in Chinese economic and technological development zones must export 75% of output or bring in advanced technologies as verified by governmental authorities.

Sociopolitical Factors

1. *Political instability:* This factor reflects uncertainty over the continuation of present political and social conditions and government policies that are critical to the survival and profitability of a firm's operations in the host country. Changes in government policies may create problems related to repatriation of earnings or, in extreme cases, expropriation of assets. Although international lobbying on foreign country policies has become pervasive, the magnitude of politically induced environmental uncertainty still overwhelms transaction-related risks affecting MNE operations.

2. *Cultural barriers:* Differences in culture between the home and host countries can become other triggers of uncertainty. This cultural factor determines a firm's receptivity and adaptability to the social context of a host country.[5] Language barriers are also an important consideration underlying location selection. Although every foreign business can recruit local people, communications with headquarters as well as between employees within the company are crucial to business success (see also Chapter 6).

3. *Local business practices:* Culture-specific business practices often constitute key forms of knowledge that MNEs must acquire. In fact, a prominent logic behind formation of international cooperative ventures with developing country enterprises is to gain such country-specific knowledge. Superior technological and organizational skills cannot guarantee the success of international operations unless the firm is able to integrate country-specific knowledge with its firm-specific knowledge. The ability to integrate these two types of knowledge often determines the survival and growth of MNEs in foreign markets.

4. *Government efficiency and corruption:* International managers often perceive the "soft" infrastructure (e.g., regulatory environment and government efficiency) as having a greater and more enduring impact on firm operations than the "hard" infrastructure (e.g., transportation and communication). Efficient governments are more responsive to an MNE's requests or complaints, take shorter time periods for ratifying projects, and provide superior assistance and support in various matters. Governmental corruption implies not only low efficiency and excessive red tape but also high costs of bribery in setting up governmental linkages to get project approval, infrastructure access, and acquisition of scarce resources (see Chapter 19).

5. *Attitudes toward foreign business:* Social and governmental attitudes toward foreign businesses often have visible or invisible influences on MNE operations and management. If the society and government of a host country are somewhat friendly to foreign business, MNEs will benefit from the congenial environment. This attitude has an enduring effect on both firm operations and the commitment of employees to the foreign firm. Burger King selected the Dominican Republic as its major site in the Caribbean (22 restaurants as of July 2001) because Dominicans (both government and the public) have a very positive view of the United States and American products. The country is now the Caribbean's largest democratic country and has a long-standing and close relationship with the United States (where many Dominicans legally immigrate).

6. *Community characteristics:* Site selection must include considerations of community environment aspects such as community size, educational facilities, housing facilities, police and fire protection, climate, suitability for expatriates and their families, facilities for children, the social environment for spouses, hotel accommodations, crime level, and other quality-of-life indicators. This environment is highly relevant because it affects costs, quality, and security of living for foreign expatriates and their families.

7. *Pollution control:* Environmental protection laws and regulations in the target location influence the choice and cost of investments. Before making a location decision, an MNE should appraise these laws and regulations, assess whether the firm is able to comply with them, and evaluate whether it is financially feasible to invest in pollution control. Rubbermaid entered Poland in 1995 and now views the country as its central site in Eastern Europe. A relatively low standard in pollution control (thus lower costs to comply with this standard) is one of the factors that attracted Rubbermaid to invest there.

Exhibit 10.1 summarizes the major locational determinants explained previously. Overall, site selection within a diverse country should be based on microcontext factors, whereas country selection should be made after a careful analysis of both microcontext and macrocontext factors.

Exhibit 10.1   Locational Determinants

Microcontext	Macrocontext
Cost and Tax Factors	*Regulatory Factors*
Transportation costs	Industrial policies
Wage rate	FDI policies
Land availability and costs	Availability of special zones
Construction costs	
Costs of raw materials and	*Sociopolitical Factors*
resources	Political instability
Financing costs	Cultural barriers
Tax rates	Local business practices
Investment incentives	Government efficiency and
Profit repatriation	corruption
	Attitudes toward foreign business
Demand Factors	Community characteristics
Market size and growth	Sustainable development
Customer presence	(e.g., pollution control and
Local competition	recycling requirements)
Strategic Factors	
Investment infrastructure	
Manufacturing concentration	
Industrial linkages	
Workforce productivity	
Inbound and outbound logistics	

COUNTRY BOX

FEDERAL EXPRESS SELECTS SUBIC BAY

In December 1992, the United States closed down its naval shipyard in Subic Bay, the Philippines, which was its largest overseas base. The departure of the military put Subic Bay in a deep economic slump and left 47,000 Filipinos unemployed. It also left an $8 billion facility unused, so the Philippine government decided to turn Subic Bay into a self-sustaining commercial investment center. It was immediately declared a free-trade zone area with unlimited duty-free imports and a hassle-free export system. In 1993, the management team from Federal Express went to Subic Bay to investigate the area for its central hub location. The government presented many investment incentives to FedEx, offering liberal air traffic rights, streamlined customs clearance procedures to accommodate the quick turnaround time of express carriers, and help in dealing with the bureaucracy. This all happened in a nation known for bureaucratic red tape and favoritism toward local companies. In September of 1995, FedEx opened its Pacific Asian hub facility in Subic Bay at a cost of about US$100 million. This strategic event enabled it to obtain a 24-hour use of airport facilities and employ the low-paid, well-educated, English-speaking laborers already located there. Hong Kong and Taipei did not have the 24-hour airport facilities critical to hub operations. Singapore was too far south, and Osaka, in Japan, was too far north. Federal Express's decision to open the regional hub in Subic Bay created an excellent strategic advantage for the company. It now connects 13 major economic and financial centers in the region.

Decision Framework

The preceding section presented locational determinants that must be assessed in the course of choosing a location. These determinants constitute the core in the framework of a location decision-making process. Aside from this core, MNEs also need to take into account their strategic objectives, global integration, and market orientation.

Location and Strategic Objectives

If an MNE wishes to pursue market growth and a competitive position in a host country, demand factors and strategic factors appear to be its most critical considerations. Because these factors generally concern long-term investments and operations, macroeconomic and sociopolitical factors also have a moderate impact on location selection. If an MNE seeks short- or midterm profitability, it should attach more value to cost and taxation factors. Infrastructure conditions and investment incentives may also play a role. The costs of production factors and operational expenses will determine the gross profit margin, whereas income tax rates will affect the net return. Remittance taxes or profit repatriation restrictions have a great impact on the level of dividends that the parent firm finally receives. If an MNE strives to diversify risks or operate in a stable environment, sociopolitical factors become fundamental to the decision. Because some macroeconomic factors such as exchange rate and the inflation rate are related to environmental uncertainty, they should also be included in the analytical framework. Finally, if an MNE intends to secure innovation, learning, and adaptation from international expansion, strategic factors often outweigh other groups of factors in affecting location choice. Nevertheless, industrial linkages, competition intensity, cultural distance, and attitudes toward foreign businesses may also influence the accomplishment of this goal.

Location and Global Integration

The location decision should be framed within the design of global integration. As the world economy becomes increasingly regionalized (see Chapter 8), MNEs may first decide which regional bloc they should enter. In this situation, location selection involves regional bloc selection, country selection, and site selection. In considering regional bloc selection, managers can review the preceding determinants at the integrated bloc level (e.g., the EU vs. NAFTA) and find out how removed or lessened intercountry barriers within the bloc reduce cost and tax burdens and change regulatory and economic environments (thus identifying new opportunities and new threats). Other groups of determinants such as demand and strategic and sociopolitical factors are less affected by the formation of a regional bloc. Today, MNEs use host country sites to achieve global or regional integration. MNEs tend to locate labor-intensive processes in sites that are relatively well endowed with abundant labor or locate an R&D facility in an area where abundant technological capabilities exist. Linking activities across locations is fundamental to capturing international scale and scope. It is important for international managers to locate projects in such sites that provide an ideal environment for integrating operations with the rest of the MNE network. When Cisco entered France, it built distribution centers in Toulouse, which serve not only France but also the Middle East. Today Cisco sells its products in approximately 115 countries, distributed mostly through consolidated sites in respective regions.

Location and Market Orientation

Market orientation is concerned mainly with whether an MNE primarily targets a host country market, export market (home or other foreign markets), or both. Naturally, different market orientations vary in their relationship with locational determinants. Local market-oriented projects are highly sensitive to demand and strategic factors in the local environment. Some regulatory and economic factors are also relevant because they affect a firm's stability and the exposure of its operations to environmental turbulence. Certain sociopolitical variables including cultural distance, government efficiency or corruption, and political stability are likely to have a stronger effect on a local market orientation than on an export orientation. The latter, by contrast, relies more on cost and tax factors. Plants producing for an export market can be located with little regard for domestic demand. Therefore, cost and tax factors, together with strategic factors such as investment incentives, input logistics, labor productivity, and infrastructure, are prominent microcontextual determinants underlying this location strategy. For example, many U.S. companies relocate their production facilities just south of the U.S.–Mexico border. These factories, called *maquiladoras,* assemble imported, duty-free components into finished goods, most of which are then reexported to the United States. In addition to benefiting from lower labor costs, these companies enjoy reduced transportation costs, eliminated tariff burdens, and logistics convenience. Currently, approximately 4,000 maquiladoras with over 1.2 million employees operate along the border zone, accounting for nearly one-third of Mexico's industrial jobs and 45% of its total exports (see Exhibit 10.2).

Finally, the dual-emphasis orientation may be influenced by all five group factors. In other words, the dual-emphasis orientation necessitates the most comprehensive scheme in the appraisal of locational determinants. Levi Strauss & Company's three manufacturing facilities in Mexico, located in Aguascalientes, Naucalpan, and Teziutlan, are ideal for this dual pursuit. All these facilities are close to Mexico City and physically close to California (the U.S. headquarters). About a half of the jeans made in these facilities are exported back to the United States while the other half targets local consumers (about 25% market share in Mexico).

Interim Summary

1. When selecting a foreign location, managers need to consider not only cost and tax factors but also market demand, investment infrastructure, regulatory and economic environments, and sociopolitical factors.

2. Managers should choose a foreign location that not only provides a favorable investment environment but also helps fulfill the firm's objectives underlying international entry.

TIMING OF ENTRY (*WHEN*)

Timing of entry involves the sequence of an MNE's entry into a foreign market vis-à-vis other MNEs (i.e., first mover, early follower, and late mover). Timing of entry is important because it determines the risks, environments, and opportunities the MNE may confront.[6] In today's increasingly integrated global marketplace, where demand level, consumption sophistication, and rivalry intensity are all changing drastically, the decision on when to embark on international expansion is critical for transnational operations. Transnational investors are likely to have more preemptive investment opportunities in foreign markets than in their home markets. This is largely because of the different market and industry structures between home and host economies. By investing in a foreign market, a later mover in the home country could become an early entrant in the host country. It could enjoy more favorable business opportunities in sectors that are in early stages of the industry life cycle in the host country market or in industries in which it has distinctive competitive advantages. Aside from noticing an opportunity, the decision on when to invest is broadly based on an entrant's assessment of entry barriers erected by a host government and existing firms, relative to the factors promoting entry. Potential entrants weigh the expected benefits and costs of entry; entry occurs when the former outweigh the latter.

Exhibit 10.2   Maquiladoras in the Mexico–U.S. Border Zone

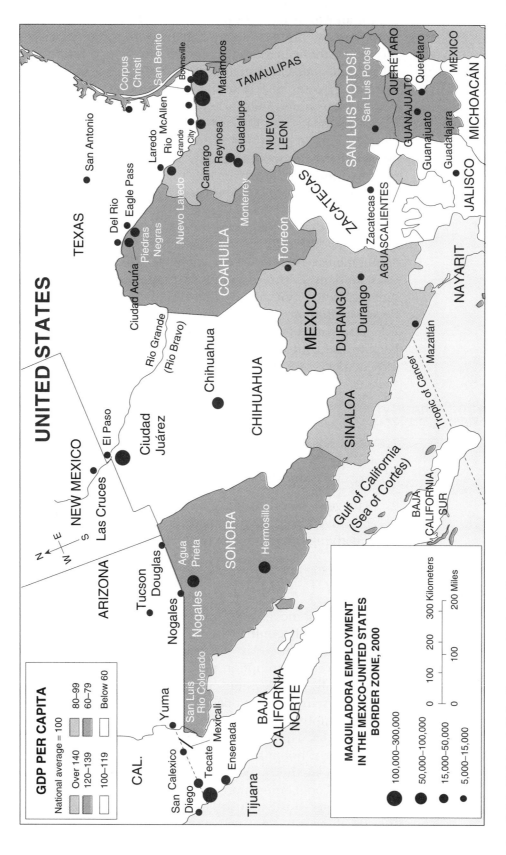

SOURCE: From H. J. de Blij & Peter R. Muller. *Concepts and Regions in Geography*, 1st ed., figure 4–11, p. 142. Hoboken, NJ: John Wiley & Son. Copyright © 2003 John Wiley & Sons. Reprinted with permission of John Wiley & Sons, Inc.

Early-Mover Advantages

When entering a foreign market, pioneering MNEs (**first mover** or **early followers**) generally have advantages such as greater market power, more preemptive opportunities, and more strategic options over late entrants. These advantages might be ultimately reflected in higher economic returns compared with later movers. First, pioneering investors tend to outperform later entrants in acquiring *market power*. Early movers are able to invest strategically in facilities, distribution networks, product positioning, patentable technology, natural resources, and human and organizational expertise. If imitation of its product is expected to be expensive or involve a long time lag, a preemptive investment can be leveraged into significant long-run benefits for early movers. Moreover, market pioneers may benefit from the advantages of holding technical leadership, seizing scarce resources, and creating buyer switching costs.[7] Because of such switching costs, and because most customers are more loyal to an early mover's successful products and services, customer loyalty tends to be stronger for early-mover products than for late-mover products. This loyalty fortifies an early mover's market power and competitive position. Citibank and Bank of America were both early movers into Latin America in both the pre-war and postwar periods, relative to other foreign banks such as Barclays from Britain and the Bank of Nova Scotia from Canada. By 1929, for example, Citibank and Bank of America had branches or offices in Mexico City, Buenos Aires, São Paulo, and Santiago. By the 1970s, these two U.S. banks had branches or offices in almost every Latin American country. They have dominated these markets largely because of the market power they obtained from an early-entry position (loyal customers, close relations with local banks and governments, and established technological and service standards). This market power was further strengthened when they erected entry barriers against later movers in the form of acquiring local banks, partnering with Visa International, creating innovative banking approaches such as Internet banking and banking services via cable TV, and extending their network-type presence almost everywhere.

Second, early movers gain from *preemptive opportunities*. Early movers have the right to preempt marketing, promotion, and distribution channels, while gaining product image, organizational reputation, and brand recognition. Toys "R" Us entered Japan in May 1990 right after MITI (The Japanese Ministry of International Trade and Industry) relaxed regulations and restrictions in the retail toy industry. By the end of 1996, it had opened 35 stores throughout Japan, with approximately $20 million annual sales per store compared with $10 million per U.S. store. The company's success involves, in part, the first-mover opportunities it seized, such as preemptive marketing and promotion as well as brand recognition and pioneer reputation. Similarly, Otis entered Russia as the first mover in the elevator industry and preempted the distribution channels previously built by the Russian government and used by local state-owned enterprises. It is incorrect to assume that foreign market opportunities are limitless, however. The window of opportunity opens only for a time and is therefore available only to early movers.[8] For example, to pursue economic reform and political stability, China's State Council set up a ceiling on the number of FDI projects in the automobile industry. Today, Volkswagen dominates China's small car market while GM does well in the luxury sedan market. They were all first movers in their respective categories.

Third, early movers benefit from many *strategic options*. Pioneer investors often have more strategic options in selecting industries, locations, and market orientations (e.g., import substitution, local-market oriented, export-market oriented, infrastructure oriented). In addition, early movers are often given priority access to natural resources, scarce materials, distribution channels, promotional arrangements, and infrastructure. As early movers into Poland, Matsushita and Philips were better able to access scarce or governmentally controlled resources such as local financing and state-instituted wholesale networks than later movers such as Toshiba and Samsung. Moreover, early investors have a superior option to select better local firms for equity/contractual joint ventures or for supply-purchase business relations. Thailand's Charoen Pokphand (CP), one of the world's largest agro-industrial MNEs, entered China in 1979 as the first mover into the Chinese agriculture sector. By 2000, the company had set up 170 projects throughout 28 provinces. Most of these projects are joint ventures with the best local firms in respective regions. Further, early movers enjoy low competition before late movers come in. The only competition comes from local firms (if any). Wal-Mart was among the first foreign superstores established in Korea, China, Costa Rica, Argentina, Germany, Puerto Rico, and Brazil, to name a few. The only competition the company faced during early years was from some indigenous department stores in major metropolitan areas. When later movers are about to enter, early movers and local firms tend to establish alliances to drive out new entrants or maintain strong competitive power in the industry. Even when not forming alliances, early movers are still in a better position to deal with competition from local firms than late entrants. They can position their competitive advantage in businesses, industries, and markets where competition from local firms is weak or where they have better technological and organizational competencies.

Early-Mover Disadvantages

Early movers, however, also suffer from some disadvantages compared with late entrants. Pioneer investors may be confronted with greater environmental uncertainty and operational risks. Environmental uncertainty generally comes from (a) underdeveloped FDI laws and regulations in a host country, (b) the host government's lack of experience in dealing with MNEs, and (c) infant or embryonic stages of the industry or market in a host country. Operational risks originate from (a) a shortage of qualified supply sources and other production inputs such as talented managers and R&D workers; (b) underdeveloped support services such as local financing, foreign exchange, arbitration, consulting, and marketing; (c) poor infrastructure in transportation, utilities, and communications; and (d) an unstable market structure in which market demand and supply are misaligned and local governments often interfere with MNE operations.

In contrast with early movers, **late investors** do not suffer, or suffer less, from the preceding uncertainties and risks.[9] When late movers arrive, the host-country environment is usually more stable, regulatory conditions are more favorable, and the market infrastructure is already developed. Korean MNEs (*chaebol*) are all late movers entering China relative to Western MNEs. They did not enter until 1994, when Hyundai, Samsung, LG, and Daewoo started their FDI in China, especially on the Shandong Peninsula. In that year China significantly deepened economic reforms and liberalization, broadened the industries and geographical areas for MNE operations, and enacted various laws and regulations concerning inbound FDI. As late movers, Korean MNEs benefited greatly from these improved environments. Facing reduced uncertainty and a more stabilized environment, Korean chaebol were aggressive late movers who waited patiently until the best time but committed aggressively after entry to seize emerging opportunities. LG Group, for example, built 20 projects in China, amounting to $688 billion in the first two years after entering the country in 1994.

Early movers also tend to pay higher costs in learning about and adapting to local environments and in countervailing imitation. Many early movers are compelled to invest more in building industrial infrastructure (e.g., supply bases and distribution networks) and technological or service standards. When Sharp and Hitachi entered China in the early 1980s to produce fax machines, they had to establish these standards and construct supply bases because the fax machine industry had not yet emerged in the country prior to their entry. It also cost early movers more in training local workers, technicians, and managers. Such human resources might be unavailable or lack skill before early FDI is undertaken. Late entrants, however, can benefit greatly from a pool of skilled laborers and favorable industrial infrastructure established by early entrants. In addition, early movers pay more to learn about the local environment (cultural, social, economic, legal, and political), unique business practices, social norms and customs, and consumer behavior. Conversely, later movers who use a wait-and-see strategy gain from lessons from early movers. In particular, they benefit from mimicking an early mover's business policies and strategies that have proved to be successful in a host country. For example, when the Franklin Templeton Group, a U.S. financial service company, entered Brazil in 1998 as a late mover, it learned a great deal about viable strategies from early movers such as Citibank. As of December 2000, its mutual fund assets in Brazil reached $1.17 billion.

Finally, early movers may have to fight followers who imitate their strategies or innovations, counterfeit their products, or infringe on their industrial (e.g., trademark and brand) or intellectual property rights (e.g., patent, expertise, software). This cost is especially high when early movers invest in a country with underdeveloped and underenforced legal systems for protecting these rights. Philip Morris entered Russia's tobacco market (Russians consume 300 billion cigarettes per year) in 1974 as a first mover. However, it has proved to be very costly for the company to protect its leading brands such as Marlboro and Parliament because about 30% of these brands sold on the street are now counterfeits. When followers imitate a first mover's products or strategies, the latter needs to commit more to new innovations, new developments, and new strategies. When followers infringe on a first mover's property rights, the latter has to spend on litigation, investigation, lobbying, or arbitration. In addition to direct costs of anti-imitation, early movers have to pay higher switching and start-up costs. Later movers can piggyback on early investment if imitation is easy, thereby gaining profit without having to pay as much as innovators.

Because of the preceding uncertainties, risks, and costs, pioneer MNEs tend to select the joint venture mode for FDI entry. In the joint venture business, however, the objectives of local partners usually diverge from those of their foreign partners. The pursuit of self-interest rather than common goals, as well as lack of autonomy among local partners, can result in significant uncertainty for joint venture operations. This internal uncertainty is generally difficult for MNEs to control. Since late investors can usually choose to establish wholly owned subsidiaries, this uncertainty is less substantial than that faced by early movers.

Exhibit 10.3 summarizes the advantages and disadvantages of being an early mover. In general, the advantages of early movers are the disadvantages of late movers, and vice versa.

Decision Framework

Entry decisions must be based on rigorous cost–benefit analysis and then prudently timed. After assessing the advantages and disadvantages of the timing choice (e.g., early mover), international managers consider other factors in formulating timing

Exhibit 10.3   Advantages and Disadvantages of Being an Early Mover

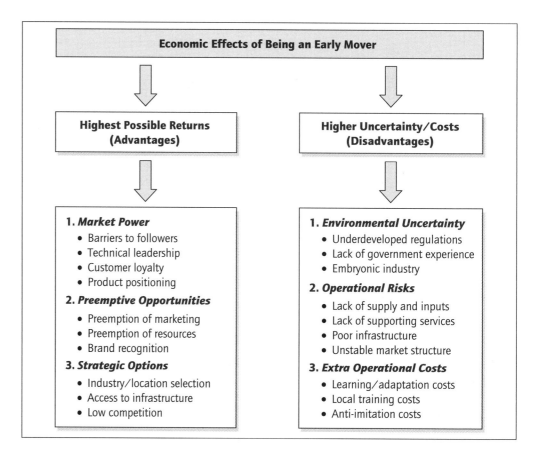

strategy. These include (a) the MNE's technological, organizational, and financial resources or capabilities; (b) the host-country environment in terms of infrastructure, industry structure, market demand, and governmental policies; and (c) potential competition from late foreign entrants as well as local entrants.

An MNE's resources and capabilities determine its ability to reduce early-mover risks and seize preemptive investment opportunities. A pioneer entrant must wait for a feasible opportunity for investment, the appearance of which depends on the investor's foresight, skills, resources, and good fortune. Not every MNE is competent to be a pioneer mover. One prerequisite, for instance, is the firm's international experience and its ability to cultivate relationships with local authorities and handle environmental changes overseas. Motorola has been capable of being the first mover into many emerging markets owing to its accumulated experience in a large number of developing countries, especially its experience in dealing with local governments and communities.

The real balance between costs and benefits or between risks and returns for a timing decision depends on actual dynamics and specific characteristics of the host-country environments. As explained in Chapter 5, the microeconomic business environment (industrial conditions and market situations) often affects MNE activities more directly than the macroeconomic environment. The host-country conditions in infrastructure, technology, factor endowments, market demand, industry structure, and government policies are all likely to affect an MNE's timing of entry and its eventual success. Moreover, anticipated first-mover opportunities may disappear, or unanticipated new opportunities may emerge, because of environmental changes in a host country. The transformation of national economies, market structures, and government policies is often so uncertain in foreign countries that pioneer MNEs may need to have second or even third backup plans. When Philip Morris (PM) entered Russia as a first mover, it built two projects, PM Izhora in Leningrad and PM Kuban in Krasnodar. The two projects were set in such a way that PM Kuban would switch from producing cigarettes to processing raw tobacco for PM Izhora if local suppliers were unable to supply processed tobacco or if the local market became more restricted.

The option of being a first mover is not entirely under the firm's control. Preemptive investment opportunities may be observed and acted on by local rivals as well as foreign competitors. The responses and actions of the firm's competitors need to be carefully examined. The MNE must study the strengths and weaknesses of potential rivals in areas such as technology, production, marketing, and capital. When an opportunity presents itself, the investor must decide whether it should enter the foreign territory as a first mover or early entrant and then whether it has the capacity to build a sustainable advantage from its entry timing. If the answers are yes, the firm must then decide how to enter the host market and best exploit the opportunity, the critical issue being discussed next. Once a pioneering strategy is chosen, the investor must react faster than its rivals, commit to its own pioneering opportunities, and take measures to sustain its first-mover advantages. If the investor chooses not to be an early mover, or if a rival has preempted this position, then the investor must decide whether, how, and when to follow.

Interim Summary

1. Compared with late entrants, early movers benefit from stronger market power, greater preemptive opportunities, and more strategic options but suffer more from environmental uncertainty, operational risks, and extra operational costs.

2. Not every early mover can succeed abroad, nor should every firm be the first mover. The timing decision depends not only on the opportunity–risk balance but also on the firm's capabilities, the local environment, and new competition.

ENTRY-MODE SELECTION (*HOW*)

Entry-Mode Choices

An MNE seeking to enter a foreign market must make an important strategic decision concerning which entry mode to use. **Entry modes** are specific forms or ways of entering a target country to achieve strategic goals underlying international presence in that country. Entry-mode choices fall into three categories: *trade related, transfer related,* and *FDI related.* Along this sequence, the levels of resource commitment, organizational control, involved risks, and expected returns all increase. Within each category, these levels differ somewhat between specific modes.

Trade-Related Entry Modes

Trade-related entry modes include exporting, subcontracting, and countertrade.

Exporting. It is natural for most firms to get their start in international expansion through exporting, in which the firm maintains its production facilities at home and sells its products abroad. Through exporting, the firm gains valuable expertise about operating internationally and specific knowledge concerning the individual countries in which it operates. Export offers the advantage of not requiring a very substantial presence in foreign countries. Generally, exporting is a type of international entry open to virtually any size or kind of firm, whereas other types of entry modes tend to demand greater resources and involve more risks. Over time, accumulated experience with exporting often prompts a firm to become more aggressive in exploiting new international exporting opportunities or consider FDI in the country to which it previously exported.

A firm can export goods to foreign customers or buyers either directly or through export intermediaries. **Export intermediaries** are third parties that specialize in facilitating imports and exports. These intermediaries may offer limited services such as handling only transportation, documentation, and customs claims, or they may perform more extensive services, including taking ownership of foreign-bound goods or assuming total responsibility for marketing and financing exports. Typical export intermediaries are export management companies. An **export management company** (EMC) is an intermediary that acts as its client's export department. Small firms may use an EMC to handle their foreign shipments, prepare export documents, and deal with customs offices, insurance companies, and commodity inspection agencies. EMCs are generally more knowledgeable about the legal, financial, and logistical details of exporting and importing and thus free the exporter from having to develop such expertise in-house.

Managers involved in exporting must know the terms of sale (or terms of price). **Terms of sale** are conditions stipulating rights and responsibilities and costs and risks borne by exporter and importer. These terms have been harmonized and defined by the International Chamber of Commerce as standards and thus are widely used in export transactions. Major terms of price include the following:

- *FOB* (Free on Board): A term of price in which the seller covers all costs and risks up to the point whereby the goods are delivered on board the ship in a designated shipment (export) port, and the buyer bears all costs and risks from that point on. This means that the buyer is responsible for the insurance and freight expenses in transporting goods from the shipment port to the destination port.
- *FAS* (Free Alongside Ship): A term of price in which the seller covers all costs and risks up to the side of the ship in a designated shipment (export) port. The buyer bears all costs and risks thereafter.
- *CIF* (Cost, Insurance, and Freight): A term of price in which the seller covers cost of the goods, insurance, and all transportation and miscellaneous charges to the named foreign port in the country of final destination.
- *C&F* (Cost and Freight): Similar to CIF except that the buyer purchases and bears the insurance.

Export managers should also be familiar with key documentation in exporting. The key documents frequently used include the letter of credit, the bill of lading, the bank draft, the commercial invoice, the insurance certificate, and the certificate of origin. **A letter of credit** (L/C) is a contract between an importer and a bank that transfers liability for paying the exporter from the importer to the importer's bank (for details, see the first section of Chapter 14). A **bill of lading** (B/L) is the document issued by a shipping company or its agent as evidence of a contract for shipping the merchandise and as a claim to ownership of the goods. In Chapter 14, we explain in detail how export managers deal with international payment, import and export financing, foreign exchange risk reduction, and collection of export accounts receivable.

International Subcontracting. Subcontracting has been used extensively by MNEs seeking low labor costs in a host country. Generally, **subcontracting** is the process in which a foreign company provides a local manufacturer with raw materials, semifinished products, sophisticated components, or technology for producing final goods that will be bought back by the foreign company. In most subcontracting businesses, local manufacturers are responsible only for processing or assembly in exchange for processing fees. In this situation, the local manufacturer does not own the property rights of materials or parts supplied by the foreign counterpart. Nike, for example, is still using subcontracting as its primary mode in China, Vietnam, Thailand, Indonesia, and Bangladesh. The company provides raw materials and technology, maintains proprietary rights over materials and products, controls production processes and product quality, and pays processing fees to local factories.

In the beginning of the 21st century, when falling trade barriers and increasing competition prompted large firms to cut costs, many MNEs producing sophisticated products began shrinking their manufacturing function by using the **original equipment manufacturing (OEM)** method. OEM is one specific form of international subcontracting, in which a foreign firm (i.e., the original equipment manufacturer) supplies a local company with the technology and sophisticated components so that the latter can manufacture goods that the foreign firm will market under its own brand in international markets. During the 1990s, Flextronics, a Singapore-based company, was a small contract assembler of circuit boards, but it is now the world's third largest subcontractor in electronics, providing cost-efficient manufacturing services that free its OEM clients (e.g., Honeywell, GE, Pratt & Whitney, Compaq, Nortel) to concentrate on design, engineering, R&D, and global marketing. I-Berhad, a Malaysian subcontractor in PC assembly, has assembly plants in Shah Alam, Selangor, and Perak that provide subcontracting services (manufacturing and assembling) for many international brands such as Sanyo, Sharp, Toshiba, and Singer. China's Kelon now serves as GE's largest subcontractor for its household appliance products. This subcontracting helps Kelon utilize its existing production capacity, benefit from technology transfer from GE, and learn managerial skills from the foreign firm. It helps GE reduce production costs, rationalize its production process, and expedite large-volume productions. Today, other MNEs, such as Motorola, Ericsson, Siemens, Acer, HP, IBM, Boeing, Alcatel-Lucent, and Northern Telecom, are using the OEM method to cut costs while maintaining their competitive edge in the global marketplace.

Countertrade. Countertrade is a form of trade in which a seller and a buyer from different countries exchange merchandise with little or no cash or cash equivalents changing hands. Because of its nature, it is also viewed as a form of flexible financing or payment in international trade. Informed estimates suggest that countertrade accounts for about 20% of world trade.[10] Countertrade has evolved into a diverse set of activities that can be categorized as four distinct types of trading arrangements:

- Barter
- Counterpurchase
- Offset
- Buyback (or compensation)

Barter is the direct and simultaneous exchange of goods between two parties without a cash transaction. Barter trade occurs between individuals, between governments, between firms, or between a government and a firm, all from two different countries. Barter may be the oldest form of trade, but it is certainly not history. For example, France shipped 138,067 tons of soft wheat to Cuba during the first quarter of 2001, half of which was through the wheat-for-sugar barter arrangement under which French trading companies purchase sugar and agricultural commodities from Alimport, Cuba's government-run food trading company. Because firms using barter run the risk of having to accept goods that may be difficult to market or earn a satisfactory profit margin from, it is important for a party to ensure that trading-in products are heavily demanded in its own market.

A **counterpurchase** is a reciprocal buying agreement whereby one firm sells its products to another at one point and is compensated in the form of the other's products at some future time (e.g., Russia purchased construction machinery from Japan's Komatsu in return for Komatsu's agreement to buy Siberian timber). Counterpurchase is more flexible than barter in facilitating many transactions because the volume of trade does not have to be equal—that is, the dollar amount of goods exported need not be equal to the dollar amount of goods taken back. In this situation, two parties can either set up an escrow account or use cash to finally settle the differences. Unlike barter, which involves a single contract, a counterpurchase agreement usually involves three separate contracts—the sales contract, the purchase contract, and the protocol contract. The protocol contract serves as a protection contract, which explains what each party will do and what each party should expect.

An **offset** is an agreement whereby one party agrees to purchase goods and services with a specified percentage of its proceeds from an original sale. Like counterpurchase, offset involves three contracts, including sales, protocol, and purchase. Unlike counterpurchase whereby exchanged products are normally unrelated, products taken back in an offset are often the outputs processed by this party in the original contract. For example, the Shanghai Aircraft Manufacturing Corp., China, may buy jets from Boeing using its proceeds from manufacturing the tail sections of the jets for Boeing. Offset is particularly popular in sales of expensive military equipment or high-cost civilian infrastructure hardware. General Dynamics sold several hundred F-16 military jets to Belgium, Denmark, Norway, and the Netherlands by agreeing to allow those countries to offset the cost of the jets through co-production agreements whereby 40% of the value of the aircraft was produced in those countries.

Finally, **buyback** (or compensation arrangement) occurs when a firm provides a local company with inputs for manufacturing products (mostly capital equipment) to be sold in international markets and agrees to take a certain percentage of the output produced by the local firm as partial payment. A buyback agreement involves two contracts, including the sales contract and the purchase contract. In a buyback arrangement, the equipment supplier gets a cash portion in addition to the goods. For example, a steel producer might send its goods to a foreign company, which would use the steel to manufacture a product such as shelving. The steel producer would then buy back the shelves at a reduced price, in effect partially paying the manufacturer with the raw steel. Buybacks help developing-country producers upgrade technologies and machinery and ensure after-sale service. Chinatex, a Shanghai-based clothing manufacturer, and Japan's Fukusuke Corp., arranged a buyback whereby the latter sold 10 knitting machines and raw materials to the former in exchange for 1 million pairs of underwear to be produced on the knitting machines. Because the buyback links payment with output from the purchased goods, Chinatex benefited from Fukusuke's instructions on how to use the equipment and its excellent after-sale services.

Transfer-Related Entry Modes

Transfer-related entry modes are those associated with transfer of ownership or utilization of specified property (technology or assets) from one party to another in exchange for royalty fees. They differ from trade-related entry modes in that the user in a transfer-related mode "buys" certain rights of transacted property (e.g., use of technology) from the other party (owner). These modes are extensively employed in technology-related or intellectual/industrial property rights–related transactions. This category includes the following entry modes:

- International leasing
- International licensing
- International franchising
- Build-operate-transfer (BOT)

International Leasing. International leasing is an entry mode in which the foreign firm (lessor) leases out its new or used machines or equipment to the local company (often in a developing country). International leasing arises largely because developing country manufacturers (lessees) do not have the financial capability or lack foreign currency to pay for the equipment. In many cases, the leased equipment sits idle but is in good operational condition, thus having a market in developing countries. In this mode, the foreign lessor retains ownership of the property throughout the lease period, during which the local user pays a leasing fee. The major advantages of this mode for MNEs include quick access to the target market, efficient use of superfluous or outmoded machinery and equipment, and accumulating experience in a foreign country. From the local firm's perspective, this mode helps reduce the cost of using foreign machinery and equipment, mitigates operational and investment risks, and increases its knowledge and experience with foreign technologies and facilities. In the late 1970s, Japan's Mitsubishi leased 100 new and used heavy trucks to Chinese companies in such industries as construction, mining, and transportation.

International Licensing. International licensing is an entry mode in which a foreign licensor grants specified intangible property rights to the local licensee for a specified period of time in exchange for a royalty fee. Such property rights may include patents, trademarks, technology, and managerial skills. They allow the licensee to produce and market a product similar to the one the licensor has already been producing in its home country without requiring the licensor to actually create a new operation abroad.

Generally, an MNE may use international licensing to (a) obtain extra income from technical expertise and services, spread around the costs of company research, and development programs or maximize returns on research findings and accumulated expertise; (b) retain established markets that have been closed or threatened by trade restrictions, reach new markets not accessible by export from existing facilities, or expand into foreign markets quickly with minimum effort or risk; (c) augment limited domestic capacity and management resources for serving foreign markets, provide overseas sources of supply and services to important domestic customers, or develop market outlets for raw materials or components made by the domestic company; (d) build goodwill and acceptance for the company's other products or services, develop sources of raw materials or components for the company's other operations, or pave the way for future investment; or (e) discourage possible infringement, impairment, or loss of company patents or trademarks or acquire reciprocal benefits from foreign expertise, research, and technical services.

Income from licenses, however, is generally lower than from franchising and FDI entry modes. Loss of quality control can be another major disadvantage of this entry mode. It is often difficult for the licensor to maintain satisfactory control over the licensee's manufacturing and marketing operations. This can result in damage to a licensor's trademark and reputation. Moreover, a licensee overseas can also become a competitor to the licensor. If the original licensing agreement does not stipulate the region within which the licensee may market the licensed product, the licensee may insist on marketing the product in third-country markets in competition with the licensor. Further, a local licensee may benefit from improvements in its technology, which it then uses to enter the MNE's home market.

International Franchising. International franchising is an entry mode in which the foreign franchisor grants specified intangible property rights (e.g., trademark or brand name) to the local franchisee, which must abide by strict and detailed rules as to how it does business. Compared with licensing, franchising involves longer commitments, offers greater control over overseas operations, and includes a broader package of rights and resources, which is why service MNEs such as KFC often elect franchising (whereas manufacturing firms often use licensing). Production equipment, managerial systems, operating procedures, access to advertising and promotional materials, loans, and financing may all be part of a franchise. The franchisee operates the business under the franchisor's proprietary rights and is contractually obligated to adhere to the procedures and methods of operation prescribed in the business system. The franchisor generally maintains the right to control the quality of products and services so that the franchisee cannot damage the company's image. In exchange for the franchise, the franchisor receives a royalty payment that amounts to a percentage of the franchisee's revenues. Sometimes the franchisor mandates that the franchisee must buy equipment or key ingredients used in the product. For example, Burger King and McDonald's require the franchisee to buy the company's cooking equipment, burger patties, and other products that bear the company name.

The merits and limitations of international franchising are similar to those of licensing. The main advantages include little political risk, low costs, and fast and easy avenues for leveraging assets such as a trademark or brand name. For example, McDonald's was able to build a global presence quickly and at relatively low cost and risk by using franchises. Nevertheless, the franchisee may damage the franchisor's image by not upholding its standards. Even if the franchisor is able to terminate the agreement, some franchisees still stay in business by slightly altering the franchisor's brand name or trademark.

Build-Operate-Transfer (BOT). BOT is a "turnkey" investment in which a foreign investor assumes responsibility for the design and construction of an entire operation and, upon completion of the project, turns the project over to the purchaser and hands over management to local personnel whom it has trained. In return for completing the project, the investor receives periodic payments that are normally guaranteed. BOT is especially useful for very large-scale, long-term infrastructure projects such as power generation, airports, dams, expressways, chemical plants, and steel mills. Managing such complex projects requires special expertise. It is thus not surprising that most are administered by large construction firms such as Bechtel (the United States), Hyundai (Korea), or Friedrich Krupp (Germany). Large companies sometimes form a consortium and bid jointly for a large BOT project. Iran's first BOT power plant, the 900MW combined cycle/gas-fired Parehsar project, was launched in 2001 through an international consortium consisting of Italy's Sondel, Germany's Dillinger Stahl (DSD), and Iran's Mapna International. The foreign partnership has a 70% stake in the project. Like other big BOT projects, a part of the financing for this project was sourced from export credit agencies instituted by the German and Italian governments. The Iranian government ensured that sovereign guarantees would be in place for repayment of loans and payment for electricity delivered locally. The plant opened in 2004 and will be operated by the consortium for 20 years, before being handed back to Iran's state power company Tavanir.

Owing in part to the difficulties of working out financing and equity arrangements, the BOT approach is often used in combination with other entry modes. Foreign businesses may set up BOT project firms by means of either equity or cooperative joint ventures with local partners. Because of their ability to provide foreign investors with returns in excess of their proportional contributions to the venture's total registered capital, contractual joint ventures have been the vehicles of choice for BOT infrastructure projects. For example, in 2001, Germany's Frankfurt Airport Corp. was awarded by the Philippine government a BOT contract for the construction of the third passenger terminal at the Ninoy Aquino International Airport. It then formed a contractual joint venture, named Fraport, with Philippines International Airport Transport Company, to construct this project.

FDI-Related Entry Modes

In contrast to the preceding trade-related and transfer-related entry modes, FDI-related entry modes involve ownership of property, assets, projects, and businesses invested in a host country. Accordingly, firms undertaking FDI will control overseas operations and economic activities. FDI-related entry modes are more sophisticated than trade-related modes and involve higher risk and longer-term contribution than both trade- and transfer-related choices. Compared with the latter, FDI-related modes underline the firm's long-term strategic goals of international presence and necessitate continuous contribution and commitment to investments and operations abroad. FDI-related entry modes include the following:

- Branch office
- Cooperative joint venture
- Equity joint venture
- Wholly owned subsidiary
- Umbrella holding company

The Branch Office. A branch office is a foreign entity in a host country in which it is not incorporated that exists as an extension of the parent and is legally constituted as a branch. Corporate law in many countries allows foreign companies to open branches that engage in production and operating activities. Unlike representative offices, which by law are prohibited from engaging in direct, profit-making business activities (they instead serve as liaisons, establishing contacts with governments and handling market research and consulting activities), branch offices are entitled to run businesses within a specified scope or location. A foreign subsidiary can also open a branch office in another region of the host country to expand its operations there. Branch offices are particularly utilized by transnational banks, law firms, and accounting or consulting companies. For example, Standard Bank had 1,000 branches in South Africa in 2001 and was ranked the largest foreign bank in that country. It also had branch offices in 14 other sub-Saharan countries. Because of South Africa's traditionally strong financial infrastructure, and its long-established presence in the major financial centers of Africa, the bank is a match for foreign entrants in retail banking technology as well as wholesale payments, clearing, and custody. In most cases, branch offices may offer a relatively simple means for establishing or expanding a presence in a target country, but since they do not have legal-person status, the foreign parent company is liable if civil charges are brought against the branch. To shield the parent company from unlimited damage claims, foreign companies interested in establishing branch offices may designate an offshore subsidiary as the parent. For instance, the first McDonald's restaurant in Russia was launched by its Canadian subsidiary.

The Cooperative (or Contractual) Joint Venture. The cooperative joint venture (also known as a contractual joint venture) is a collaborative agreement whereby profits and other responsibilities are assigned to each party according to a contract. These do not necessarily accord with each partner's percentage of the total investment. Each party cooperates as a separate legal entity and bears its own liabilities. Most cooperative joint ventures do not involve constructing and building a new legally and physically independent entity. As such, cooperative joint ventures normally take the form of a document (cooperative agreement), whereas equity joint ventures take the form of a new entity.

Many cooperative programs today involve joint activities without the creation of a new corporate entity. Instead, carefully defined rules govern the allocation of tasks, costs, and revenues. Joint exploration (e.g., offshore oil exploration consortia), research partnership, and co-production are typical forms of cooperative joint ventures. Others include joint marketing, long-term supply agreements, or technological training and assistance. Boeing entered China in the late 1970s through a co-production agreement with the Xi'an Aircraft Manufacturing Company, which co-produced 737 vertical fins, horizontal stabilizers, and forward access doors, and another co-production agreement with the Shenyang Aircraft Manufacturing Company, which co-produced 737 tail sections and 757 cargo doors. Chapter 12 details forms and features of various cooperative arrangements.

The Equity Joint Venture. The most common foreign entry for MNEs has been through equity joint ventures. An equity joint venture entails establishing a new entity that is jointly owned and managed by two or more parent firms in different countries. To set up an equity joint venture, each partner contributes cash, facilities, equipment, materials, intellectual property rights, labor, or land-use rights. According to joint venture laws in most countries, a foreign investor's share must exceed a certain threshold of the total equity (25% in many nations). Generally, there is no upward limit in deregulated industries in most countries, whether developed or developing. However, in governmentally controlled or institutionally restricted sectors, foreign investors are often confined with respect to equity arrangements.

Broadly, cooperative joint ventures and equity joint ventures are together called global strategic alliances (GSAs). The proliferation of such alliances among MNEs from different countries is transforming the global business environment. These alliances are gaining importance worldwide as global competition intensifies for access to markets, products, and technologies. Most large MNEs such as Motorola, Siemens, Sony, GM, DaimlerChrysler, and Toyota have built such alliances. In Japan alone, for example, Royal Dutch Shell has established more than 30 joint ventures. As a means of survival and growth, GSAs have become a fundamental element of many MNEs' key global business strategies. GSAs are explained further in Chapter 12.

The Wholly Owned Subsidiary. The wholly owned subsidiary is an entry mode in which the investing firm owns 100% of the new entity in a host country. This new entity may be built from scratch by the investing firm (i.e., greenfield investment) or by acquiring a local business (i.e., cross-border acquisition). This mode offers foreign investors increased flexibility and control. It allows international managers to make their own decisions without the burden of an uncooperative partner. Wholly owned subsidiaries also allow foreign investors to set up and protect their own processes and procedures, which leads to more careful strategic and operational oversight. During the 1990s, Japan's Kao Corporation established a large number of wholly owned manufacturing and marketing subsidiaries overseas. For example, it established a wholly owned subsidiary in Singapore for the following reasons:

- Coming out of a deeply rooted Japanese corporate culture, Kao's head office prefers tight control over its subsidiaries. Kao's preference for wholly owned operations clearly follows from this cultural bias.
- A wholly owned subsidiary gives a firm the tight control over operations in different countries that is necessary for global integration, thus leading to greater global value.
- A wholly owned subsidiary reduces the risk of losing control of a firm's technological expertise.
- A wholly owned mode better ensures that Kao's foreign operations will benefit from the detergent-producing skills that its domestic operation has possessed for decades.

Nevertheless, the establishment of a large, wholly owned project abroad, such as the Mercedes-Benz plant in Alabama, can be a complex, costly, and lengthy process. MNEs must choose between the importance of protecting core technology and manufacturing and marketing processes on the one hand, and the costs of establishing a new operation on the other. Many MNEs choose this alternative only after expanding into markets through other modes that have helped them accumulate host-country experience.

Wholly owned subsidiaries have traditionally been viewed by many host-country governments, particularly those of developing economies, as offering little in the way of technology transfer or other benefits to local economies. Recently, this entry mode has become more attractive to them. When domestic credit is tight, this mode provides host countries with a means of attracting foreign investment. Nevertheless, governmental support for this mode often trails far behind that of joint ventures in many countries.

Some notes of caution should be stated. First, wholly owned subsidiaries must rely on indigenous agents to make liaisons on their behalf and help procure land, materials, and services. Second, wholly owned foreign subsidiaries may not be allowed to invest and operate in industries that are vital to the host-country economy. Third, since wholly owned subsidiaries operate without the control of local partners, investment approval authorities often hold them to higher standards on pollution control, technological level, capital contribution, foreign exchange administration, and the like. Finally, wholly owned subsidiaries are more vulnerable to criticism relating to cultural and economic sovereignty. Managers in wholly owned subsidiaries should recognize and address this concern. One way is to localize production—that is, to buy as many parts and components as possible from local suppliers and to localize human resources (i.e., hire local managers).

The Umbrella Holding Company. The umbrella holding company is an investment company that unites the firm's existing investments such as branch offices, joint ventures, and wholly owned subsidiaries under one umbrella to combine sales, procurement, manufacturing, training, and maintenance within the host country. Many foreign companies are now seeking better integration of these functions for a broad range of products and services within a single but important country (such as China and Brazil). Such coordination becomes necessary as each production division sets up its own foreign subunits separated from other divisions' foreign subunits in the same host country. DuPont faced this problem in China because some joint ventures there belong to, and are controlled only by, its pharmaceutical division, whereas others belong to its plastic or petroleum divisions. In 1989 it established DuPont China Ltd. as its holding company to unite and integrate existing investments originally undertaken by respective production divisions. The umbrella model is thus particularly useful for MNEs that are multidivisional, where each division enters and runs differently while the holding company coordinates them. The umbrella mode helps improve the cash flow and capital structure of various investments by acting as a clearinghouse for intragroup financing. With a holding company in a host country, profits can be more easily transferred among different strategic business units and taken out of the country. It can also smooth the establishment of new investments. Like all legally independent subsidiaries, an umbrella company has legal-person status in a host country. To establish an umbrella company, MNEs may need to comply with certain conditions set by the host-country government. In China, for example, the foreign investor must have established a minimum of 10 subunits in the country and engaged in manufacturing or infrastructure construction to which it has contributed at least $30 million in registered capital.

A foreign investor may consider establishing an umbrella enterprise to achieve some or all of the following objectives: (a) investment in subsidiary projects; (b) facilitation of cash flow or foreign exchange balance for all local activities; (c) centralized purchase of production materials for subsidiary projects; (d) provision of product maintenance services and technical support; (e) training of subsidiary project personnel and end users of products; (f) coordination and consolidation of project management; and (g) marketing of subsidiary products.

Exhibit 10.4 highlights the implications of various entry modes in terms of risk, return, control, and commitment. These dimensions serve as base points for MNE managers considering various entry modes. Overall, risk, return, control,

Exhibit 10.4   International Entry Modes

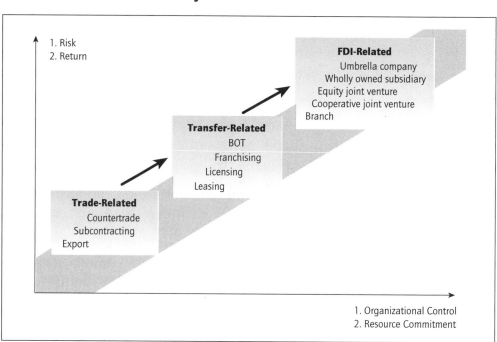

and commitment all increase along this sequence with the exception that BOT may involve even more commitment (especially capital and technology) and take even longer to build a new project than some FDI-related entry modes such as branch offices and joint ventures.

Decision Framework

To select an appropriate entry mode, MNEs should make sure they know all possible options for the entry into a target country before determining the best one. Once a foreign investor decides to pursue an FDI project, its choice of entry mode will depend on a wide range of considerations. Broadly, these can be classified into *country, industry, firm,* and *project* factors.

Country-Specific Factors

A number of host-country-specific factors have an impact on entry-mode choice. First, *government FDI policies* may directly or indirectly influence entry-mode selection. The laws in some countries mandate that foreign firms must choose joint ventures, as opposed to wholly owned subsidiaries, as an entry mode.[11] Second, *infrastructure conditions* affect the extent to which an MNE plans to commit distinctive resources to local operations and the degree to which it perceives operational uncertainty and contextual unpredictability. These in turn influence the entry-mode option. Third, *property right systems* and other legal frameworks in a host country appear to be increasingly important to entry-mode selection. Without sufficient legal protection, an MNE's property rights such as trademarks, brand names, expertise, patents, and copyrights will be exposed to possible infringement and piracy by local firms. In such circumstances, the MNE may have to use a high-control entry mode such as a wholly owned subsidiary or dominant equity joint venture. Fourth, *host-country risks,* including general political risks (e.g., instability of political system), ownership/control risks (e.g., price control, local content requirements), and transfer risks (e.g., currency inconvertibility, remittance control), may affect entry mode.[12] Licensing and joint ventures may be favored when country risk is high. Finally, *cultural distance* between home and host countries influences foreign entry decision and process. The greater the perceived distance between home and host countries, the more likely it is that the MNE will favor licensing/franchising or a joint venture over a wholly owned subsidiary.

Industry-Specific Factors

Several industry-specific factors are important considerations underlying entry-mode selection. First, *entry barriers* into a target industry in the host country constitute a significant impediment to entry-mode selection. Contractual or equity joint ventures may be an effective vehicle to bypass these barriers. Second, *industrial uncertainty and complexity* may lead MNEs to use high control or low commitment entry modes such as representative or branch offices, licensing, franchising, loosely structured cooperative joint ventures with little resource commitment, or minority equity joint ventures. Last, *availability and favorability of supply and distribution* in the industry will determine the rationalization of value-chain linkages needed for an MNE's local operations and the vertical integration of other units within the MNE network. When an MNE relies more on local resource procurement or emphasizes the local market, it is more vulnerable to industrial linkages with suppliers and distributors. Entry modes involving partners are superior when the MNE needs but lacks such linkages in the host country.

Firm-Specific Factors

Entry-mode selection is contingent on several firm-specific traits as well. First, a firm's *resource possession* influences the firm's ability to explore market potential and earn a competitive edge in the global marketplace. A firm that lacks distinctive resources (technological, organizational, operational, and financial), but wishes to share in the risks associated with having them, is often compelled to enter the market through a joint venture through which its resource commitment will be minimized.[13] Second, *the leakage risk of technologies* may affect entry mode. If this risk is high, a wholly owned subsidiary mode increases the firm's ability to use and protect these technologies. Third, a firm's *strategic goals* for international expansion are one of the foremost determinants underlying entry-mode selection. When an MNE attempts to pursue local market expansion, high commitment choices such as cooperative or equity joint ventures, wholly owned subsidiaries, and umbrella companies are preferable because they enable the firm to have a deeper, more diverse involvement with the indigenous market, creating more opportunities to accumulate country-specific experience. If an MNE aims only to exploit factor endowment advantages, low-commitment entry modes such as subcontracting, compensation trade, co-production, cooperative arrangement, and minority equity joint ventures may be superior to other options because risks and costs are low. Finally, *international or host country experience* influences entry-mode selection. MNEs with little or no experience with international or host-country business may prefer low control/low resource commitment entry modes such as export, subcontracting, international leasing or franchising, or countertrade.[14] In contrast, MNEs with significant multinational experience prefer high control/high resource commitment entry modes such as cooperative or equity joint ventures, wholly owned subsidiaries, and umbrella investment companies.

Project-Specific Factors

In the course of entry-mode selection, MNEs also need to consider some attributes of the FDI project itself. First, firms may shy away from a wholly owned entry mode in favor of a joint venture when the *project size* is large. A large investment implies higher start-up, switching, and exit costs, thus involving higher financial and operational risks. Second, *project orientation* influences an MNE's resource dispersal and entry mode. MNEs investing in import-substitution projects may be inclined to establish partnerships with local government agencies or state-owned enterprises holding monopoly positions because this type of FDI project is vulnerable to host-government control. If a project is local market oriented, the MNE may choose the cooperative or equity joint venture mode, because the local partner can provide distinctive supply and distribution channels, governmental networks, and culture-specific business knowledge and experience. If a project is technologically advanced, the firm may opt for a wholly owned subsidiary mode to protect its expertise or a joint venture mode if it needs complementary technologies or knowledge from a partner firm. Finally, when a project is infrastructure oriented, the MNE may apply the build-operate-transfer (BOT) mode if it plans on having only a short-term run or a majority joint venture mode if it has a long-term strategic plan and is willing to take risks. Finally, *the availability of proper local partners* for a particular project may affect an MNE's entry ability and choice. An MNE's ability to establish a joint venture or any other form of nonintegrated entry mode depends on the availability of capable, trustworthy partners. In the absence of acceptable local partners, the MNE may be forced to start a wholly owned subsidiary.

Greenfield Investment, Acquisition, and Merger

An MNE can set up a wholly owned subsidiary, through either greenfield investment or international acquisition. A **greenfield investment** is an initial establishment of fully owned new facilities and operations undertaken by the company alone. An **international acquisition** is a cross-border transaction in which a foreign investor acquires an established local firm and makes the acquired local firm a subsidiary business within its global portfolio. International acquisition of a local firm or another foreign company with local ventures is the quickest way to expand one's investment in the target country. An acquisition is particularly useful for entering sectors formerly restricted to state-owned enterprises. Moreover, cash flow may be generated in a shorter time than in the case of greenfield investment, since the acquired firm, by definition, does not have to be built from scratch. Furthermore, acquisition deals may be more attractive than greenfield investment because acquisitions offer immediate access to a local acquiree's existing resources such as land, manufacturing facilities, distribution channels, supply networks, skilled labor, and customer base. Foreign investors generally target enterprises with strong market niches in sectors with potential for growth. MNEs interested in acquisition must evaluate various risks. Gaining government approval for the transfer of ownership and clearance of property titles is often a difficult hurdle. Foreign investors should be careful to obtain accurate information, particularly concerning existing liabilities, when buying into an indigenous entity.

An **international merger** shares the logic of equity joint ventures and is a cross-border transaction in which two firms from different countries agree to integrate their operations on a relatively equal basis because they have resources and capabilities that together may create a stronger competitive advantage in the global marketplace. An example is the 1998 merger between Daimler-Benz of Germany (Stuttgart) and Chrysler of the United States (Detroit), the largest international corporate marriage in history (although this, too, as in many mergers, eventually turned out to be an acquisition by the German firm). Like joint ventures, cross-border mergers can generate many positive outcomes:

- Interpartner learning and resource sharing
- Elevating economies of scale or scope
- Reducing costs by eliminating expenditures for redundant resources
- Capturing greater market share by providing more comprehensive offerings
- Increasing revenue by cross-selling products to cross-border customers

The major difference between equity joint ventures and mergers is that the former involves formation of a third entity (equity joint venture) whose duration is often limited and specified in the contract, whereas the latter does not form any third party nor does it specify any duration. Joint venture parents remain independent after forming a venture, but two parties are integrated into a single organization after a merger. Also, mergers combine all of the partners' assets (although some may be spun off later), while a joint venture involves only some of those assets.

International mergers and acquisitions inevitably confront many challenges, especially during early operations. The fundamental challenges are often rooted in cross-national differences in culture, managerial styles, and corporate values (the Industry Box illustrates Unilever's experience in Brazil). To overcome these challenges, international managers should develop a new corporate mission and vision and new strategic objectives. It is also imperative to integrate communications and human resources. The new organization must develop mechanisms to identify the most appropriate organizational structures and management roles to enhance administrative efficiency and operational effectiveness.

The Evolutionary Entry Path

In many circumstances, international entry is not a one-step action but rather an evolutionary process involving a series of incremental decisions during which firms increase their commitment to the target market by shifting from low- to high-commitment entry modes.[15] Although some firms may bypass some steps or speed up the entire process, many MNEs follow the learning curve of accumulating competence, knowledge, and confidence in the international entry process. They move sequentially from no international involvement to export, to overseas assembly or sales subsidiaries (subcontracting, branches, or franchising), to overseas production via contractual or equity joint ventures (also from minority to majority), and, ultimately, to overseas penetration and integration through wholly owned subsidiaries or umbrella companies.[16] Increasing levels of involvement in foreign markets relate to a firm's accumulation of experiential and local knowledge. While relevant knowledge and experience are acquired predominantly through actual presence and activities in a foreign market, joint ventures with local firms represent bridges between no equity involvement and equity involvement in a host country. In fact, many MNEs start an equity joint venture and a wholly owned subsidiary in sequence. This way, a foreign investor will obtain initial entry as part of an equity joint venture for a fixed period stipulated in the duration clause of the contract. Then, at the end of the stipulated term, it can take over the assets from the local partner and continue to run the operation as a wholly owned subsidiary. This is an attractive alternative if the added value of the local partner is significant but limited to the early stages of the venture. Some equity joint ventures have included this option in the termination clause of the joint venture contract.

Large and experienced MNEs may combine several entry modes at the same time. For instance, selecting between an equity joint venture and a wholly owned subsidiary is not necessarily an either-or decision. Sometimes a local partner has a strong distribution network or operates in a restricted sector that is attractive to a foreign investor. In such situations, foreign companies can, for instance, surround their wholly owned subsidiary production operation with equity joint ventures that supply resources or market and sell their products in the host market. Siemens did exactly that in Brazil, where it owned four wholly owned manufacturing plants, surrounded by seven joint ventures with either local firms or other MNEs such as Bosch GmbH or Philips as supply bases, and had 13 sales and service branch offices throughout the nation as of the end of 2001.

INDUSTRY BOX

UNILEVER'S ACQUISITIONS IN LATIN AMERICA

Unilever, the Anglo–Dutch conglomerate and one of the world's oldest MNEs, describes itself as a purveyor of products ranging from tea and ice cream to shampoo and toothpaste. Unilever's acquisition of Kibon (Brazil) in 1997 marked another expansion of the company's already strong presence in Latin America. Its management of human resources illustrates the firm's ability to mix internationally savvy executives with the best local talent and practices. The company's approach is a mix of taking the best of the local culture and combining it with the firm's global intentions. Its success with Kibon stems from a deliberate but gradual integration process, particularly with regard to personnel changes. Rather than immediately imposing control from the top, Unilever's strategy centered on two important initial stages. It promoted dialogue with Kibon's staff during the initial period after the acquisition, then defined its priorities and assumed leadership. Management zeroed in on two priority areas: the ice-cream manufacturing process and R&D. Its preliminary studies of Kibon's best operations helped management make appropriate decisions about future layoffs and restructuring. Despite removing Kibon's entire board of directors, Unilever made a special effort to keep key personnel in priority areas—namely, production and R&D. Once the groundwork was laid, Unilever did not hesitate to make changes. After carefully studying the acquired company, it quickly set out to forge a new identity and strategy and to rationalize production.

Interim Summary

1. Entry modes available to international companies include trade related (exporting, subcontracting, and countertrade), transfer related (leasing, licensing, franchising, and BOT), and FDI related (branch, cooperative joint venture, equity joint venture, wholly owned subsidiary, and umbrella holding companies). The levels of involved risks, anticipated returns, resultant control, and required commitment generally increase along the preceding sequence.

2. International acquisition is a way to form a wholly owned subsidiary. Compared with greenfield investment, international acquisition generates some advantages such as quicker access, bypass of entry barriers, and utilization of an acquiree's existing resources.

CHAPTER SUMMARY

1. International entry strategies concern where, when, and how firms should enter in their international expansion. Location selection concerns not only country selection but also project location within this country. Managers need to consider various locational determinants such as cost and tax factors, demand factors, strategic factors (e.g., investment infrastructure, manufacturing concentration, industrial linkage, workforce productivity, and inbound and outbound logistics), regulatory and economic factors, and sociopolitical factors.

2. The decision on location selection is also contingent on the firm's strategic objectives of expansion, required global integration between this location and the rest of the MNE network, and the project's market orientation (local market vs. export market). The firm may also take into account its familiarity with the location, geographical market coverage, competitors' location pattern, and regional block effects (e.g., the European Union).

3. Each timing option, whether early mover or late entrant, has distinct advantages and disadvantages. Entry occurs when the firm anticipates gains to exceed risks or costs. Early movers benefit from greater market power (barriers for followers, technological leadership, customer loyalty, and product positioning); greater preemptive opportunities in

marketing, resources, and branding; and greater strategic options (site selection, infrastructure access, and low competition).

4. Early-mover disadvantages are late-mover advantages. Early movers tend to face greater uncertainty derived from variable regulations and rules and unstable industrial and market structures; greater operational risks as a result of less developed infrastructure and a lack of supporting services and resources; and greater operational costs arising from adaptation, training, learning, and anti-imitation.

5. Firms can enter a target country through numerous entry modes, ranging from trade-related modes (export, subcontracting, and countertrade), to transfer-related modes (leasing, licensing, franchising, and BOT), to FDI-related modes (branch, cooperative joint venture, equity joint venture, wholly owned subsidiary, and umbrella company). Levels of risk, control, and commitment vary significantly across categories and across entry modes within each category.

6. Most international companies, whether large or small, still actively participate in import and export businesses. Export intermediaries specialize in import and export management. Managers should familiarize themselves with key concepts such as terms of price (e.g., FAS, CIF, C&F, and FOB) and key documents (e.g., L/C and B/L) involved in import and export processes.

7. Original equipment manufacturing (OEM) is an increasingly popular mode used by many large MNEs looking for cheaper production overseas. Countertrade methods such as barter, counterpurchase, offset, and buyback offer more flexibility than conventional import and export since the former do not involve hard currency cash flows. Transfer-related entry modes are widely used in technological, intellectual, or industrial property right transfers or transactions.

8. Joint venture and wholly owned subsidiary are the two major entry modes embedded in FDI. The joint venture enables the firm to share risks and costs with others, acquire new knowledge from others, bypass entry barriers in a host country, and capitalize on the partner's reputation, experience, networks, and marketing skills. The wholly owned entry mode provides the firm with stronger organizational control and knowledge protection.

Chapter Notes

1. J. H. Dunning. *Multinational Enterprises and the Global Economy.* Reading, MA: Addison-Wesley, 1993.

2. M. E. Porter. *Competition in Global Industries.* Boston: Harvard Business School Press, 1986.

3. C. G. Culem. "The locational determinants of foreign direct investments among industrial countries." *European Economic Review,* 1988, *32,* 4: pp. 885–894; J. Friedman, D. A. Gerlowski, and J. Silberman. "What attracts foreign multinational corporations: Evidence from branch plant location in the United States." *Journal of Regional Science,* 1992, *32,* 4: pp. 403–418.

4. J. F. Hennart and Y. R. Park. "Location, governance, and strategic determinants of Japanese manufacturing investment in the United States." *Strategic Management Journal,* 1994, *15,* 6: pp. 419–436.

5. W. H. Davidson. "The location of foreign direct investment activity: Country characteristics and experience effects." *Journal of International Business Studies,* 1980, *11,* 2: pp. 9–22.

6. M. Lambkin. "Order of entry and performance in new markets." *Strategic Management Journal,* 1988, 9: pp. 127–140; M. B. Lieberman and D. B. Montgomery. "First-mover advantages." *Strategic Management Journal,* 1988, 9: pp. 41–58.

7. B. Mascarenhas. "Order of entry and performance in international markets." *Strategic Management Journal,*

1992, 13: pp. 499–510; W. Mitchell. "Whether and when? Probability and timing of incumbents' entry into emerging industrial subfields." *Administrative Science Quarterly,* 1989, 34: pp. 208–230.

8. Y. Luo. "Timing of investment and international expansion performance in China." *Journal of International Business Studies,* 1988, 29: pp. 391–408.

9. P. J. Buckley and M. Casson. "The optimal timing of a foreign direct investment." *The Economic Journal,* 1981, 91: pp. 75–87.

10. D. West. "Countertrade." *Business Credit,* 2001, *103,* 4: pp. 64–67.

11. B. Gomes-Casseres. "Firm ownership presences and host government restrictions: An integrated approach." *Journal of International Business Studies,* 1990, 21, 1: pp. 1–21.

12. F. R. Root. *Entry Strategies for International Markets.* Washington, DC: Lexington Books, 1994.

13. S. Agarwal and S. N. Ramaswami. "Choice of foreign market entry mode: Impact of ownership, location, and internalization factors." *Journal of International Business Studies,* 1992, *23,* 1: pp. 1–27.

14. C. W. L. Hill, P. Hwang, and W. C. Kim. "An eclectic theory of the choice of international entry mode." *Strategic Management Journal,* 1990, 11: pp. 117–128; J. Johanson and J. E. Vahlne. "The internationalization

process of the firm: A model of knowledge development and increasing foreign market commitments." *Journal of International Business Studies,* 1977, *8,* 1: pp. 23–32.

15. S. J. Chang. "International expansion strategy of Japanese firms: Capability building through sequential entry." *Academy of Management Journal,* 1995, 38: pp. 383–407.

16. E. Anderson and H. Gatignon. "Modes of foreign entry: A transaction cost analysis and propositions." *Journal of International Business Studies,* Fall 1986, 17: pp. 1–26.

ELEVEN

ORGANIZING AND STRUCTURING GLOBAL OPERATIONS

DO YOU KNOW?

1. Is the organizational design of the MNE (or international firm) a function of its strategy or vice versa?

2. Why does the MNE need to organize and coordinate global operations?

3. Do you expect an MNE subsidiary in Mexico to be similar in strategic importance, knowledge flow, and authority to subsidiaries of the same MNE in England, Singapore, or China? Why or why not?

4. What types of organizational structure can an MNE select from, and what are the criteria for making the choice?

5. If you were an executive at Sony, how would you integrate the firm's global activities?

OPENING CASE

Citigroup: Managing a 100-Country Business

Formed in 1998 from the merger of Citibank, founded in 1812, and the Travelers Group (which was later spun off), today's Citigroup is a world leader in financial services, with assets totaling $1.5 trillion, which offers an array of financial products in 100 countries around the world. In 2005, Citigroup was the most profitable financial services conglomerate in the world, with revenue exceeding $86 billion and net income of $24.6 billion, most of it coming from its three mainline product divisions: the Global Consumer Group, Corporate & Investment Banking, and Global Wealth

Management (its Alternative Investment Group is managed as a standalone business). While operating around the globe, the United States is Citigroup's major market. In the third quarter of 2006, net income from U.S. operations reached more than $3 billion, more than all other regions combined.

Citigroup views its global presence and intimate local knowledge (it has operated in some of its foreign markets for over a century) as a key competitive advantage. "We have the most global presence: the best international footprint of any U.S. financial services company and the best U.S. presence of any international financial services company," notes CEO Charles Prince in the company's 2005 Annual Report. Tapping the advantage embedded in this global spread depends, however, on the ability of Citigroup to organize its activities efficiently and effectively to ensure that they are well coordinated, that information flows across the entire network, and that executives are in a position to make decisions that will reflect local conditions but at the same time support the overall strategic and operational direction of the company as a whole. For that, they rely, among other vehicles, on their organizational structure.

Citigroup utilizes a matrix structure with a dual product/geography reporting structure. The product element is based on the company's major products within each of its mainline divisions (e.g., credit cards in Consumer Banking). The geographic element is represented in Citigroup's regional divisions, including the United States, Mexico, EMEA (Europe, the Middle East, and Africa), Japan, Asia-Pacific (excluding Japan), and Latin America. The dual matrix structure makes for a complex system, which became clear when the group encountered serious problems in its Japan operations, leading to the loss of its private banking business there.

SOURCE: Adapted from Citigroup 2005 Annual Report, Web site, and press releases.

Authors' Note: This chapter borrows from various Conference Board reports. We are grateful to the Conference Board for permission to use this material.

INTERNATIONAL STRATEGY AND ORGANIZATIONAL DESIGN

The objective of organizational design is to provide, maintain, and develop the organizational structure that can serve as the best vehicle for achieving the company's strategic goals. The structure selected is aimed at providing a blueprint with which to translate the firm's vision and strategic objectives into a workable distribution and dissemination of rights, duties, and responsibilities for each of the various units and individual positions that make up the organizational apparatus. Although organizational structures are driven by strategy, they also drive it. In other words, the structure represents a constraint on the firm's mode of operations and in turn on its strategic thinking and strategy implementation. For instance, when Japan emerged as an economic power in the 1980s, it was noted that having a Japanese unit report to an Asia-Pacific regional division distracted corporate attention to this market; suggestions have hence been made to separate Japan from the regional division, with direct reporting to corporate headquarters as a way to elevate its strategic visibility.[1] Similar suggestions have been made vis-à-vis China in the new millennium.

Why is it important for MNEs to globally organize, structure, and coordinate geographically dispersed businesses? First, the complexity and rapid change of global business necessitates paying close attention to different sources of knowledge and expertise (e.g., intimate knowledge of a region, close understanding of a product line). Second, once an organization has been divided into separate divisions and units, each subunit becomes subject to its own interests, goals, and environmental demands, which will often lead the unit to develop and pursue its own strategies rather than implement those of the firm as a whole. To overcome these forces, the MNE should have a structure that maximizes contributions to corporate performance while allowing subunits flexibility to adapt to their particular environment. Third, in many industries, the MNE is no longer able to compete as a collection of independent subsidiaries. Heightened requirements for economies of scale and technological developments have led many MNEs to integrate the value-chain activities performed in their subsidiaries around the world. Integrating these activities means raising the level of interdependence among subsidiaries, requiring global coordination. Fourth, interunit sharing, learning, and resource flow necessitate extensive coordination, including the assignment of different mandates to various subsidiaries. For example, Siemens's subsidiary in Japan, in partnership with Asahi Medical, has worldwide responsibility for modeling compact magnetic resonance imaging (MRI) machines, while the Singapore subsidiary has worldwide responsibility for the distribution and marketing of these machines. To execute such globally interdependent operations, parent firms must have organizing and integrating mechanisms in place. Fifth, financial management for global operations such as the use of transfer pricing (to reduce taxation) and the use of an internal bank (for intracorporate financing, foreign exchange hedging, and cash-flow management) necessitates global coordination and integration. Finally, as the opening case illustrates, MNEs need to balance often contradictory product and regional demands, all the while maintaining group oversight, coordination, and control.

Global Integration and Local Responsiveness

Given the increasing globalization of the competitive environment, the dual imperatives of global integration (I) and local responsiveness (R) (also known as I–R balance) are more critical than ever for the survival and growth of the MNE. **Global integration** refers to the coordination of activities across countries in an attempt to build efficient operational networks and take maximum advantage of internalized synergies and similarities across locations. **Local responsiveness** concerns the attempt to respond to specific needs within each host country. Local responsiveness needs stem from diversity of market conditions and social and political environments in the various countries in which the firm operates. Responsiveness is necessary to react to diverse consumer tastes, distribution channels, advertising media, and government regulations and constraints. MNEs can choose to emphasize integration over responsiveness or vice versa or compete on both dimensions, resulting in three basic responses: integrated, multifocal, or locally responsive. Firms that perceive a high level of pressure to integrate use a strategy of global integration. Globally integrated businesses link activities across nations in an attempt to minimize overall costs, reduce taxes, or maximize income. Locally responsive businesses are more tuned to local characteristics and needs. Multifocal businesses attempt to respond simultaneously to pressures for integration and responsiveness.

The relative strength of global integration and local responsiveness pressures can be analyzed at different levels, such as industry, division, or subsidiary. Levels of global integration and local responsiveness vary among MNEs and even across different divisions or subsidiaries within the same MNE. It is important that international managers identify factors that determine these levels. In general, pressures to integrate globally derive from industrial and organizational forces that necessitate worldwide resource deployment. Strategic decisions are made to strengthen the collective organization so that activities are integrated across national boundaries. In contrast, local responsiveness pressures are industrial, national, and objective forces that necessitate context-sensitive strategic decisions. Among market and industrial characteristics, the following features tend to trigger global integration: (a) Customer needs tend to be the same or similar across borders or require relatively low responsiveness, (b) major competitors are few but global, and (c) economy of scale is essential to global success. Features leading to higher local responsiveness include (a) diversity in market structures, (b) nation-specific distribution channels, (c) heterogeneous market demand and customer needs, and (d) strong requirements for product differentiation and customer responsiveness. Among sociopolitical characteristics, the following tend to boost local responsiveness: (a) The host environment is volatile and complex; (b) government regulations are opaque, cumbersome, or arbitrarily changed; and (c) there is a strong and unique local business culture.

Among organizational characteristics, the level of global integration is likely to be high if the firm (a) attempts to use transfer pricing, tax minimization, or transaction cost savings; (b) focuses on risk reduction or internalized financing; (c) emphasizes global vertical integration and global value-chain control; (d) needs to control key functions such as global branding, R&D, global distribution, and engineering; and (e) requires extensive sharing between corporate members in information, resources, and knowledge. In contrast, local responsiveness is likely to be high if the firm (a) targets local market expansion or building presence in highly uncertain markets, (b) aims to seize market opportunities overseas or develop a sustained competitive position in the host country, (c) seeks acquisition of local firms' knowledge and experience, or (d) tries to improve organizational legitimacy through localization and adaptation.

MNE Strategy and Design

For the MNE, which operates in a highly complex, diverse, and rapidly changing environment, the organization design challenge is to configure a structure that works well in diverse locations but also brings units together in a coordinated fashion with the capability for rapid redeployment. Since organization design is a vehicle for strategy formulation and implementation, MNE strategy in organizing global operations is the key input in devising its structure. The type of international strategy used by MNE headquarters to organize and coordinate worldwide businesses is threefold. A **multidomestic** strategy is one in which strategic and operational decisions are delegated to strategic business units in each country. This permits customization but interferes with economies of scale and intraorganizational learning and sharing. A **global strategy** indicates relative standardization across national markets, allowing strategic and operational control. A global strategy leverages economies of scale and can quickly disseminate innovations across borders; however, it lacks in responsiveness to local markets. A **transnational** (or **hybrid**) **strategy** seeks to achieve both global efficiency and local responsiveness. It requires shared vision and commitment through an integrated network. Under this strategy, the roles and responsibilities of subsidiaries are varied to reflect differences in their external environment, internal capabilities, and strategic role.

The MNE maintaining a high level of overall global integration follows a global strategy, whereas the MNE maintaining a high level of local responsiveness over various overseas subunits exercises a multidomestic strategy. The MNE maintaining high levels of both overall integration and overall responsiveness follows a transnational strategy. Under a global strategy, foreign subunits operating in each country are assumed to be interdependent, and the home office attempts to achieve integration among these businesses. Thus, a global strategy is one in which standardized products are offered internationally, whereas the competitive strategy is dictated by the home office. A multidomestic strategy focuses on competition within each country, tailoring products and services to each local market in a bid to maximize competitive response to idiosyncratic requirements. The transnational strategy, in which the roles and responsibilities of subsidiaries are varied to reflect differences in external environments and internal objectives, provides an asymmetrical treatment in coordinating worldwide businesses within the MNE network.

Subsidiary Roles and Imperatives

Subsidiary Autonomy

Subsidiary roles play a key part in balancing integration and local responsiveness. In an **autonomous role**, the subsidiary performs most activities of the value chain independently of headquarters, selling most of its output in the local market. In a **receptive role**, subsidiary functions are highly integrated with headquarters or with other business units (e.g., exporting most of the subsidiary production to the parent company or other subsidiaries, while importing multiple products or components from them). In an **active role**, many activities are located locally but carried out in close coordination with other subsidiaries. The autonomous role is typical of MNE subsidiaries employing a multidomestic strategy. The receptive role is common in MNE subsidiaries using global strategy. The active role is often assigned to MNE subsidiaries that follow a transnational strategy, with a strong mandate from headquarters and leeway for adaptation.[2] Among different subsidiaries of the same MNE, the level of autonomy may vary owing to the different roles or mandates assigned to each. It is possible, for instance, that most subsidiaries in a firm (using a global strategy) will be receptive while a subsidiary serving as the center of excellence in design will be active or autonomous.

Subsidiary Knowledge Flow

Another way of looking at subsidiary role is in terms of knowledge flow across the MNE units.[3] The expertise transferred can be input (e.g., purchasing skills), throughput (e.g., product, process, and packaging design), or output (e.g., marketing knowledge, distribution expertise) oriented. MNE subsidiaries can be classified by the extent to which each (a) receives knowledge inflow from the rest of the corporation and (b) provides knowledge outflow to the rest of the corporation. Four generic subsidiary roles are created from combining these two bases: the global innovator (high outflow and low inflow), the integrated player (high outflow and high inflow), the implementer (low outflow and high inflow), and the local innovator (low outflow and low inflow). In the **global innovator** role, the subsidiary is the fountainhead of knowledge for other units. The **integrated player** role implies responsibility for creating knowledge that can be utilized by other subsidiaries; the subsidiary exchanges knowledge with headquarters and with other subsidiaries on an ongoing basis. In the **implementer** role, the subsidiary engages in very little knowledge creation and relies heavily on knowledge inflows from either the parent or peer subsidiaries. Finally, the **local innovator** role implies that the subsidiary has almost complete local responsibility for the creation of relevant expertise; however, this knowledge is too idiosyncratic to be used outside its local market.

Subsidiary Importance and Competence

The strategic importance of the local environment and the capabilities of the foreign subsidiary are two key considerations in determining subsidiary roles.[4] The **strategic leader** role is played by a highly competent national subsidiary located in a strategically important market. The subsidiary serves as partner to headquarters in developing and implementing strategy. **Contributor subsidiaries** operate in small or strategically less important markets but have distinctive capabilities. **Implementer subsidiaries** operate in less strategically important markets but are competent to maintain local operations. Their market potential is limited, as reflected in corporate resource commitment. The efficiency of an implementer is as important as the creativity of its strategic leaders because it provides the strategic leverage that affords MNEs their competitive advantage. Implementers create opportunities to capture economies of scale and scope that are crucial to global strategies. Finally, **black hole subsidiaries** operate in important markets where they barely make a dent, but their strong local presence is essential for maintaining global position.

In subunits with lead roles, the head office ensures that strategies fit the overall goals and priorities of the MNE, while the headquarters' function is to provide strategic leadership by giving subsidiaries the resources and freedom needed for the innovative, entrepreneurial role they have been asked to play. If the unit is placed in a contributory role, the head office should redirect local resources to programs outside the unit's control. If a unit is in an implementer role, the head office needs to maintain tight control to capture the benefits of scale and learning. Finally, if a unit acts as a black hole, corporate management develops resources and capabilities to make it more responsive to the local environment.

Interim Summary

1. MNEs need to organize, structure, and coordinate their global operations because each subunit may have its own interests, competing goals, and unique demands. Heightened requirements for economies of scale, technological advancement, and intracorporate resource sharing also propel this need.

2. The dual imperatives of global integration and local responsiveness are becoming more critical than ever, requiring appropriate balance between the two. Firms in different industries or environments and with different strategies or capabilities may have varying levels of integration and responsiveness.

3. Subsidiaries may differ in their strategic role, a result of their specific capabilities as well as corporate vision and strategy.

MNE ORGANIZATIONAL STRUCTURES

The organization design decision can be summarized as a series of choices concerning differentiation and integration and the proper balance between them. The need for differentiation is rooted in the diverse requirements and circumstances of different locales and business units. The need for integration comes from the managerial imperative to maintain overall coordination and control to ensure strategy implementation and to reap synergies via optimal resource deployment. In electing an optimal design, firms position themselves along the globalization–localization continuum and select among different forms of differentiation and various mechanisms for coordination, integration, and control. In addition to their business environment, firm capabilities and resources are taken into account in making and implementing design choices.

The large MNE maintains multiple forms of differentiation. For example, it may utilize a product structure for manufacturing operations and a geographic design for sales and marketing. Below the primary lines of differentiation, other forms usually exist. For instance, when Procter & Gamble switched from a geographic to product structure it retained geographical differentiation, albeit at a lower level. Typically in such changes, executives with specific international specialization (e.g., Central Europe) are either retained in staff capacity, providing advice to line personnel, or report to a product or a divisional manager. The one exception to such prioritization is the matrix structure, where two or three bases of differentiation intersect to form a matrix of responsibilities, as the Opening Case illustrates.

As a company becomes more global, its structure changes to accommodate the higher volume and scope of business as well as the increasing diversity of its constituencies. However, a firm's phase of international evolution is only one of the factors affecting its choices of organizational structure. Strategy, home and host country environments, projected market growth, the nature of business, and the human resources available to the firm are among the factors influencing the choice. Thus, it is not uncommon to find different structures among firms otherwise similar in product and geographical spread. MNE management has considerable leeway in making design choices, and it continually monitors the suitability of the structure as its operations evolve and as its business environment or strategy change.

The National Subsidiary Structure

Until the early 1970s (earlier than that for European MNEs), many U.S. MNEs used a national subsidiary structure. In this arrangement, also called a mother–daughter design, national subsidiaries reported directly to headquarters and were in a position to attract the firm's attention without having information filtered through an intermediary unit. This was the case, for instance, for the German subsidiaries of General Motors and Ford. Once a firm had expanded beyond a handful of subsidiaries, however, coordination and control in this structure became difficult. Each subsidiary developed its own way of conducting business, and corporate headquarters were hard-pressed to guide them in line with their overall corporate objectives. It also became increasingly clear that such a structure did not permit an efficient and effective utilization of corporate resources.

The International Division Structure

The international division structure lets the firm's core structure focus on domestic business by shifting all foreign operations into a semi-independent division. The international division is in turn organized by function, product, or again by geography (e.g., country units within a region). In some firms, the international division was cast in a staff capacity—that is, it played an advisory role supporting line operations. The establishment of the international division was the result of the growing scope of international activities and a realization that foreign markets often offered the most promising growth opportunity. It also reflected a shortage of capabilities: With few employees having knowledge and experience in international operations, it made sense to cluster them together rather than have them spread throughout the organization.

The international division format was used mainly by firms with a low ratio of foreign to domestic revenues and low foreign product diversity, and it was replaced when the proportion of international operations grew or when corporate vision changed. For instance, Aetna ditched its international division structure in favor of a global product structure in 2000, when the company leadership came to believe in the importance of global operations. Still, the international division, or a variation thereof, can still be found today. Wal-Mart gave its Arkansas-based International Support Division such responsibilities as new store development but has now delegated this task to its foreign subsidiaries. Wal-Mart has combined international and domestic buying in order to increase its bargaining power with suppliers. Japanese and Korean firms maintain an international division devoted to marketing, sales, and distribution. The division maintains responsibility for new business development and sales in the firm's foreign outposts. However, other foreign activities (e.g., finance) report to functional counterparts in the home country.

European MNEs such as Nestlé, Royal Dutch Shell, and Unilever were among the first to shift away from an international division structure, with U.S. MNEs following suit later, the result of the much larger U.S. domestic market. However, the international division structure is still quite common in developing country multinational enterprises (DMNEs) that are in the first phases of internationalization.

The Global Functional Structure

Functional compartmentalization into research and development, marketing, production, human resources, and such can be found in all organizations, including those differentiated primarily along product line, customers, or geography. However, in firms using function as a primary differentiation mode, functional divisions maintain responsibility for worldwide operations, with functional managers reporting directly to headquarters. This allows for centralized control and the accumulation of functional expertise. Functional structures are usually adopted by MNEs with narrow, integrated product lines (e.g.,

Caterpillar). The design was widely used in the automobile industry, but as firms grew internationally they were replaced by geographic and product line designs that place functional responsibilities at lower organizational levels.

The Global Geographic Structure

In a geographic structure, regional divisions or headquarters are responsible for all products or services rendered within an area. Corporate headquarters retain responsibility for worldwide planning and control, whereas coordination is handled by central staff. Geographic divisions are based not only on political borders but also on cultural similarities, economic realities, business prospects, regional integration (e.g., the EU), and tax and logistic considerations. Regional units are in turn segmented into geographic (i.e., country units within a region), product, or functional subunits. Regional and country managers can also operate in a staff capacity. In the early 1970s, geographic structures accounted for two-thirds of MNEs, but the number was down to one-third by the mid-1980s. Persistent cultural, social, and economic diversities continue to underpin the geographic structure, and many MNEs with other structures incorporate geographical elements within their design. Regional integration may alter the boundaries of geographic units but does not necessarily challenge their necessity. Indeed, geographic structures are enjoying renewed popularity today as companies discover that differences among localities are not about to disappear. Martin Sorrell, CEO of advertising MNE WPP Group, explained why his company was reintroducing a geographic element:

> I think we're losing country focus, which is why we're creating country managers in Holland, Italy and China. . . . Our clients are doing the same thing. If you don't have someone leading the business [locally], you don't get government contact, education contacts and political contacts.[5]

In addition to facilitating key contacts with local stakeholders, geographic structures enable rapid response to changing local tastes, regulatory regimes, and volatile rates of exchange and tariffs. The format is useful for a company that is marketing oriented and requires substantial adaptation of its product or service to local markets. Firms that are relatively new to international markets or are in the midst of expansion into such markets will also benefit from that structure.[6] Although in the past they were used mostly by firms with homogeneous, mature, and stable product lines, today's geographic structures also appeal to firms with differentiated product lines, those in a changing technological environment, and those further down the internationalization route.[7]

Nestlé is a world leader in foods and beverages and is also engaged in the production and distribution of pharmaceuticals and cosmetics. Showing profitability in all but two of its close to 130 years of existence, this Swiss-based company gets almost all of its revenues from foreign markets. Hailing from a small domestic market, Nestlé started on the internationalization route early on, opening a factory in Brazil in 1921. Nestlé's geographic structure reflects the vital importance of localization in its core food business, in which customer preferences in taste, presentation, packaging, and the like vary across national boundaries, as does their emotional link to a given product. Nestlé deviates from this geographic departmentalization when it comes to businesses in which product adaptation requirements are much smaller, such as pharmaceuticals and pet food. Nestlé also centralizes across all businesses such functions as R&D, finance, purchasing, and back-office operations, where scale advantages are especially substantial (see Exhibit 11.1).

Exhibit 11.1   Nestlé's Organization Chart

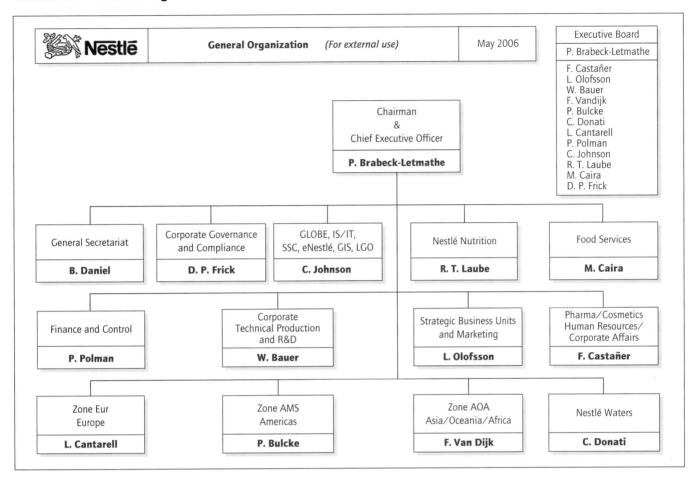

SOURCE: Nestlé 2006 Annual Report, Web site.

Underneath Nestlé's three main geographic regions are subregions encompassing countries that are geographically contiguous and, most important, share culture, language, and historical ties. Examples include Scandinavia (Sweden, Denmark, Norway, and Finland) and Iberia (Spain and Portugal) in the European region and Canada and the United States in the Americas region. Below the subregions are country units, each headed by the all-important country manager. The country manager directs all food and beverage operations in his or her region in coordination with Nestlé's strategic business units of Dairy, Coffee & Beverages, Chocolate, Confectionary & Biscuits, Ice Cream, Food, Pet Care, and Food Services. As in all geographic structures, however, the major operational responsibility rests with the country manager.

The geographic structure simplifies regional strategy and defines accountability. Lines of authority are logical and provide easier channels for communication and evaluation of individual performance. This structure also facilitates coordination of technical and functional capability across countries within a region. The structure facilitates consolidation of regional knowledge and expertise with executives becoming highly familiar with the region under their jurisdiction. Regions are easily expanded to accommodate new acquisitions, a key advantage in today's business environment. From a career development perspective, geographic structures provide opportunities for broad management training. Charles Strauss, president and CEO of Unilever U.S., describes how his geographical responsibilities prepared him for his current leadership role:

My last job [was] group president in Latin America. I was heading an operation across a wide geography, and the many product categories required that I focus on the strategy portfolio, the people and the development of organizational capability.[8]

The major disadvantages of the geographic structure are operating problems in a context of diverse product lines and marketing characteristics. Product emphasis is weak, which interferes with information flow between manufacturing and marketing. It is also difficult to transfer technology and ideas across regions. Systems and policies diverge and lose consistency, and there is costly duplication of functional and product specialists. The result may be less than optimal deployment of resources and core competencies. Scale and synergy are reduced, although they can be maintained at the regional level.

A number of conditions need to be looked at when considering a geographical structure. For example, what is the value-to-transport cost ratio? When the ratio is low, a geographic structure makes more sense. Similarly, a geographic design is more desirable when the firm needs to deliver service and support on-site, when it wants to be perceived as a local entity (e.g., owing to nationalistic sentiments), and where geographical boundaries coincide with market segmentation.[9] The Otis Elevator Company sells and services its products in more than 200 countries, which differ in market characteristics, regulatory requirements, and the like. The majority of its employees (51,000 of its 60,000 emloyees, as of 2007) are located outside the United States and are subject to different labor laws and economic and technological conditions.

Combined Forms Using Geographic Areas

Some regional structures are run in line capacity as profit and loss centers, whereas others are run in staff capacity and provide vision and more informal coordination. Companies can also opt for mixed formats. Union Carbide (before being acquired by Dow Chemical) used product structure at home and regional structure abroad to deal with the increasing interdependence between function, regional area, and product.

Another mixed geographic structure is the front–back design that separates sales and service from R&D, manufacturing, and logistics. Such structures become more appealing when back-office operations are transferred to lower-cost locations. In India, local workers perform billing for British Airways and auditing for Ford's Asian subsidiaries and call General Electric customers in the United States who are late making their payments.[10] The combined form maintains internal cohesion while permitting firms to tap market opportunities, accommodate local regulatory environments, and coordinate and control multiple sources of diversity. In recent years, however, such activities have been increasingly outsourced to independent providers who contract with the MNE for those services.

Region-Specific Factors in Geographic Structures

Effective drawing of regional boundaries minimizes duplication of functional and product efforts and facilitates interregional coordination, allowing the MNE to maintain most of the advantages of a national subsidiary structure while pursuing a globally coordinated course. To achieve local responsiveness, regions are drawn to include countries that share political, economic, and logistic attributes while reflecting strategic considerations in terms of scale and product diffusion. Visa includes Central and Eastern Europe, the Middle East, and Africa (CEMEA) in a regional division encompassing 92 countries on three continents. In contrast, Visa's other international regions—Asia-Pacific, the European Union, Canada, Latin America, and the Caribbean—are by and large contiguous. Visa's Miami-based Latin American and Caribbean region contains 44 countries and territories. Using employee attitudes to draw divisional boundaries improves knowledge flow between regional headquarters and subsidiaries. In Chapter 6, we introduced the clustering of countries on the basis of employee attitudes, which can help in the drawing of regional boundaries in a geographic structure.

A related decision in geographic structures is the location of regional headquarters. For instance, firms with an Asia-Pacific division can choose between Hong Kong, Singapore, Tokyo, Sydney, and Honolulu, among others, as locations for their regional headquarters. In making the decision, firms consider multiple factors—among them, proximity to major markets (e.g., Hong Kong is much closer to the Chinese mainland than the other cities), cost of doing business (cheaper in Sydney), communications, quality of life, and cultural barriers.[11] The success of Singapore, home to 170 regional MNE headquarters,[12] shows the importance of infrastructure and human resources relative to geographic proximity. Even though the island nation is in Southeast Asia, it attracts firms whose main operations are in East Asia, many miles away.

COUNTRY BOX

THE ROLE OF REGIONAL HEADQUARTERS

The advent of the European Union created powerful forces toward standardization and homogenization. This makes a European divisional structure more feasible and facilitates coordination and control among country units. It is also in line with other developments in the region—for example, the consolidation of distribution centers (see Chapter 16). Still, companies now decry the decline in general management knowledge that country managers brought into their ranks under prior geographic structures. In Asia, the level of integration remains much lower. ASEAN is only a free trade area, and it excludes some of the most important Asian economies. APEC is not scheduled to eliminate barriers to trade and FDI until 2020. This fragmentation and the large distances create pressures toward maintaining regional differentiation. Indeed, Asia is the one world region in which MNEs are not abandoning regional headquarters.

The Conference Board reports a number of factors responsible for success in using Asia-Pacific regional designs: an appropriate strategic and operational role for the regional headquarters; effective use of country managers, whose authority is adjusted to a country's uniqueness; balanced differentiation and integration; use of joint ventures; and attendance to staffing and other human resource issues. Interestingly, information technology was not found to play an important role in the Asia-Pacific area, possibly because of the primacy of personal relations in the region (see Chapter 6).

The leading location for regional headquarters in the EU is the United Kingdom, while Hong Kong and Singapore lead in Asia, although Sydney maintains a respectable position and Shanghai is rapidly ascending in line with the rise of China. In the Middle East, the United Arab Emirates is the leading location for regional headquarters, while Brazil is the preferred location in Latin America (although Miami also serves as a base for Latin American regional headquarters for many U.S. MNEs).

SOURCES: The Conference Board. "Organizing for global competitiveness: The Asia-Pacific regional design." Report #1133-95-RR, 1995; The Conference Board. "Regional headquarters: Roles and organization." Report #330-03-ES, 2003; UNCTAD. "World market for corporate HQ emerging." Press release, Sept. 2003; Hong Kong and Singapore government communications, 2005–2007.

The Global Product Structure

A firm embarks on a global strategy when it decides to locate manufacturing and other value-creation activities in the most appropriate global location to increase efficiency, quality, and innovation. In seeking to obtain gains from global learning, a company must cope with greater coordination and integration problems. It has to find a structure that can coordinate resource transfers between corporate headquarters and foreign divisions while providing the centralized control that global strategy requires.

The Global Product Design

In this format, global product divisions are responsible for developing, producing, or marketing a product (or group of products) worldwide. Similar designs may be organized along customer groups or markets. Product units are responsible for planning, design, production, and sales and hence must contain all functional resources, although they may occasionally pool resources across product lines. Product managers report to their corresponding divisions, which allows for integration of development, production, and marketing. MNEs that utilize product structures typically accommodate country-specific knowledge as staff capacity sometimes within a staff international division and at other times in a combination of line and staff within corporate headquarters. A product group headquarters coordinates the activities of the domestic and foreign divisions within the product group. Product group managers in the home country are responsible for organizing all aspects of value creation on a global basis.

The product group structure allows managers to decide how best to pursue a global strategy. For example, they decide which value-creation activities, such as manufacturing or product design, should be performed in which country to increase efficiency. Increasingly, U.S. and Japanese companies are moving manufacturing to low-cost countries like India or China but establishing product design centers in Europe or the United States to take advantage of their respective capabilities. In contrast, Japanese and South Korean MNEs have tended to avoid the global product design altogether, although some of them have introduced global product line elements.

The global product format is a response to the growing need to serve customers across borders. Skyrocketing investment in product development that firms wish to spread across the largest possible number of markets and customers is also driving global product structures. The format is considered especially useful for diversified companies managing a portfolio of businesses in a rapidly changing environment. Advances in communication technologies and decline in travel cost have made global product structures more attractive by making it possible to establish multinational teams consisting of individuals who are physically separated.

Types of Global Product Structure

The three basic types of product structures are the **related divisional format**, the **cluster format**, and the **unrelated holding company** format. In the related divisional format used in such firms as Interpublic (United States) and Sandvik (Sweden), product divisions report directly to headquarters. In the cluster format, used by AlliedSignal (later acquired by Honeywell) (United States) and Rhone-Pulenc (France; prior to its merger), a business reports to a cluster headquarters that is accountable to corporate headquarters for business results. In the unrelated holding company or conglomerate format, businesses are managed as investment rather than profit centers with wide reporting variations.[13]

Fiat, a diverse industrial enterprise that is Italy's largest private-sector enterprise, is organized in a conglomerate-type structure, with divisions (operational sectors) reporting to a corporate head office that defines and oversees group strategy and resource deployment. Corporate headquarters also controls financial resources and is responsible for relations with internal and external constituencies. For Fiat, the holding-company format is an advantage as it reorganizes in the face of growing competition at home and abroad. This structure makes it relatively easy to dispose of noncore assets while strengthening core assets.

The main advantages of product-based structures are a global vision and the ability to leverage resources across regions. This encourages strategic focus and flexibility. Other advantages are simplicity, clear accountability, standardized product introduction, and enhanced speed and quality of decisions. New product lines are introduced on a self-contained basis, reducing interference in other operations. From a human resource perspective, product structures support the early testing of talented individuals.

On the negative side, a global product structure makes it difficult for different product groups to trade information and knowledge and thus obtain the benefits of cooperation. The structure is costly to maintain because its self-contained nature generates duplication, fragments organizational resources, and erodes functional specialization. Communications become difficult; for example, when Procter & Gamble shifted to a global product structure, establishing five global business units such as "food and beverage," it created a setting where Cincinnati-based employees report to a Venezuela-based manager. Employees complained about lack of communication with their bosses, having to hold videoconferences at inconvenient times, and so on.[14]

Ominously, product designs are slow to adapt to local conditions. Firms can compensate for that deficiency by establishing a staff international division to handle business development, interact with key constituencies, and support line divisions. U.S.-based General Electric maintains an international division in London headed by a vice-chairman to support its product structure and engage in new business development, including search for potential alliance partners. The division places country executives in more than 40 countries, although these are not full-fledged country managers, which is the option sought by some other product-based MNEs. Still another solution to enhance the geographical sensitivity within a product structure is to establish a mixed product/geography format.

INDUSTRY BOX

"FORD 2000"

Effective January 1, 1995, Ford Motor Company shifted from a geographic structure to a global product design. The company established five Vehicle Program Centers (VPCs): one in Europe split between Dunton, UK, and Merkenich, Germany, for small front-wheel drive, and four in Dearborn, Michigan, for large front-wheel drive cars, rear-wheel drive cars, personal-use trucks, and commercial trucks. Each VPC was assigned worldwide responsibility for the design, development, and engineering of the vehicles assigned to it. In changing its structure from geographic to product based, Ford was hoping to avoid duplication and cut costs. As Alex Trotman, chairman and CEO at that time, suggested: "By integrating all our automotive processes and eliminating duplication of effort, we will use our creative and technical resources most effectively in our pursuit of total customer satisfaction.... This new way of doing business...through simplification of engineering, supply, technical and other processes, will substantially reduce the cost of operating the automotive business."

While integrating North American and European product development processes, Ford decided to maintain separate Asian and Latin American operations for the time being. Apparently, these two markets were considered not only substantial in their future potential but also sufficiently unique to merit the continuation of a geographical structure where country and regional adaptation are more easily obtained. Ford also maintained Jaguar and Aston Martin (the latter was sold in 2007), its two acquisitions up to that time, as separate corporate entities, underlying the importance of maintaining their brand-name appeal.

"Ford 2000" encountered many challenges. Integration and coordination proved more difficult than expected, and technical expertise was spread thin across the five centers. British product developers had little understanding of the American consumer and found it difficult to come up with products that would appeal to that customer. For instance, they wondered why anyone would want a car with a red interior when that was long out of vogue in Europe. Similarly, the Ford Transit, a product sold mainly in the European market, was now under the responsibility of a vehicle center based in the United States. In 2002 Ford changed its structure, reintroducing geographical elements side by side with product line differentiation (e.g., the creation of the premium model group).

SOURCE: Adapted from various Conference Board reports. We are grateful to the Conference Board for permission to use this material.

The Global Matrix Structure

Matrix designs are unique in that they contain simultaneous, intersecting differentiation bases, with many employees reporting to two or more supervisors simultaneously. MNEs that use global matrix structures select either a two-dimensional (e.g., Caterpillar, ABB) or a three-dimensional design (e.g., IBM). Two-dimensional designs involve combinations of product and geography or product and function. Once thought the wave of the future, the matrix structure has lost some of its luster over the years; it has been criticized for its complexity and ambiguity.[15] The design is costly because it involves duplication of functions across units. Coordination difficulties undermine strategic focus and divert many resources to coordination tasks. Multiple, intersecting levels of authority slow decision making and undermine accountability and performance evaluation, reducing the incentive for executives to undertake risks. The complexity of operation is especially manifested in an international context because of employee diversity across country units. Yet, companies such as Ford Motor have developed the proficiency to run matrix structures effectively.

Matrix structures provide a way for an MNE to simultaneously handle globalization and localization. The structure is designed "to help management cope with a highly complex, constantly changing global business environment by allowing the marshaling of diverse resources in multiple ways."[16] Among the advantages of the matrix structure are economies of scale and ease of transfer of technology to foreign operations and of new products to foreign markets and hence superior foreign sales performance. The matrix can also be used as an interim structure for a firm moving from an international division to a global structure. For instance, Deutsche Bank adopted a matrix structure to ease its shift from a geographic to a global product design.

Several large European (e.g., ABB, Royal Dutch Shell) and U.S. (Caterpillar) MNEs use the matrix structure successfully. With the exception of ABB, these firms are not highly diversified and have product lines based on similar technologies. This is one reason why Japanese and Korean firms do not use the matrix structure, opting for functional structures combined with an international sales division. Successful matrix firms make sure they have coordinating mechanisms in place. ABB's motto is "delegation without abdication." While decisions are pushed down the line as much as possible, corporate headquarters monitors, advises, and "steers" operational units. A common reporting system and intense effort at communications compensate for the matrix weakness. In addition, most matrix-structured MNEs are led by strong CEOs with solid international business experience. With a related business portfolio (ABB being the exception) and international experience, they regard the matrix as a worthwhile investment whose return is a superior response to the complexity and diversity of global business. With the exception of ABB, most matrix-structured MNEs have a large cadre of executives who have spent most of their careers in both foreign and domestic assignments with the same firm.

Exhibit 11.2 shows the matrix structure of the Ford Motor Company in 2007. Since the company manufactures essentially one type of product (motor vehicle), the two axes of the matrix are function (left side of the matrix) and region. Similarly to the regional divisions found in many multinationals, the regions include the Americas (see Exhibit 11.3 for a detailed chart of this region), Europe (which is becoming more internally differentiated as Eastern and Central European nations join the EU), and Asia-Pacific, Africa, and the rest of the world as a single region with tremendous differences but one where scale, at least until recently, did not justify creating a separate region (this is changing, however, with the rapid growth of Asian markets, especially China and India). Still, a close look reveals some product and ownership elements. Thus, Ford's Premier Automotive Group pulls together the operations of the group's luxury brands in Sweden (Volvo) and England (Jaguar and Land Rover) and is placed in the European region, where these cars are manufactured, while Mazda, which Ford controls but retains a minority equity in, is placed in the Asia-Pacific region as a separate entity.

To prevent problems typical of matrix structures, Ford assigns clear responsibilities to the regions, which operate as profit and loss centers, and to the functions, which maintain professional and technical oversight. CEO Alan Mullaly, who before coming to Ford ran Boeing's commercial aircraft business, notes that he rarely has to adjudicate disagreements and conflicts between the two axes of the matrix, although the structure requires intense interaction between and across functions and regions. As in other matrix organizations, Ford executives will often have two bosses, a functional and a regional head, their long-term career more often tied to the professional side where supervisors are more likely to be familiar with their area of specialization and with their career progression.

Interim Summary

1. As MNEs internationalize, they shift their structure from national subsidiary to international division and finally to various global designs.

2. MNEs select between functional, geographic, global product, and matrix structures. Over the last decades, MNEs have gradually shifted away from geographic to global product structures. However, geography continues to play a key role in MNE structure and is seeing a partial comeback.

3. Two-dimensional matrix structures in MNEs involve interfacing geographic/product or function/product combinations, while three-dimensional structures are based on function/geographic/product differentiation. The matrix structure is the most complex to manage of all structural forms.

INTEGRATING GLOBAL OPERATIONS

The integration of subunits in foreign countries in a large MNE relies on processes of control, coordination, and orientation. **Control** is direct intervention in the operations of subsidiaries to ensure conformity with organizational goals. **Coordination** provides the appropriate linkage between different

Exhibit 11.2   The Organization Chart of the Ford Motor Company (2007)

Ford

President & Chief Executive Officer

The Americas
President

Europe and Premier Automotive Group
Chairman

Asia Pacific, Africa & Mazda
Group Vice President

Ford Credit
Chairman and CEO

Product Development
Group Vice President

Chief Technical Officer
Group Vice President

Purchasing
Senior Vice President

Quality & Advanced Mfg. Engineering
Vice President

Information Technology
Vice President

Finance
Executive Vice President

Human Resources and Labor Affairs
Group Vice President

General Counsel
Senior Vice President

Government and Community Relations
Group Vice President

Communications
Vice President

Marketing
Vice President

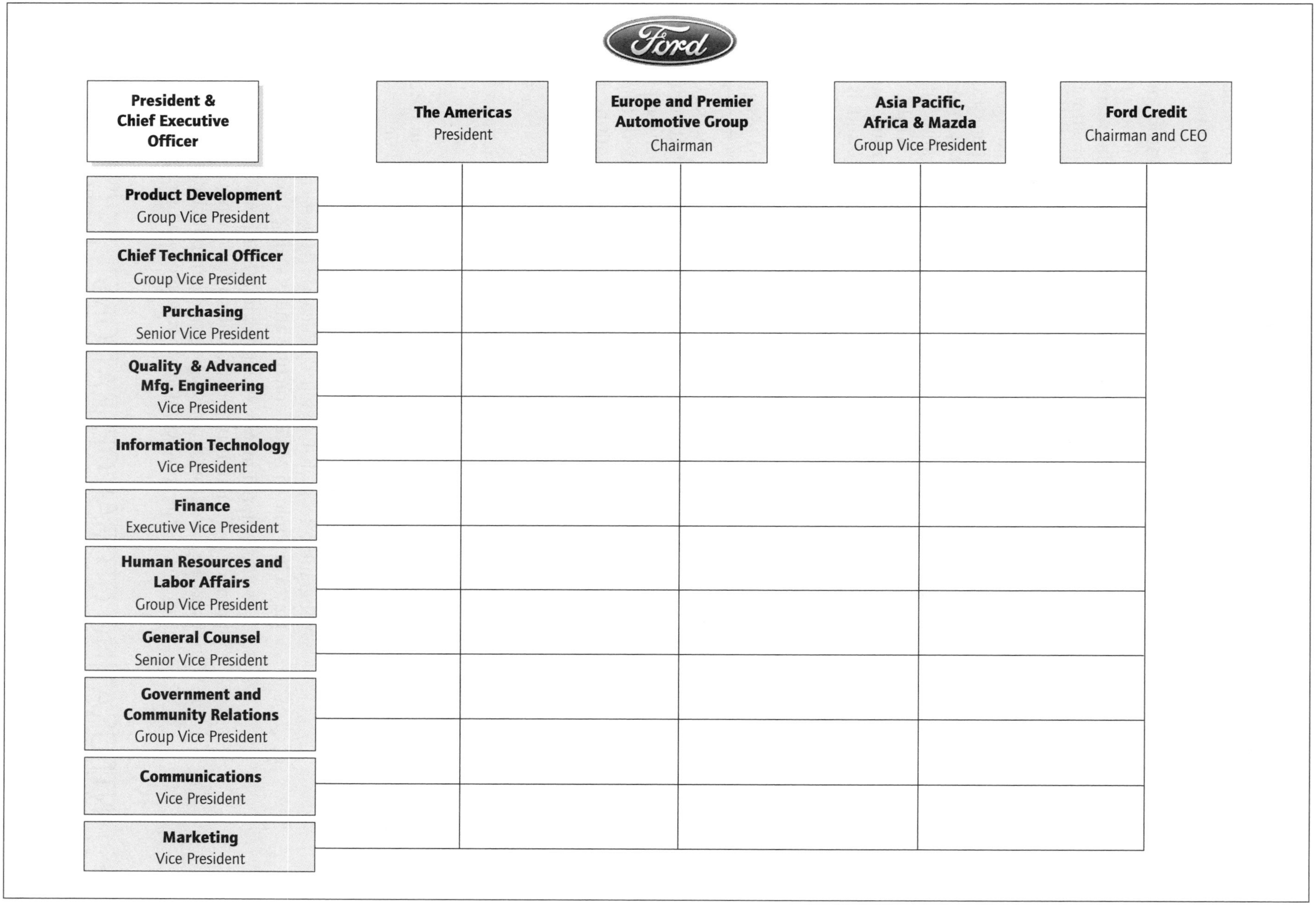

SOURCE: The Ford Motor Company, 2007.

Exhibit 11.3 Ford Americas (2007)

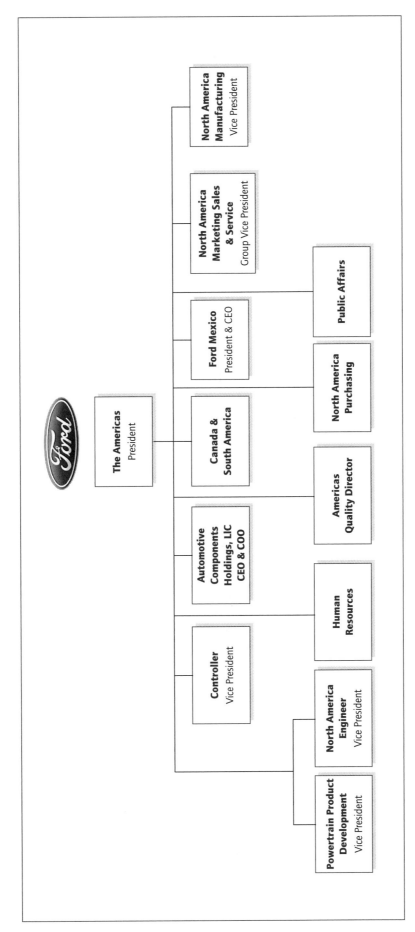

SOURCE: The Ford Motor Company, 2007.

task units within the organization. It is associated with integrating activities dispersed across subsidiaries and is less direct and less costly and has a longer time span than control. MNE headquarters are often unable to use centralized decision-making processes to maintain global control. Finally, **strategic orientation** is the indirect exercise of corporate direction.

To control its subsidiaries, the MNE uses output (e.g., performance targets), bureaucratic (e.g., codified rules), and cultural (e.g., the dissemination of corporate values) mechanisms. The diversity of countries, functions, and products makes centralized control difficult, however, making continuous monitoring necessary. Coordination helps the MNE deal with breadth (the number of units in the coordination network) and diversity (the number of functions coordinated). Formal coordination mechanisms include centralization, formalization, planning, output control, and behavioral control. Informal mechanisms include lateral relations, informal communication, and organizational culture. Coordination needs tend to be higher when international activities are more geographically dispersed. MNEs increasingly use strategic orientation in lieu of conventional controls to monitor the operation of foreign subsidiaries. Strategic orientation is less direct and less costly than control and coordination and has the most sustained effect.

Tools for Global Integration

Delegating decision making to subsidiary managers abroad or product executives at headquarters without structuring processes and rules will reduce the effectiveness and efficiency of international expansion. Major tools that can be used to maintain global integration include (a) data management and information systems, (b) managerial mechanisms and human resource administration, (c) communication intensity, (d) socialization practices, (e) expatriate dispatching, and (f) entry-mode selection and sharing arrangements.

Data management tools can be used to control the kinds of information gathered systematically by members of the organization; how such information is aggregated, analyzed, and interpreted; how, in which form, and to whom it circulates; and how it is used in major decisions. Information systems must have a dual focus. Accounting and strategic data must be aggregated both for analytical purposes and to support integration (a portfolio of countries within a business) and responsiveness (a portfolio of businesses within a country). The flow of information can also be structured with sufficient asymmetry so that individual managers will be encouraged to identify strongly with either responsive or integrative strategies, while others will develop more balanced perspectives.

Management tools can be used to set norms and standards of behavior as well as subunit objectives that are consistent with a desired strategic direction. Such tools work both directly, through their actual impact on managers, and indirectly, through the precedents they set and the meanings they assign to specific situations and choices. Management tools also include more usual human resource management components, such as shaping careers, reward systems, and management development. Less formal tools help develop norms, standards, and personal objectives. They help create an internal advocacy process that reflects the conflicting external needs for responsiveness and integration. Several managerial mechanisms can be used integrally. Planning processes can catalyze the process of strategic convergence and consensus building among executives whose initial perceptions and priorities differ. Management tools may create a climate in which managers will be encouraged to interact and will be motivated to undertake successful lateral relationships. Rewards may be based more on participation and contribution than on individual results. Managerial development activities may emphasize a corporate-wide perspective and flexible attitudes. Career paths create alternations between geographic- and product-oriented responsibilities for individual managers, so that they develop an empathy for both responsiveness and integration priorities.

Intensity of communication may be employed to balance integration–responsiveness relations. The intensity of communication between a focal subsidiary and the rest of the corporation can be treated as a positive function of the frequency, informality, openness, and density of communications between the subsidiary, the other units, and the head office. Frequent interunit communications facilitates the diffusion of innovations across subsidiaries. More intense communication patterns create higher information-processing capacity. This is especially desirable when subunits use differentiation strategies rather than harvest or cost-leadership strategies. Effective adaptation to environmental uncertainty requires unstructured decision-making processes involving open communications. Overall, frequency, informality, openness, and density of communication between a focal subsidiary and the rest of the corporation should be higher for subunits that play a greater part in global integration.

Corporate socialization of subsidiary managers can be an effective tool for global integration. **Corporate socialization** is the processes through which subsidiary managers' values and norms are aligned with those of the parent corporation. Such socialization is a powerful mechanism for building identification with and commitment to the organization as a whole, as distinct from the immediate subunit in which the manager is operating. Some of the key processes through which such socialization occurs are job rotation across foreign subsidiaries and management development programs involving participants from several subunits. Global corporate socialization of a subsidiary's top management team should vary across subsidiary strategic roles. Socialization should be high for integrated players, medium for global innovators and implementers, and low for local innovators.

Dispatching expatriates to foreign subsidiaries and manipulating the ratio of expatriates in the top management team of subsidiaries are also important for maintaining global integration. Host-country nationals are generally more familiar with the local environment, develop stronger rapport with local managers, and have a stronger identification with and commitment to the local subsidiary than to the parent MNE. Cognitively, host-country nationals are likely to have a more comprehensive understanding of the local sociocultural, political, and economic environments. By contrast, expatriate managers are likely to have a more comprehensive understanding of the MNE's overall global strategy. The local commitment of host-country nationals results from very limited prospects for their career progression outside of the local subsidiary. Expatriate managers do not operate under such a constraint. Therefore, the ratio of expatriates as a percentage of the top management team should be higher for those subsidiaries that play a bigger role in the MNE's global integration.

Entry-mode selection affects the MNE's ability to control local operations and integrate these businesses into its global network during subsequent operational stages. Other things being equal, the umbrella investment, wholly owned subsidiary, and dominant joint venture modes enable the MNE to maintain greater control and integration than minority joint venture or other cooperative arrangements in which the MNE is a minority owner. Among other entry modes, franchising and build-operate-transfer modes enable the MNE to better control foreign operations than licensing and leasing. MNEs should align their entry-mode selection with their needs for organizational control and global integration. In the case of joint ventures, the equity distribution between partners can make a substantial difference in control and integration. Majority equity ownership helps the MNE not only to protect its proprietary knowledge and control joint venture activities but also to mitigate the partner firm's possible opportunism while strategically orienting the joint venture to comply with the MNE's global mission.

The Transition Challenge

Changing an organization design is never easy. First, the change requires many resources. For instance, for its transition to the "Ford 2000" structure (see Industry Box), Ford assigned 27 senior executives to a transition team and embarked on a communications and training program for 1,700 senior and mid-level executives. The formal transition period lasted for eight months, although many of the change and integration processes continued for years. Second, during the transition many companies suffer reduced performance as employees and outside constituencies (e.g., suppliers) are not sure about duties and responsibilities. Competitors will often take advantage of such vulnerability by going after the firm's customers.

The Role of Corporate Headquarters

An essential component of organizational structure in MNEs is the corporate headquarters. While relatively small—a Conference Board report ("Organizing for global competitiveness: The role of corporate headquarters and its leadership in organizational intergration," Research Report 1291-01-RR, 2001) suggests that well-managed firms cap their headquarters staff at 2% of total head count—the board is a key player in MNE management. It is from its headquarters that the firm leverages and manages its resources, controls and coordinates its far-flung international operations, and balances scale and standardization with needs for local adaptation. The corporate headquarters provides leadership and contributes to the development of company identity and vision. Even at ABB, where decisions are pushed down the line as much as possible, corporate headquarters monitors, advises, and "steers" operational units. In research and development, traditionally one of the most centralized functions, corporate headquarters now sets a general direction while shifting more and more responsibilities, including product development, to laboratories in foreign locations (see also Chapter 13).

Corporate headquarters' employees can be found not only at headquarters but also in divisional centers and in international locations, where they provide added guidance to foreign subsidiaries and affiliates. Such guidance is especially important in the case of strategic alliances that are an increasingly popular mode through which firms enter or defend their position in a foreign market.

Interim Summary

1. MNE headquarters (or regional headquarters) integrate global operations through several mechanisms including output, bureaucratic mechanisms, and cultural mechanisms. Corporate culture (including values and philosophies) and information systems play an increasing integration role.

2. Global integration tools are diverse (e.g., reporting system, communication intensity, expatriate policy, and parent service). To choose the right tools, MNEs need to ensure that they possess the organizational infrastructures to implement them effectively.

CHAPTER SUMMARY

1. Organizational design is driven by strategy but is also a driver of strategy. The basic strategies driving MNE design are the multidomestic, global, and transnational, which indicate levels of global integration and local responsiveness.

2. The multidomestic strategy involves a decentralized system in which foreign subsidiaries are virtually independent. Under global strategy, international subunits are under centralized control from corporate headquarters, which seeks out standardized products suitable for a variety of markets. Under transnational strategy, subunits coordinate their activities with headquarters and with one another; they also share knowledge and resources.

3. A subsidiary's role can be (a) autonomous, in which case it enjoys a great deal of leeway; (b) receptive, in which case it is closely integrated with headquarters; or (c) active, in which case it coordinates with other subsidiaries. Subsidiary roles can also be classified by knowledge flow (global innovators, integrated players, implementers, and local innovators) and by subsidiary

importance and competence (strategic leaders, contributors, implementers, and black holes).

4. MNE designs include the national subsidiary structure, the international division structure, the global functional structure, the global geographic structure, the global product structure, and the global matrix structure.

5. The main challenge of MNE design is to provide the proper balance in terms of differentiation and integration across functional, product, and regional lines. To do this properly, the MNE should also devise effective mechanisms for global coordination and integration, without hindering the subsidiaries in their roles.

6. Global integration tools include data management, information systems, communication, entry mode, expatriate assignment, planning, human resource management, and socialization. Information and culture-based control are becoming more important than rigid or bureaucratic control.

Chapter Notes

1. J. C. Abegglen and G. Stalk, Jr. *Kaisha: The Japanese Corporation.* New York: Basic Books, 1985.

2. J. C. Jarillo and J. I. Martinez. "Different roles for subsidiaries: The case of multinational corporations in Spain." *Strategic Management Journal,* 1990, *11,* 7: pp. 501–512.

3. A. K. Gupta and V. Govindarajan. "Knowledge flow and the structure of control within multinational corporations." *Academy of Management Review,* 1991, *16,* 4: pp. 768–792.

4. C. A. Bartlett and S. Ghoshal. *Managing Across Borders.* Boston: Harvard Business School Press, 1989; C. K. Prahalad and Y. Doz. *The Multinational Mission: Balancing Local Demands and Global Vision.* New York: Free Press, 1987.

5. E. Hite and J. A. Trachtenberg. "One size doesn't fit all." *Wall Street Journal,* October 1, 2003, B1.

6. The Conference Board. "Organizing for global competitiveness: The business unit design." Report #1110-95-RR, 1995.

7. R. A. Daft. *Essentials of Organization Theory and Design.* New York: Thomson, 2000.

8. "Getting ahead." *Wall Street Journal,* August 22, 2000, B14.

9. J. R. Galbraith. *Designing Organizations.* New York: Wiley, 1995.

10. D. Filkins. "Punching in the future: Technology puts India to work from afar." *International Herald Tribune,* April 8–9, 2000, 1.

11. D. McClain and O. Shenkar. "Corporate downsizing, telecommunications and culture: Influence on Hawaii's competitiveness as a regional headquarters location." Report to the Department of Business, Economic Development and Tourism, State of Hawaii, 1995.

12. B. Gordon. "Singapore in quest to lure Israeli talent." *Jerusalem Post Internet Edition,* August 29, 2000.

13. The Conference Board. "Organizing for global competitiveness: The product design." Report #1063-94-RR, 1994.

14. E. Nelson. "Rallying the troops at P&G." *Wall Street Journal,* August 31, 2000, B1.

15. T. J. Peter and R. H. Waterman. *In Search of Excellence.* New York: Grand Central Publishing, 1982.

16. The Conference Board. "Organizing for global competitiveness: The matrix design." Report #1088-94-RR, 1994.

TWELVE

BUILDING AND MANAGING GLOBAL STRATEGIC ALLIANCES

DO YOU KNOW?

1. Why have so many firms chosen global strategic alliances (GSAs) to expand globally, and why have many GSAs failed? What types of GSAs can firms choose? Can you distinguish between equity joint ventures and nonequity (cooperative) joint ventures? Do you think allying between two competitors such as Toshiba and Philips is advisable?

2. How should firms select appropriate partners in another country? If you are planning to initiate an international joint venture, what criteria will underlie your partner selection, and how should you prepare for negotiating joint venture contracts?

3. How will you decide the ownership level in an equity joint venture? Is a majority status necessarily better than minority or a 50–50 status? If your company is the minority party, what

measures could you take to have more control over the joint venture?

4. In what ways can interpartner cooperation be nurtured to maximize joint payoff? How do you balance the tension between cooperation and control? If you are in charge of Xerox's alliance with Fuji in Japan, how do you safeguard your proprietary knowledge? If you want to exit from this alliance, how should it be done?

OPENING CASE

Motorola and Siemens AG in Germany

Semiconductor 300 is a global strategic alliance (GSA) in Germany established by Siemens AG and Motorola, Inc. Siemens AG, one of the world's largest and oldest electrical engineering and electronics companies based in Germany, is the market leader for the Chipcard IC. Motorola is a leading provider of wireless communications, advanced electronics, two-way radios, and data communications. Given the strengths of each partner—Siemens's chip making and Motorola's semiconductor abilities—it is not surprising that these two companies joined forces to increase productivity and gain more advantages through the Semiconductor 300 GSA. This is not the first time the two have joined together for a project. In 1995, for example, Siemens and Motorola signed a memorandum of understanding to form a $1.5 billion GSA to establish a state-of-the-art plant for building eight-inch semiconductors in White Oak, Virginia. Siemens's and Motorola's successes in past cooperative relationships aided this new partnership. They were able to accelerate the

Photo 12.1   Rhine River.

SOURCE: Jupiterimages.

decision-making process concerning issues such as ownership allocation and organizational form.

Semiconductor 300 is a 50–50 GSA (i.e., equal ownership). It seeks to develop the next generation of 300-mm 12-inch wafers, an important innovation for the semiconductor industry, which constantly requires more powerful integrated circuits at lower prices. The GSA provides both companies with first-mover advantages in the 300-mm memory chip technology arena. The Siemens and Motorola GSA also creates a valuable resource synergy. While Siemens provides Motorola with world-class technology, service, and global reach, Motorola brings expertise in advanced logic products and leading-edge manufacturing equipment development. In addition, Siemens provides leadership in dynamic-random-access memory and logic products along with state-of-the-art 0.25-micron process technology. Teaming with Motorola, Siemens is able to expand its capacity to challenge the top five chipmakers and expand its telecommunications portfolio.

DEFINING GLOBAL STRATEGIC ALLIANCES

Types of GSAs

As the preceding case illustrates, the global strategic alliance (GSA) has become a popular vehicle for MNEs to expand globally and improve their global competitive advantage. Through Semiconductor 300, Siemens and Motorola each gain more than they would by working individually. **Global strategic alliances** are cross-border partnerships between two or more firms from different countries with an attempt to pursue mutual interests through sharing their resources and capabilities. Broadly, there are two basic types of GSAs: *equity joint ventures* and *cooperative* (or *contractual*) *joint ventures*. The former involve equity contributions; the latter do not.

The **equity joint venture (EJV)** is a legally and economically separate organizational entity created by two or more parent organizations that collectively invest financial as well as other resources to pursue certain objectives. In an international setting, these parent firms are from different countries. To set up an EJV, each partner contributes cash, facilities, equipment, materials, intellectual property rights, labor, or land-use rights. An EJV, can be structured on a 50–50 ownership arrangement (e.g., the Prudential–Mitsui EJV, in which both Prudential Insurance and Mitsui Trust & Banking each have 50% ownership), or a majority–minority basis (e.g., the U.S.'s Corning–Mexico's Vitro EJV, in which Corning assumes majority ownership, 51%, whereas Vitro owns 49%).

The **cooperative joint venture** is a contractual agreement whereby profits and responsibilities are assigned to each party according to stipulations in a contract. Although the two firms entering into a contractual partnership have the option of forming a limited liability entity with legal person status, most cooperative ventures involve joint activities without the creation of a new corporate entity. Nonequity cooperative ventures have freedom to structure their assets, organize their production processes, and manage their operations. This flexibility can be attractive for a foreign investor interested in property development, resource exploration, and other projects in which the foreign party incurs substantial up-front development costs. Further, this type of venture can be developed quickly to take advantage of short-term business opportunities and then dissolved when its tasks are completed.

Cooperative joint ventures include several subforms: *joint exploration, research and development consortia,* and *co-production,* all of which are typical forms of contractual partnerships. Others include *co-marketing, long-term supply agreements,* and *joint management.*

Joint exploration projects (e.g., Atlantic Richfield's offshore oil exploration consortia in Brazil, Ecuador, and Indonesia) are a special type of nonequity cooperative alliance whereby the exploration costs are borne by the foreign partner, with development costs later shared by a local entity. Although such explorations allow the foreign firm to manage specific projects, this type of alliance does not necessarily result in the establishment of new limited liability enterprises. By comparison, the costs of a **research and development consortium** (e.g., Microsoft's R&D consortium with Cambridge University, England) may be allocated according to an agreed-upon formula, but the revenue of each partner depends on what it does with the technology created. In **co-production, or co-service, agreements**, such as the Boeing 767 project involving Boeing and Japan Aircraft Development Corporation (itself a consortium of Mitsubishi, Kawasaki, and Fuji), each partner is responsible for manufacturing a particular part of the product. Each partner's costs are therefore a function of its own efficiency in producing that part. However, revenue is a function of successful sales of the 767 by the dominant partner, Boeing. In the co-service arrangement between Delta Air Lines and Air France, the focus is on aligning commercial policies and procedures, coordinating transatlantic operations, and combining frequent-flier programs. Although Delta and Air France each retain independent fleets, together they look for ways to improve operating efficiencies.

The **co-marketing arrangement** provides a platform in which each party can reach a larger pool of international consumers. For example, Praxair (U.S.) and Merck KGA (Germany) established their global alliance in 1999 through which each uses the other's distribution channels to provide an offering combining Praxair's gases and Merck's wet chemicals to semiconductor customers. This co-marketing alliance gives each party entry into the other's main markets. Praxair has a strong distribution infrastructure in North America but is a minor player in Europe and Asia. Merck, in contrast, is strong in Europe and Asia but absent from the U.S. wet chemical market. In a typical **long-term supply agreement**, the manufacturing buyer provides the supplier with updated free information on products, markets, and technologies, which in turn helps ensure the input quality. Ikea, for example, offers such information to its dozens of foreign suppliers and also provides them with free periodic training. As a result, many of Ikea's foreign suppliers are committed to becoming its long-term exclusive suppliers. Finally, a **co-management arrangement** is a loosely structured alliance in which cross-national partners collaborate in training (technical or managerial), production management, information systems development, and value-chain integration (e.g., integrating inbound logistics with production or integrating outbound logistics with marketing). Partnership provides a vehicle for firms to quickly and efficiently acquire skills that cannot be bought from a public market. Co-management arrangements occur because international companies often realize that they lack the managerial skills necessary for running foreign operations, while local companies often find that they can benefit from foreign counterparts' international experience and organizational skills. Therefore, foreign and local companies can benefit from complementary managerial expertise contributed through an alliance.

Rationales for Building GSAs

Although GSAs take several different forms, they share some common rationales. Firms team together seeking some synergy. **Synergy** means additional economic benefits (financial, operational, or technological) arising from cooperation between two parties that provide each other with complementary resources or capabilities. In practice, these synergies and related economic benefits can be the result of *risk reduction, knowledge acquisition, economies of* *scale and rationalization, competition mitigation, improved local acceptance,* and *market entry.*[1]

First, *a GSA allows a company to enter into activities that might be too costly and risky to pursue on its own.* If an investment project is too expensive or too risky for single firms to handle alone, they may join forces to share the risk. This is the case with oil exploration and commercial aircraft manufacturing where large, risky projects call for interfirm collaboration. Having considered the fact that the design, development, and production of a new aircraft engine require more than 10 years at a cost of close to $2 billion, General Electric (U.S.) and Snecma (France) established CFM International, a 50–50 joint venture, to share the risks and costs involved in new aircraft engine development. Moreover, if the business environment in a host country is highly uncertain or unfriendly to foreign firms, a GSA with a local firm may allow an MNE to share political risks and defuse hostile local reactions. Finally, alliances can be used to cut the costs of leaving a business. Exiting an industry via an alliance also permits management to withdraw with the company's reputation intact. Minimizing exit costs is one of the considerations underlying Siemens's alliance with Toshiba and IBM to develop the 256-megabit dynamic-random-access memory (DRAM) chip.

Second, *a GSA allows a firm to acquire partner knowledge or resources to build competitive strength.* This knowledge acquisition may occur at significantly reduced costs—with capital investment much lower than if the firm developed it alone or via an acquisition.[2] Access to a partner's technology enables a firm to enjoy the fruits of research and development while avoiding rapidly escalating R&D costs. Royal Dutch Shell and ICI (Imperial Chemical Industries) share their complementary resources in producing rigid foam through a global alliance. ICI is highly regarded in the polyurethane market for its technical support and ability to bring new products to market, whereas Royal Dutch Shell is a world leader in the technology for rigid polyether polyols.

Third, *a GSA allows a firm to enhance economies of scale or scope and to improve product rationalization.* By sharing financial resources that otherwise are not available to each individual partner, two smaller companies in an industry can form an alliance to achieve economies of scale similar to those that are enjoyed by their larger competitors. GSA partners may also cooperate to take advantage of pooled nonfinancial resources. The joint use of complementary resources, competencies, and skills possessed by different organizations can create synergistic effects, which none of the companies is able to achieve if acting alone. For example, Airbus aircrafts are manufactured under a consortium composed of France's Aerospatiale and Germany's Daimler-Benz Aerospace, British Aerospace, and Spain's Construcciones Aeronauticas. Because most aerospace projects require huge capital outlays, pooling both technological and financial resources is a rational step.

Fourth, *a GSA allows a firm to prevent or reduce competition (potential or existing) with a major rival.* Clark Equipment and Volvo formed an alliance producing earth-moving equipment; alone, neither could generate enough volume in their traditional home markets (United States and Europe) to survive against such global industry leaders as Caterpillar and Komatsu. Meanwhile, a GSA may be used in a more aggressive strategy. Caterpillar Tractor linked up with Mitsubishi in Japan to put pressure on the profits and market share that their common competitor Komatsu enjoyed in its Japanese market (about 80% of Komatsu's global cash flow was generated from Japan). Thus, while the alliance may be quite beneficial to Caterpillar, it may act as a thorn in Komatsu's side and reduce its competitiveness outside Japan.

GSAs can also be used to develop technological standards that help control the competition within an industry. For example, Sematech, a GSA among several electronic and semiconductor firms, facilitated the adoption of the UNIX standard operating system for workstation computer producers. Intel and Hewlett-Packard cooperated to offer a new chip that would have a greater capacity to process data than Intel's Pentium. The chip would be able to run today's Windows software as well as programs written for HP's version of UNIX, without modification. This innovation could take the microprocessor revolution to a new level, providing the partner firms obtain a controlling position in the industry.

Fifth, *a GSA allows a firm to boost local acceptance as perceived by foreign consumers*. A foreign firm can piggyback on a local partner to gain access to the local market. The Ford Motor Company estimates that 60% of the automotive growth over the next 20 years will be in markets where Ford now has little or no presence. Ford's alliance with Mazda of Japan illustrates its efforts toward local acceptance in Asian markets. Without fully understanding the consumer behavior, distribution network, and effective marketing strategies and practices in a specific country, a foreign wholly owned subsidiary has a substantial potential for failure. The distinctive marketing and distribution practices in Japan encourage foreign companies to set up partnerships with Japanese companies as the most practical means of getting into the market. Similarly, many Japanese MNEs with little or no direct presence in Europe have moved aggressively to establish partnerships with their European counterparts.

Finally, *a GSA allows a firm to bypass entry barriers into a target foreign country*. Many governments, particularly in developing countries, pressure MNEs to conduct FDI in the form of equity joint ventures rather than wholly owned subsidiaries. To the foreign firm, an alliance with a local organization, either business or governmental, may be required to enter these countries. With Coca-Cola out, Pepsi entered India in the mid-1980s through a joint venture with the government-owned Punjab Agro Industrial Corporation (PAIC) and Voltas India Ltd. During that time, the Indian government imposed many restrictions on profit repatriation, technology transfer, and product distribution. Pepsi managed to overcome these obstacles through cooperation with local partners that contributed their market power, marketing channels, and strong ties with officials to the joint operations.

Challenges Facing GSAs

Not every firm should build GSAs to expand globally, nor is building GSAs necessarily a superior strategy to other investment choices under all circumstances. According to a survey by McKinsey & Company and Coopers & Lybrand, about 70% of GSAs fall short of expectations.[3] More complex than the single organization, GSAs involve multiple interorganizational relationships (between the parent firms, between alliance managers and the foreign parent, between alliance managers and the local parent, and between alliance managers nominated by different parents). Each of these relationships can be extremely difficult to manage. GSAs represent an intercultural and interorganizational linkage between two separate parent companies that join forces with different strategic interests and objectives. Interpartner conflict may arise from sources such as cross-cultural differences, diverging strategic expectations, and incongruent organizational structures. These conflicts in turn can lead to instability and poor performance of the alliance.

The aforementioned complexity generates problems and risks for using GSAs. First, *loss of autonomy and control* often creates interpartner conflicts and alliance instability. Each partner may want to control the alliance's operations, so coordination and governance costs are generally higher. Cross-cultural partners may disagree on long-term objectives, time horizons, operating styles, and expectations for the alliance.

Second, the *risk of possible leakage* of critical technologies may be high and often difficult to avoid. Committing distinctive resources is often necessary for gaining a competitive edge in a foreign market. This, however, may lead to leakage of valuable intellectual property (known as *appropriability hazard*). Because distinctive resources are relatively difficult to specify, contract, and monitor, hazards associated with limited protection of such rights are particularly high for these resources, especially in developing countries where intellectual property rights systems have not yet been fully established. In the absence of strong control over alliance activities and self-protection mechanisms, local partners may disseminate the foreign investor's critical knowledge to third parties.

Third, interpartner *differences in strategic goals* often lead to cumbersome decision-making processes, which may in turn cause strategic inflexibility. This may be compounded when the alliance managers do not share strategic directions and goals set by parent firms. In the absence of sufficient organizational control over alliance activities, GSAs may even be considered impediments to the flexibility of an MNE's global strategy. The MNE may need to maintain global integration of all parts of its network (outside the GSA) for strategic or financial purposes, but because of the inflexibility of the GSA, global optimization may not be possible for outsourcing, capital flows, tax reduction, transfer pricing, and rationalization of production.

Finally, local partners may *become global competitors* in the future, after developing skills and technology via the alliance. Japanese firms, for example, often plan ahead to increase the benefits they extract from a GSA, leaving the European or American partners in an inferior strategic position. In other words, they may look upon partnerships as a strategic competitive move, based on tactical expediency.[4] Reflecting on its GSA with NEC, one senior executive in Varian Associates (a U.S. producer of advanced electronics including semiconductors) concluded that "all NEC had wanted to do was to suck out Varian's technology, not sell Varian's equipment."[5]

Because of the preceding drawbacks, international managers should make a strategic assessment of the necessity of building GSAs in the course of a feasibility study. This assessment emphasizes value creation and thus is more beneficial than conducting a cost–benefit analysis. This is especially true when the alliance is used to learn about a new environment and thereby reduce the uncertainties present in a new territory. This calls for a strategic, rather than financial, view to capture value creation. Along with the increasing competition and technological development, a GSA is increasingly engaging multiple sophisticated businesses, calling for distinctive resources from multiple partners. This makes value-creation analysis for building GSAs more important and more difficult at the same time. Following this assessment, managers need to plan carefully for partner selection, contract negotiations, and alliance structuring (see Exhibit 12.1).

Interim Summary

1. There are two basic types of GSAs: equity joint ventures and nonequity (cooperative or contractual) joint ventures. Cooperative joint ventures include joint exploration, R&D consortium, co-production, co-marketing, joint management, and long-term supply agreement. Major advantages of building GSAs include cost/risk sharing, knowledge acquisition, product rationalization, competition reduction, local acceptance, and market access.

Exhibit 12.1   Key Issues Underlying Building GSAs

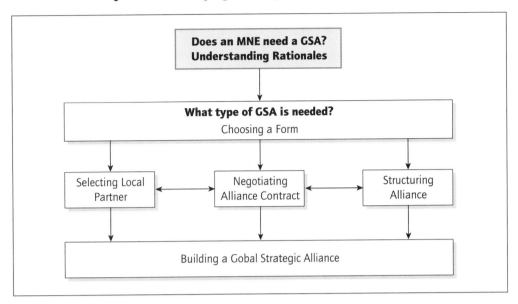

2. Many GSAs have failed, owing to inability to overcome inherent challenges such as loss of control, knowledge leakage, goal incongruence, cultural clashes, differences in managerial philosophies, and emerging competition between partners.

BUILDING GLOBAL STRATEGIC ALLIANCES

Selecting Local Partners

Partner selection is widely recognized as a vital factor in GSA success. All the benefits articulated in the preceding section may or may not be achieved, depending on who has been selected as the partner. Benefits will accrue only through the retention of a partner that can provide the complementary skills, competencies, or capabilities that will assist the firm in accomplishing its strategic objectives.[6] Partner selection determines a GSA's mix of skills, knowledge, and resources as well as its operating policies, processes, and procedures.[7] During the process of GSA formation, foreign companies must identify what selection criteria should be employed as well as the relative importance of each criterion. Generally, five criteria (five C's) should be considered in partner selection:

- Compatibility of goals
- Complementarity of resources
- Cooperative culture
- Commitment
- Capability

Exhibit 12.2 highlights these five C's for selecting appropriate local partners.

Goal Compatibility

Goal compatibility refers to the congruence of strategic goals set for an alliance between its parent firms. Goals for individual parents can be different, but goals

Exhibit 12.2   The Five-C's Scheme of Partner Selection

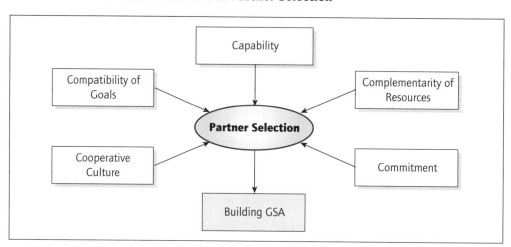

set for the alliance must be compatible or congruent, because they represent collective gains for all parents involved. The success of the consortium between Boeing and three Japanese heavy-industry companies to design and build the 767 is partially attributable to goal compatibility. Boeing sought foreign partners to ease its financial burden and operational risks, while the Japanese firms tried to expand their role in the aerospace industry. The Japanese are now significantly increasing their participation in the industry, providing an ever-increasing portion of production parts and assembly. Boeing has reduced the risks of development by adding more partners and by lowering the financial commitment required for production. When a GSA's collective goals set by different parents are incongruent, interpartner conflicts are inevitable in the subsequent phases of operations. In this case, firms are more likely to use opportunistic rather than cooperative strategies during joint operations. For instance, foreign parents want joint ventures in China to target the local market, whereas Chinese parents may want these ventures to emphasize international markets or to act as a channel to acquire foreign technologies. This incongruence creates conflicts, as reflected in Peugeot's divorce with its local partner, Guanzhou Automotive Manufacturing Company.

To ensure goal compatibility, MNEs often partner with companies that have been cooperative in the past. For example, the GSA between Mitsubishi Electric and Westinghouse Corp. proceeded in an orderly fashion partly because ties between the two companies date back to the 1920s. Previous relationships were also behind the partner selection process when LOF Glass and Nippon Sheet Glass (NSG) each spotted an opportunity in the nascent Korean auto industry. Similarly, NSG and Hankuk—which became the venture's local Korean partner— had technical and capital ties for 15 years. IBM and Siemens have also built on early ties to broaden and strengthen their alliance. Their cooperation dates back to a 1989 agreement to develop 16-megabit chips. This project was followed by joint manufacturing pacts in 1991 to launch volume production of these chips.

Resource Complementarity

Resource complementarity is the extent to which one party's contributed resources are complementary to the other party's resources, resulting in synergies pursued by both. The greater the resource complementarity between foreign and local parents, the higher the new value added owing to superior integration of complementary resources pooled by different parents. Resource complementarity also reduces governance and coordination costs and improves the learning curve.[8] For example, JVC was dependent on many different GSAs in its successful effort to make VHS (rather than Betamax) the industry standard for video. JVC stocked RCA with machines carrying the RCA label, set up licensing agreements with Japanese manufacturers, and formed alliances with Germany's Telefunken and Britain's Thorn–EMI Ferguson to help with manufacturing the video recorders. JVC's alliance with Thompson afforded it the knowledge necessary to succeed in the fragmented European market, while Thompson benefited from JVC's product technology and manufacturing prowess. As a result of these myriad GSAs, Sony conceded defeat in 1988, discontinued its production of Betamax, and began manufacturing VHS machines.

Complementary strengths were a major driving force behind the formation of Clark Equipment and Volvo's 50–50 GSA. The companies intended to operate and compete worldwide in the construction equipment business, but individually, neither partner had sufficient geographic presence and distribution capabilities to compete with the market leaders, Komatsu and Caterpillar. Volvo had roughly 70% of its sales in Europe and the Middle East, where Clark was very weak; Clark had 70% of its sales in North America, where Volvo had virtually no presence. Pooling their marketing resources resulted in a much broader geographic scope.

Cooperative Culture

Cooperative culture concerns the extent to which each party's corporate culture is compatible, thus leading to a more cooperative atmosphere during GSA operations. Normally, maintaining cooperation can become difficult for partners from different cultures. For instance, Americans tend to be individualistic, which is in sharp contrast to the Japanese emphasis on the group (see also Chapter 6). Such differences can be neutralized if each party tries to learn about the other's unique culture. Because Toyota and GM were committed to learning about each other's corporate culture, the mix of Toyota's team approach and GM's corporate focus on innovation contributed significantly to enhanced productivity at their California-based GSA, NUMMI (New United Motor Manufacturing Company).

A company must take a close look at compatibility in organizational and management practices with a potential partner. For instance, it should ask the following questions: Are both companies centralized or decentralized? If not, are managers from these two parties flexible and committed enough to overcome potential conflict? How compatible are customer service policies and philosophies? To mitigate the differences in managerial and marketing practices with local Chinese partners, Hewlett-Packard hired as middle managers local people well versed in Chinese business culture.

Commitment

Commitment concerns the extent to which each party will constantly and continually contribute its resources and skills to joint operations and be dedicated to enhancing joint payoff. Without this commitment, complementary resources, compatible goals, and cooperative culture are no guarantee of a GSA's long-term success. A partner's commitment also affects ongoing trust building. Commitment counters opportunism and fosters cooperation. When GSAs face unexpected environmental changes, commitment serves as a stabilizing device offsetting environmental uncertainties. Commitment is therefore even more critical in a volatile environment. Daewoo and GM each blamed the other for the lackluster performance of the Pontiac LeMans in the United States. Daewoo accused GM of failing to market the LeMans aggressively, while GM maintained that the initial poor quality of the LeMans and the unreliability of supplies soured dealers on the car. Lack of commitment ended this GSA in 1992.

Capability

In the context of GSAs, capability concerns three categories: strategic (including technology), organizational, and financial. **Strategic capabilities** of a partner firm generally include such areas as market power, marketing competence, technological skills, relationship building, industrial experience, and corporate image. A partner's market power often represents its industrial and business background, market position, and established marketing and distribution networks. Market power also enables the firm to mitigate some industrywide restrictions on output, increase bargaining power, and offer economies-of-scale advantages. A local partner's market experience and accumulated industrial knowledge are of great value for the realization of MNE goals. A local partner's history and background in a host market often results in a good reputation or high credibility in the industry. Lengthy industrial/market experience signifies that the local firm has built an extensive marketing and distribution network.

Organizational capabilities include organizational skills, previous collaboration, learning ability, and foreign experience. In a GSA, people with different cultural backgrounds, career goals, and compensation systems begin working together with little advance preparation. This "people factor" can halt the GSA's progress, sometimes permanently. Organizational skills are reflected not only in the ability to blend cultures and management styles but also in job design, recruitment and staffing, orientation and training, performance appraisal, compensation and benefits, career development, and labor–management relations. Among these, the ability to overcome cultural barriers, recruit qualified employees, and establish incentive structures is especially important. The international experience of partners is critical to the success of intercultural and cross-border venturing activities. International experience affects the organizational fit between partners in the early stages of joint venturing and the changes of fit over time as the alliance evolves.

Financial capabilities are reflected in risk management, exposure hedging, financing, and cash-flow management. A partner's risk management ability affects a GSA's vulnerability to external hazards and internal stability. Risk reduction in the form of hedging and risk sharing largely determines a GSA's stability and pattern of growth. During the host-country operations, currency fluctuations can accentuate the volatility of earnings and cash flows. Such volatility can in turn distort management information systems and incentives, hinder access to capital markets, jeopardize the continuity of supplier and customer relationships, and even force the company into bankruptcy. In many foreign markets, MNEs are constrained in obtaining local financing resources. A local partner who maintains superior relationships with local financial institutions and knows how to secure local financing is an important asset to both the venture and the MNE. This ability determines optional composition of debt and equity that will minimize costs and risks. It also affects the GSA's profitability, liquidity, working capital structure, leverage, and cash positions, all of which influence a firm's financial position and structure.

Negotiating Alliance Contracts

Familiarity with general terms negotiated and specified in an alliance contract is important. Major terms stipulated in an equity joint venture agreement are summarized in Exhibit 12.3.

Exhibit 12.3   Major Issues and Terms During Alliance Contract Negotiations

1. Joint venture name and its legal nature (e.g., limited liability company or not)

2. Scope and scale of production or operations

3. Investment amount, unit of currency, and equity (ownership) distribution

4. Forms of contribution (e.g., cash, technology, land, or equipment)

5. Responsibilities of each party

6. Technology or knowledge transfer

7. Marketing issues (e.g., focusing on export market or local market)

8. Composition of the board of directors (in EJVs)

9. Nomination and responsibilities of high-level managers

10. Joint venture project preparation and construction

11. Labor management (e.g., various human resource issues)

12. Accounting, finance, and tax issues (e.g., the currency unit of accounting)

13. Alliance duration

14. Disposal of assets after expiration

15. Amendments, alterations, and discharge of the agreement

16. Liabilities for breach of contract or agreement

17. *Force majeure* (i.e., force or power that cannot be acted or fought against)

18. Settlement of disputes (e.g., litigation or arbitration)

19. Obligatoriness of the contract (e.g., when it will take effect) and miscellaneous issues

Negotiating tactics affect the bargaining process as well as outcomes. Assembling the negotiating team is a critical element in creating a workable alliance. Qualified negotiators must be able to effectively convey what their parents expect to achieve from the GSA, the plans for structuring and managing the alliance, the value of the contributions each partner brings to the table, and practical solutions to potential problems. Good negotiators are also aware of the culturally rooted negotiating styles of the parties. Negotiations about forming a GSA become much easier when the discussions involve negotiators experienced in dealing with diverse cultures.

MNEs often include alliance manager candidates in the negotiating teams. For example, in the alliance activities of ICL, Fujitsu, Westinghouse, GlaxoSmithKline, Tanabe, Philips, Montedison, and Hercules, the companies usually bring their alliance executive candidates to the negotiating table. This kind of inclusion offers several benefits. First, it provides the executives with an opportunity to learn whether they are compatible with their potential partners. Second, it provides continuity; a GSA manager involved in structuring the deal will be aware of its objectives, its limitations, and the partner's strengths and weaknesses. Third, the expertise of the individuals who will manage the alliance can be valuable in structuring a workable contract. Finally, an alliance manager who takes part in creating the alliance is more likely to be committed to its success than one who has had the responsibility thrust upon him or her.

Another successful strategy for MNEs negotiating large, sophisticated alliance projects is to have two levels of negotiations. On one level, senior executives meet to define the general goals and form of cooperation. The negotiations concern broad strategy and whether the partners are committed to working together. At the second tier, operational managers or experts meet to work out the details of the alliance contract. Siemens, Toshiba, and IBM followed this strategy when they negotiated an R&D alliance to develop the 256-megabit DRAM chip. Senior executives at the three companies met and agreed on the principal objectives of the alliance contract. The three partners then organized a team to address many structural and managerial issues. Engineers and lower-level managers from each partner formed a single team to iron out the specifics of the development project and map out the work schedule and goals for the project.

Structuring Global Strategic Alliances

A critical decision underlying building GSAs, especially EJVs, is the ownership structure. The **ownership structure** is generally defined as the percentage of equity held by each parent. It is often interchangeably termed *equity ownership, sharing arrangement,* or *equity distribution.* This structure is particularly important for EJVs because the equity level determines the levels of control and profit sharing during the subsequent operations. Depending on contractual stipulations, the levels of control and profit sharing in nonequity cooperative alliances may or may not be the product of equity contribution. In the case of a two-party alliance (as earlier cases noted, alliances can have more than two partners), the joint venture is named a *majority-owned joint venture* when a foreign investor has a greater than 50% equity stake. It is a *minority-owned joint venture* if the investor owns less than a 50% equity stake. If ownership is equal to 50%, the joint venture is considered *co-owned* or *split-over.* Although there are other forms of joint ventures including those established between affiliated home-country-based firms, between unaffiliated home-country-based firms, or between home-country- and third-country-based firms, joint ventures that are launched by home-country-based (foreign) and host-country-based (local) firms are the dominant form of joint venture partnership.

A majority equity holding means that the partner has more at stake in the alliance than the other partner(s). Normally, the equity position will be associated with an equivalent level of management control in the venture. In other words, control based on equity ownership is often direct and effective. Nevertheless, the correlation between holding equity and managerial control is not always precise. It is possible for a partner to have a small equity holding but exercise decisive control. This often occurs when a minority party maintains greater bargaining power vis-à-vis the other party. For instance, because the other party depends on its resources, Burger King is able to control its joint venture operations in Moscow as a minority holder because the Russian partner relies on its expertise and experience in managing a large fast-food chain.

The ownership structure may end up equally split when both partners want to be majority equity holders. A 50–50 ownership split ensures that neither partner's interests will be compromised, other things being constant. A 50–50 split best captures the spirit of partnership and is particularly desirable in high-technology joint ventures as insurance that both partners will remain involved with technological development. In fact, equal ownership accounts for more than half of joint ventures in developed countries.[9] Split ownership can ensure equal commitment from each partner. Nevertheless, decision making must be based on consensus. This often means a prolonged decision process that can lead to deadlocks. The success of 50–50 equity ventures relies strongly on the synergy between partners over issues ranging from strategic analyses to daily management. It is important that partners speak a common language, have similar backgrounds, and share a set of short- and long-term objectives. By contrast, partners coming from diverse market environments, with different business backgrounds and conflicting goals, often have a harder time making a 50–50 venture a success.

In a minority position, the partner may transfer expertise to the local partner without sufficient returns. More important, the ability to control alliance operations is weakened. Generally, the number of votes in board meetings is in equal proportion to actual equity stake. Thus, key decisions made by the board might be more favorable to the majority party. Protecting proprietary resources contributed to the venture also becomes more difficult for the minority party. Nonetheless, minority status involves lower levels of risks, resource commitment, and start-up or exit costs compared with a majority state.

Different MNEs attach varying importance to equity ownership level in joint ventures, depending on their strategic goals, global control requirements, resource dependence, firm experience, and alternatives for bargaining power, among other factors. A firm may not be interested in equity level because it has many other alternatives for gaining bargaining power and thus controlling joint venture activities. A firm lacking these alternatives, however, has to rely on equity arrangement for control purposes. Of course, high-equity ownership itself cannot ensure a party's satisfaction with joint venture performance. Venture performance depends more on successful management by both parties. This management, however, is challenging owing to interparty differences in culture, language, philosophy, goals, and managerial style, as shown in Fujitsu's alliance in Spain (see Country Box).

COUNTRY BOX

FUJITSU IN SPAIN: BARRIERS TO ALLIANCE MANAGEMENT

Japan-based Fujitsu established a majority joint venture, SECOINSA (Sociedad Española de Communicationes e Infomática, S.A.), partnering with the National Telephone Company of Spain and various Spanish banks. Fujitsu soon found that alliances are not a panacea. Communication proved to be difficult, and both firms had to rely on English as the common language, although it is the second language for both. The Japanese felt they could not disclose their true feelings in written English; they favored a more personal and fluid rapport that adapted to issues as they arose. The Spanish managers, on their side, believed the Japanese were too business oriented and were hiding behind a barrage of company talk that prevented friendships or personal rapport. They also felt that the Japanese were not well-rounded because their at-work and after-work personas merged into one. Spanish people favor a distinct separation between job and leisure. The Japanese rarely adapted to the ways of the Spanish, which made the Spanish believe that the Japanese looked down on local ways.

Disharmony also existed in management. Decision making at Fujitsu was through the *ringi-sho* system, in which an idea is documented and distributed to all relevant parties for approval. Ringi-sho is a conservative approach that could minimize risks but is time-consuming. Further, the Spanish are inclined to assume that authority is earned through ability and merit and that authority automatically leads to power, whereas the Japanese treat age as the determining factor in earning power and authority. Finally, Fujitsu wanted to maintain stringent control over its products and prevent imitation. It wanted all the components tested at its facilities in Japan, but because manufacturing was done in Spain, SECOINSA favored Spanish-made components. SECOINSA suggested that the work could be done in Europe if Fujitsu would supply the specifications, testing, and quality-control methods. Fujitsu was willing to provide the needed information but refused to reveal it to any outside parties and would not pass along any information in writing, thus making quality control difficult to ensure.

Interim Summary

1. Five criteria must be considered in partner selection (five C's): compatibility of goals, complementarity of resources, cooperative culture, commitment, and capability. As the key criterion, capability should be assessed along strategic capabilities (e.g., market power, marketing competence, technological skills, corporate image), organizational capabilities (e.g., foreign experience, organizational skills, learning ability, and previous collaboration), and financial capabilities (e.g., risk management, exposure hedging, local financing, and cash management).

2. Many relatively standardized terms and clauses should be specified in joint venture contracts. Preparing for negotiations includes choosing a negotiating team, planning for multilevel negotiations, and knowing a partner's intentions, strengths, and weaknesses.

3. Setting the ownership level in an equity joint venture is important because it infers, in part, control over the venture. Three strategic options are majority, minority, and equally split. If the minority party has strong bargaining power, it can still dominate the venture.

MANAGING GLOBAL STRATEGIC ALLIANCES
The management issues involved in global strategic alliances include managing interpartner learning, exercising managerial control, accentuating cooperation and trust, and thinking ahead of exit (Exhibit 12.4).

Managing Interpartner Learning

In bringing together firms with different skills, knowledge bases, and organizational cultures, GSAs create unique learning opportunities for the partner firms.[10] By definition, alliances involve a sharing of resources. This access can be a powerful source of new knowledge that, in most cases, would not have been possible without the GSA. Learning opportunities are manifested in two areas: operational and managerial. *Operational knowledge* includes knowledge of technology, processes (including quality control), production, marketing skills, and operational expertise (e.g., relationship-building expertise). *Managerial knowledge*

Exhibit 12.4   Managing Global Strategic Alliances

comprises organizational and managerial skills (e.g., leadership, human resource management, organizational structure, managerial efficiency, and employee participation); market (international and host country), industrial, and collaborative experience; and financial management (e.g., cost control, tax reduction, capital utilization, financing, risk reduction, resource deployment, and asset management).

To acquire partner knowledge, a firm needs to first identify what knowledge it needs and then extract and transfer this knowledge from its partner to its own organization. Germany's Bosch established "strategy meetings," which focus on what and how the firm can learn from its Japanese partners. Bosch sends trained German technicians and marketing managers to the Japanese joint ventures to help acquire partner skills and knowledge, including tips on how to improve customer satisfaction in Japan. The acquired knowledge is then shared by all members of the Bosch group who are trying to get access to Japanese clients. Similarly, when Chrysler joined forces with Mitsubishi Motors in 1986 to create Diamond Star Motors, its major objective was to gain firsthand knowledge of Japanese management and manufacturing principles. Chrysler deliberately ceded management control for daily operations to Mitsubishi to learn how that firm handled the complex engineering, functional, and operational tasks involved in launching and manufacturing a new range of midsized models.

Each party is expected to learn a certain amount about the other's capabilities. *Openness* is thus crucial to knowledge sharing or transfer between partners, because much of what the parties are trying to learn from each other or create together is difficult to communicate. This information is often embedded in a firm's practices and culture, and it can only be learned through working relationships that are not hampered by constraints. To enhance interpartner trust, commitment from each party is necessary. However, to the party whose knowledge is very sensitive or constitutes its core competence (e.g., Coca-Cola's formula), knowledge protection becomes necessary. There are several ways to protect core knowledge from uncompensated leakage to partner firms.

First, *the design, development, manufacture, and service of a product manufactured (or a service rendered) by an alliance may be structured to protect the most sensitive technologies.* For example, in the GSA between GE and Snecma to build commercial aircraft engines, GE tried to reduce the risk of excess transfer by keeping certain sections of the production process secret. This modularization cut off the transfer of what GE felt was key competitive technology, while permitting Snecma access to final assembly. Similarly, in the GSA between Boeing and the Japanese to build the 767, Boeing walled off research, design, and marketing functions (considered more central to Boeing's competitive position) but allowed the Japanese to share production technology. Boeing also separated those technologies not required for 767 production.

Second, *contractual safeguards can be written into an alliance agreement.* For example, TRW has three strategic alliances with large Japanese auto component suppliers to produce seat belts, engine valves, and steering gears sold to Japanese-owned auto assembly plants in the United States. TRW has clauses in each of its GSA contracts that bar the Japanese companies from competing by introducing component parts. These protect TRW against the possibility that the Japanese companies may enter into alliances to gain access to TRW's home market and become its competitor.

Third, *both parties to a GSA can agree in advance to exchange specific skills and technologies that ensure equitable gain.* Cross-licensing agreements are one way of achieving this goal. For example, in the case of the alliance between Motorola and Toshiba, Motorola has licensed some of its microprocessor technology to Toshiba and in return Toshiba has licensed some of its memory chip technology to Motorola.

Finally, *avoiding undue dependence on an alliance can help mitigate the leakage risk.* This is particularly important when an MNE establishes GSAs with competitors or uses its own core knowledge in alliances. GM limited its dependence on its Asian allies in its Saturn project in an attempt to independently replenish the knowledge critical to its business. When GSAs do involve core knowledge, managers must guard against shifts in the balance of power, maneuvering by other parties, and the taking of vital knowledge. Moreover, an MNE may reduce dependence on an alliance by creating several similar GSAs or by seeking to be the senior partner in each relationship. For instance, Toyota and Daewoo provided GM with different versions of high-quality, low-cost small cars. Toyota exercises a dominant influence over its family of suppliers; it usually buys a large portion of their output, often helps finance them, and provides equipment and managerial advice.

Exercising Managerial Control

Parent control is the process through which a parent company ensures that an alliance is managed in a way that conforms to its own interest. The partners often have differing agendas for forming the alliance, and their strategic objectives are not identical. In this case, the alliance's efforts and outcomes valued by one partner are not necessarily appreciated by the other. Therefore, for each partner, achieving hands-on control over the alliance's operation confers the right of participation in the alliance's decision making, through which it ensures its strategic goals will be vigorously pursued by the alliance management.[11]

Parent control is realized through equity control and managerial control. We explained earlier that the majority equity holder is generally able to maintain greater equity control over the GSA and that this equity control is often reflected in voting power in board meetings. In routine management, however, it is managerial control rather than equity control that matters. **Managerial control** is the process through which a party influences alliance activities or decisions in a way that is consistent with its own interests through various managerial, administrative, or social tools. The really dominant party in alliance management is the one that dominates managerial control. As noted earlier, the minority equity holder may be able to exercise greater managerial control if it holds a stronger bargaining power over the majority counterpart.[12]

As Exhibit 12.5 shows, mechanisms of managerial control include the following:

1. *Nomination and appointment of key personnel:* Control requires knowledge of events and circumstances. Such knowledge is most readily available to the alliance's parents if it supplies key personnel to run or monitor operations or critical functions such as marketing, R&D, or corporate finance. The appointment of key staff as a control mechanism is especially important to parents that are geographically remote or occupy a minority position.

2. *Meetings of board of directors:* Although a majority equity holder is in an advantageous position in terms of composition and representation on the board, a minority partner can manipulate the frequency of meetings and agenda coverage. In addition, a majority parent cannot consistently overrule or refuse to compromise with its partner without building ill will and risking the long-term survival of the relationship. Further, minority parents can prevent the majority partner from implementing unilateral decisions by negotiating the inclusion in

**Exhibit 12.5   How to Maintain Managerial
Control Over Alliance Activities**

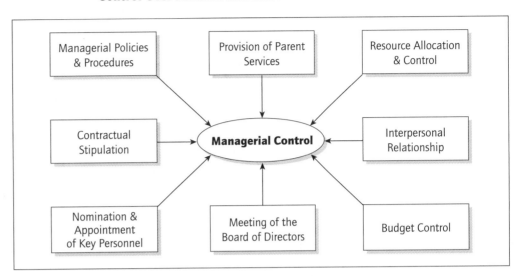

the alliance contract of veto rights over decisions important to their interests (e.g., dividend policy, new investment, transfer pricing, divestment, and selection of key managers). Finally, control at the board level is not simply a matter of votes. It also results from the ability to influence other board members on important issues. This is to a large extent a matter of bargaining power and negotiation skills.

3. *Managerial policies and procedures:* The behavior of executives in a GSA is influenced by various managerial policies and procedures devised by the owners. Since an alliance contract usually does not stipulate these policies and procedures, a minority partner can be more proactive by playing a larger part in formulating and adjusting such policies and procedures. Reward and report systems are particularly effective for the purpose of control. The former determines the incentive structure and performance evaluation and the latter the information flow, dissemination, and accuracy.

4. *Budget control:* Five aspects of budget control can be implemented: (a) emphasis on the budget during performance evaluations—that is, using quantitative criteria in evaluating divisional manager performance; (b) participation in the budget process—that is, the partner's degree of involvement during budget development; (c) budget incentives—that is, linking pay and promotion prospects to meeting budget goals; (d) budget standard setting difficulty—that is, the difficulty surrounding the setting of budget goals; and (e) budget controllability filters—that is, extenuating factors that are brought into the performance evaluation process. In general, minority partners can use all five budget control mechanisms to increase their overall or specific control over GSA operations and management.

5. *Provision of parent services:* To increase the likelihood that specific tasks in the alliance are performed in conformity with their expectations, parent firms may offer staff services and training, sometimes at no cost to the alliance. Such services can be provided irrespective of equity ownership level. Increased control accrues to parent firms in the following ways: (a) greater awareness of the parent to conditions within the GSA because of enhanced dialogue with the alliance employees, (b) increased loyalty from alliance employees who identify more with the parent and have assimilated its ethos, and (c) increased

predictability of behavior in the GSA because its managers are more likely to use the guidelines within which they have been trained.

6. *Contract stipulations:* As one of the major mechanisms by which conflicts may be overcome and performance enhanced, contract stipulations serve to reduce managerial complexity in coordinating activities for collective goals; this is an institutionalized mechanism for mitigating opportunism and increasing forbearance. A minority partner can maintain greater control over subsequent GSA operations and management if terms and clauses in the contract are more favorable to that firm. Greater bargaining power and superior negotiation skills result in such favorable conditions. Of various terms and conditions, RRB (responsibility-rights-benefits), managerial rules, and strategic goals are of particular relevance for the minority party that aims to increase control using this approach.

7. *Resource allocation and control:* While resource competence leads to bargaining power, resource allocation and utilization contribute to managerial control. In other words, allocation and control of key resources needed by the GSA are an effective mechanism for a minority party attempting to exert control over the GSA's business activities and management process. This control mechanism is often sustained because control of key resources makes both the GSA's success and the partner company's goal accomplishment dependent on the firm. Local knowledge is the contribution most consistently associated with a minority share in the original GSA agreement.

8. *Interpersonal relationship:* An MNE can increase its control if it builds and maintains a trustworthy, enduring personal relationship with upper-level managers representing the partner firm. This approach has helped many MNEs, as minority parties, successfully control their GSAs in developing countries. By arranging for managers from local firms to work at foreign headquarters, helping solve personal difficulties they face, or offering favors as needed, foreign companies are able to solidify relationships with local executives who will, in turn, remain loyal to the foreign company. This will eventually promote the foreign company's managerial effectiveness.

Heightening Cooperation

When a GSA is formed, alliance success will depend largely on interpartner cooperation during subsequent operations and management. Cooperation, however, requires organizational commitments from both parties. Two important mechanisms nurturing cooperation include personal attachment and conflict reduction.

Personal Attachment

Governance mechanisms such as contractual stipulations and managerial control systems are insufficient for controlling opportunism and increasing cooperation. Ongoing business relationships often intermingle with social content, which generates strong expectations of trust. **Personal attachment** reflects socialization and personal relations between senior GSA managers from each party during their involvement in exchange activities. Personal attachment counters the pressure for dissolution, improves trust, and increases alliance duration and stability. Personal attachment is driven by interpersonal relationships as well as interpersonal learning of individual skills and knowledge. Personal attachment can be developed in the following ways:

First, *it is important that friendly personal contact be maintained between the leaders of the cooperating organizations.* This means planning for personal visits between partner chief executives at least once a year. Apart from the intrinsic merit such visits have in ironing out any differences between the partners and laying down broad plans for the future, they are very important in setting an example and establishing a climate of cooperation for the people working within the alliance.

Second, *careful consideration should be given to the length of appointment of key personnel to an alliance.* If this is short, say two years or under, the chances of achieving mutual bonding are reduced. Not only is there personal unfamiliarity to overcome, but if a language has to be learned or improved, this clearly takes time as well. Personnel with longer-term appointments are also more likely to invest in establishing relationships within the alliance, for they see it as a more significant part of their overall career path. Western, and especially American, companies tend to assign people to alliances on contracts of four years maximum, whereas Japanese companies tend to appoint their people for up to eight years.

Third, *careful selection of people who are to work in an alliance will also improve the prospects for mutual bonding.* They should be selected not merely on the basis of technical competence, important though this is, but also on an assessment of their ability to maintain good relationships with people from other organizational and national cultures. Track records can reveal a lot in this respect. Some global companies have, for this reason, now created opportunities for successful alliance and expatriate managers to be able to remain in interorganizational and international assignments without detriment to their long-term advancement within the home corporation.

Finally, *it is important for the alliance to encourage socializing between the partners' personnel.* Activities such as sports and social events as well as charitable and sponsorship activities in the local community can be helpful in overcoming social barriers. They help to bring about an acceptance of the alliance within its local community and a strengthening of its external identity.

Reducing Conflicts

Most MNEs concede that conflict in GSAs is inevitable, given the rich diversity of capabilities, cultures, and constraints of each partner. There is likely to be a string of disputes over "hard" financial or technological issues and frictions of a "softer" cultural and interpersonal nature. In both cases, it is important to have mechanisms in place for resolving such conflicts from the very outset of the alliance's existence.

First, it is important to understand and analyze the actions and positions of the partner firm from their perspective, rather than from one's own. This helps one better appreciate the partner's position on issues and options available to that partner. This approach helped Fuji and Xerox overcome the common dividend dilemmas between the U.S. and Japanese firms. U.S. MNEs generally prefer high dividend payout because of pressure from Wall Street and institutional investors, whereas Japanese shareholders accept low payout in return for profits reinvested for growth. So, by understanding the constraints of both sides, each partner was more willing to opt for the middle ground: Fuji Xerox dividends generally hover around 30% of earnings.

Second, having alliance executives jointly set milestones and principles helps mitigate possible conflicts. Because many conflicts stem from unclear or misread signals between partners, it is important to jointly develop a set of operating principles for the alliance and establish effective communication systems.

The communications system in Fuji Xerox includes a co-destiny task force, presidential summit meetings, functional meetings, resident directors meeting, and personnel exchanges. Such communication channels bridge the differences between Fuji and Xerox. Having regular meetings is an important step to jointly set principles for alliance operations. These meetings should establish the facts of any matters at issue and record the discussion and any solutions proposed. The records of such meetings provide a basis on which problems can be addressed at a higher level between the partners.

Third, *parent firms should steer the alliance clear of the goals and strategies of the parents*. Many executives view conflicts between an alliance and its parent organizations as a potential minefield. A GSA should steer clear of its parents' strategies, geographic expansion, and product lines. For example, many of the difficulties and tensions in the Rolls-Royce–Pratt & Whitney (P&W) venture of forming International Aero Engines to manufacture V2500 engines stemmed from competitive conflicts with the parents. The V2500, a competitor of CFM International's own products, also competes directly with two P&W engines— the JTAT 200 series and the P&W 2037, as well as Rolls-Royce's RB211 engine.

Fourth, *maintaining flexibility is crucial for avoiding conflicts*. It is important to have a formal specification of rules and guidelines that clarify important issues such as financial procedure and technology sharing for those working within the alliance. However, because market and environment conditions change, partners must be adaptable. Although a contract may legally bind partners together, an adherence to a rigid agreement may hamper adaptations. Cultivating a corporate culture that embraces adaptation is important.

Finally, *an understanding of human resource groups in alliances and their typical concerns is key to preventing or mitigating conflicts*. This understanding motivates alliance managers with different cultural backgrounds to be more committed to joint operations and more cooperative with their counterparts. Chapter 17 provides a detailed account of those issues.

Thinking Ahead of Exit

Because GSAs are not required to continue indefinitely, GSA divorce does not necessarily signal failure. It may mean in some cases that the business logic for the alliance no longer applies. Thus, the best scenario of alliance dissolution is that the *venture has already met its strategic goals set by both parties*. In particular, when each party aims to acquire knowledge from the other, this alliance does not have to maintain its longevity. For instance, Hercules and Montedison, two former competitors in polypropylene products, established an alliance and pooled together $900 million in assets to create Himont in November 1983. Each side enjoyed a competitive advantage in the industry that the other lacked and wanted. Through research and technological breakthroughs, Himont added new properties and applications for polypropylene and grew worldwide to include more than 3,000 employees, 38 manufacturing plants, and distribution capabilities in 100 countries. As a leader in the chemical industry with a return on equity of 38%, Himont earned at least $150 million per annum from new products. After successfully fulfilling its objectives (i.e., learning technologies), Hercules sold its equity stake in Himont to its partner.

In many other cases, nevertheless, GSAs are terminated owing to conflicts or failure to achieve alliance goals. *Differences in strategic or operational objectives often lead to divorce*. In several U.S.–Japanese alliances producing auto parts, U.S. partners often have a narrow focus—to gain access to the Japanese auto transplants in the United States. Their counterparts, however, have broader goals—to secure a foothold in the U.S. market. Similarly, a former alliance between Corning and Ciba-Geigy of Switzerland derailed because of growing differences in the two partners' ambitions and operational objectives.

Differences in managerial styles can be a cause for termination. In the case of the Corning–Vitro alliance, the two partners had different ideas about how to define and provide "service" to customers. Corning was concerned about prompt service to retailers, such as Wal-Mart and Kmart. Vitro, having operated for years in a closed Mexican economy with little competition, was concerned only with product reliability.

Exit may also be attributed to differences in conflict resolution. In many alliances in China, for instance, the Chinese partners prefer not to prespecify explicit conflict-resolution terms, especially judiciary or arbitration resolutions, in an alliance contract. From their perspective, leaving these terms ambiguous may encourage interpartner cooperation in the long term. When partnering with Western firms, however, this ambiguity can lead to alliance termination. For example, in 1994, Lehman Brothers sued Sinochem and Sinopec, two giant state-owned Chinese firms, for failing to honor their obligations in swap transactions. This accusation, however, was rejected by the Chinese partners, who argued that there was no explicit stipulation on these transactions in the agreement. As a result of this open confrontation, the partnership between Lehman Brothers and the two Chinese giants ended.

Other reasons underlying the end of GSAs include *inability to meet shifting targets* (e.g., DuPont and Philips terminated their alliance in optical media for this reason), *inability to meet financial requirements* (e.g., financial strains prompted Chrysler to sell its stake in Diamond Star Motors to Mitsubishi), *inability to predict partner competencies* (e.g., AT&T ended its partnership with Philips when it found that Philips NV's clout did not extend far beyond the Dutch market), and *inability to predict regulatory policies* (e.g., Rohm and Hass terminated its electronic chemical alliance with Tokyo Okha Kogyo to accommodate European regulatory concerns about possible overlaps with its pending acquisition of Morton International).

There are generally three forms of termination—*termination by acquisition* (equity transfer), *termination by dissolution,* and *termination by redefinition* of the alliance. In the first case, the alliance is terminated with one of the partners acquiring the stake of the other partner. Termination by acquisition could also take the form of one partner selling its equity stake in the alliance to another company (e.g., British Aerospace selling its equity stake in Rover to BMW), or both partners selling their shares to a third company. Most MNEs prefer reallocation of alliance ownership between existing parent firms. These changes in ownership and resource commitments are a function of both firms' evolving relationships to the venture. Termination by acquisition is most common in international equity alliances. For instance, New Japan Chemical recently agreed to buy out its partner Hercules's share in their alliance, Rika Hercules. After this acquisition, the two partners intend to maintain a friendly relationship, including technological exchanges.

In lieu of termination, partners to a GSA may agree to redefine or restructure their original agreement. For example, Matsushita Electric Industries of Japan (MEI) and Solbourne Computer, Inc., of Colorado entered into an ambitious partnership in 1987 to compete with Sun Microsystems's SPARC computers. When the venture failed, MEI and Solbourne agreed in 1992 to redraft their initial agreement into a more limited partnership arrangement. In this case, redefinition or restructuring of an old alliance may imply creation of a new alliance. In other words, the life cycle of the old alliance has ended while the life cycle of the new alliance has just begun.

To end this chapter, see the Industry Box, where CEOs of Corning Incorporated and Emerson Electric detail their experiences involving GSAs.

INDUSTRY BOX

EXPERIENCE IN BUILDING GSAs IN CORNING AND EMERSON

James R. Houghton, chairman and CEO of Corning Incorporated, identified seven criteria that have helped Corning reach decisions to enter into alliances:

1. Start with a solid business opportunity.

2. Both partners should make comparable contributions to the new alliance.

3. The new alliance should have a well-defined scope and no major conflicts with either parent.

4. Trust is the most important ingredient of the alliance.

5. Management of each parent firm should have the vision and confidence to support the alliance.

6. An autonomous operating team should be formed.

7. Responsibility for alliances cannot be delegated. It must include the CEOs or board-level individuals from one or both partners who can make decisions.

Charles F. Knight, chairman and CEO of Emerson Electric, suggested five rules as pre-venturing guidelines:

1. Do not go into business with a company in a turn-around situation.

2. Do not do business with a company that does not have good management.

3. Stick to core competencies.

4. Do a lot of due-diligence work.

5. Involve the alliance management in every business plan and deal, and have them report annually to the board of directors.

SOURCE: The Conference Board. *Making International Strategic Alliances Work.* Report #1086-94-CH, 1994.

Interim Summary

1. A GSA is, among other things, a learning tool enabling the investing firms to acquire knowledge from foreign partners. Firms must identify what knowledge they seek and how complementary it is to existing knowledge. To protect sensitive technology from leakage, firms can use walling-off, contractual specification, and cross-licensing techniques.

2. Firms can execute non-equity-based control to influence GSAs. The tools of this control include appointment of key personnel, board meetings, managerial policies and procedures, budget control, provision of parent services, contract codification, resource control, and interpersonal relationships.

3. Cooperation can be facilitated by personal attachment between key managers from the parties. Firms should plan ahead for exit strategies with such options as termination by acquisition, termination by dissolution, and termination by redefining the alliance.

CHAPTER SUMMARY

1. GSAs have become a pervasive vehicle for MNEs to further their globalization. Whether in the form of equity joint ventures or cooperative joint ventures, GSAs provide MNEs with possible gains such as access to foreign markets, learning from foreign firms, sharing start-up costs and project risks, reducing global

competition, and improving local acceptance. Nonetheless, there exist many challenges in forming and managing GSAs.

2. GSAs cannot succeed in the absence of good partners. In selecting local partners, firms must seek a fit between a candidate's capabilities (strategic, organizational, and financial) and their own. Goal compatibility, resource complementarity, cooperative culture, and commitment are also important criteria underlying partner selection.

3. Many GSAs are unstable owing to governance problems. Contract specifications and ownership arrangement are two critical *ex ante* mechanisms counteracting this problem. To what extent a joint venture contract should be specified and covered and in what level the equity ownership should be sought depend on the firm's strategic needs, bargaining power, and market uncertainty.

4. GSAs are like game fields in which both cooperation and control coexist. Firms exercise managerial control to direct GSAs to suit their needs. The minority equity holder can elevate its managerial control as long as it has bargaining power vis-à-vis the other party. Managerial control is achieved through both formal methods (e.g., appointing key personnel, managerial policies, budget control, and contract stipulation) and informal methods (e.g., interpersonal relations and setting board meeting agendas and locations).

5. Interpartner learning is sometimes an overriding intention behind GSAs, especially those in developed countries. After acquiring a partner's knowledge, the firm must integrate it with its own knowledge base. No firm can build a sustained competitive advantage solely on the basis of acquired knowledge.

6. Joint payoffs from GSAs depend in part on trust building and ongoing cooperation. Continued commitment, parent support, and mutual compromise and understanding as well as satisfactory resolution of conflicts are necessary steps toward this end. Informal steps such as socialization (e.g., personal attachment between senior managers from different parties) also encourage cooperation.

7. GSAs are transitional, not permanent, in nature. Thus, firms should be prepared in advance with exit options and procedures. GSAs may be terminated as a result of achieving initial goals for all parties or failing to achieve these goals owing to differences in managerial styles, conflict resolution, or strategic orientation. Equity transfer from one party to the other (or a third party) is a common approach for termination.

Chapter Notes

1. A. See Yan and Y. Luo. *International Joint Ventures: Theory and Practice*. Armonk, NY: M. E. Sharpe, 2000; F. J. Contractor and P. Lorange. *Cooperative Strategies in International Business*. Lexington, MA: Lexington Books, 1988; and Y. L. Doz and G. Hamel. *Alliance Advantage*. Boston: Harvard Business School Press, 1998.

2. Y. L. Doz and G. Hamel. *Alliance Advantage: The Art of Creating Value Through Partnering*. Boston: Harvard Business School Press, 1998; J. Bleeke and D. Ernst. "The way to win in cross-border alliances." *Harvard Business Review*, 1991, *69*, 6: pp. 127–135.

3. R. M. Kabterm. *When Giants Learn to Dance*. New York: Simon & Schuster, 1989; Y. L. Doz. "The evolution of cooperation in strategic alliances: Initial conditions or learning processes?" *Strategic Management Journal*, Summer 1996, 17: pp. 55–85.

4. R. B. Reich. "Japan Inc., U.S.A." *New Republic*, November 26, 1984: pp. 19–23; F. J. Contractor and P. Lorange. "Competition vs. cooperation: A benefit/cost framework for choosing between fully-owned investment and cooperative relationships." *Management International Review*, 1988 (Special Issue): pp. 5–18; G. Hamel. "Competition for competence and interpartner learning within international strategic alliances." *Strategic Management Journal*, 1994 (Summer Special Issue), 12: pp. 83–103.

5. S. Goldenberg. *International Joint Ventures in Action: How to Establish, Manage, and Profit From International Strategic Alliances*. London: Hutchinson Business Books, 1988; G. Hamel, Y. L. Doz, and C. K. Prahalad. "Collaborate with your competitors and win." *Harvard Business Review*, January–February 1989: pp. 133–139.

6. G. Hamel. "Competition for competence and interpartner learning within international strategic alliances." *Strategic Management Journal*, 1991 (Summer Special Issue), 12: pp. 83–103; K. R. Harrigan. *Managing for Joint Venture Success*. Lexington, MA: Lexington Books, 1986.

7. K. R. Harrigan. *Strategies for Joint Ventures*. Lexington, MA: D. C. Heath, 1985; J. P. Killing. *Strategies for Joint Venture Success*. New York: Praeger, 1983.

8. P. Lorange and J. Roos. *Strategic Alliances: Formation, Implementation, and Evolution*. Cambridge, MA: Blackwell, 1992; B. Kogut. "Joint ventures: Theoretical and empirical perspectives." *Strategic Management Journal*, 1988, *9*, 4: pp. 319–332; A. C. Inkpen. *The Management of International Joint Ventures: An Organizational Learning Perspective*. London: Routledge, 1995.

9. P. W. Beamish. "The characteristics of joint ventures in developed and developing countries." *Columbia Journal of World Business,* Fall 1995; pp. 13–19: P. W. Beamish. *Multinational Joint Ventures in Developing Countries.* London: Routledge, 1988.

10. J. L. Badaracco. *The Knowledge Link: How Firms Compete Through Strategic Alliances.* Boston: Harvard Business School Press, 1991; G. Hamel. "Competition for competence and inter-partner learning within international strategic alliances." *Strategic Management Journal,* 1991, 12: pp. 83–103; D. Lai, J. W. Slocum, and R. A. Pitts. "Building cooperative advantage: Managing strategic alliances to promote organizational learning." *Journal of World Business,* 1997, *32,* 3: pp. 203–223.

11. J. M. Geringer and L. Hebert. "Control and performance of international joint ventures." *Journal of International Business Studies,* 1989, *20,* 2: pp. 235–254; A. Parkhe. "Strategic alliance structuring: A game theoretic and transaction cost examination of interfirm cooperation." *Academy of Management Journal,* 1993, 36: pp. 794–829.

12. A. See Yan and Y. Luo. *International Joint Ventures: Theory and Practice.* Armonk, NY: M. E. Sharpe, 2000; Y. Luo. *Entry and Cooperative Strategies in International Business Expansion.* Westport, CT: Quorum Books, 1999; S. H. Park. "Managing an inter-organizational network: A framework of the institutional mechanism for network control." *Organization Studies,* 1996, 17: pp. 795–824.

THIRTEEN

Managing Global Research and Development

DO YOU KNOW?

DO YOU KNOW?

1. Why do firms increasingly globalize research and development (R&D)? What benefits and challenges can you outline for firms that locate and operate R&D laboratories in different countries?

2. What types of foreign R&D units are available for firms to choose from? If you work at Honeywell's corporate technology center in Minneapolis, what type do you think this center belongs to? If this center plans to build a new but specialized lab in Asia, what factors should you consider in opting for its location?

3. How should firms structure and integrate global R&D activities? Can you differentiate, for instance, between the polycentric decentralized structure model and the global central lab model? If you are a senior manager at Ericsson, which model may you recommend for the company?

4. How do managers of MNEs define autonomy of global R&D units, and what areas of human resource management are particularly important for managing global R&D?

OPENING CASE

Intel's R&D Network in Developing Countries

I ntel has over 20,000 R&D employees located in more than 30 countries. Some of the facilities are owned by the parent firm while others are managed in collaboration with universities or through venture-capital investments in technology-intensive companies. Intel's R&D investments in

developing countries, especially in China, India, and Russia, are growing faster than elsewhere. That expansion is motivated by the availability of an educated and skilled workforce with specific competencies in relevant areas. In these countries, Intel owns laboratories that conduct key research in a variety of fields; it has also signed a series of collaboration agreements with universities.

Intel China Research Center (ICRC) in Beijing was established in 1998 as the company's first research lab in the Asia–Oceania region. ICRC has conducted applied research in the areas of human–computer interface, computer architecture, future workloads, and compilers and runtime. In early 2005, it had a staff of 75 researchers, most of whom held a PhD or an MSc from a Chinese university. Among the research innovations that have emerged from ICRC are the Open Research Compiler, developed jointly with the Chinese Academy of Science; Audio Visual Speech Recognition, a system using computer vision to assist speech recognition; and Microphone Array and audio-signal-processing technology. A second Chinese R&D laboratory with over 150 employees is operating in Shanghai, developing software for Intel.

The Intel India Design Center in Bangalore employs more than 800 employees and delivers software solutions to the company. In comparison, the Nizhny Novgorod (Russia) software development center is home to 340 specialists and engineers who are developing software tools and applications for Intel.

Cooperation with universities abroad is an important aspect of Intel's global R&D strategy. The Intel Research Council, an internal group of technical experts, awards university research grants worldwide for projects in key areas. A final vector of Intel's global strategy is Intel Capital, Intel's strategic investment program. Its mission is to make and manage financially attractive investments that support Intel's strategic objectives. Its overseas presence grew from less than 5% of the value of the deals in 1998 to about 40% in 2003. Of these overseas investments, about half were in companies based in Asia (including Japan) and the rest in Europe, Israel, and Latin America.

SOURCE: Abbreviated from UNCTAD. The World Investment Report, 2005.

WHY GLOBALIZE R&D?

Like Intel, many MNEs are increasingly dedicating their important resources (financial, technological, and human) to global research and development (R&D) in search of sustained competitive advantages in the global marketplace. At the dawn of the 21st century, R&D has been fundamentally globalized, with core innovative capabilities remaining close to corporate headquarters in the home country. Many Western MNEs are extending their R&D activities not only in other developed countries but also in developing countries, especially emerging markets (e.g., IBM's R&D center in Beijing, China). At the same time, MNEs from newly industrialized nations such as Asia's mini-dragons (South Korea, Singapore, Taiwan, and Hong Kong) have begun to relocate many R&D activities abroad.

Globalizing R&D is a process of locating and operating R&D laboratories in different countries, under a coordinated and integrated system by the company's headquarters, in order to leverage the technical resources of each facility to further the company's overall technological capabilities and competitive advantage. For example, ExxonMobil developed a synthetic base stock for formulating high-performance engine oils through the collaboration of process research laboratories in Canada and Louisiana and a product development laboratory in the United Kingdom. While the two terms are often used interchangeably, *globalizing R&D* differs from *internationalizing R&D*. The former requires global integration of geographically dispersed R&D laboratories or centers, but the latter does not. From this standpoint, internationalizing R&D is an early stage of globalizing R&D, which evolves as a firm's international expansion grows larger and more complex in scale and scope. The R&D function serves as the key avenue for building and sustaining a company's global competitive advantage. MNEs with a well-designed strategy on globalizing R&D tend to achieve superior sales and profit performance.[1]

R&D intensity (i.e., total R&D expenditure relative to total sales during the same period) has been steadily increasing in many industries such as electronics, pharmaceuticals, chemicals, and medical equipment. For instance, the average R&D intensity relative to sales by global pharmaceutical MNEs was about 4.7% in 1977 but 14% in 2000. While American MNEs lead in innovation in many high-technology industries such as automobiles, computers, software, health care, and advanced materials, MNEs from Europe, Canada, Japan, and newly industrialized countries such as Korea, Taiwan, and Israel also demonstrate high R&D level and inventive productivity. Some large MNEs each spend over $6 billion annually (see Exhibit 13.1). The main thrust of global firms has been to increase the patent output per unit of R&D spending and sharpen their global competitiveness.[2]

Managing global R&D receives greater attention by international business managers for these reasons: First, *technology is recognized as a major source of global competitive advantage*. International R&D expands and augments the overall R&D process of the firm. Second, *the nature of the technological innovation process has changed*. Technological innovations are often the result of the integration of technologies from different disciplines (an example is the convergence of electronic, telecommunications, and information technologies). As illustrated in Chapter 5, countries differ in their competitive advantage, and the globalization of R&D

Exhibit 13.1   The Top 20 MNEs, by R&D Expenditures in the World, 2003 (Millions of Dollars)

World Rank	MNE Name	Home Economy	R&D Spending
1	Ford Motor	U.S.	6,841
2	Pfizer	U.S.	6,504
3	DaimlerChrysler	Germany	6,409
4	Siemens	Germany	6,340
5	Toyota Motor	Japan	5,688
6	General Motors	U.S.	5,199
7	Matsushita Electric	Japan	4,929
8	Volkswagen	Germany	4,763
9	IBM	U.S.	4,614
10	Nokia	Finland	4,577
11	GlaxoSmithKline	UK	4,557
12	Johnson & Johnson	U.S.	4,272
13	Microsoft	U.S.	4,249
14	Intel	U.S.	3,977
15	Sony	Japan	3,771
16	Honda Motor	Japan	3,718
17	Ericsson	Sweden	3,715
18	Roche	Switzerland	3,515
19	Motorola	U.S.	3,439
20	Novartis	Switzerland	3,426

enables firms to tap these various sources of strength. Third, *time is a critical competitive factor in a number of industries.* R&D activities are decentralized to accelerate the process of innovation and adaptation. Finally, *the growth of network and information exchange systems facilitates long-distance communication,* which lowers coordination costs associated with globalizing R&D activities.

Globalizing R&D is also a strategic response to changes in international markets. Along with a shortened product life cycle in many industries, foreign customers demand higher levels of technical service and customized products. Targeting and developing regional markets, such as the European Union, LAFTA (Latin American Free Trade Association), and CACM (Central American Common Market), may offer greater rewards for modifying products to meet market requirements. To gain access to cutting-edge technologies developed by foreign companies or improve the adaptability of their own innovations, MNEs send their own engineers and scientists to on-site laboratories. The globalization process is moving up the R&D value chain from technology support to product development and further to technology development. This indicates the increasingly important role assumed by foreign facilities in the creation of knowledge. Leading MNEs such as IBM, Philips, and Matsushita are expanding their networks worldwide. IBM, for instance, recently announced that it will open a new center of excellence in India that will focus on key technologies such as electronic commerce, cellular and mobile telephony, and distance learning.

Two distinctive patterns pertaining to globalizing R&D have emerged. First, while in the past the technology flow was unidirectional from the parent company to the affiliate abroad, *firms are now considering foreign R&D units as a critical source of knowledge and technology.* These units are assigned new tasks associated with the parent firm's global strategy. A part of these new tasks may involve deriving distinctive new product variants as part of a regional or world product mandate or, if a unique global product is envisaged, providing research input into its development. Second, *interorganizational technology cooperation has become a widespread practice.* Such cooperation exists not only between the firms but also between firms and academic institutions at home and abroad. Apart from cost and resource sharing rationale, such cooperation is compelled by the increasing demand for skilled scientists and R&D personnel who are in short supply in the home countries (e.g., Japan).

Benefits and Challenges of Global R&D

The following benefits may be generated from globalizing R&D:

First, globalizing R&D may provide a vehicle for access to, or extract benefits from, a target country's technical resources, scientific talent, or local expertise. Israel, for instance, counts twice as many scientists (as a percentage of the population) as the United States and is a very attractive country for companies that seek skilled engineers and researchers. MNEs such as IBM have established joint ventures or set up labs there, despite a fairly small local market for their products. MNEs may also receive benefits such as tax breaks and low-interest financing offered by host governments (e.g., Indonesia, Malaysia, and Thailand) when they set up R&D centers overseas. The Country Box (page 360) illustrates how India's rich pool of software engineers has lured many world-class MNEs to build global R&D centers there.

Second, globalizing R&D may enhance a firm's global competitive advantage. Building and maintaining a competitive position abroad necessitates localizing R&D in target countries, which improves proximity and responsiveness to local customers. Setting up research facilities in a host country signals long-term commitment to the local economy. For example, General Motors was selected, from among several world-class automakers, by the Chinese government to build mid-size cars in a joint venture with the Shanghai Automotive Industry Corporation because the U.S. company offered to set up a technology institute in China. Today, GM's R&D center in Warren, Michigan, coordinates and integrates the work being conducted at six Chinese universities and seven joint ventures. By locating R&D activity abroad, an MNE is able to improve its responsiveness to local needs in terms of both time and relevance. Hoffmann-LaRoche, the Swiss-based pharmaceutical company, established an R&D facility in Japan to become more aware of and responsive to consumption differences in Asia. Increased investments by MNEs in India, Brazil, Poland, and Mexico created a strong need for technical support and local adaptation abroad, which in many cases requires the presence of a permanent R&D group for expanded operations.

Finally, globalizing R&D may enable the MNE to enjoy the benefits arising from international division of labor in R&D among multiple foreign countries or regions. A well-coordinated MNE is able to allocate specific responsibilities to different yet integrated R&D subsidiaries depending on their expertise, knowledge, and external resources. This multilateral cooperation enables the firm to obtain a more varied flow of new ideas, products, and processes, providing greater input into a firm's innovation process. This also creates a synergy earned from comparative advantages in R&D resources from each participating nation. Canon, for example, built technical centers in Shanghai (China), interactive systems in Surrey (United Kingdom), software systems in California (United States), imaging technology in Sydney (Australia), telecommunications in Rennes

(France), and process development centers in Japan. This individually specialized yet globally integrated network nurtures synergy creation from global research and development.

Globalizing R&D is a complex process involving a series of challenges and difficulties. Globalizing R&D generally creates the following challenges:

First, *maintaining minimum efficient scale in foreign R&D operations is not always easy*. It may be difficult to staff the foreign labs with enough qualified people to achieve the minimum efficient scale. In addition, splitting up an MNE's most qualified people over numerous international R&D sites might dilute the critical mass at the home-based, centralized R&D facility. Further, government controls and political risks in a host country may increase the uncertainty of R&D operations. It may create a schism between an MNE's motivations and those of a local government. In certain developing countries where import restrictions exist, it may also be difficult to import the necessary research materials. Hiring local employees may also be subject to governmental control.

Second, *the leakage of proprietary knowledge poses a serious threat when R&D is globalized*. This may arise because of the presence of a foreign joint-venture partner, lax patent laws in the country, or perhaps the likelihood of foreign nationals being hired away by indigenous firms after they have acquired much of the MNE's expertise. McDonnell Douglas and Boeing faced such leakage risks when they partnered with Japanese firms on the F-15 Eagle fighter and the Boeing 767. Maintaining the confidentiality of technical information and knowledge is difficult and costly.

Finally, *globalizing R&D inevitably increases coordination and control costs*. An MNE may face coordination issues such as allocating research tasks among dispersed R&D centers, exchanging information among different R&D centers, and developing products that are responsive to market needs in different countries. The more decentralized and distant an MNE's R&D facilities, the more costly the coordination and control necessary for the arrangement to succeed. If R&D is done in just one country, there are fewer language and cultural barriers to surmount as well as a shorter distance to be covered to hold face-to-face meetings. Lack of coordination and control can easily lead to costly duplication of effort since different facilities may not be fully aware of what others are doing. In addition, cultural and business differences between home and host countries may intensify the difficulty in running R&D activities overseas. For example, the relationship between engineers and managers is very different in the United States, Japan, and Europe. In the United States, managers traditionally hold less authority over engineers working under them than is the case in Japan and Europe. Problem solving also differs across countries. In Europe, it is customary to discuss problems and solutions before cost figures are considered, whereas Americans first wish to know whether a program is financially feasible.

Despite these challenges, we have witnessed increased globalization of R&D activities as MNEs become more internationalized. To most of them, overseas R&D activities have added net value to their growth in the global marketplace and created sustained competitive advantages over local and international competitors.[3] To obtain the advantages of global R&D while attenuating its disadvantages requires well-prepared design and structuring in the building phase and well-established systems of management, coordination, communication, and control in the operational phase. Managing global R&D activities is difficult and complex, requiring the consideration of multiple factors in formulating strategies and policies concerning R&D dispersion and control. These factors include not only the dynamics of external environments, such as market demands and governmental policies, but also the requirements of organizational development, such as the firm's strategic goals and internal rationales behind research and development. A firm's global R&D system should be structured to fulfill organizational needs while taking advantage of external opportunities. Internally, the R&D function faces an ongoing task of managing coordination and control across the company's international network of R&D laboratories. Externally, corporate R&D is increasingly called upon to create and manage technological cooperation with universities, research consortia, and even competitors in order to stay abreast of leading-edge developments. It is equally essential for the firm to manage such critical areas as communication and coordination, human resource management, technology transfer, and collaboration with local firms, among others. Without such management, the economic return of R&D dispersion cannot be ensured. We elaborate on these issues in the following section.

Interim Summary

1. An increasing number of MNEs have globalized R&D to take advantage of the expertise available in foreign markets as well as to be responsive to the demands of those markets. Firms view foreign R&D units as a critical source of knowledge and an important vehicle for intra-MNE knowledge sharing and utilization.

2. Globalizing R&D involves challenges such as high costs, knowledge leakage, and coordination difficulty. Overcoming these challenges necessitates a well-designed global structure and a carefully planned organizational scheme.

COUNTRY BOX

INDIA: R&D CENTERS OF GLOBAL COMPANIES IN INDIA

Since 1997, a large number of global firms, especially those in the information technology (IT) industry, have started R&D centers in India to access research resources there, particularly a large pool of software engineers. Most global R&D centers are concentrated in Bangalore (e.g., IBM, Lucent, HP, Sony, Siemens, Telesoft, Philips, Texas Instruments, LG, Sun Micro, Verifone, SAP, and Huawei), with several others located in Hyderabad (e.g., Motorola, Nokia, Bell Labs, and Microsoft), Mumbai (e.g., Gateway, Informix, Shimadzu, and E-gain), and Delhi (e.g., Oracle and Adobe). MNEs in Bangalore serve as both producers and consumers of software, turning the city into an international gateway for trained manpower. Bangalore has become the largest IT cluster in India, attributable to the presence of educational institutions, state support, venture capital, and an extensive network of technology developers and providers. Many prestigious research institutes such as the Indian Institute of Science, Jawaharlal Center for Advanced Scientific Research, National Aerospace Laboratory, Central Manufacturing Technology Institute, Aeronautical Research Center, and Central Power Research Institute are located in Bangalore.

The growth of Bangalore as an IT cluster was catalyzed by the founding of the first global R&D center by U.S. firm Texas Instruments (TI). Originally founded in 1985, the center consists of 500 engineers specially trained in the design of circuits. In 1998 this center began to design digital signal processors (DSPs), the fastest growing sector of the global semiconductor market. It also designs chips, specifically Application Specific Integrated Circuits (ASICs). Fabrication is carried out in TI's U.S. facility, with the designs being encrypted and transmitted from India through a dedicated satellite link. The establishment of the TI India R&D center was one of the reasons for Bangalore becoming a software hub, since TI gave R&D contracts to other firms such as Wipro and Sasken, thus acting as a catalyst for knowledge networking. Wipro is a leading Indian IT firm and a major exporter of software from India. Wipro has an R&D division consisting of 3,000 engineers exclusively working on telecom.

DESIGNING AND STRUCTURING GLOBAL R&D

Types of Foreign R&D Units

Defining the type of a planned foreign R&D program is the first step in globalizing R&D. In relation to the role of foreign R&D units, R&D subsidiaries can be categorized into (a) corporate technology units, (b) specialized or regional technology units, (c) global technology units, (d) technology transfer units, and (e) indigenous technology units.

A *corporate technology unit* is designed to generate basic, long-term technology of an exploratory nature for use by the corporate parent. A *specialized technology unit* is set to develop specialized technologies, products, or processes predefined by headquarters to serve either the global or regional market. A *global technology unit* is generally established for developing new products and processes for major world markets. A *technology transfer unit* focuses on facilitating the transfer of the corporate parent's technology to a subsidiary and providing local technical services. Finally, an *indigenous technology unit* is formed overseas to develop new products specifically for the local market.

Technology transfer units and indigenous technology units are both locally adapting laboratories. The major function of these two units is to help the production and marketing facilities in a host country make the most efficient use of the MNE's existing technology. They may also assist the process of technology transfer by advising on necessary adaptation of the manufacturing technology. They may act as technical service centers by examining why a product may not fully satisfy a local market and by adapting it to better meet local needs. ExxonMobil, CPC International, and Otis, for example, used this technique in the development of products for the European market. When indigenous technology units are designed to serve a key foreign market, they become locally integrated laboratories and involve some fundamental development activities. The particular host market (e.g., China) may be large, diverse, and fast-growing and may necessitate a nationwide R&D head office to coordinate and integrate host-country R&D activities. IBM's R&D center in Beijing and Xerox's R&D center in Shanghai are playing such a role.

Corporate technology units and global technology units are both globally interdependent laboratories. These two types of labs provide inputs into a centrally defined and coordinated R&D program, with no necessary connection with host-country production operations. Their major function focuses on research and development, rather than improvement and adaptation. They link mainly to corporate and divisional R&D, not local manufacturing. CPC International's R&D affiliates in Italy and Japan and Eastman Kodak's R&D unit in Australia are examples of successful corporate technology units. IBM, on the other hand, has established several global technology units worldwide (each focusing on a certain product-technology area) developing a product or process that will have universal applicability in all major foreign and domestic markets. This approach has served IBM well since the 1970s.

Specialized technology units are globally controlled yet individually differentiated laboratories. Each of these specialized units is focused on specific technological areas defined by headquarters. Daimler-Benz (now DaimlerChrysler), for example, has its corporate research center in Stuttgart, Germany. Its R&D center in Palo Alto, near Stanford University in Silicon Valley, focuses on applying the latest communication technologies to the company's vehicles. Its R&D center in Bangalore, India, emphasizes the development of multimedia, telematics, and manufacturing solutions. In Shanghai, the automaker's joint R&D center was established to focus on microelectronics and electronic packaging. These R&D activities are tightly coordinated with microelectronics research in Germany, and scientists are exchanged between China and Germany on a regular basis. Regional technology units are regionally integrated laboratories. In contrast to specialized units that focus on specific technological areas, regional units are responsible for respective geographical areas. Both specialized and regional units are subject to the control and coordination of headquarters.

R&D unit designation may change over time as international expansion increases, the R&D subsidiary grows, or the MNE's strategy changes. The global R&D function may evolve in stages, along with the degree of the MNE's internationalization. In the initial stage, firms may dedicate few technical resources overseas and maintain domestically oriented management structures and a highly ethnocentric management group. As their commitment to overseas markets grows, companies build up technical capabilities abroad to respond to local market conditions, either by modifying the parent's products or by generating products for sale only in the local market. When the headquarters realizes that the overseas labs have achieved a level of technical competence beyond that of the rest of the company, it may switch its overseas laboratories' orientation from the host-country markets to the world market. The headquarters may assign new product-development projects to overseas labs to take advantage of their specialized technical skills. In this situation, foreign R&D units benefit simultaneously from a wide variety of environmental conditions that stimulate new product development as well as from intracompany collaborations that create synergetic returns for the company as a whole.

Selecting an R&D Location

Choosing an R&D location is an important and complex decision because external parameters such as market conditions, resource availability, and governmental policies vary across countries and even locations within a country. Once a laboratory is built, the costs of switching from one location to another are enormous. The location selection framework presented in Chapter 10 is generally applicable to the R&D site decision. Nevertheless, the following factors are specific to the location choice of overseas R&D:

First, *location selection depends on an R&D subsidiary's strategic role set by the parent company.* If the subsidiary is designed to serve a home market, managers should consider the availability of scientific knowledge and talent from foreign universities. For a subsidiary targeting the world market, location factors include accessibility to foreign scientific communities and availability of adequate infrastructure and universities.[4] When the subsidiary serves only as a technology transfer center, it should be located in a country in which the company already has a substantial investment in marketing or manufacturing. R&D generally follows marketing and manufacturing in the globalization process. In cases where the labs are established to perform basic research or develop new products for the global market, they should be situated in places in which there is a concentration of advanced innovation and technology resources. This concentration is an important reason why MNEs tend to cluster their technology development centers in several hot spots, as illustrated by the examples in Exhibit 13.2.

Exhibit 13.2   Hot Spots in the United States for Technology Development

Location	Technology	Major Companies
Albuquerque, NM	Chips	Intel, Motorola, Philips, Honeywell
Austin, TX	Computers, software, biotechnology	IBM, Samsung, Motorola, Texas Instruments, 3M
Boston, MA	Computers, telecom, biotechnology	Hundreds of start-ups
Orange County, CA	Computers, electronics	Over 300 high-tech start-ups
Huntsville, AL	Aerospace	Cummings, Honeywell, Hughes Lockheed Martin, United Technologies Corp.
Portland, OR	Electronics	Intel, Tektronix, US West
Research Triangle Park, NC	Pharmaceuticals, microelectronics, computer, telecom, biotechnology	98 research companies
San Francisco Bay	Software, computers, electronics	HP, Intel, Xerox, Oracle, Sun, Silicon Graphics
Seattle, WA	Aerospace, communications, biotechnology, software	Boeing, Microsoft

SOURCE: Adapted from V. Comello. "Hot high-tech locations." From www.rdmag.com, 1998.

Second, *host governmental policies may influence location decisions.* Some of these policies include government requirements to increase the local technological content of the firm's activities; work permit regulations for expatriate scientists, engineers, and managers; efficient patent laws; and tax subsidies to support the foreign firm's R&D activities. In the 1990s, many developing countries established high-tech development zones to attract MNEs' R&D investments. These zones offer a series of incentives to foreign companies such as tax exemption for a certain number of years, financing support from government-owned banks, reduction of land rent expenses, and priority in acquiring local resources. Government itself may also organize some high-profile research consortia soliciting foreign participation. In the United States, for example, the Microelectronics and Computer Technology Corporation, Semiconductor Research Corporation, and Semateck consortia focus on technologies in microelectronics and semiconductors. In Europe, broader consortia were fostered through the European Strategic Program for Research and Development in Information Technology (ESPRIT), Research Development in Advanced Communications Technology for Europe (RACE), and European Research Coordinating Agency (EUREKA), to name a few.

Third, *the local infrastructure and technological level of a foreign country are critical.* A threshold of technological capability must exist in the country to permit R&D to take place. Some MNEs may wish to start tapping into technology that is more advanced. For example, Germany is a world leader in such areas as chemistry, physics, metallurgy, and medicine, while Britain has traditionally spent heavily in chemicals and pharmaceuticals. The presence of research universities or local firms with advanced technology becomes important in these circumstances (see the Industry Box about Ford in Aachen).

Finally, *sociocultural factors may affect location selection.* MNEs have shown a preference for locating R&D facilities in nations with a similar culture and language,[5] which makes sense considering the difficulties associated with operating any business in a different cultural and social environment. It can be frustrating to operate in an environment where the most basic cultural, social, and business practices (which are taken for granted in one's home country) are quite different. Furthermore, the decision makers in headquarters should consider the attractiveness of the foreign country's lifestyle to the staff that will be assigned overseas. If the general consensus is that the location is undesirable, it may be difficult to find qualified people willing to work abroad. Because R&D development largely depends on the creativity and efficiency of human resources, the working and living conditions overseas may determine the expatriates' incentives and commitments (see also Chapter 17).

INDUSTRY BOX

FORD RELOCATES ITS R&D CENTER IN AACHEN, GERMANY

Ford chose Aachen in Germany as its new European R&D location partly because of its proximity to one of the most industrialized regions in Europe. Aachen is centrally positioned in the heart of Europe, allowing for close cooperation with more than 40 universities in 16 different countries. Aachen is also home to one of the major prestigious technical universities in Europe (RWTH Aachen), enabling Ford to easily recruit highly qualified scientists and engineers. Technical cooperation with local universities and institutes facilitates the acquisition of new technologies and supports strategic technology monitoring. Aachen, which is located close to the Netherlands, Belgium, and France, serves as an ideal listening post for the notoriously diverse European tastes and expectations. Ford finds it easier to design and develop product variants or to monitor European politics from Aachen than from other locations. Today, there are about 130 researchers, from 20 different countries, working on sophisticated technologies to meet the growing demand for personal mobility, safety improvement, and emission control.

Structuring Global R&D Activities

To ensure global R&D success, MNEs must design an appropriate organizational structure governing R&D activities. Two critical factors should be considered in structuring global R&D operations: (a) *the level of authority an MNE plans to provide to its foreign R&D activities* and (b) *the scope of the geographical market to be covered.* Building on these two axes (autonomy level and market breadth), five models can be identified, namely the (a) ethnocentric centralized, (b) polycentric decentralized, (c) specialized lab, (d) global central lab, and (e) globally integrated network structures. Exhibit 13.3 displays these five forms. You may note that these are choices about overall organizational structure governing an MNE's worldwide R&D, whereas the five types of global R&D units illustrated earlier are choices about a role played by a specific R&D laboratory within an MNE's global R&D network. A specific R&D lab is positioned within this network to help fulfill an MNE's overall goal in research and development. Each of these forms serves as an organizational framework in which different R&D units may be designed with different roles and types.

In the *ethnocentric centralized* R&D structure, all major R&D activities are concentrated in one home country. This structure contains a corporate technology unit at home and may also include a few technology transfer units to distribute centralized R&D results to local operations. In this model, the core technologies are viewed as a national treasure in the home country base, designing products that are subsequently manufactured in other locations and distributed worldwide. This structure ensures technology protection and

Exhibit 13.3   Organizational Models for Global R&D

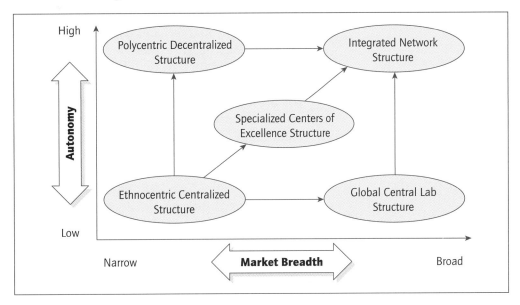

enhances returns to scale in R&D. Its disadvantage is the lack of sensitivity to signals from foreign markets and insufficient consideration of local market demands. MNEs choose this structure only if they manufacture global, standardized products and do not consider differentiating between foreign markets. Nippon Steel of Japan, for example, has adopted this structure because its products are highly standardized in international markets. The company has four centralized R&D laboratories near Tokyo (about 1,000 researchers). This structure helps the company reduce costs considerably.

The *polycentric decentralized* R&D structure is characterized by a decentralized federation of R&D sites with no supervising corporate R&D center. This structure contains a number of indigenous technology units in major foreign markets. Foreign R&D laboratories are highly autonomous with little incentive to share information with other R&D units or central R&D. Overseas R&D laboratories emphasize product or process development in response to localization requests and local consumer demands. Royal Dutch Shell, for example, used this structure during 1984–1997 to develop Carilon, a multiple-application polymer, in Shell's three decentralized R&D units, including the Amsterdam R&D center, the Westhollow Research Center in Houston, and the Belgium R&D laboratory. In this structure, efforts to preserve autonomy and national identity may impede cross-border coordination and therefore lead to inefficiency on a corporate level and to duplication of R&D activities. The company may also lose its focus on a particular technology. Shell, therefore, restructured this R&D system in 1998 and authorized the Westhollow Research Center in Houston to lead in developing Carilon, with other centers focusing on commercialization.

In the *specialized laboratory* structure, foreign R&D units are assigned global mandates. The aim is to improve the global efficiency of the product development process, concentrating in a single location the resources relevant to development operations in a particular product category. This structure contains several specialized technology units in respective product areas. When there exists a leading market in terms of size and presence of customers, the MNE will assign the global responsibility for developing and manufacturing the product to the laboratories and plant in that country. This approach makes it possible to achieve economies of scale in R&D and to place the product-development operations close to the company's key customers. For example, Alcatel acquired Rockwell Company's R&D laboratory in the United States, the most sophisticated telecom market, and used it as the primary research base for its transmission systems. Because there are costs in transferring R&D to a manufacturing plant that is farther away from the R&D center, global development laboratories are often selected on the basis of their proximity to the manufacturing plants. For instance, Ericsson specializes its R&D facilities on the basis of their historical background and major area of technical specialization; its R&D on silicon technology and chip design is done in Australia, Italy, and Finland, while its R&D on mobile telephone systems is carried out in Germany, France, Spain, and Greece. Similarly, the organization of R&D at Siemens is based on worldwide centers of competence laboratories selected on the basis of their traditional scientific specialization and competence and given worldwide responsibilities. Siemens's Italian subsidiary is a worldwide competence center for microwave radio systems and cellular telephones.

The *global central lab* structure is used to leverage a company's centralized technical resources to create new global products. Although it is also centralized, R&D under this structure covers a much broader market domain than R&D in the ethnocentric centralized model. In this structure, there may be more than one global technology unit to generate worldwide innovation. Also, companies concentrate their technical resources in their country of origin. To make this structure work, it is important to create an effective market information network that provides a flow of information from the decentralized production or marketing units to the parent company. This enables the central development laboratories to generate products suitable for the global market or to adapt different product versions to individual markets. Nissan, for example, implemented this model in the early 1990s. In the development of the Primera automobile, targeted for the European market, Nissan formed a core project team in Western Europe. Back in Japan, this team was supported by some 100 engineers who had all experienced European culture during numerous visits.

The *globally integrated network* structure may be filled by a number of foreign R&D units with different roles and types, such as the global technology unit, the corporate technology unit, the specialized technology unit, and the indigenous technology unit. In this model, home R&D is no longer the center of control for all R&D activities but rather one among many interdependent R&D units that are closely interconnected by means of flexible and varied coordination mechanisms. A central coordinating body exercises the necessary supervision to prevent duplication and to integrate the diverse contributions. Development processes whose results can be exploited across a number of markets involve resources from the different facilities whose work is coordinated according to a common plan. Each unit in the network specializes in a particular product, component, or technology area and perhaps a set of core capabilities. At times, this unit takes over the lead role as a competence center and is then responsible for the entire value generation process, not just for product-related R&D. Schindler Lifts, the worldwide leader in escalators and second in elevators, established its integrated R&D network in 1996. Its R&D is dispersed over several units in Switzerland, France, Spain, Sweden, and the United States. To avoid duplication and to realize synergy, its management has started to identify its core competencies in R&D. Each of the designated competence centers in the integrated R&D network assumes strategic roles for the entire company and is engaged in defining strategies and business development. Various MNEs, including Nestlé, Philips, and Bayer, moved from a polycentric decentralized organization toward an integrated R&D network.

Interim Summary

1. Foreign R&D units can be divided into the following five types: corporate technology units, specialized or regional technology units, global technology units, technology transfer units, and indigenous technology units. To select an R&D location, managers must consider an intended role of the R&D unit, host government policies, and infrastructural, technological, and socio-cultural conditions.

2. Structuring global R&D depends on the level of decentralization offered to foreign R&D activities and the scope of the geographical market covered by foreign units. Five structuring models are the ethnocentric centralized model, polycentric decentralized model, specialized lab model, global central lab model, and globally integrated network model.

MANAGING AND OPERATING GLOBAL R&D

The increasing dispersion of R&D laboratories in foreign markets forces MNEs to take a global view in managing their research operations through such areas as human resource management, autonomy specification, global planning, and communications improvement.

Human Resource Management

Chapter 17 discusses human resource management policies, many of which are applicable to managing human resources in global R&D. Nevertheless, R&D human resources should be managed in a way that fulfills the unique needs of global research and development. First, *selecting key personnel should be linked to the role or type of the foreign R&D unit.* If the laboratory belongs to an indigenous technology unit, for example, then well-qualified local talents should be considered for both R&D and management positions. If the lab is to accept technology from the parent company or belongs to a specialized or global technology unit, then qualified expatriates are preferable. Second, *personnel policies for foreign labs should be relatively standardized to the extent allowed by local laws and customs.* Promotions, titles, and reward and recognition programs should be as similar as possible. Because there should be frequent contact between home and overseas lab personnel, this uniformity of titles and managerial positions can help make foreign labs feel they are equal partners with the parent laboratories. Reward and recognition programs that are instituted at headquarters should be extended to include all the overseas laboratory personnel. Third, *maintaining some regular contacts and visits between foreign R&D units and the home lab center is useful.* This can take several forms: a visit to exchange information, an extended visit to work out a particularly difficult problem or to exploit a new discovery, or a regularly scheduled planning conference. 3M, for example, schedules regular conferences between U.S. R&D and Japanese engineering groups. In addition, 3M's Japanese R&D subsidiary often sends its laboratory and production personnel to their counterpart labs and factories in the United States for up to six months of training on equipment similar to what is being built in Japan.

Autonomy Setting

In the context of this chapter, autonomy means an R&D unit's decision-making power concerning R&D activities.

The autonomy of a foreign R&D unit depends largely on the role it plays within the MNE network. For example, management in a lab that serves as a specialized global competence center should be delegated greater power. In general, autonomy should be higher if the lab's technical resources are scarce, need to be located together in a center of excellence to attain critical mass, or should be put to use where they would create the most leverage for the company as a whole. When a foreign R&D unit serves as a technology transfer unit for the MNE network, its autonomy will be low and the decision-making authority will be centralized at headquarters. In this situation, the unit plays a role as effective adopter of new products and processes created by the parent company. If the unit functions as an indigenous, specialized technology laboratory, or global technology center, it requires a high level of autonomy and a low level of formalization (i.e., specifying the necessary behaviors in the form of rules, procedures, or programs). The subsidiaries require increased degrees of freedom and more resources dispensed by the parent companies. Some R&D subsidiaries of companies such as Unilever, ITT, and Philips enjoy considerable strategic and operational autonomy, although headquarters exercises administrative control through the budgeting and financial reporting systems. These relatively autonomous subsidiaries were found to be generally more productive than other R&D units in these companies.[6]

The autonomy of a foreign R&D unit is subordinating an MNE's strategic needs for global integration. There are positive associations between the creation, adoption, and diffusion of innovations by a subsidiary and the extent to which the subsidiary is normatively integrated with the parent company and shares its overall strategy, goals, and values. Such integration is typically the result of a high degree of organizational socialization and is achieved through extensive travel and transfer of managers between the headquarters and the subsidiary and through joint work in teams, task forces, and committees. Ericsson, Procter & Gamble, and NEC are convinced that these activities have helped them in developing a common context that significantly improves subsidiary contributions to the entire innovation processes.

Resource allocation is a crucial vehicle in balancing global integration and local autonomy for managing dispersed R&D units abroad. Generally, resources allocated to global technology units or specialized technology units may be those involved in a core competency, strategic and exploratory research, global market coverage, or significant investment areas. Resources likely to be duplicated in regional R&D centers are those that focus primarily on product development as opposed to technology development. In addition to technological factors, considerations such as financial and geopolitical factors play a large role in determining proper allocation of resources. For example, Philips has set up an R&D facility in Palo Alto, California, as a window on Silicon Valley for all of its divisions and business units. Finally, in aligning resources, it is important to consider the interface between human resources and physical resources in a new information technology environment. Networks connecting a company's facilities throughout the world enable researchers to work on one project from many locations. The major innovations that have been made in modeling and simulation technology allow more development and testing to be done in simulation, reducing the time and money spent on manufacturing prototypes or running tests on finished products.

Global Planning

The corporate R&D office has the important task of coordinating an increasingly dispersed global network of R&D laboratories. Global planning serves as a primary means of information exchange among decentralized R&D laboratories and projects. In the planning process, corporate headquarters outlines a strategic intent to globalize R&D and communicate it to foreign R&D units. Matshushita, for example, established a three-pillars blueprint, including the following:

- Construction of a tripolar R&D *network* between laboratories in North America and Europe and domestic research laboratories to establish advanced technological bases and create products for the global market
- Improved *efficiency* of R&D activities through expansion of collaborative relationships with international research institutions
- Increased *speed* of R&D globalization through effective communications and superior management across borders

R&D planning activities can also contribute to learning throughout the MNE if they routinely solicit the participation of all scientists and technicians. The central R&D office can transform planning into an educational process. For example, Lucent holds biennial internal scientific conferences in which scientists exchange information with one another and with strategic planning and business units. Planning activities can also facilitate global integration. Johnson & Johnson's Global Product Category Planning Groups provide a mechanism for incorporating foreign markets' product-development priorities, which were often ignored in the past. Although budgeting is considered increasingly difficult because development cycles are five years long or more, global planning is easier owing to the ability to disseminate information and establish priorities.

Planning can help align the technological and business strategies of a company. Once the technology strategy is set, this alignment can be carried into specific project areas. A key aspect of R&D alignment on business objectives is cross-functional planning and execution. With the participation of marketing, manufacturing, and sales, R&D groups can optimize their process of project assessment, selection, and portfolio balancing. Progress on R&D projects can also be evaluated more regularly and reported to multifunction teams. Nestlé's research center at its Swiss headquarters sets budget and planning priorities through multifunctional strategic business units in close collaboration with operating businesses. After evaluating incoming development and product proposals through extensive information sharing, strategic business units set short- and medium-term priorities. Annual R&D work programs are updated and corrected on a rolling basis throughout the year.

It is usually impractical to combine product development, manufacturing, and R&D within the same organizational unit. This is particularly true in very large companies. Corporations such as IBM, General Foods, and Xerox have established committees or boards with coordination responsibility throughout the entire corporation. Membership in these committees is composed of representatives from business units, manufacturing, and R&D. AT&T has begun to experiment with having research managers at AT&T Labs report to both research management and product units. This new alignment is intended to improve the coupling between business and research. It is also designed to reduce the "time to market" between invention and product introduction.

Communication Improvement

Geographic distance poses a major challenge for communication across an international network of R&D labs. Cross-border communication breakdowns occur frequently, lowering R&D productivity. Moreover, the role of informal communication is especially important because much of the work can be accomplished only in teams. An effective communication system is needed not only within the R&D function but also between R&D and other functional activities such as marketing, manufacturing, and sales. To improve communication within a global R&D network, international managers need to be aware of the following issues.

Rules and Procedures

For overseas laboratories, careful reporting and documentation of research progress can help keep R&D personnel aware of research activity across the company. At Nestlé, progress reports are filed every six months and circulated to interested parties. In any given year, several hundred reports enter into the reporting system. Research progress reports supplement the communication flows related to the planning cycle, which can also serve an educational purpose.

Electronic Communication

Videoconferencing images, facsimiles of visual and written material, electronic mail, and computer conferencing all offer greater possibilities for communication than a simple telephone call. They provide an essential infrastructure for accomplishing cross-border teamwork. However, they cannot replace the face-to-face informal communication that builds trust. Misunderstandings and excessively slow contact or feedback of information erode the climate of trust necessary for teamwork. Along with electronic means of communication, periodic meetings through direct, face-to-face contact are necessary.

Boundary Spanners

Headquarters R&D staff often perform the role of boundary spanners between the dispersed R&D laboratories. They travel frequently to each site location to share development elsewhere in the global R&D network and to discuss progress at the particular site. They may also divulge sensitive information across the network about developments with customers, joint-venture partners, or suppliers. At Johnson & Johnson, the head office R&D group consists of "internal scouts" who are always on the lookout for opportunities to cross-fertilize research project ideas from one laboratory to another. At Nestlé, the corporate R&D staff visits foreign laboratories to optimize long-term research priorities, to develop personal contacts, and to identify potential key personnel.

Informal Networks

Communication through informal networks is often an efficient means for teamwork. The central R&D group can stimulate informal networks, which may be created both inside and outside the company, locally or internationally.[7] An external local network consists of local suppliers, customers, and research institutions that provide the opportunity for learning from foreign environments. The central office R&D group can organize an external international network of academics who work on company projects. Private conferences bring these academics together to present their research and to exchange information. Locating and funding outside academic researchers can be supervised by the central office. Johnson & Johnson finances R&D projects in universities through their Focused Giving Program. The program funds $3 million of academic research in and outside of the United States and gathers the recipients together once a year to deliver findings. An MNE's internal network can be activated most directly with international project teams. Project team members stay in their respective laboratories most of the time and collaborate on projects using electronic means and personnel transfers.

Cultural Adaptation

Often, international R&D project teams must overcome cultural differences. Although many researchers can speak English, there is no assurance that the members of a multicultural R&D team understand one another. Research shows significant cross-cultural differences among R&D professionals on the dimensions of power (respect for hierarchy), risk avoidance, individualism, and masculinity/femininity (see also Chapter 6).[8] The Japanese believe that a manager who champions an innovation should work within the organizational rules, procedures, and hierarchy, whereas Americans do not hold this belief. Often, an effective means of reducing cultural differences is to socialize R&D professionals through a wide range of activities. International training seminars help create a shared corporate culture as well as a network of colleagues who can communicate on a much more informal basis. Not only do international assignments deepen the understanding of the individual transferred; the host and home laboratories also gain a much clearer picture of the internal workings of other laboratories through this individual.

Interim Summary

1. Incentive systems such as recognition and reward should be as uniform as possible among different R&D units. Also, it is useful to maintain a regular program of exchange and visitation between global R&D units to foster unity and cooperation. Communication is important not only within an R&D unit and between R&D units but with other functional divisions such as marketing and sales as well.

2. Autonomy of foreign R&D units should be based on their strategic roles in overall corporate strategy and requirements for global integration. Having clear business and technology strategies within the company makes integration of research much easier. Once the technology strategy is set, it can be carried into specific project areas, giving everyone a common frame of reference.

TECHNOLOGY TRANSFER ACROSS BORDERS

A popular alternative to establishing foreign-based R&D labs or centers is to use technology transfers and collaborative agreements with foreign partners. This approach is especially attractive to those firms or projects that require large investments and involve high uncertainties. In Chapter 12 we illustrated a number of issues related to building and managing global alliances. The discussion in this section focuses only on technology transfer.

International technology transfer is a process by which one firm's technology or knowledge is passed on to another firm in a different country for economic benefits. Through technology transfer, a firm can acquire needed technology or knowledge from a foreign provider. Frequently used methods of technology transfer include international licensing, nonequity or equity joint ventures, turnkey operations, and countertrade (see Chapter 10, which explains these modes). Generally, firms acquiring technology through international transfer seek increasing competitiveness, increasing profits by reducing development costs, enhancing technological position in the market, or reducing prices while maintaining quality. If firms want to transfer their own technology to foreign companies, they need to consider such factors as protection of proprietary technology, competition, impact on a firm's existing market power, and earning of royalties from remote markets.

Technology transfer is a complex, ongoing activity, as demonstrated by the fact that many license relationships have been in effect for more than 50 years. Moreover, variations prevail across industry, company, or market lines. Even within an MNE network, policies and management of technology transfer differ according to subsidiaries, type of technologies, and stages of the technology life cycle. As such, it would be inappropriate for a firm to try to police technology transfer through uniform rules.

A frequent problem with technology transfer across borders is that much of the technological capability is not easily transferable from one partner to another. This is simply because the successful operationalization of many technologies depends to a great extent on the acquired experiences and expertise of critical personnel such as key scientists, engineers, equipment operators, and suppliers. The ways in which interdependent technologies are fine-tuned to work effectively within a complex system are often implicit or tacit in nature, relying on overall experiences, skills, and understandings that have been learned over time and internalized. Because of this, it is essential to check the absorptive capability of a transferee (e.g., a buyer of the technology). The **absorptive capability** concerns a firm's ability to acquire, assimilate, integrate, and exploit knowledge and skills that are transferred from others. This capability often depends on the level of the firm's related technology or skills already developed, the effectiveness of organizational learning systems, and the ability to combine a firm's own skills with newly acquired skills.

Effective technology transfer, especially via a joint venture, requires coordinating mechanisms linking two parties, which are often labeled "bridges." There are three categories of bridges—procedural bridges, human bridges, and organizational bridges.[9] *Procedural bridges* involve the joint planning and joint staffing of activities, particularly around the time of the transfer of the technology. The emphasis in procedural bridges is on collaboration through joint planning, problem solving, and implementation. *Human bridges* rely on establishing direct interaction between individuals from different organizational areas, typically through the transfer and rotation of personnel. Such personal contact allows both responsibility and enthusiasm to be transferred from one person to another, and it establishes a common social and work-related context that should facilitate more learning and cooperative efforts. The success of the joint-venture technology-transfer project between British GEC Sensors and French Alcatel is attributable to formal communication and informal social networks at the senior manager, project manager, and operational staff levels. *Organizational bridges* use dedicated transfer teams to establish more formal ties between organizational areas. These groups are created to build a more formal structure and common context for the effective transfer of experience. When British Celltech and American Cyanamid cooperated through joint-venture-based technology transfer, for example, they faced many communication problems. Cyanamid is a vast, complex organization, and it took Celltech a number of years to understand where executive power lay and with whom to negotiate to get decisions made. These problems were later solved by forming several transfer teams to build formal ties between project managers from the two parties.

Interim Summary

1. Cross-border technology transfer between different firms is an alternative to foreign R&D projects that involve large investments or high uncertainty. Licensing and joint ventures are especially common ways of achieving this transfer.

2. Effective technology transfer requires coordinating mechanisms linking two parties. These linkages include human bridges, procedural bridges, and organizational bridges.

CHAPTER SUMMARY

1. Globalizing R&D is a process of distributing and operating R&D facilities in different countries under a coordinated system by headquarters. It is an important strategic response to changes in foreign market demands and global competition. Globalizing R&D provides access to other countries' technical or scientific resources or talents, strengthens competitive advantage and local adaptation, and facilitates interfirm knowledge sharing.

2. Globalizing R&D is a complex process involving many challenges, including high costs and risks. Counteracting these challenges requires appropriate design, coordination, and management of various foreign R&D units. These units can be structured as corporate technology units, global technology units, specialized or regional technology units, technology transfer units, or indigenous technology units. Of these, the first two are more centralized and globally interdependent laboratories, whereas the last two are more decentralized and locally adapting units.

3. Carefully selecting locations for foreign R&D units can lower the levels of risks, costs, and uncertainties. Location choice depends on an R&D unit's strategic role, foreign government policies, local infrastructure and technological level, and sociocultural considerations.

4. The governance of global R&D often determines how much it contributes to global success. If an MNE adopts an ethnocentric structure, all major R&D activities will be concentrated in its home country. If it follows a polycentric structure, these activities will be scattered overseas with no supervising corporate R&D center. If it uses a specialized laboratory structure, each foreign R&D unit will be assigned global mandates. If it adopts a global central lab structure, major R&D activities will be centralized in the home center, which serves a broad range of markets. Today, more MNEs follow a globally integrated network structure, which entails many interconnected foreign R&D units with different roles and types.

5. Personnel policies affect the productivity of foreign R&D units. These policies should be standardized to the extent allowed by local laws and customs. Unit members should be motivated to develop, share, and commercialize new knowledge. Parent firms should delegate sufficient autonomy to R&D units such that the latter can fulfill their goals effectively. Both formal and informal communication systems should be developed to spur interunit sharing of information, experience, and technology.

6. International technology transfer enables MNEs to acquire technology from foreign providers. This lowers R&D costs and expedites knowledge acquisition. Firms must develop absorptive capability and foster a learning environment for technology to be effectively transferred, exploited, and integrated with their own.

Chapter Notes

1. V. Chiesa. "Strategies for global R&D." *Research Technology Management*, 1996, *39*, 5: pp. 19–25.

2. B. Bowonder and S. Yadav. "R&D spending patterns of global firms." *Research Technology Management*, November–December, 1999: pp. 44–55; The Conference Board. *The Changing Global Role of the Research and Development Function*, 1995: p. 7.

3. M. E. Porter. "Competition in global industries: A conceptual framework." In M. E. Porter (ed.), *Competition in Global Industries*, pp. 15–60. Boston: Harvard Business

School Press, 1986; J. H. Dunning. "Multinational enterprises and the globalization of innovatory capacity." In O. Granstrand, L. Hakanson, and S. Sjolander (eds.), *Technology Management and International Business: Internationalization of R&D and Technology*, pp. 19–51. Sussex, UK: John Wiley & Sons, 1992.

4. J. N. Behrman and W. A. Fischer. *Overseas R&D Activities of Transnational Companies*. Cambridge, MA: Oelgeschlager, Gunn & Hain, 1980; S. D. Julian and R. T. Keller. "Multinational R&D siting." *Columbia Journal of World Business*, Fall 1991: pp. 47–57.

5. S. D. Julian and R. T. Keller. "Multinational R&D siting, corporate strategies for success." *Columbia Journal of World Business*, 1991, *26*, 2: pp. 46–57; J. Howells. "The location and organization of research and development: New horizons." *Research Policy*, 1990, 19: pp. 133–146.

6. A. De Meyer. "Management of an international network of industrial R&D laboratories." In R&D Management Conference Proceedings, "Managing R&D Internationally." Manchester, UK: Manchester Business School, July 1992; R. Nobel and J. Birkinshaw. "Innovation in multinational corporations: Control and communication patterns in international R&D operations." *Strategic Management Journal*, 1998, 19: pp. 479–496.

7. W. Kuemmerle. "Building effective R&D capabilities abroad." *Harvard Business Review*, March–April 1997: pp. 61–70; R. D. Pearce. *The Internalization of Research and Development by Multinational Enterprises*. New York: St. Martin's Press, 1989.

8. S. A. Shane. "Cultural influences on national rates of innovation." *Journal of Business Venturing*, 1993, 8: pp. 59–73; R. D. Pearce and S. Singh. *Globalizing Research and Development*. New York: St. Martin's Press, 1992.

9. R. Katz, E. S. Rebentisch, and T. J. Allen. "A study of technology transfer in a multinational cooperative joint venture." *IEEE Transactions on Engineering Management*, 1996, *43*, 1: pp. 97–105.

PART FIVE

Functional IB Areas

FINANCIAL MANAGEMENT FOR GLOBAL OPERATIONS

DO YOU KNOW?

1. In what ways does financial management influence the global success of MNEs? What are the major financial management issues that are especially important for global operations?

2. How do payment methods differ between domestic and international transactions? By what means are global payments most commonly conducted?

3. Where does financing for global business and export projects come from? If you are a manager of Siemens, which plans to list its stocks on the NASDAQ, what are the major stages and procedures you ought to know?

4. What steps do MNEs take to reduce risk from foreign exchange fluctuations? Can you distinguish between foreign exchange risk and foreign exchange exposure? If you work for GE, whose operations often involve foreign exchange risks, by what measures, internally or externally, can you reduce or eliminate such risks?

OPENING CASE

Minimizing Exposure in RTZ

RTZ, a $10 billion international mining company based in Britain, has revamped its foreign exchange policies following a radical review of the relationship between exchange risk management and shareholder value. After realizing that currency

fluctuations can erode shareholder wealth, the company decided to abandon traditional short-term hedging strategies in favor of a dynamic, forward-looking focus on long-term results. Although RTZ's costs are largely denominated in the currencies of the countries where it operates, an analysis of its revenue structure showed that the U.S. dollar, the Japanese yen, and the euro were the major currencies determining the price of its products. RTZ views its global net exposure as a portfolio of currency positions similar to a fund manager's treatment of a portfolio of equities. It tries to avoid excessive concentration of risk in any single currency. RTZ maintains a positive exposure in currencies that affect its revenues directly and a negative exposure in currencies in which it denominates its costs. When the firm needs liquidity, it borrows (usually long-term, to balance long-term exposure) in currencies where it has the greatest positive exposure, while holding surplus cash in currencies in which it has large negative exposure. In addition, some of RTZ's positive exposure offsets imports of commodities such as diesel fuel, which are denominated in major currencies. To facilitate implementation of this approach to foreign exchange risk management, corporate headquarters sets debt policies and handles most of the firm's borrowing operations. This centralized borrowing practice allows the corporate finance group and treasury to hedge the company's strategic exposure. Moreover, treasury controls the day-to-day management of the company's exposure. The finance director, a member of the executive committee, informs the CEO and other top executives about RTZ's exposure and actions taken to reduce risk.

WHY LEARN FINANCIAL MANAGEMENT?

International business decisions today are hardly associated with financial management. Financial management should not be viewed as the domain of financial managers alone but rather as required knowledge for all international business managers. For example, what does "exposure" mean? Is it true that foreign exchange risks involve only foreign currencies, and that domestic currency is risk free in international business? Why did RTZ centralize its foreign exchange risk-exposure management associated with worldwide business? If you are a marketing manager in an overseas subsidiary, how would you deal with headquarters' requirement for using currencies that may not be attractive to your clients? To answer these questions, we need to know the major functions of financial management for global operations.

Financial management is one of the major business functions. Financial management for global operations is, however, much more complex than its domestic equivalent because management must cope with different financial environments, markets, and systems. As the RTZ case shows, effective financial management for international business has become more significant as a result of greater risks and more opportunities. Financial management of MNEs' global operations occurs in an environment characterized by volatile foreign exchange rates, a variety of restrictions on capital flows, various levels of country risk, different tax systems, and a wide spectrum of institutional settings.

Increasing globalization of financial markets, the rise of global e-commerce, and heightened pressure for acting locally while thinking globally have fundamental implications for MNE corporate finance. In this environment, management's ability to seize opportunities and avoid unnecessary risk depends on its knowledge of the international environment and its financial management skills. Increasing global competition is causing senior financial managers such as CFOs (chief financial officers) to review the cost structure, orientation, and strategic role of the finance function. Many are taking steps to reduce the cost of financial work, including automating the collection and processing of information, developing shared financial service facilities with higher transaction volumes, and improving automated systems. By emphasizing service over enforcement, they also initiate and motivate a role change from corporate policeman to business advocate and strategic partner. They often lead the global strategy process through their priority activities such as budgeting and planning, acquisition, and investment decisions.

As MNEs continue to expand globally, their assets are increasingly widely dispersed and specialized. Philips Electronics (Europe's largest electronics company), for example, has operating units in 60 countries, some of which are large, fully integrated companies developing, manufacturing, and marketing a diverse range of products from lightbulbs to defense systems. Although other companies may be less diversified, the trend toward a broader configuration of assets continues. As a result, headquarters management in many MNEs is obligated to shift from exercising centralized control toward managing a network of established foreign subsidiaries. Accordingly, formal financial coordination and control processes are now being supplemented by investment analysis, risk reduction, global mobilization of financial resources, and optimization of capital structure.

Knowledge of international financial management helps a global business in two important ways. First, it helps the financial manager decide how international events (e.g., changes in foreign exchange rates) will affect a firm and what steps can be taken to exploit positive developments and insulate the firm from harmful ones. Second, it helps the manager anticipate events and make profitable decisions before the events occur. Today, it is difficult to think of any firm, international or domestic, that is not affected in some way by the international financial environment. A wide variety of firm decisions are tied to exchange rates and other developments in the global financial environment. Financial management for global operations deals with the following major issues:

- International trade finance
- Financing global operations
- Managing foreign exchange risk and exposure
- Working capital management

Interim Summary

1. Modern international business is inextricably linked to financial management. For MNEs, financial management is much more complex than for other companies since they face multiple financial environments, systems, and markets.

2. Adequate international financial management helps an MNE maneuver past international events in the most beneficial way possible as well as to anticipate these events. This is important because many decisions are tied to exchange rates, which can have serious effects on the real income of a company.

INTERNATIONAL TRADE FINANCE

International Trade Payment

The widely used payment methods in international trade include (a) cash in advance, (b) letter of credit, (c) documentary collection, and (d) open account terms. For an exporter, the risk of being unable to receive an importer's payments increases along this sequence.

Cash in Advance

Cash in advance affords the exporter the greatest protection because payment is received either before shipment or upon arrival of the goods. It is often used in a country where there is political instability or where the buyer's credit is shaky. Political crises or foreign exchange controls in the purchaser's country may cause payment delays or even prevent fund transfers, leading to a demand for cash in advance. In addition, in a circumstance where production of contracted products requires a vast amount of capital investment, prepayment is usually demanded, both to finance production and to reduce marketing risks.

Letter of Credit (L/C)

The majority of international trade uses letter of credit (L/C) as the payment method. The **letter of credit** is a letter addressed to the seller, written and signed by a bank acting on behalf of the buyer. In the letter, the bank promises it will honor drafts drawn on itself if the seller conforms to the specific conditions set forth in the L/C. These conditions usually conform to those stipulated in an export contract or sales agreement. If they are not in conformity, the exporter must comply with conditions specified in the L/C. Through an L/C, the bank substitutes its own commitment to pay for that of its customer (the importer). The letter of credit, therefore, becomes a financial contract between the issuing bank and a designated beneficiary that is separate from the commercial transaction.

The advantages of the L/C method for an exporter include the following:

- An L/C *eliminates credit risk* if the bank that opens it is of good standing. It also reduces the risk that payment will be delayed or withheld owing to exchange controls or other political acts.
- An L/C *reduces uncertainty.* The exporter knows all the requirements for payment because they are clearly stipulated in the L/C.
- An L/C can help *stabilize production.* The exporter that manufactures under contract a specialized piece of equipment runs the risk of contract cancellation before shipment. Opening a letter of credit will provide protection during the manufacturing phase.
- An L/C *facilitates financing* because it ensures the exporter a ready buyer for its product.

While the L/C issuance often requires an importer to pre-deposit or have a savings account in the issuing bank (and thus to forgo interest earnings in another investment), the importer also gains some benefits from this method, including the following:

- Because payment is made only under compliance with the L/C's conditions, the importer is able to ascertain that the merchandise is actually shipped on or before a certain date by requiring an on-board bill of lading (B/L). An L/C also helps ensure that the quality and quantity of exporting merchandise conform to regulations described in the L/C.
- The bank bears responsibility for any oversight on checking the documents that are required in the L/C (a phenomenon known as *document discrepancies*). In commercial L/C transactions, banks deal in documents and not in goods. The importer can refuse to accept the bill of lading and decline to pay if it finds any, and even very minor, oversight in any of the requirement documents.
- Using an L/C heightens the importer's bargaining power and allows the importer to ask for a price reduction from the exporter.
- If prepayment is required, the importer should deposit its money with a bank rather than with the seller because it is then easier to recover the deposit if the seller is unable or unwilling to make a proper shipment.

Exhibit 14.1 shows the process of using an L/C in an export business from a Chinese trading company to a U.S. importer. After a Chinese exporter in Shanghai has shipped the goods, it draws a draft against the issuing bank (Citibank) and presents it, along with the required documents, to its own bank, the Bank of China. The Bank of China, in turn, forwards the bank draft and attached documents to Citibank in New York; Citibank pays the draft upon receiving evidence that all conditions set forth in the L/C have been met.

Because there are several types of L/Cs, each export contract must specify which type should be used. Most L/Cs issued in connection with commercial transactions are **documentary**—that is, the exporter must submit, together with the draft, any necessary invoices and other documents such as the customs invoice, certificate of commodity inspection, packing list, and certificate of country of origin. L/Cs without the requirement for presentation of documents are called **clean L/Cs.** A clean L/C may be used for overseas bank guarantees,

Exhibit 14.1   Process of Using Letter of Credit (L/C)

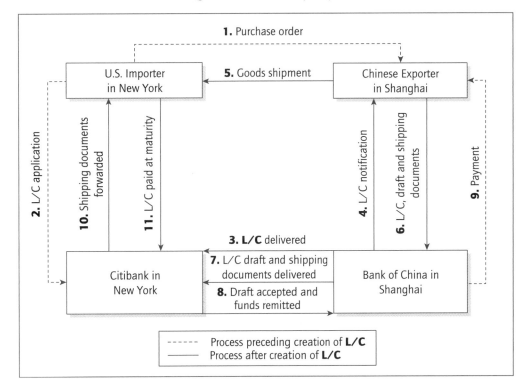

escrow arrangements, and security purchases. However, it is rarely used in import/export business.

The letter of credit can be revocable or irrevocable. A **revocable** L/C is a means of arranging payment, but it does not carry a guarantee. It can be revoked, without notice, at any time up to the time a draft is presented to the issuing bank. An **irrevocable** L/C, in contrast, cannot be revoked without the specific permission of all parties concerned, including the exporter. Most credits between unrelated parties are irrevocable.

A letter of credit can also be confirmed or unconfirmed. A **confirmed** L/C is issued by one bank and confirmed by another, obligating both banks to honor any drafts drawn in compliance. An **unconfirmed** L/C is the obligation of only the issuing bank. Naturally, an exporter will prefer an irrevocable letter of credit by the importer's bank with confirmation by another (domestic or foreign) bank. In this way, the exporter needs to look no further than a bank in its own country for compliance with terms of the letter of credit. For example, if the Bank of China had confirmed the letter of credit issued by Citibank, and Citibank, for whatever reason, failed to honor its irrevocable L/C, a Chinese exporter could collect its accounts receivable from the Bank of China.

There are also special types of L/Cs that are used for specific purposes of an exporter. A **transferable** L/C is one under which the beneficiary has the right to instruct the paying bank to make the credit available to one or more secondary beneficiaries. No L/C is transferable unless specifically authorized in the letter of credit; moreover, it can be transferred only once. The stipulated documents are transferred along with the L/C. In effect, the exporter is the intermediary in a transferable credit and usually has the credit transferred to one or more of its own suppliers. When the credit is transferred, the exporter is actually using the creditworthiness of the opening bank, thus avoiding having to borrow or use its own funds to buy the goods from its own suppliers.

A **back-to-back** L/C exists where the exporter, as beneficiary of the first L/C, offers its credit as security to finance the opening of a second credit in favor of the exporter's own supplier of the goods needed for shipment under the first or original credit from the advising bank. The bank that issues a back-to-back L/C not only assumes the exporter's risk but also the risk of the bank issuing the primary L/C. If the exporter is unable to produce documents or the documents contain discrepancies, the bank issuing the back-to-back L/C may be unable to obtain payment under the credit because the importer is not obligated to accept discrepant documents of the ultimate supplier under the back-to-back L/C. Thus, many banks are reluctant to issue this type of L/C.

A **revolving** L/C exists where the tenor (maturity) or amount of the L/C is automatically renewed pursuant to its terms and conditions. An L/C with a revolving maturity may be either cumulative or noncumulative. When cumulative, any amount not utilized during a given period may be applied or added to the subsequent period. If noncumulative, any unused amount is simply no longer available. If a revolving L/C is used, it must be explicitly stipulated in the export contract.

Documentary Collection

The **documentary collection** is a payment mechanism that allows exporters to retain ownership of the goods until they receive payment or are reasonably certain that they will receive it. In a documentary collection, the bank, acting as the exporter's agent, regulates the timing and sequence of the exchange of goods for value by holding the title documents until the importer either pays the draft—termed **documents against payment** (D/P)—or accepts the obligation to do so—termed **documents against acceptance** (D/A). The introduction of D/P and D/A is detailed in the "Uniform Rules for Collections" enacted by the International Chamber of Commerce (ICC).

The two principal control documents in a documentary collection are a draft and a bill of lading (B/L). The *draft* is written by the drawer (exporter) to the drawee (importer) and requires payment of a fixed amount at a specific or determinable date to the payee (usually the exporter himself). A draft is a negotiable instrument that normally requires physical presentation as a condition for payment. A draft may be either a *sight draft* (i.e., payable upon presentation) or a *time draft* (i.e., payable at a determinable future date as specified in the draft). As introduced in Chapter 10, *bill of lading* is the document of title (property rights of the shipped products), the document for shipment (usually ocean transportation), and the carrier's receipt for the goods being shipped. Exhibits 14.2 and 14.3 present a step-by-step procedural flow for D/P and D/A, respectively.

A sight draft is commonly used for D/P payment. Nevertheless, for export sales that take several months in ocean transportation, exporters and importers may agree to use D/P at 30, 60, 90, or 180 days, and the like. Bear in mind that sight drafts are not always paid exactly at presentation, nor are time drafts always paid at maturity. Firms can get bank statistics on the promptness of sight and time draft payments, by country, from bank publications such as Chase Manhattan's Collection Experience Bulletin.

In practice, D/A at sight is seldom used. D/A is usually accompanied with a time draft ranging from 30 days up to perhaps two years, which is why time draft-based collections are also viewed as an important commercial or corporate financing approach that is granted by the exporter to the importer. The flip side of this method is the high risk of receivable collection for the exporter. D/A is a riskier collection method than D/P because the importer can claim the title of

Exhibit 14.2   Documents Against Payment (D/P) Flow

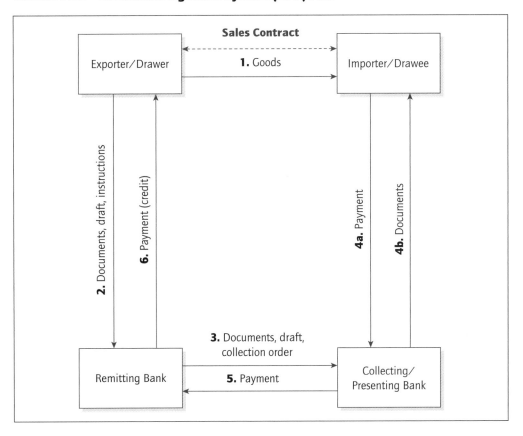

Exhibit 14.3   Documents Against Acceptance (D/A) Flow

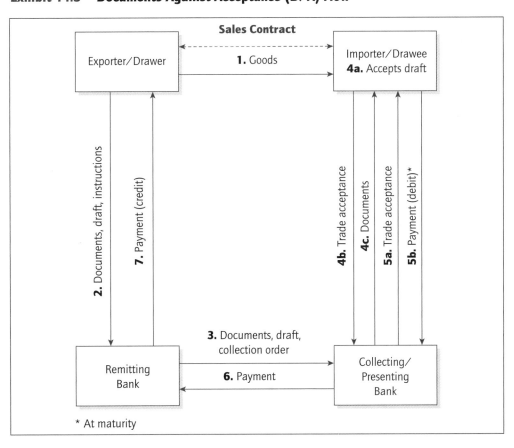

goods under the "promise" of payment rather than actual payment. For this reason, most bad debts accumulated in international trade have resulted from transactions that used D/A as terms of payment.

Open Account

Open account selling involves shipping goods first and billing the importer later. The credit terms are arranged between the importer and the exporter, but the exporter has little evidence of the importer's obligation to pay a certain amount at a certain date. Sales on open account, therefore, are made only to a foreign affiliate or to a customer with which the exporter has a long history of favorable business dealings. However, open account sales have greatly expanded because of the major increase in international trade, more accurate credit information about importers, and the greater familiarity with exporting in general. The benefits include greater flexibility (no specific payment dates are set) and lower costs, including fewer bank charges than with other methods of payment. As with shipping on consignment, the possibility of currency controls is an important factor because of the low priority in allocating foreign exchange normally accorded this type of transaction.

Means of Payment Remittance

Remittance can be made by several means. In documentary L/Cs or collections, the primary means of remittance is by airmail payment order, in which an instruction is mailed from an importer's bank to an exporter's bank. These banks may also use Telex/SWIFT (Society for Worldwide Information and Funds Transfer) capabilities to settle the payment. For cash in advance or open account terms, the importers/buyers may use company check, bank draft, or bank money order to remit the payment. Company check is also widely used for goods purchased on cash with order (CWO) or cash on delivery (COD). Today, interbank e-mail systems have been extensively applied in lieu of airmail payment orders between cross-border banks (especially between those in developed countries).

Export Financing

Export financing is important because many export projects have large start-up costs. External sources of export financing are twofold: private sources and governmental sources. Of private sources, the institutions that provide trade financing include commercial banks, export finance companies, factoring houses, forfait houses, international leasing companies, in-house finance companies, and private insurance companies. These sources offer different types of financing for exporters.

Private Sources

Bank Financing. Commercial bank financing for foreign trade business includes bank guarantees, bank lines of credit, and buyer credit. A **bank guarantee** is a financial instrument that guarantees a specified sum of payment in the event of nonperformance by an exporter or by a foreign importer in the event of a payment default for goods purchased from a foreign supplier. Apart from regular bank guarantees, there are three other types of guarantees involved with commercial banks. These include (a) the *loan guarantee,* which grants a loan conditional on security provided by the borrower; (b) a *distraint guarantee,* which helps a debtor recover control over its seized assets; and (c) a *bill of lading guarantee,* which ensures that the carrier will hand over the goods to the consignee when individual bills of lading are lost.

Bank line of credit is a sum of money allocated to an exporter by a bank or banks that the exporter can draw from to finance its export business. This could also be structured to finance an export transaction from the foreign customer's side. In effect, the bank line of credit allows the exporter to extend competitive credit terms to foreign customers. **Buyer credit** exists where one or more financial institutions in an exporter's country extend credit to a foreign customer of the exporter. Although most buyer credit financing is arranged to finance capital equipment purchases, other goods with payment terms of up to one year can be financed by buyer credits. Buyer credits are normally arranged under an export credit insurance program.

Export Factoring and Forfaiting. Export factoring is particularly suited for small and medium-sized exporters. This technique proceeds through factoring houses. **Factoring houses** not only provide financing but can perform credit investigations, guarantee commercial and political risks, assume collection responsibilities, and finance accounts receivable. In addition, these houses can perform such services as letters of credit, term loans, marketing assistance, and all other necessary services a small to medium-sized exporter cannot afford to handle. Often, a factoring house's service charges are quoted on a commission basis. Commissions can range anywhere from 1% to 3% of total transaction value.

Although factoring is a well-known export financing technique in the United States, forfaiting has been widely used for export financing in Europe. **Forfaiting,** a term derived from the French term *a forfeit,* is a transaction in which an exporter transfers responsibility of commercial and political risks for the collection of a trade-related debt to a forfaiter (often a financial institution), and in turn receives immediate cash after the deduction of its interest charge (the discount). The forfait market consists of a primary and secondary market. The primary market consists of banks and forfait houses that buy properly executed and documented debt obligations directly from exporters. The secondary market consists of holders of these forfait debt obligations trading them among themselves.

In general, a forfait financing transaction involves at least four parties to the transaction: an exporter, the forfaiter, the importer, and the importer's guarantor. The financial instruments in forfaiting are usually time drafts or bills of exchange and promissory notes. Forfaiting is used to finance the export of capital equipment where transactions are usually medium term (i.e., three to eight years) at fixed-rate financing. The discount used by the forfaiter is based on its cost of funds plus a premium, which can range anywhere from 0.5% to 5% depending on the country of importation and level of risks involved.

Banker's Acceptance. The banker's acceptance (BA) is a time draft drawn on and accepted by banks. It is a two-armed instrument with one branch in financing and the other in investment. The bank first creates the BA by stamping "accepted" on the face of a draft presented by its customer (i.e., the drawer), then discounts the BA (i.e., it pays the drawer a sum less than the face value of the draft), followed by selling (rediscounting) the BA to an investor in the acceptance market. At maturity the bank settles the BA when it debits the drawer for the full amount of the BA and pays the full value to the investor who presents it. By definition, a BA is a time draft (30, 60, 90, or up to 180 days after sight or date) drawn on and accepted by a bank. The fee charged by the accepting bank varies depending on the maturity of the draft as well as the creditworthiness of the borrower. The BA is mainly used for the export trade in raw materials, components, and general commodity financing. A deep secondary market for BA combined with the lack of reserve requirements often enables the bank to obtain funding for eligible transactions at a cost significantly lower than alternative sources.

Corporate Guarantee. A corporate guarantee is where one company undertakes to pay if the principal debtor does not pay a matured debt obligation to a creditor. Typically in global business, creditors will ask the corporate or parent company to guarantee an obligation of one or more of its overseas subsidiaries or offshore affiliates that the creditor may consider not creditworthy for the export-related financing or credit limit. Because the parent company is often located outside of the exporting country, it is important to state in the financing contract by which country's law the guarantee will be governed.

Governmental Sources

Export–Import Bank Financing. Many countries have put in place export–import financing programs that are similar in most respects to programs of the Export–Import Bank of the United States (Eximbank). Japan's Eximbank, for instance, is an independent governmental financial institution providing yen financing for exports, imports, and overseas investments. Exports are supported by parallel lending with these banks in the form of yen loans for major borrowing with medium to long terms. South Korea Eximbank provides direct loans to both foreign and domestic firms. The loans are low cost with medium- to long-term financing arranged in conjunction with larger commercial banks throughout the world. Their purpose is to encourage the export of capital goods and services, overseas investment, and major resource development. South Korea's Eximbank offers such services as direct lending to both suppliers and buyers, relending facilities to foreign financial institutions, and the issuance of guarantees and export insurance.

In the United States, the primary function of its Eximbank is to give U.S. exporters the necessary financial backing to compete in other countries. Today this is done through a variety of different export financing and guarantee programs (e.g., direct loans, discount loans, guarantees, and export credit insurance) to meet specific needs. All are designed to be in direct support of U.S. exports, whether the eventual recipient of the loans or guarantees are foreign or domestic firms. Generally, export-import banks do not compete with private sources of export financing. Their main purpose is to step in where private credit is not available in sufficiently large amounts at low rates or long terms, to allow home-country exporters to compete in a foreign market.

Foreign Credit Insurance. Many industrialized and developing countries have set up foreign credit insurance or guarantee programs to assist their exporting companies. Even branches of foreign companies located in these countries are often eligible for assistance. These programs are usually run by and dependent on the government. In the United States, such insurance programs are offered by both Eximbank and the Foreign Credit Insurance Association. In Canada, these services are provided by Export Credits Insurance Corporation (ECIC). In Asia, Japan's International Trade Bureau (Export Insurance Section), Hong Kong's Export Credit Insurance Corporation, India's Export Credit & Guarantee Corporation Ltd, and Taiwan's Central Trust of China all oversee and offer these programs. In Latin America, similar programs can be found (e.g., in Compania Argentina de Seguros de Credito in Argentina and Instituto de Resseguros do

Brasil in Brazil). Europe has an even longer history in providing export credit insurance. Les Assurances du Credit in Belgium, Export Credit Council in Denmark, Export Guarantee Board in Finland, Compagnie Francaise D'Assurance pour le Commerce Exterieur in France, Hermes Kreditversicherungs in Germany, and Instituto Nazionale delle Assicurazioni in Italy, for example, are all leading institutions offering foreign credit insurance and backed by their respective governments.

Because the services provided by these institutions are basically similar, let us use the case of the United Kingdom to illustrate the process and scope of these services. In the United Kingdom, commercial credit and political risks connected with exports can be insured with the Export Credits Guarantee Department (ECGD), a separate department of the British government. Even though ECGD is an arm of the British government, it is commercially independent. Risks covered by ECGD include commercial credit and political risk. More specifically, commercial credit risks include insolvency of the buyer, the buyer's failure to pay within six months of due date for goods already accepted, and the buyer's failure to accept goods that have been shipped (provided this non-acceptance was not caused by an action or noncompliance on the part of the exporter). Political risks covered by ECGD include government action that blocks payment to the exporter, cancellation of a valid import license in the buyer's country, war or any cause of loss not within the control of the exporter or the buyer, or cancellation of an export license or imposition of new licensing restrictions. Generally, ECGD covers 95% of any loss resulting from political risk and 90% of the loss arising from most commercial risks.

Interim Summary

1. There are a number of accepted payment forms in international trade, ranging from cash in advance, to letter of credit (L/C), to documentary collection (e.g., D/P and D/A), to open account terms. The L/C method is particularly desirable for the exporter because it eliminates credit risk, reduces uncertainty, and facilitates financing, whereas it ascertains the quality and quantity of a purchase for the importer.

2. Documentary collection is a riskier payment form than L/C for the exporter. In this system, a draft is delivered either upon receipt of goods or with a time-based maturity clause. The International Chamber of Commerce details uniform rules for documentary collection.

3. There are various means of acquiring bank financing. For smaller exporters, factoring, whereby a financing house fronts money for transactions on a commission basis, is a good choice. Capital may also be acquired from governmental sources, which offer many of the same services as private banks but are specifically intended to aid traders from their home country.

FINANCING FOR GLOBAL BUSINESS

Compared with financing for foreign trade activities, financing for MNEs' global productions, investments, and operations involves more choices and is more complex. Broadly, the sources of financing for global investments and operations include intercompany financing, equity financing, debt financing, and local currency financing (see Exhibit 14.4).

Exhibit 14.4   Sources of Financing for Global Operations

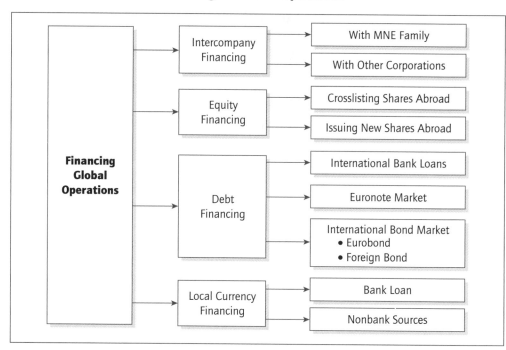

Intercompany Financing

Intercompany financing from the parent company or sister subsidiaries is a common means of financing for overseas subsidiaries or affiliates, which is done in the following ways:

- Allowing the subsidiary to keep a higher level of retained earnings
- Obtaining financing from the parent company in the form of equity, loans, trade credit (e.g., longer maturity or extension for accounts payable), or borrowing with a parent guarantee
- Arranging trade credit from other subsidiaries to this affiliate

Parent loans are sometimes preferable to parent equity financing by MNEs, for several reasons. First, intercompany loan payments may be more readily remittable in the future than dividends. Second, loan interest reduces the tax burden. A subsidiary borrowing these loans will pay lower local corporate income tax after deducting interest expenses from its total taxable income. Third, the loan provided to the parent or a sister subsidiary and the loan received from the parent or another subsidiary are eliminated on consolidation. Cash has moved within the corporation without affecting the consolidated debt or equity accounts. Finally, short-term intercompany loans may be used to stabilize the subsidiary's working capital structure, and long-term intercompany loans may be used to reduce its dependence on external banks. **Working capital** is the net position whereby a firm's current liability is subtracted from its current assets.

Equity Financing

Financing through equity markets can be realized in an MNE's home country, a foreign affiliate's host country, or a third country. An MNE's equity financing can take the form of either crosslisting shares abroad or selling new shares to foreign investors. Many U.S.-based MNEs, for instance, have secured listing of their companies on foreign stock exchanges.

Crosslisting an MNE's shares on foreign stock exchanges may provide many benefits. For example, it may

- Improve the liquidity of existing shares by making it easier for foreign shareholders to trade in their home markets and currencies
- Increase the share price by overcoming mispricing in a segmented, illiquid home capital market
- Increase the firm's visibility and political acceptance to its customers, suppliers, creditors, and host governments
- Create a secondary market for shares that can be used to compensate local management and employees in foreign affiliates[1]

Crosslisting is frequently accompanied by depository receipts. In the United States, foreign shares are usually traded through **American depository receipts** (or **ADRs**). These are negotiable certificates issued by a U.S. bank in the United States to represent the underlying shares of stock, which are held in trust at a foreign custodian bank. ADRs are sold, registered, and transferred in the United States in the same manner as any share of stock. Because ADRs can be exchanged for the underlying foreign shares, or vice versa, arbitrage keeps foreign and U.S. prices of any given share the same. To crosslist stocks abroad, an MNE must be committed to full disclosure of operating results and balance sheets. Today, the major liquid markets are London, New York (NYSE and NASDAQ), Tokyo, Frankfurt, and Paris. To decide where to crosslist, an MNE should consider its ownership expansion objectives, the size of the target stock market, the sophistication of market-making activities, and host-governmental regulations.

An alternative to seeking international ownership through parent listings is the issuance of equity by local subsidiaries. Some countries require levels of minority or even majority ownership by local nationals. Firms typically have difficulty in achieving a broad-based ownership of their subsidiaries in the very thin capital markets of most developing countries. U.S. MNEs, in particular, prefer the flexibility of operations that sole ownership affords. Firms that are technology based are concerned with the loss of control over proprietary technology that taking on an equity partner or partners might portend. MNEs of other countries, however, sometimes want to take on local equity, especially in their U.S. subsidiaries, thereby taking advantage of the remarkably broad and sophisticated U.S. equity market. Exhibit 14.5 illustrates what foreign MNEs must know when selling stocks in the United States, the largest capital market in the world.

Debt Financing

Chapter 9 introduced international capital markets, which are in fact the major source of MNEs' debt financing. Debt financing for global operations can be made through international bank loans, the Euronote market, and the international bond market. International bank loans are often sourced in the **Eurocurrency markets**—that is, in countries not using the denomination currency (e.g., a Japanese firm may obtain yen loans from banks in the United States and Europe). As such, international bank loans are often called **Eurocredits**. Because of the large size of these loans, the lending banks usually form a syndicate to diversify their risk. The basic borrowing interest rate for Eurocurrency loans has long been tied to the London Interbank Offered Rate (LIBOR), which is the deposit rate applicable to interbank loans within London.

Exhibit 14.5 Tapping Wall Street: Three Stages for Non-U.S. MNEs to Be Traded in the United States

- *Set up an ADR program.* With ADRs (American depository receipts), U.S. depository banks maintain custody of deposited foreign securities at their overseas branches and issue receipts as proof of ownership. The receipt is transferable in the United States. Registration is made under either the Securities Act of 1933 or the Securities Exchange Act of 1934, or both.

- *Listing.* Some MNEs permit their ADRs to be traded in the pink sheets, which list quotes for ADRs of nonlisted companies. Others are listed on the NASDAQ or on an exchange from the outset. Firms listing on the NYSE or NASDAQ face the same legal requirements. NYSE listings have two separate standards for domestic and foreign entities, with the latter facing more stringent requirements.

- *Public offerings.* In a public offering, the foreign firm turns over its ordinary shares to its depository bank. The depository bank then issues ADRs, and it delivers them to the underwriters for resale and distribution.

The **Euronote market** is the collective term used to describe short- to medium-term debt instruments sourced in the Eurocurrency markets. The Euronote is generally a less expensive source of short-term funds than syndicated loans, because the notes are placed directly with the investor public. Euronotes can be *underwritten* or *nonunderwritten.* In an underwritten Euronote, there are normally one to three lead banks that organize a group of participating banks to take shares of the total commitment. The lead and participating banks stand ready to buy the borrower's notes in the event the notes could not be placed in the market at previously guaranteed rates. The nonunderwritten Euronotes include Euro-Commercial Paper (ECP) and Euro-Medium-Term Notes (EMTNs). ECP is a short-term debt obligation of a corporation or bank. Maturity is typically one, three, and six months, while EMTNs' typical maturity ranges from as short as nine months to a maximum of 10 years.

The international bond market comprises Eurobonds and foreign bonds. A **Eurobond** is underwritten by an international syndicate of banks and other securities firms and is sold exclusively in countries other than the country in whose currency the issue is denominated (e.g., a bond issued by a Japanese firm residing in Tokyo, denominated in Japanese yen but sold to investors in Europe and the United States). Most Eurobonds use the straight fixed rate, with a fixed coupon, set maturity date, and full principal repayment upon final maturity. Recently, convertible Eurobonds have emerged. These bonds resemble the straight fixed-rate issue in practically all price and payment characteristics, with the added feature that they are convertible to stock prior to maturity at a specified price per share. A **foreign bond** is underwritten by a syndicate composed of members from a single country, sold principally within that country, and denominated in the currency of that country (a Japanese firm issued corporate bonds in U.S. dollars and sold to U.S. investors by U.S. banks). Foreign bonds sold in the United States are also known as **Yankee bonds**, those sold in Japan as **Samurai bonds**, and those sold in the United Kingdom as **Bulldogs.**

Local Currency Financing

The preceding description focused on corporate-level financing. Local currency financing in a host country opens an avenue for subsidiary financing. Access to various local financial markets in which an MNE operates can be advantageous in lowering the overall cost of capital and reducing financial risks. Thus, international managers should evaluate local financing choices as well as opportunities for investing the firm's surplus funds.

Financing in a host country generally includes two sources: bank loans and nonbank sources. *Bank loans* contain overdrafts, discounting, and loans. In countries other than the United States, banks tend to lend through overdrafts. An **overdraft** is a line of credit against which drafts (checks) can be drawn (written) up to a specified maximum amount. **Discounting** is a short-term financing technique by which a local bank discounts a firm's trade bills. These bills can often be rediscounted with the central bank. Discounting is particularly popular in Europe and Latin America because, according to the commercial laws in these countries (i.e., Code Napoleon in Europe), the claim of the bill holder is independent of the claim represented by the underlying transaction, which makes the bill easily negotiable. Loans can be term loans, lines of credit, or revolving credit agreements. **Term loans** are straight loans that are made for a fixed period of time and repaid in a single lump sum. Term loans are relatively expensive, so frequent borrowers may instead seek a line of credit. A line of credit, which is usually good for one year with renewals renegotiated every year, allows the company to borrow up to a stated maximum amount from the bank. Similar to a line of credit, a revolving credit agreement permits the company to extend credit up to the stated maximum. The difference is that under this agreement the bank is legally committed to providing credit up to the specified maximum. The company has to pay interest on its outstanding borrowing plus a commitment fee on the unused portion of the credit line.

Nonbank sources of funds include commercial paper, factoring (see the preceding section), and local bond or equity markets and parallel loans with a foreign company. Stanley Works, the $1.9 billion U.S. manufacturer of hand and power tools, has seven joint ventures in Japan. Its local financing is made via listing on the Tokyo Exchange assisted by Nikko Securities Co. Goldman Sachs also assists Stanley to be listed in Hong Kong and Singapore, where the company operates three manufacturing plants and several distribution centers. A **parallel loan** (also known as a back-to-back loan) involves an exchange of funds between firms in different countries, with the exchange reversed at a later date. For example, a U.S. MNE's subsidiary in Brazil may need Brazilian reals while a Brazilian company's subsidiary in the United States may need dollars. The Brazilian firm can lend reals to the U.S.-owned subsidiary in Brazil while it borrows an equivalent amount of dollars from the U.S. parent in the United States.

Financing Decisions

Several considerations affect the financing decisions and choices for MNEs. These considerations include minimizing taxes, managing currency risk and political risk, and exploiting financial market distortions to raise money at below-market rates.

Financing choices designed to minimize corporate taxes are often concerned with selecting the tax-minimizing currency, jurisdiction, and vehicle for issue and selecting the tax-minimizing mode of internal transfer of currency or profit. Many MNEs prefer parent loans rather than parent investment for funding subsidiaries because interest payments on debt are tax deductible but dividends are not. Nevertheless, the debt-to-equity ratio of subsidiaries must be maintained within a reasonable limit. This is necessary to fulfill operating needs as well as local government requirements in certain countries.

In general, an MNE should seek financing in such a way that it balances the currency risks inherent in the operation. For instance, firms may reduce the risk of currency inconvertibility by appropriate interaffiliate financing. Parent funds may be invested as debt rather than as equity. Back-to-back loans may be arranged, and as much local financing as possible may be sought. To reduce political risk, financing may be sought directly from the host and other governments, international development agencies, and overseas banks. When an MNE's offshore projects are financed by these government-based financial institutions, the firm may benefit from both financing and networking. Kennecott, for example, used this approach to finance its copper mine project in Chile.

Given the uncertainty in international financial markets, MNEs should ensure that their financing is not dependent on any one single source. Diversity of financing sources can help the MNE gain more from differences between capital markets across nations.[2] These differences are largely attributable to government credit and capital controls, which is why the cost of international borrowing is likely to be lower than that of domestic funding. Novo, a Danish MNE that produces industrial enzymes and pharmaceuticals, for example, has crosslisted in both the Copenhagen Stock Exchange and the NYSE and has used a multitude of other financing tools such as Eurobonds, Euronotes, local currency loans, and intercompany financing. This strategy enables Novo to escape the shackles of its segmented national capital market and make the company more visible to foreign investors. Novo eventually reaped the full benefit of dramatic share price increase by selling a directed equity issue in the United States.

Interim Summary

1. MNEs have a broad range of choices in financing their global investment projects, including intercompany financing, equity financing, debt financing, and local currency financing. These choices are often more complex than export financing.

2. Equity financing involves either crosslisting shares on foreign exchanges or selling new shares to foreign investors. Many U.S. MNEs finance their global operations through crosslisting their shares abroad. Three stages for non-U.S. MNEs to be traded on Wall Street include (a) setting up an ADR program, (b) listing, and (c) public offerings.

3. Debt financing is made through international bank loans, the Euronote market, and the international bond market. Subsidiaries can also obtain local currency financing through local banks or local bond or equity markets.

MANAGING FOREIGN EXCHANGE RISK AND EXPOSURE

Foreign Exchange Risk and Exposure

Exchange risk is a critical issue in international business. Any company that operates in more than one nation or currency area or has cash flows across nations will face foreign exchange risk and foreign exchange exposure. Foreign exchange risk and exposure are two different concepts. **Foreign exchange risk** concerns the variance of the domestic-currency value of an asset, liability, or operating income that is attributable to unanticipated changes in exchange rates.[3] This definition implies that foreign exchange risk is not the unpredictability of foreign exchange rates themselves but rather the uncertainty of values of a firm's assets, liabilities, or operating incomes owing to uncertainty in exchange rates. Therefore, volatility in exchange rates is responsible for exchange-rate risk only if it translates into volatility in real values of assets, liabilities, or operating incomes. This makes foreign exchange risk dependent on foreign exchange exposure. A firm may not face foreign exchange risks unless it is "exposed" to foreign exchange fluctuations. For example, General Electric (GE) and Hitachi both invest and operate in Mexico. Unlike Hitachi, which imports many parts for its production plants in Mexico, GE has built up its own supply base within Mexico. In this case, GE faces lower foreign exchange risks than Hitachi because GE is not exposed to fluctuations of the Mexican peso in the process of supply procurement.

Foreign exchange exposure refers to the sensitivity of changes in the real domestic-currency value of assets, liabilities, or operating incomes to unanticipated changes in exchange rates.[4] This implies that exposure involves the extent to which the home currency value of assets, liabilities, or incomes is changed by exchange rate variances. The "real" domestic currency value means the value that has been adjusted by the nation's inflation. Domestic-currency-denominated assets can be exposed to exchange rates if, for example, unanticipated depreciation of the country's currency causes its central bank to increase interest rates.

Foreign exchange risk is a positive function of both foreign exchange exposure and the variance of unanticipated changes in exchange rates. Uncertainty of exchange rates does not mean foreign exchange risk for items that are not exposed. Similarly, exposure on its own does not mean foreign exchange risk if exchange rates are perfectly predictable. The levels of foreign exchange risk and exposure often differ between asset and liability items and operating income. Because current asset and current liability items, especially accounts receivable and payable, have fixed face value and are short-term oriented, they are extremely sensitive to the uncertainty of foreign exchange rates. Unlike these asset or liability items, operating incomes do not have fixed face values. Exposure of operating incomes depends not only on unexpected changes of exchange rates but also on such factors as the elasticity of demand for imports or exports, the fraction of input prices that depend on exchange rates, and the flexibility of production to respond to market demand changes induced by exchange rate movements.

Transaction and Economic Exposures

Because foreign exchange risk is determined by foreign exchange exposure (along with the uncertainty of foreign exchange rates), managers must analyze and monitor foreign exchange exposure. MNEs encounter three types of foreign exchange exposure:

- Transaction exposure
- Economic (or operating) exposure
- Translation (or accounting) exposure (discussed in Chapter 15)

Transaction exposure concerns how changes in exchange rates affect the value, in home currency terms, of anticipated cash flows denominated in foreign currency relating to transactions already entered into. It arises when commitments in foreign currency are subject to settlements of exchange rate gains and losses owing to changes in currency rates. A change in exchange rates between the home or functional currency and the currency in which a transaction is denominated increases or decreases the expected amount of the functional or reporting currency cash flow on settlement of the transaction. For example, a U.S. exporter expects to receive a payment of £200,000 in two months after it ships the products to the importer in London. With a current spot rate of £1 = $1.5, this export is worth $300,000. Two months later, however, the actual spot rate changes to £1 = $1.3, which reduces the actual dollar value to $260,000. This U.S. exporter thus will suffer a $40,000 foreign exchange loss if it does not take steps to hedge its foreign exchange exposure and risk.

Transactions that give rise to foreign exchange exposure include the following:

- Purchasing or selling on credit goods and services whose prices are stated in foreign currencies (thus recorded as accounts payable or accounts receivable)
- Borrowing or depositing funds denominated in foreign currencies (reflected in foreign debt and credit)
- Transacting a foreign-exchange contract
- Various transactions denominated in foreign exchange

Accordingly, transaction exposure can be a variety of foreign-currency-denominated assets (export receivables or bank deposits), liabilities (accounts payable or loans), revenues (expected future sales), expenses (expected purchase of goods), or income (dividends).

Economic exposure, also called operating exposure, measures the change in the present value of the firm resulting from any change in the future operating cash flows caused by an unexpected change in exchange rates and macroeconomic factors. The change in value depends on the effect of the exchange rate change on future sales volume, prices, or costs. Unlike **translation exposure**, which refers to the potential for accounting-derived changes in owners' equity to occur because of the need to consolidate foreign currency financial statements, both transaction exposure and economic exposure exist because of unexpected changes in future cash flows. In contrast to transaction exposure, which is concerned with preexisting cash flows that will occur in the near future, economic exposure emphasizes expected future cash flows that are potentially affected by unanticipated changes of exchange rates and macroeconomic conditions (e.g., unexpected changes in interest rates and inflation rates). Thus, economic exposure derives largely from economic analysis, which requires integrated strategies in finance, marketing, outsourcing, and production.

An MNE's economic exposure is determined by several economic factors. First, it is influenced *by pricing flexibility* (i.e., a firm's ability to raise its foreign currency selling price sufficiently to preserve its home currency profit margin in the case of foreign currency depreciation).[5] This price flexibility depends mainly on price elasticity of demand, which is in turn determined by the level of competition in the market and the degree of product differentiation provided by the firm. For example, Motorola's subsidiaries in Indonesia and Thailand successfully maintained their U.S. dollar gross profit margin for producing and selling cellular phones in these markets during the Asian financial crisis because of a local price increase, which was made possible by the high quality and superior innovation of their products. Similarly, with about 45% of the world's liquid-crystal-display market, Japan's Sharp Inc. increased its export price in 1995 by 5% in countries where it did not face real competition.

Second, economic exposure is influenced *by production/outsourcing flexibility*— that is, the ability to shift production and outsourcing of inputs among different nations. MNEs with worldwide production systems can cope with currency changes by increasing production in a nation whose currency has undergone a real devaluation and decreasing production in a nation whose currency has revalued in real terms. For example, to cope with *endaka* (which means the strong Japanese yen period), many Japanese MNEs used the yen's strength to quickly and inexpensively set up integrated manufacturing bases in Asian countries with currencies pegged to the dollar. In addition, their earlier investments in the United States, Mexico, and Europe allowed them to play both sides of the yen–dollar swings, using cheaper dollar-denominated parts and materials to offset higher yen-related costs. For instance, 75% of the parts for the Toyota Camry built in Georgetown, Kentucky, were from the United States, up from 60% when Toyota started manufacturing the car there in 1988. The Honda Accord built in Marysville, Ohio, had local content rise from 70% before 1993 to about 85% in 1995.

Finally, economic exposure is influenced *by an MNE's localization structure and export orientation.* The negative impact of host-country (local) currency devaluation will be lower if an MNE's localization of production inputs there is higher. The harmful effect of host-country currency depreciation is reduced in this situation because this depreciation lowers the subsidiary's dollar production costs, particularly those attributable to local inputs. In contrast, the higher the import content of production inputs, the less dollar production costs will decline. An MNE using its foreign subsidiary as an export platform will benefit from a host-country currency depreciation. Thus, exporting products made of localized supplies is preferable to targeting a local market using local supplies, as far as risk minimization is concerned. For risk minimization, targeting a local market using local supplies is in turn better than targeting a local market but using imported supplies. Home currency depreciation also affects the operations of companies that focus on the home market using home supplies. This is because home currency depreciation reduces the competitive threat from foreign companies that may have a cost-leadership advantage. Exhibit 14.6 highlights major approaches that manage transaction exposure and economic exposure, respectively, which are further detailed below.

Managing Transaction Exposure

Hedging With Financial Instruments

Forward Market. Forward markets are available in most major currencies of the world. The period of forward contract coverage could extend to more than five years. Exhibit 14.7 shows how hedging via a forward contract works.

By the forward mechanism in this example, the UK exporter's accounts receivable is hedged, no matter what happens to the Canadian dollar/sterling spot and forward rates over the next two months. Once contracted, the forward is irrevocably fixed. In general, the expected cost of hedging is equal to the risk premium in the forward exchange rate plus forward transaction costs. The level of risk premium is reflected in the difference between the spot rate and the forward rate. The level of transaction cost is reflected in the spread on the particular forward rate.

Exhibit 14.6   Framework of Managing Foreign Exchange Exposure

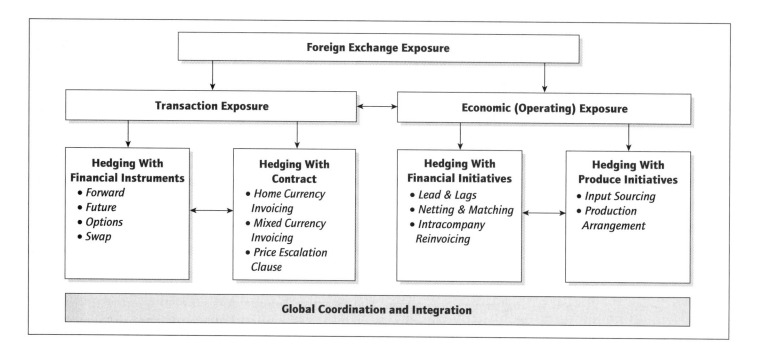

Exhibit 14.7   Forward Hedging Example

Contract data	
Exporter	United Kingdom exporter
Importer	Canadian importer
Contract date	January 1, 2001
Expected payment date	March 1, 2001
Invoice amount	C$1 million
Exchange rate (C$/£) quotes on January 1, 2001	
Spot rate	2.2765–2.2775
1 month forward/future	2.2730–2.2751
2 months forward/future	2.2705–2.2728
3 months forward/future	2.2681–2.2705
Mechanism of forward contract	
January 1, 2001	UK exporter sells C$1 million two-month forward at 2.2728 in the forward market (a bank handling foreign exchange transactions).
March 1, 2001	UK exporter receives C$1 million from Canadian importer, delivers C$1 million to the bank, and in return receives £439,986 at C$2.2728 per pound sterling.

Since the forward rate is fixed in a completed forward contract, it is important for financial managers to accurately forecast currency appreciation or depreciation. The UK exporter sells the forward under the assumption that the Canadian dollar will depreciate or sterling will appreciate around the settlement date. If the realized spot rate actually moves in an opposite direction, this exporter will lose foreign exchange gains that it would otherwise have obtained.

Futures Market. Hedging via the futures market shares major principles with forward hedging. The difference is that in the forward market all the payment is made at the end, whereas with the futures market some of the payment is made through the margin account before the end. In the preceding example, the expected two-month future spot rate is 2.2728. If it turns out at the maturity date of the futures contracts that the actual spot rate is 2.1728, then the UK exporter will find it has contributed £20,250 to its margin/future account. It will, of course, receive £460,236 (C$1 million/2.1728) at the due date, rather than the £439,986 that would have been received with a forward contract. However, after compensating for its contribution in the margin account, the UK exporter will be receiving £439,986, the same as if the Canadian dollar had been sold on the forward market. On the other hand, if the actual spot rate ends up at 2.3728, then the UK exporter will find it has gained £18,543 in its margin account. With this actual spot rate, it will receive £421,443. After adding its gains from the margin account, it will still receive £439,986. Thus we find that no matter what happens to the spot rate, the UK exporter still receives £439,986 from its C$1 million. In practice, the addition or subtraction to the margin account is done on a daily basis and is called *marking-to-market.* Because interest rates vary over time, it is unlikely that the amount in the margin account at the maturity of the futures contract will bring the eventual price of C$1 million to exactly £439,986. If interest rates are low when the margin account has a large amount in it, it is possible that slightly less than £439,986 is received. This is the marking-to-market risk of futures contracts.

Options Market. In the options market, a **call option** is an option to purchase a stated number of units of the underlying foreign currency at a specific price per unit during a specific period of time. Alternatively, a **put option** is an option to sell a stated number of units of the underlying foreign currency at a specific price per unit during a specific period of time. The *strike* (or *exercise*) *price* in this market refers to the price at which the option holder has the right to purchase or sell the price-underlying currency. A call whose strike price is above the current spot price of the underlying currency, or a put option whose strike price is below the current spot price of the underlying currency, is termed *out-of-the-money.* The reverse situation is called *in-the-money.* Although out-of-the-money options have no intrinsic value, in-the-money options have intrinsic value. Intrinsic value reflects the extent to which an option would currently be profitable to exercise. Similar to forward and futures markets, an option holder has to pay risk premium and transaction costs to the banks offering the options service. Buying options, however, is more costly than using forwards and futures.

Consider the case in which Dow Corning has to pay £1 million in three months for materials imported from the United Kingdom and thus needs to hedge this account payable. If Dow Corning buys call options on pounds at a strike price of $1.5/£, the options will be exercised if the spot rate for the pound ends up above $1.5/£ but will not be exercised if the spot rate for the pound is below $1.5/£. This makes sense because it will cost Dow Corning less to buy the pounds at the actual spot rate when it is below $1.5/£. In other words, a call option provides an *option* that will be exercised if the pound becomes more expensive to buy or will not be exercised (using the actual spot rate instead) if the pound becomes cheaper. In a put option as in the example of the preceding UK exporter, which needs to hedge its accounts receivable amounting to C$1 million, the put option will be exercised if the actual spot rate ends up below C$2.2728/£ or will not be exercised if the actual spot rate is above 2.2728, whatever generates more cash flow in pounds for the UK exporter.

Swaps. A swap involves the exchange of interest or foreign currency exposures or a combination of both by two or more borrowers. It is a transformation of one stream of future cash flows into another stream of future cash flows with different features. An interest rate swap is an exchange between two parties of interest obligations (payments of interest) or receipts (investment income) in the same currency on an agreed amount of the principal for an agreed period of time. Currency swaps involve counterparty A exchanging fixed-rate interest in one currency with counterparty B in return for fixed-rate interest in another currency. Swaps can be used for different purposes such as investment, speculation, and hedging.

When a firm needs to hedge its accounts payable (as in the situation of Dow Corning above), swaps hedging involves (a) borrowing, if necessary, in home currency; (b) buying the foreign exchange on the spot market; (c) investing the foreign exchange; and (d) repaying the domestic currency debt. For example, Dow Corning can hedge its import of £1 million of denim fabric with payment due in three months by borrowing dollars, buying pounds spot with the dollars, and investing the pounds for three months in a pound-denominated security in London. If this is done, then in three months Dow Corning repays a known number of dollars of domestic debt and pays accounts payable in pounds using its investment principal and earnings.

Hedging With Contract Invoicing and Clause

Home Currency Invoicing. Transaction exposure associated with international accounts receivable or payable can also be hedged via internal techniques. One of these techniques has to do with invoicing trade in their own (home) currency or a third-country currency whose value is stable and also acceptable to both parties. For example, if Dow Corning from the United States can negotiate the price of its imported denim fabrics in terms of U.S. dollars, or the UK exporter can manage the export contract by invoicing at sterling, they need not face any foreign exchange transaction exposure on their imports or exports. In general, when business convention or the power that a firm holds in negotiating its purchases and sales results in agreement on prices in terms of the home currency, the firm that trades abroad will not face foreign exchange risk and exposure.

Mixed-Currency Invoicing. It is not unusual for both parties in an import/export contract to prefer invoicing the transaction using their own home currencies. As a compromise, both parties may agree to denominate the contract partly in an importer's currency and partly in an exporter's currency. For example, Dow Corning's £1 million import contract may be invoiced as £500,000 and $750,000. If this were done and the exchange rate between dollars and pounds varied, Dow Corning's transaction exposure would involve only half of the funds payable—those that are payable in pounds. Similarly, the British exporter would face exposure on only the dollar component of its receivables. Additionally, international trading companies often use composite currency units such as the special drawing right (SDR) and the European currency unit (ECU) to denominate the export contract. Because these composite units are constructed by taking a weighted average of a number of major world currencies, their values are considerably more stable than that of any single currency. Because they offer some diversification benefits, the composite currency units will reduce transaction risk and exposure, though not completely.

Price Escalation Clause. If using currency invoicing is not realistic for the two parties of an export contract, both parties may consider including and specifying a special term in the contract, known as a price escalation clause. Under this special clause, both parties agree to adjust the sales price in full or in a certain proportion of fluctuations of the invoice currency. When the weak currency denominated in the contract depreciates 1%, for example, the contract price will automatically increase by 1% or another percentage agreed upon by both. This clause is often applied in export contracts denominated in an importer's currency that is highly volatile and will continue to depreciate in the global foreign exchange market. To reduce the transaction exposure, an exporter uses this clause to fully or partially transfer foreign exchange risk to an importer. Another technique similar to this clause is a risk-sharing arrangement between a buyer and a supplier for long-term collaborations. Both parties agree to adjust the price or share the foreign currency risk when the contracted currency fluctuates beyond a certain reasonable range. For example, Ford (United States) and Mazda (Japan) may agree that all purchases by Ford will be made in yen at the current exchange rate, as long as the spot rate on the date of invoice is between, say, ¥105/US$ and ¥125/US$. If the exchange rate remains within this range, Ford may agree to accept whatever transaction exposure exists. If, however, the rate falls beyond this limit, Mazda may agree to share the difference equally.

Managing Economic (Operating) Exposure

Financial Initiatives

Several financial initiatives, such as using leads and lags, risk-sharing arrangements, and intracompany netting, are extensively employed to minimize foreign exchange risk and exposure. Because transaction exposure and economic exposure are sometimes inseparable, these financial initiatives can also be used to lower transaction exposure in some circumstances. Nevertheless, they are designed mainly to manage operating exposure to protect the net present value of the firm resulting from any change in the future operating cash flows caused by exchange rate changes and macroeconomic factors.

Leads and Lags. By timing or retiming the transfer of funds, firms can reduce operating exposure. To lead is to pay early; to lag is to pay late. **Leads** exist when a firm holding a soft currency with debts denominated in a hard currency accelerates the debt payment by using the soft currency to pay the hard currency debts before the soft currency drops in value. **Lags** exist when a firm holding a hard currency with debts denominated in a soft currency decelerates the payment by paying those debts late. Leads and lags may also be used to reduce transaction exposure. An international trading company can collect soft foreign currency receivables early or collect hard foreign currency receivables later. For instance, if the UK exporter mentioned previously expects that the Canadian dollar will depreciate against the pound sterling, it may ask its Canadian importer to lead in paying its export sales. Similarly, if Dow Corning in the preceding case predicts that the pound sterling will drop in value vis-à-vis the U.S. dollar, it may decelerate paying its accounts payable to its UK importer. This practice should proceed within the permitted range by a host government. Italy, for example, has placed a 180-day limit on export and import lags on trade payments with non-EU countries.

Intracompany leads and lags within an MNE network are easier to implement than those between two independent companies. Under parent control and by sharing common goals, MNE subsidiaries can rely on this financial technique to improve their respective foreign exchange positions and optimize local currency cash flow. On the other hand, headquarters treasury managers must ensure that the timing of the intracompany settlement is functional from a group perspective rather than merely from a local one. They should also be aware that performance measurement may be affected if some subsidiaries are asked to lead and some to lag. The subsidiary that does the leading loses interest receivable and incurs interest charges on the funds led. To overcome this problem, evaluation of performance may be done on a pre-interest, pretax basis.

Netting and Matching. Netting is a practice by which subsidiaries or affiliates within an MNE network settle intersubsidiary indebtedness for the net amount owed during the posttransaction period. Gross intra-MNE trade receivables and payables are netted out. This approach not only reduces transaction and fund transfer cost and provides an opportunity for subsidiaries to manipulate their financial position but also helps foreign subsidiaries surpass the foreign exchange control barriers in respective countries. Netting occurs in either bilateral or multilateral form. *Bilateral netting* exists when two sister subsidiaries cancel out their receivables and payables and settle only the net payment. *Multilateral netting* involves three or more sister subsidiaries' intergroup debt and virtually necessitates the coordination of the headquarters treasury. For example, Pepsi's UK subsidiary buys $6 million worth of goods from the Swiss sister subsidiary, and the UK subsidiary sells $2 million worth of goods to the French sister subsidiary. During the same netting period, the Swiss subsidiary buys $2 million worth of goods from the French subsidiary. In this triangular case, the settlement of the intersubsidiary debt within the three subsidiaries ends up involving a payment equivalent to $4 million from the UK subsidiary to the Swiss subsidiary.

For diversified MNEs, it is important to establish the netting center supervised by the headquarters treasury. Philips, for example, established what is called the Philips Multilateral Clearing System (PMC) in its headquarters to facilitate netting among affiliates (see Industry Box, p. 402). Participating subsidiaries report all intra-MNE balances to the group treasury on an agreed date and the treasury subsequently advises all subsidiaries of amounts to be paid to and received from other subsidiaries on a specified date. Whether such netting operations function well largely depends on the effectiveness of information and communication systems and established discipline on the part of foreign subsidiaries.

Similar to netting, matching is often used for balancing accounts receivable and payable. However, it differs from netting in that matching may be used to match currency cash flows with firms outside the MNE network and occurs on the basis of the same foreign currency (netting may occur for different currencies). Specifically, **matching** is a mechanism whereby a company matches its foreign currency inflows with its foreign currency outflows in respect to amount, timing, and currency unit. The prerequisite for a matching operation, either within or beyond the MNE network, is a two-way cash flow in the same foreign currency. For example, the U.S. firm focusing on exports to Canada can acquire its debt capital in the Canadian dollar markets and use the relatively predictable Canadian dollar cash inflows from export sales to service the principal and interest payments on Canadian dollar debt. This U.S. exporter has thus hedged an operational cash inflow by creating a financial cash outflow and so does not have to actively manage the exposure with contractual financial instruments. This technique is effective in eliminating operating exposure when the exposed cash flow is relatively constant and predictable over time. In addition to acquiring Canadian debt, there are several other ways to create cash outflow in the same foreign currency stated in the firm's cash inflow. For instance, the U.S. exporter could seek out potential suppliers in Canada to provide a substitute for raw materials or components previously procured from the United

States. Another alternative is to pay foreign suppliers in a third country (e.g., Mexico or Venezuela) with Canadian dollars.

Intracompany Reinvoicing. This practice involves the establishment of a reinvoicing center within an MNE. The center is a separate corporate subsidiary that may be located in the MNE headquarters or in the country that is the center of financial intelligence for the MNE. Like the netting center, a reinvoicing center manages in one location all currency exposure from intracompany transactions. Thus, the reinvoicing center may be combined with or migrated into the netting center for some MNEs. The reinvoicing center often takes legal title of products but does not get involved in the physical movement of goods. In other words, it handles paperwork but has no inventory. For example, Acer's Korean subsidiary may ship goods directly to the Japanese sales affiliate. The invoice by the Korean subsidiary, which is denominated in Korean won, is passed on to Acer's reinvoicing center located in Singapore. The Singapore reinvoicing center takes legal title to the goods and then subsequently invoices the Japanese sales affiliate in Japanese yen. As a result, all operating subsidiaries deal only in their own currency, and all operating exposure lies with the reinvoicing center. In practice, such reinvoicing centers not only manage foreign exchange exposure for intracompany sales from one place but also oversee intracompany cash flows, including leads and lags. With a reinvoicing center, all subsidiaries settle intracompany accounts in their local currencies. The reinvoicing center needs only to hedge residual exposure for the entire MNE. Finally, to avoid some taxes such as interest withholding taxes or capital formation taxes, reinvoicing centers should avoid doing business with local suppliers or customers in the country of location. It is necessary for this special financial subsidiary to qualify for nonresident status, which helps the firm gain greater access to external foreign exchange markets and open bank accounts in foreign countries.

Production Initiatives

Input Outsourcing. A firm can mitigate its economic exposure through input outsourcing in the same currency as the one used in export sales. To mitigate the risk from *endaka* in the 1990s, Japanese automakers protected themselves against the rising yen by purchasing a significant percentage of intermediate components from suppliers in Taiwan and South Korea. Because the currencies of Taiwan and South Korea are closely linked to the U.S. dollar, the yen-equivalent prices of the intermediate supplies tended to decline with the dollar and thus lessen the impact of a falling dollar on the cost of Japanese cars sold in the United States. In using this approach, MNEs should consider flexibility in making substitutions among various sources of goods and services. Maxwell House, for example, can blend the same coffee whether using coffee beans from Brazil, the Ivory Coast, or other producers. The more outsourcing flexibility, the easier it is for the firm to reduce operating exposure through offsetting accounts receivable against accounts payable in the same currency. This strategy, of course, must be weighed against the extra costs and the requirements of product differentiation in different markets.

Production Arrangement. By production arrangement we mean that an MNE with worldwide production systems can adjust the quantity of its production in a specific location to respond to foreign exchange risk and exposure. An MNE may increase production in a nation whose currency has been devalued and decrease production in a country whose currency has been appreciated. For example, with a well-developed portfolio of plants worldwide, Westinghouse Electric (United States) may ask its subsidiary in Spain to increase production of generators in response to a weakening peseta while arranging for another subsidiary in Canada to reduce generator production in response to a rising Canadian dollar. Similar examples can also be found at Ford and GM. These two companies have substantial leeway in reallocating various stages of production among their several plants in different countries, in line with relative production and transportation costs. Ford can shift production among the United States, Spain, Germany, the United Kingdom, Brazil, and Mexico. Obviously, this production initiative works better for MNEs whose products are standardized in the global market (see Chapter 16). Using the multiple production plants strategy to reduce currency risk must be weighed against the extra capital investment and operating costs. Standardized products benefit more from economies of scale and require fewer extra operating costs than specialized products.

INDUSTRY BOX

NETTING IN PHILIPS

Philips, the Dutch lighting and electronics giant, uses what is known as the Philips Multilateral Clearing System (PMC) to facilitate cash movements cross-border among its affiliates. This system is managed by the Amsterdam-based bank Mendes Cans. Intersubsidiary cross-border payments are made monthly through the PMC. Units worldwide notify the treasury in Eindhoven of expected payments beginning 20 days prior to settlement. The system then generates payment instructions automatically several days before the settlement date. Although most major international banks provide competent multilateral netting systems, Mendes Cans has long enjoyed a reputation as an innovator and high-quality partner in this regard.

Philips uses an internal, worldwide information exchange system called IFIS for purchase orders, invoices, and other communications related to intersubsidiary transactions. IFIS is in effect an internal EDI (electronic data information) system. Externally, Philips uses EDI for purchase orders and invoices with just a few trade partners; ironically, related payments and collections are still processed with different systems. Having spent a large part of his time in centralizing and improving funding and foreign exchange management, corporate treasurer Jean-Pierre Lac is now focusing on improving Philips's cash management. He is particularly concerned with the company's disbursement and collection methods. About 6,000 people in the company spend their time cutting checks, cashing checks, and doing related activities. Today, Philips is shifting from checks to electronic payments wherever possible. How quickly it can move depends on each country's payments system. In the Netherlands, for example, Philips delivers all of its payment orders to banks by tape; Germany and the Scandinavian countries have similar systems.

Global Coordination of Exposure Management

Most of the techniques highlighted in Exhibit 14.6 cannot be instituted without headquarters coordination and guidance. Organizationally, an MNE's currency exposure should be coordinated and overseen by its netting and reinvoicing center, which may or may not be located at headquarters. For MNEs without these centers, the treasurer's office at headquarters should play these roles. While most MNEs today are delegating more power in production and operations to overseas subsidiaries, they are using a centralized structure to manage currency exposure. Because of opportunities for offsetting exposures from different product divisions or different foreign subsidiaries, centralization of exposure management ensures offsetting and self-hedging, which in turn reduces transaction costs and hedging expenses.[6] Centralization also increases benefits from economies of scale in purchasing financial instruments for hedging. It further facilitates the integration of hedging with other important aspects of international financial management such as global mobilization of cash flow, working capital management, and financing for global operations.[7] Finally, centralization does not diminish the importance of having valuable insights and necessary feedback from local managers. Incorporating a local perspective into the decision framework for exposure management helps diffuse conflicts between subsidiaries and headquarters. In situations where hedging can only be available at a local level, the role of the treasury at headquarters should transform from centralization to assistance. The electronic systems available today can greatly assist the management of currency exposure in terms of both strategy formation and ongoing control. Financial EDI systems have already been used by some MNEs such as Merck, GlaxoSmithKline, Xerox, GE, and PepsiCo. EDI systems significantly improve the effectiveness of information flows within an MNE network. At the same time, EFT (electronic funds transfer) systems as applied by Philips, Siemens, and BMW have made cash flow shifts within an MNE network quicker and easier. The improved effectiveness of both information and cash flows in turn reduces the costs for exposure management and hastens the management process. Finally, global coordination should not rule out the importance of unique hedging techniques used in specific host countries. Local practices in exposure management may be more cost-effective. In Latin America, for example, many firms maintained a portion of excess cash in either gold- or dollar-related government bonds to hedge operating exposure during an inflationary period. The Country Box summarizes these techniques in Latin America.

Interim Summary

1. MNEs with resources built up in foreign countries encounter transaction exposure, economic (operating) exposure, and translation (accounting) exposure. Transaction and operating exposures are caused by real changes in the value of a company's cash flows or assets, whereas accounting exposure is not caused by this real change but by the use of differing exchange rates when financial statements in multiple currencies are consolidated.

2. There are a number of ways of handling risks related to transaction exposure. These include hedging with financial instruments (forward, futures, options, and swaps) and hedging with contract invoicing and special clauses. Managing operating exposure is achieved through financial initiatives (leads and lags, netting and matching, intracompany reinvoicing) and production initiatives (input outsourcing and product arrangement).

COUNTRY BOX

EIGHT HEDGING TECHNIQUES IN LATIN AMERICA

1. Investing in dollar-related government assets, such as Argentina's bonex, Mexico's petrobonds, or Brazil's ORTN bonds

2. Opening central bank dollar accounts, which normally pay monthly interest at LIBOR

3. Using intercompany loans—that is, hedging excess cash by lending local currency to another company

4. Investing in real estate, especially purchasing prime location office space as a long-term hedge

5. Maintaining a portion of excess cash in gold

6. Purchasing other commodities such as coffee and soybeans and exporting them to a home or third country

7. Setting up a trading company there, which also handles risk management and receivables collection

8. Converting debt and blocked funds to equity

WORKING CAPITAL MANAGEMENT

Quantitatively, working capital is equal to the amount of current assets minus the amount of current liabilities. In practice, working capital management concerns the efficiency enhancement of current assets such as cash, accounts receivable, and inventory. Because cash and accounts receivable are particularly vulnerable to the impact of currency fluctuations, potential exchange controls, and multiple tax jurisdictions, this section highlights the management of cash and accounts receivable.

Cash Management

Ideally, a global treasury would be a single finance company with the ability to disburse or collect all financial reserves worldwide instantaneously, with the absolute minimum risk and transaction costs. In reality, however, there are many limits such as financial regulations, cash-flow restrictions, and idiosyncratic tax structures in foreign territories in which operations take place. The global cash management system includes three elements: home-country cash management, host-country cash management, and cross-border cash management. Most MNEs centralize at home such activities as borrowing, global liquidity management, international banking relations, and foreign exchange exposure management. Meanwhile, local disbursement and collection, local banking relationships, payroll, or management of trade credit and purchasing are generally managed overseas.

MNE cash concentration, known as *pooling,* generally occurs in two stages. First, cash is collected and pooled in local currency and used for local expenses. If a company has several subsidiaries in a single country, it is very efficient to use cash surpluses from one to fund the cash deficits of another. As introduced in Chapter 10, these activities are generally undertaken by the MNE's umbrella company, which plays a role as headquarters in the host country. Periodically, as net cash surpluses grow, unneeded funds are remitted. Siemens, for example, carefully manages national cash pools in each currency, using cash excesses from some units to fund the cash needs of others within the same host country. Treasury looks at balances and short-term cash projections for each national cash pool and decides how much to lend or draw out. Central borrowing is generally cheaper, but a special loan program or a high tax rate at the subsidiary level can sometimes make local borrowing more attractive. It is hence necessary to consider interest rates, tax rates, and the profitability of local operations when determining the most efficient funding route.

Another approach to global cash management is to build an efficient account structure, which also helps reduce banking fees and float. For example, Merck, a major U.S. pharmaceutical producer, uses a network of accounts held within a single bank's global network to transfer funds between national pools and the Merck treasury center in London. The system works in this way: The global bank maintains branches in each country of Merck's operation. At each branch, there is now both a national pool account and a treasury center account, with the treasury center wielding authority over both accounts. If a French subsidiary has "long" French francs, it can place the funds with the treasury center in the form of a deposit (a loan to the treasury). This subsidiary first transfers those funds into the French national pool account with the global bank's Paris branch. Then the treasury center debits the national pool account and moves the funds into its own account at the Paris branch. By transferring funds in this way, the company can avoid lifting charges levied by many European banks for transfers from resident to nonresident accounts.

Today, many diversified large MNEs have found that their financial resources and needs are either too large or too sophisticated for the financial services available in many locations where they operate. In response, many have established *in-house banks* to manage not only currency exposure but also cash flows. Such an in-house bank is not a separate corporation; rather, it is a set of functions performed by the existing treasury department. Acting as an independent entity, the central treasury of the firm transacts with its various business units. The purpose of the in-house bank is to provide banklike services to the various units of the firm. The in-house bank may be able to provide services not available in many country markets, and it may do so at lower cost when available. In addition to providing financing benefits, in-house banks allow for more effective currency risk management. Foreign subunits may sell their intra-MNE receivables to the in-house bank. The in-house bank is better equipped to deal with currency exposure and has a greater volume of international cash flow, allowing foreign subunits as a whole to gain from more effective use of netting and matching. This approach frees the units of the firm from struggling to manage transaction exposures and allows them to focus on their primary business activities. Volvo Construction Equipment's treasury center in Brussels acts as an in-house bank that maintains a network of bank accounts for all intraorganizational transactions. This network of accounts is used primarily for intersubsidiary payments, and subsidiaries are responsible for making third-party payments and collections through local banks.

Foreign Receivables Management

A firm's operating cash flow comes primarily from collecting its accounts receivable. Managing foreign receivables requires appropriate measures in three stages: pretransaction stage, transaction stage, and posttransaction stage. In the *pretransaction stage,* a firm must investigate the buyer or importer's corporate credibility and financial capability. This is particularly imperative when dealing with a new client from a foreign country. Many large international companies categorize foreign clients into several clusters such as superior customers, priority customers, normal customers, and risky customers. This categorization and related client information are then disseminated to sales managers and treasury managers. Such clustering is usually built on a client's previous record, company size, corporate image, financial strengths, and targeted markets. An exporter can obtain this information from previous collaboration, bank reports, archival research, or credit investigation agents. In general, the selection of currency unit, terms of payment, and length of credit are all contingent on a foreign buyer's creditability and repayment ability.

In a *transaction stage,* the exporting company needs to decide in what currency the transaction should be denominated and what the terms of payment (including the length of time draft) should be. Ideally, the exporting transaction should be denominated in a hard currency together with a letter of credit at sight. In practice, however, this is largely determined by the exporter's bargaining power vis-à-vis the importer. The hedging instruments, hedging clauses, and invoicing techniques introduced earlier are useful in this stage.

International firms must establish organizational systems for tracking, managing, and collecting foreign accounts receivable in a *posttransaction stage.* In these systems, managers in the accounting or treasury department should be able to track the collection record and coordinate with the international sales or marketing department (when documents against payment [D/P] or documents against acceptance [D/A] are used) or the bank (when a letter of credit [L/C] is used). They should also share the information concerning the foreign exchange gains or losses and uncollected due receivables with the sales or marketing managers so that the latter can better evaluate past transactions and better prepare future businesses. In many firms, collecting foreign accounts receivable is linked with the reward system for sales managers. The level of bonus, commission, or reward does not depend on the amount of sales but rather on the actual revenues collected.

Interim Summary

1. Cash and accounts receivable are particularly vulnerable to currency fluctuations, exchange controls, and multiple tax jurisdictions. Many MNEs have established in-house banks to manage cash flows and accounts receivable.

2. Most MNEs centralize at-home borrowing, global liquidity management, international banking relations, and foreign exchange exposure management while leaving the management of local cash disbursement and collection, local banking relations, payroll, and trade credit management to local managers.

CHAPTER SUMMARY

1. Financial management for global operations occurs in an environment with foreign exchange risks, capital flow restrictions, country risks, and different tax systems. It deals with foreign trade finance, global financing, managing foreign exchange risk and exposure, and working capital management.

2. Payment for international transactions differs markedly from that for domestic transactions. To the exporter, bad-debt risks ascend along the cash in advance, letter of credit (L/C), documentary collection (D/P or D/A), and open account methods. Many uniform documents such as draft, bill of lading (B/L), and commercial invoice are needed in international payment.

3. Smaller international firms play an active part in international trade. To obtain export financing, they can use several channels, including private sources (commercial banks, factoring or forfait houses, and corporate guarantee) and government sources (export–import banks and foreign credit insurance).

4. FDI involves yet more complex financing choices, including intercompany financing, equity financing, debt financing, and local currency financing. Intercompany loans from parent or peer subsidiaries can also be used for the purpose of avoiding taxation or foreign exchange control. Crosslisting firm stocks on exchanges in different countries is a major financing source for large MNEs because it increases liquidity and visibility.

5. Eurocurrency markets are the major source of international bank loans (i.e., Eurocredits). Yankee bonds are foreign bonds sold in the United States and Samurai bonds are foreign bonds sold in Japan. All financing decisions must consider currency risks, source diversity, taxation implications, and interest rates.

6. Foreign exchange risk and exposure are two related yet distinct concepts. The former concerns the variance of the home-currency value of an asset, liability, or income affected by unanticipated changes in exchange rates. The latter refers to the sensitivity of changes in the home-currency value of an asset, liability, or income to unanticipated changes in exchange rates. Risk is an increasing function of exposure and the variance of unanticipated changes in exchange rates.

7. MNEs encounter three types of foreign exchange exposure—transaction exposure, translation (accounting) exposure, and economic (operating) exposure. Transaction exposure can be hedged through financial instruments such as forward and options and production initiatives such as input sourcing.

8. Firms need to create a global management system for working capital, especially cash flow. Headquarters managers must clearly define what aspects of cash management are centralized and what should be decentralized. Meanwhile, they should formalize policies managing international accounts receivable.

Chapter Notes

1. See S. M. Saudagaran. "An empirical study of selected factors influencing the decision to list on foreign stock exchange." *Journal of International Business Studies,* Spring 1988: pp. 101–128; D. K. Eiteman, A. I. Stonehill, and M. H. Moffett. *Multinational Business Finance.* New York: Addison-Wesley, 1998.

2. J. J. Choi. "Diversification, exchange risk, and corporate international investment." *Journal of International Business Studies,* Spring 1989: pp. 145–155; M. Adler and B. Dumas. "International portfolio choice and corporate finance: A synthesis." *Journal of Finance,* June 1983: pp. 925–984.

3. See M. D. Levi. *International Finance,* p. 302. New York: McGraw-Hill, 1996.

4. See M. Adler and B. Dumas. "Exposure to currency risk: Definition and measurement." *Financial Management,* Summer 1984: pp. 41–50; C. R. Hekman. "Measuring foreign exchange exposure: A practical theory and its application." *Financial Analysts Journal,* September/October 1983: pp. 59–65.

5. C. C. Y. Kwok. "Hedging foreign exchange exposures: Independent vs. integrative approaches." *Journal of International Business Studies,* Summer 1987: pp. 33–52; L. Oxelheim. "Managing foreign exchange exposure." *Journal of Applied Corporate Finance,* 1991, *3,* 4: pp. 73–82.

6. L. Oxelheim. *Managing in the Turbulent World Economy—Corporate Performance and Risk Exposure.* New York: Wiley, 1997; L. A. Soenen and J. Madura. "Foreign exchange management—A strategic approach." *Long Range Planning,* 1991, *24,* 5: pp. 119–124.

7. D. R. Lessard and S. B. Lightstore. "Volatile exchange rates can put operations at risk." *Harvard Business Review,* July/August 1986: pp. 107–114; R. M. Stulz. "Rethinking risk management." *Journal of Applied Corporate Finance,* 1996, *9,* 3: pp. 8–24; W. R. Folks Jr. "Decision analysis for exchange risk management." *Financial Management,* Winter 1972: pp. 101–112.

INTERNATIONAL ACCOUNTING FOR GLOBAL OPERATIONS

DO YOU KNOW?

1. What forces lead to different national accounting systems? How many accounting zones are there internationally, and what are these zones based on? If you were a manager at Nokia, would you like to see international harmonization of such differing systems? Why or why not?

2. Why is foreign currency translation so important yet difficult for MNEs? What are the major translation methods? Can U.S. companies such as Honeywell choose a specific method they like or switch methods every year?

3. What are the main benefits of intra-MNE transfer pricing practices, and how do taxation agencies ensure that these transactions are fair? If you are a manager in a large MNE such as 3M, what do you take into account in choosing a transfer pricing practice?

OPENING CASE

Glaxo to Settle Tax Dispute With IRS for $3.4 Billion

Pharmaceutical giant GlaxoSmithKline PLC will pay the U.S. government $3.4 billion to settle a nearly two-decade-long dispute over how to tax dealings between the British company and its American subsidiary, in a case that underscores the Internal Revenue Service's resolve to confront corporate tax avoidance. The settlement, which the IRS said was the largest ever, covers taxes the agency said Glaxo owed for 1989 through 2005 because the company's American unit improperly overpaid its British parent for drugs,

mainly the antiulcer blockbuster Zantac. It said those overpayments reduced the company's profit in the United States, thus lowering its U.S. tax bill.

Glaxo's decision to settle the dispute, which was headed for a trial in U.S. Tax Court in February 2007, was particularly sweet for the IRS because it has a poor track record of winning disputes involving the accounting practice at stake in the Glaxo case. That practice, called "transfer pricing," is the art of attaching a monetary value to trademarks, patents, research, and other intangibles that one arm of a multinational company transfers to another. Transfer pricing determines how costs are distributed between the far-flung arms of a multinational company and thus what profit is booked in what country. Higher costs cut into profit, lowering a company's tax bill, while lower costs do the opposite.

Disputes over transfer pricing tend to be among the biggest fights between the IRS and corporate taxpayers, and they are of growing importance since more than 60% of world trade occurs inside multinational companies. Every country wants to maximize the tax revenue on goods and services produced within its borders, and every company has an incentive to book profits where taxes are lowest. That has bred a slew of disputes between companies and tax authorities over the proper pricing.

Symantec Corp., a Cupertino, California, software maker, is currently in a $1 billion transfer-pricing tax court dispute with the IRS involving an Irish subsidiary of Veritas Software Corp., a company it acquired in 2005. The IRS is arguing that licensing fees paid by the subsidiary to Veritas in the U.S. were too low and that Veritas credited the U.S. business with too much of the cost of developing some technology. That wound up increasing the income of the subsidiary in Ireland—a lower-tax country—at the expense of income in the

United States, lowering the company's overall tax bill. Symantec has sued the IRS in U.S. Tax Court.

SOURCE: Abbreviated from "Glaxo to settle tax dispute with IRS over U.S. unit for $3.4 billion." *Wall Street Journal*, September 12, 2006, A3.

COUNTRY DIFFERENCES IN ACCOUNTING

The Glaxo case illustrates that MNEs should deal appropriately with accounting and tax issues that affect the firms' net incomes and cash flow. The aim of an accounting system is to identify, measure, and communicate economic information to allow informed judgments and decisions by users of the information. Today, the explosive expansion of cross-border transactions and the rapid growth of companies seeking capital in international markets have made international accounting issues a daily concern for international managers. **International accounting** involves accounting and taxation issues for companies that have internationalized their economic activities across countries in which accounting standards and practices vary. Four fundamental issues need to be understood by international business managers: (a) country differences in accounting and international harmonization; (b) foreign currency translation; (c) cross-border transfer pricing; and (d) tax havens, treaties, and strategies. We explain country differences in the next section.

Why Accounting Systems Differ Among Countries

To a large extent, accounting is a product of its external environment. It is shaped by, reflects, and reinforces characteristics peculiar to its national environment. No two countries have identical accounting systems. In a few cases—such as that of the United States and Canada, or the United Kingdom and Ireland—the differences are relatively few and minor. In other instances—for example, Germany and France, or China and India—the differences are much more fundamental.[1] In general, a country's accounting system is shaped by institutions, societal culture, and external relations with other countries. The institutions of the country, in particular how it organizes its economic, political, legal, taxation, and professional systems, are the central forces determining the development of the accounting system.

Institutions

Economic System. A country's economic system factors, such as the level of inflation, economic and industrial structures, and the complexity of business organizations, affect the accounting system. As inflation rates increase, the problems of historical cost accounting also increase. Developed countries rarely suffer severely from high inflation and thus tend to view inflation accounting with suspicion. Inflation continues to be a serious problem in countries such as Mexico, Chile, and Brazil. Obviously, when inflation is running at high levels, the historical cost of an asset quickly becomes irrelevant. Therefore, various forms of inflation accounting have been found in these countries. In Brazil, for example, a revised Corporation Law, introduced in 1976, regulated that official monthly price indices be employed to update the values of all assets, depreciation, cost of goods sold, and owner's equity.

Economic structure influences how such accounting issues as pensions, retained earnings, dividends, depreciation, and research and development (R&D) cost amortization are handled. For example, accounting for pensions is an important issue in the United States, which has a very complex and concrete pension standard. This reflects the particular institutional arrangements of the United States, where many companies oversee employee pension plans. In other regions such as Chile, Hong Kong, and Singapore, pensions are run by the state or through private arrangements, and accounting for pensions becomes less important. In some transitional economies such as China, Russia, and Hungary, accounting for owner's equity items such as initial capital, retained earnings, and dividends vary according to ownership form (i.e., state-owned, collectively owned, privately owned, and foreign-owned enterprises). Similarly, accounting for depreciation and R&D expense amortization differs across countries that have different levels of economic development. More advanced economies such as Japan and the United States tend to use a faster amortization schedule.

Industrial structure affects the consistency of accounting standards and practices among different industries. Whether a country stipulates industry-specific accounting principles depends on the relative importance of that industry to the economy. For example, in Vietnam, accounting standards governing the foreign trade sector differ significantly from those governing other sectors. Similarly, accounting for the oil and gas industry has been a crucial and contentious issue in the United States and subject to unique accounting rules and practices. In the United Kingdom, the standard on research and development was strongly influenced by the potential impact of alternative accounting methods on companies in the aerospace and other R&D-dependent industries.

The complexity of the business organizations that dominate an economy affects the complexity of the internal accounting information system and management accounting in general. For instance, if most companies in a country are small or family owned, then there is little need for sophisticated external reporting systems, and there should be relatively few accounting regulations. As a company increases in size and complexity, the demand for sophisticated management accounting systems heightens, with problems of control, performance evaluations, and decision making gaining center stage. Typically, when business organizations become more complex, firms will start to arrange themselves into groups, with subsidiaries, branches, joint ventures, or strategic alliances all gaining in importance. Accounting standards and practices must reflect these changes. For example, greater focus will be placed on the regulation of group financial statements and extra disclosure requirements.

Political System. The political system is a critical determinant of national accounting because the accounting system will reflect political philosophies and objectives. The most common system found in Western Europe, North America, Japan, and Australia, for instance, is the *liberal–democratic system.* A second important system is the *egalitarian–authoritarian political system* (e.g., North Korea and Cuba). Most transition economies such as Russia and Eastern European countries fall somewhere in between. In the egalitarian–authoritarian form, all production and operations are owned and controlled by governmental institutions. Accounting serves two roles in this circumstance: to help in centralized planning and to help in controlling the economy. Profit is essentially retained by the government instead of the firm. Therefore, "owner's equity" in state-owned enterprises actually reflects "state's equity" or "governmental equity." While dividend policy is important in Western countries, it is meaningless in central-planning systems.

Legal System. The legal system determines the extent to which company law governs the regulation of accounting. In countries such as France, Germany, and

Argentina, in which codified Roman law dominates, accounting regulations and rules appear to be concrete and comprehensive. This contrasts with countries using common law such as the United Kingdom and the United States. As such, many split the accounting world into two groups based on the pervasiveness of the legal approach: *legalistic orientation* toward accounting (i.e., using codified Roman law) and *nonlegalistic orientation* (i.e., using common law). Laws in codified Roman law countries are a series of "thou shalts" (you shall) that stipulate the minimum standard of behavior expected. In most countries with a legalistic orientation, accounting principles are national laws and accounting practices are codified. Accounting rules tend to be prescriptive, detailed, and procedural. Because accounting standards and practices are set by legislators, whether they are adaptive and effective depends largely on the legislators' knowledge of accounting principles, practices, and implications.

By contrast, laws in countries with a nonlegalistic orientation are a series of "thou shalt nots" (you shall not) that establish the limits beyond which an activity or practice is unlawful. Within these boundaries, latitude and judgment are allowed and encouraged. Accounting practices in common law countries are in large part decided by accountants themselves. Thus they tend to be more flexible, innovative, and adaptive. Nevertheless, the legalistic approach may be used in a particular sector or a special circumstance in common law countries. For example, tax laws and the regulations enacted by the U.S. Securities and Exchange Commission represent the legalistic approach to accounting. In addition, certain laws not directly related to accounting may have strong implications for accounting practices. For example, the major accounting effect of the Foreign Corrupt Practices Act in the United States is that U.S. MNEs must establish a system of internal controls and an internal audit staff to ensure that bribes are not being offered (see Chapter 19).

Taxation System. The taxation system is an important factor in situations where accounting systems are strongly influenced by state objectives. In countries such as France and Germany, public accounting reports are used to determine tax liabilities. In the United States and the United Kingdom, published accounts are adjusted for tax purposes and submitted separately from the reports to shareholders. Overall, there are three types of tax systems that correspond to different financial reporting rules:

- Tax rules and financial reporting rules are kept entirely, or mostly, independent of each other (e.g., the United Kingdom and the United States).
- There is a common system, with many of the financial reporting rules also being used by the tax authorities (e.g., less developed British Commonwealth countries).
- There is a common system, with many of the tax rules also being used for financial reporting purposes (e.g., Austria and Western Europe).

Professional System. The accounting profession is influential because the way in which it is organized, and society's attitude toward accountants, affects their ability to control or audit companies and their reporting systems. The extent to which auditors are independent and hold power relative to the companies they audit influences the perceived value of financial statements. The accountant's role in formulating regulations also affects the national accounting system. Even though this role is largely contingent on the country's legal system, accounting regulations can be influenced by the professional who may act as an adviser to the government, provide input into the regulatory process, and issue standards or recommendations in areas where there are no legal regulations. The French profession in the form of the OEC (Ordre des Experts Comptables) provides a good example of this approach.[2]

Societal Culture

Societal culture influences the accounting system. For example, the detailed accounting procedures instituted by the French government reflect France's statistical tradition. Australia's accounting requirements for public firms are generally permissive, reflecting the distrust of government power embedded in that country's individualistic, frontier culture. Cultural dimensions at the national level, initially identified by Hofstede,[3] which are particularly relevant to accounting development, are "uncertainty avoidance" and "individualism." As outlined in detail in Chapter 6, in a high-uncertainty-avoidance country, institutions will be organized in ways that minimize uncertainty. Rules and standards tend to be explicit, prescriptive, all-embracing, and rigid. Individualism affects preferences for earnings measurement rules and disclosure practices and influences the willingness to accept uniform accounting rules in preference to a more permissive system involving the use of professional discretion. Recent studies by accounting scholars suggest that countries with low-uncertainty-avoidance cultures (e.g., the United Kingdom, the United States, and Sweden) tend to have strong independent auditing professions that audit a firm's accounts to ensure they comply with GAAP (Generally Accepted Accounting Principles).[4]

External Relations

External relations, economic and political, with other countries influence accounting practices and regulations through colonialism or regionalization. Historically, colonies adopted or were forced to adopt the accounting system of the colonial power, even though it may not have been particularly appropriate at the colony's stage of development. Thus, the accounting standards and practices in the British colonies were significantly influenced by British accounting, and the influence remains today in Hong Kong, Australia, New Zealand, India, and Jamaica. The same can be said for former French colonies, Spanish colonies, and others. Regionalization harmonizes national differences in accounting systems. For example, since the passage of NAFTA, the accounting systems in the United States, Canada, and Mexico have converged on a common set of norms. Similarly, the member nations of the European Union and the Central American Common Market (CACM) have expended great effort toward integrating their accounting systems.

As shown in Exhibit 15.1, the preceding forces—namely, institutions, societal culture, and external relations—jointly affect or explain a country's accounting system, especially accounting objectives, regulation mode, and regulation strictness. Accounting objectives reflect the ways in which the system is intended to meet the needs of investors, creditors, the government, or other users. The mode of regulation concerns whether accounting rules and standards are regulated by government, the profession, or other groups. Finally, the strictness of regulation is the extent to which accounting rules and standards are strict and comprehensive. The Industry Box exhibits accounting diversity in Volvo during its global expansion and operations.

The characteristics of a national accounting system influence many company decisions, especially those concerning R&D expenditure, fixed assets, inventory valuation, accounting for income taxes, and foreign currency translation. For example, Germany and the United States require immediate expense recognition for R&D expenditures under all circumstances since they believe that there is a great deal of uncertainty as to whether the R&D will benefit future

Exhibit 15.1   Forces Shaping a Country's Accounting System

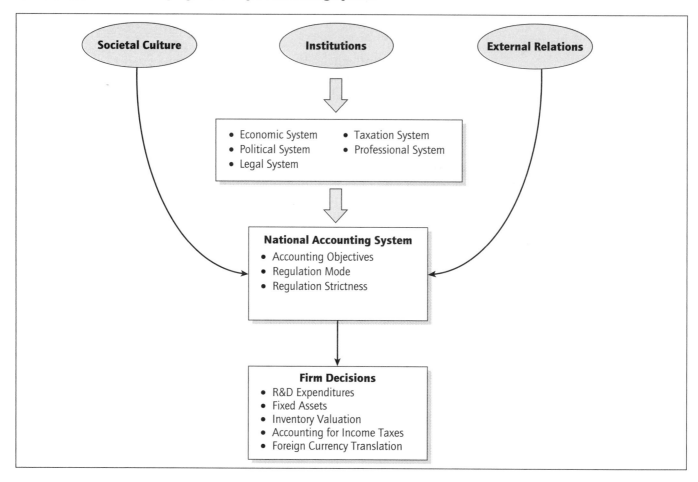

periods. Canada, France, the Netherlands, Switzerland, the United Kingdom, and IAS (International Accounting Standards), however, allow this recognition only when the technical feasibility of a product or process has been established.[5]

INDUSTRY BOX

ACCOUNTING DIVERSITY IN VOLVO

Volvo is one of the largest industrial groups in the Nordic region. More than 80% of its sales occur outside Sweden. For a large MNE from a relatively small country, raising capital on foreign stock markets is an essential vehicle to access international capital and improve publicity. Currently, Volvo's shares (except those of its cars division, acquired by Ford) are traded on the stock exchange of eight foreign countries, including the United Kingdom, Germany, Norway, France, the United States, Belgium, Japan, and Switzerland. The largest foreign market was London, where 17.8 million shares were traded in 2003, while in the United States 2.0 million ADRs were traded on the NASDAQ. The London Stock Exchange requirements for listing demand that a company produce financial statements that are prepared and independently audited in accordance with standards appropriate for companies of international standing and repute. Any financial statements that comply with International Accounting Standards or UK or U.S. standards would automatically meet these requirements. In contrast, the SEC in the United States requires all foreign corporations to disclose, in their annual Form 20-F report, a U.S. GAAP reconciliation of their reported net income and shareholders' equity. Volvo, along with many other corporations subject to these requirements, voluntarily reproduces some financial information in its annual report and accounts together with an explanation of the U.S. GAAP differences.

National Accounting Zones

Although no two countries share perfectly identical accounting standards and practices, countries can be grouped into a few clusters based on critical similarities. This is possible because factors that shape a country's accounting system, as discussed earlier, can be similar to those facing another country. In light of dramatic changes in both external environment and accounting systems in many countries, especially emerging economies, we list five accounting zones. This is a modified list, building on a recent study by Mueller and his associates.[6] As highlighted in Exhibit 15.2, these five models, or zones, are as follows:

1. British–American (or Anglo-Saxon)

2. Continental

3. South American

4. Transitional economy

5. Centrally planned economy

In *Anglo-Saxon nations,* accounting is oriented toward the decision needs of investors and creditors. Countries in the *Continental zone* include most of Continental Europe and Japan. Financial accounting is legalistic in its orientation, and practices tend to be highly conservative. Most countries in South America belong to the *South American zone,* with the exception of Brazil. A distinct feature in this zone is the persistent use of accounting adjustments for inflation. In the *transitional economy zone,* accounting standards vary according to ownership types. For collectively owned (e.g., township or village enterprises that are jointly owned by the local community, management, and workers) and privately owned enterprises, the accounting orientation moves toward a capitalist market, emphasizing information for investors, bankers, and taxation departments. State-owned enterprises (SOEs) that are no longer dominating their national economies operate under dual accounting systems. One provides information for managers used to the former system oriented toward a command economy that retains a heavy proportion of net profits earned by SOEs; the other employs a capitalist market orientation, trying to emulate the British–American accounting model. China is included in this zone because its SOEs no longer play a dominant role in shaping its growing economy. Chinese SOEs in many sectors have already adopted new accounting principles that are very similar to GAAP in the United States. Finally, the accounting system in the *centrally planned economies,* in which central governments control production and resources of most enterprises, is characterized by high uniformity. Uniform accounting is necessary for tight central economic control. The primary users of financial statements are government planners. Assets are state owned, and liabilities accrue through governmental arrangements via state banks. Initial or increased capital contribution is made and owned by the government. The overwhelming majority of net profits are either turned over to the state (often upper-level governmental authorities) or owned by the government. "Owner's equity" in a private sense does not exist.

International Accounting Harmonization

Having discussed national differences in accounting systems earlier, we can better appreciate the benefits that can be obtained from international harmonization

Exhibit 15.2   Selected Economies Using the Five Major Accounting Models

British–American Model

Australia	India	Panama
Bahamas	Indonesia	Papua New Guinea
Barbados	Ireland	Philippines
Benin	Israel	Puerto Rico
Bermuda	Jamaica	Singapore
Botswana	Kenya	South Africa
Canada	Liberia	Tanzania
Cayman Islands	Malawi	Trinidad & Tobago
Central America	Malaysia	Uganda
Colombia	Mexico	United Kingdom
Cyprus	Netherlands	United States
Dominican Republic	New Zealand	Venezuela
Fiji	Nigeria	Zambia
Ghana	Pakistan	Zimbabwe
Hong Kong		

Continental Model

Algeria	France	Norway
Angola	Germany	Portugal
Austria	Greece	Senegal
Belgium	Italy	Sierra Leone
Burkina Fasso	Ivory Coast	Spain
Cameroon	Japan	Sweden
Denmark	Luxembourg	Switzerland
Egypt	Mali	Togo
Finland	Morocco	Zaire

South American Model

Argentina	Chile	Paraguay
Bolivia	Ecuador	Peru
Brazil	Guyana	Uruguay

Transitional Economy Model

Armenia	Hungary	Russia
Azerbaijan	Kazakhstan	Serbia
Belarus	Kyrgyzstan	Slovak Republic
Bosnia-Herzegovina	Latvia	Slovenia
Bulgaria	Lithuania	Tadzhikistan
Croatia	Moldova	Turkmenistan
Czech Republic	Poland	Ukraine
Estonia	Romania	Uzbekistan
Georgia	China	

Centrally Planned Economy Model

Cuba	North Korea	Vietnam

and standardization. **Harmonization** is a process of increasing the compatibility of accounting practices by setting limits on how much they can vary. Harmonized standards minimize logical conflicts and improve the comparability of financial information from different countries.[7] The terms *harmonization* and *standardization* are often used interchangeably. Although highly related, these two concepts are not identical. **Standardization** means the imposition of a rigid and narrow set of rules and may even apply a single standard to all situations. Unlike harmonization, standardization does not necessarily accommodate national differences. As such, *harmonization* is a more appropriate term than *standardization* in the reconciliation of national differences in accounting standards. Accounting harmonization comprises three main components:

- Harmonization of accounting standards that deal with measurement and disclosure
- Disclosures made by publicly traded companies in connection with securities offerings and stock exchange listings
- Auditing standards

Not everyone agrees that national differences in accounting standards should be harmonized. Some argue that international standards setting was too simple a solution for a complex problem. They suspect that these standards could be adaptive enough to handle differences in social traditions, political systems, and economic environments among different countries. Along with the increasing integration of the world economy, however, the pressure for internationalizing and harmonizing accounting and auditing practices has been intensified. A growing body of evidence suggests that the need for international harmonization of accounting, disclosure, and auditing has been so widely accepted that the trend will accelerate. The globalized business community requires transparent, internationally comparable accounting practices consistent across borders. The two most notable developments that increase the necessity for harmonization are the evolution of MNEs and the development of international capital markets. For many MNEs, more than half of sales, profits, assets, or investments come from overseas operations. The heterogeneity of applicable accounting, auditing, and tax rules hampers an MNE's ability to prepare reliable financial information necessary for a careful analysis of various strategies. Meanwhile, the vast global capital market requires a common accounting language for the communication of financial information. In the absence of this common language, it is difficult to develop and maintain a truly efficient global capital market.

The major benefits of harmonization are threefold. First, comparable and transparent financial information helps enhance the reliability of foreign financial statements. It also helps in making informed decisions, which, in turn, reduce risk for investors. Second, harmonized accounting reduces the costs of preparing financial statements and facilitates the task of investment analysts, investors, and other users in assessing business results. This saves on both the time and money currently spent consolidating divergent financial information. Third, many emerging and transitional economies regard uniform accounting as an efficient way of conforming to global norms. This is because they can avoid creating burdensome national standard-setting bodies of their own. For instance, China is about to issue a core set of accounting standards that are based on, and broadly comply with, International Accounting Standards (IAS).

International Accounting Standards

Harmonization proceeds through formulating and implementing international accounting standards. These standards have now been widely recognized and accepted in many countries throughout the world. For instance, a special television program was recently broadcast in Japan covering new accounting rules developed by the IAS Committee and their impact on corporate financial reporting in Japan. The key players in setting international accounting standards and in promoting international accounting harmonization include the following:

1. International Accounting Standards Committee (IASC)

2. Commission of the European Union (CEU)

3. International Organization of Securities Commissions (IOSCO)

4. International Federation of Accountants (IFAC)

5. International Standards of Accounting and Reporting (ISAR), which is under the United Nations Conference on Trade and Development (UNCTAD)

6. Organization for Economic Cooperation and Development Working Group on Accounting Standards

IASC, the most dominant player in setting international accounting standards, was founded in 1973 by representatives of professional bodies in Australia, Canada, France, Germany, Japan, Mexico, the Netherlands, the United Kingdom, Ireland, and the United States. As of July 2007, IASC had 140 member bodies from 104 countries, representing more than 2 million accountants. IAS are used as a result of either international or political agreement (e.g., the European Union accounting-related directives) or voluntary compliance. When national and international standards differ, national standards usually take precedence. Companies that adopt more than one set of accounting standards must often issue one set of reports for each set of accounting standards they adopt. At the national level, some countries now use IAS as the basis for national standards, whereas others use them as a benchmark against which to compare national practices. The standard-setting bodies in many developing countries are now using IAS as the basis for national requirements, although there are some who question the desirability of wholesale adoption without regard to differing economic circumstances. The Country Box offers an example in Australia.

An increasing number of MNEs report their accounting results by reference to IAS. When the accounting standards in a home country conform with IAS, accounting managers need not provide separate sets of financial statements; they just need to offer an explicit statement of conformity with IAS as well as national standards. Groupe Saint Louis (a French MNE), for example, provides such a note attached to its consolidated financial statements:

> The Saint Louis consolidated financial statements have been prepared in accordance with French accounting principles relating to consolidated accounts. The principles and methods used are also in conformity with the pronouncements of IAS Committee. [per company documents]

When national and international standards differ, MNEs often include in the financial report a reconciliation showing the differences between national accounting practices and the requirements of IAS. Profit before taxation and shareholders' equity are usually reported twice, with one based on IAS and the other on the home country's standards. Some other companies provide full financial statements in conformity with IAS, either as the main financial statements or in addition to the financial statements complying with national accounting practices. Nokia (Finland), for example, prepares its financial statements according to IAS. At the same time, it provides a reconciliation between U.S. GAAP and IAS results.

Core standards as set forth by IAS include the following categories:

- General, which involves disclosure of accounting policies, changes in accounting policies, and information disclosed in financial statements
- Income statement, which deals with such issues as revenue recognition, construction contracts, production and purchase costs, depreciation, taxes, government grants, retirement benefits, R&D, interest, and hedging
- Balance sheet, which covers various issues such as leases, inventories, deferred taxes, foreign currency, investments, joint ventures, business combinations, intangible assets, and goodwill
- Other standards, which involve how to account for consolidated financial statements, subsidiaries in hyperinflationary economies, equity financing, earnings per share, discontinued operations, fundamental errors, and segment reporting[8]

Interim Summary

1. Accounting practices in each nation are shaped by that country's institutions, culture, and external relations. Institutions include economic, political, legal, taxation, and professional systems. Legal systems divide accounting practices into two broad groups: the legalistic orientation, based in countries with codified Roman law, and the nonlegalistic orientation, found in countries with common law systems.

2. Based on national accounting systems and practices, countries can generally be grouped into five accounting zones: Anglo-Saxon, Continental, South American, transition economies, and centrally planned economies. Within each group, countries share not only similar accounting systems but also similar economic and organizational structures.

COUNTRY BOX

ACCOUNTING IN AUSTRALIA

The Australian Accounting Standards Board (AASB), the main body governing accounting policies in Australia, has issued ED 102, *International Harmonization and Convergence Policy*. The proposal reflects the AASB's statutory responsibility to participate in, and contribute to, the development of a single set of worldwide accounting standards. The AASB's objective is to pursue, through participation in the activities of the International Accounting Standards Committee (IASC) and the International Federation of Accountants' Public Sector Committee (PSC), the development of an internationally accepted single set of accounting standards that can be adopted in Australia for both domestic and worldwide use. In the short term, however, the AASB aims to converge the Australian standards with those issued by the IASC, but only where such standards are "in the best interests of both the private and public sectors in the Australian economy."

As part of its work program, the AASB intends to work with the IASC and PSC to remove incompatibilities between international standards and the corresponding Australian standards. For instance, the AASB's ED 49 somewhat differs from IAS 38 in measuring, amortizing, and recognizing intangible assets (including R&D expenditures). When the AASB harmonizes with IAS 38, it results in a value decrease of many existing intangible assets, fewer new intangibles being recognized as assets, and lower costs that can be recognized as expenses in developing intangible assets. IAS 38 imposes many more restrictions in recognizing internally generated intangibles such as goodwill, brand names, mastheads, and publishing titles than does the AASB's ED 49.

SOURCES: Adapted from Jim Dixon. "Harmonization policy." *Accountancy*, October 1, 2001 (Vol. 128, Issue 1298): pp. 1–2; Colin Parker and Daen Soukseun. "IAS 38: How tangible is the intangible standard." *Australian CPA*, December 1998 (Vol. 68, Issue 11): pp. 32–33.

FOREIGN CURRENCY TRANSLATION

Foreign currency translation is perhaps the most prominent accounting issue that directly and significantly affects the results revealed in MNEs' financial statements. MNEs, regardless of their home countries, cannot prepare consolidated financial statements unless their accounts and those of their subsidiaries are expressed in a same, single currency. For instance, one cannot add Chinese yuan (RMB) or Japanese yen to U.S. dollars without a proper conversion of different currencies. Without foreign currency translation, MNE headquarters cannot appropriately plan, evaluate, integrate, and control overseas activities that should be coordinated within the network. The expanded scale of international investment activities also necessitates foreign currency translation. This occurs particularly when an MNE's subsidiary wishes to list its shares on a foreign stock exchange, contemplates a foreign acquisition or joint venture, or wants to communicate its operating results and financial position to its foreign stockholders.

Translation is the process of restating accounting data recorded in one currency (e.g., the currency of a foreign subsidiary in Italy) into another currency (e.g., the currency of the parent company in the United States) for the purpose of aggregating data from different reporting entities. Translation differs from conversion; **conversion** refers to the physical exchange of one currency for another, whereas translation is simply a change in monetary expression, as when a balance sheet expressed in Italian lira is restated in U.S. dollar equivalents. No physical exchange occurs in the course of translation. Exhibit 15.3 outlines the definitions of other terms that are associated with foreign currency translation.

Countries are in different stages with respect to the financial statement consolidation requirement. Consolidation has long been a common practice in countries such as the Netherlands, the United Kingdom, and the United States, whereas it is a relatively recent phenomenon in many other European and Asian countries. For example, German MNEs have been required to present global

Exhibit 15.3   Glossary of Foreign Currency Translation Terms

Conversion The exchange of one currency for another.

Current Rate The exchange rate in effect at the relevant financial statement date.

Discount When the forward exchange rate is below the current spot rate.

Exposed Net Asset Position The excess of assets that are measured or denominated in foreign currency and translated at the current rate over liabilities that are measured or denominated in foreign currency and translated at the current rate.

Foreign Currency Transactions Transactions (e.g., sales or purchases of goods or services or loans payable or receivable) whose terms are stated in a currency other than the entity's functional currency.

Foreign Currency Translation The process of expressing amounts denominated or measured in one currency in terms of another currency by use of the exchange rate between the two currencies.

Functional Currency The primary currency in which an entity conducts its operation and generates and expends cash. It is usually the currency of the country in which the entity is located and the currency in which the books of record are maintained.

Historical Rate The foreign exchange rate that prevailed when a foreign currency asset or liability was first acquired or incurred.

Local Currency Currency of a particular country; the reporting currency of a domestic or foreign operation.

Monetary Items Obligations to pay or rights to receive a fixed number of currency units in the future.

Reporting Currency The currency in which an enterprise prepares its financial statements.

Translation Adjustments Translation adjustments result from the process of translating financial statements from the entity's functional currency into the reporting currency.

Unit of Measure The currency in which assets, liabilities, revenue, and expense are measured.

consolidated financial statements only since 1990. In Japan, consolidation is also quite recent, with most companies not reporting full consolidated statements before the early 1980s. Today, consolidation has become much more widespread as a result of increasing globalization and heightened needs for information flow within and beyond the boundary of the MNE.

Commonly Used Translation Methods

There are four internationally accepted and commonly used translation approaches:

- Current rate method
- Current/noncurrent method
- Monetary/nonmonetary method
- Temporal method

The primary distinction among these methods is the classification of assets and liabilities that would be translated at either the current or historical rate. All four methods, which can be found today in various countries, produce considerably different foreign currency translation results. At present, the IAS Committee and U.S. GAAP both mandate use of the current rate method for translating the financial statements of a foreign entity.

Current rate method. A feature of this approach is that all assets and liabilities, both monetary and nonmonetary, are translated at the current or closing rate. Foreign currency revenues and expenses are generally translated at exchange rates prevailing when these items are recognized (typically translated by an appropriately weighted average of current exchange rates for the period). All resulting exchange differences are classified as a separate component of equity of the reporting enterprise until disposal of the net investment in a foreign entity. The basis of this method is the "net investment concept," wherein the foreign subsidiary is viewed as a separate entity that the parent invested into, rather than being treated as part of the parent's operations. As an important consequence of this method, translating all foreign currency balances gives rise to translation gains and losses every time exchange rates change. Reflecting such exchange adjustments in current income could significantly distort reported measures of performance.

Current/noncurrent method. Current assets and liabilities are translated at the current rate, and noncurrent assets and liabilities at the applicable historical rates. Income statement items, with the exception of depreciation and amortization charges, are translated at average rates applicable to each month of operation or on the basis of weighted averages covering the entire period to be reported. A major weakness under this method is the treatment of inventory and long-term debt. As a current asset, inventory is translated at its current cost, which is a major departure from traditional GAAP. The translation of foreign-denominated long-term debt under this approach may be misleading to users, because it is translated at its historical value. For example, from the perspective of a U.S. reporting entity, if the dollar weakens internationally, it will take more dollars to repay this obligation, a fact that would not be apparent from the reporting entity's financial statements.

Monetary/nonmonetary method. This method translates monetary assets and liabilities at the current rate. Nonmonetary items such as fixed assets, long-term investments, and inventories are translated at historical rates. Income statement items are translated under procedures similar to those described for the current/noncurrent approach. Under U.S. GAAP, if the foreign entity's local currency is the functional currency, it requires the current rate method. If the U.S. dollar is the functional currency, U.S. GAAP requires the remeasurement method, which is essentially the same as the monetary/nonmonetary framework. A limitation of this method is that not all items can be classified as monetary or nonmonetary.

Temporal method. Monetary items such as cash, receivables, and payables are translated at the current rate. Nonmonetary items are translated at the rates that preserve their original measurement bases. In other words, nonmonetary assets carried on foreign currency statements at historical cost are translated at the historical rate. Nonmonetary items carried abroad at current values are translated at the current rate. Revenue and expense items are translated at rates that prevailed when the underlying transactions occurred. The temporal method was the required method in the United States under SFAS (Statement of Financial Accounting Standards) No. 8 until it was superseded by SFAS No. 52, which requires the current rate method. The major points of the preceding four methods are summarized in Exhibit 15.4.

All translations of foreign currencies will inevitably result in gains or losses associated with translation adjustment. The way in which such gains or losses are accounted for affects the operating results as perceived, particularly by the stockholders of a parent company. Approaches to accounting for translation adjustment include deferral, partial deferral, and no deferral. With a deferral approach, translation adjustments are excluded from the income statement and are instead accumulated separately as a part of equity in the consolidated balance sheet. Under the partial deferral approach, translation losses are recognized in a consolidated income statement as soon as they occur, whereas translation gains are recognized only as they are realized. A final method is to recognize instantly

Exhibit 15.4   Foreign Currency Translation Methods

Items/ Methods	Current	Current/ Noncurrent	Monetary/ Nonmonetary	Temporal
Cash	CR	CR	CR	CR
Accounts receivable	CR	CR	CR	CR
Inventories				
Cost	CR	CR	HR	HR
Market	CR	CR	HR	CR
Investments				
Cost	CR	HR	HR	HR
Market	CR	HR	HR	CR
Fixed assets	CR	HR	HR	HR
Other assets	CR	HR	HR	HR
Accounts payable	CR	CR	CR	CR
Long-term debt	CR	HR	CR	CR
Common stock	HR	HR	HR	HR

CR = current rate; HR = historical rate.

NOTE: Example economies using the current method include Austria, Canada, France, Taiwan, Sweden, the United States, and the United Kingdom; Japan is an example using the current/noncurrent approach; Germany is an example using the monetary/nonmonetary method; before 1981, the United States used the temporal approach.

translation gains or losses in the income statement. Inclusion of such "paper" gains or losses in current income brings up a random element to earnings that could generate substantial earning gyrations whenever exchange rates fluctuate. Nevertheless, it is a widespread view that if the reporting currency of the parent company is the unit of measure for the translated financial statements, immediate recognition of translation gains or losses in income is advisable. From a parent company point of view, translation gains or losses reflect changes in the domestic currency equity of the foreign investment and should be recognized.

Harmonization of Translation Methods

MNEs employing different translation approaches could produce divergent consolidated financial statements, which in turn would hinder financial comparison and strategic decision making. Because most countries have no strict standards, the practice is mainly left up to the MNEs themselves. To harmonize the use of such methods, IAS 21, prepared by the IASB (International Accounting Standards Board), and SFAS No. 52, prepared by the FASB (Financial Accounting Standards Board), are presently the two most important standards widely applied by international companies. Although they are basically compatible, IAS 21 differs from SFAS No. 52 in that the former advocates the current rate method in all circumstances (as explained earlier), whereas the latter emphasizes functional currency, which will determine an applicable translation method. Today, an increasing number of internationally listed MNEs are following IAS, and the world's stock exchanges are pressured to allow IAS in lieu of domestic standards for foreign company listings. While domestic MNEs in the United States are asked to follow SFAS No. 52, foreign MNEs in the United States are permitted to follow IAS 21.

The core premise of SFAS No. 52 centers on *functional currency*. SFAS No. 52 stipulates that the assets, liabilities, and operations of a foreign entity shall be measured using the functional currency of that entity. An entity's functional currency is the currency of the primary economic environment in which it operates; normally, that is the environment in which an entity primarily generates and expends cash. For an entity with operations that are relatively self-contained and integrated within a particular country, the functional currency generally would be the currency of that country (e.g., RMB for a Shanghai subsidiary of a U.S. parent). If a foreign entity keeps its accounts in a currency other than the functional currency (e.g., the German accounts of a U.S. subsidiary whose functional currency is actually British pounds), its functional currency is the third-country currency (pounds). If a foreign subsidiary is merely an extension of a U.S. parent company (e.g., Nike's assembly subsidiary in Thailand whose main function is to assemble shoes that will be exported to the United States), its functional currency is the U.S. dollar.

According to SFAS No. 52, if a foreign entity's books of record are not maintained in its functional currency, remeasurement into the functional currency is required before translation into the reporting currency. If a foreign entity's functional currency is the reporting currency, remeasurement into the reporting currency obviates translation. The remeasurement process is intended to produce the same result as if the entity's books of record had been maintained in the functional currency. This means that an entity needs to maintain two sets of records: one in the local currency and one in the functional currency, when these two are different. To help understand the preceding issues, see the process tree (Exhibit 15.5) on currency translation accrued in a foreign subsidiary of a U.S. MNE.

Exhibit 15.5   Process Tree in Foreign Currency Translation

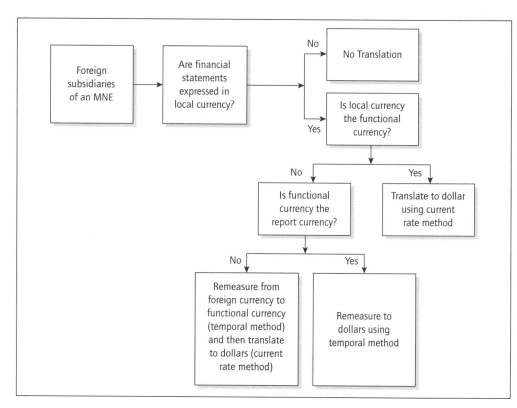

International Accounting Information Systems

Consolidating financial statements is only one aspect of international financial reporting. As MNEs act more locally, accounting and financial reporting systems become increasingly critical. Global coordination has shifted from the previous rigid control mechanisms such as budget and bureaucratic control to information-based coordination, which is why international accounting information systems become fundamental. **International accounting information systems (IAIS)** involve accounting-related reporting systems, data management, and communication between various units of the same MNE. Financial controllers in MNE headquarters find themselves under increasing pressure to bring information to market more quickly, to deliver more extensive information than previously required, and to proactively manage business risk at a corporate level. Preparation of detailed MNE group information on a monthly basis is now the norm—with the result that headquarters' accountants and financial managers often spend most of their time preparing and monitoring information rather than working with the output or reformulating accounting plans. Many MNEs have set up computerized accounting information systems with overseas affiliates to furnish the accounting information needed to plan, evaluate, and coordinate all business activities. Microsoft, with 54 financial groups charged with providing financial support to more than 85 global subsidiary operations, has struggled with these challenges. Its answer is the financial *digital nerve system,* an intranet-based environment that links all of the company's financial groups into a single, coherent system that provides its employees with real-time access to information and financial reports through the Internet. An effective IAIS provides an MNE with a competitive advantage arising from operational flexibility and transnational coordination in this increasingly competitive and complex global environment.

In general, MNEs tend to make internal reporting systems in their foreign subunits uniform. This allows easy comparison of corporations throughout the world and augments the consolidation process at the home office. A uniform reporting system, however, must accommodate the following differences:

- Different managerial styles of users may impose different standards on the design. European managers are more conservative decision makers than most U.S. managers, which means European managers need more detailed accounting information to make decisions.
- Intraorganizational interdependence in information flow, capital flow, resource flow, and product flow is a key factor determining design. The greater the interdependence, the greater intense communication and information exchange is indispensable.
- Legislative and legal developments in both home and host countries may influence uniform reporting. For example, the Freedom of Information Act and Fair Credit Reporting Act in the United States prohibit the improper use of personal data. European countries with data protection legislation do not allow name-linked data to be transmitted outside national boundaries.

Interim Summary

1. Translation is not the actual exchange of hard currency, but a reexpression in another currency (e.g., an MNE's home-country currency) for the purpose of consolidating financial statements.

2. The major translation approaches are the current rate method, in which all assets and liabilities are translated at the current rate; the current/noncurrent method, by which current assets and liabilities are translated at the current rate, noncurrent assets and liabilities at the historical rates, and income statements at average rates; and the monetary/nonmonetary method, whereby monetary assets and liabilities are translated at the current rate, and nonmonetary assets and liabilities at historical rates.

TRANSFER PRICING AND TAXATION STRATEGIES

Why Transfer Pricing?

As one of the major international tax issues facing MNEs, **transfer pricing** refers to the pricing of goods and services transferred between members of an MNE network. These transfers are also termed intra-MNE transactions. The essence of transfer pricing is to earn economic benefits such as tax avoidance by manipulating the price of intra-MNE transactions. Transfer pricing can achieve the following benefits for the MNE.

Tax and Tariff Reduction

Tax minimization is the main driver behind transfer pricing policies. When tax rates are different in two countries, MNEs favor low transfer prices for goods and services bought by, and high transfer prices for goods and services sold by, an affiliate in a low-tax jurisdiction. Consider this example: Subsidiary A assembles shoes in China, whose corporate income tax is 33%, and needs to sell $10,000 worth of shoes to its sister subsidiary B in Japan, where the income tax is 55%. If these shoes were overpriced at $12,000, then it could lower subsidiary B's tax by $1,100 ($2,000 × 55%). Although subsidiary A had to pay $660 ($2,000 × 33%) more in taxes, the MNE network saved $440 ($1,100 – $660). Transfer pricing can also be used in a similar fashion to minimize import duties. The effect of tariffs could be reduced if the selling company underprices the goods it exports to the buying unit. For example, a product that normally sells for $100 has an import price of $120 because of a 20% tariff. If the invoice price were listed as $80 rather than $100, however, it would be imported for $96.

Avoiding Exchange Controls

Transfer pricing may be used to offset the volume effects of foreign exchange quotas. For example, if a government allocates a limited amount of foreign exchange for importing particular goods, a parent company may underprice products shipped to its subsidiary, thereby allowing a greater volume of imports. If an MNE wishes to move funds out of one country, it may consider charging higher prices on goods sold to its local affiliates. Similarly, an MNE may indirectly finance an affiliate by lowering the prices on goods sold to it.

Increasing Profits From Joint Ventures

Transfer pricing enables the party to gain unilateral profit from controlling the joint venture's import and export activities. For example, some Hong Kong investors are not overly concerned with the reporting profits in their joint ventures in Mainland China. This is because they have already made noticeable returns from overpricing materials imported for the joint ventures or by underpricing joint venture outputs exported to headquarters. They normally control the material importation and products export for the ventures as specified in joint venture agreements.

Internally, the underlying problem of transfer pricing is possible conflict between the goals of subsidiaries and those of the parent when subsidiaries are evaluated as separate profit or investment centers. Overpricing outputs or underpricing inputs for subsidiaries in high-tax countries reduces their accounting-based profits. Therefore, MNEs should prepare corporate policies on internal transfer pricing and use different criteria to assess subsidiary performance when this practice has been used. Furthermore, if a transfer price is too high, tax authorities in the purchasing affiliate's country forgo income tax revenues. MNEs should check anti-taxation evasion measures adopted by related countries. This is explained below.

Transfer Pricing Techniques

From the tax authority perspective, intra-MNE transfer pricing must proceed following the arm's-length principle. The **arm's-length principle** in this context means that the transfer price struck between related companies should be the same as that negotiated between two independent entities acting in an open and unrestricted market. In the process of using transfer pricing, MNEs must become familiar with the methods used by taxation authorities in host and home countries to determine whether transfer pricing practices comply with the arm's-length principle. These methods delineate the legitimate range of transfer pricing that is allowed by tax authorities. Knowing these methods helps an MNE prepare appropriate transfer pricing policies. These methods are as follows:

- *Current open market prices:* Tax authorities generally view using comparable open market prices as the most satisfactory method because it requires the fewest adjustments. If this method cannot be applied, they may compare the gross margin or operating profit the company earns from intercompany transactions with gross margins or operating profit earned in the open market. Differences between the terms of intercompany transactions and the terms of open-market transactions require adjustment before a true comparison can be made for taxation purposes.

- *Gross margin method:* This method relies on a certain range of gross margins achieved in comparable transactions between independent companies. The gross margin methods include (a) the resale price method and (b) the cost-plus method. The *resale price method* is used for transfers of goods to distributors, which sell them without further processing. The price paid for a final product by an independent party is used as a baseline, on which a suitable markup is deducted to allow for the seller's expenses and reasonable profit. The *cost-plus method* is used when one group company transfers items that need additional processing by the other group company before they can be sold to a final customer. Cost-plus simply marks up the cost of producing the transferred goods and services commensurate with functions performed by the transferring company. In this case the effective comparison is with the margin earned on similar transactions occurring at arm's length. In effect, the procedure is the opposite of the resale price method.

- *Operating profit methods.* The difficulty of finding comparable transactions or gross margins often leads companies to use operating profit methods that include (a) the comparable profits method, (b) the transactional net margin method, and (c) the profit split method. The *comparable profits method,* as its name suggests, simply compares the period percentage operating profit (e.g., return on sales or return on assets) in the controlled subsidiary with percentages in similar uncontrolled entities on a whole-company basis. The *transactional net margin method* is similar to the comparable profits method but compares operating profit on transactions rather than on a whole-company basis. Often, intragroup trading of goods and services is unique to a particular group. In this situation, no external operating profit comparisons can exist, so the *profit split method* may have to be used. Group companies simply reach an agreement on how profits from the final product will be shared between them, based on a considered assessment of the contribution made by each party to the transaction.

Transfer Pricing Regulations and Penalties

Concurrent with the increase in transfer pricing is an increase in scrutiny by cross-border tax authorities who want to ensure that their countries receive their fair shares of tax revenues. Tax authorities are acutely aware of the potential revenue losses associated with intercompany transfer pricing policies. For this purpose, tax authorities are requiring more reporting and documentation, carrying out more comprehensive audits, and introducing harsher penalty regimes. For example, the U.S. Tax Court fined DHL for misstatement of income for the tax years 1990–1992 because of the trademark royalty paid by its Hong Kong affiliate, DHL International. The IRS had sought more than $160 million in back taxes, plus penalties. DHL and the IRS varied widely on the value of the DHL trademark. DHL estimated the value as low as $20 million to $50 million. The IRS said the DHL trademark was worth as much as six times that amount when DHL sold its trademark to DHL International at what the tax agency said was not an "arm's-length" transaction.

The issue of the 1995 OECD guidelines and the U.S. Section 482 regulations are the two most important guidelines regulating transfer pricing practices. The *OECD transfer pricing guidelines* (1995 version) provide information on the application of the arm's-length principle that the OECD hopes can be used by MNEs and tax authorities in all member countries. The OECD guidelines reject the use of splitting profits between jurisdictions on the basis of revenue and payroll. This latter method is considered to be against the arm's-length principles and is therefore considered an invalid transfer pricing method. *The U.S. Section 482 guidelines* are similar to the OECD model. The arm's-length standard is affirmed as the basis of the Section 482 regulations but requires that the best method be used. Taxpayers must demonstrate that their chosen method produces the most reliable arm's-length result. This means that MNEs will have to give full and documented consideration to all possible methods before settling on the most appropriate. Unlike the OECD model, the U.S. rules accept the profit-based methods.

Both the OECD and U.S. guidelines require the taxpayer to provide the supporting documentation for its transfer price on a timely basis, or suffer, at worst, a nondeductible penalty of up to 40% in the United States and up to 100% in the United Kingdom. The strict U.S.-initiated transfer pricing model (with accompanying documentation requirements, penalties, and enforcement) is spreading quickly to other nations around the globe and adding to the strain. Since 1997, new legislation and rulings have taken effect in many countries, including Australia, Brazil, Canada, Denmark, France, Korea, Mexico, and the United Kingdom. Most of these countries focus on the need to document adherence to the arm's-length standard, with the accompanying threat of large penalties for failure to do so.

To reduce the risk arising from transfer pricing and tax audit, many MNEs adopt an advance pricing agreement (APA) with the tax authorities of the countries in which they generate taxable income. An **advance pricing agreement** is an agreement between the tax authority and the taxpayer on the transfer pricing methodology to be applied to any apportionment or location of income, deductions, credits, or allowances between two or more members within an organization. An APA allows an MNE to negotiate an understanding with one or more tax authorities that approves a transfer pricing methodology for a given term, resolving the uncertainty about its acceptability and reducing audit risk. An APA may be unilateral (least preferred by most tax authorities), bilateral, or multilateral. Bilateral and multilateral agreements are more easily negotiated with tax authorities in countries that have existing tax treaties. The APA is also an alternative dispute-resolution process that can reduce the number of transfer pricing cases requiring legal resolution, saving both time and money for the MNE and for the tax authority.

Interim Summary

1. Transfer pricing aims at gaining benefits through manipulation of prices of intra-MNE transactions on exchange controls and increased profits from joint ventures. These benefits include tax and tariff reduction, foreign exchange control avoidance, and profit increase from joint ventures. Tax avoidance is the overriding intention behind this practice.

2. The legitimate range of transfer pricing allowed by tax authorities is determined by (a) current open market prices, (b) the gross margin method, or (c) operating profit methods.

TAX HAVENS, TREATIES, AND STRATEGIES

Intra-MNE transfer pricing on tangible goods or intangible services is only one of the major vehicles to reduce worldwide taxation burdens for MNEs. Using tax havens and taking advantage of tax treaties between home and host countries have also served as important instruments for MNEs seeking tax reduction. Tax reduction or avoidance differs from tax evasion in that the latter is considered illegal but the former is acceptable, aimed at keeping tax burdens to the minimum.

Tax Havens

High tax rates in many countries have forced MNEs to seek refuge in tax havens. **Tax havens** are geographical locations in which taxation is substantially lower than that in a home country. To avoid high taxation in a home country, an MNE may incorporate or register a company in a tax haven that may impose little or no corporate income taxes. For example, Bermuda has become a home to 75% of Fortune 100 companies, owing to virtually zero income taxes (plus meetings and conventions in Bermuda are 100% U.S. tax deductible for American corporations and associations). Because of low or no taxes on certain classes of income, thousands of so-called mailbox companies have sprung up in such exotic places as Liechtenstein, Vanuatu, and the Netherlands Antilles. Tax havens have the following categories:

- Traditional tax havens with virtually no taxes whatsoever: the Bahamas, Bermuda, the Cayman Islands, Andorra, Bahrain, Campione, Monaco (except for French citizens), Tonga, and Vanuatu.
- Tax havens that impose a relatively low rate: the British Virgin Islands, the Channel Islands, Gibraltar, Liechtenstein, Switzerland (except a few regions), Angola, the Netherlands Antilles, Kiribati and Tuvalu, Montserrat, Norfolk Island, the Solomon Islands, and several other small islands.
- Tax havens that tax income from domestic sources but exempt all income from foreign sources, such as Hong Kong, Liberia, and Panama.
- Tax havens that allow special privileges, such as Brazil, Luxembourg, and the Netherlands.

To benefit from a tax haven, an MNE would ordinarily set up a subsidiary in the tax haven country through which different forms of income would pass. The goal is to shift income from high-tax to tax haven countries. For example, a U.S. manufacturer could sell goods directly to a dealer in Japan and gather the profits in the United States, or it could sell the goods to its Bermuda subsidiary at cost and then sell the goods to the Japanese dealer, thus concentrating the profits in the Bermuda subsidiary. Specifically, MNEs can use tax havens by setting up holding companies, offshore banking, captive insurance companies, shipping companies, free-port manufacturing, or export and management companies. Most manufacturing MNEs seeking tax havens prefer the holding company mode. Companies can avoid taxes in their home country by transferring assets to a holding company over which they have control. The holding company then collects the income arising from the relevant assets (investments, loans, parent royalties, etc.). Ideal locations for such holding companies are countries that do not tax, or only lightly tax, the income in question. In the finance sector, a remarkable phenomenon is that the international banking industry does not remain in well-established finance centers such as London, New York, Tokyo, Zurich, and Luxembourg but has moved offshore in search of more favorable climates for international banking operations (e.g., low tax rates, freedom from exchange controls, and freedom from withholding tax on interest). For example, the value of operations generated by U.S., Canadian, and European banks channeled through the Bahamas and Cayman Islands is still rising. Most banking institutions in the islands have highly reputable international connections. The majority are cubicle operations with neither offices nor staff of their own, but the amount of funds booked through these subsidiaries is phenomenal. For example, international banks in the Bahamas had $1 trillion under management in 2002, while mutual funds had assets of about $100 billion.

Tax Treaties

Where income earned and taxed in one country is remitted to investors in other countries, the income may be subject to multiple taxation. This is a particular, but not peculiar, problem to U.S. investors, because the United States follows the worldwide concept of taxation. Two common approaches are used to avoid multiple taxation: foreign tax credits and tax treaties. The idea of the *tax credit* is that a company can reduce its tax liability by the amount of the credit. In determining the tax credit in the United States, for example, the predominant nature of the foreign tax must be that of an income tax as defined in the United States. With the spread of business worldwide, most nations in the world, both developed and developing, have signed numerous bilateral tax treaties. Accordingly, tax treaties have become the primary device for avoiding multiple taxation today.

The major purpose of international *tax treaties* is to eliminate international double taxation and render mutual assistance in tax enforcement (e.g., preventing tax evasion) and in reducing barriers to trade and investment. Many countries avoid international double taxation by not taxing their taxpayers on foreign source income (e.g., China). To a large extent, the income tax treaties determine the amount of tax to be paid to the country where the income is produced and the amount to be paid to the taxpayer's country of residence. They do this by offering reduced rates of tax or complete exemptions from tax for certain specified items of income. For example, under U.S. law, interest paid by a U.S. company to a foreign recipient is subject to a 30% U.S. withholding tax. Under the UK–U.S. income tax treaty, this tax is eliminated. Each treaty may also differ from the others and results from negotiation between the two countries. To prevent a resident of a nontreaty country from using, for example, the UK treaty to invest in the United States, anti-conduit provisions were also included. If a Saudi Arabian investor were to lend money to a UK corporation that lent it to the U.S. subsidiary, the anti-conduit provisions would treat the loan as coming directly from Saudi Arabia.

Other Tax Strategies for MNEs

Setting Up a Holding Company in a Host Country

This technique for repatriating cash and reducing future taxes involves setting up a holding company in the same host country as a high-tax operating subsidiary. Funding is provided to that holding company to buy the shares of the operating company from the U.S. parent, allowing direct future earnings to be repatriated without withholding taxes. The consolidation of the return of the holding company and the operating company allows not only deduction of the new interest but also reduction of future foreign taxes. The U.S. law, through Section 304 of the Internal Revenue Code, considers this taxation as a dividend distribution rather than a sale, because the ultimate ownership of the operating company has not changed. Foreign countries generally levied this as a sale by a foreign corporation, with no foreign tax on any capital gain.

Establishing a Holding Company in an Integrated Region

This approach involves a regional or other multicountry holding company. Given that intercompany dividends between European Union countries are tax free, a subsidiary in the country (e.g., the Netherlands) would borrow to buy shares of another subsidiary in another European country (e.g., Belgium). For this reason, MNEs need a holding company in a country that does not tax dividend income or capital gains and that has a low withholding rate on dividends back to the United States.

Building a Finance Corporation

In view of the tax incentives given to finance companies in some countries such as Belgium and Ireland, U.S. MNEs may establish finance companies in these countries to manage group cash and currency exposure and to channel funds within Europe without bringing them back to the parent. For example, if an MNE has excess cash in Germany, it may want to finance a subsidiary in exchange for preferred shares in the finance company. The German company reduces its cash, which may be particularly useful if it cannot pay dividends because of an insufficiency of earnings or reluctance to pay withholding tax.

Locating Projects in a Low-Tax Region Within a Host Country

A large proportion of MNEs entering developing countries invest their projects in special technological, investment, or trade zones that impose substantially lower tax rates or provide preferential tax terms. China provides an excellent example. MNE manufacturing projects located in Shenzhen, one of the five special economic zones in China, enjoy a reduced 15% rate on corporate income tax (as opposed to 33% in normal cases). They also receive an exemption of income tax for the first two years and a 50% reduction of income tax during the third to fifth years, starting from the first profit-making year. MNEs located in coastal cities such as Tianjin, Shanghai, Dalian, Qingdao, and Guangzhou are entitled to a 24% corporate income tax levied on general manufacturing projects and a 15% corporate income tax for those MNEs that are technologically intensive. Similarly, if projects are hosted in an Economic and Technological Development Zone designated by the central government, MNEs will enjoy a 15% corporate income tax. If the project is more than 10 years in duration, it enjoys a two-year exemption, a subsequent three-year 50% reduction of corporate income tax, and a 10% corporate income tax for MNEs with 70% of output exported, after a stipulated term.

In sum, there are several tax strategies used by MNEs in addition to transfer pricing or using tax havens and tax treaties. To deal with the complex international tax systems efficiently, MNEs set up holding companies or finance corporations in a foreign region (or country) or locate investment projects in special zones within a target foreign country. Because the taxation burden directly affects net profit that can be retained by the firm, these strategies add value to the firm's wealth and influence the firm's ability to reinvest overseas. Although the international taxation environment is much more complex than the domestic one, MNEs can benefit from opportunities arising from the differences in taxation rates and systems between countries. These benefits will not accrue unless MNEs have adopted realistic and viable strategies on taxation reduction.

Interim Summary

1. High tax rates in many countries often compel MNEs to incorporate or register a company in a tax haven. Bermuda is especially popular for American MNEs. Tax treaties and foreign tax credits are also used to avoid double taxation on the same income.

2. Other tax reduction strategies exist, dealing primarily with setting up holding companies to avoid taxation, creating finance firms in countries with tax incentives, and locating new projects in low-tax regions of host countries.

CHAPTER SUMMARY

1. Accounting is fundamental to MNEs because their ultimate success needs to be reflected in accounting reports and because their key decisions are often made based on accounting information. Some accounting practices such as transfer pricing, accounting information systems, and cash-flow management can add important value to an MNE.

2. When firms expand globally, they face different accounting systems in different nations. Such differences exist because of different economic, political, legal, cultural, and taxation systems. These differences can affect a firm's decisions on R&D expenditure, fixed assets, inventory valuation, foreign currency translation, and accounting for income taxes.

3. MNEs will benefit from harmonizing accounting standards and practices between nations. The International Accounting Standards Committee (IASC) is the leading institution in setting international accounting standards. Increasing numbers of MNEs now report their accounting results by reference to the IASC's standards.

4. Foreign currency translation can significantly affect the results in MNEs' consolidated financial statements. Widely accepted translation approaches include the current rate method, the current/noncurrent method, the monetary/nonmonetary method, and the temporal method. The IASC and U.S. GAAP now both mandate use of the current rate method. SFAS No. 52 details how this method is advanced.

5. Transfer pricing provides MNEs with several gains, especially reducing corporate income taxes in heavily taxed countries in which MNE subsidiaries are located. However, firms must conform to various restrictions and rules imposed by home- or host-country taxation authorities. Tax havens and treaties offer additional opportunities for tax avoidance.

Chapter Notes

1. See C. Roberts, P. Weetman, and P. Gordon. *International Financial Accounting*, pp. 8–9. London: Financial Times Management, 1998.

2. H. H. E. Fechner and A. Kolgore. "The influence of cultural factors on accounting practice." *International Journal of Accounting*, 1999, *29*, 4: pp. 265–277.

3. G. Hofstede. *Culture's Consequences: International Differences in Work-Related Values*. Beverly Hills, CA: Sage, 1980. For details, refer to Chapter 6.

4. S. J. Gray. "Towards a theory of cultural influence on the development of accounting systems internationally." *Abacus*, 1988, *24*, 1: pp. 1–15; S. B. Salter and F. Niswander. "Cultural influences on the development of accounting systems internationally." *Journal of International Business Studies*, 1995, 26: pp. 379–397; R. J. Kirsch. "Towards a global reporting model: Culture and disclosure in selected capital markets." *Research in Accounting Regulation*, 8: pp. 71–110.

5. For a detailed discussion on these accounting issues, see W. E. Becker and P. Brunner. "A summary of accounting principle differences around the world." In F. D. S. Choi (ed.), *International Accounting and Finance Handbook*, 3rd ed., pp. 1–33. New York: Wiley, 1997; International Accounting Standards Committee. *International Accounting Standards 1996*. London: IASC.

6. See G. G. Mueller, H. Gernon, and G. Meek. *Accounting: An International Perspective*. New York: Business One Irwin, 1994.

7. F. D. S. Choi, C. A. Frost, and G. K. Meek. *International Accounting*. Upper Saddle River, NJ: Prentice-Hall, 1999.

8. For details, see B. J. Epstein and A. A. Mirza. *IAS 2000*. New York: Wiley, 2000.

GLOBAL MARKETING AND SUPPLY CHAIN

DO YOU KNOW?

1. What determines the potential of a foreign market?

2. What adaptations, if any, are necessary for a product to sell in another country? For instance, if you were to sell a Ford Focus in Vietnam, what adjustments would you make in the car's appearance and technical specifications?

3. What influence does the country of origin of a manufacturer (or a service provider) have on the customer's decision to buy a product? Would you buy a Malaysian-made Proton car?

4. How do you make channel decisions in a foreign market? What should you do when your main channel—for example, direct marketing—is deemed unlawful?

5. What transportation modes dominate international trade?

6. If you were a manager at Mattel, how would you prepare for a slowdown or shutdown at California's ports?

OPENING CASE

Domino's Pizza

Founded in 1960 in Ypsilanti, Michigan, Domino's Pizza opened its first foreign store in 1983 in Winnipeg, Canada. It added Japan in 1984, the United Kingdom in 1985, and Mexico in 1989. Domino's successfully entered Hong Kong and Taiwan in 1984 and 1987, respectively, although it was not clear whether pizza would sell given the lack of milk-product tradition among Chinese; Domino's has since applied the lessons it has learned in those markets, entering the Chinese mainland in 1994. In 2000, Domino's acquired a controlling stake in a Dutch pizza company that operated 52 of its stores. International expansion continued in the new millennium, with international same store sales registering uninterrupted growth from 2002 onward. In 2005 alone, the company added 238 new international stores versus 168 domestic stores (both franchise and company owned).

Domino's has learned that country environments can vary substantially. The menu in the Chinese stores is adapted to local tastes, with shrimp, scallops, and squid added to the conventional toppings. The pepperoni pizza is called the American Pizza, and print advertising demonstrates how to eat pizza with your hands. While prices in China are slightly lower than in the United States, store sales volume is more than double the U.S. average. Unlike in the United States, where

Photo 16.1   **Most international merchandise trade is conducted via maritime transportation.**

SOURCE: Jupiterimages.

home delivery is dominant, in China it accounts for only 10% to 15% of volume, with most orders placed in restaurants open from 9 A.M. to 11 P.M. However, competitive pressures from Pizza Hut and local outlets are pushing Domino's toward an expansion of home delivery in the Chinese market.

Master franchisees in each country are keys to Domino's marketing strategy. Many master franchisees and general managers are veterans of the U.S. market; for example, Taiwan's general manager was a Domino's employee who spent many years in the United States. Master franchisees contribute to product adaptation, determine pricing, and devise national promotion and advertising. In Japan, the master franchisee came up with the idea of using a customized scooter for delivery in narrow alleys. The franchise concept was developed in the United States before being extended overseas, first in the form of overseas franchisees of U.S. firms and subsequently also in the form of U.S. franchisees of foreign businesses. The latter include, for instance, Bark Busters, a dog behavior-control business headquartered in Australia, and Japan-based Kumon, a children's supplemental education business started by Toru Kumon in Japan some 50 years ago, which now operates in 43 countries. Kumon of America has grown to become the largest foreign franchise in the United States.

SOURCES: Domino's Pizza International, Inc. HEC case, 1998 and Company Updates to 2006; "Foreign franchise concepts find growth opportunities in the U.S. market." *Wall Street Journal,* March 8, 2004, B8; 2005 Annual Report; 2006 personal communications.

THE INTERNATIONAL MARKETING CHALLENGE

International markets offer vast opportunities for firms with a product or a service potentially in demand abroad. As the Domino's case shows, even when the imported product deviates from local tastes and customs, it can penetrate a market. Novelty, cultural attractiveness, and appropriate marketing strategies can get a product through the door in some international markets. Some U.S. products are even more successful abroad than at home. For example, U.S.-based Kenny Rogers Roasters filed for bankruptcy in 1998 and was purchased the following year by Nathan's Famous; however, Kenny Rogers China, led by the former head of Kentucky Fried Chicken's (KFC) operations there, continues to operate and expand in that country. Unfortunately, this is the exception, not the norm.

International markets are full of pitfalls and littered with failed attempts at foreign expansion. Dunkin' Donuts closed its China operations in 1999, as did Tex-Mex. Office Max closed its doors in Japan four years after its initial entry. Gateway Computers divested its foreign operations altogether. Many otherwise successful brands do not sell well in foreign markets; for instance, Campbell's Soup did not do well in Brazil, and McDonald's failed to find a following in Barbados. Initial success often proves elusive, evaporating when the novelty of the product wears off or when pent-up demand slackens.[1] British wireless provider Vodafone retreated from Japan in 2006, having failed to find a following among Japanese consumers. For years, U.S. and Japanese manufacturers attempted unsuccessfully to sell dishwashers in Japan; however, local housewives felt guilty not washing the dishes by hand and found the machine too bulky for their small kitchens and inadequate when it came to Japanese staples such as sticky rice, raw eggs, and fermented soybeans. Manufacturers have been working on a smaller dishwasher, but it is not yet clear whether demand for the machine will be there.[2]

In addition to local adaptation, firms increasingly face the intense competition associated with globalization. Markets that in the past have been insular or have relied on a single source of imports now have a bewildering array of offerings from multiple source countries. Indeed, the essence of international marketing, especially in more global industries, is that competition can come from anywhere on the globe. Being the country in which the product originated (e.g., a spaghetti noodle maker from Italy) can help but is no guarantee of success.

Success in international markets depends on meeting many challenges: accurate assessment of market potential, selection of the right product mix, and appropriate adjustments in distribution, pricing, packaging, and advertising. Cultural values and social mores, rules and regulations, economic conditions, and political realities constitute the context within which international marketing takes place. The increasing diversity within many national environments (e.g., the growth of the Hispanic sector in the United States) represents an additional challenge but also an opportunity: Upstart Alo Vatan has become the third largest provider of phone service for the large Turkish community in Germany by being tuned in to the Turk's linguistic, cultural, religious, and social sensitivities.[3]

Assessing Market Potential

To assess the potential of a foreign market, firms seek to identify the aggregate demand for a product (or a service) and estimate the costs associated with product introduction and distribution as well as with adapting the product to a new environment. Accessibility, profitability, and market size all play a role in deciding market priority. In and of itself, population size reveals little about short-term market potential. When China embarked on economic reforms in 1978, MNEs salivated at the prospect of "selling a toothbrush to every Chinese" in a country of well over a billion, only to discover that most Chinese had neither the desire nor the money to buy foreign products at that time. It has taken more than 20 years for China to become the substantial consumer market it is today.

Probably the single most important indicator of market potential is economic development and its correlate, disposable income.[4] Nominal income figures say little, however, about consumers' ability to afford certain products and services. Thus, economists use Purchasing Power Parity (PPP) to adjust nominal figures to the purchasing power of local consumers. The Big Mac Index, published by the *Economist*, shows what a McDonald's Big Mac costs in selected locations around the world in both unadjusted and PPP terms[5] (see Exhibit 16.1).

In addition to income figures, per capita GDP figures are often used to gauge the potential in a given market. In Exhibit 16.2, the relationship between GDP levels and car ownership is shown for a variety of countries.

While GDP and disposable income provide a preliminary measure of market potential, the actual opportunity will vary greatly based on local idiosyncrasies, way of life, and consumption patterns. For instance, research by the Boston Consulting Group showed that in some developing economies such as Colombia or the Philippines, Coca-Cola is a substitute for potable water. Other research shows that the French drink six times more wine than the British, whereas Germans consume six times the amount of beer as Italians,[6] and that Venezuelans, Mexicans, Russians, Turks, and South Africans (in that order) care most about their appearance.[7] Venezuelans also spend as much as 20% of their household income on personal care products and hold the world record for deodorant use.[8] One-Hour Martinizing, a dry-cleaning franchise, decided to open its first foreign franchise in Ecuador after discovering that businessmen there changed their shirts as much as three times a day because of the hot, sticky weather.[9]

Demographics also play a role in estimating future market potential. For instance, Japan and many EU countries face low and even negative population growth and an aging population, whereas most Asian nations are forecasted to grow and maintain relatively youthful populations (China is an exception owing to the One Child policy). These forecasts spell, for example, strong market demand for toys in Indonesia and, at the same time, increased demand for health care products and services in the EU and Japan.

Exhibit 16.1   Big Mac Prices in Selected Markets

	Big Mac Prices		Implied PPP* of the Dollar	Actual Dollar Exchange Rate (5/22/06)	Under-(−) or Over-(+) Valuation Against the Dollar (%)
	In Local Currency	In Dollars			
United States[†]	$3.10	3.10	–	–	–
Argentina	Peso7.00	2.29	2.26	3.06	−26
Australia	A$3.25	2.44	1.05	1.33	−21
Brazil	Real6.40	2.78	2.06	2.30	−10
Britain	£1.94	3.65	1.60[†]	1.88[†]	+18
Canada	C$3.52	3.14	1.14	1.12	+1
Chile	Peso1,560	2.94	503	530	−5
China	Yuan10.5	1.31	3.39	8.03	−58
Czech Rep	Koruna59.05	2.67	19.0	22.1	−14
Denmark	DKr27.75	4.77	8.95	5.82	+54
Euro area[§]	£2.94	3.77	1.05**	1.28**	+22
Hong Kong	HK$12	1.55	3.87	7.75	−50
Hungary	Forint560	2.71	181	206	−12
Indonesia	Rupiah14,600	1.57	4,710	9,325	−49
Japan	¥250	2.23	80.6	112	−28
Malaysia	Ringgit5.50	1.52	1.77	3.63	−51
Mexico	Peso29.00	2.57	9.53	11.3	−17
New Zealand	NZ$4.45	2.75	1.44	1.62	−11
Peru	New Sol9.50	2.91	3.06	3.26	−6
Philippines	Peso85.00	1.62	27.4	52.6	−48
Poland	Zloty6.50	2.10	2.10	3.10	−32
Russia	Rouble48.00	1.77	15.5	27.1	−43
Singapore	S$3.60	2.27	1.16	1.59	−27
South Africa	Rand13.95	2.11	4.50	6.60	−32
South Korea	Won2,500	2.62	806	952	−15
Sweden	SKr33.00	4.53	10.6	7.28	+46
Switzerland	SFr6.30	5.21	2.03	1.21	+68
Taiwan	NT$75.00	2.33	24.2	32.1	−25
Thailand	Baht60.00	1.56	19.4	38.4	−50
Turkey	Lire4.20	2.72	1.35	1.54	−12
Venezuela	Bolivar5,701	2.17	1,839	2,630	−30

SOURCE: "McCurrencies." *Economist,* May 7, 2006. Copyright © 2006 The Economist Newspaper Ltd. All rights reserved. Reprinted with permission. Further reproduction prohibited. www.economist.com.

* Purchasing-power parity—local price divided by price in United States; [†] average of New York, Chicago, San Francisco, and Atlanta; [‡] dollars per pound; [§] weighted average of prices in euro area.
** Dollars per euro.

Exhibit 16.2   Relationship Between GDP per Capita and Vehicle Ownership

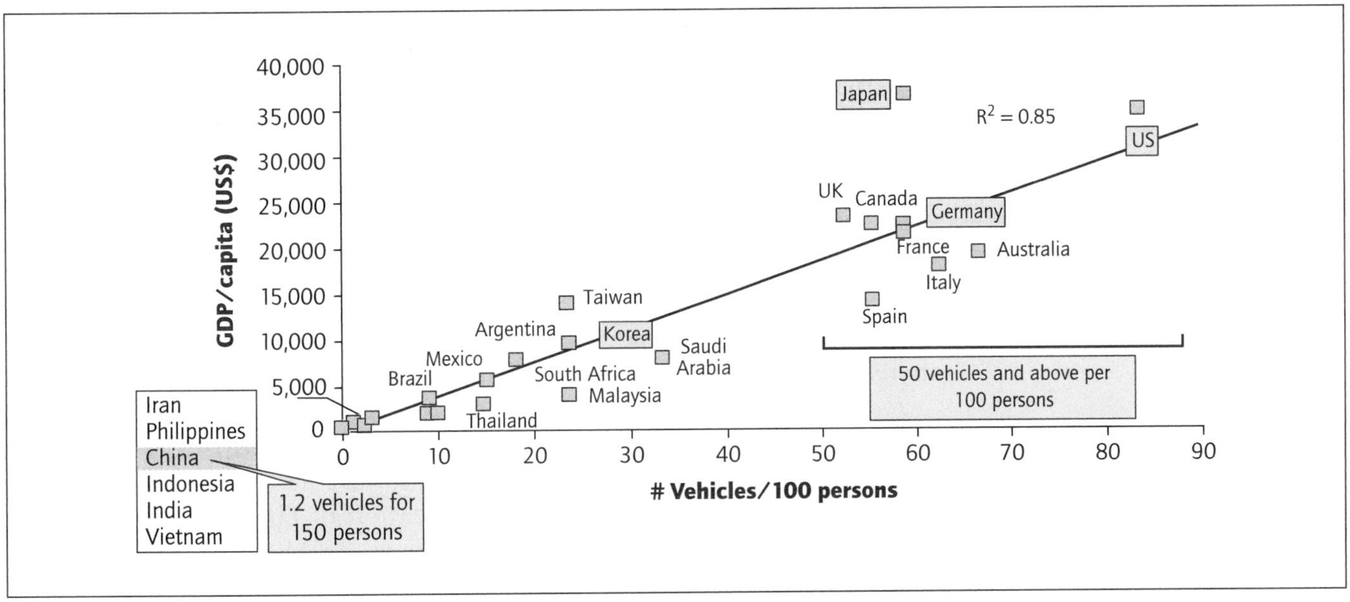

SOURCE: Mercer Management Consulting.

To explore those opportunities systematically, firms undertake international marketing research. The research is aimed at answering the following questions:[10] (a) What objectives should the firm pursue in the foreign market? (b) What foreign market segments should the firm pursue? (c) What are the best product, distribution, pricing, and promotion strategies for the foreign market? (d) What should be the product–market–company mix in order to take advantage of foreign marketing opportunities?

GLOBALIZATION AND LOCALIZATION IN INTERNATIONAL MARKETS

As in other areas of international business, striking a balance between globalization and localization is a key challenge in international marketing. Lack of marketing globalization has proved to be detrimental to performance;[11] however, the same is true for indiscriminate standardization of marketing practices without attention to localization factors.[12] Here is how the globalization-versus-localization dilemma is described in a Conference Board report citing General Motors Europe:

Generally, the more closely defined the market segment, the less important are national stereotypes (Germans focus on ecology, Italians on performance). Across national markets, there is a trend toward greater similarity on product specifications, price, and packaging. On the other hand, cultural and national differences exist and require flexibility in communication with customers.

Globalization, in a marketing sense, is the standardization of products (or services), brands, marketing, advertising, and the supply chain across countries and regions. Localization, in contrast, is the adjustment of one or more of the above elements to be idiosyncratic characteristics of a given national market. Determining and fine-tuning the globalization–localization balance is a major challenge for the MNE. The challenge is approached and handled in different ways. Cees van der Hoven, CEO of Ahold NV, the number-three supermarket chain globally behind Wal-Mart and French Carrefour, summarizes his firm's strategy succinctly: "Everything the customer sees we localize, everything they don't see, we globalize." Carrefour, while preferring brand uniformity and substituting global brands for the local brands it acquires, also tailors its products to local markets.[13]

Globalization Forces

Once the most localized and decentralized business function, marketing is increasingly coordinated on a global basis. Regional blocks such as the EU and ASEAN accelerate the trend. For instance, Dell Computer utilizes a Pan-European office to take advantage of increasing standardization of European rules and requirements, as do Microsoft and other leading companies.

Photo 16.2   **Like other firms, McDonald's adapts its menu and operations to local circumstances.**

SOURCE: Jupiterimages.

Global Brands

Behind the globalization trend is an assumption that despite local variations, many industrial and (to a lesser extent) consumer products can be standardized. "There are pipes all over the world and there are water leaks all over the world," says Richard Rennick, owner of American Leak Detection, whose franchises span more than 60 countries.[14] Kellogg designated Corn Flakes, Special K, Frosted Flakes, Fruit Loops, and Nutri-Grain bars as "global brands" because of their wide name recognition and global sales volume.[15] Avon launched its "Far Away" fragrance as a global product, reflecting inputs from most of its foreign subsidiaries, retaining positioning, pricing, packaging, and advertising uniformity to the extent possible.[16]

Global products are products that enjoy worldwide recognition and are relatively unaltered in terms of brand and appearance when offered abroad. AC Nielsen, the marketing research firm, created a ranking of global brands. To be designated global, products had to be sold throughout the world under the same name with more than $1 billion in sales and more than 5% of those sales outside the home market (see Exhibit 16.3).

Why Global Brands?

The primary motivation toward product and service globalization is to gain scale economies. Selling an identical product using the same promotional message and distribution channels reduces cost and complexity. JC Penney closed its home-furnishing stores in Japan because so many products had to be made differently for the Japanese market that it became unprofitable to operate there.[17] Globalization permits firms to leverage experience accumulated in one market toward another, using communications technologies to facilitate coordination

Exhibit 16.3   2005 Top Global Brands

Rank	Company	Headquarters	Brand	Brand Value ($Mil)
1	The Coca-Cola Company	Atlanta, GA	Coca-Cola	67,525
2	Microsoft	Redmond, WA	Microsoft	59,941
3	International Business Machines Corporation	White Plains, NY	IBM	53,376
4	GE	Fairfield, CT	GE	46,996
5	Intel	Santa Clara, CA	Intel	35,588
6	Nokia	Finland	Nokia	26,452
7	Walt Disney Company	Burbank, CA	Disney	26,441
8	McDonald's Corporation	Oak Brook, IL	McDonald's	26,014
9	Toyota Motor Company	Japan	Toyota	24,837
10	Altria Group	New York	Marlboro	21,189
11	DaimlerChrysler AG	Germany	Mercedes-Benz	20,006
12	Citigroup	New York	Citi	19,967
13	Hewlett-Packard	Palo Alto, CA	Hewlett-Packard	18,866
14	American Express	New York	American Express	18,559
15	Gillette (P&G)	Cincinnati, OH	Gillette	17,534

SOURCE: Adapted from *BusinessWeek*, 2005.

and integration. In addition, the allure of a "global" product can be an important selling point for some consumers.

Marketing Repercussions of a Global Approach

What does the current trend toward globalization mean to the marketing function? Here are some of the key ramifications:[18]

Rapid rollout of new products across major markets, preempting competitors from introducing similar products

Product prioritization and targeting across markets, blocking local product offerings

Globally uniform branding and advertising to create a consistent message, reassure customers of global reach, and reduce cost and duplication; this improves the probability of entry into the increasingly crowded shelves of retailers that display only bestselling brands

Manufacturing relatively standardized products to scale economies

Transfer of marketing best practices across borders

A Conference Board survey suggests that the greatest increase in globalization is set to occur in advertising, brand positioning, and package design.

Further, such coordination seems to distinguish the successful from the less successful firms. Successful firms also coordinate pricing to some extent, but not new product development.[19]

A by-product of the increased globalization of the marketing function is the erosion in the authority of country managers (see Chapter 11 for a description of the country manager role). Today's country managers find themselves exercising lesser control over marketing budget, pricing, and other key marketing decisions. Although they usually maintain control over local brands and have some say in new product development, their influence over the marketing of global brands in their country of jurisdiction is on the wane. National brand managers, where they exist, report directly to a global marketing group rather than the country manager.[20] An innovative design solution is AMP's global account group, which assigns marketing executives to work directly with key clients in the United States, Japan, and Europe.[21]

Localization Forces

As earlier noted, localization forces are pressures toward adjustment in product marketing or distribution to make it more appealing or to meet requirements particular to a foreign market. Following a spate of alleged product contamination and other problems in foreign markets, Coca-Cola executives noted that the firm's motto "Think globally and act locally" needed to be changed to "Think locally and act locally." Indeed, despite globalization, local conditions remain paramount. In the global music market, the share of recording by local artists has risen from 58% in 1991 to 68% in 2000.[22] U.S. cable channels such as HBO acknowledge that they grossly underestimated the need for adjustment in Asian markets. Among other customization requirements, HBO has to satisfy Malaysian and Singaporean censors, who demand editing out sensitive material.[23] Firms in other industries do not fare better. Metro Cash and Carry was "taken to the cleaners" when it tried to import its South African wholesale model in Israel.[24] Carrefour, the French supermarket giant, suffered huge losses in Japan, where it never adjusted to the Japanese habit of purchasing small daily quantities of food.[25] Carrefour eventually pulled out of the country. Similarly, Wal-Mart, the world's largest retailer, has sold its South Korean stores to a Korean competitor who proceeded to remake them in Korean style. Wal-Mart also withdrew from Germany, where its store greeting, product mix, and store location model did not fare well.

Cross-national variations have a significant impact on sales and marketing. Differences in income levels create different consumer requirements. Diverse regulatory regimes put different constraints on product design, packaging, and promotion. Even in the EU, where logotype and trademarks are relatively standardized, promotion, pricing, and media mix are far from uniform.[26] For instance, regulations regarding vitamins in foodstuffs such as cereal force manufacturers to produce multiple versions of the same product, substantially increasing cost.[27] Social attitudes and public opinion also make a difference. Kellogg's Nutri-Grain, successful in the United States, did not do nearly as well in the United Kingdom, where health consciousness had not been raised prior to the time it was introduced.[28] Opposition to genetically modified foods, muted in the United States, has been vocal in the EU and Canada, although many suggest that the limitation on the sales of such foods, where the U.S. is the global leader, are a protectionist measure, a nontariff trade barrier (see Chapter 2).

Culture also has a major influence on marketing. Cultures high on power distance and uncertainty avoidance place more emphasis on appearance as a way to reaffirm one's status and to reduce uncertainty regarding others' positions. Members of high-power-distance cultures are more likely, for instance, to buy expensive watches, a status symbol. In cultures with high uncertainty avoidance, consumers buy more bottled water but fewer used cars because they want to minimize surprises. Jewelry purchase has been found to be more related to high masculinity scores than to purchasing power.[29] In high-power-distance cultures, a sales pitch will be made in a formal manner and advertisements are likely to showcase a model "in control" of a situation,[30] whereas the pitch is likely to be personalized in individualistic countries.[31]

Cultural and social mores also shape the context in which a product is used. In Hong Kong, Taiwan, and Mainland China, McDonald's restaurants serve as space for social activity for seniors in the late morning and for schoolchildren in the afternoon.[32] In this case, cultural rankings on collectivism are supplemented by physical realities: With residential space scarce, the restaurants provide an opportunity for social gathering. This affects everything from restaurant design to hours of operation and product preference.

Product Adaptation

Faced with a foreign market with different characteristics, a firm may choose not to offer a product or a service in that market, offer the same product it offers in other markets, or adapt it to regional or country requirements. To make the decision, firms use "benefit/cost" and "user/need" models. Benefit/cost models assess the advantages and disadvantages of a product or distribution mode in a given market. User/need models test the needs of potential customers, including the circumstances in which the product or service is likely to be used. The analysis yields a decision to standardize or customize the product or its promotion and distribution.

Following disappointing sales in India, Ford decided to develop "an Indian car," the first designed and built for a developing market. While using the Ford Fiesta platform to lower development costs, the car shows little resemblance to the Fiesta. Extras were cut to make possible a price tag that would appeal to value-conscious consumers and local content beefed up to reduce costs and meet government requirements. Ford's designers and engineers drove many miles on India's roads with families of five, a key customer group, making the following adjustments to customer requirements:

> Rear headroom was raised to make way for men in turbans, doors were adjusted to open wider than normal to avoid catching the flowing saris of women, air intake valves were fitted to avoid flooding during monsoon season, shock absorbers were toughened for pock-marked city streets, and air conditioning was revved up for summer heat.[33]

With the Indian market increasingly attractive, more companies make sure their product is adapted to local conditions. Nokia, for instance, sells in India cell phones with a dust-resistant touch pad an antislip grip for humid conditions, and, of course, the ability to support Hindi.[34]

The Volkswagen Beetle (not the New Beetle), manufactured in Mexico, is not exported to the United States because compliance with U.S. safety and emission standards would make it prohibitively expensive. Mitsubishi gave up building a "global car" and redesigned its cars sold in the United States to be "more American." Toyota and Nissan increased engine size and interior space in their U.S.

models and moved much of the design and development to the United States to be closer to the market. Honda credits its U.S. market research with the addition of a third row of seats on its sport-utility vehicle, something to which Japanese designers initially objected.[35] Coca-Cola, the quintessential global brand, tinkers with its formula to suit local taste. Its Diet Coke is sold in France as Coke Light. Kraft Foods sweetens the flavors of Tang for sale in Latin America. In Israel, Pizza Hut features special toppings not offered elsewhere in the world, including imitation shrimp. In Egypt, Chili's offers a version of the Sohur (a special midnight buffet) during the month of Ramadan when Moslems fast from daylight to sunset.[36] *Time* magazine, whose first international edition dates back to 1942, publishes different editions for the U.S., Asian, and European markets, among others, as does the *Wall Street Journal*. In both cases, regional editions share some common material but use local content as appropriate. As in other cases, this customization has been greatly aided by technological advances that enable simultaneous printing in different locations.

While making adjustments to local tastes and customs, it is equally important for the MNE to leverage its name recognition and global reputation. McDonald's is the largest fast-food chain in the world, with more than 30,000 restaurants, about 17,000 of these in 121 foreign countries, employing over 314,000 people. With 60% of its profits coming from international sales, the firm's motto is "All business is local." As its then head of international operations said, "We don't run Spain out of Portugal." McDonald's is selling Big Macs around the world, but in Seoul it also offers roast pork on a bun with garlicky soy sauce.[37] In selected Jerusalem outlets, Big Macs (minus the cheese) are kosher. In India, where cows are sacred, Veggie McNuggets are served. When the Indonesian rupee collapsed during the Asian financial crisis, rice was added to the menu as a substitute for expensive fries. While offering local variants, as shown in Exhibit 16.4, McDonald's makes full use of its scale and spread. It serves a global brand which customers can find in multiple locations.

The adaptation challenge extends to all marketing aspects. In Japan, manufacturers' relationships with suppliers and distributors often last for decades. Despite a growing proliferation of larger stores and retail chains, Japanese retail trade continues to be fragmented, dominated by small, family-owned merchants, with half of the retail establishments employing one or two people.[38] When Office Depot and Office Max launched their Japanese outlets as replicas of the firms' U.S.-based large, warehouse-type discount stores, they soon discovered that the global efficiencies derived from this strategy were insufficient to compensate for high rents and for the reluctance to buy in an impersonal, warehouse-type store. The firms changed their strategies accordingly.[39] Office Max eventually exited the Japanese market. Still, a decade of Japanese economic stagnation has encouraged the entry of discount chains into the market, with many of those carrying imported merchandise, often from China.

Exhibit 16.4   Product Adjustments at McDonald's

Country	Adjustment
Switzerland	Veggie Mac, and ski-thru window in some restaurants
Singapore	Chicken rice, also reduced fat in foods, switched to vegetable oil in food preparation and in french fries
Saudi Arabia	Traditional first floor, family section on the second floor; all Muslim employees; nonpork menus

Country	Adjustment
Portugal	Traditional bica (like espresso) served in porcelain instead of foam cups. Pasties de nata (Portuguese style cakes) added to menus alongside traditional muffins and brownies
Paraguay	Use of computers and Internet in select restaurants, McMacos, McFiesta added to menus (lower price and smaller size)
Netherlands	McKroket (100% beef ragout with crispy layer around it, topped with fresh mustard and mayonnaise sauce)
Mexico	McNifica, McBurrito à la Mexicana
Japan	Teriyaki McBurger (sausage patty on a bun with teriyaki sauce)
Italy	Salads featuring Mediterranean flavors. Marinara (shrimp and salmon in fresh lettuce), Vegetariana (veggie), Mediteranea (cheese and olive), Fiordiriso (rice, tuna, ham, mushrooms)
Ireland	Shamrock shake (available during St. Patrick's Day celebrations)
Hong Kong	Curry potato pie, shake fries, red bean sundae
Germany	Translating Quarter Pounder to metric system is difficult, so they named it McRoyal and Hamburger Royal
Argentina	McCafe (a variety of coffees, pastries, desserts), McSwing (ice cream with various toppings)
Australia	McCafe with formal cutlery, special napkins, china cups, chocolate desserts, uniforms of black and gold
Chile	McPalta (made from avocados)

SOURCE: Used with permission from McDonald's Corporation.

COUNTRY BOX

KIMCHI WARS

Kimchi is a Korean national dish of fermented cabbage, which is also popular in Japan and a number of other East Asian countries. The dish received mixed reviews in foreign markets, with many customers complaining about strong taste and offensive smell. A group of Korean food scientists was recently recruited by Doosan, South Korea's leading kimchi producer, to develop a version that would appeal to Americans and displace imports from Japan, which currently dominate international markets with a 70% share.

The South Korean team (known as the "kimchi doctors") faced a challenge similar to that of other international marketers: How to develop a product that is attractive in a foreign market yet retains the unique characteristics and allure of its country of origin, and how to differentiate its product from its major competitors. The team succeeded in developing kimchi with longer shelf life and a smell more appealing to Westerners. In the summer of 2001, Korean kimchi manufacturers won an important victory when the Codex Alimentarius, which sets international food standards accepted by the WTO, adopted a global standard for kimchi that corresponds to the Korean method of preparing the dish.

Doosan also faces competition from other domestic manufacturers, among them a company previously allied with a kosher food manufacturer in New York that is now developing kimchi kraut for the European market and a kimchi-topped burger for McDonald's. Meanwhile, Pizza Hut has introduced a kimchi topping for its pizza that now accounts for 30% of its Korean sales.

This was not the end of the kimchi war, however. In 2005, the South Korean authorities said they found parasite eggs in kimchi imported from China and halted all kimchi imports from that country, which was about to pass the 100,000-tons mark (versus just 90 tons in 1999). Accusing the Koreans of protectionism, China promptly retaliated, stopping all kimchi imports from South Korea. Among those hurt by the move was Doosan, which established kimchi production in China in 2003.

SOURCES: Adapted from J. Solomon. "Stinking national dish seeks smell of success and a global market." *Wall Street Journal,* August 17, 2001, A1; T. I. Tsai. "Korea swallows its pride in Chinese kimchi war." *China Business,* November 22, 2005.

Country-of-Origin Effect

Country-of-origin effect is the influence of the country of manufacturing's image on the buying decision. The effect consists of these perceptual dimensions: innovativeness—namely the use of new technology and engineering advances; design—namely appearance, style, color, and variety; prestige (i.e., exclusivity), status, and brand name reputation; and workmanship, including reliability, durability, craftsmanship, and manufacturing quality.[40] There is strong evidence that country of origin influences buyers' perceptions, regardless of reality.[41] For instance, British firms are not associated in the consumer's mind with products and innovations they have actually created.[42]

Country-of-origin effect can change over time. In the 1960s, Japanese products had a reputation of shoddy quality, and it was decades before the country established a reputation for quality manufacturing. The same evolution occurred for products from South Korea and, more recently, for those made in China; however, as the recent scare regarding made-in-China products illustrates, that reputation can be tarnished almost overnight, especially where safety is a concern. Since products from developed nations tend to receive higher evaluation,[43] a country moving into the ranks of developed economies is also likely to enhance the reputation of its products. In the interim, firms from emerging economies often engage in reputation-enhancing activities. Giant Manufacturing, a Taiwanese bicycle maker, sponsors professional racing teams to build a reputation as a company staying on the leading edge of technology.[44]

Leveraging a Positive Country Image

Country image varies across product categories.[45] German automotive firms take advantage of the country's reputation for advanced engineering, quality, and reliability; however, BMW, owner of the Rolls-Royce brand, assembles the car in England and touts its British origin because of the vehicle's association, in the consumer's mind, with British high class. Japanese automotive and electronics makers are known for the quality and reliability of their products and will often highlight the country of origin in their product promotion. Other countries may be noted for a single product—for example, Iranian carpets or Russian caviar. Here, a British publication laments the country's top ranking in merely one industry:

> The United States is rated best for many key sectors, including retail, computers, and telecom; Germany is top for sectors such as engineering, cars, and beer; France for cosmetics, food, health care, spirits; Japan for consumer electronics and domestic appliances; Britain is rated top for just one commercial area: air travel.[46]

A positive country image may lead to minimized customization that is not inherent to product use. The original appearance and packaging will be preserved to the extent permitted by law so as to highlight the product's national origin. An example is Ikea, the Swedish furniture retailer, which highlights its national origin to leverage the positive image of Scandinavian furniture as stylish, practical, well designed, and reasonably priced. At other times, the image may lead a company to customize a product, so it will remind the customer of a different locale; for instance, Anheuser-Bush has launched in the U.S. beers that intentionally look like imports.[47]

Leveraging Nationalist Sentiments

Sometimes, the country of origin serves as a patriotic call to arms to buy domestic products or services. Many countries have seen campaigns in which consumers are encouraged to "buy local" as a way of supporting local industry and employment. For example, a prospective car buyer may be reminded that by buying a Chevrolet he or she will prevent further deterioration of the U.S. trade deficit with Japan, or that buying a Ford will keep jobs in the United States. To counterbalance the appeal of such calls, foreign car makers like Toyota and Honda who manufacture in the U.S. take full-page advertisements touting the number of American jobs they create and their support of various community activities in the country.

Support of domestic products will sometimes deteriorate to vilification of foreign products. For example, Japanese farmers had placed ads in local newspapers accusing U.S. orange growers of spreading "agent orange" on their fruit (Agent Orange was a chemical used by the U.S. armed forces in Vietnam to retard vegetation growth and has no relation to the fruit). In India, angry protesters attacked Coke and Pepsi facilities after it had been alleged that their beverages contain pesticides (the companies retort that the water they use is safe and meets all international and local standards). Because of their visibility, companies such as Coca-Cola and McDonald's are often identified with their home country and hence vulnerable to backlashes related to its acts. When Serbian students demonstrated against U.S. interests during NATO's military campaign, McDonald's and Coca-Cola topped the target list.[48] In the aftermath of the invasion of Iraq, McDonald's restaurants were targeted by terrorists in Turkey and Italy. Overall, the standing of U.S. brands had initially suffered as a result of opposition to the Iraq War, but by 2006 their reputation appeared to have rebounded. Still, negative attitudes toward the United States have been leveraged in the launch of Meca Cola, Arab Cola, and Muslim-Up to compete with the quintessential American brand in Arab countries as well as in Europe, which has a substantial Moslem minority.

Some foreign firms attempt to disarm nationalist sentiment by emphasizing the local content in their product. Local content is the portion of a product (or service) that includes locally made and procured inputs. Airbus, in its ads in the United States, lists its many U.S. suppliers. The aim is to "localize" the product, helping people feel that by buying the foreign product they are, in fact, supporting their countrymen. Finding a local angle is not always easy in an age when many products involve multiple nations and when the national flags of many countries are made abroad. Take, for example, the ad placed by German automaker Mercedes-Benz in a Canadian newspaper for its M-Class car manufactured in the United States. The firm touts that the plant's president is a Canadian. Still others may downplay the foreign origin of the product, using brand names and packaging that embed local heritage. In Russia, "the beloved taste of real Russian butter" appears on the package of butter from New Zealand, while Zlato vegetable oil, featuring a Russian peasant family in its TV commercials, originates in Argentina. The phenomenon does not extend, however, to products not held in high esteem by local consumers.[49]

MNEs often point out that local firms do not necessarily suffer from their entry. Burger Ranch, an Israeli burger chain, continued to prosper following the entry of McDonald's and Burger King, which greatly increased the overall market. In Latvia, Kvas, a traditional fermented drink, initially disappeared from the market under pressure from Coca-Cola and PepsiCo. Then, using modern production and marketing techniques and boasting of its healthy benefits, Kvas recaptured a third of the local market.[50] In Japan, locally based Askul successfully competed against Office Depot and Office Max with marketing that is better suited to the local environment.[51] With some creativity, a local player can even piggyback on the investment made by an MNE: A Russian detergent manufacturer took advantage of Procter & Gamble's campaign promoting its Ariel detergent over "ordinary powder" by introducing its "Ordinary Powder" brand. The local product, priced at about 15% of the import, managed to quickly capture a slice of the market.[52]

Branding

Branding is the process of creating and supporting positive perceptions associated with a product or service. In global markets, branding is especially complex, given varying demand and environmental characteristics. Procter & Gamble entered China in 1988 with one product. Today, the company has dozens of brands and a multibillion-dollar volume in profitable sales there. Here is how the former head of P&G's China operations views the principles that led P&G to create successful brands in China:

Selecting the right (Chinese) name

In-depth understanding of the local market and willingness to make the necessary adaptations

Fine-tuning the right size/price/value formulation of offerings

Providing quality and reliability at a competitive price

Holistic marketing using a variety of channels

Turning trademarks into "trust-marks"

Establishing leadership brands, changing social habits if necessary

Selecting the right allies and partners [Presentation at Ohio State University, 2000]

Companies that enjoy overall prestige and reputation are in an especially advantageous position to leverage their branding power. Exhibit 16.5 contains the rankings of *Fortune*'s Global Most Admired Companies. The list is dominated by U.S. firms (which also happen to have the highest "brand equity" globally), but the top 20 includes such firms as Toyota (Japan), BMW (Germany), Singapore Airlines, and Nokia (Finland).

Exhibit 16.6 lists some of *Business Week*'s top 100 global brands (only brands with at least 20% foreign revenues were included). Note that all but two of the top 10 are U.S. brands, but this is up from one five years ago.

The global reach of some brands should not distract attention from the power of local brands. Ahold's CEO notes that discarding the Dutch company's Swedish brand ICA would be "ridiculous" since this brand ranks together with Volvo as one of the best-known brands in Sweden.[53]

Channel Decisions

Channel decisions involve the length (the number of levels or intermediaries employed in the distribution process) and width (the number of firms in each level) of the channel used in linking manufacturers to consumers.[54] In business-to-business sales, channel decisions are often more important than brand name,

Exhibit 16.5   *Fortune's* Global Most Admired Companies

2006 Rank	2001 Rank	Company	Country
1	1	General Electric	U.S.
2	10	Toyota Motor	Japan
3	26	Procter & Gamble	U.S.
4	74	FedEx	U.S.
5	17	Johnson & Johnson	U.S.
6	3	Microsoft	U.S.
7	7	Dell	U.S.
8	14	Berkshire Hathaway	U.S.
9	N/A	Apple Computer	U.S.
10	5	Wal-Mart Stores	U.S.
11	N/A	IBM	U.S.
12	N/A	Target	U.S.
13	N/A	BMW	Germany
14	24	United Parcel Service	U.S.
15	9	Home Depot	U.S.
16	61	PepsiCo	U.S.
17	N/A	Costco Wholesale	U.S.
18	4	Intel	U.S.
19	31	Singapore Airlines	Singapore
20	8	Nokia	Finland
21	18	Citigroup	U.S.
22	15	Coca-Cola	U.S.
23	33	BP	Britain
24	N/A	Bank of America	U.S.
25	35	ExxonMobil	U.S.

SOURCE: *Fortune* magazine. 2001 and 2006.

* Indicates a tie in rank.

advertising, and pricing.[55] A study of United Kingdom, Japanese, and German subsidiaries in the United States shows that they are more likely to localize channel decisions than product or pricing decisions. Localization is especially pronounced among UK affiliates, perhaps owing to the assumption of cultural similarity.[56]

Intermediation

Many international sales are not made directly by companies but by export intermediaries. Export intermediaries are firms that mediate between firms, especially SMIEs, and their export markets, by providing logistic, documentation, and related services. While intermediaries play a central role for smaller firms, their function is sometimes outsourced by large MNEs. When SED International, a leading international distributor of microcomputer and wireless communication products throughout the United States and Latin America, was designated a "Certified HP Top Value Reseller," it was given exclusive rights to offer top-selling HP products in several international markets.[57] SED resells HP products, charging customers up to 5% over competitors in the direct distribution channel. Because

Exhibit 16.6 **The Global Brand Scoreboard**

Rank	2005 Brand Value	$Billions	Country of Ownership
1	COCA-COLA	67.53	U.S.
2	MICROSOFT	59.94	U.S.
3	IBM	53.38	U.S.
4	GE	47.00	U.S.
5	INTEL	35.59	U.S.
6	NOKIA	26.45	Finland
7	DISNEY	26.44	U.S.
8	McDONALD'S	26.01	U.S.
9	TOYOTA	24.84	Japan
10	MARLBORO	21.19	U.S.
11	MERCEDES-BENZ	20.01	Germany
12	CITI	19.97	U.S.
13	HEWLETT-PACKARD	18.87	U.S.
14	AMERICAN EXPRESS	18.56	U.S.
15	GILLETTE	17.53	U.S.
16	BMW	17.13	Germany
17	CISCO	16.59	U.S.
18	LOUIS VUITTON	16.08	France
19	HONDA	15.79	Japan
20	SAMSUNG	14.96	S. Korea
21	DELL	13.23	U.S.
22	FORD	13.16	U.S.
23	PEPSI	12.40	U.S.
24	NESCAFE	12.24	Switzerland
25	MERRILL LYNCH	12.02	U.S.

SOURCE: Data adapted from Interbrand Corp., JPMorgan Chase & Co., Citigroup, Morgan Stanley; *BusinessWeek*, August 1, 2005.

of the amount of business it generates, HP prefers to deal with SED instead of handling multiple consumers.

Direct Marketing

Direct marketing involves selling directly to customers via individual agents who typically make a commission not only on their sales but also on the sales of other agents that they have recruited. The model was pioneered by cosmetics makers Avon and Mary Kay and was eventually adopted by manufacturers of other products. Amway has become the world's largest direct seller, with operations in many countries. Direct marketers face many problems abroad. The image of direct selling is quite low, especially in Asia. In China, the government initially ruled that direct sales constituted a "pyramid scheme" and banned such sales, although it has since retracted its position. In Japan, Avon found that its system of selling to random groups was ineffective, because people were reluctant to invite strangers into their homes. However, once Avon tinkered with the system to rely on groups of friends and acquaintances, the operation prospered.

Niche Marketing

Niche marketing is narrowly directed toward a predefined segment of the market. In international markets, niche marketing may be directed not only to a product category (e.g., low end) but also to an ethnic or geographical segment. Big Boy in Thailand, Schlotzky's Delicatessen in Malaysia, Shakey's Pizza Restaurant in the Philippines, and Carl's Jr. in Mexico all target a specific niche in their target market.[58] Convencao, a small Brazilian soft-drink company, cut into the market share of industry giants Coke and Pepsi by offering lower priced soft drinks in its home market.[59] A niche play can also serve as a base for expansion. Timberland, known for its weather-proofed boots, now exports casual wear to more than 50 (mostly developed) countries, including Italy.[60]

Pricing

Pricing is the decision and process of setting a price to a product or a service. In international markets, pricing is more complex owing to varying cost structures (e.g., transportation costs, tariffs) and variable market positioning. An equally equipped car will sell for substantially different prices in different EU markets. A British buyer seeking to buy a car in Belgium will not only find the steering wheel on the wrong side but could also face a reluctant dealer, deterred by exclusive distribution agreements. The European Commission fined German automaker Volkswagen for turning back German customers who sought to buy their cars from Italian dealers.

Price differentials facilitate market segmentation, allowing a firm to position its products differentially in different markets. Firms may hike prices where there is little competition and where consumer resistance to price increases is low. Or they may price a brand higher so it can be positioned as "premium." Belgian brewer Interbrew markets its Stella beer in the United States under the slogan "Reassuringly expensive."[61] Even if desirable, price consistency is not easy to achieve. For instance, some subsidiaries provide a higher level of service than others.[62] Prices are also influenced by host government decisions. The Turkish government imposes an 80% import tax on all vehicle imports to protect domestic vehicles manufactured in Turkey. In the United States, pharmaceutical manufacturers have been lobbying to prevent cheaper medicine imports, mostly from Canada, arguing that cheaper drugs lower the incentives for domestic manufacturing and expose consumers to the risk of fakes.[63]

Predatory Pricing

Predatory pricing is the selling of goods below real cost so as to drive competitors out of the market (which enables the predator firms to eventually raise prices). Matsushita allegedly priced its Panasonic TV sets below cost in the United States, subsidizing sales with its high margins in the Japanese market and driving U.S. manufacturers out of business.[64] A complaint by Zenith was dismissed on the grounds that if Matsushita had priced its products below cost, it would have gone out of business in the 20 years the case took to resolve.[65] A similar complaint was filed by Republic Engineered Steels and Timken, which argued that Brazilian exporters were selling steel at 40% below their home-market price, or the cost of manufacturing the product in Brazil.[66] In recent years,

Chinese products have become the subject of predatory pricing complaints in the United States (see also the description of "dumping" in Chapter 2).

Promotion

Globalization can yield substantial savings in product promotion. When United Distillers (now Diageo) bought control of its distributors it consolidated more than 50 campaigns worldwide into one.[67] General Motors Europe uses a unified promotional approach to drive brand identity; however, it recognizes the need for adaptation in some markets. When it launched its Omega sedan, it created a single European campaign but held a separate campaign for Germany and Switzerland. Still, the savings must be assessed vis-à-vis existing local variations that may lower the effectiveness of global promotion.

Advertising

Like other marketing functions, if not more, advertising needs to be adjusted to local tastes, norms, and regulations if it is to be effective in international markets. When Lego introduced an advertising campaign that had been successful in the United States into Japan, it quickly flopped.[68] Like other firms, Lego discovered that moving advertising across borders is difficult linguistically, culturally, and socially.[69] Missteps are common. DHL Worldwide Express had to apologize for an ad that Indonesians felt likened then-president Suharto to a courier. Nike was criticized for an ad showing the Brazilian national team playing a soccer match against the devil, which viewers found blasphemous rather than humorous.[70] In another incident, Nike sold shoes with an imprint that reminded some Moslems of the Arabic script for "God." The perceived insult was especially severe because a shoe sole is considered by Moslems to be impure (e.g., it should not be shown to a counterpart to a conversation), and Nike had to pull 37,000 shoes off the shelves. Even savvy MNEs such as Coca-Cola, which announced that it would stay away from controversial topics such as religion, politics, and disease,[71] encounter difficulty. When a rumor spread in Egypt that the Coca-Cola logo contained the Arabic words for "no Mohammed, no Mecca," the firm countered with a decree from Egypt's Mufti, the country's top religious authority, that the logo did not defame Islam.[72] Some firms, in contrast, thrive on controversy: Benetton purposely includes religion and subjects such as the death penalty and the aids epidemic in its global advertising campaigns.

The temptation to standardize advertising is considerable. Standardization provides a coherent and consistent message and greatly reduces production cost by spreading it across multiple markets. McKinsey calculated that Gillette saved $20 million by creating a global campaign for its Sensor razor in 19 markets, out of a total advertising expense of $175 million.[73] Cable television and the Internet make a global campaign more feasible today than in the past. Coca-Cola, Benetton, and, more recently, Ford have all launched global advertising campaigns. However, as the Conference Board notes, advertising uniformity depends on "the similarity of consumer buying motivations and of competitors' messages; the existence of specific government restrictions on content; and the availability of desired media channels."[74] In Canada, for example, infomercials can only be aired after midnight. Other countries prohibit the use of brand names during programs. Indeed, Coca-Cola has recently abandoned its global ad campaign, although it maintains central "guidance, process, and strategy" for its advertising efforts.[75]

As they globalize their marketing, firms increasingly seek advertising agencies with the global reach to provide a one-stop shop. Kellogg assigned responsibilities for three of its global brands to Leo Burnett and assigned two others to J. Walter Thompson. This is one reason for the consolidation of advertising agencies into global networks. Network members share the reach and brand recognition of the network while offering in-depth knowledge of the local market. At the same time, advertising agencies tap locations such as Canada and Mexico to lower their production costs for TV commercials, among other promotions.

Marketing Alliances

International strategic alliances are a major market entry venue. Such alliances as well as mergers and acquisitions allow a firm to quickly establish itself in a foreign market (see also Chapters 10 and 12). Leuven (Belgium)-based Interbrew grew through a series of acquisitions from a small family-owned brewery to the world's second largest brewer and the owner of more than 200 brands. Its typical strategy: Retain the existing local brands while leveraging distribution channels to market high-margin specialty brands.[76] Similar moves by Coca-Cola to acquire smaller rivals and link their distribution channels with its own have raised concerns among competition authorities in the EU and Mexico.[77] Marketing alliances are also established between large firms; for example, IBM and Dai Nippon Printing cooperate in database marketing. Swiss food giant Nestlé and French retailer Casino cooperate in marketing, logistics, and sales. The two share and analyze bar code information to learn how to enhance customer loyalty while reducing costs.[78]

Interim Summary

1. Market potential is a function of economic (e.g., disposable income), cultural, and social factors.

2. Globalization forces include the emergence of global brands, the prospect of cost savings and efficiencies, technological advances, and lower trade barriers. Localization forces include a variety of country-level factors that affect product appeal and adaptation requirements not only for the product itself but also for marketing channels, pricing, and promotion.

3. Country of origin exerts substantial influence on consumer purchasing decisions.

4. Branding, channel decisions, and promotion all reflect the globalization–localization tension.

THE GLOBAL SUPPLY CHAIN

The term *global supply chain* covers both logistics and operations. It includes such activities as sourcing and outsourcing, procurement, order processing, manufacturing, warehousing, inventory control, servicing and warranty, customs clearing, wholesaling, and distribution. Supply chain management is a key component in a firm's global strategy, influencing major decisions such as plant and service location. A report published by the Conference Board states: "in today's world, it is supply chains that compete, not companies."[79] A survey of major U.S. companies found that three-quarters of respondents believed that having an effective supply chain had a major impact on their company's ability to meet its strategic objectives. A reduced operating cost, improved sales and market share, and enhanced customer service have all been noted as being closely tied with supply chain effectiveness.[80] Not surprisingly, having an effective global supply chain can be a key competitive advantage.

In real terms, the cost of logistics has been falling for years,[81] although fluctuations (for example, the extra cost associated with the rise in oil prices and enhanced security since 9/11) are expected to continue. Intercountry variations remain substantial: Whereas logistics represent roughly 8% of U.S. GDP, the corresponding numbers are 11% for Europe, 13% for India, and 21% for China, but all these numbers have been going down for years.[82] The overall decline in logistic costs reflects increased efficiencies—for example, the incorporation of just-in-time production systems and the resulting decrease in inventory levels.[83] Stride Rite Corp., a retailer of athletic and casual footwear, cut by one-third the shipping time of shoes manufactured in Asia to its distribution center in Kentucky. The retailer cut 30% of its transportation cost and improved inventory turnaround time by 25%.[84]

Still, even e-commerce has so far failed to create a "seamless" supply chain. Among the 600 e-marketplaces seeking to match corporate buyers and suppliers in early 2000, "virtually none is capable of handling international logistics, credit verification, and payment between companies in different countries." Issues such as international shipping costs, language, currency translation, customs documentation, and cross-border financial settlement are only beginning to be addressed.[85] Forrester Research found that most companies failed to calculate the total cost of shipping an international order, and many were losing money on shipments for failing to adjust pricing to reflect real costs (see also Chapter 18). Additionally,

> Eighty-five percent of the companies noted that they could not fill overseas orders because of the complexity of shipping across borders. Of those that had problems shipping overseas, 75% cited their system's inability to register international addresses accurately or to price total delivery cost.[86]

The Globalization of Supply Chains

This shift from domestic to global supply chains is driven by rapidly escalating capital costs and enhanced technologies as well as by regional integration. To deliver a product or service effectively, firms increasingly consolidate production and distribution in a few strategic locations. The evolution of flexible manufacturing systems enables mass customization to meet customer demands at reasonable cost. Transport industry consolidation facilitates seamless transportation (e.g., Canada National Railways and Illinois Central plan to merge [as of mid-2007] to provide direct shipping between Canada, the United States, and Mexico). Developments in management information systems permit accurate tracking of variable customer demands and material flow. Suggests a logistics executive,

> In the past, for technical reasons, it was impossible to enter an order in one country, process it in another, and ship the goods from a third country. Now with the installation of a new client/server-based order management system, all this is possible.[87]

Where integration has progressed as in the EU, standardized regulations have been replacing national rules, enhancing the case for consolidation. French tire maker Michelin shifted from local plants manufacturing a variety of products to regional or global plants specializing in one type of product. The company now manufactures a given type of tire in just one or two European sites.[88] Nike consolidated its distribution operations in Belgium, and Energizer (the European arm of Eveready Battery) consolidated its 60 distribution systems into six. Becton Dickinson, a medical technology provider, developed a global supply chain as part of a broader shift from a decentralized geographical structure to a global design (see also Chapter 11). Other repercussions of supply chain globalization are extended supply and distribution chains, increased transportation from and to transportation centers, and more small-volume transactions.[89] These developments create opportunities for locals at the hub of logistic systems, especially if they manage to develop the requisite infrastructure.

The Challenge for SMIEs

SMIEs usually do not have the requisite economies to justify a specialized facility in a single location. One solution is mutualization—the sharing of logistic facilities by two or more partners.[90] SMIEs also form alliances with other firms, especially local companies. The local partner may already have a logistic component or a long-term logistic provider, which makes it difficult for the foreign firm to consolidate its supply chain locally. For instance, foreign investors in China found that their Chinese partner was not as helpful in resolving distribution obstacles they had initially believed.[91] Sourcing logistic services from third parties is another solution for the SMIE that is also used by large firms such as Marks & Spencer and Phillips Semiconductors. In such alliances, the shipper takes the lead in strategy formulation while the provider leads day-to-day operations. There is a sole key provider (although some of those purchase services from subcontractors) with whom the manufacturer has a close working relationship.[92]

Global Sourcing

Global sourcing is the procurement of production or service inputs and components in international markets. Global sourcing provides the MNE with the opportunity to leverage its scale and competitive advantage in spotting procurement opportunities around the globe for use in its various divisions and locations. For example, because of its scale, Wal-Mart uses its huge volume to extract lower prices from suppliers; Ford uses component parts produced in its Chinese joint ventures in its Brazilian assembly plants. Toronto-based Canadian Tire sources in the United States and Asia, importing 8,000 and 4,000 container loads annually from these respective locations.[93] Fashion house Donna Karan International sources more than half of its raw materials and finished products in Asia. MNEs also increasingly use outsourcing, or the buying of inputs outside their network. Firms may even outsource the logistic function itself.

Logistic Providers

While one-stop, international provision of logistic provision remains an ultimate goal, national services are more likely to be replaced by regional providers. Texas Instruments Semiconductors Group contracts with a key logistic provider to manage forwarding and distribution in each region of the world.[94] TNT Logistics distributes parts for Italian carmaker Fiat throughout Europe, while Fritz Companies handles warehousing and distribution for General Motors' after-sale parts and accessories in Taiwan.[95] Consolidation among providers is also apparent, as in the merger between U.S.-based AEI and Switzerland's Danzas. However, in other countries the number of logistic providers is actually increasing—for example, the number of logistic service providers in Brazil has tripled in three years.[96]

Customizing the Supply Chain

While the globalization of supply-chain management proceeds, various factors require continuous attention to localization and customization. Three sets of factors underpin localization: The first is variation among national environments. The second is product customization that triggers logistic adjustments. The third is the existence of national borders that constrain the free flow of goods and services and hence limit global product flow. Manufacturing advances—for example, the incorporation of suppliers' input at the product design phase—heighten dependencies and the logistic challenges that accompany the need to coordinate manufacturers and suppliers.

National Variation

World regions vary in size, terrain, and other characteristics that impact the supply chain. For example, the NAFTA land area is more than six times that of the EU, implying different logistic requirements and challenging the use of global "best practices." Skill level, quality of supplies, availability of process equipment and technologies, and the level of transportation and communications infrastructure vary substantially among regions. Asia, Africa, large parts of the Middle East, and Latin America suffer from poor infrastructure. Yet, although overall Asian infrastructure is relatively weak, Singapore has superb infrastructure in terms of both air and shipping. China has built remarkable infrastructure, especially in its coastal region, while India's infrastructure remains weak (which of course spells opportunities for infrastructure developers).

"We have ordered a lot of bicycles with cool boxes," says Paul Wright, the general manager for Commercial Development at TNT Logistics Asia, who noted that in many Asian locations "neither the technology nor the regulatory environment support logistics integration."[97] Energizer maintains Central and Eastern European operations separate in an otherwise integrated European supply chain, reflecting the significant differences in development levels and the lack of integration with the EU. Even among developed nations, conditions often vary. For instance, in the United States it takes three weeks from the time of manufacturing for breakfast cereals to reach retailers' shelves, but it takes 11 weeks in France.[98] This may explain why domestic supply chains continue to dominate the transfer of goods. Furthermore, increased FDI in local production bases creates even more reliance on domestic supply chains.[99] Fragmented supply chains and a great number of intermediaries add to the problem.[100]

Product and Logistic Customization

Product customization challenges supply-chain management characteristics because of its impact on modularity, packaging, transportation, tracking, shipping, and distribution. A "postponement" strategy, designed to delay customization to the latest possible value-adding phase, is not always feasible without compromising product variety.[101] Meritor, which used to provide a variety of automotive parts (mostly in North America), now manufactures only roofs, doors, and suspension systems but provides them to car manufacturers across the globe from 28 facilities in 13 countries.[102] When McDonald's started operations in Russia, it consolidated all its processing operations in one large facility. This was a radical departure from McDonald's operations around the globe but was necessary to overcome bottlenecks and supply disruptions.

Packaging

Standardization of packaging is appealing for logistic ease and because it promotes brand recognition. Kodak's yellow film box is recognized across the globe as is Fuji Film's green. Coca-Cola uses similar color and logo (albeit in different alphabets and characters) to enhance its brand. Package standardization also produces savings in design and promotion costs.[103] Mattel reduced the number of packages it prints for a single product from 14 to 3 to save on cost. The firm is now able to ship toys from one market to another in midseason.[104]

Some adaptations are necessary for logistic reasons, such as sturdier packaging to shield a product from outside elements in a harsh environment. Packaging size must often be adapted as well. Where space is scarce, as in the typical Japanese household, bulk packaging is less attractive to customers. Other adaptations are necessary to meet legal requirements. The 1991 German Packaging Ordinance requires manufacturers to use environmentally friendly, recyclable packaging material where feasible.[105] A similar law went into effect in Japan in 1996.[106] Various laws also govern safety (e.g., use of nonflammable material) requirements. Other packaging adaptations are necessary for cultural or religious reasons. For example, Hogla-Kimberly, a joint venture between Kimberly-Clark and an Israeli manufacturer, sells diapers to the religious sector in Israel in specially designed, easy-to-prop-open packaging that meets religious requirements for avoiding work on the Sabbath.

Labels in most countries must be printed in the local language (in Canada, labels must be printed in English and French), adding time and cost. The United States requires all food products to carry labels indicating their nutritional value. Most countries also require clear labeling of the country source of the product. In the United States, U.S. content must be disclosed on cars, textile, wool, and fur products. Other producers need not specify U.S. content but must comply with Federal Trade Commission guidelines if they choose to do so. For instance, to merit a "Made in the USA" label, a product must be "all or virtually all" made in the United States with no, or "negligible," foreign content.[107]

Transportation Modes

Meeting customer demand in a timely and cost-effective fashion depends on effective transportation. Globalization has been one of the driving forces behind intermodal transportation, a term denoting the combination of ocean vessels (including short sea shipping), river transport, rail, road links, and air transport within a seamless supply chain. Intermodality poses many challenges, however. Comparing the price of alternative transportation modes is difficult because price is based on many product (e.g., weight, value, space) and nonproduct (e.g., port of shipment, customs administrative procedures) factors. Intermodality also requires modularity and standardization to permit frequent transfer of goods from one mode to another.[108] Still, new technological developments, which facilitate the monitoring of goods as they pass through the supply chain, support intermodality. Additional obstacles to intermodality and seamless logistics lie at the legal and political level. For instance, Thai regulations require transport and warehousing to be handled by separate companies. In China, approval must be obtained from authorities in each province along the supply chain.[109]

Different transportation modes vary greatly by price and shipping time. For instance, sending a 40-foot container from Shanghai to New York via an all-water route would cost $3,500 to $3,900 and take 30 to 35 days to arrive. Sending the same goods via a ship to Los Angeles and from there by truck would cost $4,700 to $5,000, but the delivery time would be shortened to 20 to 25 days. Finally, sending the same goods by air will take only 2 to 3 days but the cost will be $50,000.[110] And, depending on location, not all modes will be available.

Maritime Transportation

Maritime transportation serves well over 90% of international trade.[111] Of the 29 border crossing points between the United States and Mexico, nine ports handle most of U.S.–Mexico trade.[112] Mexico-based Frigotux is building a refrigerated terminal in the hope of diverting some of the 90% share of Mexican agricultural exports now handled by trucking into marine shipping from Tuxpan to Philadelphia–Camden and Rotterdam (the Netherlands).[113] Historically global in use and regulation, impediments to further globalization of maritime transport include the issuance of "flags of convenience"—that is, the registering of ships in countries with less stringent regulations, such as Liberia and Panama. Such registries not only provide for less stringent safety standards but also confer labor and tax benefits; however, they do raise opposition in some of the countries where MNEs operate.

Port Facilities. Port facilities represent a crucial ingredient in the cost and convenience of maritime transport, which, among other reasons, explain the trend toward foreign investment in port facilities as a way to facilitate seamless transportation. For instance, many of the port facilities in Mexico and the United States are operated by foreign firms (you may recall the recent uproar in the United States when a company from the United Arab Emirates acquired a British company that was handling American port facilities).

Port facilities vary in quality. According to the Conference Board, the most competitive ports provide speed processing (cargo handling and administration), low cost, and superb intermodal links (road, rail, and air). Ports also vary according to their main function in the global supply system. There are four types of ports: (a) the maritime hub—dedicated to transshipment from an ocean vessel to another or to a feeder vessel; (b) the gateway port—an interchange between the maritime hub and maritime and/or land transport; (c) the logistic–industrial port—interchange between transport modes combined with logistic support; and (d) the trade port—logistic activities combined with other value-added international trade services.

Nonhub ports compete mostly by adopting niche strategies—for example, specializing in a single product line to achieve expertise and economies of scale. For instance, the Port of Barcelona handles more than 500,000 cars a year. One of the main challenges for ports as key links in the global supply chain has been to accommodate local distribution—for example, to integrate domestic and international shipping (now mostly separated) to accommodate situations such as when the final destination is closer to the port rather than to rail transportation.[114] Some ports try to take advantage of congestion in established ports; for instance, as a result of the surge in U.S.–Asian trade, Prince Rupert, British Columbia, plans to offer rapid logistic services despite its remote location and the fact that there is hardly any local demand for the shipped goods. [115]

Exhibit 16.7 ranks nations based on their water transport infrastructure (including internal waterways such as canals).

The Inland Port. "Port Columbus" in landlocked central Ohio is an "inland port." It utilizes 86 million square feet of warehousing and distribution facilities on the grounds of a former air force base located "within a 10-hour drive of over 50% of the United States and Canadian populations" (per port literature). The port has transportation arteries reaching to airports, highways (there are 130 trucking firms in the area), and rail and coastal ports via agreements with the ports of New York–New Jersey, Virginia, and Los Angeles. Countries with vast, underdeveloped hinterland such as China are interested in the inland port concept as a way of improving access to less developed, hinterland regions that are located far from port facilities.

Trucking. Trucking plays an important role in international trade, particularly in Europe where distances are relatively short and economic integration expedites transportation time. Central European countries, such as Hungary and the Czech Republic, are major beneficiaries of the trend toward European integration, especially the flow of goods between Western and Eastern Europe, developing warehousing facilities and roads. Trucking is also a key means of transportation in other cross-border but geographically contiguous areas, such as Texas–Mexico and Hong Kong–Shenzhen in southern China. Trucks also play an important role in the domestic distribution of products delivered internationally by ship, rail, or air; the use of containers has made such intermodality substantially easier.

While the United States, Europe, and other, mostly developed countries have moved to standardize safety and other regulations pertaining to trucking, there remain substantial impediments to the globalization of truck transportation.[116] For example, there are different safety standards, a reason the United States gave at the time to justify its refusal to comply with NAFTA and let Mexican trucks cross into the United States. Pressure from existing joint ventures between U.S. and Mexican trucking firms as well as opposition from U.S. organized labor also played a role in the decision.[117] Traffic congestion is costly to trucking in terms of deteriorating service quality, delayed shipments, higher energy costs, and lower productivity of vehicles and workforce. The problem is especially pronounced in densely populated areas such as Europe. Developing countries have less of a congestion problem but a higher proportion of unpaved roads than do the United States and other developed countries, imposing serious constraints on the domestic transportation of goods (see Exhibit 16.8).

Exhibit 16.7   Water Transportation Infrastructure (harbors, canals, etc.)

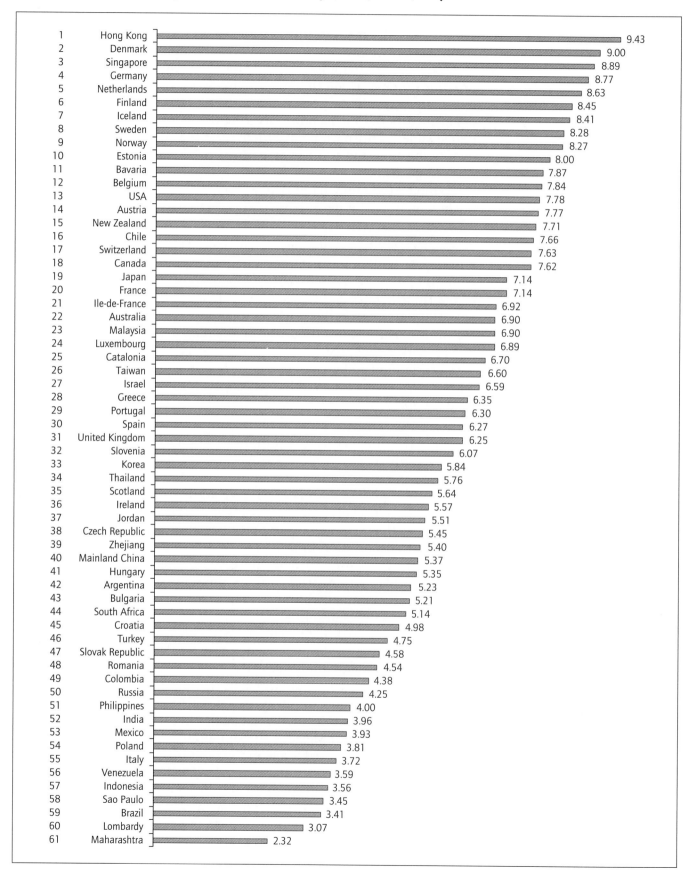

1	Hong Kong	9.43
2	Denmark	9.00
3	Singapore	8.89
4	Germany	8.77
5	Netherlands	8.63
6	Finland	8.45
7	Iceland	8.41
8	Sweden	8.28
9	Norway	8.27
10	Estonia	8.00
11	Bavaria	7.87
12	Belgium	7.84
13	USA	7.78
14	Austria	7.77
15	New Zealand	7.71
16	Chile	7.66
17	Switzerland	7.63
18	Canada	7.62
19	Japan	7.14
20	France	7.14
21	Ile-de-France	6.92
22	Australia	6.90
23	Malaysia	6.90
24	Luxembourg	6.89
25	Catalonia	6.70
26	Taiwan	6.60
27	Israel	6.59
28	Greece	6.35
29	Portugal	6.30
30	Spain	6.27
31	United Kingdom	6.25
32	Slovenia	6.07
33	Korea	5.84
34	Thailand	5.76
35	Scotland	5.64
36	Ireland	5.57
37	Jordan	5.51
38	Czech Republic	5.45
39	Zhejiang	5.40
40	Mainland China	5.37
41	Hungary	5.35
42	Argentina	5.23
43	Bulgaria	5.21
44	South Africa	5.14
45	Croatia	4.98
46	Turkey	4.75
47	Slovak Republic	4.58
48	Romania	4.54
49	Colombia	4.38
50	Russia	4.25
51	Philippines	4.00
52	India	3.96
53	Mexico	3.93
54	Poland	3.81
55	Italy	3.72
56	Venezuela	3.59
57	Indonesia	3.56
58	Sao Paulo	3.45
59	Brazil	3.41
60	Lombardy	3.07
61	Maharashtra	2.32

SOURCE: The International Institute for Management Development (IMD). *The World Competitiveness Yearbook, 2006.* Lausanne, Switzerland: IMD. Reprinted with permission.

Exhibit 16.8   Road Density

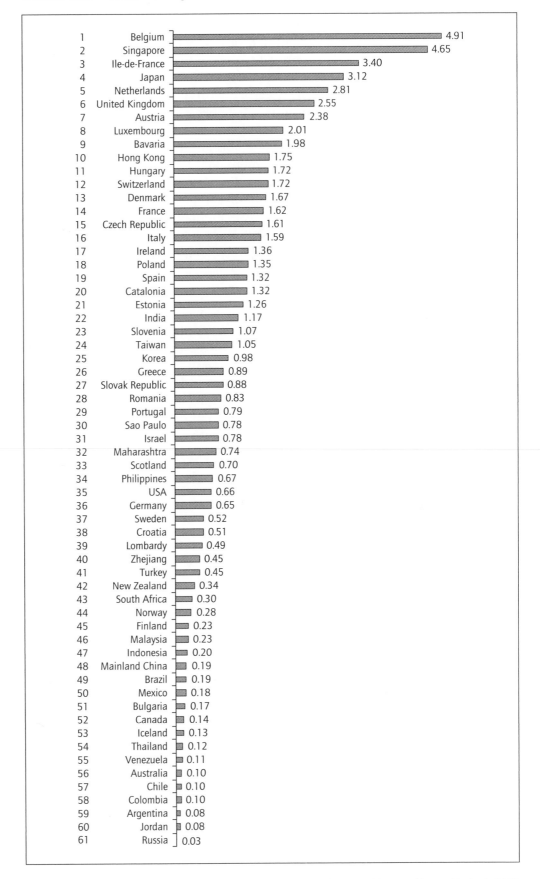

1	Belgium	4.91
2	Singapore	4.65
3	Ile-de-France	3.40
4	Japan	3.12
5	Netherlands	2.81
6	United Kingdom	2.55
7	Austria	2.38
8	Luxembourg	2.01
9	Bavaria	1.98
10	Hong Kong	1.75
11	Hungary	1.72
12	Switzerland	1.72
13	Denmark	1.67
14	France	1.62
15	Czech Republic	1.61
16	Italy	1.59
17	Ireland	1.36
18	Poland	1.35
19	Spain	1.32
20	Catalonia	1.32
21	Estonia	1.26
22	India	1.17
23	Slovenia	1.07
24	Taiwan	1.05
25	Korea	0.98
26	Greece	0.89
27	Slovak Republic	0.88
28	Romania	0.83
29	Portugal	0.79
30	Sao Paulo	0.78
31	Israel	0.78
32	Maharashtra	0.74
33	Scotland	0.70
34	Philippines	0.67
35	USA	0.66
36	Germany	0.65
37	Sweden	0.52
38	Croatia	0.51
39	Lombardy	0.49
40	Zhejiang	0.45
41	Turkey	0.45
42	New Zealand	0.34
43	South Africa	0.30
44	Norway	0.28
45	Finland	0.23
46	Malaysia	0.23
47	Indonesia	0.20
48	Mainland China	0.19
49	Brazil	0.19
50	Mexico	0.18
51	Bulgaria	0.17
52	Canada	0.14
53	Iceland	0.13
54	Thailand	0.12
55	Venezuela	0.11
56	Australia	0.10
57	Chile	0.10
58	Colombia	0.10
59	Argentina	0.08
60	Jordan	0.08
61	Russia	0.03

SOURCE: The International Institute for Management Development (IMD). *The World Competitiveness Yearbook, 2006.* Lausanne, Switzerland: IMD. Reprinted with permission.

Rail

A competitive time-to-cost ratio as well as road and sky congestion makes rail an attractive transportation mode domestically and internationally. For instance, about half of U.S. grain exports to Mexico are transported by rail. One problem with rail transportation is variation in rail gauges, which means that goods need to be transferred from one system to another. In some countries, rail gauges even vary internally. This is the case, for instance, for Brazil and Argentina. Still, the two countries, together with Bolivia and Chile, have a substantial part of their system in standard, one-meter gauges, facilitating transport within MERCOSUR.[118]

Where rails are not contiguous, railways can still play an important role as part of intermodal transportation. The Baltic state of Estonia wants to connect Europe and East Asia via the Trans-Siberian railroad. It believes that it can cut the current marine shipping time of 33 days to 17 to 24 days using intermodal containers, thus tapping into the huge trade volume between Asia and Europe.[119]

Exhibit 16.9 shows the density of rail networks, with Hong Kong, Singapore and Europe showing the highest densities.

Air Transport

Air transportation has grown rapidly in recent years. Expensive but generally more reliable, air shipments were initially confined to perishable or high-value items but are increasingly in use. One impediment to globalization of air transport is the stringent safety standards imposed by developed nations, especially the United States and the EU, compared with the relatively lax regimes common in many developing countries. The United States does not permit the landing of foreign aircraft that do not comply with certain safety standards, although U.S. authorities have not always been effective in enforcing these standards.

INDUSTRY BOX

GLOBAL LOGISTICS AT WAL-MART

The largest retailer in the world, Arkansas-based Wal-Mart, started its international operations in 1991, when it opened in Mexico, where it is now the largest retailer. Today, Wal-Mart has more than 2,700 stores in 13 countries, including the United Kingdom, Argentina, Brazil, and China, which has been targeted for rapid expansion and where the company has agreed to accept union representation, something it has resisted in the United States and all its other foreign locations. In some locations—for example, Germany and South Korea—the Wal-Mart business model did not work at all, leading the company to retreat from those markets in 2006.

Efficient, large-scale supply-chain management has long been a Wal-Mart competitive advantage, which the firm sought to leverage in its foreign operations. Still, the firm faced the need to adjust to the different environments in which it operated. In Argentina, Wal-Mart expanded aisle size initially set to U.S. standards to accommodate higher than expected customer traffic. As Joe Menzer, president and CEO of Wal-Mart International, suggested, "it wasn't such a good idea to stick to the domestic Wal-Mart blueprint in Argentina, or in some of the other international markets we've entered, for that matter." As 2000 drew to a close, Wal-Mart was fighting a bill introduced in the Buenos Aires legislature to limit hypermarkets' size to 20,000 square feet, a tenth of Wal-Mart's Supercenters. In England, Wal-Mart had to adjust to ASDA's (its acquired chain) 65,000-square-foot stores, roughly a third of Wal-Mart's domestic average. The different store size and product composition required adjustments in store layout and display, as well as in transportation, warehousing, and distribution. Wal-Mart also replaced ASDA's information system with its own to benefit from worldwide sourcing, buying power, and distribution scale.

SOURCES: Wal-Mart Annual Report, 2000; Y. Ono and N. N. Zimmerman. "Wal-Mart enters Japan with Seiyu stake." *Wall Street Journal*, March 15, 2002, B5; Company press releases and media reports, 2004–2006.

Exhibit 16.9   Railroad Density

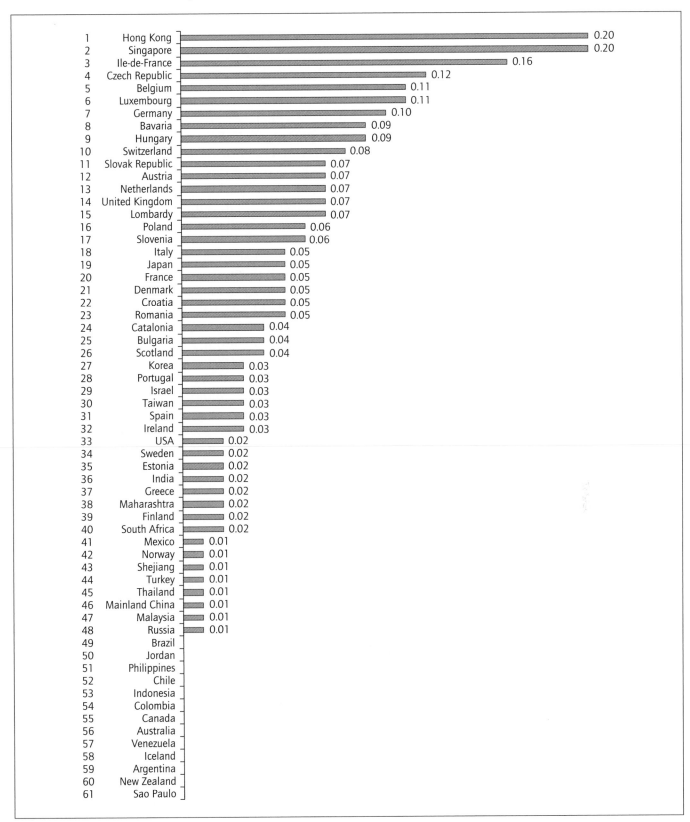

1	Hong Kong	0.20
2	Singapore	0.20
3	Ile-de-France	0.16
4	Czech Republic	0.12
5	Belgium	0.11
6	Luxembourg	0.11
7	Germany	0.10
8	Bavaria	0.09
9	Hungary	0.09
10	Switzerland	0.08
11	Slovak Republic	0.07
12	Austria	0.07
13	Netherlands	0.07
14	United Kingdom	0.07
15	Lombardy	0.07
16	Poland	0.06
17	Slovenia	0.06
18	Italy	0.05
19	Japan	0.05
20	France	0.05
21	Denmark	0.05
22	Croatia	0.05
23	Romania	0.05
24	Catalonia	0.04
25	Bulgaria	0.04
26	Scotland	0.04
27	Korea	0.03
28	Portugal	0.03
29	Israel	0.03
30	Taiwan	0.03
31	Spain	0.03
32	Ireland	0.03
33	USA	0.02
34	Sweden	0.02
35	Estonia	0.02
36	India	0.02
37	Greece	0.02
38	Maharashtra	0.02
39	Finland	0.02
40	South Africa	0.02
41	Mexico	0.01
42	Norway	0.01
43	Shejiang	0.01
44	Turkey	0.01
45	Thailand	0.01
46	Mainland China	0.01
47	Malaysia	0.01
48	Russia	0.01
49	Brazil	
50	Jordan	
51	Philippines	
52	Chile	
53	Indonesia	
54	Colombia	
55	Canada	
56	Australia	
57	Venezuela	
58	Iceland	
59	Argentina	
60	New Zealand	
61	Sao Paulo	

SOURCE: The International Institute for Management Development (IMD). *The World Competitiveness Yearbook, 2006.* Lausanne, Switzerland: IMD. Reprinted with permission.

Crossing National Borders

French tire maker Michelin calculates that 45.3% of its European sales come from import flows, meaning that almost half of the products it sells in one country are imported from another. For example, the vast majority of Michelin sales in the United Kingdom are imports.[120] It is difficult to establish a seamless supply chain spanning national borders, as customs inspection, processing, and other barriers associated with border crossing create unpredictable and costly delays.[121] In the aftermath of September 11, 2001, delays have increased despite the revamping of import procedures to better handle the security of their supply chain, including the prescreening of certain shipments.[122] In 2005, a labor action in California's ports created long delays and a nightmare for U.S. retailers waiting for their Asian imports to arrive before the busy Christmas season.

The NAFTA agreement provides for nontariff movement of goods across Canada, the United States, and Mexico on the condition that the goods in question originate in one of the three countries. This requires substantial documentation to establish country-of-origin source. In addition, shortage of border-crossing points, bridges, rails, and docks undermine traffic expansion.[123] Paperwork and the need to switch trailers have been identified as key reasons for delays in crossing the U.S. borders with Mexico and Canada (delays have been worse on the Mexican border).[124] Most U.S.–Mexico trade passes through border-crossing points between the two countries, mostly in Texas but also in Arizona and California. One border crossing—Laredo—accounts for almost 40% of all trade and half of the U.S. agricultural, fishery, and forestry exports to Mexico.[125] Yet, crossing Laredo can take upward of three hours as shipments are handled through an antiquated system.[126]

Every day, close to $2 billion worth of goods cross the U.S.–Canadian border, a number that has been increasing by 13% annually since 1994; 2,000 trucks pass through the Blaine border crossing between Washington and British Columbia daily. The cost associated with crossing the U.S.–Canadian border is estimated at 5% to 10% of product cost. In an effort to reduce the cost, constituencies on both sides of the border have been pushing for increased integration, with some going as far as proposing the elimination of the border altogether.[127] Such calls have been largely silenced since 9/11, as concerns over the transfer of potential terrorists and their ware across the border have risen.

Exhibit 16.10 ranks countries on the extent to which the bureaucracy of customs hinders the efficient transit of goods. Hong Kong, Denmark, and Singapore are ranked best with the smallest hindrance, whereas the Philippines, Russia, and Indonesia close the list.

Interim Summary

1. Supply chains have undergone substantial globalization in recent years with firms consolidating sourcing and distribution; however, the trend has been more pronounced in some regions (e.g., the EU) than in others (e.g., Asia).

2. Customization remains an issue in product packaging and promotion, although here too there is an attempt to reduce the number of variants.

3. Transportation modes need to be considered in terms of their cost and efficacy, with special attention given to intermodal transportation.

4. Border-crossing has become more cumbersome in the aftermath of 9/11.

Exhibit 16.10   Customs' Authorities Bureaucracy

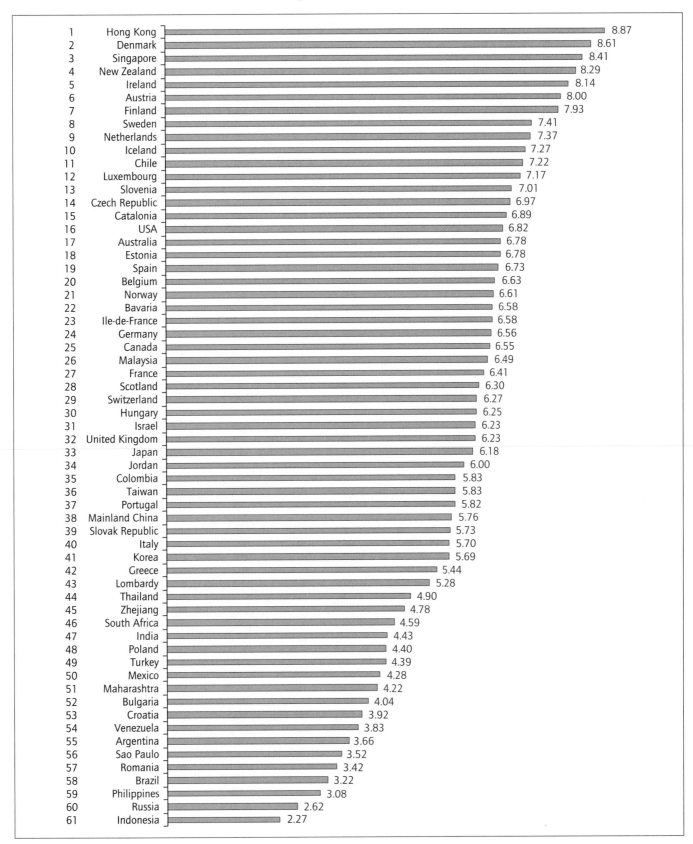

1	Hong Kong	8.87
2	Denmark	8.61
3	Singapore	8.41
4	New Zealand	8.29
5	Ireland	8.14
6	Austria	8.00
7	Finland	7.93
8	Sweden	7.41
9	Netherlands	7.37
10	Iceland	7.27
11	Chile	7.22
12	Luxembourg	7.17
13	Slovenia	7.01
14	Czech Republic	6.97
15	Catalonia	6.89
16	USA	6.82
17	Australia	6.78
18	Estonia	6.78
19	Spain	6.73
20	Belgium	6.63
21	Norway	6.61
22	Bavaria	6.58
23	Ile-de-France	6.58
24	Germany	6.56
25	Canada	6.55
26	Malaysia	6.49
27	France	6.41
28	Scotland	6.30
29	Switzerland	6.27
30	Hungary	6.25
31	Israel	6.23
32	United Kingdom	6.23
33	Japan	6.18
34	Jordan	6.00
35	Colombia	5.83
36	Taiwan	5.83
37	Portugal	5.82
38	Mainland China	5.76
39	Slovak Republic	5.73
40	Italy	5.70
41	Korea	5.69
42	Greece	5.44
43	Lombardy	5.28
44	Thailand	4.90
45	Zhejiang	4.78
46	South Africa	4.59
47	India	4.43
48	Poland	4.40
49	Turkey	4.39
50	Mexico	4.28
51	Maharashtra	4.22
52	Bulgaria	4.04
53	Croatia	3.92
54	Venezuela	3.83
55	Argentina	3.66
56	Sao Paulo	3.52
57	Romania	3.42
58	Brazil	3.22
59	Philippines	3.08
60	Russia	2.62
61	Indonesia	2.27

SOURCE: The International Institute for Management Development (IMD). *The World Competitiveness Yearbook, 2006.* Lausanne, Switzerland: IMD. Reprinted with permission.

CHAPTER SUMMARY

1. International markets are typically more difficult to enter than domestic markets yet represent tremendous potential for firms.

2. There are various ways to assess the potential of a foreign market. First and foremost is economic development and its correlate of disposable income; however, consumption patterns are determined by a myriad of other factors, including culture.

3. Companies standardize products and services as well as the methods in which they are advertised, sold, distributed, and serviced, in an attempt to reduce costs and increase efficiencies. At the same time, there remain strong pressures to adapt products and services to the local environment in which they are offered.

4. Country of origin remains a powerful force in marketing and consumer behavior. It can lead consumers to purchase a product or a service (even if higher priced) from a country with a positive image and avoid a product or a service from a country with a negative image.

5. Pricing pressures and economic integration push companies to consolidate their global supply chains from sourcing to delivery. Logistic providers respond by consolidating their own operations.

6. A trend toward "intermodal" transportation involves the simultaneous use of multiple transportation modes—namely, rail, sea, and air.

Chapter Notes

1. Micklethwait. "Washed up?" *Economist,* 338, 1996: pp. S23–S27.

2. Ono. "Overcoming the stigma of dishwashers in Japan." *Wall Street Journal,* May 19, 2000, B1.

3. W. Boston and K. Richter. "Telecom firms battle to serve Germany's Turks." *Wall Street Journal,* November 6, 2000, B7.

4. W. J. Keegan. *Global Marketing Management.* Englewood Cliffs, NJ: Prentice-Hall, 2001.

5. "Burgernomics beats reading the tea leaves." *Economist,* April 29, 2000.

6. H. Riesenbeck and A. Freeling. "How global are global brands?" *European Business Report,* Summer 1993: p. 13.

7. *Economist,* September 2, 2000, p. 98.

8. *Economist,* September 2, 2000, p. 98.

9. "Franchises head overseas." CNNfn.com, September 11, 2000.

10. M. R. Czinkota and I. A. Ronkainen. *International Marketing.* Orlando, FL: Harcourt Brace, 1998.

11. The Conference Board. *The Changing Global Role of the Marketing Function.* Report #1105-95-RR, 1995.

12. The Conference Board. *The Changing Global Role of the Marketing Function.* Report #1105-95-RR, 1995; S. Samie and K. Roth. "The influence of global marketing standardization on performance." *Journal of Marketing,* April 1992: pp. 1–17.

13. Ellison. "Carrefour and Ahold find shoppers like to think local." *Wall Street Journal,* August 31, 2001.

14. "Franchises head overseas." CNNfn.com, September 11, 2000.

15. A. Baar and A. McMains. "Kellogg realigns global brands." Adweek.com, May 29, 2000.

16. The Conference Board. "Launching a mass-market fragrance worldwide at Avon." Report #1105-95-RR, 1995: p. 15.

17. Y. Ono. "U.S. superstores find Japanese are a hard sell." *Wall Street Journal,* February 14, 2000, B1.

18. The Conference Board. *The Changing Global Role of the Marketing Function.* Report #1105-95-RR, 1995.

19. The Conference Board.

20. The Conference Board.

21. The Conference Board. "Global accounts at AMP." Report #1105-95-RR, 1995: p. 19.

22. "Domestic recording artists boost share of market to 68%." *Wall Street Journal,* September 7, 2001, B6.

23. M. Flagg. "Asia proves unexpectedly tough terrain for HBO, Cinemax channels." *Wall Street Journal,* August 23, 2000, B1.

24. S. Bereger. "Expert: Metro Cash and Carry 'taken to the cleaners' in Israel." *Jerusalem Post* (Digital Israel), September 14, 2001.

25. M. Tanikawa. "French supermarket struggles to fit it." *Wall Street Journal,* October 5, 2001.

26. J. N. Kapferer. "How global are global brands? ESOMAR seminar." Cited in M. van Mesdag, "Culture-sensitive adaptation or global standardization—the duration of usage hypothesis." *International Marketing Review,* 1999, *17,* 1: pp. 74–84.

27. G. T. Sims. "Corn Flakes clash shows the glitches in the European Union." *Wall Street Journal,* November 1, 2005, A1.

28. H. Riesenbeck and A. Freeling. "How global are global brands?" *McKinsey Quarterly,* 1991, 4: pp. 3–18.

29. M. De Mooij. "Masculinity/femininity and consumer behavior." In G. Hofstede, with W. A. Arrindell, *Masculinity and Femininity: The Taboo Dimension of National Cultures.* Thousand Oaks, CA: Sage, 1998, 55–73.

30. G. A. Fowler. "Marketers take heed: The macho Chinese man is back." *Wall Street Journal,* December 18, 2002, B1.

31. K. F. Winsted. "Evaluating service encounters: A cross-cultural and cross-industry exploration." *Journal*

of Marketing Theory and Practice. Spring 1999: pp. 106–123.

32. J. L. Watson. "China's Big Mac attack." *Foreign Affairs,* 2000, *79,* 3: p. 130.

33. J. E. Hilsenrath. "Ford designs Ikon to suit Indian tastes." *Wall Street Journal,* August 8, 2000, A17; also cited in *Globe & Mail,* April 8, 2000.

34. "From top to bottom." *Economist,* June 3, 2006: p. 17.

35. N. Shirouzu. "Tailoring world's cars to U.S. tastes." *Wall Street Journal,* January 15, 2001, B1.

36. R. Martin. "Religion reshapes realities for US restaurants in Middle East." *Restaurant News,* February 16, 1998.

37. D. Barboza. "Market place: Pluralism under golden arches." *New York Times,* 1999, C1.

38. Euromonitor. *Retail Trade International, 2000,* 11th ed. Euromonitor PLC.

39. Y. Ono. "U.S. superstores find Japanese are a hard sell." *Wall Street Journal,* February 14, 2000, B1.

40. M. S. Roth and J. B. Romeo. "Matching product category and country image perceptions: A framework for managing country-of-origin effects." *Journal of International Business Studies,* 1992, 3rd quarter: pp. 477–497.

41. R. A. Peterson and A. J. P. Jolibert. "A meta-analysis of country-of-origin effect." *Journal of International Business Studies,* 1995, 4th quarter: pp. 883–900.

42. C. Powell. "Why we really must fly the flag: Being cool isn't enough." *Observer,* April 25, 1999, 4.

43. R. Daedeke. "Consumer attitudes towards products 'made in' developing countries." *Journal of Retailing,* Summer 1973: pp. 13–24.

44. J. Baum. "Riding high: A Taiwanese bicycle maker races to success in the West." *Far Eastern Economic Review,* May 7, 1998: pp. 58–59.

45. M. S. Roth and J. B. Romeo. "Matching product category and country image perceptions: A framework for managing country-of-origin effects." *Journal of International Business Studies,* 1992, 3rd quarter: pp. 477–497.

46. C. Powel. "Why we really must fly the flag." *Observer,* April 25, 1999, 4, citing a BMP DDB survey.

47. C. Lawton. "Pushing foreign—and faux foreign—beer in the U.S." *Wall Street Journal,* June 27, 2003, B1.

48. J. L. Watson. "China's Big Mac attack." *Foreign Affairs,* 2000, *79,* 3: p. 120.

49. G. Vchazan. "Foreign products get Russian makeovers." *Wall Street Journal,* January 16, 2001, A23.

50. B. Smith. "In Latvia, a traditional drink takes on Western production and Pepsi generation." *Wall Street Journal,* September 8, 2000, A17.

51. Y. Ono. "U.S. superstores find Japanese are a hard sell." *Wall Street Journal,* February 14, 2000, B1.

52. "Spin cycle." *Economist,* August 14, 1999: p. 52.

53. S. Ellison. "Carrefour and Ahold find shoppers like to think local." *Wall Street Journal,* August 31, 2001, A5.

54. M. R. Czinkota and I. A. Ronkainen. *International Marketing,* 5th ed. Orlando, FL: Harcourt Brace, 1998.

55. J. Kim and J. D. Daniels. "Marketing channel decisions of foreign manufacturing subsidiaries in the U.S.: The case of metal and machinery industries." *Management International Review,* 1991/1992, 31: pp. 123–138.

56. J. Kim and J. D. Daniels.

57. "SED International, Inc. announces status as certified HP top value reseller." *Business Wire,* April 9, 1998.

58. R. Frank. "Big Boy's adventures in Thailand." *Wall Street Journal,* April 12, 2000.

59. G. Dyer. "Brazil's regional drink makers *slake* thirst for value." *Financial Times,* June 16, 1999, 5.

60. D. Summers. "Boots for global trip." *Financial Times,* October 12, 1995, 13.

61. "This Euro brew's for you." *Business Week,* July 24, 2000: pp. 120–122.

62. T. Burt and D. Hargreaves. "Crackdown pledge as VW fine is upheld." *Financial Times,* July 7, 2000.

63. L. McGinley. "Drug industry seeks to prevent importation of cheaper medicines." *Wall Street Journal,* July 19, 2000, A8.

64. C. W. L. Hill. *International Business: Competing in the Global Marketplace.* Boston: McGraw-Hill, 1999.

65. R. Belderbos and P. Holmes. "An economic analysis of Matsushita revisited." *Antitrust Bulletin,* 1995, 40: pp. 825–857.

66. "Trade barriers." *Journal of Commerce,* June 10, 1992: p. 5A.

67. H. Riesenbeck and A. Freeling. "How global are global brands?" *European Business Report,* Summer 1993.

68. K. Kashani. "Beware the pitfalls of global marketing." *Harvard Business Review,* September/October 1989: pp. 92–93.

69. J. Lafayette. "Marketing: Picking the right ad agency." *International Business,* 1992, 5: pp. 106–110. D. Guthery and B. A. Lowe. "Translation problems in international marketing research." *Journal of Language for International Business,* 1992, 4: pp. 1–14.

70. L. Himelstein. "The swoosh heard round the world." *Business Week,* May 12, 1990: p. 76.

71. S. Donaton. "Not always Coca-Cola's policy threatens integrity of magazines." *Advertising Age,* 1999, 70: p. 36.

72. M. Gjalwash. "In Egypt, rumors of blasphemy swirl around Coca-Cola." *Online Athens,* July 25, 2000.

73. H. Riesenbeck and A. Freeling. "How global are global brands?" *European Business Report,* Summer 1993: p. 7.

74. The Conference Board. *The Changing Global Role of the Marketing Function.* Report #1105-95-RR, 1995: p. 14.

75. B. McKay. "Coke hunts for talent to re-establish its marketing might." *Wall Street Journal,* March 2002, B4.

76. "This Euro brew's for you." *Business Week,* July 24, 2000: pp. 120–122.

77. "Unquenchable thirst." *Financial Times London,* April 30, 1999, 19.

78. The Conference Board. *The changing global role of the marketing function.* Report #1105-95-RR, 1995.

79. The Conference Board. "Meeting the Challenge of Global Logistics." Europe Report #1207-98-CR, 1998.

80. Harris Interactive. Chicago '06 Longitudes Supply Chain Management survey. April 2006.

81. P. P. Dornier, R. Ernst, M. Fender, and P. Kouvelis. *Global operations and logistics.* New York, Wiley, 1998.

82. "The physical Internet: A survey of logistics." *Economist,* June 17, 2006: p. 8.

83. Prologis company information, 1999.

84. E. Chabrow. "Supply chains go global." Informationweek.com, April 3, 2000.

85. "Exchanges fall short on global e-commerce." Internetweek.com, May 8, 2000.

86. UNCTAD. "Electronic commerce and development." 2000.

87. The Conference Board, Report #1105-95-RR, 1995.

88. P. P. Dornier, R. Ernst, M. Fender, and P. Kouvelis. *Global Operations and Logistics,* p. 62. New York: Wiley, 1998.

89. The Conference Board. Report #1105-95-RR, 1995.

90. P. P. Dornier, R. Ernst, M. Fender, and P. Kouvelis. *Global Operations and Logistics,* p. 180. New York: Wiley, 1998.

91. S. M. Shaw and J. Meier. "Second generation MNCs in China." *The McKinsey Quarterly,* 1993, 4: pp. 3–16.

92. S. Lal, P. Van Laarhoven, and G. Sharman. "Current research: Making logistics alliances work." *McKinsey Quarterly,* 1995, 3: pp. 188–190.

93. The Conference Board. Report #1105-95-RR, 1995.

94. B. Radstaak and M. H. Ketelaar. *Worldwide Logistics.* Holland International Distribution Council, 1998.

95. P. P. Dornier, R. Ernst, M. Fender, and P. Kouvelis. *Global Operations and Logistics,* p. 180. New York: Wiley, 1998.

96. R. Morton. "Latin American business is looking up." *Transportation & Distribution,* October 2000: p. 52.

97. P. Wright. "Logistics in Asia." The Conference Board. Report #1105-95-RR, 1995: p. 20.

98. The Conference Board. "Nestlé on the win-win partnership with the retail trade." Report #1105-95-RR, 1995.

99. The Conference Board. Report #1105-95-RR, 1995.

100. P. P. Dornier, R. Ernst, M. Fender, and P. Kouvelis. *Global Operations and Logistics,* p. 226. New York: Wiley, 1998.

101. P. P. Dornier, R. Ernst, M. Fender, and P. Kouvelis, pp. 120–121.

102. M. Yost. "Innovation lifts Meritor's profile in auto-parts business." *Wall Street Journal,* November 15, 1999, B4.

103. The Conference Board. Report #1105-95-RR, 1995: p. 14.

104. L. Bannon. "New playbook: Taking cues from GE, Mattel's CEO wants toy maker to grow up." *Wall Street Journal,* November 14, 2001, A1.

105. S. Livingstone and L. Sparks. "The new German packaging laws: Effects on firms exporting to Germany." *International Journal of Physical Distribution & Logistics Management,* 1994, 24: pp. 15–25.

106. P. L. Grogan. "European influence." *BioCycle,* 1997, 38: p. 86.

107. U.S. Department of Commerce. "Complying with the Made in the USA standard."

108. The Conference Board, Report #1105-95-RR, 1995.

109. P. Wright. "Logistics in Asia." The Conference Board, Report #1105-95-RR, p. 19.

110. N. King. "Panama Canal at crossroads." *Wall Street Journal,* January 7, 2004, B1.

111. S. Mankabady. *The International Maritime Organization.* London: Croom Helm, 1984.

112. T. Drennan. "Where the action's at: The U.S.-Mexican border." FAS on-line, U.S. Department of Agriculture, 1999: p. 2.

113. D. McCosh. "A cool place for Mexican shippers." *Journal of Commerce,* April 28, 1999: p. 1.

114. "Improving interchange management." *Intermodal Insights,* September 1999: p. 179.

115. D. Machlaba. "Tiny British Columbia port aims to be new venue for China trade." WallStreetJournal.com, August 8, 2006.

116. J. Braithwaite and P. Drahos. *Global Business Regulation.* New York: Cambridge University Press, 2000.

117. R. Gold. "Mexican trucks won't fill the U.S. soon." *Wall Street Journal,* February 16, 2001, A2; H. Cooper and K. Chen. "U.S. is told to let Mexican trucks enter." *Wall Street Journal,* February 7, 2001, A2.

118. W. Zinn. "Obstacles to supply chair efficiency in a trade block environment: Three cases in MERCOSUR." Working paper, Fisher College of Business, The Ohio State University.

119. B. Smith. "Estonia mulls Beijing-Baltic rail link in bid to be gateway for Asian exports." *Wall Street Journal,* November 13, 2000, B19.

120. P. P. Dornier, R. Ernst, M. Fender, and P. Kouvelis. *Global Operations and Logistics,* p. 63. New York: Wiley, 1998.

121. P. P. Dornier, R. Ernst, M. Fender, and P. Kouvelis. *Global Operations and Logistics.* New York: Wiley, 1998.

122. G. R. Simpson. "U.S. to revise dealings with importers, reward those with enhanced security." *Wall Street Journal,* November 27, 2001, A24.

123. A. W. Mathews. "On the borderline. NAFTA reality check: Trucks, trains, ships face costly delays." *Wall Street Journal,* June 3, 1998, A1.

124. 1991 Intermodal Association of North America (IANA) Intermodal Index.

125. T. Drennan. "Where the action's at: The U.S.-Mexican border." FAS on-line, U.S. Department of Agriculture, 1999.

126. R. Gold. "Mexican trucks won't fill the U.S. soon." *Wall Street Journal,* February 16, 2001, A2; H. Cooper and K. Chen. "U.S. is told to let Mexican trucks enter." *Wall Street Journal,* February 7, 2001, A2.

127. B. Cameron. "Just blow it up." *National Post* (Canada), August 18, 2001, B3.

GLOBAL HUMAN RESOURCE MANAGEMENT

SEVENTEEN

DO YOU KNOW?

1. What are the staffing stages that an MNE goes through on its globalization route?

2. What are the reasons for assigning expatriates to MNE affiliates?

3. What are the elements of expatriate compensation?

4. How does human resource management differ between a WOS (wholly owned [foreign] subsidiary) and an IJV (international joint venture)?

5. Would you like to work for a foreign firm? Why or why not?

OPENING CASE

Managing Global Human Resources at HSBC

Founded in Asia in 1865 by a Scottish national, the Hong Kong and Shanghai Banking Corporation (HSBC) is the world's largest by assets, with more than 280,000 employees around the globe. Until two decades ago, the bank's top managerial ranks drew exclusively on an elite group of up to 800 international managers (IMs), all of them British men enjoying lucrative expatriate terms on their foreign postings. Today, the company, which has greatly expanded since, and which prides itself on its combination of local knowledge and global savvy, looks radically different. HSBC now has roughly 380 IMs, but these top executives hail from no fewer than 33 nations. The head of Asia-Pacific operations, for instance, is of Indian origin. The same trend of human resource globalization can be observed in numerous other MNEs, from U.S.-based Citigroup to Swedish packaging firm Tetra Pack.

In addition to its IMs, HSBC employs about 1,600 employees as "secondees," "contract executives," and short-term assignees (mostly technical staff) in international postings. Each of the three groups has its own compensation package, but generally speaking the terms of employment for members of those groups are not nearly as generous as those for the IMs. The bulk of HSBC's workforce (e.g., individuals working as bank tellers, data coders, and the like) are local residents who work under so-called local terms—that is, under similar (though usually competitive) terms to employees of local businesses in each of the countries where the bank operates without any of the perks reserved for the other groups, such as housing and children's education.

SOURCE: Adapted from "Traveling more lightly." *Economist,* June 24, 2006: p. 27.

International human resource management (IHRM) is the procurement, allocation, utilization, motivation, and compensation of human resources in the international arena. IHRM is critical to the strategy and success of global operations. A Conference Board survey identified "culture and people issues" as the biggest roadblocks to global success.[1] Research by Booz, Alen, and Hamilton found that the problem of hiring quality personnel ranked as one of the main factors inhibiting expansion of U.S. foreign investment in Japan. The Japanese, on their part, named conflict between expatriates and the local workforce as their main globalization concern.[2] Appointing people with significant experience in international operations is one way for companies to avoid those problems and improve integration and corporate performance worldwide.

The distinct features of IHRM are multiculturalism and geographic dispersion[3] as well as the need to address issues such as international taxation, relocation, and foreign culture orientation. IHRM also generates more involvement in personal life (e.g., expatriate housing and educational assistance in the host country).[4] IHRM implies multiple constituencies, including a great variety of employee groups. The challenge for Johnson & Johnson, Bombardier, Teva, and other MNEs is to make proper adjustments in each of the markets in which they operate yet maintain systemwide consistency and equity that will enable global deployment of talent in line with the firm's strategy.

From a career perspective, it is useful to note that international experience increasingly opens doors from initial entry up to the CEO suite. HSBC is by no means the only MNE to instill global know-how and experience in its executives. Johnson & Johnson (J&J) seeks candidates with international experience (e.g., participation in a college exchange program) on the assumption that such individuals are better suited to the demands of a global business environment. J&J executives also go through Executive Development and Executive Conference programs, which further develop their global mindset.[5]

STRATEGIC IHRM

Strategic International Human Resource Management (SIHRM) is defined as "human resources, management issues, functions, and policies and practices that result from the strategic activities of MNEs and that impact the international concerns and goals of these enterprises."[6] Compared with strategic human resource management in a domestic context, SIHRM is more complex because it concerns multiple environments and employee groups and because it must be aligned with the multifaceted strategic considerations of the MNE. The SIHRM model has three possible orientations.

- The adaptive system imitates local HRM practices.
- The exportive system replicates the HRM system in the home country and other affiliates.
- The integrative system emphasizes global integration while permitting some local variations.

An optimal SIHRM system is capable of balancing the different forces in the firm's environment, in particular, the tension between local responsiveness and global integration.[7] The overall SIHRM strategy chosen by the parent—together with the affiliate's specific conditions, for example, the cultural distance from the parent—will determine the degree of similarity in SIHRM between the affiliate and headquarters. This, in conjunction with the criticality of the group, will determine the similarity of HRM practices for each employee group (see Exhibit 17.1).

Exhibit 17.2 shows the evolution in the firm's SIHRM system based on product life-cycle theory.[8] IHRM changes as firms go through the domestic, international, multinational, and global phases of internationalization. Exhibit 17.2 shows the phases and associated IHRM activities.[9]

Exhibit 17.1   Model of Strategic International Human Resource Management (SIHRM)

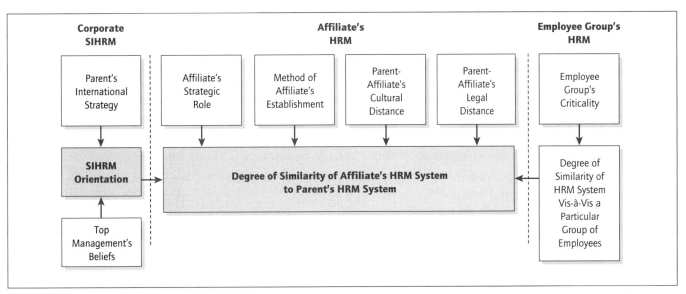

SOURCE: S. Taylor, S. Beechler, and N. Napier. "Toward an integrative model of strategic international human resource management." *Academy of Management Review, 21,* 4: p. 965.

Exhibit 17.2   Phases of Internationalization and IHRM

Phase I—Domestic: focus on home market and export
- Incidental brief visits to foreign agents/sales offices or short assignment on a project basis.
- Product and technical competence are the most important factors.
- Can scarcely speak of international HRM.

Phase II—International: focus on local responsiveness and transfer of learning
- Managers are assigned to posts in foreign markets to provide general management, technical expertise, and financial control.
- In addition to technical competence, language skills, cross-cultural sensitivity, and adaptability are also important.
- Host-country nationals are frequently recruited for management positions in the areas of sales, marketing, and personnel.

Phase III—Multinational: focus on global strategy, low cost, and price competition
- Selection focuses on recruiting the best managers for international positions, regardless of country of origin.
- Training and developing all members to share corporate values and norms.
- Management development, career counseling, and periodic transfers to different assignments.

Phase IV—Global: focus on both local responsiveness and global integration
- The major issue is how to satisfy the requirements for global integration and national responsiveness.
- Large measure of cultural diversity.
- Offering promising managers the opportunity to grow and gain experience so that an environment for continuous learning will be created throughout the entire organization.

SOURCE: Adapted from N. J. Adler. "Strategic human resource management: A global perspective." In R. Pieper (ed.), *Human Resource Management: An International Comparison.* Berlin: DeGruyter, 1990. Reprinted with permission of Verlag Walter de Gruyter & Co. GmbH.

Interim Summary

1. As the MNE shifts from domestic to global strategy, the criteria by which it selects management as well as its general HR policies will change to reflect the new strategy.

2. In advanced phases of internationalization, growth opportunities for managers expand both vertically and geographically.

INDUSTRY BOX

AIRLINE PILOTS GO GLOBAL

With the entire U.S. airline industry mired in recession in the aftermath of September 11, 2001, many U.S. pilots who were furloughed and have been unable to find employment at home have turned to foreign airlines from China and Vietnam to Bolivia and Qatar. They are following in the footsteps of their British and Australian colleagues, who, facing limited opportunities at home, have for decades sought employment in other markets, from Singapore to Hong Kong. In Qatar, four out of five pilots are foreigners. The flow is likely to continue. Boeing estimates that China alone will need more than 35,000 new pilots in the next 20 years (1,786 a year), while the rest of Asia will require 56,500 new pilots during the same period. Most developing nations lack the training capacity to meet their pilot needs and do not have enough ex-military pilots to fill the void, at least in the foreseeable future.

The global mobility of pilots has raised some safety concerns. For instance, having a captain who does not share a native language with a copilot or a traffic controller can lead to confusion, and language problems have been identified as contributing factors in a number of plane crashes, including that of an American Airlines jet in Colombia. Cultural values have also caused problems, for instance, in terms of the relationship between the captain and the copilot (as described in Chapter 6, copilots from high-power-distance cultures often do not question the judgment of the captain). In 2008, the International Civil Aviation Organization, a UN agency, will start English proficiency tests for pilots. In the meantime, firms and entrepreneurs have been rushing to open flight training schools to address the pilot shortage.

SOURCE: Adapted from S. Carey, B. Stanley, and J. Larkin. "With jobs scarce, U.S. pilots sign on at foreign airlines." *Wall Street Journal*, May 5, 2006, A1.

COUNTRY BOX

KOREAN COMPANIES SEEK GLOBAL TALENT

South Korean firms once employed almost exclusively Korean nationals as executives and engineers. No more. With the ranks of many Korean MNEs spread thin as they expand across the globe, and as global competition intensifies, these firms are increasingly looking for foreign nationals to fill the ranks not only in local affiliates but also in their Korean home base. LG Electronics, Korea's leading home appliance maker, recently hosted a recruitment fair in Russia to attract Russian talent to its R&D center. "Discovering young talent from every corner of the globe is not a matter of choice," says the company, "it is now essential for survival." The Korean government now offers a special technology visa that allows qualified foreigners multiple entries over three years and makes it easier for them to work.

South Korean companies also attract foreign workers to their overseas subsidiaries, where they are increasingly likely to conduct sophisticated, high-value work. For instance, 12 of LG's 27 R&D centers are situated outside Korea, in countries that include India, Russia, and China.

SOURCE: Adapted from J. A. Song. "South Korean technology companies fill skill vacuum." *Financial Times*, June 15, 2006, p. 22.

STAFFING THE MNE

The Globalization of Boards of Directors

A global survey conducted by the Conference Board found that the percentage of firms with nonnational directors increased between 1995 and 1998 from 39% to 60%. The percentage of companies with three or more nonnational directors increased from 11% to 23%, with the majority of directors recruited in the last three years. By 1998, 10% of directors of surveyed firms were nonnationals, up from 6% three years earlier. Today, the numbers are much higher. Danone, which did not have any foreign directors in 2002, now has two. Other firms are way ahead. Take a look, for instance, at the following composition of Nestlé's board, where only four out of 14 board members are Swiss, and one of them is Swiss American (see Exhibit 17.3).

The Conference Board survey found that entering new markets and exposure to new demands from customers and investors are the primary internal drivers for seeking nonnational board members. The initiative often comes from new managers wishing to expand international operations where the credibility and expertise

Exhibit 17.3   Nestlé's Board of Directors, 2006

Peter Brabeck-Letmathe	Francisco Castañer	Lars Olofsson	Werner Bauer	Frits van Dijk	Paul Bulcke	Carlo Donati
Austrian	Spanish	Swedish	German	Dutch	Belgian	Swiss
Chairman and CEO (Chief Executive Officer)	*Executive Vice President*	*Executive Vice President*	*Executive Vice President*	*Executive Vice President*	*Executive Vice President*	*Executive Vice President*
	Pharmaceutical & Cosmetic Products, Liaison with L'Oréal, Human Resources, Corporate Affairs	Strategic Business Units and Marketing	Technical, Production, Environment, Research & Development	Asia, Oceania, Africa, Middle East	United States of America, Canada, Latin America, Caribbean	Nestlé Waters
Luis Cantarell	**Paul Polman**	**Chris Johnson**	**Richard Laube**	**Marc Caira**	**David Frick**	**Bernard Daniel**
Spanish	Dutch	American	American and Swiss	Canadian	Swiss	Swiss
Executive Vice President	*Executive Vice President*	*Deputy Executive Vice President*	*Deputy Executive Vice President*	*Deputy Executive Vice President*	*Senior Vice President*	*Secretary General*
Europe	Finance, Control, Legal, Tax, Purchasing, Export	GLOBE Program, Information Systems, Strategic Supply Chain, eNestlé, Group Information Security	Nestlé Nutrition	Food Services Strategic Business Division	Corporate Governance, Compliance *Ex officio* member of the Executive Board	

SOURCE: Nestle

of nonnational directors makes a difference. Firms that initially took on non-nationals for "cosmetic" reasons learned to appreciate their added value over time. For Deutsche Telekom, the addition of France Telecom CEO Michel Bon to its supervisory board cemented the ties between the two firms, raised Deutsche Telekom's profile in the French market, and brought a new business perspective.

Selecting Global Board Members

Firms seeking to internationalize their boards typically begin by selecting some-one with the same nationality but with an international perspective. In the next phase, firms look for individuals with in-depth cultural and business experience in a given part of the world. Even then, the majority of appointments are made from among employees with experience working or living in the home (head-quarters) country. For example, U.S.-based DuPont appointed Percy Barnevik, then CEO of the Swedish–Swiss concern ABB, and Goro Watanabe, an executive vice president of Japan's Mitsui, to its board. Both executives have had substantial experience in the U.S. market.

Searches for nonnational directors are difficult, resulting, on average, in 9 to 10 rejections for one acceptance. The extra time commitment (U.S. and UK firms hold eight or nine annual board meetings; the average in Continental Europe is four), difference in time zones, and lack of language and culture proficiency are barriers to the appointment of nonnational directors, as is the board evaluation process. While Americans have had difficulty adjusting to a Japanese board that is seldom staffed by independent directors, Japanese directors serving on U.S. boards find them "frighteningly open" in terms of the information flow between management and board. The Conference Board recommends accommodating nonnationals by reducing the number of annual meetings, rotating meeting locations, setting up orientation programs, and widening the definition of nonnational director to include nonnationals living and working abroad who maintain strong ties with their home country.

Another obstacle to the appointment of nonnational directors is representation. U.S. institutional investors are concerned with having nonnational directors in domestic firms as well as with having national directors in non-U.S. firms. Since institutional investors have a fiduciary duty to protect shareholder interests, they must consider representation of shareholders in the decision to elect directors. This works well in the United States or the United Kingdom, but not in Continental Europe or Japan, where shareholders are only one of many constituencies represented by the board. Representation is more difficult when significant shareholders sit on the board, especially if they are family members, board members of companies with significant cross-shareholdings, board members of major suppliers, or labor or pension fund representatives. While U.S. share-holders are relatively dispersed, shareholders with major control blocks are common in Europe, Latin America, and Asia.

Staffing the MNE Ranks

Factors that affect MNE staffing (recruitment and selection) include firm strategy, organizational structure, and subsidiary-specific factors such as how long the subsidiary has been in business, the production and marketing technologies employed, and host-country characteristics such as the level of development, political stability, regulation, and culture. The MNE can draw employees from the home country (parent-country nationals, or PCNs, who are by definition expatriates), from the country in which the overseas operation is located (host-country nationals, or HCNs), or from a third country that is neither a home country nor a host country (third-country nationals, or TCNs). For instance, Brazilian-born Carlos Gohsn is CEO of French carmaker Renault and its Japanese affiliate Nissan.

Alternative philosophies of staffing abroad are ethnocentric, polycentric, regiocentric, and geocentric.[10] In *ethnocentric* staffing, PCNs are appointed to key positions regardless of the location of their assignment, as HSBC did until 20 years ago or so. Japanese companies tend to follow this mode more than European and U.S. firms.[11] South Korean firms and most other developing countries' MNEs (DMNEs) utilized ethnocentric staffing (Samsung, for instance, not only had an all-Korean senior management team until 1999, but 90% of those people graduated from Seoul National University);[12] however, Korean firms are now rapidly increasing the ranks of non-Koreans as part of their globalization drive. LG Electronics is recruiting technological talent in Russia, among other regions, utilizing a new Korean government program providing foreign technology experts with a three-year work visa.[13] In China, recruitment of foreign executives is also on the rise. For instance, in 2006 Shanghai Automotive (SAIC) hired the former head of GM's China operations. For many U.S. firms, the greater the cultural distance to the host nation, the greater the proportion of U.S. nationals in the subsidiary.[14]

In *polycentric* staffing, HCNs are hired to key positions in subsidiaries but not at corporate headquarters. In *regiocentric* staffing, recruiting is conducted on a regional basis (e.g., Asian candidates are recruited for a position in Thailand). In *geocentric* staffing, managers are recruited worldwide based solely on their qualifications and regardless of their nationality. The value of this approach is not only in obtaining the best candidates but also in introducing new perspectives into the company. Indeed, firms that consider themselves to be the most successful in globalization have had a significantly higher proportion of foreign citizens in senior management—20% to 25% versus 10% for other firms.[15] Nestlé and Johnson & Johnson are examples.

Most of the MNE workforce abroad consists of HCNs or, as they are sometimes called at the subsidiary level, "local employees." The reason is simple: HCNs are, in most instances, the most widely available and the easiest to employ as they are normally (unless illegal immigrants) permitted to work and are likely to have local certification where needed (e.g., in the case of nurses, accountants, and lawyers). HCNs also know more about the local environment and are generally cheaper to employ, especially in developing and emerging markets, although this is not necessarily the case for DMNEs investing in developing markets—say, the operations of Chinese appliance maker Haier in the United States.

You may recall from Chapter 3 on foreign direct investment that labor cost is an important consideration in location decisions, especially for labor-intensive activities. Exhibit 17.4 provides comparative compensation costs for manufacturing workers in selected countries, showing considerable differences between countries. Such differentials explain, among other factors, why an MNE might choose to invest in a particular location, although this will be especially pronounced for labor-intensive industries, such as garments and toys.

In 2000, roughly one of eight manufacturing employees in the United States was employed by a foreign affiliate. Today, the ratio is closer to one in six. Honda alone employs more than 25,000 U.S. employees in all 50 states. U.S. firms, on their part, employ millions of people in foreign countries. The availability of qualified

Exhibit 17.4   Hourly Compensation Costs in U.S. Dollars for Production Workers in Manufacturing, 2004

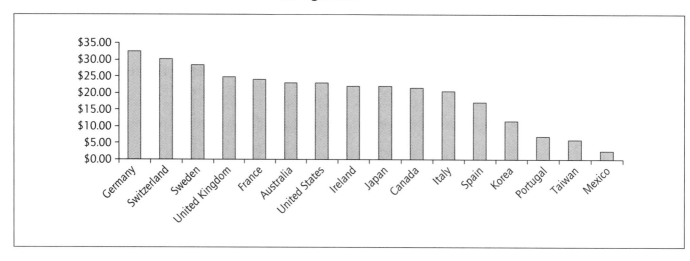

SOURCE: U.S. Bureau of Labor Statistics, June 2006.

candidates is often a decisive factor in selecting a manufacturing or service location.[16] For years, foreign MNEs in Japan have found it difficult to hire qualified Japanese employees, although this situation is now changing. In some countries, hiring requires a government-controlled labor bureau that may assign employees to work for the MNE. In Singapore, high on the cultural dimensions of power distance and masculinity, it is legal to specify race, age, and sex requirements in job advertisements, which would violate American Equal Employment Opportunity law.

Once an employee is hired, the MNE needs to deal with communication and integration challenges. Sixty percent of Citigroup's workforce lacks knowledge of English, a key obstacle to the firm's effort to leverage its global reach.[17] A formal career planning system in which people are evaluated in terms of skills, abilities, and traits that will be tested, scored, and computerized may appear to be impersonal in collective cultures. Individualistic societies use more cognitive testing because they emphasize performance, individual rights, and individual interests, whereas collective cultures emphasize loyalty and organizational compatibility that cannot be assessed via cognitive tests.[18] Personality profiles generated in the United States may be meaningless in Japan, where assertiveness is not appreciated.

Finally, the MNE is expected to monitor employment conditions not only at home but also in its subsidiaries and among its subcontractors. Wal-Mart has been accused of buying from vendors that use child labor in Bangladesh, whereas Nike recently admitted to worker abuse occurring in its Indonesian factories ranging from verbal abuse to sexual coercion.[19] More recently, Apple has committed to rectify what it defined as minor deviations from the labor code in its Chinese supplier. Even letting go of an errant supplier will no longer satisfy many of the NGOs (Nongovernmental Organizations) that monitor worker treatment, as Disney found in early 2007 when a Hong Kong–based group protested its retreat from a mainland factory.

Country-Specific Issues

As in other functional realms, the need for adjustment in corporate policies and practices is anchored in variations across labor markets. In transition economies like Vietnam and Romania, older employees who have grown accustomed to a central planning system often have difficulty adjusting to the higher productivity expected in an MNE. Concerning the supply of younger, highly skilled employees, the problem is different. Despite having large workforces, transition economies often have relatively few skilled employees owing to the lack of an educational infrastructure. In China, for example, one of the greatest problems facing MNEs is very high turnover, a problem that undermines investment in recruitment and training and limits growth prospects. To overcome the problem, Ford Motor Company offers retention incentives to its Chinese workers in the form of a housing loan that is forgiven after seven years of service and tuition reimbursement for those pursuing an MBA degree. China is also the only country in which Ford operates that individuals who have left the company can be rehired.

Interim Summary

1. Boards of directors increasingly include nonnationals as a way to deal with growing globalization and introduce new perspectives.

2. Ethnocentric, polycentric, regiocentric, and geocentric staffing are the main staffing strategies of the MNE.

3. For reasons of local knowledge and cost, host-country nationals constitute the bulk of the MNE workforce abroad.

THE EXPATRIATE WORKFORCE

Types and Distribution of Expatriates

Expatriate numbers are small relative to total MNE employment. Many MNEs (e.g., Ford and Johnson & Johnson) have attempted to reduce the number of their expatriates as a cost-reduction measure as well as to create career opportunities and tap the skills of local employees. Yet, with the growth of global operations and increased demand for their skills, expatriate numbers are growing. A 2006 Mercer survey found that 38% of the firms surveyed have increased the number of international transfers over the previous two years, while 47% maintained the same number. Forty-four percent reported an increase in international transfers between firm locations other than headquarters.[20]

There are different types of expatriates.[21] The traditional expatriate, typically an experienced executive, is selected for his or her managerial or technical skills for a period that usually lasts between one and five years. Some members of this group become international cadres who move from one foreign assignment to another, seldom returning to their home country, sometimes becoming permanent expatriates who stay in overseas assignments for extended periods of time, or even permanently. Young, inexperienced expatriates are sent for six months to five years, usually on local hire terms. Temporaries go on short assignments, up to one year. Organization Resource Counselors (ORC) reports that 77% of 500 MNEs it surveyed expect to increase temporary assignments.[22] Still another type is the expatriate trainee, who is placed abroad for training purposes as part of initiation into an MNE. For instance, Johnson & Johnson places new executive recruits in another country for an 18-month period.[23] A PricewaterhouseCoopers (PWC) survey of 270 European organizations employing 65,000 expatriates found a significant increase in "short-term, commuter, and virtual assignments" over the past two years. Short-term assignment increased by 54% whereas virtual assignments increased by 44%.

Two-thirds of the firms in the PWC survey employ virtual expatriates, up from 44% earlier. The virtual expatriate takes on foreign assignments without physically relocating. A frequent flier, the virtual expatriate uses videoconferencing and telecommunications to stay in touch. Examples include Ian Hunter, who manages the Middle East and Pakistan for London-based GlaxoSmithKline, and Gerals Lukomsli, who manages Central Eastern Europe, the Middle East, and Africa for Motorola. Both manage from England. Rajiv Bhatia oversees hotels in Mexico and other countries from his New Jersey base for Cendant Corp., a franchisee for Howard Johnson and other U.S. hotel chains. Arte Nathan, the senior human resource officer for Las Vegas–based Wynn Resorts, oversaw the recruitment of 5,000 employees for his company's new (2006) casino in Macau (a Special Administrative Region of China) mostly using electronic communications. Among the allures of the virtual expatriate are low cost, avoiding family adjustment, and not having to relocate.[24]

Using Expatriates: Pros and Cons

MNEs use expatriates "to get the business off the ground, put in the infrastructure, as well as to prepare a plan to eventually change the mix of expatriates versus nationals."[25] Still, expatriates continue to be necessary in many locations and not only as a means to control operations and instill corporate culture. In many developing nations, locals are not yet ready to assume senior management positions. In addition to contributing essential knowledge and experience, expatriates serve as a mechanism of control and as a way to transmit corporate culture and goals.[26] By rotating expatriates, MNEs establish and maintain informal networks that are conducive to the sharing of knowledge and coordination among units. Expatriation creates a global perspective and is essential to knowledge and technology transfer. A senior Corning executive observed the following:

> Five to ten years ago, companies were using expatriates largely for command and control or to transfer specific knowledge. Today, in an effective local organization we are looking for learning that the expatriates can use in their jobs as they move around the globe.[27]

In addition to the high cost, reasons against using expatriates include the disincentive to the local workforce whose promotion is blocked and who would feel relatively deprived owing to their lower wage levels. Excessive use of expatriates can rob a company of the skills, insight, and initiative of local nationals. Another strike against expatriates is their high rate of failure, discussed in the next section.

Expatriate Failure

Expatriate failure can usually be observed in the case of a premature return to the home country (although the return can also be triggered by personal reasons) or when performance does not meet expectations and cannot be attributed to objective business reasons (e.g., an economic downturn). The expatriate failure rates reported by companies range widely, with some as low as 15% and others as high as 80%; it is also known that many expatriates who stay on the job perform inadequately.[28] Japan and China show the highest failure rates for U.S. expatriates, probably a result of differences in culture and business environment.[29] Failure rates for European and Japanese expatriates are reportedly lower than for U.S. expatriates.[30] The relative success of Japanese expatriates may be attributed to the country-specific training they receive for an entire year prior to their assignment; however, the gap may also reflect differences in evaluation method. Unlike their U.S. counterparts, Japanese expatriates are commonly evaluated on adjustment and host-country knowledge rather than on professional results. Also, because of culture (loss of "face") and other factors, Japanese firms are less likely to repatriate a low-performing expatriate.

The financial cost of expatriate failure is substantial, ranging from $55,000 to $150,000[31] and more in direct costs. The real cost of expatriate failure is considerably higher, however. It includes not only the cost of selection, training, preparation, and moving but also the consequences of poor performance in lower revenues, lost business opportunities, and damage to the firm's reputation, which may undermine future ventures in the host country. Thus, it is important for companies to reduce the failure rate to the extent possible.

The reasons for expatriate failure include spouse's unhappiness (including dual-career issues which today involve almost three-quarters of expatriates), inability to adjust to an unfamiliar environment, personality or emotional immaturity, inability to cope with the responsibilities and stress posed by overseas work, and lack of technical competence.[32] Lack of motivation to work overseas, especially in a location to which the firm attaches little value, is also a problem.[33] More than 80% of firms surveyed by PWC had employees who refused overseas assignments because of dual-career and family concerns or the perceived career risk of being away from headquarters ("out of sight, out of mind"). Still, more than half of the firms surveyed reported an increase in the overall number of international assignments. More willing to relocate are executives who have relocated domestically, who find the host country culturally or otherwise appealing, and who see a match with their career plans. Spouse willingness to relocate also plays a major role. Older, better-educated spouses, often members of minority groups and with fewer children, are more likely to relocate.[34]

Despite the dramatic strides made by women up the corporate ladder, they remain underrepresented in the expatriate workforce. This is sometimes the result of an assumption that women will be ineffective in foreign cultures, especially in those high on masculinity, where women rarely occupy senior management positions (e.g., Saudi Arabia, where women are kept away from management positions for religious reasons, or Japan). The view that women will not be effective in high-masculinity locations is not empirically supported, as evidence suggests expatriate women are viewed first and foremost as foreigners; still, the perception persists.[35]

Expatriate Selection

Among the attributes MNEs are looking for in an expatriate are cultural empathy, adaptability and flexibility, language skills, education, leadership, maturity, and motivation.[36] Adler specifies these competencies: a global perspective, local responsiveness, synergistic learning (integrating learning from multiple cultures), transition and adaptation, cross-cultural interaction, collaboration, and foreign experiences. Especially important is the ability to exercise discretion in choosing when to be locally responsive and when to engage in global integration.[37]

Successful expatriates need three sets of skills. The first set includes personal skills that facilitate mental and emotional well-being—for example, stress orientation, reinforcement, substitution, physical mobility, technical competence, dealing with alienation and isolation and realistic expectations prior to departure. The second set consists of people skills such as relational abilities, willingness to communicate, nonverbal communication, respect for others, and empathy for others. The third set includes perception skills—namely, the cognitive process that helps executives understand the behavior of foreigners. This includes flexible attribution and breadth as well as being open-minded and nonjudgmental.[38] Extroversion and being culturally adventurous are important for expatriate success in culturally distant countries.

Expatriate Selection Instruments

A number of instruments assist in the selection of expatriates. The Prospector assesses the potential of aspiring international executives on 14 dimensions:

1. Cultural sensitivity
2. Business knowledge
3. Courage
4. Motivational ability
5. Integrity
6. Insight
7. Commitment
8. Risk taking
9. Seeking feedback
10. Using feedback
11. Being culturally adventurous
12. Seeking learning opportunities
13. Openness to criticism
14. Having flexibility[39]

Another instrument is the Overseas Assignment Inventory (OAI), developed by Tucker International. This instrument uses these predictors of success on a foreign assignment: expectations, open-mindedness, respect for others' beliefs, trust in people, tolerance, locus of control, flexibility, patience, social adaptability, initiative, risk taking, sense of humor, and spouse communication.[40]

Role-based simulations have become especially popular in recent years as a selection tool. These simulations are either generic or country specific, such as Motorola's China program. They have proved quite effective. Danone, the French food giant, was able to reduce the failure rate among its expatriates from 35% to 3% in the three years it began using such evaluation and selection programs.[41]

Preparing for a Foreign Assignment

Expatriates entering a foreign country must adjust to new job responsibilities and to a new environment, including a different culture. The first adjustment phase is anticipatory and takes place before departure. In-country adjustment follows.

Adjustment varies by individual factors (self-efficacy, relation, and perception skills), job-related factors (role clarity, role discretion, role novelty, and role conflict), organization culture (culture novelty, social support, and logistical help), organization socialization, nonwork factors, and family–spouse adjustment. Language fluency and previous assignments also influence adjustment.[42]

Adjusting to a new culture is an especially challenging task for expatriates. Five determinants of cross-cultural adjustment have been identified:[43] Predeparture cross-cultural training; previous overseas experience; multiple-candidate, multi-criteria selection; individual skills including self-dimension skills (to maintain mental health, psychological well-being, self-efficacy, and effective stress management), relational skills (to interact with host nationals), and perceptual skills (to correctly perceive and evaluate the host environment); and nonwork factors such as cultural distance and spouse and family adjustment. Matching expatriates' previous cross-cultural experiences with the target countries and moving expatriates gradually from culturally similar countries to culturally distant countries have also been found to mitigate cultural adjustment.[44] The U-curve theory suggests that individuals exposed to a new culture go through four stages of adjustment: In Stage 1, "honeymoon," they are fascinated by the new culture. In Stage 2, "culture shock," infatuation with the new culture is replaced by disillusionment and the frustration of having to cope with it on a daily basis. In Stage 3, "adjustment," individuals gradually adapt to the new culture and learn how to behave appropriately. In Stage 4, "mastery," individuals incrementally learn how to function smoothly in the new culture.[45]

Expatriate Training

Although such training has been proved to reduce expatriate failure,[46] only 30% of U.S. firms conduct cross-cultural training, compared with 70% of European and Japanese firms. The reasons for the low U.S. rate include a belief that cross-cultural training programs are ineffective, trainee dissatisfaction, a short span between selection and relocation, and a perception that the short-term nature of many overseas assignments does not warrant the expense of cross-cultural training.[47]

Training for an overseas assignment has two components.[48] The first is information giving, consisting of (a) practical information on living conditions in the destination country; (b) area studies—namely, facts about the country's environment; and (c) cultural awareness information. There are no empirical studies that measure the effectiveness of practical information. Evidence suggests that areas studies training is generally useful, although it is not very helpful in terms of equipping expatriates with the skills necessary to work effectively in the destination culture. Similar evidence applies to cultural awareness programs. The second set of activities in cross-cultural training consists of experiential learning, which combines cognitive and behavioral techniques. The goal is to acquire intercultural effectiveness skills that include transition stress management, relationship building, cross-cultural communication, and negotiation techniques.[49] A number of studies suggest that such training is especially valuable.[50]

Effective cross-cultural training requires an integrated approach consisting of both general cultural orientation and specific cultural development. Content and sequencing of training content are critical for success. Yoshida and Brislin[51] list five cultural training guidelines: First, *identify*—become aware of which skills you need to function well in the target culture. Second, *understand*—know why, where, when, to whom, and how the behavior is appropriate. Third, use *cultural informants to understand specifics*—observe and consult people from the target culture to make sure you are using the behaviors in the proper context and are delivering them appropriately. Fourth, *practice*—it is only through practice that proficiency in a new skill is gained. Fifth, *deal with emotions*—trainees should anticipate strong emotional reactions to cultural differences, as well as to the new behaviors they will be using.

Harrison proposes a two-stage cultural orientation.[52] The first stage is designed to focus trainees' attention and prepare them for cross-cultural encounters in general. This stage consists of (a) self-assessment of factors that may influence one's receptiveness to and propensity for effective cross-cultural assignments and (b) cultural awareness of the general dimensions on which most cultures differ and the potential impact of these differences for expatriates. The second stage, specific cultural orientation, is designed to develop a trainee's ability to interact effectively within the specific culture to which he or she will be assigned. This stage also includes two phases: (a) knowledge acquisition (e.g., *retention*) of the language and customs in the specific culture and (b) skill training (*reproduction*) in the application of appropriate behaviors in the specific culture.

Choosing a Training Method. Tung proposes a contingency framework for determining the nature and level of rigor of training based on the degree of interaction required in the overseas position and the cultural distance between the expatriate's native and new culture. If the expected interaction between expatriates and HCNs is low and the cultural distance is low, training should focus on task-related rather than culture-related issues, and the level of rigor required is relatively low. If expected interaction and cultural distance are high, training should focus on the new culture and on cross-cultural skill development as well as on the new task, and the level of rigor should be moderate to high.[53]

Another training model is based on social learning theory and is focused on the degree of cognitive involvement by the trainee. The model distinguishes between processes–symbolic modeling, which is based on observation of modeled behavior, and participative modeling, which requires observation and participation in the modeled behaviors.[54] In addition to training methods, the model includes level of training rigor, the duration of training relative to the degree of interaction, and cultural novelty. For example, if the level of interaction and the cultural distance are low, the length of training should be less than a week and such methods as area or cultural briefings, films, and books are appropriate. If the individual is going overseas for a period of 2 to 12 months and is expected to have some interaction with host nationals, training should be more rigorous and last longer (one to four weeks), and role-play would be appropriate. If the individual is leaving for a novel culture and the expected interaction with host nationals is intense, training should be rigorous and last as long as two months. Sensitivity training and some field experiences would be appropriate.

Compensation

MNE compensation programs are geared to attract and retain qualified employees, facilitate transfer between HQ and affiliates, create consistency and equity in compensation, and maintain competitiveness.[55] Compensation systems derive from MNE international strategies (multidomestic, international, global, and transnational) as well as the MNE's product or organizational life cycle. They also reflect the host-country's laws, regulations, and cultural traditions. Research suggests that an appropriate compensation package should reduce expenses while enhancing commitment to the employer, job satisfaction, and willingness to relocate internationally.[56]

An effective compensation system starts with accurate performance appraisal. Challenges in conducting performance appraisal for expatriates include choosing the evaluator, difference in performance perceptions between home and host countries, communication difficulties with headquarters, inadequate recording of performance objectives, home (parent)-country ethnocentrism, and indifference to the foreign experience of the expatriate. Other problems are difficulty in balancing local responsiveness and global integration, noncomparability of data from different subsidiaries or regions, and environmental variations across subsidiaries. Decisions need to be made regarding raters' location (home or host country) and their expatriate experience and regarding the use of standard, customized, or hybrid evaluation forms.[57] Studies found that a balanced set of raters from host and home countries and more frequent appraisals relate positively to perceived accuracy of evaluation; however, most respondent firms did not follow these practices.[58] The use of a balanced set of raters from host and home country increased accuracy as did the use of host-country raters.

Cost and Elements of Expatriate Compensation

The cost of employing expatriates is high, up to three to five multiples of domestic salary for a local hire.[59] The cost can easily reach US$350,000 and more for the first year and much more in high-cost locations such as Japan or Norway. Recent data show an effort to reduce expatriate pay packages (rather than benefits) while retaining end-of-term bonuses.[60]

Expatriate compensation comprises these elements:

- Salary—Base pay plus incentives (merit increases, profit sharing, bonus plans), determined via job evaluation or competency-based plans. Incentives—in the form of cash or deferred payment—may be based on home- country plans, host-country plans, or both. Payment may be deferred until return if the home country's tax rate is lower.
- Housing—Most MNEs pay allowances for housing or provide company-owned housing for expatriates. A housing allowance is provided to maintain expatriates' living standard at their home-country level.
- Services allowance and premiums—These are paid to compensate expatriates for differences in expenditures between the home and host country. Allowances are provided for higher cost of living in the host country, home leave (home-country visits), education (children's tuition, language classes), and relocation (moving, shipping, and storage, temporary living quarters). The balance sheet approach is the most widely used technique for equalizing the purchasing power of home- and host-country employees and to offset qualitative differences between locations.[61] The housing allowance is a function of the expected hardship in the host country and the job type, but it takes into account the fact that the expatriate represents the employer in the host country. A hardship allowance is paid to compensate the expatriate for a variety of factors that make expatriate assignment difficult. Exhibit 17.5 shows a hardship evaluation for an expatriate in Santiago, Chile.
- Tax equalization—Expatriates face two potential sources of income tax liability—home and host. The United States, like Israel and North Korea but unlike most other nations, taxes its citizens on foreign income, although it exempts the first $82,000 (inflation adjusted) of foreign wages. In 2006, Congress effectively increased taxation on U.S. expatriates by including housing benefits within the allotted exemption. Depending on tax treaties

Exhibit 17.5   Hardship Evaluation: Santiago, Chile

Review Date: January 2006
Publication Date: January 2006

	Maximum Score	Location Score
I: Assessment of Physical Threat to Employee and Family		
A. Potential or actual violence in area	15	4
B. Hostility of local population	10	2
C. Prevalence of disease	15	3
D. Limited medical facilities and services	10	3
Total threat category	50 pts	12 pts
II: Assessment of Discomfort to Employee and Family		
A. Difficult physical environment	10	2
B. Geographic isolation	10	3
C. Cultural or psychological isolation	10	2
Total discomfort category	30 pts	7 pts
III: Assessment of Inconvenience to Employee and Family		
A. Shortcomings in local education system	5	1
B. Restricted availability or low quality of local housing	5	1
C. Limited recreational or community facilities	5	2
D. Poor availability, quality, or variety of consumer goods	5	1
Total inconvenience category	20 pts	5 pts
TOTAL (all categories)	100 pts	24 pts

SOURCE: Copyright © 2006 AIRINC Associates for International Research, Inc.

and duration of stay, the host country may tax the expatriate as well, but the tax is credited on the U.S. tax return. Tax equalization is an adjustment to expatriate pay to reflect tax rates in the home country.[62] Exhibit 17.6 shows a sample of how foreign compensation is calculated. Note that total foreign compensation is 60% higher than base pay.

Approaches to Expatriate Compensation

There are three basic approaches to expatriate compensation: home based, host based, and hybrid. All three approaches assume that the employee will remain vested in home-country social security, pensions, and other retirement programs. All three motivate employees to take the assignment, successfully complete it, and return without extraordinary loss or gain. A home-country compensation system links base expatriate salary to the salary structure of the home country. For instance, the salary of a U.S. executive transferred to Sweden will be based on the United States rather than Swedish level. In a host country–based (localized) compensation system, base salary for an expatriate is linked to the pay structure in the host country; however, supplemental compensation provisions are often linked to home-country salary structures. The combination produces an international compensation approach oriented toward the higher of host or home gross salary level and the lowest of host-, home-, or third-country taxes.[63] Elements related to the home country will be gradually

Exhibit 17.6   Individual Report: Sample Company

EMPLOYEE	Unknown		EXCHANGE RATE	EUR = TWD 41.8
HOME COUNTRY	Germany		ANNUAL BASE SALARY	EUR 100,000
HOST LOCATION	Taipei, Taiwan		FAMILY SIZE AT HOST	5
DATE	August 2004		HOME COUNTRY TAX EXEMPTIONS	5

Computation of Host Compensation

Calculation of Net Pay

	EUR	TWD
Base Salary	100,000	4,180,000
+ Hardship (*15% of base salary where applicable*)	15,000	627,000
− Home Country Income Tax (*Germany + SS, on base salary only*)	(15,226)	(636,447)
= **Net Home Pay**	84,774	3,543,553

Equalization Component

Conservative

	EUR	TWD
Host Expenditure on Goods & Services	59,210	2,474,978
− Home Country Spending on Goods & Services	(45,550)	(1,903,990)
= **Goods & Services Differential**	13,660	570,998

Index: 130

Host Expenditure on Rent & Utilities

	EUR	TWD
Rent TWD 109,294; Utilities TWD 27,392 per month provides a 3 BR House in Peitou, Yangmingshan	39,240	1,640,232
− Home Country Spending on Rent & Utilities (Norm)	(14,500)	(606,100)
= **Rent & Utilities Differential**	24,740	1,034,132

	EUR	TWD
Net Host Compensation (*Net home pay + G&S differential + R&U differential*)	123,174	5,148,673
Estimated Foreign Tax—grossed up	39,026	1,631,303
Total Foreign Compensation	162,220	6,779,976

SOURCE: Copyright © 2006 AIRINC Associates for International Research, Inc.

phased out from the fourth to the sixth years in the host country. A study by Watson Wyatt Worldwide found that of the U.S.-based foreign subsidiaries studied, 66% departed from their home-country compensation plans to offer U.S.-style executive compensation plans.

Finally, a hybrid compensation system blends features from the home- and host-based approaches. The purpose is to create an international expatriate workforce that, while not hailing from a single location, is paid as if it were.[64] The simplest form of a hybrid system assumes that all expatriates, regardless of country of origin, belong to one nationality. Other derivatives of this system involve the application of identical cost-of-living allowances to all nationalities, uniform premiums, and uniform housing and other local allowances.

Exhibit 17.7 summarizes the features, advantages, and disadvantages of the three approaches.

Exhibit 17.7   Expatriate Compensation Systems

	Home-Based	Host-Based	Hybrid
Features	☐ Consistent treatment of expatriates of same nationality ☐ Link with home-country structure/economy ☐ Different pay levels for different nationalities ☐ No relationship to local employees	☐ Equity with local nationals ☐ All nationalities paid the same ☐ Simple administration ☐ Variation in "value" by localities ☐ No link to home-country structure/economy	☐ All nationalities paid equitably ☐ Some link to home-country structure/economy ☐ No relationship to local employees
Applicable Conditions	☐ Temporary international assignment (2–5 years) ☐ Expatriates will ultimately be repatriated to their country of origin ☐ The number of different nationalities in any one host location is relatively low ☐ International staff predominate in higher-level host location jobs	☐ International assignments are of indefinite duration ☐ Expatriates tend to be assigned to high-pay countries and will ultimately be repatriated to their country of origin ☐ The number of different nationalities in any one host location is relatively high ☐ Host-country local staff predominate in higher-level host location jobs	
Advantages	☐ Expatriates neither gain nor lose financially ☐ Facilitates mobility ☐ Eases repatriation	☐ All employees operate on equivalent pay ☐ System is easy to administer ☐ All employees, including expatriates, are paid the same ☐ Most suitable for international assignments of indefinite duration	☐ All expatriate nationalities are paid equitably ☐ Assists transfers and development of an international management cadre
Disadvantages	☐ Expensive ☐ No link to local pay structure ☐ Expatriates of the same seniority from different origins will be paid differently ☐ Administration can be complex	☐ Complicates reentry ☐ Most applicable when salary and living standards improve, thereby becoming expensive ☐ Unprotected fluctuations in the exchange rate puts company and employee at additional risk ☐ Certain host-country benefits are not applicable to expatriates ☐ Difficult to transfer to lower-paying location	☐ Complicated administration ☐ Sometimes difficult to communicate ☐ No link to local pay structure

SOURCE: G. T. Milkovich and J. M. Newman. *Compensation.* Chicago: Irwin/McGraw-Hill, 1999. Reprinted with permission of The McGraw Hill Companies.

Other expatriate compensation approaches include lump-sum/cafeteria and negotiation. The lump-sum or cafeteria approach offers expatriates more choices. Salary is set according to the home-country system, but instead of breaking compensation into its component parts, firms offer a total allowance package and each expatriate makes his or her own selection of pay and benefits. The logic is to avoid paying for items that expatriates do not need or value. The negotiation approach assumes that employer and employee find a mutually acceptable package and is most common in smaller firms with very few expatriates. This approach creates comparability and potentially inequity perceptions.

Culture and Compensation

Business performance improves when HRM practices are consistent with national culture (see also Chapter 6).[65] In masculine cultures, work units with more merit-based reward practices were found to perform better, while in feminine cultures, work units with fewer merit-based reward practices were higher performers. The propensity to use both seniority-based and skill-based compensation systems was positively correlated with uncertainty avoidance. Compensation practices based on individual performance were correlated with individualism. High masculinity was associated with lesser use of flexible benefits, workplace child-care programs, career-break schemes, and maternity-leave programs.[66] High collectivism was found to be negatively related to individual- and equity-based rewards and merit-based promotion systems.[67] However, there are occasions where collectivists compromise cultural traditions to help their organization survive.[68]

The following recommendations have been made vis-à-vis compensation in different cultures:[69]

- In high-power-distance cultures, MNEs should pursue hierarchical compensation for local managers, pay and benefits should be tied to position, and a large pay differential between echelons is desirable.
- In cultures with high individualism, performance-based pay and extrinsic rewards are important. In cultures with low individualism, group-based pay and compensation packages that reflect seniority and family needs are more acceptable.
- In cultures with high masculinity, MNEs should pursue a compensation strategy for local managers that recognizes and rewards competitiveness, aggressiveness, and dominance. In cultures with low masculinity, compensation should focus on social benefits, quality of work life, and equity.
- In cultures with high uncertainty avoidance, structured and consistent pay plans are preferred. Salary and benefits decision making should be centralized, with no variable pay plans or discretionary salary allocation. Where uncertainty avoidance is low, pay should be closely linked to performance.
- In high-uncertainty-avoidance cultures it is better to have centralized pension systems with multiple controls and safeguards.
- Low-uncertainty-avoidance cultures are more open to defined contribution pensions with flexible plan implementation.
- Separate pension plans for different classes of employees are acceptable in high-power-distance cultures.
- In masculine cultures with moderate to high uncertainty avoidance, policies designed to protect job security are more welcome.
- Employees from feminine cultures with moderate to high uncertainty avoidance prefer policies designed to protect income security.
- Employees from feminine cultures prefer family-friendly management practices as well as other policies designed to maximize quality of work life.
- Employees in low individualistic and low-power-distance cultures prefer flexible benefit programs.
- Health programs in low-power-distance cultures should be uniform for all, while employee choice of health insurance providers works better in individualistic cultures.

Performance evaluation also varies across cultures. Management by Objectives (MBO), where subordinates and supervisors agree to measurable goals, tends to fail in high-power-distance cultures, as in East Asia. Employees in such cultures also tend to shun "360 degrees" evaluation, in which subordinates participate in the evaluation of their superiors. In cultures with high uncertainty avoidance, it is hard to get subordinates to commit to risky goals. Cultural differences also affect the relative importance of different performance dimensions; for example, in collectivist cultures, group harmony and cohesiveness tend to be more important than performance.

Repatriation

The repatriation of expatriates represents an adjustment that is equally if not more difficult than the adjustment to the overseas assignment.[70] Some of the problems are mundane, from the inability to borrow owing to lack of credit history to limitations regarding housing that got more expensive during one's absence, and others are emotional, including, surprisingly, cultural adjustment. Returning expatriates do not expect their repatriation to be problematic because they are coming back to familiar turf; however, they do not take into account the fact that their home environment has changed during their stay abroad and that they themselves have changed. Most returning employees are dissatisfied with the repatriation process. Most U.S. firms do not provide a written guarantee of reassignment prior to departure, and most returnees do not know what their next assignment will be prior to repatriation. Even those with a suitable reassignment often feel that their employers fail to make effective use of their foreign experience. With the exception of housing assistance, most firms do not provide spousal career counseling or other forms of family repatriation assistance. It is therefore not surprising that one quarter of repatriated employees leave their firm within one year of repatriation[71] and that many decline to undertake subsequent international assignments.

Interim Summary

1. MNEs use expatriate staff to get businesses off the ground, disseminate knowledge and corporate culture to the foreign subsidiary, develop their staff, and control and coordinate their subsidiaries.

2. Many expatriates have difficulty adjusting to a new country and to an unfamiliar business environment, and failure rates are high.

3. Adaptability and a nonjudgmental stance toward other cultures help expatriates succeed in their mission.

4. Proper selection and training reduce expatriate failure rates.

5. Repatriation is a significant challenge that many firms have yet to address.

HRM IN INTERNATIONAL AFFILIATES

Human resource issues and problems vary depending on the type of foreign affiliate involved. Although wholly owned subsidiaries (WOSs) employ up to three employee groups (PCNs, HCNs, and TCNs), international joint ventures (IJVs) employ multiple employee groups, as follows:

- Foreign parent expatriates (i.e., nationals of the country in which the headquarters of the foreign parent is located, assigned by that parent to the affiliate)
- Host parent transferees (host-country nationals employed by the host parent and transferred to the affiliate from the host-parent headquarters or one of its subsidiaries)
- Host-country nationals (nationals of the host country, hired directly by the affiliate)
- Third-country expatriates of the host parent (third-country nationals who are neither nationals of the host country nor of the foreign parent's country and who are assigned by the host parent to work in the affiliate)
- Third-country expatriates of the foreign parent (third-country nationals assigned by the foreign parent to work in the affiliate)
- Third-country expatriates of the affiliate (third-country nationals recruited directly by the affiliate, who are neither nationals of the parent country nor of the country in which the affiliate operates)
- Foreign headquarters executives (i.e., policymakers at the headquarters of the foreign parent, who play a major role in the functioning of the affiliate at headquarters or are board members of the affiliate)
- Host headquarters executives (i.e., policymakers at the headquarters of the host parent, who play a major role in the functioning of the affiliate at headquarters or are board members of the affiliate)

Human Resource Problems in Foreign Affiliates

The following human resource problems can be expected in WOSs and IJVs.[72]

- *Staffing Friction.* Parent companies prefer to appoint their own transferees or expatriates to key positions in the affiliate as a control measure. When the staffing policy is not contractually specified, friction often ensues. In many cases, friction also develops regarding the level of staffing, with the host parent looking at the IJV as a way of "unloading" extra staff. In both WOSs and IJVs, HCNs are often deprived of opportunities to staff the most senior positions.

- *Blocked Promotion.* In both types of affiliates, local employees can be frustrated by the lack of promotion opportunities if senior positions are reserved for "outsiders." This problem is especially serious in IJVs where the "outsiders" may be not only the foreign expatriates but also transferees of the host parent. When such "outsiders" are abundant, local staff may be reluctant to join, stay, or contribute their best efforts to the affiliate.

- *Exile Syndrome and Reentry Difficulties.* Feeling "exiled" in an overseas assignment because of fear of interruption of one's career track back home occurs in both WOSs and IJVs. WOSs are more closely integrated, however, so an assignment to a subsidiary might be less disruptive. Assignees in an IJV, on the other hand, may be working with, or supervised by, employees of another company. They will not report directly to their parent headquarters, nor will their supervisors be in a position to assess their performance. Exile syndrome may be damaging to the foreign affiliate because it may lead employees to bypass their supervisors in the affiliate, report achievements rather than failures, and take a short-term perspective.

- *Split Loyalty.* Split loyalty is unique to IJVs. Employees recruited by the host or the foreign parent may remain loyal to that parent rather than shift their allegiance to the IJV. This happens especially where employees expect to return to the parent firm at the end of their assignment or when the IJV has a predetermined life span. The result is suspicion and a low level of cooperation that prevents the venture from attaining its potential.

- *Compensation Gaps.* The problem of compensation gaps (e.g., HCNs receiving much lower pay than expatriates) occurs in both types of affiliates. For example, many U.S.-based executives of foreign MNEs earn more than their superiors in Europe or Asia. IJVs suffer from an additional problem of relative deprivation, however, where employees receive compensation packages that are not necessarily based on universal criteria, such as skills and experience, but on affiliation with a particular parent or the IJV itself. Each MNE has an established compensation policy, and in many cases, the differences are significant. Moreover, each employee group has a different perception about what the most desirable package of benefits is. The result is a feeling of deprivation and consequently reduced motivation and morale.

- *Blocked Communication.* Effective communication among parent firms and between a parent and an affiliate can be hampered by a combination of cultural differences and variations in organizational procedures and norms. Because of differences in parents' objectives, communications may be distorted or withheld by their respective employees. Such communication blockages represent an impediment to decision making. The problem is especially serious in IJVs with a 50–50 equity distribution.

- *Limited Delegation.* Many parent firms try to maintain control of their affiliate by limiting the scope of authority and decision-making power they delegate. This is especially true where parents have conflicting goals, where they depend on the affiliate for scarce and vital resources, and when they feel that the affiliate's staff is loyal to the other parent. Under these conditions, the affiliate's management finds it difficult to operate effectively, especially in a fast-changing environment.

- *Screening of Information.* Many firms are hesitant to pass information and technology to an affiliate, especially in an IJV when the partner might be a present or a future competitor. The result is self-defeating, with the other parent(s) limiting information as well. The venture is then unable to operate effectively.

- *Unfamiliarity.* Expatriates who join a foreign affiliate are unfamiliar, in most cases, with the environment in which the venture operates. In IJVs, most employees are also unfamiliar with the unique structure of this organization and with its conflict-prone nature.

Research provides some suggestions for alleviating some of the human resource problems in foreign affiliates. Among the solutions are organization development and training, identifying and rewarding leadership, improving interpersonal and negotiation channels, and career planning that takes account of the overlapping yet diverse tracks among the member organizations. Still, relatively little is known about the training and preparation required for operating effectively in a specific foreign affiliate. At the same time, we are only beginning to consider the adjustments when moving, say, from a WOS to an IJV. Exhibit 17.8 provides a starting point.

Interim Summary

1. Wholly owned subsidiaries (WOSs) and international joint ventures (IJVs) share many human resource problems, although IJVs tend to be more problematic owing to such problems as split loyalty.

Exhibit 17.8   Management Education Requirements in Two Types of Foreign Affiliates

Educational Focus	Wholly Owned Subsidiary	International Joint Venture
Cultural sensitivity/national	High	High
Cultural sensitivity/org. level	Low	High
Interpersonal skills	Low	High
Negotiation/bargaining skills	Med	High
Entrepreneurial skills	High	High
Leadership skills	High	High
Knowledge/global environment	High	High
Knowledge/regional	High	High
Knowledge/firm-specific	Med	Low
Knowledge/functional area	High	Med

SOURCES: Adapted from E. Bailey and O. Shenkar. "Management education for international joint venture managers." *Leadership and Organization Development Journal*, 1993, 14: pp. 15–20.

2. Firms should preempt and actively manage human resource problems in their international affiliates before they adversely affect performance.

CHAPTER SUMMARY

1. Strategic international human resource management (SIHRM) determines the degree of similarity between the HRM practices of the parent company and those of its foreign affiliates. IHRM changes as the firm develops its international presence and capabilities.

2. Boards of directors are becoming more global, with a significant increase in the proportion of non-native members.

3. Although small in numbers, expatriate employees play a vital role in the operations of MNEs. Since expatriate failure rates are high, companies need to pay attention to the recruitment, selection, training, and compensation of their expatriate employees.

4. Approaches to expatriate compensation can be home based, host based, or a hybrid of both systems. Lump-sum/cafeteria and negotiation are additional approaches that offer more flexibility, but they are difficult to administer.

5. Companies pay close attention to their local workforce and need to adapt practices to local environments within their overall strategic focus.

6. Significant correlations exist between cultural dimensions and human resource practices.

7. HRM problems in foreign affiliates vary by the type of affiliate (e.g., a wholly foreign-owned subsidiary versus an international joint venture), among other factors.

Chapter Notes

1. The Conference Board. "How the CEOs drive global growth." Report #1184-97-RR, 1997.

2. "Citing Towers Perrin." *Wall Street Journal*, November 24, 1992.

3. N. J. Adler. "Cross-cultural management: Issues to be faced." *International Studies of Management and Organization*, 1983.

4. F. Acuff. *International and Domestic Human Resources Functions: Innovations in International Compensation.* New York: Organization Resources Counselors, 1984.

5. "Developing a Global Mindset at Johnson & Johnson—1998." IMD case #GM791, January 6, 1999.

6. S. Taylor, S. Beechler, and N. Napier. "Toward an integrative model of strategic international human

resource management." *Academy of Management Review,* 1996, *21,* 4: pp. 959–985.

7. R. Schuller, P. Dowling, and H. DeCieri. "An integrative framework of strategic international human resource management." *International Journal of Human Resource Management,* 1993, 1: pp. 717–764.

8. R. G. Vernon. "International investment and international trade in the product cycle." *Quarterly Journal of Economics,* 1996: pp. 190–207.

9. N. J. Adler and F. Ghadar. "Strategic human resource management: A global perspective." In R. Pieper (ed.), *Human Resource Management: An International Comparison.* Berlin: DeGruyter, 1990.

10. H. V. Perlmutter. "The tortuous evolution of the multinational corporation." *Columbia Journal of World Business,* 1969, 4: pp. 9–18.

11. R. L. Tung. "Selection and training procedures of U.S., European, and Japanese multinationals." *California Management Review,* 1982, 25: pp. 57–71.

12. "Won Choi Hae, Korea's Samsung seeks a bit more worldliness." *Wall Street Journal,* March 22, 2002.

13. J. A. Song. "South Korean technology companies fill skills vacuum." *Financial Times,* June 15, 2006, 22.

14. N. Boyacigiller. "The role of expatriates in the management of interdependence, complexity and risk in multinational corporations." *Journal of International Business Studies,* 1990, 3rd quarter: pp. 357–381.

15. The Conference Board. "How the CEOs drive global growth." Report #1184-97-RR, 1997.

16. R. Kopp. "International human resource policies and practices in Japanese, European, and United States multinationals." *Human Resource Management,* 1994, 33: pp. 581–599.

17. P. Beckett. "Citigroup's Menezes plays key game to lift growth via emerging markets." *Wall Street Journal,* February 21, 2001, C1.

18. N. Ramamoorthy and S. J. Carroll. "Individualism/collectivism orientations and reactions toward alternative human resource management practices." *Human Relations,* 1998, 51: pp. 571–588.

19. "Nike admits worker abuse." CNNfn.com, February 22, 2001.

20. "Traveling more lightly." *Economist,* June 24, 2006: p. 77.

21. D. R. Briscoe. *International Human Resource Management.* Englewood Cliffs, NJ: Prentice-Hall, 1995.

22. Cited in the *Wall Street Journal,* January 16, 2001, B12.

23. "Developing a global mindset at Johnson & Johnson—1998." IMD case #GM791, January 6, 1999.

24. J. Flynn. "E-mail, cellphones and frequent flier miles let 'virtual' expats work abroad but live at home." *Wall Street Journal,* October 25, 1999, A26; J. Millman. "Exporting management savvy." *Wall Street Journal,* October 24, 2000, B1; J. S. Lublin. "Global experience doesn't have to mean going to live overseas." *Wall Street Journal Online,* August 29, 2006.

25. The Conference Board. "How the CEOs drive global growth." Report #1184-97-RR, 1997.

26. M. S. Fenwick, H. L. D. DeCieri, and D. E. Welch. "Cultural and bureaucratic control in MNEs: The role of expatriate performance appraisal." *Management International Review,* 1999, 39: pp. 107–124.

27. The Conference Board. "How the CEOs drive global growth." Report #1184-97-RR, 1997.

28. L. Copeland and L. Griggs. *Going International.* New York: Plume, 1985; D. R. Briscoe. *International Human Resource Management.* Englewood Cliffs, NJ: Prentice-Hall, 1995.

29. R. L. Tung. "Selecting and training of personnel for overseas assignments." *Columbia Journal of World Business,* 1981, 16: pp. 68–78; R. L. Tung. "Expatriate assignments: Enhancing success and minimizing failure." *Academy of Management Executive,* 1987, 1: pp. 117–126.

30. Windham International 1995 survey. Cited in the *China Business Review,* May–June 1997: p. 30.

31. M. E. Mendenhall, E. Dunbar, and G. R. Oddou. "Expatriate selection, training and career pathing: A review and critique." *Human Resource Management,* 1987, 26: pp. 331–345.

32. R. L. Tung. "Expatriate assignments: Enhancing success and minimizing failure." *Academy of Management Executive,* 1987, 1: pp. 117–126.

33. M. E. Mendenhall and G. R. Oddou. "The overseas assignment: A practical look." *Business Horizons,* 1988, *31,* 5: pp. 78–84.

34. J. M. Brett and L. K. Stroh. "Willingness to relocate internationally." *Human Resource Management,* 1995, 34: pp. 405–424.

35. N. Adler and D. N. Izraeli. "Women managers: Moving up and across borders." In O. Shenkar (ed.), *Global Perspectives of Human Resource Management,* pp. 165–193. Englewood Cliffs, NJ: Prentice Hall, 1994.

36. K. E. Baumgarten. "A profile for international managers and its implications for selection and training." Thesis, faculty of applied educational science, University of Twente, Enschede, The Netherlands, 1992.

37. N. J. Adler and S. Bartholomew. "Managing globally competent people." *Academy of Management Executive,* 1992, 6: pp. 52–65.

38. M. E. Mendenhall and G. R. Oddou. "The overseas assignment: A practical look." *Business Horizons,* 1988, *31,* 5: pp. 78–84.

39. G. M. Spreitzer, M. W. McCall Jr., and J. D. Mahoney. "Early identification of international executive potential." *Journal of Applied Psychology,* 1997, 82: pp. 6–29.

40. M. S. Schell and C. M. Solomon. *Capitalizing on the Global Workforce: A Strategic Guide to Expatriate Management.* Chicago: Irwin Professional Publications, 1997.

41. D. Woodruff. "Distractions make global manager a difficult role." *Wall Street Journal,* November 21, 2000, B1.

42. J. S. Black, M. Mendenhall, and G. Oddou. "Toward a comprehensive model of international adjustment: An integration of multiple theoretical perspectives." *Academy of Management Review,* 1991, 16: pp. 291–317.

43. M. E. Mendenhall and G. R. Oddou. "The overseas assignment: A practical look." *Business Horizons,* 1988, *31,* 5: pp. 78–84.

44. S. Ayree, Y. W. Char, and J. Chew. "An investigation of the willingness of managerial employees to accept an expatriate assignment." *Journal of Organizational Behavior,* 1996, 17: pp. 267–283.

45. J. S. Black and M. Mendenhall. "The U-curve adjustment hypothesis revisited: A review and theoretical framework." *Journal of International Business Studies,* 1991, 22: pp. 225–247.

46. R. L. Tung. "Expatriate assignments: Enhancing success and minimizing failure." *Academy of Management Executive,* 1987, 1: pp. 117–126.

47. M. E. Mendenhall, E. Dunbar, and G. R. Oddou. "Expatriate selection, training and career pathing: A review and critique." *Human Resource Management,* 1987, 26: pp. 331–345.

48. D. J. Kealey and D. R. Protheroe. "The cross-cultural training for expatriates: An assessment of the literature on the issue." *International Journal of Intercultural Relations,* 1996, 20: pp. 141–165.

49. D. J. Kealey and D. R. Protheroe. "The cross-cultural training for expatriates: An assessment of the literature on the issue." *International Journal of Intercultural Relations,* 1996, 20: pp. 141–165.

50. D. J. Kealey and D. R. Protheroe. "The cross-cultural training for expatriates: An assessment of the literature on the issue." *International Journal of Intercultural Relations,* 1996, 20: pp. 141–165.

51. T. Yoshida and R. W. Brislin. "Intercultural skills and recommended behaviors: The psychological perspective for training program." In O. Shenkar (ed.), *Global Perspectives of Human Resource Management,* pp. 112–113. Englewood Cliffs, NJ: Prentice-Hall, 1995.

52. J. K. Harrison. "Developing successful expatriate managers: A framework for the structural design and strategic alignment of cross-cultural training programs." *Human Resource Planning,* 1992, 17: pp. 17–35.

53. R. L. Tung. "Expatriate assignments: Enhancing success and minimizing failure." *Academy of Management Executive,* 1987, 1: pp. 117–126.

54. M. E. Mendenhall, E. Dunbar, and G. R. Oddou. "Expatriate selection, training and career pathing: A review and critique." *Human Resource Management,* 1987, 26: pp. 331–345.

55. D. R. Briscoe. *International Human Resource Management.* Englewood Cliffs, NJ: Prentice-Hall, 1995.

56. H. B. Gregersen and L. K. Stroh. "Coming home to the Arctic cold: Antecedents to Finnish expatriate and spouse repatriation adjustment." *Personnel Psychology,* 50: pp. 635–654; R. A. Guzzo, K. A. Noonan, and E. Elron. "Expatriate managers and the psychological contract." *Journal of Applied Psychology,* 1994, 74: pp. 617–626.

57. H. B. Gregersen, J. S. Black, and J. M. Hite. "Expatriate performance appraisal: Principles, practices, and challenges." In J. Selmer (ed.), *Expatriate Management:*

New Ideas for International Business. Westport, CT: Quorum Books, 1995.

58. H. B. Gregersen and J. M. Hite. "Expatriate performance appraisal in U.S. multinational firms." *Journal of International Business Studies,* 1996, 4th quarter: pp. 711–738.

59. The Conference Board. Report #1148-96-RR, 1996.

60. *Benefits Canada,* 1966, *20,* 11: p. 11.

61. Milkovich and Newman. *Compensation.* Chicago: Irwin/McGraw-Hill, 1999.

62. Milkovich and Newman. *Compensation.* Chicago: Irwin/McGraw-Hill, 1999.

63. J. B. Anderson. "Compensating your overseas executives, Part 2: Europe in 1992." *Compensation and Benefits Review,* 1995.

64. M. S. Schell and C. M. Solomon. *Capitalizing on the Global Workforce: A Strategic Guide to Expatriate Management.* Chicago: Irwin, 1997.

65. S. Schneider. "National vs. corporate culture: Implications for human resource management." *Human Resource Management,* 27: pp. 231–246.

66. R. S. Schuller and N. Rogovsky. "Understanding compensation practice variations across firms: The impact of national culture." *Journal of International Business Studies,* 1998, 29, 1: pp. 159–177.

67. N. Ramamoorthy and S. J. Carroll. "Individualism/collectivism orientations and reactions toward alternative human resource management practices." *Human Relations,* 1998, 51: pp. 571–588.

68. C. C. Chen. "New trends in reward allocation preferences: A Sino-U.S. comparison." *Academy of Management Journal,* 1995, 38: pp. 408–424.

69. P. S. Hempel. "Designing multinational benefits programs: The role of national culture." *Journal of World Business,* 1998, 33: pp. 277–294.

70. N. J. Adler. "Re-entry: Managing cross-cultural transitions." *Group & Organization Management,* 1981, 6: pp. 341–356.

71. J. S. Black, H. B. Gregersen, and M. E. Mendenhall. "Toward a theoretical framework of repatriation adjustment." *Journal of International Business Studies,* 1992, 23: pp. 737–760.

72. Based on O. Shenkar and Y. Zeira. "Human resource management in international joint ventures: Directions for research." *Academy of Management Review,* 1987, 12: pp. 546–557.

Emerging Issues in International Business

Photo Part 6   Distribution can be an obstacle to e-commerce in many markets.

SOURCE: Jupiterimages.

THE INTERNET AND GLOBAL E-COMMERCE

EIGHTEEN

DO YOU KNOW?

1. When shopping online, do you know, or mind, in what country the seller is located?

2. Would having a Web site make your firm international? Why or why not?

3. Would global e-commerce remove barriers to trade, both tariff and nontariff?

4. What are the prospects for global e-commerce in the years ahead? What are the opportunities and threats posed by e-commerce to the MNE and the SMIE?

OPENING CASE

eBay in China

The "e-commerce darling" of analysts and the world's leading electronic auctioneer, eBay has struggled in the lucrative and rapidly growing Chinese market. Having earlier failed in the promising Japanese market, which the company exited in 2002, eBay turned its attention to South

Korea and China, especially the latter, which by 2006 had the second largest number of Internet users after the United States. Initially the market leader in China and South Korea, by 2006 eBay had slipped to second place in both countries. In China, the U.S.-based company has fallen behind Alibaba's Tao Bao unit, despite repeatedly cutting listing fees and offering listing waivers. In early 2006, after criticizing Alibaba by saying that "free is not a business model," eBay was forced to stop charging listing fees on its auction site altogether. Analysts note that the eBay China site has also been slow to adopt new applications and was considered less friendly by users, although the company vigorously denies those claims.

In late 2006, eBay reached a cooperation agreement with Baidu, a leading Chinese Internet provider. The partnership targets the model of multiple services utilized by market leader Alibaba. Through its partnership with Baidu, eBay is hoping to regain a leadership position in the China market. The company is also hoping that a turnaround in China will signal a departure from its rather mediocre financial results overseas, which have been a considerable drag on its stock price.

SOURCES: Adapted from M. Nangalindan. "China may be eBay's latest challenge as local rivals eat into market share." *Wall Street Journal*, October 12, 2006, C1; S. Lemon. "Baidu, eBay, expand partnership in China." *Infoworld*, November 9, 2006.

INTERNET AND E-COMMERCE INFRASTRUCTURE

Internet Diffusion

Exhibit 18.1 presents the percentage of Internet users in the different regions of the world. It shows the high growth rates of the number of users around the world. The exhibit shows significant differences between world regions, with the developed world—North America and Europe—leading, while Asia, the Middle East, and, in particular, Africa are trailing. This picture masks, however, substantial differences within regions; for instance, in the Asian continent, South Korea has a very high usage rate, whereas Vietnam has a very low rate. The number of users is obviously not only a function of the penetration rate but also of population size and is also changing fast. For instance, as noted in the opening case, China is already the second largest Internet market and is forecast to become number one within the next few years.

Exhibit 18.1a   Internet Penetration by World Region, 2007

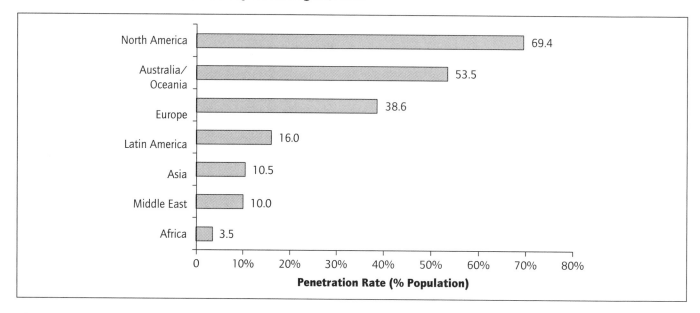

SOURCE: www.internetworldstats.com (updated on January 11, 2007).

Exhibit 18.1b   Internet Users Around the World, 2007

World Regions	Population (2007 Est.)	% of World Population	Internet Usage, Latest Data	% Population (Penetration)	% of World Usage	Usage Growth 2000–2007
Africa	933,448,292	14.2%	32,765,700	3.5%	3.0%	625.8%
Asia	3,712,527,624	56.5%	389,392,288	10.5%	35.6%	240.7%
Europe	809,624,686	12.3%	312,722,892	38.6%	28.6%	197.6%
Middle East	193,452,727	2.9%	19,382,400	10.0%	1.8%	490.1%
North America	334,538,018	5.1%	232,057,067	69.4%	21.2%	114.7%
Latin America/Caribbean	556,606,627	8.5%	88,778,986	16.0%	8.1%	391.3%
Oceania/Australia	34,468,443	0.5%	18,430,359	53.5%	1.7%	141.9%
WORLD TOTAL	6,574,666,417	100.0%	1,093,529,692	16.6%	100.0%	202.9%

SOURCE: www.internetworldstats.com (updated on January 11, 2007).

Exhibit 18.2   Top Country-Level Domains, 2007

United States	50,022,310
Germany	4,356,683
United Kingdom	3,040,414
Canada	2,633,432
China	2,294,734
France	1,828,439
Australia	1,427,770
Japan	933,274
Spain	917,148
Korea	855,267
Hong Kong	787,912
Italy	748,619

SOURCE: webhosting.info, 2007.

Another indicator of the level of Internet penetration is the abundance of country-level domain names. Exhibit 18.2 presents country rankings by the total number of domains registered in that country (including the suffixes *com, net, info, org,* and *biz*).

COUNTRY BOX

THE UNITED STATES LAGS BEHIND IN HIGH-SPEED INTERNET ACCESS

High-speed Internet access is not only about downloading music and movies but rather is a major determinant of productivity growth and a facilitator of e-commerce, among other contributions. Surprisingly to many, the United States, where the Internet was envisioned and launched, lags behind many other nations in high-speed Internet access. An OECD (Organisation for Economic Co-operation and Development) survey of that organization's 30 member states ranked the United States in 12th place among industrialized nations, with 16.8 broadband subscribers per 100 inhabitants. By comparison, Iceland had 26.7 subscribers per 100 residents, followed by South Korea, the Netherlands, Denmark, Switzerland, Finland, Norway, Canada, and Sweden, all with rates exceeding 20 subscribers per 100 inhabitants. In 2001, the United States ranked fourth in a similar survey. Further, the United States is behind many industrialized nations in introducing next-generation Internet access, which runs through fiber-optic cable rather than telephone lines or conventional cable.

The U.S. government complains that the OECD survey is unfair because it does not take into account the large size of the country and its dispersed population, noting that the United States still has more broadband subscribers than any other country in the world; however, countries such as Norway and Iceland have even lower population density. In many of the high-ranking countries, the government has taken an active role in building next-generation Internet access, something the U.S. government has been reluctant to do.

SOURCES: Adapted from Abboud, Leila. "U.S. lags behind in high-speed Internet access." *Wall Street Journal,* April 12, 2006, B2; OECD. *Working Party on the Indicators for the Information Society, ICT Access and Use by Households and Individuals.* 2006.

E-READINESS

E-readiness refers to the degree to which a country has developed the infrastructure necessary to facilitate electronic transactions, which are at the heart of e-commerce. This refers not only to technical infrastructure but also to such factors as government regulations and the availability of skilled personnel. The Economist Intelligence Unit (EIU) calculates e-readiness in terms of five criteria: connectivity and technology infrastructure (e.g., broadband penetration), business environment (e.g., regulation), consumer and business adoption (e.g., quality of logistics), social and cultural environment (e.g., innovation), and supporting e-services (e.g., back-office support).

Exhibit 18.3 displays the top 10 and bottom 10 nations in terms of their e-readiness in the EIU survey. Note that three of the top 10 nations are in Scandinavia and four are Anglo-Saxon (not counting Hong Kong, a former British colony). The bottom group, as expected, is populated by developing nations in Asia and Africa, with a single European representative, Ukraine. In that case, as well as in the case of Iran, one suspects that low readiness is correlated not only with development level but also with a regime that for years was bent on tight control of its population via control of information. The same may be true for Kazakhstan and Azerbaijan, which, like Ukraine, were part of the former Soviet Union.

Exhibit 18.3   E-Business Readiness Rankings

Top Ten		Bottom Ten	
1	Denmark	59	Sri Lanka
2	United States	60	Nigeria
3	Switzerland	61	Ukraine
4	Sweden	62	Indonesia
5	UK	63	Algeria
6	Netherlands	64	Kazakhstan
7	Finland	65	Iran
8	Australia	66	Vietnam
9	Canada	67	Pakistan
10	Hong Kong	68	Azerbaijan

SOURCE: Economics Intelligence Unit, 2006.

One aspect of e-readiness is a "wired" government. A government that is prepared to handle electronic communications helps to create more users who are tuned in to Internet-provided information and who are comfortable with electronic transactions. An e-ready government also facilitates the working of firms, especially SMIEs (small to medium-sized international enterprises), who engage in e-commerce and need to interact with the government for purposes of regulation and taxation or to bid for government business. Exhibit 18.4 shows the top 25 countries in terms of their government e-readiness, an index consisting of site development, telecommunications infrastructure, and human capital. As in the prior year surveys, the top 25 group is dominated by highly developed economies, led by the United States and Western European nations. Only two Asian nations—Japan and South Korea—are in the top 25 group.

Exhibit 18.4   E-Government Readiness Index Rankings, 2005 (Top 25 Nations)

	Country	Index
1	United States	0.9062
2	Denmark	0.9058
3	Sweden	0.8983
4	United Kingdom	0.8777
5	Republic of Korea	0.8727
6	Australia	0.8679
7	Singapore	0.8503
8	Canada	0.8425
9	Finland	0.8231
10	Norway	0.8228
11	Germany	0.8050
12	Netherlands	0.8021
13	New Zealand	0.7987
14	Japan	0.7801
15	Iceland	0.7794
16	Austria	0.7602
17	Switzerland	0.7548
18	Belgium	0.7381
19	Estonia	0.7347
20	Ireland	0.7251
21	Malta	0.7012
22	Chile	0.6963
23	France	0.6925
24	Israel	0.6903
25	Italy	0.6794

SOURCE: Department of Economic and Social Affairs. *United Nations Global E-Government Readiness Report, 2005.* © 2005 United Nations. Reprinted with the permission of the United Nations.

Interim Summary

1. Internet usage level, which is dramatically lower in poorer countries, is a crucial (though not the only) component of e-commerce readiness.

2. Government's e-readiness, one indicator of infrastructure for e-commerce activity, is much higher in developed nations.

CROSS-BORDER E-COMMERCE

Electronic commerce (e-commerce) is the conduct of transactions to buy, sell, distribute, or deliver goods and services over the Internet. E-commerce transactions are business-to-business (B2B), business-to-customer (B2C), or customer-to-customer (C2C). B2B, which currently drives much of the growth in global e-commerce, involves interfirm transactions, including government procurement. B2C transactions are between firms and individuals purchasing goods or services over the Internet. Ordering a book online from a vendor is an example of a B2C transaction. C2C transactions involve individual transactions—for example, sales via online auction. All three types now occur globally as well as domestically. Global e-commerce is the conduct of electronic commerce, whether B2B, B2C, or C2C, across national boundaries (e.g., a U.S. customer purchasing pharmaceuticals from a Canadian site), although, as we will see later in this chapter, the definition of borders is not always clear-cut in that environment (think, for instance, about the location of a server versus the location of a distribution center from which goods are sent to the final customer). Compared with the other types, B2B represents a considerably bigger share of the e-commerce pie.

While e-commerce activities still constitute a small portion of overall commercial activities, they are growing fast. For instance, in early 2004, B2C e-commerce sales represented 1.9% of overall retail sales; this percentage was twice as large as in 2001, according to the U.S. Census Bureau.

The Impact of E-Commerce on International Business

Initially, the emergence of the Internet and e-commerce created expectations for exploding global electronic trade. The assumption was that "a firm marketing its products or services through the Internet is, by definition, a global firm because consumers worldwide can access it."[1] Others acknowledged that "the Internet won't magically ensure overseas success, but it can ease some of the pain of going global."[2] Today, we have developed a more balanced view, where the Internet and e-commerce are making important inroads into global trade but the progression is incremental and does not necessarily imply the demise of "brick-and-mortar" retailers.

Exhibit 18.5 shows the potential impact of "information and communication technology" (ICT), a somewhat broader class of phenomena than the Internet and e-commerce, on MNE competitiveness, according to de la Torre and Moxon. Among the possible changes are a fundamental change in the cost of market transactions versus internalization and a change in location parameters.

Photo 18.1   **In some countries, the Internet café is the main point of access for users.**

SOURCE: Jupiterimages.

Prospects for Large MNEs

For the larger MNE, the Internet and e-commerce create an opportunity for rapid global dissemination of products, but they also enable quicker imitation on the part of competitors. In theory, the Internet creates pressure toward price parity, posing a problem for the MNE with different distributors charging different prices in different markets. There is evidence, however, that e-commerce may actually encourage collusion. Sony and Philips were faced with legal problems in Germany when they tried to stop online sales of Primus Online, offering less expensive Sony and Philips products.[3]

Exhibit 18.6 shows how the motivation to locate activities internationally might change under Internet and e-commerce. Note that the traditional motivations have been discussed in Chapters 2 through 4. Among the potentially

Exhibit 18.5   Potential Impact of Information and Communications Technology (ICT) on MNE Competitiveness

Topic/ Construct	Elements Sensitive to ICT-Driven Transformation	Potential Direction of Change
Internalization advantages		
■ market failure resulting in transacting costs that exceed coordination costs	■ search costs diminished ■ alternative sources of resources enlarged ■ increased value of intangible assets ■ lower coordination costs within network	Indeterminate, since forces acting in different direction; drop in coordination costs may result in greater internalization and concentration simultaneous with more outsourcing
■ risk and uncertainty favors internalization ■ externalities, scope economies, etc.	■ market information easier to access and of higher quality ■ increased availability of alternative channels ■ greater resource availability and sources	Favors increases in outsourcing and market-based transactions Favors disintegration and market-based transactions
Locational advantages		
■ differences in factor endowment and costs ■ transport costs and distance (physical and cultural)	■ information content of tasks more transferable ■ logistics, coordination and communications facilitated by ICTs	Favors greater dispersion of economic activities Fewer changes with respect to physical products; larger changes for intangibles
■ artificial barriers and market impediments	■ border controls increasingly difficult for digital products	Little change for physical products; large impact on digital products and content
■ infrastructure and incentives	■ critical role of infrastructure and protection of intellectual property	The digital divide will favor locations with good infrastructure and IP protection
Ownership advantages		
■ structural or asset-based, e.g., technology, trademarks, and other monopolistic advantages	■ digital piracy and greater availability of technical information shortens life cycles ■ increased permeability of borders to information ■ greater returns to scale	These effects would seem to enhance the relative power of MNEs and lead to greater concentration and integration in global industries
■ knowledge and organizational capabilities ■ political connections	■ virtual and internal communication networks expand capabilities ■ increased transparency and availability of political information	Increases the value of intangible assets and internal capabilities Should lead to a reduced advantage from "insider" positions or knowledge
The liability of foreignness		
■ foreign firm faces higher operating costs due to lack of knowledge	■ increased availability of public and private information reduces liability of foreignness	Market integration and lower foreignness costs will lead to higher competitive advantage for MNEs

SOURCE: J. de la Torre and R .W. Moxon. "Introduction to the symposium e-commerce & global business: The impact of the information and communication technology revolution on the conduct of international business." *Journal of International Business Studies*, 2001, *32*, 4: pp. 617–639.

important impacts noted by Zaheer and Manrakhan are a reduction in transaction costs and improvement of monitoring and coordination by the MNE and the ability to export human skills without incurring immigration and brain drain. Note also the differential impact on resource-, market-, efficiency-, and capability-seekers, discussed earlier in this book. All in all, we are looking at the possibility of "virtual FDI," which could challenge basic assumptions about location decisions, among others.

Prospects for SMIEs

The reduction in barriers should, in theory, open doors to SMIEs, especially from developing countries that have been shut out of international trade and investment. It should lower transaction costs for such firms and improve their international competitiveness.[4] Many SMIEs have taken advantage of the new opportunities. Small Latin American start-ups became SMIEs almost overnight, opening local offices in Spain, Portugal, Mexico, Hispanic areas in the United States, and Latin America.[5] Latinexus is a Latin American electronic marketplace that aims to provide an even playing field for SMIEs by providing the same cost benefits and broad audiences available to blue-chip firms.[6] Other SMIEs piggybacked on intermediaries such as Amazon or L.L. Bean to reach international customers.

For physical goods, however, barriers in the form of logistic challenges in dealing with multiple, dispersed customers remain significant for the smaller firm. There are indications that size and volume may matter even more in an e-commerce operation. The handling of a large and diverse number of customers may lie beyond the ability of many SMIEs that lack strategic and managerial capabilities. Shanghai Online Information Mailing (SOIM) is a Chinese start-up that serves local Chinese Internet users. With its 400,000 subscribers, it provides its clients e-mails of e-zines, allowing them to read articles off the Internet inexpensively. Phil Ren, founder of SOIM, acknowledges he does not know how to manage his workforce or strategize for the growing Chinese market.[7] OECD data show that in most countries, Internet penetration is substantially lower in smaller businesses, putting them at a disadvantage in B2B applications as well.[8] A 2004 UNCTAD report ("E-commerce and development report," New York and Geneva, 2001) notes that the SMIE's low brand visibility is a considerable negative in e-commerce, where customers rely on brand names as a substitute for a retailer they do not know or see.

Prospects for Intermediaries

Although it was initially believed that the Internet would make intermediaries superfluous, the impact diverged. The number of intermediaries has indeed been reduced for digitalized products (e.g., software, music, movies, and certain educational and training programs) as well as for services such as brokerage, retail, and auctions; however, intermediaries have remained entrenched in other areas. Further, a new breed of value-adding intermediaries has emerged, no longer principally involved in the physical distribution of goods, but in the collection, collation, interpretation, and dissemination of vast amounts of information.[9] One such intermediary is planetarysales.com, a division of SinoMetrics International, Inc. The company offers to deliver—from Web content to product delivery—in the target country language.

Other Impacts

E-commerce's impact extends to other realms. For example, it has made it more difficult to determine the origin of a product or service, with concomitant implications for customs, tariffs, and taxation. This is because the server, the manufacturer,

Exhibit 18.6   Motivations to Locate Activities Internationally: Impact of Remote Electronic Access

	Traditional motivations for physical location in specific countries or markets	*Fundamental assumptions on why physical co-location is necessary*	*How do assumptions change with remote electronic access?*
Resource Seekers	To acquire specific resources at lower real costs. Resources could include: ■ Physical resources ■ Labor ■ Technological capability, management skills, knowledge, and intellectual capital	■ Immobility of resources ■ Cheaper to engage in FDI than import ■ Extractive type industries; preemptive lock-in ■ Capability cannot be acquired in market ■ Knowledge spillover and agglomeration effects are localized	■ Resources delivering digitized content can be remotely accessed (e.g., animation or graphic design labor) ■ Requires new forms of employment contracts and control mechanisms for remote telecommuters
Market Seekers	Locate production and/or marketing to supply country or region, to: ■ Achieve sales growth, scale economies ■ Service global customers ■ Facilitate local adaptation, learning ■ Minimize production and transaction costs (2) Have a physical presence in leading markets served by competitors, for strategic blocking and knowledge spillovers	■ For locating downstream activities: Building customer relationships and servicing global customers requires physical co-location with them ■ For locating upstream activities: Access to markets, restricted (e.g., tariff barriers), transportation costs, low scale economies ■ Strategic benefits and knowledge spillovers only derived from co-location	■ Customer relationships for simple products may be better built through digital channels (e.g., Amazon versus brick-and-mortar bookstore), as may digitizable service elements, such as help desks ■ How local are knowledge spillovers? Tacit knowledge spillovers likely to remain localized, codified knowledge less so. Rate of knowledge spillovers likely to be higher in local than in global arena
Efficiency Seekers	■ Rationalize structures to take advantage of differences across countries in cost of traditional or created factor endowments ■ Tends to take place in countries of broadly similar economic levels	■ Differential locational advantages (e.g., tax, performance incentives, labor market, living conditions) ■ Low coordination costs ■ Optimizing location portfolio ■ Cross-border markets are well developed and open ■ Knowledge spillover effects	■ Physical and regulatory locational advantages cannot be remotely accessed ■ Coordination costs lower ■ More opportunities to optimize location portfolio (e.g., global relay strategies) ■ Extent of regulation of Internet commerce? ■ Again, how local are knowledge spillovers?
Strategic Asset or Capability Seekers	■ Aim to capitalize on the benefits of common ownership of diversified activities/capabilities	■ Arise from market imperfections in asset markets in which the MNE operates	■ Information as a strategic asset ■ Will asset/capability markets become less susceptible to market failure?

SOURCE: S. Zaheer and S. Manrakhan. "Concentration and dispersion in global industries: Remote electronic access and the location of economic activities." *Journal of International Business Studies*, 2001, *32*, 4: pp. 667–686.

and the physical distributor may be located in different countries (see also the section Taxation Issues). E-commerce should also accelerate the mobility of people as a production factor. Jobs in back-office and customer service are likely to shift to lower-cost countries, especially where language is no obstacle (e.g., from the United States to Canada, Ireland, and India). For instance, Washington-based Talisma Corporation outsources customer service functions to Bangalore, India, where an abundance of highly educated workers can be found at a fraction of the U.S. cost.[10]

Interim Summary

1. Cross-border e-commerce can alter the location decisions of MNEs.

2. Cross-border e-commerce has the capability to reduce but not eliminate friction in international business transactions.

3. Although e-commerce opens new opportunities for SMIEs, many lack the resources to capitalize on its promise.

GLOBAL E-COMMERCE CHALLENGES

Entering into global e-commerce is not easy. Dominant portals such as AOL found that penetrating Germany, the United Kingdom, and other European markets is difficult. In a departure from past patterns of MNE entry, AOL found that domestic competition on the part of European newcomers flared up almost immediately. As in other realms of international business, finding the right balance between globalization and localization has proved difficult. The next section illustrates how.

Standardization Forces

Many consumers from other nations reach into U.S. sites. This is true for Canadians, who do much of their online shopping on U.S. Web sites (although many resent buying from a U.S. firm and seem to shift purchases to Canadian e-sellers where possible).[11] (Canadian sites, on their part, have been quite successful in selling pharmaceuticals to U.S. citizens.) Latin Americans prefer to use U.S. e-commerce sites over those developed in their own countries because of trust, convenience, and lower prices.[12] Yahoo found out that its U.S. site posted more traffic from China than its Chinese site.[13]

Standardization at times appears appealing. The position of English as a lingua franca has been considerably strengthened on the Internet, supported by the prevalence of English as a second language and by the dominance of U.S.-hosted Web sites. However, as Exhibit 18.7 shows, English may be the leading Internet language, but 70% of Web pages are *not* in English.

Localization Challenges

As with other international business activities, the risks of neglecting customization are substantial. Many U.S. firms underestimated the customization they would need to undertake in e-trading with foreign markets, whether tangible (tax, currencies, tariffs) or intangible (culture, buying habits).

Web Site Localization

Despite the promise of "instant globalization," MNEs engaged in e-commerce soon discover that the "liability of foreignness" persists. AOL has struggled behind local providers in the Latin American market and has failed to become the primary provider in the many Latin American markets it serves,[14] and eBay

Exhibit 18.7   Language Used on Internet Web Pages, 2007 (Percentage of Users)

English	29.9%
Chinese	14.0%
Spanish	8.0%
Japanese	7.9%
German	5.4%
French	5.0%
Portuguese	3.1%
Korean	3.1%
Italian	2.8%
Arabic	2.6%
Other languages	18.2%

SOURCE: InternetWorldStats.com, 2007.

had to withdraw from the potentially lucrative Japanese market, admitting such missteps as emphasizing collectibles rather than new goods on the belief that the Japanese market would mirror the development of the U.S. site.[15] And, as the opening case showed, eBay lost ground in the South Korean and Chinese markets despite initial success.

Let's start with demographics. Exhibit 18.8 shows the varying levels of Internet access across gender in different countries. Figures vary from about 50% in the United States and Canada (but also the developing nations of the Philippines and Thailand) to 6% in Jordan, where religious mores limit women's access to the Internet as well as their ability to make decisions on major purchases. This means that women are also less likely to be customers for e-goods.

In addition to demographic disparities, cultural "faux pas" are as common in e-commerce as in traditional trade. Auction house eBay posted prices in dollars on its British site. Language blunders are also common. "Getgift.com" may make sense in the United States, but its Swedish translation is "go get poison for goats." When U.S. sites use American spelling for words such as *favorite, behavior, theater, liter,* and so on, some British consumers perceive these as misspellings.

Other variations also apply. For instance, European laws give Internet users more protection than do U.S. laws.[16] The European laws are based on "safe harbor" principles requiring that a company seek explicit agreement before transferring personal data to another company. Also under European law, the data subject must receive reasonable access to personal data to review and possibly correct it. Data collection is permitted when (a) the subject has unambiguously given consent; (b) the data are needed to complete a contract, such as billing; (c) the data are required by law or needed to protect the subject's vital interests; or (d) the data are needed for law-enforcement purposes. Under a tentative agreement negotiated by the U.S. Department of Commerce, U.S. firms can (a) subject themselves to the data-protection authority in one of the EU nations; (b) show that they are subject to similar U.S. privacy laws, such as those covering credit applications or videocassette/DVD rentals; (c) sign up with a self-regulatory organization, such as BBBOnline (Better Business Bureau), which provides an adequate level of privacy protection and is subject to oversight by the U.S. Federal Trade Commission; or (d) agree to refer privacy disputes to a panel of European regulators.

Exhibit 18.8   Women as Percentage of Internet Users, Selected Countries

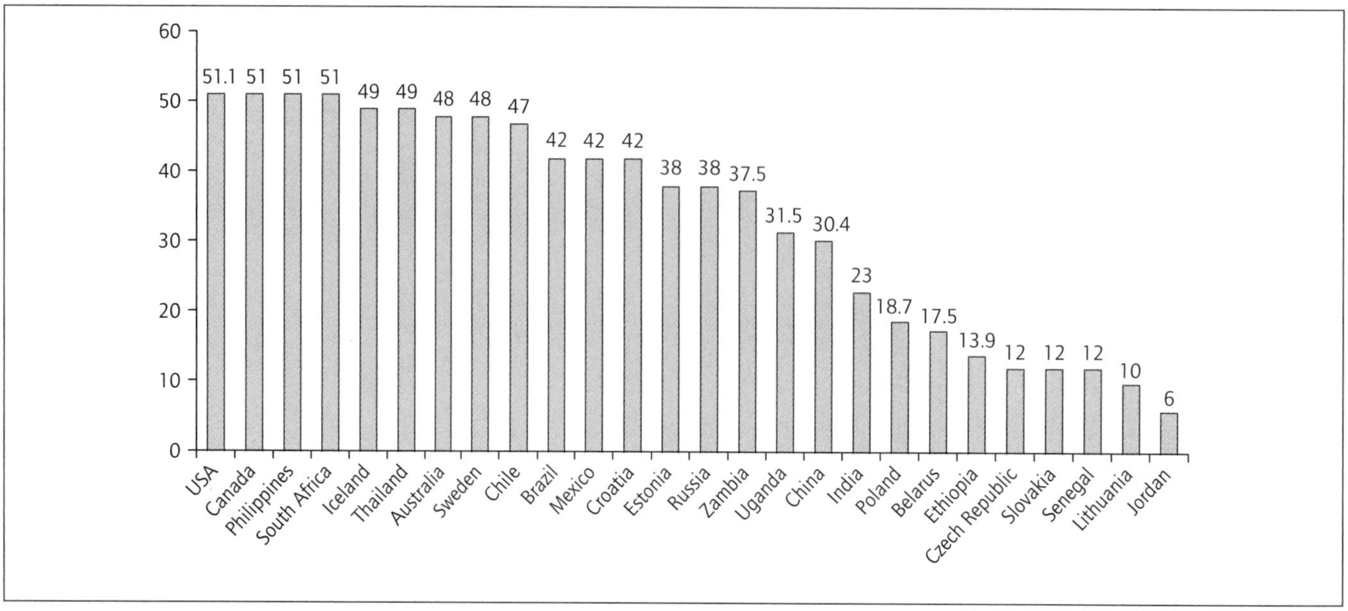

SOURCE: Department of Economic and Social Affairs. *United Nations Global E-Government Readiness Report 2005*. © 2005 United Nations. Reprinted with the permission of the United Nations.

A key response to localization pressures has been to establish local Web sites. It is here that Internet and e-commerce companies make a difference for MNEs—they need not establish physical premises to have local presence. Yahoo! has 21 international online properties in 12 languages, including localized English versions in Asia, Australia and New Zealand, Brazil, Canada, China, Denmark, France, Germany, Hong Kong, Italy, Japan, Korea, Mexico, Norway, Singapore, Spain, Sweden, Japan, the United Kingdom, and Ireland. It also has guides in Spanish and Chinese. As far back as 1997, Sony had 13 country-specific sites. UPS offers its services around the globe in multiple languages. Reebok has done the same after tracking its Web traffic.[17] A study found that firms with localized Web sites abroad were distinctly different from those without them. Among other differences, those with localized Web sites had higher revenues, higher media visibility, wider global reach, and more alliances.[18]

Some vendors have taken pains to localize their Web sites. Ikea, the Swedish furniture maker, designs its sites with an eye to national tastes. Its Italian site is stylish, the German site is more traditional, and the Saudi Arabian site shows a reassuring family shopping scene. For its Danish site, the firm substituted red and white for its customary blue and yellow (the Swedish flag colors).[19] McDonald's adds pink and brown to its trademark red and gold on its Japanese Web sites. E-tailers such as Amazon established European operations with local partners who have helped them with the necessary customization. Yahoo! did the same in Japan.[20] Others have turned to specialists for help in tailoring their sites and sales practices to foreign nations. E-commerce globalization and customization has become a multibillion-dollar-a-year consulting industry. A number of start-ups promise to help firms, especially small or medium-sized companies (SMEs), in customizing their Internet ware. Thinkamerican.com helps small U.S. apparel brands sell in Japan. In addition to language translation, the company translates sites into Japanese while watching for cultural errors. It also aims to cut costs by consolidating the shipments of multiple small vendors.[21] Yet, according to Forrester Research, many Fortune 100 firms have failed to tailor their sites to different world markets.[22]

Logistics

Logistics represents a key area where many companies have failed to make the necessary adjustments in terms of global e-commerce in general or in terms of customizing the system to deal with the requirements in a given country. A Forrester study suggested the following:

> Eighty five percent of the companies noted that they could not fill overseas orders because of the complexity of shipping across borders. Of those that had problems shipping overseas, 75 percent cited their system's inability to register international addresses accurately (one European customer had his on-line order rejected because he could not fill the "state" section on the U.S. order form)[23] or to price total delivery cost.[24]

Taxation Issues

In the international arena, the implications of e-commerce taxation are potentially ominous. While cross-border catalog sales have existed for many years, they were never substantial enough to generate a strong interest among governments. E-commerce has changed that.[25] In the EU, value-added taxes (VAT) ranging from 15% to 25%—representing a key portion of government revenues—are at risk. In itself, a Web site is not considered a fixed place of business that would trigger taxation, but it could be considered as such in conjunction with server location and other company operations in that country. However, Web and server locations as well as other components of e-commerce operations are increasingly difficult to pinpoint. Furthermore, e-commerce makes it increasingly easy for MNEs to shift their domicile to low-tax locations and to offshore tax havens, as it becomes difficult if not impossible for other nations to claim physical presence of the company in their territory. Problems such as transfer pricing become much more acute in this environment.

The Internet raises many other taxation issues. For instance, the traditional distinction between income and royalty taxation may be impossible to determine when a consumer downloads software from a vendor.[26] Individual income tax may be largely avoided in countries with a territorial tax base, whereas the few countries with a global taxation base, such as the United States, may find it increasingly difficult to enforce their tax legislation.

To the MNE as well as the SMIE, e-commerce taxation represents a significant challenge. In Chapter 15, we discussed the tax strategies employed by MNEs, including tax havens, tax treaties, and the creation of a holding or a finance corporation. Global e-commerce creates additional strategic opportunities, such as placing servers in low-tax jurisdictions. However, it also creates additional risks: For instance, most tax treaties do not refer to e-commerce activities, and they may be open to challenge.

INDUSTRY BOX

E-TRADE GOES GLOBAL

In February 2007, E-Trade Financial announced the launch of a pilot platform allowing U.S. investors to buy, sell, and trade foreign stocks and currencies online. The service, which will commence in the second quarter of 2007 and take two months to complete, will initially include six foreign markets—namely, Canada, Germany, the United Kingdom, France, Japan, and Hong Kong. The company expects to eventually expand the service to 36 additional international markets, which will initially be open to broker-assisted trading. To customers, this will mean not only faster execution but also lower fees. Instead of $100, they will now pay a $20 fee for an international trade.

E-Trade said the move was in response to customer demand. The company noted that a survey it conducted found that 67% of its customers were interested in direct trading on foreign exchanges. E-Trade predicted that its competitors (e.g., Charles Schwab and TDAmeritrade) will soon mimic the move as global markets become increasingly important in individual portfolios. According to analysts, both competitors have put less attention on international markets and will now have to play catch-up with E-Trade.

SOURCES: Adapted from "E-Trade goes global." CNNmoney.com, February 20, 2007; "E-Trade unveils global trading platform." The Associated Press/MSNBC.com, February 20, 2007.

Interim Summary

1. The localization challenge in global e-commerce entails customization of Web sites as well as of the supply chain and distribution network.

2. Country of origin is especially difficult to determine in global e-commerce transactions. Both MNEs and SMIEs have to deal with the challenges and opportunities posed by this reality in taxation as well as in other realms.

CHAPTER SUMMARY

1. E-commerce could change some of the fundamental assumptions pertaining to trade and foreign investment, although it is too early to determine whether, for instance, it will "even the playing field" between the SMIE and the large MNE.

2. E-commerce is unlikely to terminate the role of global intermediaries, but it is likely to shift their positioning toward knowledge analysis and dissemination. For instance, with their role as ticket issuers eliminated, travel agencies will need to focus on advice, niche, or wholesale activities.

3. As in other international business realms, international e-commerce requires a balance of globalization and localization. With foreign customers often logging on to U.S. sites, firms attempt to localize their Web sites in terms of language, culture, and currency units while also adding multiple country sites.

4. Taxation is looming large as an obstacle to the promise of free flow of goods and services on which e-commerce thrives. In the global arena, taxation could affect the competitiveness of U.S. purveyors.

5. MNEs must take account of the repercussions of global e-commerce in such realms as competitive advantage, location, and taxation.

Chapter Notes

1. J. A. Quelch and L. R. Klein. "The Internet and international marketing." *Sloan Management Review,* Spring 1996: pp. 60–75.

2. A. LaPlante. *Computerworld* online, October 1997.
3. N. E. Boudette. "Germany's Primus Online faces legal challenge." *Wall Street Journal,* January 6, 2000, A17.

4. UNCTAD. "Building confidence: Electronic commerce and development." 2000.

5. P. Druckerman. "Latin American Web concerns fight to stay in business." *Wall Street Journal*, October 9, 2000, A20.

6. "Latin firms build online marketplace for business in major e-commerce push." *Wall Street Journal*, July 14, 2000.

7. "Big brother and e-revolution." *BusinessWeek*, October 4, 1999: p. 132.

8. OECD. Cited in the *Economist*, November 11, 2000.

9. J. A. Quelch and L. R. Klein. "The Internet and international marketing." *Sloan Management Review*, Spring 1996: pp. 60–75.

10. *Wall Street Journal*, November 21, 2000, A1.

11. R. Ricklefs. "U.S. e-tailors expand efforts north of the border." *Wall Street Journal*, January 31, 2000, A21.

12. E. Rasmusson. "Targeting global e-customers." *Sales & Marketing Management*, 2000: p. 78.

13. K. L. Stout. "Yahoo! Asia top exec calls it quits." cnn.com, February 19, 2001.

14. J. Karp. "AOL hangs tough in the dicey Latin market." *Wall Street Journal*, September 5, 2001, A22.

15. N. Wingfield. "EBay, admitting missteps, will close its site in Japan." *Wall Street Journal*, February 27, 2002, B4.

16. B. Mitchener and D. Wessel. "U.S. in tentative pact protecting Europeans' privacy." *Wall Street Journal*, February 24, 2000, B11; "EU rejects U.S. data privacy protection as inadequate. cnn.com, July 7, 2000.

17. S. Kalin. "The importance of being multiculturally correct." *Computerworld*, October 6, 1997.

18. S. Koth, V. R. Rindova, and F. T. Rothaermel. "Assets and actions: Firm specific factors in the internationalization of U.S. Internet firms." *Journal of International Business Studies, 32*, 4: pp. 769–791.

19. B. Giussani. "Europe's Internet lag: An American fabrication?" *New York Times*, September 14, 1999.

20. R. A. Guth. "Yahoo! Japan learns from parent's achievements, errors." *Wall Street Journal*, December 11, 2000, A28.

21. L. Vickery. "Cultural portal could translate way to profit." *Wall Street Journal*, February 12, 2001, B6.

22. B. Vivkers. "Firms give global Web businesses local appeal." *Wall Street Journal*, December 4, 2000, B17A.

23. E. Rasmusson. "E-commerce around the world." *Sales & Marketing Management*, 1999: p. 94.

24. Forrester Research. "Mastering e-commerce logistics." 1999. Cited in *Building Confidence*, p. 50.

25. R. Dorenberg and L. Hinnekens. *Electronic Commerce and International Taxation*. The Hague: Kluwer Law International, 1999.

26. R. Dorenberg and L. Hinnekens. *Electronic Commerce and International Taxation*. The Hague: Kluwer Law International, 1999.

SOCIAL RESPONSIBILITY AND CORRUPTION IN THE GLOBAL MARKETPLACE

DO YOU KNOW?

1. Why does the MNE face a greater array of social responsibility issues than a domestic firm?

2. What are the main elements of the MNE code of conduct?

3. What characteristics of a nation predispose it to corruption?

4. What are some of the major macroeconomic consequences of corruption, and what are its implications for the foreign investor?

5. What are the most common corrupt practices in international business?

6. How would you react if the only way to close a deal would involve violating a company code of ethics?

OPENING CASE

Shell's Brent Spar Project

The Royal Dutch Shell Group, known as Shell, grew out of an alliance between the Royal Dutch Petroleum Company of the Netherlands and the Shell Transport and Trading Company of the UK, in 1907. One of today's largest multinational oil companies, Shell invested heavily in the exploration and subsequent extraction of major oil and gas deposits in the North Sea, including at the Brent Field. Oil extracted from that field has been stored on the Brent Spar, a large floating oil platform. Unlike most other North Sea installations, the Brent Spar had most of its huge storage tanks

underwater. It weighed 14,500 tons, the equivalent of 2,000 double-decker buses. After 15 years of operation, the Spar was decommissioned in 1991, when a review of refurbishment costs showed that further use would not be economical.

After the Spar's decommission that October, Shell's subsidiary in the United Kingdom initiated a number of decommissioning studies to find out how to dispose of it. Owing to its size, the platform could not be moved around easily, and except for the water to the North of Orkney, most of the North Sea was not deep enough to accommodate it. In a search for the best practicable environmental option (BPEO), Shell considered six options: (a) horizontal dismantling and onshore disposal, (b) vertical dismantling and onshore disposal, (c) infield disposal, (d) deepwater disposal, (e) refurbishment and reuse, and (f) continued maintenance. From these initial options, after a preliminary study, Shell chose to limit feasibility studies to the options of horizontal onshore dismantling and deepwater disposal. It eventually opted for the deepwater disposal option and submitted a request to the UK government, which has endorsed it. However, Greenpeace, a nongovernmental global environmental organization, opposed the deepwater disposal option, which it saw as a dangerous precedent, given the 130 offshore spars still operating in the North Sea. The opposition prompted an outcry on the part of European political and various social groups, resulting in boycott campaigns and even the torching of Shell gas stations. Finally, on June 20, 1995, Shell reversed its decision to sink the Spar.

The Brent Spar experience and an outcry following the execution of a Nigerian environmentalist a few years earlier (for which Shell has been criticized because it did not try to stop it) brought about soul-searching in the company, which decided it wanted to become a better global citizen. The Shell Report now provides full disclosure of social responsibility challenges, and the company uses a Social Impact Statement to assess the environmental impact of its decisions around the globe (see Industry Box in this chapter). It also provides cheap heating and cooking oil in poor communities. Still, Shell continued to run into troubles. In 2004, it agreed to pay $150 million to U.S. and UK regulators who alleged that the company had greatly overstated its oil reserves. The debacle led to corporate governance changes, among them, in 2005–2006, the unification of its century-old dual-board structure.

SOURCES: Excerpted from S. C. Zyglidopoulos. "The social and environmental responsibilities of multinationals: Evidence from the Brent Spar case." *Journal of Business Ethics*, 2002, *36*,1–2: pp. 141–152; E. Becker. "At Shell, grades for citizenship." *New York Times*, November 30, 2003, A2; Shell publications, 2004–2006.

CORPORATE SOCIAL RESPONSIBILITY IN INTERNATIONAL BUSINESS

Corporate social responsibility encompasses the economic, legal, ethical and philanthropic, and discretionary expectations that society has of an organization at a given point in time. For the MNE, like other business firms, economic responsibilities are paramount, including, for instance, principles that determine how and where profit may be derived and disbursed. Such principles often vary from one country to another, as do the legal systems that govern company operation. For example, labor laws in China often are not enforced, and foreign investors there discover that China's legal system resolves few disputes. Ethical responsibilities include activities and practices that are expected or prohibited by society even though they may not be codified into law. Such responsibilities encompass norms, standards, and expectations that reflect what employees, consumers, shareholders, and the global community regard as fair, just, and consistent with respect for and the protection of stakeholders' moral rights.

The ethical category is where divergent views traceable to different cultures are likely to be most significant. Global business ethics are essentially about the reconciliation of home- and host-country ethical standards and the identification of norms that will satisfy both. The practice of moral relativism, wherein companies simply adapt to local norms, can create an untenable situation because many countries, especially those with emerging and developing economies, do not have articulated ethical standards that protect vulnerable stakeholders. Consider, for instance, the case of Google, which agreed to comply with the Chinese government's demand to censor politically sensitive terms. Moral universalism, a response or remedy to this deficiency, involves the identification of a particular set of ethical standards that has broad international support, such as the U.N. Global Compact or the Global Reporting Initiatives.

Finally, philanthropic responsibilities reflect expectations that business will engage in social activities that are neither mandated by law nor generally expected of business in an ethical sense. Philanthropy today is more often than not strategic in nature, with businesses playing an active role in global corporate citizenship. As in the case of law and ethics, philanthropic expectations vary widely by country, and savvy executives will carefully research expectations in each host country.

MNE Social Responsibilities

Generally speaking, the MNE bears greater social responsibility than its domestic counterparts. Globalization has increased calls for MNEs to use their resources to alleviate a wide variety of social problems. The pharmaceutical industry, for example, is asked to donate free drugs and vaccines to developing nations. MNEs engaged in manufacturing are encouraged to apply developed nations' laws and norms to issues such as child labor and environmental pollution in less-developed countries, regardless of local laws and customs.

Globalization has resulted in the proliferation of new laws and regulations that direct business activities to address diverse social problems. In recent years, MNEs such as Wal-Mart and Nike have come to recognize the importance of social responsibility at the global level. Developing country multinational enterprises (DMNEs) such as India's Tata Group and Mittal Steel are showing similar concern, often displaying even higher sensitivities because of the paternalistic expectations in their home environment. For instance, in India, Tata channels some profit back to the community via major philanthropic trusts. Nearly 80% of the capital of the holding company, Tata Sons Limited, is held by these trusts, which helped establish leading institutions in the sciences, medicine, atomic energy, and the performing arts.

An MNE's corporate social responsibility is typically focused on its relationships with several major stakeholders—namely, host governments, the public (including Nongovernmental Organizations, or NGOs), business partners, and consumers and employees. Getz summarized 15 areas of international standards for MNEs dealing with host governments, which are listed below:[1]

Economic and Development Policies

MNEs should consult with government authorities and national employers' and workers' organizations to assure that their investments conform to the economic and social development policies of their host countries.

MNEs should not adversely disturb the balance of payments or currency exchange rates of the countries in which they operate. They should try, in consultation with government officials, to resolve exchange rate difficulties when possible.

MNEs should cooperate with government policies regarding local equity participation.

MNEs should not dominate the capital markets of the countries in which they operate.

MNEs should provide necessary information to host government authorities so they can correctly assess taxes due.

MNEs should not engage in transfer pricing policies that modify the tax bases on which their entities are assessed.

MNEs should reinvest some profits in the countries in which they operate.

Laws and Regulations

MNEs are subject to the laws, regulations, and jurisdictions of the countries in which they operate.

MNEs should respect the right of every country to exercise control over its natural resources and to regulate the activities of entities operating within its territory.

MNEs should use appropriate international dispute-settlement mechanisms, including arbitration, to resolve conflicts with the governments of the countries in which they operate.

MNEs should not request the intervention of their home governments in disputes with host governments.

MNEs should resolve disputes arising from expropriation by host governments under the domestic laws of the host countries.

Political Involvement

MNEs should refrain from improper or illegal involvement in local political affairs.

MNEs should not pay bribes or render improper benefits to any public servant.

MNEs should not interfere in intergovernmental relations.

Environmental Responsibilities. MNEs operating in environmentally sensitive industries, such as the chemical, pharmaceutical, petroleum, mining, and natural resource exploration industries, to name a few, and are expected to establish a viable sustainability program. Pollution, in its various forms, has been given a great deal of attention in recent years. While pollution in emerging economies such as China has become a key concern, so have the worries that industrialized nations will export their own environmental problems to developing markets. Basel Action Network (BAN), an environmental NGO, found out that many developing countries have become "digital dumps" for discarded computers. In Nigeria, more than 400,000 old computers and monitors arrive annually, and up to three-quarters of those are beyond repair and are simply dumped in informal rubbish dumps, creating an environmental hazard. Although the practice violates the Basel Convention on the Control of Transboundary Movements of Hazardous Waste as well as other international agreements, the practice continues unabated.[2] In 2006, an illegal dumping of toxic waste in the waters of Nigeria by a foreign ship sickened thousands of people there.

ISO 14000, the new European Union pollution guidelines, was established in 1996 to regulate global environmental concerns. This standard contains six components, each of which is relevant to MNEs: (a) environmental management systems, (b) environmental auditing, (c) performance evaluation, (d) environmental labeling, (e) life cycle assessment, and (f) environmental product assessment. Here are some examples of what is required in a business environment governed by ISO 14000:

Adopt management strategies that will enable firms to obtain ISO 14000 certification in their industry.

Reduce pollution and conserve resources as a means of meeting stringent environmental regulations.

Shift from product changes to behavioral and manufacturing process changes, so as to manufacture products in a more environmentally sound manner.

Reduce solid waste by incorporating recycling into the manufacturing process.

Baxter International, a manufacturer of pharmaceutical and biomedical products with production facilities in almost 30 countries, has a viable sustainability program in place. The external verification aspect of Baxter's program got its start in the mid-1990s in response to a stockholder group seeking assurance that environmental data presented to the public were accurate. Initially, Baxter only used its own staff to verify environmental data. External auditors were drawn into the verification process as a result of the stockholder group's concerns. Over time, the external report evolved to incorporate the reporting of health and safety data as well as environmental data. Currently, an external consultant, ERM Certification and Verification Services (ERM CVS), and Baxter have an arrangement by which they jointly verify select data at every facility audited. ERM CVS retains overall quality control of the process through verification protocols. Another firm that is taking sustainable development seriously is French telecommunications concern Alcatel (which merged with U.S.-based Lucent in 2006). Alcatel's sustainable development strategy is based on strict published guidelines as well as social, environmental, and economic objectives defined by the company. Alcatel's sites around the world have benefited from an environmental management system, and through its "Digital Bridge" initiative, Alcatel technologies serve development in scores of countries. In 2003, the company joined the UN Global Compact, reinforced its corporate governance practices, updated its "Statement on Business Practices," and elaborated on its Social Charter, which emphasizes Alcatel's commitment to socially responsible practices.

Consumer Protection. Consumer protection is another important requirement in a global setting. MNEs are expected to respect the consumer protection laws and regulations of host countries and preserve the safety and health of consumers by disclosing appropriate information, applying proper labeling, and using accurate advertising. Consumers also increasingly ask how "green" the company is before buying its products. Attributes such as corporate reputation, women and minority employment and board membership, company participation in weapons production and use of nuclear power, product safety, employee safety and health, and environmental protection record have become important dimensions of corporate social responsibility for the MNE.

Corporate Governance. Another vital area of social responsibility for the MNE is corporate governance, of which financial governance is one of the major responsibilities. Financial governance focuses on the structures and processes necessary for the pursuit of shareholder value. Key elements in this category are shareholder rights, protection of minority shareholders, and transparency and disclosure issues (e.g., disclosing the composition of the board, the number of independent directors, and special board committees). Here, too, variations across countries present a major challenge for the MNE. For instance, in Japan, women's board membership is almost nonexistent, while in the United States women now represent about 15% of board members. A U.S. MNE with a Japanese subsidiary or a joint venture might therefore face a dilemma when considering appointing a woman to the board in that affiliate. According to a 2004 Conference Board survey, Japan is also the only industrialized country where boards of directors do not have a defined role in ethics.

Global Guidelines and Mandates

There are many global guidelines by which MNEs measure their social responsibility. Many of those guidelines have been issued in the last decade by NGOs. The more prominent types of guidelines include the environment, supply-chain management, hiring practices, community relations, internal management, information disclosure, and charitable donations. Some of the global benchmarks against which corporate performance on those issues is being measured include the United Nations Declaration of Human Rights, the International Labor Organization's (ILO's) labor standards, and several globally recognized voluntary standards, such as the Organization for Economic Co-operation and Development's guidelines for multinationals and the United Nations Global Compact, to name just a few.

Perhaps the most widely accepted reporting guideline is the Global Reporting Initiative (GRl), based in Amsterdam. Launched in 1997 and billed as a common framework for sustainable reporting, the GRI was developed by a group of organizations known for responsible business reporting. Among them were representatives of the Association of Chartered Certified Accountants, the United Nations Environment Program, and the World Business Council for Sustainable Development. The GRI took the best practices in the area of human rights, labor relations, environmental management, and sustainable development and crafted them into guidelines that enable any corporation to produce one comprehensive report.

Many global guidelines, such as the OECD Guidelines for Multinational Enterprises, are voluntary. These initiatives involve the issuance of codes of corporate conduct setting forth commitments in such areas as labor relations, environmental management, human rights, consumer protection, information disclosure, and corruption. The codes are often backed up by management systems that help firms fulfill their commitments in their day-to-day operations. More recent developments include guidelines on management, reporting and auditing standards, and the emergence of supporting institutions (e.g., professional societies, consulting and auditing services). While the initiatives are often referred to as voluntary, MNEs are under increasing pressure to adopt them. Pressures stem from legal and regulatory institutions, employees, and public opinion.

A Culture of Social Responsibility

Levi Strauss & Co. illustrates the importance of corporate culture in improving an MNE's social responsibility. The company's core values—empathy, originality, integrity, and courage—underlie how the company competes in the global marketplace and how its executives, directors, and employees are expected to behave. These values guide its foundation's giving programs, the support it provides to communities where it has a business presence, and its employee community-involvement programs. In 1991, Levi Strauss became the first worldwide company to establish a comprehensive ethical code of conduct for manufacturing and finishing contractors working with the company. Over the period 2001–2004, the company was ranked one of "America's 50 Best Companies for Minorities" by *Fortune* magazine. Its philanthropy includes a focus on strengthening workers' rights and ultimately improving working and living conditions in communities where third-party contractors make Levi Strauss's products. The Levi Strauss Foundation provides innovative "sourcing" grants to local, regional, and global nonprofit organizations to support programs that do the following:

Educate policymakers on the need to include human rights protections in trade agreements

Increase local monitoring and enforcement of labor and health and safety laws

Educate workers about their rights and increase their knowledge of financial literacy and health issues

Create positive partnerships between nonprofit organizations and contractors

Exhibit 19.1 shows Levi Strauss's detailed guidelines for global sourcing, including its expectations from itself and its providers in each of the countries in which the company operates.

Exhibit 19.1   Levi Strauss's Global Sourcing Guidelines

I. Country Assessment Guidelines

The numerous countries where Levi Strauss & Co. has existing or future business interests present a variety of cultural, political, social and economic circumstances. The Country Assessment Guidelines help us assess any issue that might present concern in light of the ethical principles we have set for ourselves. The Guidelines assist us in making practical and principled business decisions as we balance the potential risks and opportunities associated with conducting business in specific countries. Specifically, we assess whether the

Health and Safety Conditions would meet the expectations we have for employees and their families or our company representatives;

Human Rights Environment would allow us to conduct business activities in a manner that is consistent with our Global Sourcing and Operating Guidelines and other company policies;

Legal System would provide the necessary support to adequately protect our trademarks, investments or other commercial interests, or to implement the Global Sourcing and Operating Guidelines and other company policies; and

Political, Economic and Social Environment would protect the company's commercial interests and brand/corporate image. We will not conduct business in countries prohibited by U.S. laws.

II. Terms of Engagement

Ethical Standards

We will seek to identify and utilize business partners who aspire as individuals and in the conduct of all their businesses to a set of ethical standards not incompatible with our own.

Legal Requirements

We expect our business partners to be law abiding as individuals and to comply with legal requirements relevant to the conduct of all their businesses.

Environmental Requirements

We will only do business with partners who share our commitment to the environment and who conduct their business in a way that is consistent with Levi Strauss & Co.'s Environmental Philosophy and Guiding Principles.

Community Involvement

We will favor business partners who share our commitment to improving community conditions.

Employment Standards

We will only do business with partners who adhere to the following guidelines:

Child Labor: Use of child labor is not permissible. Workers can be no less than 15 years of age and not younger than the compulsory age to be in school. We will not utilize partners who use child labor in any of their facilities. We support the development of legitimate workplace apprenticeship programs for the educational benefit of younger people.

Prison Labor/Forced Labor: We will not utilize prison or forced labor in contracting relationships in the manufacture and finishing of our products. We will not utilize or purchase materials from a business partner utilizing prison or forced labor.

Disciplinary Practices: We will not utilize business partners who use corporal punishment or other forms of mental or physical coercion.

Working Hours: While permitting flexibility in scheduling, we will identify local legal limits on work hours and seek business partners who do not exceed them except for appropriately compensated overtime.

(Continued)

Exhibit 19.1 (Continued)

While we favor partners who utilize less than sixty-hour workweeks, we will not use contractors who, on a regular basis, require in excess of a sixty-hour week. Employees should be allowed at least one day off in seven.

Wages and Benefits: We will only do business with partners who provide wages and benefits that comply with any applicable law and match the prevailing local manufacturing or finishing industry practices.

Freedom of Association: We respect workers' rights to form and join organizations of their choice and to bargain collectively. We expect our suppliers to respect the right to free association and the right to organize and bargain collectively without unlawful interference. Business partners should ensure that workers who make such decisions or participate in such organizations are not the object of discrimination or punitive disciplinary actions and that the representatives of such organizations have access to their members under conditions established either by local laws or mutual agreement between the employer and the worker organizations.

Discrimination: While we recognize and respect cultural differences, we believe that workers should be employed on the basis of their ability to do the job, rather than on the basis of personal characteristics or beliefs. We will favor business partners who share this value.

Health and Safety: We will only utilize business partners who provide workers with a safe and healthy work environment. Business partners who provide residential facilities for their workers must provide safe and healthy facilities.

SOURCE: Levi Strauss. http://www.levistrauss.com/Downloads/GSOG.pdf

Auditing and Assessing MNE Social Responsibility

Many MNEs have implemented programs that help them respond to societal concerns about the economic, social, and environmental impacts of their activities. These programs assist them in managing compliance with legal or regulatory requirements and formulating responses to "soft" forms of social conduct—in which they commit to norms for appropriate conduct in a variety of areas of business ethics. Some MNEs have chief audit executives who ensure that social responsibility is on the board's agenda and that the various codes and standards are upheld.

Even with the best of internal monitoring, however, MNEs sometimes turn to outside organizations to gauge and verify their social responsibility performance. There are four categories of organizations that provide external monitoring and verification services: (a) global accounting firms such as KPMG and PricewaterhouseCoopers; (b) monitoring firms or NGOs focusing their efforts specifically on inspecting work sites for code of conduct violations; (c) forensic and investigation firms, which typically use a network of professionals to investigate allegations of impropriety or perform due-diligence assessments of potential or existing suppliers' ability to comply with codes; and (d) quality assurance or quality registrar or ISO certification firms. Building on the platform established by the International Standards Organization (ISO), an NGO established to promote the development of voluntary standards that govern quality and environmental impact, several quality registrars or quality certification firms have started performing workforce monitoring on codes of conduct and human rights issues.

CORRUPTION IN INTERNATIONAL BUSINESS

While social responsibility has been on the radar screen of MNEs for many years, corruption—perhaps the most blatant form of deviation from social responsibility laws and norms—is an issue seldom discussed. For instance, for almost three decades the United States was virtually the only country to criminalize bribe paying when doing business abroad. Other nations looked the other way, viewing bribe paying as a necessary if unpleasant part, and cost, of international business. Many nations treated corruption outside their national borders differently than at home, condoning the use of corrupt practices abroad while banning them at home. Some nations continue to do so today. Drawing the line at one's borders is increasingly tenuous, however. As noted in the *Economist*, "companies have learned the hard way that they live in a CNN world, in which bad behavior in one country can be seized on by local campaigners and beamed on the evening news to customers back home."

Definition and Magnitude of Corruption

By nature, corruption defies a precise definition,[3] and definitions also vary from one country to another. However, most definitions of corruption view it as the illegitimate exchange of power into material remuneration mostly on the part of officeholders who take advantage of their position to grant undeserving favors. Not all corruption violates the law. Some corrupt activities merely defy "accepted norms" or "customs."[4] In this chapter, we will use the following definition of corruption:

> An exchange between two partners (the "demander" and the "supplier"), which (a) has an influence on the allocation of resources either immediately or in the future, and (b) involves the use or abuse of public or collective responsibility for private ends.[5]

Understandably, corruption is difficult to measure. Most nations do not gauge corruption levels, and companies are reluctant to divulge information on corrupt activities that may put them in harm's way; they are also reluctant to jeopardize their government contacts or embarrass their home and or host governments. Nevertheless, estimates of corrupt activities and their economic impact are available. The *Economist* puts the "shadow" or "underground" economy at $9 trillion annually.[6] Even in some developed economies (e.g., Italy and Belgium), underground economic activity represents a quarter of GDP,[7] a figure comparable to that of the emerging economy of China.[8] World Bank figures from 2005 put the annual cost of corruption at $1.5 trillion.

Some industries are especially prone to corruption. The European Court of Auditors estimates that member states have wasted $1.2 billion on fraudulent infrastructure projects.[9] Between May 1994 and April 1998, 239 international contracts totaling US$108 billion were influenced by bribes. About half of those contracts involved military procurement; the others involved aerospace, communications, infrastructure, energy, and transportation.[10] It is estimated that leading exporters, especially in the arms and construction industries, traditionally pay upward of 10% to a senior official to win a contract.[11] The U.S. government cites a case in which a European aircraft maker offered agent commissions of 20% or more in an Asian market if its product was chosen.[12]

The Origins of Corruption

A number of conditions tend to increase the probability of corruption. First, developing economies are more prone to corruption, partly because of the lack of an adequate legal framework and weak enforcement; hybrid or transitional economies are susceptible because their institutions tend to lag behind the reality of fast economic and social change. A study by Shleifer and Vishny shows that while Soviet officials extorted small bribes, officials in the transitional Russian system that followed extorted larger sums because they did not have to show concern for other bribe takers.[13] Additional factors supporting corruption, according to Transparency International (TI) data, include low public-sector pay, immunity of public officials, secrecy in government, and media restrictions. Privatization, financial liberalization, and increase in FDI and trade also play a role.[14]

A second predictor of corruption is high level and scope of government involvement in and regulation of economic activity, especially where public-official pay is low and corruption is viewed as legitimate remuneration. Nigeria represents such an example, as do certain sectors in India and Vietnam, among other countries. A lack of transparency (e.g., public disclosure of financial information), more common in developing and hybrid economies but also evident in some developed economies (e.g., Italy), is also associated with higher corruption levels.

A third predictor of corruption is culture, which was found to correlate, for instance, with receptivity toward questionable accounting principles.[15] Uncertainty avoidance and masculinity (see Chapter 6) have been found to correlate with unethical decision making.[16] Husted formed a "cultural profile" of a corrupt country, high on uncertainty avoidance, masculinity, and power distance. Corruption is associated with high uncertainty avoidance because it is an uncertainty reduction mechanism. Masculinity creates corruption potential because it implies preference for material things. Power distance is associated with paternalism, a system in which a superior grants favors to subordinates in return for loyalty, permitting arbitrary judgment and hence corruption.[17]

Drawbacks of Corruption

Ninety percent of the Asian executives surveyed by the *Far Eastern Economic Review* said that corruption slowed progress.[18] Corruption obstructs firm growth and development through the imposition of risk, the punishment suffered by violator firms, the damage to a firm's reputation, and the financial cost incurred in direct and indirect payments. According to the World Bank, the percentage of firms that see corruption as a problem for their operations and growth exceeds 40% in Ukraine and 35% in Bulgaria.[19] From an economic perspective, corruption causes misallocation of capital, diverting resources from constructive activities such as innovation and technological development. It also produces incomplete, distorted, and undisclosed information, allowing one party to take advantage of another, which undermines cooperation and potential synergies between partners. The damage is especially pronounced in emerging economies, in which internal funds often constitute the single most important source of capital, discouraging legitimate investment. As a headline describing the military coup in Pakistan read, "Pakistani stocks surge since military takeover amid hopes less corruption will lift economy."[20]

Corruption tends to undermine trade and FDI, depriving both the host countries and the investors of the benefits associated with trade and investment. One researcher calculated, for instance, that an increase in the level of corruption from the Singaporean (very low) to the Mexican (high) level would be tantamount to an increase of more than 20% in the tax burden on foreign investment.[21] Further, the prospect of obtaining personal benefits may lead officials to oppose trade liberalization. Foreign investors, on their part, may be reluctant to invest in an economy known for its corrupt practices.[22] Referring to his company's exit from Bulgaria, a Unilever official said:

> It was impossible for us to do business without getting involved in corruption. So we took the logical step and accepted the consequences. That meant packing our bags.[23]

Corruption Rankings

Established in 1993 by a former World Bank official, Transparency International (TI) publishes the Corruption Perception Index (CPI), a broad measure of corruption that is calculated from multiple survey responses. The 2006 report provides CPI scores for 163 countries studied. Exhibit 19.2 shows the least and the most corrupt economies among those, their ranking, and their CPI score. As expected, all of the least corrupt nations are developed while all of the most corrupt are developing. Still, the full rankings provide some interesting insights. For instance, among developed economies, Italy and Greece rank relatively low (45th and 54th, respectively), while among developing economies, Barbados ranks near the top, least corrupt group, at 24th place. It is also interesting to note that all of the Scandinavian countries rank in the top 10 (least corrupt) countries, reinforcing the argument regarding the cultural correlates of corruption (please refer to Chapter 6, where these nations' distinct Scandinavian culture cluster is discussed).

Exhibit 19.2   Least and Most Corrupt Countries, 2006

	Least Corrupt			Most Corrupt	
Rank	Country	CPI Score	Rank	Country	CPI Score
1	Finland	9.6	142	Angola	2.2
1	Iceland	9.6	142	Congo (Repub.)	2.2
1	New Zealand	9.6	142	Kenya	2.2
4	Denmark	9.5	142	Kyrgyzstan	2.2
5	Singapore	9.4	142	Nigeria	2.2
6	Sweden	9.2	142	Pakistan	2.2
7	Switzerland	9.1	142	Sierra Leone	2.2
8	Norway	8.8	142	Tajikistan	2.2
9	Australia	8.7	142	Turkmenistan	2.2
9	Netherlands	8.7	151	Belarus	2.1
11	Austria	8.6	151	Cambodia	2.1
11	Luxembourg	8.6	151	Ivory Coast	2.1
11	United Kingdom	8.6	151	Equatorial Guinea	2.1
14	Canada	8.5	151	Uzbekistan	2.1
15	Hong Kong	8.3	156	Bangladesh	2.0
16	Germany	8.0	156	Chad	2.0
17	Japan	7.6	156	Congo (Dem. Repub.)	2.0
18	France	7.4	156	Sudan	2.0
18	Ireland	7.4	160	Guinea	1.9
20	Belgium	7.3	160	Iraq	1.9
20	Chile	7.3	160	Myanmar	1.9
20	USA	7.3	163	Haiti	1.8

SOURCE: Transparency International.

As in other instances, it is useful to be aware of internal variations within countries. For instance, the *Economist* ranks Chechnya, Dagestan, and Primorsky as having the highest level of corruption in Russia. The Samara region has the lowest.[24]

Interim Summary

1. What constitutes corrupt business practices varies cross-nationally; still, anti-corruption norms are spreading.

2. In addition to misallocation of capital resources, corrupt countries create an artificial, usually ossified, economic atmosphere that makes firms less capable of competing in open, international markets.

3. The level of corruption varies cross-nationally with developing and transitional economies typically ranking high (i.e., they are more corrupt).

TYPES OF CORRUPT PRACTICES

International business corruption takes many forms: a request from an exporter to pay a fee to "expedite" customs clearance, a "consultant fee" demanded from a foreign investor by government officials involved in project approval, a bid awarded to regulators and their proxies. Common forms of corruption in international business are listed below.

Smuggling

Smuggling is the illegal trade and transportation of goods devised to circumvent customs duties, quotas, and other constraints on the movement of goods (e.g., safety transportation requirements that may add to cost at destination). Smuggling diminishes national control over trade policies. It damages legitimate importers that find themselves in competition with sellers offering the same or similar products at a lower cost, as well as the manufacturer whose reputation is tarnished by the sale of inferior imitations or an inability to service products that are not under genuine warranty. Smuggling is especially likely to occur in economies sharing a contiguous border across which exist substantial differences in the availability and cost of goods. A case in point: the Hong Kong border with southern China, where local mainland authorities sometimes collude with the smugglers. In the past, this was a conduit for the smuggling of stolen cars into the mainland (easily detected, because the steering wheels in Hong Kong are on the right side). Nowadays, the flow consists more of counterfeit products into Hong Kong (since 1997, Hong Kong has been a Special Administrative Region of China, but it continues to be a separate entity for trade and customs purposes).

Photo 19.1   **Smuggled designer handbags are popular counterfeit items.**

SOURCE: Jupiterimages.

Cigarettes have been especially appealing to smugglers throughout the world owing to high taxes and tariffs and the relative ease of transportation. The Canadian government alleged that cigarette makers have been exporting their Canada-made cigarettes to the United States only to have them smuggled back into Canada to avoid high taxes. The manufacturers, mostly affiliates of U.S. firms, denied involvement but acknowledge the rampant smuggling of the product.[25] A recent study suggests that MNEs have not always been unwitting participants in the smuggling of cigarettes but have often cooperated or at least did not initiate action against the phenomenon.[26] Cigarettes continued to top the list of goods seized by U.S. customs authorities in 2004 and 2005.

Particularly appealing to smugglers are contraband goods such as drugs, liquor, and guns (where prohibited), because of the lack of competition from legitimate means of importation. Smuggling also occurs in products that seem difficult to ship and conceal, such as steel. Steel smuggling involves falsifying shipping documents to conceal the product source or its classification. There are about 100 nations that export steel to the United States, and because there are almost 1,000 different types of steel—two variables that determine the tariff level—there is substantial incentive to smuggle the metal, and it is difficult for the U.S. Customs Service to monitor it.[27]

The smuggling of illegal immigrants has become especially lucrative. Driven by hardship at home and the prospect of a better life elsewhere, individuals are often lured into paying exorbitant sums to organized gangs with the promise of entry into a developed country, most notably the United States and those of the EU. It is estimated that almost half a million illegal immigrants are smuggled into the EU annually, whereas 300,000 make their way into the United States.[28] A 2006 congressional discussion suggests that the numbers are considerably higher.

Money Laundering

Money laundering involves concealing the source of ill-gotten funds by channeling them into legitimate business activities and bank deposits in other countries. Although not new, the phenomenon has been growing rapidly, partially because of a burgeoning drug trade and privatization in the former Soviet Union and other emerging economies. While it is impossible to accurately measure the extent of the problem, some estimates have put it as high as 5% of global GDP. The flow has been aided by electronic payment systems that make possible the transfer of huge sums of money at lightning speed. The chairman of the Bank of New York acknowledged that the bank's money-laundering lapse was the result of a "global payments system that put priority on speed rather than knowing whether the electronic money transfers are legal."[29] One way to launder money is through trade. This is done via the undervaluation of exports (e.g., a motor vehicle exported from the United States to Jordan for which the declared value was $377) or through overvaluation of exports (e.g., footballs imported into the United States from Pakistan for which the declared value was $142.50).[30] The events of September 11, 2001, have drawn much more attention to money laundering as a vehicle in international terrorism, triggering much closer scrutiny of the phenomenon, which continues to this day.

Piracy and Counterfeiting

Counterfeiting and piracy account for 5% to 7% of world trade, or $200 to $300 billion in lost revenues.[31] Counterfeiting and piracy are not the same. Piracy means using illegal and unauthorized means to obtain goods, such as copying software. Counterfeiting goes a step beyond, attempting to pass the copied product as an original, such as producing and selling a fake Gucci bag or a Rolex watch. Both phenomena have been growing rapidly and represent a substantial threat to the original manufacturers. In piracy, the most significant threat is probably in intellectual property, such as computer software, music, and videos.

The growth in piracy of such goods is explained by industry growth and the globalization of intellectual property products. Technological advances make pirating easier: The price of disc production machinery has declined precipitously in recent years, facilitating a cottage industry in pirated discs in China, Vietnam, and other countries. Counterfeit goods include not only videos and designer watches and handbags but, alarmingly, pharmaceuticals and aircraft spare parts. Counterfeit services can also be found in the form of unauthorized providers of automotive services, which put up the manufacturer's logo as a way to entice unsuspecting customers.

Both piracy and counterfeiting have greatly expanded in recent years, with violating products in pharmaceuticals, aircraft components, and automotive parts creating a serious threat to consumers. Both phenomena also discourage innovation by reducing the incentive for a company to invest in a new technology or product for fear they will not be able to capture the profit that comes from being a first entrant into the market. The violation of intellectual property rights, of which piracy and counterfeiting are a prime example, are currently a major friction factor in the relationship between China and the United States.

INDUSTRY BOX

SOCIAL IMPACT ASSESSMENT STEPS AT SHELL

1. Impact Identification Through Integrated Impact Assessments

Experience has shown that the greatest business and societal benefit comes from effective identification and management of operational impacts during planning and design as well as through the operational life. We require that an integrated environmental, social, and health impact assessment is carried out prior to any new project or significant modification of an existing one. Conducting environmental, social, and health impact assessments provides a structured way of looking ahead at the potential positive and negative impacts that could arise throughout the project's lifecycle. It is a tool to aid design and decision-making.

2. Stakeholder Engagement Plans

Stakeholder engagement helps us build relationships with communities, governments, NGOs, and shareholders. It is also a critical mechanism for problem solving, improving business decisions, and achieving business objectives. Given this importance, it is now a requirement for all businesses to establish and implement a Stakeholder Engagement Plan.

3. Social Performance Plans

Social Performance Plans have now been introduced as a requirement for all of Shell's businesses. Oil Products business has social performance plans in place at the 28 major facilities it operates near communities. Gas & Power will do the same in 2005 at the facilities it operates. The joint ventures where it does not have operational control are encouraged to develop social performance plans. Exploration & Production will put social performance plans in place in 2005 at operations where social impacts could be high. Plans have been in place since 2003 at our nine major Chemicals facilities, four of which surveyed community opinions in 2004 to measure social performance. These social performance plans guide our efforts to engage with stakeholders, reduce disruptive social impacts, and generate benefits for the communities where we operate.

4. Social Performance Reviews

The tools that our businesses use to manage the impact of our operations include social performance reviews to identify key stakeholders and assess responses to our main social impacts. The first four major social performance reviews have been fundamental in helping the Shell Group develop guidance on how to better and more consistently manage the key social impacts of our operations. The social performance reviews also provide a way to help assure our performance in the social arena and bolster our continuous learning.

SOURCE: Shell Oil.

Bribe Paying

Bribery, which often appears under such euphemisms as "fees," "commissions," "gratuities," and "sweeteners," is a perennial form of corruption in international business. Investigations by the Securities and Exchange Commission (SEC) during the 1970s found that more than 400 U.S. companies made questionable payments totaling more than $300 million to foreign government officials, politicians, and political parties. Between mid-1994 and mid-1996, U.S. firms lost 36 of 139 contracts, valued at $11 billion, to bribery.[32] Swiss authorities froze $100 million held by the government of Kazakhstan, allegedly used by American and European oil firms to bribe Kazakh officials in order to gain favorable exploration and use rights.[33] Among the companies discovering bribery in their overseas affiliates are Xerox, ABB, and IBM. Synchor, a U.S. pharmaceutical company, saw its acquisition price lowered when the acquirer, Cardinal Health, discovered improper payments made by Syncor in Taiwan.

TI publishes a Bribe Payers Index (BPI) that ranks countries according to their propensity to bribe abroad (see Exhibit 19.3). As in the case of the CPI, the developed economies are less likely to pay bribes in foreign markets than companies hailing from developing countries. Companies from the emerging economies of India, China, and Russia are most likely to pay bribes when operating abroad.

China, with the second lowest score, is a good illustration of the costs, patterns, and underlying reasons for bribe paying. An internal report of the Chinese government estimated the state lost well over US$50 billion in one decade from undervaluation of privatized assets by officials in return for payoffs. Hong Kong's Independent Commission Against Corruption estimated that gifts and bribes add 3% to 5% to operating costs in China.[34] The same commission also found in a survey of 50 Hong Kong companies doing business on the mainland that 35 admitted paying bribes, such as through the purchase of "inspection certificates" necessary for the exportation of goods.[35] In recent years, the Chinese government has undertaken a number of campaigns against bribery, leading to the arrest of senior officials in 2005 and again in 2006, but the government acknowledges that the phenomenon remains widespread.

The Foreign Corrupt Practices Act (FCPA)

The origin of the Foreign Corrupt Practices Act (FCPA) can be traced to the 1970s, when press reports alleged U.S. firms made questionable payments to foreign government officials. Payments were disbursed through hidden "slush funds," and financial records were often falsified to conceal them. The congressional investigations that ensued culminated in the enactment of the FCPA, which was further amended in 1988. The FCPA criminalized the payment of bribes and other forms of special payment to foreign officials for the purpose of securing or retaining a deal (liability exists whether the deal has been consummated or not). It also required issuers of securities to meet accounting, record-keeping, and corporate control standards. Criminal and civil enforcement of the antibribery provisions with respect to domestic concerns is the responsibility of the Justice Department. The SEC is responsible for civil enforcement of the antibribery provisions with respect to issuers.

Under the FCPA, the term "officials of a foreign government" includes executives in state-owned firms, foreign political parties, and candidates for office. A payment may be "in kind," such as a gratuitous trip. "Facilitating payments" made within the context of routine government operations (e.g., obtaining permits, issuance of license, providing utilities) are permissible under the act's 1988 amendment but must be reported on the company's financial statements.

Exhibit 19.3   The Bribe Payers Index

Rank	Country/Territory	Average Score (0–10)	Percentage of Global Exports (2005)	Ratification of OECD Convention	Ratification of UNCAC
1	Switzerland	7.81	1.2	X	
2	Sweden	7.62	1.3	X	
3	Australia	7.59	1.0	X	X
4	Austria	7.50	0.5	X	X
5	Canada	7.46	3.5	X	
6	UK	7.39	3.6	X	X
7	Germany	7.34	9.5	X	
8	Netherlands	7.28	3.4	X	
9	Belgium	7.22	3.3	X	
10	US	7.22	8.9	X	
11	Japan	7.10	5.8	X	
12	Singapore	6.78	2.2		
13	Spain	6.63	1.9	X	X
14	UAE	6.62	1.1		
15	France	6.50	4.3	X	X
16	Portugal	6.47	0.3	X	
17	Mexico	6.45	2.1	X	X
18	Hong Kong	6.01	2.8		X*
19	Israel	6.01	0.4		
20	Italy	5.94	3.6	X	
21	South Korea	5.83	2.8	X	
22	Saudi Arabia	5.75	1.8		
23	Brazil	5.65	1.2	X	X
24	South Africa	5.61	0.5		X
25	Malaysia	5.59	1.4		
26	Taiwan	5.41	1.9		**
27	Turkey	5.23	0.7	X	
28	Russia	5.16	2.4		X
29	China	4.94	5.5		X
30	India	4.62	0.9		

SOURCE: Transparency International.

* Hong Kong is a territory of China and covered under UNCAC.
** Taiwan is not a UN member.
The results draw from the responses of more than 11,000 businesspeople in 125 countries polled in the World Economic Forum's Executive Opinion Survey of 2006. A score of 10 indicates a perception of no corruption, while zero means corruption is seen as rampant. Leading the ranking is Switzerland, but even its score of 7.8 is far from perfect. The message: There may be variations here, but there are no real winners.

Bona fide payments (e.g., for work-related travel) that are legal in the host country and are made for the purpose of product promotion or as part of contractual obligations are also allowed under the 1988 amendment.

Subject to the FCPA are not only U.S. firms but also wholly owned U.S. subsidiaries and other U.S. entities controlled by foreign corporations, including their directors, employees, and agents. Actions taken abroad by U.S. citizens, nationals, or residents are covered under the FCPA even if conducted for a foreign corporation. The FCPA also prohibits indirect foreign payments, which can be interpreted as covering the foreign subsidiaries of U.S. corporations as well. However, it is not clear if the percentage of ownership in the subsidiary has a bearing on FCPA liability and if an international joint venture between a U.S. and a local company in a foreign country creates liability on the part of the local partner. This is an important question because firms often delegate functions with corruption potential (e.g., dealing with local government authorities) to their local partners. The FCPA also covers payment by intermediaries but requires proof that the U.S. MNE knew about the practice. It also prohibits payments to a third party with the knowledge that the payment will end up in the hands of a foreign official.

Violations of the FCPA can result in fines of up to $2 million for firms and $100,000 plus imprisonment for up to five years for individuals. Both firms and individuals are also liable to a civil fine if they violate the antibribery provisions. In suits brought by the SEC, fines can reach as much as $500,000. Under federal criminal laws other than the FCPA, individuals may be fined up to $250,000 or up to twice the amount of the gain or loss incurred. A firm or individual who violates the FCPA may also be barred from doing business with the U.S. government. Other sanctions include ineligibility to receive export licenses and being barred from the securities business.

The Globalization of the Fight Against Corruption

Immediately following the passage of the FCPA, the United States tried to expand it to other nations. The efforts were initially unsuccessful, but since then many governments (e.g., Thailand, Zimbabwe, Poland, and China's Special Administrative Region of Hong Kong) have established independent commissions against corruption. In the NAFTA-created NADBank, the United States successfully won agreement from its NAFTA partner Mexico in 1996 to require companies to certify that they have not engaged in bribery of foreign or domestic officials in projects funded by the bank. Companies must also have corporate policies that prohibit bribery and assert that they have not been convicted of bribery within five years of certification; otherwise they will be barred from future participation in a NADBank-funded or -guaranteed project.

In 1994, the United States sponsored the 1994 OECD Recommendation on Bribery in International Business Transactions, which called on member states to take "concrete and meaningful steps" to deter, prevent, and combat bribery of foreign public officials. In 1999, the OECD adopted the Combating Bribery of Foreign Officials in International Business Act (CBFOIB). The act is substantially modeled after the U.S. FCPA. It makes the payment of bribes to elected or appointed foreign officials a criminal offense and abolishes its tax deductibility. The act requires that sanctions against foreign corruption be comparable to those against public officials domestically. It also requires coordination in matters of jurisdiction, a key issue given the global nature of the phenomenon, as well as coordination in legal matters (including extradition). Effective accounting and measures against money laundering are also set.

While 31 nations have signed the Anti-bribery Convention (see also Exhibit 19.3), the results on the ground have been quite disappointing. By 2006, according to Transparency International (TI), 19 signatory nations, about two-thirds of the total, "have achieved little or no enforcement." According to the OECD, there have only been 50 prosecutions under the Convention since 1999. In the United Kingdom, Japan, and the Netherlands, there was not a single case of prosecution. While some governments have taken the results seriously (for instance, the UK announced in June 2006 the establishment of a special police task force to deal with the problem), it remains to be seen, according to TI, whether overseas bribery will be treated "as a crime, not as a business strategy."[36]

International organizations also have been increasing their anticorruption activities. Since 1996, the board of the World Bank has required that all commissions paid to agents be disclosed, giving the board the right to audit contractors and suppliers, and strengthened provisions for cancellation of bribe-tainted contracts and for debarment of violators from contracting. Antibribery amendments have been added to the Bank's loan conditions and procurement rules, and standard bidding documents were approved. The amendments require disclosure of commissions and gratuities paid or to be paid to agents relating to their bids or to contract execution on World Bank–financed contracts. The Bank will reject proposals for contract award or cancel the loan if the bidder or the borrower has engaged in fraud or corruption in the procurement or execution of the contract. Companies determined by the Bank to have engaged in corrupt or fraudulent practice will be blacklisted from participation in Bank-financed contracts, either indefinitely or for a stated period of time.

The International Monetary Fund has taken similar steps. The Council of Securities Regulators of the Americas (COSRA) adopted an antibribery resolution to ensure enforcement of and compliance with internal control and accurate books and records requirements. COSRA also agreed to facilitate closer cooperation among securities and banking regulators in investigations and in criminal prosecutions for bribery. In the WTO, the 1977 Government Procurement Agreement (GPA), while voluntary, assists in the anticorruption drive, although the signatories are predominantly industrialized countries, including the United States, Canada, the EU member states, Israel, Japan, Norway, the Republic of Korea, and Switzerland.

Interim Summary

1. Corruption in international business appears in many forms. Although bribery may be the first corrupt practice that comes to mind, it is by no means the only one. Smuggling, for instance, is a means of increasing profit margin even on legitimate goods by avoiding customs duties, tariffs, import quotas, and any other constraints on the movement of goods.

2. Violation of intellectual property rights, including piracy and counterfeiting of everything from luxury clothing to aircraft parts and pharmaceuticals, is becoming a critical problem, with countries such as China, Vietnam, and Russia the leading violators.

3. The FCPA, passed in the 1970s, made it illegal for U.S. companies to bribe foreign officials. However, this fight against corruption did not become truly global and did not see ratification in international treaties until recently.

COUNTRY BOX

MOTOROLA FACES (AND IS ACCUSED OF) CORRUPTION IN RUSSIA

On March 20, 2006, U.S.-based Motorola shipped 167,500 mobile phones worth around $17 million to Russia. The company filed all the required paperwork and obtained official approval on March 24. The phones arrived at Moscow's Sheremetyevo airport on March 29 and were promptly seized by agents of Russia's Interior Ministry. The Russian authorities first declared the phones counterfeit, then contraband, then a health hazard, and, finally, a smuggled good. Later on, the government also alleged that one model represented a health hazard to users as well as a risk to Russia's communication system. In April, the authorities announced that they had destroyed about 50,000 of the phones owing to a violation of safety standards, although the company suspects that many of those phones have found their way illicitly to store shelves. Motorola argued that any safety concerns were entirely unfounded and came from an unaccredited agency hired by the Russian authorities. Motorola has not been provided access to the data or procedure used in the testing process.

"It is a classic corruption case," said a member of Russia's Lower House, who commented on the case. "They confiscate goods from private companies and sell them for a profit." By "they" he was referring to law enforcement officials who have become themselves conduits in the illegal trade. In the meantime, a Russian company has sued Motorola for patent infringement, arguing that all of the company's phones were based on a patent registered in Russia, which this company owned. Asked why he did not file a civil suit against Motorola but chose to intervene with the prosecution instead, the head of this firm said that in Russia, "all judges cost three kopecks [a Russian money unit]."

SOURCE: Adapted from S. L. Myers. "Hang-up in Russia: 167,500 seized phones." *International Herald Tribune*, June 15, 2006, 2.

CHAPTER SUMMARY

1. The MNE Code of Conduct defines the contours of social responsibility in international business in realms such as disclosure, employment, the environment, and corruption.

2. MNEs increasingly take a proactive view of social responsibility, establishing internal control systems as well as seeking the assistance of NGOs.

3. Corruption is correlated with developing or emerging status of an economy, higher level and scope of government intervention, and certain cultural dimensions.

4. Corrupt practices in international business include smuggling, money laundering, piracy and counterfeiting, and bribe paying.

5. The Foreign Corrupt Practices Act (FCPA) penalizes U.S. firms and individuals who engage in corrupt practices. The OECD Convention, if enforced, will level the playing field for U.S. firms that until recently were the only ones to be legally deterred from corrupt practices by their home country.

Chapter Notes

1. K. A. Getz. "International codes of conduct: An analysis of ethical reasoning." *Journal of Business Ethics*, 9: pp. 567–577.

2. J. Coomson. "The digital divide becomes a digital dump." *Ghanian Chronicle*, February 8, 2006.

3. A. J. Heidenheimer, M. Johnston, and V. T. LeVine. *Political Corruption: A Handbook*. New Brunswick, NJ: Transaction Publishers, 1987.

4. R. Kahana. *Corruption in Israeli Society*. Jerusalem: Academon, 1984.

5. J. Macrae. "Underdevelopment and the economics of corruption: A game theory approach." *World Development*, 1982, *10*, 8: pp. 677–687.

6. "Black hole." *Economist*, August 28, 1999: p. 59. Citing a study by Friedrich Schneider.

7. "The termite hunter." *Economist*, October 16, 1999: p. 72.

8. O. Shenkar. *The Chinese Century*. Wharton School Publishing, 2006.

9. "Crime, corruption, and multinational business." *International Business*, July 1995.

10. G. R. Simpson. "Bribes taint contract bids overseas often." *Wall Street Journal*, February 23, 1999, A3.

11. J. Mason. "Petty corruption set to move up agenda for multinationals." *Financial Times*, January 11, 2001, 13.

12. "U.S. government report on transnational bribery." *National Export Strategy Report*, September 24, 1996.

13. A. Shleifer and R. Vishny. "Corruption." *Quarterly Journal of Economics*, Autumn 1993.

14. Transparency International Web site, September 1999. transparency.org.

15. J. R. Cohen, L. W. Pant, and D. J. Sharp. "A methodological note on cross-cultural accounting ethics research." *International Journal of Accounting*, 1996, *31*, 1: pp. 55–66.

16. S. J. Vittell, S. L. Nwachukwo, and J. H. Barnes. "The effects of culture on ethical decision-making: An application of Hofstede's typology." *Journal of Business Ethics*, 1993, 12: pp. 753–760.

17. B. W. Husted. "Wealth, culture and corruption." *Journal of International Business Studies*, 1999, *30*, 2: p. 340. A similar argument is made in terms of the lax internal control of Japanese corporations as in the infamous Sumitomo fiasco, in which one trader caused billions of dollars in losses while his colleagues by and large covered up his activities. See, for instance, S. Wudunn. "Big new loss makes Japan look inward." *New York Times*, June 17, 1996.

18. Asian Executive Poll. *Far Eastern Economic Review*, July 1, 1999: p. 31.

19. World Bank. Cited also in "Judge or be judged." *Economist*, July 29, 2006: p. 68.

20. "Pakistani stocks surge since military takeover amid hopes less corruption will lift economy." *Wall Street Journal*, February 24, 2000.

21. "Who will listen to Mr. Clean?" *Economist*, August 2, 1997: p. 52.

22. P. Mauro. "Corruption and growth." *Quarterly Journal of Economics*, 1995, *110*, 3: pp. 681–712.

23. G. P. Zachary. "Industrialized countries agree to adopt rules to curb bribery." *Wall Street Journal,* February 16, 1999, A18.

24. "Beyond the Kremlin's walls." *Economist,* May 20, 2000: p. 65.

25. "Now exhale." *Economist,* August 26, 2000: p. 19.

26. K. Gillespie. "Smuggling and the global firm." *Journal of International Management,* 2003, 9: pp. 317–333.

27. R. G. Matthews. "Evasive maneuvers: Steel smugglers find many ways to enter lucrative U.S. market." *Wall Street Journal,* November 1, 2001, A1.

28. WTO Statistics on Globalization, 2001.

29. E. Schmitt. "Chairman admits bank's 'lapse' in judgment in Russian laundering case." *New York Times,* September 23, 1999 (Internet edition).

30. John Zdanowicz. Cited in R. Block, "Policing trade to nab terrorists." *Wall Street Journal,* March 11–12, 2006, A4.

31. T. McGirk. "Chasing shadows." *Time,* June 11, 2001.

32. U.S. government. Report on Transnational Bribery: Fourth Annual National Export Strategy Report. September 24, 1996.

33. J. Tagliabue. "Kazakhstan is suspected of oil bribes in the millions." *New York Times,* July 28, 2000, A5.

34. *Business Week,* December 6, 1993.

35. "Hong Kong business reveals the price of graft." *South China Morning Post,* July 25, 1993.

36. H. Williamson and M. Peel. "Nations shamed over bribery." *Financial Times,* June 27, 2006, 4; Transparency International Web site. transparency.org.

INTERNATIONAL ENTREPRENEURSHIP

DO YOU KNOW?

1. Have you ever considered starting your own firm?

2. If yes, have you considered a foreign country as a location, a market, or perhaps a funding source for your start-up business? What country, and why?

3. What are the features of global start-ups, and how do they differ from those of established small businesses that have expanded internationally?

4. What makes a new international venture an attractive acquisition target for an MNE?

5. What countries are especially good at creating entrepreneurial firms, and what does this say about their competitive advantage?

OPENING CASE

Japanese Entrepreneurs in Hawaii

In recent years, Japanese entrepreneurs have been flocking to the U.S. 50th state, seeking an investment environment more conducive to entrepreneurship than the one they have at home. Entrepreneurship has traditionally not been very strong in Japan, whose start-up rate is the lowest among industrialized nations. Unlike the United States, where graduates of the best universities often contemplate starting their own business while still in college, most Japanese graduates aspire to join prestigious companies or leading government ministries. Many Japanese have become

entrepreneurs out of necessity, having faced limited employment and promotion prospects. Still, Japan boasts several entrepreneurial success stories, from electronics maker and media firm Sony after World War II to, more recently, Internet pioneer and investor in high-tech start-ups Softbank.

Japanese culture is high on collectivism and cherishes conformity, which does not create an atmosphere conducive to entrepreneurial activity, which breaks the rules. Starting a joint-stock company in Japan requires 10 million yen in up-front capital, the appointment of paid corporate officers, and expensive and time-consuming filing requirements. Capital is hard to come by: Japanese banks clamped down on lending during a decade-old period of economic stagnation, and venture capital is not widely available. It is no wonder that Japan's "actualization ratio"—the percentage of entrepreneurs who manage to get their businesses off the ground—is in the low 30s. To encourage entrepreneurship, Japan's Ministry of Economy, Trade, and Industry has made it possible since 2003 to establish a firm with a capitalization of one yen (less than one cent), although registration fees still amount to 250,000 yen; still, entrepreneurship rates remain very low. Hawaii, which is closer to Tokyo than to New York, represents an enticing opportunity to do business in a U.S. environment with no minimum capital requirements, in a state known for its quality of life. Most Japanese start-ups who register their firms in Hawaii still conduct their actual business from Japan. Digital Point, one of those firms, has developed another line of business—assisting other Japanese start-ups with their Hawaii registration.

SOURCES: Partially adapted from Sebastian Moffett. "Japan's entrepreneurs say Hawaii offers a better business climate." *Wall Street Journal,* October 15, 2002, A16; "One yen wonders." *Economist,* June 28, 2003: p. 66.

DEFINING INTERNATIONAL ENTREPRENEURSHIP

In recent years, interest in entrepreneurship has grown dramatically. Governments realized that entrepreneurial firms are a major source of economic growth, jobs, and competitive advantage and have been trying to form an environment conducive to their formation and prosperity. Large, established firms came to view entrepreneurial firms as a source of innovation to be tapped. Individuals discovered that entrepreneurship was a way to fulfill one's dreams and realize opportunities unavailable from traditional employment. The rising interest in entrepreneurship occurred in tandem with an accelerated globalization of the business environment (see Chapter 1) and a heightening awareness of the entrepreneurial, funding, and marketing opportunities available beyond national borders.

International entrepreneurship is defined as "the discovery, enactment, evaluation, and exploitation of opportunities—across national borders—to create future goods and services."[1] The study of international entrepreneurship consists of two thrusts, comparative and cross-border. Comparative entrepreneurship examines similarities and differences between countries on the level of entrepreneurial activity, the business environment (for example, the extent to which the regulatory environment is supportive of new business), and the motivations of would-be entrepreneurs. Cross-border entrepreneurship looks at entrepreneurial activities that leverage national differences in environment and resources—for instance, a U.S.-based venture capital (VC) fund identifying promising start-ups in India, or an Irish high-tech start-up seeking an alliance with a Chinese company to produce its newly developed technology for sale in the U.S. market.

Toward the conclusion of Chapter 4, on the MNE, we discussed the case of "born global" or "international new ventures," start-up firms that export their products or services to foreign markets even before they have sold a single product domestically. Oviatt and McDougall define the "born global" or "international new venture" (INV) as "a business organization that, from inception, seeks to derive significant competitive advantage from the use of resources and the sale of outputs in multiple countries."[2] Unlike other firms that typically undertake international expansion incrementally, the INV adopts an international mindset from day one. These firms are increasingly active on the international scene as exporters and foreign investors.

COMPARATIVE ENTREPRENEURSHIP

Comparative entrepreneurship examines the variation in entrepreneurship rates and patterns across nations; it also looks at the underlying reasons for the variation. Exhibit 20.1, taken from the Global Entrepreneurship Monitor, shows the rates of entrepreneurial activities in different countries. Nascent entrepreneurial activity, measured when resources are committed to a new venture, is led by Venezuela, Jamaica, and Thailand; in contrast, Hungary, Japan, and Sweden show very low rates. The percentage of new business owners, measured as the prevalence of new businesses that have paid salaries for more than three but less than 42 months, shows Thailand, New Zealand, and China at the top, with rates about double or more than that of the U.S. rate of 5.20%, while Hungary, Japan, and Belgium place at the bottom. Early-stage entrepreneurial activity, which combines the former two measures, places Venezuela at the top, followed by New Zealand and Jamaica, while Hungary, Japan, and Belgium are at the bottom. The rate for established business owners, who have been in business for more than 42 months, is highest in Thailand, China, and New Zealand. Finally, rates for overall business owners, a composite measure for nascent, new, and established businesses, are highest in Venezuela, New

Exhibit 20.1   Entrepreneurial Activity Across Countries

	NASCENT ENTREPRENEURIAL ACTIVITY	NEW BUSINESS OWNERS	EARLY-STAGE ENTREPRENEURIAL ACTIVITY (Nascent + New)*	ESTABLISHED BUSINESS OWNERS	OVERALL BUSINESS OWNERS (Nascent + New + Established)	NUMBER OF OBSERVATIONS
Argentina	5.90%	3.90%	9.50%	5.00%	14.10%	1,746
Australia	6.50%	4.70%	10.90%	9.60%	20.40%	2,002
Austria	3.00%	2.40%	5.30%	3.80%	8.80%	2,197
Belgium	2.90%	1.20%	3.90%	5.60%	9.40%	4,047
Brazil	3.30%	8.20%	11.30%	10.10%	21.40%	2,000
Canada	6.60%	3.60%	9.30%	7.40%	16.60%	5,519
Chile	6.00%	5.30%	11.10%	3.80%	14.40%	1,733
China	5.60%	9.40%	13.70%	13.20%	26.70%	2,109
Croatia	4.10%	2.50%	6.10%	3.70%	9.70%	1,555
Denmark	2.40%	2.40%	4.80%	4.40%	8.80%	1,968
Finland	3.10%	1.90%	5.00%	8.60%	13.50%	2,010
France	4.70%	0.70%	5.40%	2.30%	7.50%	1,603
Germany	3.10%	2.70%	5.40%	4.20%	9.40%	6,577
Greece	5.20%	1.60%	6.50%	10.50%	16.90%	2,000
Hungary	1.10%	0.80%	1.90%	2.00%	3.80%	2,878
Iceland	8.50%	2.70%	10.70%	7.30%	17.60%	2,002
Ireland	5.70%	4.70%	9.80%	8.10%	17.70%	1,541
Italy	2.90%	2.30%	4.90%	6.40%	11.30%	1,793
Jamaica	10.50%	6.70%	17.00%	9.50%	26.40%	2,031
Japan	1.10%	1.10%	2.20%	5.40%	7.40%	1,931
Latvia	4.20%	2.80%	6.60%	5.00%	11.50%	1,964
Mexico	4.60%	1.40%	5.90%	1.90%	7.60%	1,885
Netherlands	2.50%	1.90%	4.40%	5.70%	9.40%	2,706
New Zealand	9.40%	10.00%	17.60%	10.80%	28.20%	938
Norway	4.40%	5.20%	9.20%	7.30%	15.60%	1,562
Singapore	3.90%	3.70%	7.20%	4.70%	11.90%	3.876
Slovenia	3.00%	1.40%	4.40%	6.30%	10.10%	3,016
South Africa	3.60%	1.70%	5.10%	1.30%	6.00%	2,736
Spain	2.40%	3.40%	5.70%	7.70%	13.20%	18,953
Sweden	1.70%	2.50%	4.00%	6.30%	10.20%	1,717
Switzerland	2.60%	3.70%	6.10%	9.70%	15.40%	5,456
Thailand	9.70%	13.10%	20.70%	4.10%	34.80%	2,000
United Kingdom	3.40%	2.90%	6.20%	5.10%	11.20%	9,167
United States	8.80%	5.20%	12.40%	4.70%	16.20%	1,530
Venezuela	18.80%	7.50%	25.00%	8.60%	33.10%	1,856
Arerage	5.00%	3.90%	8.40%	6.60%	14.80%	108,604

*This measure corresponds to the old Total Enterpreneurial Activity (TEA) Index.

SOURCE: Global Entrepreneurship Monitor 2005 Executive Report, by Maria Minniti, with William D. Bygrave and Erkko Autio. © 2006. Reprinted with permission.

Zealand, and China. Please note that not all countries are included in this survey; for instance, Israel, which has one of the highest entrepreneurial rates in the world (see Country Box, p. 543), does not appear in the exhibit.

There are good reasons for the substantial differences in entrepreneurial rates shown in Exhibit 20.1. Countries vary on the environmental characteristics that are considered conducive to entrepreneurial activity, in entrepreneurial motivation (for instance, whether individuals choose to become entrepreneurs as a means toward self-fulfillment or riches, or rather out of necessity because substitutes for upward mobility are scarce), and in the objectives of their people (for example, do they seek to grow a firm or head for a quick exit via an IPO or an acquisition).

Exhibit 20.2 provides a framework for the study of comparative entrepreneurship. The first phase, discovery, covers the question of who discovers the entrepreneurial opportunities, which is mostly a function of the role of different social groups in the society and economy of a particular country. The evaluation phase looks at why some people will view those opportunities favorably while others do not. This is a function of the opportunity cost in their market, which, in turn, is a product of culture and institutions. Finally, the exploitation phase is a product of local ecology—namely, the availability and specificity of the resources available in a given national environment, which assists entrepreneurs in taking advantage of available opportunities.

Exhibit 20.2   National Context and Entrepreneurship

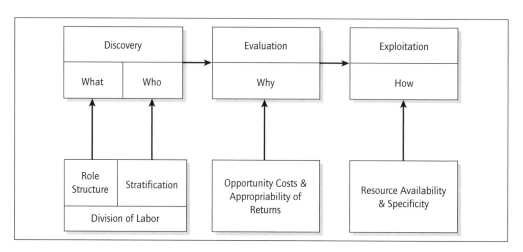

SOURCE: T. Baker, E. Gedajilovic, and M. Lubatkin. "A framework for comparing entrepreneurship processes across nations." *Journal of International Business Studies*, 2005, 36: pp. 492–504.

Entrepreneurial Motivation

There are different reasons why individuals decide to pursue entrepreneurial activities. Many would-be entrepreneurs are motivated by the prospect, for instance, of acquiring wealth or changing an industry (e.g., forming an online retailer that changes people's buying habits). However, many others decide to engage in entrepreneurship by necessity; for instance, they start their own business because they cannot find suitable and rewarding employment.

Exhibit 20.3 compares and ranks different countries on their ratio of opportunity to necessity for early-stage entrepreneurs. The exhibit shows very high ratios for Denmark and Iceland, compared with very low ratios for Brazil and China. In other words, while Danish entrepreneurs are likely to start a business as a way to tap opportunities for wealth and personal growth, Brazilians and Chinese are more likely to take the plunge as a way of overcoming limited employment opportunities. For example, many Chinese entrepreneurs in recent years have been laid-off employees from state-owned enterprises who had little prospect of securing employment in the private sector.

Exhibit 20.3   Opportunity-to-Necessity Ratio Among Early-Stage Entrepreneurs

	RATIO EARLY-STAGE OPP/ EARLY-STAGE NEC	RANK
Argentina	2.2	27
Australia	7.1	9
Austria	5.9	15
Belgium	8.7	6
Brazil	1.1	34
Canada	6.0	13
Chile	2.8	24
China	1.2	33
Croatia	0.9	35
Denmark	27.4	1
Finland	6.3	11
France	1.3	32
Germany	2.4	26
Greece	5.7	16
Hungary	1.5	30
Iceland	18.2	2
Ireland	4.2	22
Italy	5.0	19
Jamaica	1.7	28
Japan	4.2	23
Latvia	4.9	20
Mexico	4.7	21
Netherlands	11.5	4
New Zealand	12.7	3
Norway	9.8	5
Singapore	5.3	18
Slovenia	7.8	7
South Africa	1.5	31
Spain	5.9	14
Sweden	5.6	17
Switzerland	6.1	12
Thailand	2.8	25
United Kingdom	6.7	10
United States	7.2	8
Venezuela	1.6	29
Average	5.9	

SOURCE: Global Entrepreneurship Monitor 2005 Executive Report, by Maria Minniti, with William D. Bygrave and Erkko Autio. © 2006. Reprinted with permission.

Culture and Entrepreneurship

National culture is closely related to entrepreneurship levels and motivations.[3] Generally speaking, high individualism and low uncertainty avoidance encourage entrepreneurial activity, especially when opportunity based. The relationship between culture and entrepreneurship is not a simple one, however. One study has found that while high individualism was associated with generating variety through innovation and new ventures, the leveraging of resources via internal or external ties required high collectivism.[4] It is hence possible to have levels of individualism that are "too high."[5] The venture-creation decision was found to correlate with cultural dimensions in another study using a cognitive approach. Institutional features have also been found to correlate with entrepreneurial activities. In particular, normative aspects of the environment were found related to the inclination of individuals to engage in entrepreneurial activity, while the cognitive and regulatory aspects were related to their ability to raise funds from external investors.[6]

Three traits have been identified as related to entrepreneurial potential: internal locus of control, moderate risk-taking propensity, and high energy level.[7] Still, it is useful to remember that entrepreneurs share a lot in common across cultures: Baum et al. found that the difference between Israeli entrepreneurs and nonentrepreneurs was greater than the difference between Israeli and U.S. entrepreneurs.[8]

Funding New Ventures

One of the first challenges facing the entrepreneur is raising money for the new venture. Most entrepreneurs use informal financing sources, such as family, friends, and sometimes strangers and, of course, their own funds. Fewer solicit "classic" investment from professional venture capital firms, which can invest in seed, start-up, early-stage, or expansion-stage firms.[9] Exhibit 20.4 shows classic venture capital investment as percentage of GDP in various countries, with Sweden, South Africa, and Belgium at the top (around 0.3%), while Greece, China, and Japan are at the bottom with less than 0.05%. Remember that this is an overall rate across all types of ventures: When it comes to high-tech business, the United States leads the group of countries listed in Exhibit 20.4, although its numbers are still dwarfed by those of Israel (see Country Box).

Between 1991 and 2000, the amount of venture capital raised in the United States rose by a factor of 80, compared with a factor of 12 in Europe. European VC funds spend a higher proportion of their money on early-stage firms and are more likely to fund manufacturing ventures than their U.S. counterparts. European VC firms also make proportionally smaller investments in more companies. In the United States, institutional investment (e.g., investment funds) constitutes roughly two-thirds of VC investment versus about one-third in Europe.[10] U.S. funds, like their UK counterparts, have been found to require higher levels of return than those in France, Belgium, and the Netherlands. The U.S. and UK funds were also more involved in the management of enterprises and had a shorter holding period.[11] There are also substantial differences in the reliance of venture capital firms on various information sources. U.S. funds, like those in Hong Kong and Singapore, relied on accounting information culled from business plans, while those in India, for example, tended not to. Still, valuation methods did not vary much.[12]

When it comes to informal investment, the picture is quite different. Jamaica, Ireland, and China lead in the prevalence of informal investment with prevalence rates ranging from 6% to 9%. The United States is in the middle, with roughly 4.5% prevalence, while Japan and Brazil, at the bottom, have well below 1% (see Exhibit 20.5).

**Exhibit 20.4   Classic Venture Capital
                   Investment (Percentage of GDP)**

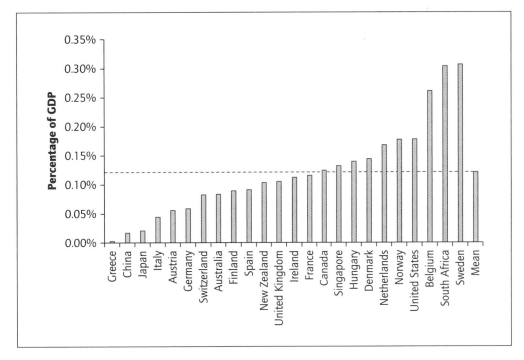

SOURCE: Global Entrepreneurship Monitor 2005 Executive Report, by Maria Minniti, with William D. Bygrave and Erkko
Autio. © 2006. Reprinted with permission.

Exhibit 20.5   Prevalence Rates of Informal Investors

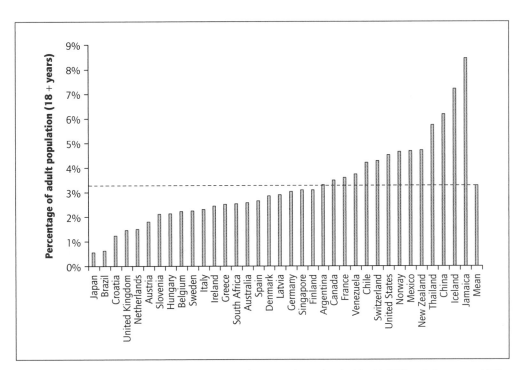

SOURCE: Global Entrepreneurship Monitor 2005 Executive Report, by Maria Minniti, with William D. Bygrave and Erkko
Autio. © 2006. Reprinted with permission.

Exhibit 20.6   Ease of Starting a Business

Easiest	Most Difficult
Canada	Mauritania
Australia	Saudi Arabia
United States	Togo
New Zealand	Haiti
Singapore	Eritrea
Hong Kong, China	Yemen
Puerto Rico	West Bank and Gaza
Romania	Congo, Dem. Rep.
United Kingdom	Chad
Jamaica	Angola

SOURCE: The World Bank, 2006.

There are additional factors that determine entrepreneurial level. For instance, being located within clusters of similar firms, suppliers, and customers makes it easier to establish new venture firms and makes their success more probable.[13] Together with funding opportunities and a supportive culture, a regulatory environment that makes starting a new business trouble free is of paramount importance to entrepreneurship. For instance, the minimum capital requirement to start a business in Syria is more than US$60,000, which represents more than 5,000% of the per capita income in the country, making it impossible for anyone but the wealthiest individuals to start a business. Similarly, in Haiti it takes more than 200 days to complete business registration versus five days in the United States and two days in Australia. Brazil requires 17 different procedures to complete business registration, while Canada requires only two and Finland three.[14] Exhibit 20.6 summarizes the ease of starting a business based on the procedures, time, cost, and paid-up minimum capital for starting a business.

Interim Summary

1. International entrepreneurship covers the similarities and differences in entrepreneurial environments, capabilities, and motivations across countries.

2. Entrepreneurship tends to be higher in cultures high on individualism and low on uncertainty avoidance.

3. Funding opportunities and regulatory environment are among the main factors that determine the level of entrepreneurship.

CROSS-BORDER ENTREPRENEURSHIP

Just as large MNEs leverage their access to multiple environments, each with its own comparative advantage, so can entrepreneurs leverage the resources, skills, and markets in various locations to tap broader opportunities and create synergies that would be impossible to create otherwise.

Accelerated globalization permits the distribution of diverse activities across borders—for example, the placement of financing in one location and sales and distribution in another. For instance, some European start-ups have chosen to do initial public offerings (IPOs) in the United States through American Depository Receipts (ADRs). This allows them not only to raise funds but also to enhance their legitimacy in the United States and better penetrate that market. Such IPOs have also been found to increase the legitimacy of start-ups in their home countries.[15]

MNEs, on their part, increasingly realize that entrepreneurial capabilities and opportunities reside not only in their home countries and are pursuing those opportunities. Since 1991, Intel has invested more than $4 billion in almost 1,000 firms in 27 countries. Of the $265 billion the company invested in start-ups in 2005, 67% went to companies based outside the United States, up from 37% in 2004. The corporate venture arm of Motorola has recently added an international office in China to the ones it already had in the United Kingdom and Israel, while Microsoft launched an international outreach initiative, including $1.7 billion for R&D and venture capital investment in India[16] and an additional R&D center in Israel.

Exhibit 20.7 presents a framework for the ingredients for the formation of INVs. These ventures internalize their activities to a much lesser extent than established MNEs, using alternatives such as strategic alliances. The entrepreneurial enterprises take advantage of technological advances that permit knowledge mobility to leverage, but to do so they must internationalize from the very beginning. To achieve that, in turn, they need to have founders and managers that possess international experience and "think globally."[17]

In the chapter on alliances, we have noted that such cooperative agreements are a good way to compensate for resource shortage, something that is typical of INVs. Yehezkel and her colleagues found that the number of Israeli medical technology start-ups that established alliances was three times greater than those who did not. Technology and R&D alliances were formed with both domestic and foreign partners at about the same ratio; however, for marketing alliances, the Israeli firms preferred a foreign over a local partner by a six-to-one ratio, not surprising for "born global" firms. Altogether, the companies that established alliances delivered lower returns than did those who did not, but did so at a lower risk level.[18]

Alliance formation was also found related to culture: One study found that firms from individualistic, uncertainty-tolerant cultures relied less on alliances in the technology area. Firms from high-masculinity cultures tended to avoid technological alliances altogether.[19] Li and Atuahene-Gima found that start-ups in China, a relatively collectivistic culture, relied on alliances for both product development and political networking.[20]

Internationalizing the Born Global Enterprise

As discussed in Chapter 4, small firms are much more likely to engage in exports than undertake foreign direct investment, a result mostly of their limited resources. The INV is no exception. Still, exporting requires good understanding of a target market as well as recognition and acceptance in that market. European firms that did an IPO in the United States increased exports into the U.S. market, especially when the listing was followed by a rising stock price.[21]

In a sense, entrepreneurial firms possess qualities that prepare them to face the vagaries of international markets. Being proactive (in other words, having a bias for action) and innovative, key features of the entrepreneurial firm, are

Exhibit 20.7   Creating Sustainable International New Ventures

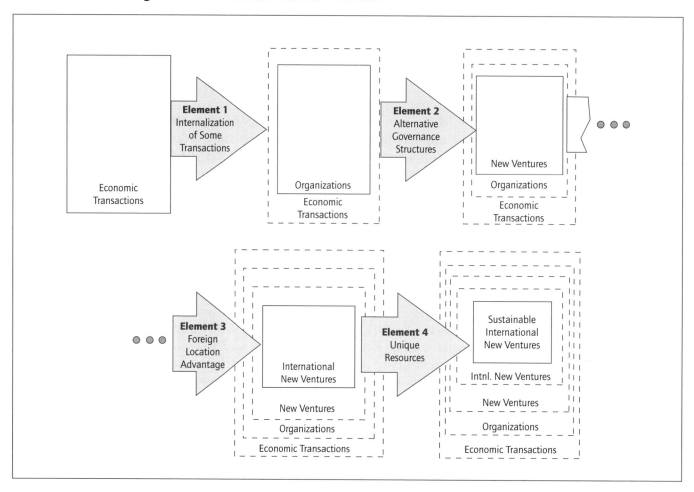

SOURCE: Benjamin M. Oviatt and Patricia P. McDougall. "Toward a theory of international new ventures." *Journal of International Business Studies,* 1994, *25,* 1: 45–64. Reprinted with permission of Palgrave Macmillan.

important assets when it comes to international activities, especially those that go beyond a firm's current operations.[22] As is the case for large MNEs, U.S.-based start-ups are less likely to reach into international markets because of the relatively large domestic market; they also benefit from ample financing and technological capabilities at home. Still, foreign markets are a draw for U.S. born-global firms as much as the United States is for foreign born-global firms. International experience of board members, larger size, and product rather than cost differentiation were found to be predictors of internationalization.[23] In particular, the international experience of the founders and managers was found to be a trigger of international expansion.[24] Such experience allows managers to identify entrepreneurial opportunities as well as have better knowledge about how to tap those opportunities. In contrast to large MNEs, new international ventures have not been found to be motivated by a desire to achieve economies of scale or cost reduction.[25]

INVs benefit from international expansion in a number of ways. By developing learning capabilities and tapping into various sources of innovation and different sets of comparative advantages, such ventures tend to extend their technological learning as well. A study by Zahra, Ireland, and Hitt found that ventures with greater country diversity increased their technological capability, but up to a point—those with the greatest diversity found their learning to go down, probably because of difficulty managing the learning process. Having high control modes, especially acquisitions, was also associated with better learning, as was having an environment with a culture similar to one's own.[26] This is not surprising. In general, knowledge of an international market was found to be an important determinant of international sales growth of entrepreneurial firms.[27]

Its advantages notwithstanding, internationalization also carries considerable risks for the entrepreneurial firm. Time, cost, and resource diversion are some of the main risks internationalization presents to new ventures.[28] Added risks appear when those firms enter risky and volatile markets. Some INVs are better able to handle those risks than are others. For example, Oviatt and McDougall found that innovative ventures with high growth objectives that served niche markets with low-cost, focused product lines were able to generate more international revenues and enter riskier markets than were other new venture firms.[29] For other firms, higher internationalization translated into a higher market share but not necessarily into superior return on investment.[30]

The INV that decides to export is still faced with entry-mode decisions (see Chapter 10)—for example, the choice between direct exporting and the use of distributors. A study by Burgel and Murray found that 68% of the technology start-ups in their sample had international sales, selling 38% of their turnover in foreign markets; 33% sold more in international markets than domestically. A majority of those firms chose to export through distributors even when they had more international experience, although having managers with personal experience in international markets has led to direct exportation.[31]

COUNTRY BOX

ISRAELI START-UPS IN THE GLOBAL MARKETPLACE

Israel has seen dramatic growth in technological start-ups, which started to take off in the early 1990s. By the year 2000, the country already shared second place with the United States (trailing Canada) in the prevalence of growth-oriented ventures; ranked second, following the United States in entrepreneurial motivation; and tied with Canada for third place in the entrepreneurial capacity of its population.[32] Today, there are more Israeli firms on the NASDAQ than those of any other non-U.S. domicile, and dozens of Israeli companies are also listed on European and, more recently, Asian exchanges, sometimes in addition to their home bourse of Tel-Aviv. Startup activity is concentrated in the high-technology sector, which accounts for the vast majority of Israel's industrial exports.

Well-equipped industrial parks provide the physical structure, as well as a supportive environment, for high-tech entrepreneurial activity. Many of those parks provide incubators that accompany the entrepreneur from idea to market and provide a network of expert advice. Private parks, such as the Weizmann Biotechnology and Genetics Park in Nes Tziona,[33] provide infrastructure in specialized areas. Israel's more than 100 venture capital (VC) funds provide critical launch capital, as do many foreign MNEs. The Global Entrepreneurship Monitor shows classic venture capital investment in Israel at 1.25% of GDP, or about seven times (!) the U.S. level. Many projects are also financed by the Chief Scientist Office of the Ministry of Industry and Trade.

At the heart of Israel's success is its human resource pool, which boasts the highest ratio of engineers and scientists in the world. The pool has been augmented by immigrants from the former Soviet Union, 40% of whom hold academic degrees,[34] as well as by Israeli Silicon Valley veterans. Today, 24% of Israeli's workforce and 35% of the 25 to 64 age-group hold university degrees, ranking the nation third in the world after the United States and the Netherlands. Trade agreements with the United States, the EU, and EFTA have increased the exposure of Israelis to the outside world. Social norms now stress individualism, materialism, and independence. In tandem, entrepreneurship is increasingly accepted as a driving force in personal lives and in market development.

CHAPTER SUMMARY

1. International entrepreneurship consists of both differences across countries on entrepreneurial levels and features and cross-national entrepreneurial activities.

2. Entrepreneurial levels are determined by economic development, cultural dispositions, and the regulatory environment, among other factors.

3. In a global/knowledge economy, entrepreneurial capabilities are increasingly a determinant of competitive advantage.

4. International new ventures display rapid internationalization often, but not always, across multiple national markets.

5. International entrepreneurship still has a long way to go, as entrepreneurs and executives are only beginning to tap the resources and opportunities available in other markets.

Chapter Notes

1. Benjamin M. Oviatt and Patricia P. McDougall. "Defining international entrepreneurship and modeling the speed of internationalization." *Entrepreneurship Theory and Practice,* September 2005: pp. 537–553.

2. Benjamin M. Oviatt and Patricia P. McDougall. "Toward a theory of international new ventures." *Journal of International Business Studies,* 1994, *25,* 1: pp. 45–64.

3. Ronald K. Mitchell, Brock Smith, Kristie W. Seawright, and Eric A. Morse. "Cross-cultural cognitions and the venture creation decision." *Academy of Management Journal,* 2000, *43,* 5: pp. 974–993.

4. James H. Tiessen. "Individualism, collectivism, and entrepreneurship: A framework for international comparative research." *Journal of Business Venturing,* 1997, 12: pp. 367–384.

5. Michael H. Morris, Duane L. Davis, and Jeffrey W. Allen. "Fostering corporate entrepreneurship: Cross-cultural comparisons of the importance of individualism versus collectivism." *Journal of International Business Studies,* 1994, 5: pp. 67–89.

6. Lowell W. Busenitz, Carolina Gomez, and Jennifer W. Spencer. "Country institutional profiles: Unlocking entrepreneurial phenomena." *Academy of Management Journal,* 2000, *43,* 5: pp. 994–1003.

7. Anisya S. Thomas and Stephen L. Mueller. "A case for comparative entrepreneurship: Assessing the relevance of culture." *Journal of International Business Studies,* 2000, *31,* 2: pp. 287–301.

8. J. R. Baum, J. D. Olian, M. Erez, E. R. Schnell, K. G. Smith, H. P. Sims, J. S. Scully, and K. A. Smith. "Nationality and work role interactions: A cultural contrast of Israeli and U.S. entrepreneurs." *Journal of Business Venturing,* 1993, 8: pp. 499–512.

9. Global Entrepreneurship Monitor, 2005: p. 49.

10. Laura Bottazzi and Marco Da Rin. "Venture capital in Europe and the financing of innovative companies." *Economic Policy,* April 2002.

11. Sophie Manigart, Koen De Waele, Mike Wright, Ken Robbie, Phillipe Desbrieres, Harry J. Sapienza, and Amy Beekman. "Determinants of required return in venture capital investments: A five country study." *Journal of Business Venturing,* 2002, 17: pp. 291–312.

12. Anday Lockett, Mike Wright, Harry Sapienza, and Sarika Pruthi. "Venture capital investors, valuation and information: A comparative study of the U.S., Hong Kong, India and Singapore." *Venture Capital,* 2002, *4,* 2: pp. 237–252.

13. Harry Matlay and Jay Mitra. "Learning, innovation and globalization: The competitive advantage of collaborative entrepreneurship." In Leo-Paul Dana (ed.), *Handbook of International Entrepreneurship.* Cheltenham, UK: Edward Elgar, 2006.

14. The World Bank. *Doing Business in 2006.*

15. Boyd D. Cohen. "Internationalizing European IPOs in the United States." In Leo-Paul Dana (ed.), *Handbook of International Entrepreneurship.* London: Edward Elgar, 2006.

16. Jonathan Shieber. "Intel increases its foreign investments." *Wall Street Journal,* February 2, 2006, B3.

17. Benjamin M. Oviatt and Patricia P. McDougall. "Toward a theory of international joint ventures." *Journal of International Business Studies,* 1994, *25,* 1: pp. 45–64.

18. Orly Yeheskel, Oded Shenkar, Avi Feigenbaum, and Ezra Cohen. "Cooperative wealth creation: Strategic alliances in Israeli medical-technology ventures." *Academy of Management Executive,* 2001, *15,* 1: pp. 16–25.

19. Kevin H. Steensma, Louis Marino, K. Mark Weaver, and Pat H. Dickson. "The influence of national culture on the formation of technology alliances by entrepreneurial firms." *Academy of Management Journal,* 2001, *43,* 5: pp. 951–973.

20. Haiyang Li and Kwaku Atuahene-Gima. "Product innovation strategy and the performance of new technology ventures in China." *Academy of Management Journal,* 2001, *44,* 5: pp. 1123–1134.

21. Boyd D. Cohen. "Internationalizing European IPOs in the United States." In Leo-Paul Dana (ed.), *Handbook of International Entrepreneurship.* Cheltenham, UK: Edward Elgar, 2006.

22. Dirk De Clercq, Harry J. Sapienza, and Hans Crijns. "The internationalization of small and medium-sized firms." *Small Business Economics,* 2005, 24: pp. 408–119.

23. James M. Bloodgood, Harry J. Sapienza, and James G. Almeida. "The internationalization of new high-potential U.S. ventures: Antecedents and outcomes." *Entrepreneurship Theory and Practice,* Summer 1996: pp. 61–76.

24. Patricia P. McDougall, Benjamin M. Oviatt, and Rodney C. Shrader. "A comparison of international and domestic new ventures." *Journal of International Entrepreneurship,* 1: pp. 59–82.

25. Candida G. Brush. *International Entrepreneurship.* New York: Garland Publishing, 1995.

26. Shaker A. Zahra, R. Duane Ireland, and Michael A. Hitt. "International expansion by new venture firms: International diversity, mode of market entry, technological learning, and performance." *Academy of Management Journal,* 2000, *43,* 5: pp. 925–950.

27. Erkko Autio, Harry J. Sapienza, and James G. Almeida. "Effects of age at entry, knowledge intensity, and imitability on international growth." *Academy of Management Journal,* 2000, *43,* 5: pp. 909–924.

28. Harry J. Sapienza, Erkko Autio, and Shaker Zahra. "Effects of internationalization on young firms' prospects for survival and growth." *Academy of Management Best Papers Proceedings,* 2003: pp. G1–G7.

29. Benjamin M. Oviatt and Patricia P. McDougall. "How new ventures exploit trade-offs among international risk factors: Lessons for the accelerated internationalization of the 21st century." *Academy of Management Journal,* 2000, *43,* 6: pp. 1227–1247.

30. Benjamin M. Oviatt and Patricia P. McDougall. "New venture internationalization, strategic change, and performance: A follow-up study." *Journal of Business Venturing,* 1996, 11: pp. 23–40.

31. Oliver Burgel and Gordon C. Murray. "The international market entry choices of start-up companies in high technology industries." *Journal of International Marketing,* 2000, *8,* 2: pp. 33–62.

32. M. Lerner and Y. Avrahami. *Global Entrepreneurship Monitor—1999 Israel Executive Report.* 2000.

33. State of Israel Export Institute Report. "Biotechnolgoy in Israel." December 1, 2000: p. 18.

34. State of Israel Investment Promotion Center Report. 2000.

GLOSSARY

A

Absolute PPP (purchasing power parity) A theory that the exchange rate is determined by the relative prices of similar baskets of goods or services.

Absorptive capability A firm's ability to acquire, assimilate, integrate, and exploit knowledge and skills that are transferred from another firm.

Active or aggressive reciprocity The withdrawal of previous commitments and concessions from, or the undertaking of retaliatory measures against, a country until it reduces or eliminates its barriers to trade.

Active role A subsidiary role in which many activities are located locally but carried out in close coordination with other subsidiaries.

Adaptive system A system that imitates local HRM (human resources management) practices.

Advance pricing agreement An agreement between the tax authority and the taxpayer on the transfer pricing methodology to be applied to any apportionment or location of income, deductions, credits, or allowances between two or more members within an organization.

Affinity How closely aligned nations are, based on both history and political reality.

American depository receipts (ADRs) A means of trading foreign shares in the United States. Negotiable certificates issued by a U.S. bank in the United States to represent the underlying shares of a foreign stock held in trust in a foreign custodian bank.

Animosity How nations are closely estranged, based on both history and political reality.

Appreciation An increase in the foreign exchange value of a floating currency.

Arbitrage Temporary discrepancies that provide profit opportunities for simultaneously buying a currency in one market (at a lower price) while selling it in another (at a higher price).

Arm's-length principle Principle stating that the transfer price struck between related companies should be the same as that negotiated between two independent entities acting in an open and unrestricted market.

Autonomous role A subsidiary role in which the subsidiary performs most activities of the value chain independently of headquarters.

Auto-stereotypes How we see ourselves as a group and as distinguished from others.

B

Back-to-back L/C (letter of credit) A letter of credit in which the exporter, as beneficiary of the first L/C (letter of credit), offers its credit as security to finance the opening of a second credit in favor of the exporter's own supplier of the goods needed for shipment under the first or original credit from the advising bank.

Balance of merchandise trade The value of a country's exports of goods minus the value of the country's imports of goods.

Balance-of-payments An accounting statement that reports the country's international performance in trading with other nations and the volume of capital flowing in and out of the country.

Balance of trade Exports minus imports of goods and services.

Bank guarantee A financial instrument that guarantees a specified sum of payment in the event of nonperformance by an exporter or by a foreign importer in the event of a payment default for goods purchased from a foreign supplier.

Bank line of credit The sum of money allocated to an exporter by a bank or banks that the exporter can draw from to finance its export business.

Banker's acceptance (BA) A time draft drawn on and accepted by banks with one branch in financing and the other in investment.

Barter The direct and simultaneous exchange of goods between two parties without a cash transaction.

Bid The exchange rate in one currency at which a dealer (e.g., a bank) will buy another currency.

Bid–ask spread The compensation for transaction cost for the dealer.

Bill of lading (B/L) A document issued by a shipping company or its agent as evidence of a contract for shipping the merchandise that lists the goods received for shipment.

Black hole subsidiaries Subsidiaries that operate in important markets where they barely make a dent, but their strong local presence is essential for maintaining global position.

Black markets Illegal markets in foreign exchange that exist as a response to business or private demand for foreign exchange.

Boycott The blanket prohibition on importation of all or some goods and services from a designated country.

Branch office A foreign entity in a host country in which it is not incorporated but exists as an office of extension of the parent and is legally constituted as a branch.

Branding The process of creating and supporting positive perceptions associated with a product or service. In global markets, branding is especially complex given varying demand and environmental characteristics.

Bribery Payments to government officials, politicians, and political parties made in order to gain favors that are otherwise not allowed by law.

Build-operate-transfer (BOT) An investment in which a foreign investor assumes responsibility for the design and construction of an entire operation and, upon completion of the project, turns the project over to the purchaser and hands over its total management to local personnel whom it has trained.

Bulldogs Foreign bonds sold in the United Kingdom.

Business-to-business (B2B) Interfirm transactions, including government procurement, that drives 90% of the projected growth in global e-commerce.

Business-to-customer (B2C) Transactions between firms and individuals purchasing goods or services over the Internet (e.g., ordering a book online from a vendor).

Buy-local campaigns Efforts to curb all imports regardless of the country of origin.

Buyback A compensation arrangement through which a firm provides a local company with inputs for manufacturing products to be sold in international markets and agrees to take a certain percentage of the output produced by the local firm as partial payment for the contract.

Buyer credit Financing that exists in which one or more financial institutions in an exporter's country extend credit to a foreign customer of the exporter.

C

Call option The purchase of a stated number of units of the underlying foreign currency at a specific price per unit during a specific period of time.

Capability building An MNE's capacity to learn and develop new capabilities.

Capability exploitation An MNE's capacity to extract economic returns from current resources.

Capital account In the balance of payments, records private and public investment or lending activities and is divided into portfolio and foreign direct investments.

Centers of excellence Foreign units equipped with the best practice of managing knowledge (e.g., GM small diesel center of excellence in Japan).

Channel decisions The length (number of levels or intermediaries employed in the distribution process) and width (number of firms in each level) of the channel used in linking manufacturers to customers.

Civil law Legal system that relies almost exclusively on the legal code and is applied universally.

Clean L/C (letter of credit) An L/C that does not require the presentation of documents.

Clearing House Interbank Payments System (CHIPS) Computerized system that provides for calculation of new balances owed by any one bank to another and for payment by 6 P.M. that same day in Federal Reserve Bank of New York funds.

Cluster When suppliers, manufacturers, and even distributors are located near each other or concentrated in the same area (e.g., Silicon Valley in California for the semiconductor and software industries).

Cluster format A format in which a business reports to a cluster headquarters that is accountable to corporate headquarters for business results.

Co-management arrangement A loosely structured alliance in which cross-national partners collaborate in training, production management, information systems development, and value-chain integration.

Co-marketing arrangement An arrangement that provides a platform in which each party can reach a larger pool of international consumers.

Commitment The extent to which each party will constantly and continuously contribute its resources and skills to joint operations and be dedicated to enhancing joint payoff.

Commodity cartel Group of producing countries that wish to protect themselves from the wild fluctuations that often occur in the prices of certain commodities traded internationally.

Common-law system Legal system, based on tradition, precedent, and custom, in which the independent judiciary relies on case precedents.

Common market A customs union that allows not only free trade of products and services but also free mobility of production factors across national member borders.

Comparative advantage The theory that a country should specialize in a good in which the opportunity cost for producing that good is lower at home than in other countries.

Comparative production cost A cost that depends on the commodity's production process (especially the state of technology) and on the prices of production factors.

Concentration ratio The proportion of FDI outward stock held by the top 10 investor countries.

Confirmed L/C (letter of credit) A letter of credit issued by one bank and confirmed by another, obligating both banks to honor any drafts drawn in compliance.

Confucian dynamism A cultural dimension renamed "long-term orientation" that is anchored in the Confucian value system.

Conglomerate FDI The activity of FDI abroad to manufacture products not manufactured by the parent company at home.

Contributor subsidiaries Subsidiaries that operate in small or strategically less important markets but have distinctive strategies.

Control A direct intervention into the operations of subsidiaries to ensure conformity with organizational goals.

Conversion The exchange of one currency for another.

Cooperative culture The extent to which each party's corporate culture is compatible, thus leading to a more cooperative atmosphere during GSA operations.

Cooperative joint venture A contractual agreement whereby profits and responsibilities are assigned to each party according to stipulations in a contract.

Cooperative (or contractual) joint venture A collaborative agreement whereby profits and other responsibilities are assigned to each party according to a contract.

Coordination Linking different task units within the organization into a unified system.

Co-production (co-service) agreement An agreement in which each partner is responsible for manufacturing a particular part of the product.

Core competence Skills within a firm that competitors cannot easily match or imitate.

Corporate guarantee The act of one company undertaking to pay if the principal debtor does not pay a matured debt obligation to a creditor.

Corporate socialization The processes through which the values and norms of subsidiary managers are aligned with those of the parent corporation. Such socialization is a powerful mechanism for building identification with and commitment to the organization as a whole.

Corruption   An exchange between two partners (the "demander" and the "supplier") that (a) has an influence on the allocation of resources either immediately or in the future, and (b) involves the use or abuse of public or collective responsibility for private ends.

Corruption Perception Index (CPI)   A broad measure of corruption that is calculated from multiple survey responses.

Counterfeiting   The attempt to pass off a copied product as an original, such as producing and selling a fake Gucci bag or a Rolex watch.

Counterpurchase   A reciprocal buying agreement whereby one firm sells its products to another at one point in time and is compensated in the form of the other's products at some future time.

Countertrade   A form of trade in which the seller and the buyer from different countries exchange merchandise without substantial cash involvement.

Country competitiveness   The extent to which a country is capable of generating more wealth than its competitors do in world markets.

Country-of-origin effect   The influence of the country of manufacturing's image on the buying decision.

Crawling peg   A system for revising the exchange rate, involving establishing a par value around which the rate can vary up to a given percentage.

Cross rate   The exchange rate between two infrequently traded currencies, calculated through a widely traded third currency.

Cultural distance   The extent to which cultures differ from each other.

Cultural or business etiquette   The manners and behavior that are expected in a given situation, be it business negotiations, a supervisor–subordinate discussion, or in situations outside the workplace and after business hours.

Culture   The art and other manifestations of human intellectual achievement regarded collectively; the customs, civilization, and achievement of a particular time or people; the way of life of a particular society or group.

Culture clustering   The grouping of cultures based on relative similarity.

Currency valuation   The extent to which a country's home currency is valued or priced properly to reflect the situation of market supply and demand pertaining to this currency.

Current account   The record of the export or import of goods and services.

Current/noncurrent method (of accounting)   Current assets and liabilities are translated at the current rate, and noncurrent assets and liabilities at the applicable noncurrent rates.

Current rate   The exchange rate in effect at the relevant financial statement date.

Current rate method (of accounting)   All assets and liabilities, both monetary and nonmonetary, are translated at the current or closing rate.

Customer-to-customer (C2C)   Individual transactions online (e.g., online an auction).

Customs union Similar to a free trade area except that member nations must conduct and pursue common external commercial relations such as common tariff policies on imports from nonmember nations.

D

Defensive   A motive that protects and holds a firm's market power or competitive position threatened by domestic rivalry or changes in government policies.

Depreciation   A reduction in the foreign exchange value of a floating currency.

Devaluation   A reduction in the foreign exchange value of a currency that is pegged to another currency.

Developing/emerging nation multinational enterprise (DMNE)   A multinational enterprise from a developing or emerging economy.

Digital divide   The difference in Internet hosts between developed countries and developing countries; developed countries have more Internet penetration.

Direct marketing   Direct sales to customers via individual agents who typically make a commission not only on their sales but also on the sales of other agents they have recruited.

Direct quote   A home currency price of a unit of foreign currency.

Discount When the forward exchange rate is below the current spot rate.

Discounting A short-term financing technique by which a local bank discounts a firm's trade bills.

Documentary collection A payment mechanism that allows exporters to retain ownership of the goods until they receive payment or are reasonably certain that they will receive it.

Documentary (L/C) In a commercial transaction, the exporter must submit any necessary invoices and other documents such as the customs invoice, certificate of commodity inspection, packing list, and certificate of country of origin.

Documents against acceptance (D/A) The act of the exporter's bank to hold the title documents until the importer accepts the obligation to pay the draft.

Documents against payment (D/P) The act of the exporter's agent (bank) to hold the title documents until the importer pays the draft.

Double-entry bookkeeping System in which every debit or credit in the account is represented as a credit or debit somewhere else.

Dumping The sale of imported goods either at prices below what a company charges in its home market or at prices below cost.

Dynamic capabilities A firm's ability to diffuse, deploy, utilize, and rebuild firm-specific resources to attain a sustained competitive advantage.

E

E-business Use of the Internet to conduct transactions of buying, selling, and distribution of goods or services.

E-business climate The institutional and regulatory frameworks that facilitate or hinder e-commerce.

E-commerce The conduct of transactions to buy, sell, distribute, or deliver goods and services over the Internet.

E-commerce readiness An index comprising the three criteria of connectivity, information security, and e-business climate, plus e-leadership (the extent to which e-commerce is a national priority) and human capital (the availability of human resources to support e-commerce).

E-leadership The extent to which e-commerce is a national priority.

E-readiness The degree to which nations are prepared for e-commerce.

Early mover Firms that enter a market shortly after the first mover.

Economic exposure Foreign exchange risk, measured in the change in present value of the firm, determined by changes in the future operating cash flows of the firm caused by unexpected changes in exchange rates and macroeconomic factors.

Economic integration The abolition of trade barriers or impediments between national economies, such as within the EU.

Economic motives The intentions of a company to benefit from the differences in costs of labor, natural resources, and capital, as well as the differences in regulatory treatments, such as taxation between domestic and foreign countries.

Economic soundness The extent to which an economy has been equipped with all the economic prerequisites for sustained economic growth.

Economy of scale The reduction of manufacturing cost per unit as a result of increased production quantity during a given period.

Effective tax rate The statutory corporate rate, adjusted for all other taxes and subsidies affecting an MNE's taxable income; determines the company's net return from its revenues.

Efficiency-seeking FDI An MNE attempts to rationalize the structure of established resource-based or marketing-seeking investment in such a way that the firm can gain from the common governance of geographically dispersed activities.

Embargo The prohibition on exportation to a designated country.

EMS (European Monetary System) A system designed to create a zone of stability in Europe.

Entrepreneurs A special group of businesspeople taking risks in the development of new products, new markets, or new technologies.

Entry mode The manner in which a firm chooses to enter a foreign market through FDI.

Environmental dynamics The diversity that exists between countries with regard to their currency, inflation and interest rates, accounting practices, cultures, social customs, business practices, laws, government regulations, and political stability.

Equity joint venture (EJV) A legally and economically separate organizational entity created by two or more parent organizations that collectively invest financial as well as other resources to pursue certain objectives.

Escape clauses Special allowances permitted by the WTO (World Trade Organization) to safeguard infant industries or nourish economic growth for newly admitted developing countries.

Ethical behavior Not only following the rule of law but also attending to the values, norms and concerns of the home and host environments.

Ethnocentric The belief that one's own ethnic group or culture is superior; showing disregard for other countries.

Ethnocentric staffing The act of selecting PCNs (parent-country nations) regardless of location.

Euro The currency of European Union countries.

Eurobond A bond that is underwritten by an international syndicate of banks and other securities firms and is sold exclusively in countries other than the country in whose currency the issue is denominated (e.g., a bond issued by a Japanese firm residing in Tokyo, denominated in Japanese yen but sold to investors in Europe and the United States).

Eurocurrency markets Countries not using the denomination currency (e.g., a Japanese firm may obtain yen loans from banks in the United States and Europe).

Eurodollars U.S. dollar deposits in non-U.S. banks.

Euronote market The collective term used to describe short- to medium-term debt instruments sourced in the Eurocurrency market.

European Central Bank (ECB) The central bank in the euro zone based in Frankfurt; sets interest rates for the euro zone.

Expatriate trainee An individual placed abroad for training purposes as part of initiation into an MNE (multinational enterprise).

Export controls Governmental limits on the type of products that can be exported to other countries, particularly those considered enemy nations or security risks.

Export–import bank financing A program whose primary function is to give U.S. exporters the necessary financial backing to compete in other countries.

Export intermediaries Third parties that specialize in facilitating imports and exports.

Export management company (EMC) An intermediary that acts as its client's export marketing department.

Exportive system A system that replicates the HRM (human resources management) system in the home country and other affiliates.

Exposed net asset position The excess of assets, which are measured or denominated in foreign currency and translated at the current rate, over liabilities, which are measured or denominated in foreign currency and translated at the current rate.

Externality The extent to which the actions of one agent directly affect the environment of another agent.

F

Factor-intensity reversal A change that occurs when the relative prices of labor and capital change over time, which affects the relative mix of capital and labor in the production process of a commodity from being capital-intensive to labor-intensive (or vice versa).

Factoring houses Institutions that provide financing, perform credit investigations, guarantee commercial and political risks, assume collection responsibilities, and finance accounts receivable for small to medium-sized importers.

Familiarity theory Theory that supports the concept that a firm would rather invest in host countries that are relatively close to it culturally and is likely to be more successful in such relatively familiar environments.

Financial capabilities Qualities of a global strategic alliance partner in risk management, exposure hedging, financing, and cash flow management.

Financial risk The variability of the rate of return on an asset over time.

First mover First MNE to enter a specific foreign market.

First to file A patent system in which the first to file a patent in a given country is awarded the patent without the need to prove it is the inventor.

First to invent A patent system in which patent protection is granted to the person or entity who first invented the technology or product.

Fixed or managed exchange rate system A system in which a country regulates the rate at which the local currency is exchanged for other currencies.

Fixed-rate system A system under which governments buy or sell their currencies in the foreign-exchange market whenever their exchange rates threaten to deviate from their stated par values.

Floating exchange rate system (or flexible exchange rate system) A system in which a rate of currency exchange is determined by the laws of supply and demand rather than government intervention.

Flow of FDI (foreign direct investment) The amount of FDI undertaken over a given time period (e.g., a year).

Foreign bond A bond that is underwritten by a syndicate composed of members from a single country, sold principally within that country, and denominated in the currency of that country (e.g., a Japanese firm issues corporate bonds in U.S. dollars and sells to U.S. investors by U.S. banks).

Foreign Corrupt Practices Act (FCPA) The act that criminalized the payment of bribes and other forms of special payment to foreign officials for the purpose of securing or retaining a deal (liability exists whether the deal has been consummated or not). It also required issuers of securities to meet accounting, record-keeping, and corporate control standards.

Foreign currency transaction Transactions (e.g., sales or purchases of goods or services or loans payable or receivable) whose terms are stated in a currency other than the entity's functional currency.

Foreign currency translation The process of expressing amounts denominated or measured in one currency in terms of another currency by use of the exchange rate between the two currencies.

Foreign direct investment (FDI) Direct investment in real or physical assets such as factories and facilities in a foreign country.

Foreign exchange The money of a foreign country, including foreign currency bank balances, banknotes, checks, and drafts.

Foreign exchange exposure The sensitivity of changes in the real domestic-currency value of assets, liabilities, or operating incomes to unanticipated changes in exchange rates.

Foreign exchange market A market where foreign currencies are bought and sold.

Foreign exchange rate The price of one currency expressed in terms of another currency.

Foreign exchange risk The variance of the domestic-currency value of assets, liabilities, or operating income that is attributable to unanticipated changes in exchange rates.

Foreign exchange transaction An agreement between a buyer and seller that a certain amount of one currency be delivered at a specified rate in exchange for some other currency.

Foreign portfolio investment (FPI) Investment by individuals, firms, or public bodies (e.g., governments or nonprofit organizations) in foreign financial instruments such as government bonds, corporate bonds, mutual funds, and foreign stocks.

Foreign sales corporations Offshore corporations that market the products or services of firms in foreign countries.

Foreign subsidiaries Overseas units or entities created as a result of FDI.

Forfaiting A transaction in which an exporter transfers responsibility of commercial and political risks for the collection of a trade-related debt to a forfaiter (often a financial institution) and in turn receives immediate cash after the deduction of its interest charge (the discount).

Forward-forward swap Swap that involves two forward transactions.

Forward rate The exchange rate for a transaction that requires delivery of foreign exchange at specified future date.

Forward transaction Transaction between a bank and a customer (company, bank) calling for delivery, at a fixed future date, of a specified amount of foreign exchange at the fixed forward exchange rate.

Free trade area Country combination in which the member nations remove all trade barriers between themselves but retain their freedom concerning policy making vis-à-vis nonmember countries.

Functional currency The primary currency in which an entity conducts its operation and generates and expends cash. It is usually the currency of the country in which the entity is located and the currency in which the books of record are maintained.

G

Geocentric staffing The act of recruiting the best managers worldwide regardless of nationality.

Global e-commerce The conduct of electronic commerce, whether B2B, B2C, or C2C, across national boundaries (e.g., a U.S. customer purchasing pharmaceuticals from a Canadian site).

Global firm A firm that integrates operations in international subsidiaries.

Global innovator A generic subsidiary role with high outflow and low inflow.

Global integration The coordination of activities across countries in an attempt to build efficient operation networks and take maximum advantage of internalized synergies and similarities across locations.

Global products Products that enjoy worldwide recognition and are relatively unaltered in terms of brand and appearance when sold abroad.

Global sourcing The procurement of production or service inputs and components in international markets. Global sourcing provides the MNE (multinational enterprise) with the opportunity to leverage its scale and competitive advantage in spotting procurement opportunities around the globe for use in its various divisions and locations.

Global strategic alliances (GSAs) Cross-border partnerships between two or more firms from different countries with an attempt to pursue mutual interests through sharing their resources and capabilities.

Global strategy Relative standardization across national markets, allowing strategic and operational control.

Global supply chain Activities in both logistics and operations, such as sourcing, procurement, order processing, manufacturing, warehousing, inventory control, servicing and warranty, customs clearing, wholesaling, and distribution.

Globalization of markets Trend toward one huge global market through the increasing volume and variety of cross-border transactions in goods, services, capital, information, and labor force.

Globalization of operations The standardization, in a marketing sense, of products (or services), brands, marketing, advertising, and the supply chain across countries and regions.

Globalization infrastructure Institutional frameworks and market efficiency that support fair and transparent transactions of products or services and streamline flows of commodities, capital, labor, knowledge, and information.

Globalizing R&D The process of distributing and operating R&D (research and development) laboratories in different countries, under a system coordinated and integrated by the company's headquarters, in order to leverage the technical resources of each facility to further the company's overall technological capabilities and competitive advantages.

Goal compatibility The congruence of strategic goals set for an alliance between parent firms.

Greenfield investment An initial establishment of fully owned new facilities and operations by the company without outside investment.

Group of Seven (G7) A group of countries consisting of the United States, Japan, West Germany, France, Britain, Canada, and Italy who meet periodically to make economic decisions.

H

Hard currency A currency that is expected to revalue or appreciate relative to major currencies.

Harmonization The process of increasing the compatibility of accounting practices by setting limits on how much they can vary.

Heckscher-Ohlin law of factor price equalization The

international equalization of the prices of production factors under free trade.

Heckscher-Ohlin theorem Theorem that states that a country exports goods that make intensive use of locally abundant factors of production. Meanwhile, it would import commodities that make intensive use of locally scarce factors of production.

Hetero-stereotypes How we are seen by others.

Historical rate The foreign exchange rate that prevailed when a foreign currency asset or liability was first acquired or incurred.

Home-country compensation system A system that links base expatriate salary to the salary structure of the home country (e.g., the salary of a U.S. executive transferred to Japan will be based on the U.S. rather than the Japanese level).

Horizontal FDI (Foreign direct investment) When a multinational enterprise (MNE) enters a foreign country to produce the same product(s) produced at home (or to offer the same service that it does at home).

Host country–based (localized) compensation system A system that links base salary for an expatriate to the pay structure in the host country; however, supplemental compensation provisions are often connected to home-country salary structures.

Host Economy Transnationality Index An UNCTAD-calculated average of FDI inflows as a percentage of gross capital formation, FDI inward stock as a percentage of GDP, value added of foreign affiliates as a percentage of GDP, and employment of foreign affiliates as a percentage of foreign employment.

Human capital Human resources that create economic value.

Human skills A factor of production in the conventional theory of trade that results in comparative advantage in terms of comparative abundance of professional skills and other high-level human skills.

Hybrid compensation system A system that blends features from the home- and host-based approaches.

Hypertext Transfer Protocol (HTTP or HTP) A set of rules for exchanging files (text, graphic images, sound, video, and other multimedia files) on the World Wide Web.

I

Imitation lag A strategy that prevents other countries from immediately duplicating the new products of the innovating country.

Implementor A generic subsidiary role with low outflow and high inflow.

Implementor subsidiaries Subsidiaries that operate in less strategically important markets but are competent to maintain local operations.

Independent float System under which an exchange rate is allowed to adjust freely to the supply and demand of a currency for another.

Indirect quote A foreign currency price of a unit of home currency.

Individualism/collectivism (I/C) One of Hofstede's four dimensions of culture: the extent to which the self or the group constitutes the center point of identification for the individual.

Industrial policies All forms of conscious and coordinated government interventions to promote industrial development.

Infant industry argument An argument for tariffs that holds that an industry new to a country, especially a developing country, needs to be protected by tariff walls or risk being squashed by global players before it can grow and develop.

Information security The existence of security and other protections pertaining to information dissemination.

Integrated player A generic subsidiary role with high outflow and high inflow.

Integrative system A system that emphasizes global integration while permitting some local variations.

Interest rate parity (IRP) theory that provides an understanding of the way in which interest rates are linked between different countries through flows of capital.

Intermodal transportation The combination of ocean vessels (including short sea shipping), river transport, rail, road links, and air transport within a seamless supply chain.

Internalization The activity in which an MNE controls its foreign operations through a unified governance structure, primarily because it is less expensive to deal within the same corporation than to contract with external organizations.

International (or foreign) trade The exchange of goods and services with consumers in another country.

International accounting A system that involves accounting and taxation issues for companies that have internationalized their economic activities across countries in which accounting standards and practices vary.

International accounting information systems (IAIS) Accounting-related reporting systems, data management, and communication between various units under an intra-MNE (multinational enterprise) structure.

International acquisition A cross-border transaction in which a foreign investor acquires an established local firm and makes the acquired local firm a subsidiary business within its global portfolio.

International bond markets Markets where government bonds or corporate bonds are issued, bought, or sold in foreign countries.

International business Business activities that involve the transfer of resources, goods, services, knowledge, skills, or information involving two or more countries.

International cadres Individuals who move from one foreign assignment to another, seldom returning to their home country.

International entrepreneurs Companies or individuals that actively invest and operate in another country without a home base.

International entry strategies Strategies that concern where (location selection), when (timing of entry), and how (entry-mode selection) international companies should enter and invest in a foreign territory during international expansion.

International firm Any firm, regardless of its size, that is engaged in international business.

International Fisher Effect The theory that addresses the relationship between the percentage change in the spot exchange rate over time and the differential between comparable interest rates in different national capital markets.

International franchising An entry mode in which the foreign franchisor grants specified intangible property rights to the local franchisee, which must abide by strict and detailed rules as to how it does business.

International human resource management (IHRM) The procurement, allocation, utilization, and motivation of human resources in the international arena.

International investment The activity that occurs when a company invests resources in business activities outside its home country.

International leasing An entry mode in which the foreign firm (leaser) leases out its new or used machines or equipment to the local company.

International licensing An entry mode in which a foreign licensor grants specified intangible property rights to the local licensee for a specified period of time in exchange for a royalty fee.

International loan markets Markets that involve large commercial banks and other lending institutions providing loans to foreign companies.

International location selection Country and regional selection (e.g., state, province, or city) for an MNE's (multinational enterprise's) foreign direct investment (FDI) project(s).

International merger A cross-border transaction in which two firms from different countries agree to integrate their operations on a relatively co-equal basis because they have resources and capabilities that together may create a stronger competitive advantage in the global marketplace.

International monetary system Set of policies, institutions, practices, regulations, and mechanisms that determine foreign exchange rates.

International money markets The markets in which foreign monies are financed or invested. MNEs (multinational enterprises) may use international money markets to finance global operations at a lower cost than is possible domestically.

International stock (or equity) markets Markets in which company stocks are listed and traded on foreign stock exchanges.

International technology transfer The process by which one user's technology or knowledge is passed on to another in a different country for economic benefits.

International trade The activity that occurs when a company exports goods or services to consumers in another country.

International transactions Activities facilitated by

companies crossing national boundaries.

Internationally committed company A firm with at least one majority-owned plant or a joint venture abroad but lacking representation in all three regions of the world (Asia, Europe, and the Americas).

Internationally leaning firm Firm with foreign sales and possibly a representative office or a licensing agreement but with no ownership of foreign production sites.

Internet A worldwide network of computer networks known as the World Wide Web.

I–R paradigm (Integration–Responsiveness) A theoretical framework that suggests that participants in global industries develop competitive postures across two dimensions (global integration and local responsiveness).

Irrevocable L/C (letter of credit) A means of arranging payment that cannot be revoked without the specific permission of all parties concerned, including the exporter.

J

Joint exploration project A nonequity cooperative alliance whereby the exploration costs are borne by the foreign partner, with development costs later shared by a local entity.

L

Lags When a firm holding a hard currency with debts denominated in a soft currency decelerates by paying those debts late.

Laissez-faire The concept of freedom of enterprise and freedom of commerce with minimal government intervention in a society's economic activity.

Language A systematic means of communicating ideas or feelings by the use of conventionalized signs, gestures, marks, and especially articulate vocal sounds.

Late investor An MNE that follows early movers into a new market.

Lawmaking treaty A multilateral treaty that ratified by many countries with a joint interest in the issue at hand.

Leads When a firm holding a soft currency with debts denominated in a hard currency accelerates by using the soft currency to pay the hard currency debts before the soft currency drops in value.

Legal jurisdiction The laws of a particular country.

Legitimacy The acceptance of the MNE as a natural organ in the local environment.

Letter of credit (L/C) A contract between an importer and a bank that indicates that the bank will give credit to the importer and agrees to pay the exporter.

Liability of foreignness The costs of doing business abroad that result in a competitive disadvantage vis-à-vis indigenous firms.

Lingua franca A means of communication shared by people of different national and linguistic origins.

Local content The portion of a product (or service) that includes locally made and procured inputs.

Local currency Currency of a particular country; the reporting currency of a domestic or foreign operation.

Local innovator A generic subsidiary role with low outflow and low inflow.

Local responsiveness The attempt to respond to specific needs within a variety of host countries.

Location advantages The benefits arising from a host country's comparative advantages accrued for foreign direct investors.

Long position A position in which the initial transaction represents an asset or future ownership claim to foreign currency.

Long-term supply agreement An agreement in which the manufacturing buyer often provides the supplier with free updated information on products, markets, and technologies, which in turn helps ensure the input quality.

Louvre Accord An agreement that calls for the G7 (Group of Seven) to support the falling dollar by pegging exchange rates within a narrow, undisclosed range.

M

Managed float System designed to eliminate excess volatility and to preserve an orderly pattern of exchange rate changes in which some currencies are allowed to float freely, but the majority are either managed by a government or pegged to another currency.

Managerial control The process in which a party influences alliance activities or decisions in a way that is consistent with its own interests through various managerial, administrative, or social tools.

Market motives   Firms conducting international business for reasons of seizing new market opportunities or protecting and holding their market power or competitive position.

Market-seeking FDI   MNEs attempt to secure market share and sales growth in the target foreign market.

Masculinity/femininity (M/F)   One of Hofstede's four dimensions of culture: the extent to which traditional masculine values such as aggressiveness and assertiveness are emphasized.

Matching   A mechanism whereby a company matches its foreign currency inflows with its foreign currency outflows in respect to amount, timing, and the currency unit.

Mental maps   Our perceptions of the world around us and of geographic realities.

Mercantilism   An economic philosophy based on beliefs that a country should simultaneously encourage exports and discourage imports in order to increase wealth.

Monetary items   Obligations to pay or rights to receive a fixed number of currency units in the future.

Monetary/nonmonetary method (of accounting)   Monetary assets and liabilities are translated at the current rate. Nonmonetary items are translated at historical rates.

Money laundering   The act of concealing the source of ill-gotten funds by channeling them into

legitimate business activities and bank deposits.

Monopolistic advantage   The benefit incurred to a firm that maintains a monopolistic power in the market.

Moral hazard   A hidden reckless action of external partners who know they will be saved if things go wrong.

Most favored nation (MFN)   A clause in most treaties that requires a trade concession that is given to one country be given to all other countries.

Most-favored-nation treatment   Any advantage, favor, or privilege granted by one country must be extended to all other member countries.

Multidomestic firms   An enterprise with multiple international subsidiaries that are relatively independent of each other.

Multidomestic strategy   A delegation of strategic and operating decisions to strategic business units in each country.

Multinational enterprise (MNE)   A firm that has directly invested abroad and has at least one working affiliate in a foreign country (e.g., a factory, a branch office) over which it maintains effective control.

Mutualization   The sharing of logistic facilities by two or more partners.

N

National treatment   The principle that foreign goods in a member country should be treated the same as domestic goods, once the foreign goods have cleared customs.

Netting   A practice by which subsidiaries or affiliates

within an MNE (multinational enterprise) network merely settle intersubsidiary indebtedness for the net amount owed during the posttransaction period.

New trade theory   Countries do not necessarily specialize and trade solely to take advantage of their differences; they also trade because of increasing returns, which makes specialization advantageous per se.

Niche marketing   Marketing that is narrowly directed toward a predefined segment of the market. In international markets, niche marketing may be directed not only to a product category (e.g., low end) but also to an ethnic or geographical segment.

Nominal exchange rate   The exchange rate before deducting an inflation factor.

Nontariff barriers   Indirect measures that discriminate against the foreign manufacturers in the domestic market or otherwise distort or constrain trade.

O

Offensive   A motive that seizes market opportunities in foreign countries through trade or investment.

Offer   The exchange rate at which a dealer will sell the other currency.

Official reserves account   A country's net holdings of the official reserves of monetary gold, special drawing rights (SDRs), reserve positions in the IMF, and convertible foreign currencies.

Offset   An agreement whereby one party agrees to purchase goods and services with a specified percentage of its proceeds from an original sale.

OLI framework (ownership, location, internalization) Framework that explains international production activities and recognizes the importance of three variables: ownership specific (O), location specific (L), and internalization (I).

Openness The extent to which a country's national economy is linked to world economies through the flow of resources, goods, services, people, technologies, information, and capital.

Operational nature Organizational principles and managerial philosophies may differ widely across nations, thus heightening the complexity of operation and management of international business.

Operational risk Any change to the "rules of the game" under which the foreign firm operates (e.g., new and arbitrary taxation), especially when foreign firms are singled out.

Opportunity cost The activity or pathway that must be given up to pursue another activity or pathway. For a good X, the opportunity cost is the amount of other goods that have to be given up to produce one unit of X.

Optimal tariff theory An assumption that governments can capture a significant portion of the manufacturer's profit margin through the imposition of a tariff.

Organizational capabilities Qualities of a global strategic alliance partner in organizational skills,

previous collaboration, learning ability, and foreign experience.

Original equipment manufacturing (OEM) A specific form of international subcontracting, in which a foreign firm supplies a local company with the technology and most sophisticated components so that the latter can manufacture goods that the foreign firm will market under its own brand in international markets.

Outflows of FDI The flow of FDI out of a country.

Outsourcing Buying of inputs outside the MNE's network.

Overdraft A line of credit against which drafts (checks) can be drawn (written) up to a specified maximum amount.

Overseas Assignment Inventory (OAI) Instrument that assists in the selection of expatriates using the following predictors of success on a foreign assignment: expectations, open-mindedness, respect for others' beliefs, trust in people, tolerance, locus of control, flexibility, patience, social adaptability, initiative, risk taking, sense of humor, and spouse communication.

Ownership risk Threat to the current ownership structure or to the ability of the MNE (multinational enterprise) to select or shift to a given structure.

Ownership structure The percentage of equity held by each parent in a global alliance.

P

Par value The rate at which a currency is fixed; the

benchmark value of a currency.

Parallel loan (also known as back-to-back loan) An exchange of funds between firms in different countries, with the exchange reversed at a later date.

Parallel market An alternative market to the official exchange market.

Parent control The process through which a parent company ensures that the way an alliance is managed conforms to its own interest.

Passive reciprocity A position taken by a country in which it refuses to lower or eliminate its barriers to trade until the other party does the same.

Pegged exchange rate system A system in which a country's currency is tied to, or fixed with, another country's currency.

People skills Skills such as relational abilities, willingness to communicate, nonverbal communication, respect for others, and empathy for others.

Perception skills The cognitive processes that help executives understand the behavior of foreigners. This includes flexible attribution and breadth as well as being open-minded and nonjudgmental.

Permanent expatriates Individuals who stay in overseas assignments for extended periods of time, or even permanently.

Personal attachment Socialization and personal relations between senior GSA managers representing each party during their involvement in exchange activities between the same interacting organizations.

Personal skills Skills needed by expatriates that facilitate mental and emotional well-being (e.g., stress orientation, reinforcement, substitution, physical mobility, technical competence, dealing with alienation and isolation, realistic expectations prior to departure).

Physical assets Factories and facilities.

Piracy The use of illegal and unauthorized means to obtain goods, such as copying software.

Political behavior The acquisition, development, securing, and use of power in relation to other entities.

Political risk The unforeseen problems for the trader and investor that will adversely affect the profit and goals of a particular business enterprise.

Polycentric staffing The act of hiring HCNs (host-country nationals) for key positions in subsidiaries but not at corporate headquarters.

Portfolio theory The behavior of individuals or firms administering large amounts of financial assets in search of the highest possible risk-adjusted net return.

Power distance (PD) One of Hofstede's four dimensions of culture: the extent to which hierarchical differences are accepted in society and articulated—for example, in the form of deference to senior echelons.

Predatory pricing The selling of goods below real cost so as to drive competition out of the market.

Preference similarity A phenomenon in which the consumers and investors of two countries that have the same or similar demand structures demand the same goods with similar degrees of quality and sophistication.

Pricing The decision and process of setting a price to a product or service. In international markets, pricing is much more complex owing to varying cost structures (e.g., transportation costs, tariffs) and market positioning.

Product origin The country in which a product was developed.

Production factors Activities involved in the production process, such as capital, labor, raw materials, and land.

Production function The amount of output that can be produced by using a given quantity of capital and labor.

Productivity The value of the output produced by a unit of labor or capital.

Prospector An instrument that assists in the selection of expatriates by assessing the potential of aspiring international executives on 14 dimensions: cultural sensitivity, business knowledge, courage, motivational ability, integrity, insight, commitment, risk taking, seeking feedback, using feedback, cultural adventurousness, seeking learning opportunities, openness to criticism, and flexibility.

Psychic distance Differences in language, culture, political systems, and such that disturb the flow of information between the firm and the market.

Purchasing power parity (PPP) A theory emphasizing the role of prices of goods and services in determining changes in exchange rates.

Put option The act of selling a stated number of units of the underlying foreign currency at a specific price per unit during a specific period of time.

Q

Quality based (deployment) The distinctiveness of the resources allocated to a foreign market.

Quantity based (deployment) The amount of critical resources deployed in a target foreign market.

Quotas Quantitative limitations on the importation of goods typically spelled out in terms of units or value.

R

R&D intensity Total R&D (research and development) expenditure relative to total sales during the same period.

Real exchange rate The exchange rate after deducting an inflation factor.

Receptive role A subsidiary role in which most subsidiary functions are highly integrated with headquarters or with other business units.

Regiocentric staffing The act of recruiting on a regional basis (e.g., recruit within Asia for a position in China).

Related divisional format A format in which product

divisions report directly to headquarters.

Relative PPP (purchasing power parity) Theory that focuses on the relationship between the change in prices of two countries and the change in the exchange rate over the same period.

Religion Key values and norms that are reflected in adherents' beliefs and way of life.

Reporting currency The currency in which an enterprise prepares its financial statement.

Research and development consortium A joint R&D project in which the costs may be allocated by an agreed-upon formula, but the revenue of each partner depends on what it does with the technology created.

Resource complementarity The extent to which one party's contributed resources are complementary to the other party's resources, resulting in synergies pursued by both parties.

Resource-seeking FDI MNEs attempting to acquire particular resources at a lower cost than could be obtained in the home country.

Revaluation An increase in the foreign exchange rate that is pegged to another currency or gold.

Revocable L/C (letter of credit) A letter of credit that can be revoked without notice, at any time up to the time a draft is presented to the issuing bank.

Revolving L/C The amount of the L/C is automatically renewed pursuant to its terms and conditions.

Risk The unpredictability of operational and financial outcomes.

Rule of origin The administration of tariffs and quotas based on the country of origin, not countries through which a product passed, unless it underwent material change in those countries.

S

Salary Base pay plus incentives (merit, profit sharing, bonus plans), determined via job evaluation or competency-based plans.

Samurai bonds Foreign bonds sold in Japan.

Services allowance and premiums Premiums paid to compensate for differences in expenditures between the home and host country.

Short position Position in which the cash market position represents a liability or a future obligation to deliver foreign currency.

Small and midsize international enterprises (SMIEs) Companies that engage in international business activities but do not have substantial FDI presence and hence do not qualify as MNEs (multinational enterprises).

Smuggling The illegal trade and transportation of goods that is devised to circumvent customs duties, quotas, and other constraints on the movement of goods (e.g., safety transportation requirements that may add to cost at destination).

Society for Worldwide International Financial Telecommunications

(SWIFT) A network of telephone, Internet, telex, and satellite communications that link banks in each country and throughout the world.

Soft, or weak, currency A currency that is anticipated to devaluate or depreciate relative to major trading currencies.

Special drawing right (SDR) A unit of account for the International Monetary Fund (IMF) to expand their official reserves bases.

Spot-forward swap Situation in which an investor sells forward the foreign currency maturity value of the bill and simultaneously buys the spot foreign exchange to pay for the bill.

Spot rate The exchange rate for a transaction that requires almost immediate delivery of foreign exchange.

Spot transactions Transactions between banks that are normally settled on the second working day after the date on which the transaction is concluded.

Standardization The imposition of a rigid and narrow set of rules; may even apply a single standard to all situations.

Statutory tax The rate that determines the general level of the tax burden shouldered by firms.

Stereotypes Our beliefs about others, their attitudes, and their behaviors.

Stock of FDI (federal direct investment) The total accumulated value of foreign-owned assets at a given time.

Strategic capabilities Expertise of a global strategic alliance partner in market power, marketing competence, technological skills, relationship building, industrial experience, and corporate image.

Strategic IHRM (SIHRM) Human resources, management issues, functions, and policies and practices that result from the strategic activities of MNEs (multinational enterprises) and affect the international concerns and goals of these enterprises.

Strategic leader The role played by a highly competent national subsidiary located in a strategically important market.

Strategic motives The intention of a company to capitalize on its distinctive resources or capabilities already developed at home (e.g., technologies and economy of scale).

Strategic orientation The indirect exercise of corporate direction.

Structural discrepancies Differences in industry structure attributes between home and host countries.

Subcontracting The process in which a foreign company provides a local manufacturer with raw materials, semifinished products, sophisticated components, or technology for producing final goods that will be bought back by the foreign company.

Subsidies Payments provided by a government or its agencies to domestic companies to make them more competitive vis-à-vis foreign competitors at home or abroad.

Surge in imports A sudden and dramatic increase in imports or in market share that can cause material damage to the domestic industry.

Swap The exchange of interest or foreign currency exposures or a combination of both by two or more borrowers.

Swap transaction Transaction in which there is a simultaneous purchase and sale of a given amount for two different settlement dates.

Synergy Additional economic benefits (financial, operational, or technological) arising from cooperation between two parties that provide each other with complementary resources or capabilities.

T

Target-zone arrangement A system arranged by a group of nations sharing some common interest and goals. Countries adjust their national economic policies to maintain their exchange rates within a specific margin around an agreed-upon, fixed central exchange rate.

Tariff Surcharges that an importer must pay above and beyond taxes levied on domestic goods and services.

Tariff barriers Official constraints on the importation of certain goods and services in the form of a total or partial limitation or in the form of a special levy.

Tax equalization An adjustment to expatriate pay to reflect tax rates in the home country.

Tax havens Geographical locations in which taxation is substantially lower than that in a home country.

Technical standards Provisions made by government agencies in various countries that pertain to a large array of areas—for example, safety, pollution, and technical performance.

Technology gaps Relative scarcity of technology in a country that determines comparative disadvantage in technology-intensive products.

Temporal method (of accounting) Monetary items are translated at the current rate. Nonmonetary items are translated at the rates that preserve their original measurement bases.

Temporaries Individuals who go on short assignments, up to one year.

Term loans Straight loans that are made for a fixed period of time and repaid in a single lump sum.

Terms of sale Conditions stipulating rights and responsibilities and costs and risks borne by exporter and importer.

Theocratic law Legal system that relies on religious codes.

Timing of entry When a firm enters a foreign market compared with other firms (e.g., early entry is when a firm enters a foreign market before the foreign MNEs and late entry when the firm enters after other international businesses have established themselves).

Traditional expatriate An older and experienced

expatriate selected for his or her managerial or technical skills for a period of one to five years.

Transaction exposure Foreign exchange risk determined by changes in exchange rates affecting the value, in home currency terms, of anticipated cash flows denominated in foreign currency, relating to transactions already entered into.

Transfer pricing The pricing of goods and services that are transferred between members of an MNE (multinational enterprise) network.

Transfer risk Impediments to the transfer of production factors.

Transferability The extent to which MNE (multinational enterprise) resources or knowledge developed at home can be transferred to a foreign subunit, resulting in competitive advantage or contributing to business success in the target foreign setting (industry, segmented market, or host country).

Transferable L/C (letter of credit) A letter of credit under which the beneficiary has the right to instruct the paying bank to make the credit available to one or more secondary beneficiaries.

Translation The process of restating accounting data recorded in one currency (e.g., the currency of a foreign subsidiary in Italy) into another currency (e.g., the currency of the parent company in the United States) for the purpose of aggregating data from different reporting entities.

Translation adjustments Translation adjustments result from the process of translating financial statements from the entity's functional currency into the reporting currency.

Translation exposure Foreign exchange risk that refers to the potential for accounting-derived changes in owners' equity to occur because of the need to consolidate foreign currency financial statements.

Transnational firm A firm that consists of subsidiaries that fulfill varying roles.

Transnational (or hybrid) strategy A strategy that seeks to achieve both global efficiency and local responsiveness.

Transnationality index The average of three ratios: (a) foreign assets to total assets, (b) foreign sales to total sales, and (c) foreign employment to total employment.

Treaties of friendship, commerce, and navigation (FCN) Treaties that provides firms from the signatory countries with the same rights and privileges enjoyed by domestic businesses in the other country.

U

Umbrella holding company An investment company that unites the firm's existing investments such as branch offices, joint ventures, and wholly owned subsidiaries under one umbrella so as to combine sales, procurement, manufacturing, training, and maintenance within the host country.

Uncertainty The unpredictability of environmental or organizational conditions that affect firm performance.

Uncertainty avoidance One of Hofstede's four dimensions of culture: the extent to which uncertainty and ambiguity are tolerated.

Unconfirmed L/C (letter of credit) A letter of credit that is the obligation of only the issuing bank.

Unit of measure The currency in which assets, liabilities, revenue, and expense are measured.

Unrelated holdings company format A format in which businesses are managed as investment rather than profit centers with wide reporting variations.

Uppsala (or Scandinavian) model A perspective that views international expansion as a process involving a series of incremental decisions during which firms develop international operations in small steps (e.g., accumulated knowledge about country-specific markets helps firms increase local commitment, reduce operational uncertainty, and enhance economic efficiency).

User/need model A model that assesses the needs of potential customers including the circumstances in which the product or service is likely to be used.

V

Vertical FDI When the MNE (multinational enterprise) enters a foreign country to produce intermediate goods that provide input into a company's domestic operations.

Virtual expatriate An individual who takes on foreign assignments without physically relocating.

W

Wholly owned subsidiary An entry mode in which the investing firm owns 100% of the new entity in a host country.

Working capital The net position whereby a firm's current liability is subtracted from its current assets.

World Bank Group International institution comprising the World Bank, the International Development Association, the International Finance Corporation, and the Multilateral Investment Guarantee Agency; raises standards of living in developing countries by channeling financial resources from developed countries to them.

World Trade Organization (WTO) Multilateral trade organization aiming at international trade liberalization and which has the authority to oversee trade disputes among countries.

World Wide Web A worldwide network of computer networks that constitutes all the resources and users on the Internet that use Hypertext Transfer Protocol (HTP or HTTP).

Y

Yankee bonds Foreign bonds sold in the United States.

Young, inexperienced expatriates Individuals sent for six months to five years, usually on local hire terms.

INDEX

ABOUT THE AUTHORS

Oded Shenkar holds the Ford Motor Company Chair in Global Business Management and is Professor of International Business at the Fisher College of Business, the Ohio State University. He is a member of several editorial boards, including those of the two leading journals in international business (*Journal of International Business Studies* and *Management International Review*), and has authored over 85 refereed articles in such journals as *Academy of Management Review, Academy of Management Journal, Journal of Applied Psychology, Strategic Management Journal,* and *Journal of International Business Studies,* among many others. He is also the author of seven books, most recently *The Chinese Century,* which appeared in 12 foreign editions. Based on major journal publications, he was ranked among the 300 most prolific management authors (*Organization Science*), the 30 top international strategy authors (*Journal of International Management*), and first among Chinese management scholars (*Journal of Business Research*). He was the first Andersen Fellow at the Judge Institute of Management, Cambridge University; and the first holder of the Ford Motor Company Chair at the Fisher College of Business. Oded is a vice president and board member of the Academy of International Business and is also on the boards of the Hang Lung Center for the Study of Chinese Management (Hong Kong University of Science and Technology) and the School of Business at Zhejiang University (China). He has taught in Hong Kong (the Chinese University of Hong Kong and HKUST), Mainland China (Peking University, the University of International Business and Economics), Japan (International University of Japan), the UK, and Israel, among other places. He has been a consultant to governments, international organizations, and multinational enterprises as well as to small and start-up global firms.

Yadong Luo is Professor of International Business and Strategy and holds the Emery Means Findley Distinguished Chair in Graduate Business Studies in the School of Business, University of Miami. He is also chairman of the mangaement department. He has authored more than 120 refereed journal articles, 90 other publications, and 15 books. His recent books include *Global Dimensions of Corporate Governance* (2006), *Coopetition in International Business* (2004), and *Multinational Enterprises in Emerging Markets* (2002). Yadong's recent articles have appeared in leading journals such as *Administrative Science Quarterly, Academy of Management Journal, Academy of Management Review, Strategic Management Journal, Journal of International Business Studies, Journal of Applied Psychology, Organization Science, Journal of Management, Journal of Management Studies, Journal of International Management, Journal of World Business,* and *Management International Review.* He is the recipient of more than a dozen teaching and research awards, including the Provost's Award for Scholarly Activity at the University of Miami and the Regents' Medal for Excellence in Research at the University of Hawaii. He holds a distinguished honorary professorship at Fudan University and Xi'an Jiaotong University, both in China. He is a consulting editor of *Journal of International Business Studies* and an editor of *Journal of World Business.* He has been a consultant to governments, law firms, and large corporations. Prior to coming to the United States, Yadong was a provincial official in charge of international business in China.